Comparative Health Systems

Global Perspectives

EDITED BY

James A. Johnson, PhD, MPA
Professor of Health Administration and International Health
Central Michigan University, Mount Pleasant, Michigan
and
Adjunct Professor of Health Policy
Auburn University, Montgomery, Alabama

Carleen H. Stoskopf, ScD, MS
Director
Graduate School of Public Health
and
Professor of Health Management and Policy
San Diego State University, San Diego, California

JONES AND BARTLETT PUBLISHERS
Sudbury, Massachusetts
BOSTON   TORONTO   LONDON   SINGAPORE

World Headquarters

Jones and Bartlett Publishers
40 Tall Pine Drive
Sudbury, MA 01776
978-443-5000
info@jbpub.com
www.jbpub.com

Jones and Bartlett Publishers
Canada
6339 Ormindale Way
Mississauga, Ontario L5V 1J2
Canada

Jones and Bartlett Publishers
International
Barb House, Barb Mews
London W6 7PA
United Kingdom

Jones and Bartlett's books and products are available through most bookstores and online booksellers. To contact Jones and Bartlett Publishers directly, call 800-832-0034, fax 978-443-8000, or visit our website, www.jbpub.com.

Substantial discounts on bulk quantities of Jones and Bartlett's publications are available to corporations, professional associations, and other qualified organizations. For details and specific discount information, contact the special sales department at Jones and Bartlett via the above contact information or send an email to specialsales@jbpub.com.

This publication is designed to provide accurate and authoritative information in regard to the Subject Matter covered. It is sold with the understanding that the publisher is not engaged in rendering legal, accounting, or other professional service. If legal advice or other expert assistance is required, the service of a competent professional person should be sought.

Production Credits
Publisher: Michael Brown
Production Director: Amy Rose
Associate Editor: Katey Birtcher
Editorial Assistant: Catie Heverling
Editorial Assistant: Teresa Reilly
Senior Production Editor: Tracey Chapman
Associate Production Editor: Kate Stein
Senior Marketing Manager: Sophie Fleck
Manufacturing and Inventory Control Supervisor: Amy Bacus
Composition: Publishers' Design and Production Services, Inc.
Art: Accurate Art, Inc.
Assistant Photo Researcher: Jessica Elias
Cover Design: Kristin E. Parker
Cover Image: © Kts/Dreamstime.com
Printing and Binding: Malloy, Inc.
Cover Printing: Malloy, Inc.

Library of Congress Cataloging-in-Publication Data
Comparative health systems : global perspectives / [edited by] James Johnson, Carleen Stoskopf.
    p. ; cm.
  Includes bibliographical references and index.
  ISBN-13: 978-0-7637-5379-5 (pbk.)
  ISBN-10: 0-7637-5379-3 (pbk.)
  1. World health. 2. Medical policy. 3. National health services. I. Johnson, James A., 1954– II. Stoskopf, Carleen.
  [DNLM: 1. Delivery of Health Care. 2. Health Policy. 3. International Cooperation. 4. World Health. W 84.1 C7373 2010]
  RA441.C663 2009
  362.1—dc22
                            2009012592

6048

Printed in the United States of America
13 12 11 10 09   10 9 8 7 6 5 4 3 2 1

DEDICATION

To James Allen Johnson IV
born June 19, 2008
and
Joseph Adam Johnson
born March 12, 2009
—J.A.J.

To Jonathan and Marissa Ann Stoskopf Venn
—C.H.S.

Table of Contents

Acknowledgments

We would like to thank all of the authors from around the world for their invaluable and insightful contributions to this book. We also want to thank Holly Shakya for her exceptional job and hard work as editorial assistant. Holly brought her own perspectives and much appreciated professionalism to this project, often serving in the valued role of third editor. Additionally, we thank Jacqueline Walker for her dedicated effort as editorial secretary to the project and Jonathan Venn for his editorial contributions. Finally, we thank Katey Birtcher and Kate Stein at Jones and Bartlett for their guidance and support as we worked our way through this multifaceted international undertaking.

Foreword

Dr. Suzan Guest

Can anyone doubt that health systems are the most complex and resource-intense network of organizations and people that have ever been invented by human beings? In country after country, responding to healthcare challenges and opportunities attracts our best and brightest researchers, thinkers, leaders, and healers. Billions of dollars are invested annually. Huge successes have been achieved and more are possible. At the same time, it is patently obvious that health systems exist in an environment where rapid, discontinuous changes of all kinds drive everyone to keep responding in new ways. Research studies, such as the one I heard presented in the summer of 2008 by one of this book's co-authors, Dr. James Johnson at the Organization Development World Congress in Sardinia, Italy, report on where health system growth and improvement is needed. Models and theories abound throughout the world. For example, in the book *Who Is Wounding the Healers*, my co-author Bill Bergquist and I look at four key internal cultures that we believe fundamentally describe the health systems in Canada and the United States. Economic, sociological, psychological, and anthropological analyses have all been carried out in an attempt to comprehend and learn what we need to know about health and health care. The level of complexity involved in all the various parts of these systems is increasing in almost every way. We are also learning that much of what has been achieved may not be sustainable.

This book contributes another important framework. It is directed at examining how our interconnected and interdependent world affects healthcare decisions and processes across many boundaries and borders. It matters that we understand how these systems work (and do not work). It matters because health care is about life on the planet. We have the capacity to do so much more by understanding the variability of our worldwide health policies and practices. The challenge is to think in new ways and come up with innovations that will enable us to develop organizations, processes, policies, and practices that can be in balance over the long term.

This book is intended to help students to think more deeply about how health care is organized and delivered. Each country has invented its system to respond to a particular set of forces. By examining each of the systems presented in the book, students will come away with new perspectives and ideas. These can then be used as a series of lens to first get new insights about each person's "home" country system. Each country has been successful in its own way. Celebrating and valuing each of these are important. In addition, examining various approaches can enable readers to understand the connections between and among the variety of health systems. We need local systems that nourish good health as well as structures that foster international sustainable health and wellness.

To achieve sustainability, we need to change our health systems. From a change perspective, success is sometimes more difficult to deal with than failure. People have a lot more difficulty letting go of what has worked or is working, especially when an alternative, appealing worldview has yet to emerge. As we consider how changes might be made to achieve both local and worldwide balance in delivering healthcare services, we need thinkers who can deeply analyze, value, and understand what exists and what might then be created to meet 21st-century needs. These chapters are intended to provide solid evidence so that readers can examine all of this complexity to generate new, persuasive ideas about what might come next. The literature on organizational change tells us that at key moments of transformation, overwhelming levels of complexity are often rethought and reorganized into more profound and useful ways of getting things done. An example has to do with how we once determined pregnancies. We used to do blood tests that involved killing rabbits and weeks of analysis. As we came to understand more about hormones and created new ways to analyze body fluids, new assessment processes emerged. Today women can simply use a urine stick. This kind of simplicity rests on a tremendous amount of research, experimentation, and innovation. That is exactly what needs to occur in order to change and improve health systems. This book represents an excellent resource for building our knowledge base so that the rest of the development process can emerge.

As a result of analyzing the various approaches to managing and organizing health care in different countries around the world, students will be able to engage in critical thinking and go beyond mere description of the various systems. Readers will gain a deeper understanding about how and what the various systems accomplish, look at their relationships to each other, and reach some conclusions about what is most important about them. These kinds of comparisons are useful for illuminating, critiquing, or challenging reader ideas about health systems. We invite readers to extend their thinking. Is the Canadian, Nigerian, or Portuguese system really what you expected or thought it was going to be? Based on what facts or evidence? What surprised you about the various approaches to health care? We invite you to think about the significance of the various parts of the systems. Where do the various healthcare systems meet, for instance? We want you to reflect about how and why you are interpreting the evidence in particular ways, and we expect you to answer the "so what" question. What is the point of all of this anyway? Finally, we want you to be able to assemble the information that is here for yourselves and interpret what it means. What is the point of this comparison? Why does this comparison matter?

I share with Drs. Johnson and Stoskopf the hope that readers will see unexpected results, similarities, and differences and come up with coherent, new interpretations and new ideas for the policies, systems, and structures that serve us all.

—Dr. Suzan Guest
International organization development consultant based in British Columbia, Canada and author of the book *Who Is Wounding the Healers—The Four Cultures of Healthcare*

Foreword

Dr. Ted Karpf

This is a book whose time has come. Drs. Johnson and Stoskopf have anticipated and documented the core concerns faced by nations. Health and health care are at the forefront of international concern, especially in a time of global financial turmoil and insecurity. This book is absolutely essential to understanding what's at stake and to charting a path through the maze of issues confronting healthcare planners and healthcare recipients, healthcare professionals and financing managers, politicians and bureaucrats. It's more than a matter of systems and approaches; it is about the security of the global community. According to Dr. Margaret Chan, Director-General of the World Health Organization:

> "Healthy human capital is the very foundation for productivity and prosperity. Equitable distribution of health care and equity in the health status of populations is the foundation for social cohesion. Social cohesion is our best protection against social unrest, nationally and internationally. Healthy, productive and stable populations are always an asset, but must especially so during a time of crisis." (November 2008, G-8 follow-up, Tokyo, Japan)

The recipients of health care must be heard above the din of competing claims of equity and effectiveness.

> "The people have the right and duty to participate individually and collectively in the planning and implementation of their health care. Primary health care...requires and promotes maximum community and individual self-reliance and participation in the planning, organization, operation and control of primary health care, making fullest use of local, national and other available resources; and to this end develops through appropriate education the ability of communities to participate." (Declaration of Alma-Ata International Conference on Primary Health Care, Articles IV and VII, Alma-Ata [Khazakstan], USSR, 6–12 September 1978)

Obtaining decent care, which acknowledges the voice of the people through the values of agency and dignity, interdependence and solidarity, subsidiarity and sustainability, raises the ante a bit higher. Political and healthcare leaders, financial managers, and medical and healthcare professionals must be reminded amidst the policy debate that where the people are invested in their own care the formulas for success and sustainability changes. Where the people are engaged in determining the levels and resource allocations for care, there is also more room than those charged with determining formulas can imagine.

The healthcare debate must finally factor in the people who it claims are to be served and sustained with improved health. Lest we miss the point—"the highest attainable level of health for all people"—leading to a just and equitable society, then the various financial models and healthcare systems will still not bring us the long-needed satisfaction and support we need today. U.S. President Barack Obama has stated repeatedly that "health care is a right." This notion, enshrined three decades ago at Alma-Ata, changes the rules and reorganizes the lines of accountability along with our thinking and expectations. Where health is a right, then social responsibility will lead to an enhanced commitment to improved health. The formula ceases to be about "those people" or "their problems" and becomes about us!

As we proceed through these pages it will be important to ask how this approach will help ensure that the people are heard and heeded.

—Dr. Ted Karpf
International health advocate,
World Health Organization, Geneva, Switzerland
and author of the book, *Restoring Hope:
Decent Care in the Midst of HIV/AIDS*

Preface

Over the past decade, I have taken graduate students to Geneva, Switzerland each summer to study global health. While there, we visit the World Health Organization (WHO), which is receiving updates on global health and interacting with senior scientists, health practitioners, and leaders in the mission of "health for all." In addition to being spellbound by descriptions of the many initiatives and great successes of the WHO, we repeatedly hear of one major limitation that continues to impede even the greater progress. That is the poor state of health systems in many parts of the world. There are models of success as well as models of absolute failure. Most health systems are oriented toward disease care, and many are underfunded and understaffed, whereas some countries expend large portions of their national resources on health. Some health systems are operated by governments, and others are more involved in the private sector. Regardless of scope or scale, every program, every initiative, every policy, and every course of treatment are imbedded within a particular country-specific health system.

Several years ago, my friend and colleague Dr. Carleen Stoskopf joined me on one of the trips to Geneva.

While there, we discussed the need for a book that would describe a range of health systems so that students could better understand the limitations and opportunities offered in the diversity that we had each seen in our own international work. We felt that one of the best ways for students to learn about the range of systems would be through comparative study. As with many invigorating sidewalk café conversations in Europe (and elsewhere), we set this idea aside and returned to the busy activities of our academic positions at the time—Carleen, a Department Chair at the School of Public Health at the University of South Carolina in Columbia and myself, a Department Chair at the Medical University of South Carolina in Charleston. A few years later, however, at a meeting of the American Public Health Association in Boston, in a conversation with publisher Michael Brown, the topic came back up and momentum for such a book grew quickly.

We conceptualized the book as a text to be used in courses in international health, comparative studies, global health, international affairs, health administration, and public health. In an increasingly interconnected and interdependent world comprised of wide variations in health delivery systems, practices, and policy, the book was developed to offer students some understanding through comparative study.

In seeking to achieve this goal, we enlisted contributors from many countries to write about the systems that they had worked in and were familiar with. Thus, every chapter that describes a health system is written by at least one person from that country. Chapters also ended up having U.S.-based co-authors, as we used our own professional network in schools of public health, medicine, administration, and policy to identify chapter contributors. Needless to say, the book project emerged as a significant multicultural undertaking involving authors from every continent and from the largest possible range of health system types.

To further the objective of comparative study, we imposed a framework on each chapter that would allow students to compare and contrast such divergent systems as Canada, India, Japan, Nigeria, Germany, Australia, Mexico, and many others. The framework used to develop each chapter included the following:

Country Description
- History
- Size and geography
- Government and political system
- Macroeconomics (GDP, OECD)
- Demographics (including religion, gender, poverty)

Brief History of the Healthcare System
- Description of health system
- Facilities
- Workforce
- Technology and equipment

Evaluation of Health System
- Cost
- Quality

- Access
- Current and emerging issues and challenges

Although these chapters were developed by in-country authors and their collaborators, Carleen and I, working with colleagues, developed other chapters that are overarching. This includes a chapter that describes health systems and one that provides an overview of disease. Dr. Walter Jones contributed a very useful chapter discussing health policy and economics, and Dr. Gerald Ledlow, Matthew Walker, and my son, Allen Johnson, contributed a chapter describing the role of nongovernmental organizations (NGOs) as an important, though sometimes overlooked, component to health systems and global health. Additionally, we included a chapter that outlines future challenges, a resource list, and a glossary that should be useful to students and professors.

Having worked in and traveled to 22 countries myself, I can say with great confidence that this book will serve to broaden the reader's understanding. It will also likely change their perspectives on global health. They will learn that although highly developed countries continue to offer profound breakthroughs in medical science and technology, as well as reform and continuous improvement of health systems, the best solutions don't always emerge in the wealthiest countries.

As stated by Dr. Barry Bloom, Dean of the Harvard School of Public Health, the huge disparities in health that exist between countries remain one of the great moral and intellectual problems of our time. This book can serve as one tool among many that will be needed to empower students to become effect change agents in this ongoing challenge.

—Dr. James A. Johnson

Contributors*

Beatrice Wiafe Addai, PhD, MD (*Ghana*)
Ministry of Health
Accra, Ghana

Ahmed Adu-Oppong, PhD, MSc, MBA, MHA
  (*Ghana*)
University of Cape Coast School of Medical Science
Cape Coast, Ghana

Omowale Amuleru-Marshall, PhD, MA, MEd, MPH
  (*Guyana*)
St. George's University
Grenada, West Indies

Pedro Pita Barros, PhD, MSc (*Portugal*)
Universidade Nova de Lisboa
Lisbon, Portugal

Joan Buckley, PhD, MBS (*Ireland*)
University College Cork
Cork, Ireland

M. Nicholas Coppola, PhD, MS, MHA (*United States*)
Texas Tech University
Health Sciences Center
Lubbock, Texas, United States

Glenn Croxton, MBA (*United States*)
Henry Ford Health System
Detroit, Michigan, United States

Linda F. Dennard, PhD, MPA (*United States*)
Auburn University
Montgomery, Alabama, United States

Clara E. Dismuke, PhD (*Portugal*)
Medical University of South Carolina
Center for Health Economics and Policy Studies
Charleston, South Carolina, United States

R. Paul Duncan, PhD, MS (*Canada*)
University of Florida
College of Public Health and Health Professions
Gainesville, Florida, United States

* Parenthetical note indicates country of birth.

Omur Cinar Elci, PhD, MD (*Turkey*)
St. George's University
School of Medicine
Grenada, West Indies

Neil Gardner, MPA (*United States*)
U.S. Department of Health and Human Services
Philadelphia, Pennsylvania, United States

Octavio Gómez-Dantés, MD, MPH (*Mexico*)
Carso Health Institute
Mexico City, Mexico

Damian E. Greaves, MSc, MPH-candidate (*Saint
    Lucia*)
St. George's University
Grenada, West Indies

Patricia Gunn, MIR (*United States/Scotland*)
Auburn University
Montgomery, Alabama, United States

Mikiyasu Hakoyama, PhD (*Japan*)
Central Michigan University
School of Human Environmental Studies
Mount Pleasant, Michigan, United States

Whiejong M. Han, PhD, MA (*Korea*)
University of South Carolina
Arnold School of Public Health
Columbia, South Carolina, United States

Joseph Ntein Inungu, DrPH, MD, MPH (*Democratic
    Republic of Congo*)
Saginaw Valley State University
University Center, Michigan, United States

James Allen Johnson III, MPH-student (*United States*)
Florida State University
Tallahassee, Florida, United States

James A. Johnson, PhD, MS, MPA (*United States*)
Central Michigan University
Dow College of Health Professions
Mount Pleasant, Michigan, United States
and Auburn University
Montgomery, Alabama, United States

Walter J. Jones, PhD, MA, MHSA (*United States*)
Medical University of South Carolina
Charleston, South Carolina, United States

Kalu N. Kalu, PhD, MBA (*Nigeria*)
Auburn University
Montgomery, Alabama, United States
and Yale University
New Haven, Connecticut, United States

Lois Kisiwaa-Ameyaw (*Ghana*)
Hospital Nutritionist
Ghana

Astrid Knott, PhD, MA (*Germany*)
Minneapolis VA Medical Center
Minneapolis, Minnesota, United States

Gerald Ledlow, PhD, MHA, EMT, FACHE (*United States*)
Georgia Southern University
Jiann-Ping Hsu College of Public Health
Statesboro, Georgia, United States

Katherine H. Leith, PhD, MPH, LMSW (*Germany*)
University of South Carolina
Center for Health Services and Policy Research
Columbia, South Carolina, United States

Carol Linehan, PhD, MA (*Ireland*)
University College Cork
Cork, Ireland

John E. Lopes, Jr., DHSc, MS (*United States*)
Central Michigan University
School of Rehabilitation and Medical Sciences
Mount Pleasant, Michigan, United States

Hala Madanat, PhD, MS, CHES (*Jordan*)
San Diego State University
School of Public Health
San Diego, California, United States

Alexander Mayer, PhD, DrRerOec (*Germany*)
Wuppertal University
Wuppertal, Germany
and Augsburg University
Augsburg, Germany

Linda McCarey, MS, BSN, RN (*Canada*)
Haliburton-Kawrtha-Pine Ridge Health Unit
Port Hope, Ontario, Canada

Puneet Misra, MBBS (MD), MPH, PDGHHM (*India*)
All India Institute of Medical Sciences
New Delhi, India

Michael E. Morris, MPH, MPA, PhD-student (*United States*)
University of Florida
Gainesville, Florida, United States

Chinelo Ogbuanu, MD, MPH (*Nigeria*)
University of South Carolina
Arnold School of Public Health
Columbia, South Carolina, United States

Ikechukwu Ogbuanu, MD, MPH (*Nigeria*)
University of South Carolina
Arnold School of Public Health
Columbia, South Carolina, United States

Elena A. Platonova, PhD, MHA (*Russia*)
University of North Carolina Charlotte
College of Health and Human Services
Charlotte, North Carolina, United States

Lisa Riste, PhD (*United Kingdom*)
University of Manchester
Manchester, England

Hani Michel Samawi, PhD, MSc, MS (*Jordan*)
Georgia Southern University
Jiann-Ping Hsu College of Public Health
Statesboro, Georgia, United States

Alexander V. Sergeev, PhD, MD, MPH (*Russia*)
Ohio University
College of Health and Human Services
Athens, Ohio, United States

Leiyu Shi, DrPH, MBA, MPA (*Taiwan*)
Johns Hopkins University
Bloomberg School of Public Health
Baltimore, Maryland, United States

Douglas A. Singh, PhD, MBA (*United States*)
Indiana University-South Bend
South Bend, Indiana, United States

James H. Stephens, DHA, MHA, FACHE (*United States*)
Georgia Southern University
Jiann-Ping Hsu College of Public Health
Statesboro, Georgia, United States

Carleen H. Stoskopf, ScD, MS (*United States*)
San Diego State University
Graduate School of Public Health
San Diego, California, United States

Michael Tatchell, PhD, MSS (*Australia*)
Pharmacy Guild of Australia
Baron, ACT, Australia

Renny Tatchell, PhD, MA (*New Zealand*)
Central Michigan University
School of Rehabilitation and Medical Sciences
Mount Pleasant, Michigan, United States

Thomas Tatchell, PhD, MA (*United States*)
T Squared Consulting
Mount Pleasant, Michigan, United States

Jenna Tsai, EdD, MAT (*Taiwan*)
Hungkuang University
Shalu, Taichung, Taiwan

Reyhan Ucku, MD, MPH (*Turkey*)
Dokuz Eylul University
School of Medicine
Izmir, Turkey

George Velcz, MBA (*United States*)
St. Jude Children's Research Hospital
Memphis, Tennessee, United States

Matthew Walker, MPH, DrPH-student (*Australia*)
Georgia Southern University
Jiann-Ping Hsu College of Public Health
Statesboro, Georgia, United States

DaNita Weddle, MBA (*United States*)
Pierce, Monroe, and Associates, LLC
Detroit, Michigan, United States

Jörg Westermann, PhD, MA (*Germany*)
Walden University
College of Health Sciences
Minneapolis, Minnesota, United States

Sudha Xirasagar, PhD, MBBS (*India*)
University of South Carolina
Arnold School of Public Health
Columbia, South Carolina, United States

About the Editors

James A. Johnson, PhD, MS, MPA, is a medical social scientist and professor of health administration and international health at the Dow College of Health Professions, Central Michigan University, and adjunct professor of health policy at Auburn University Montgomery. He was previously chairman of the Department of Health Administration and Policy at the Medical University of South Carolina. Dr. Johnson teaches courses in health organization development, international health, systems thinking, and community health. His publications include over 100 journal articles, most of which are peer reviewed, and 13 books on a wide range of healthcare and organizational issues. His most recent books include *Managing Health Promotion and Education Programs* and *Health Organizations: Theory, Behavior, and Development*, published by Jones and Bartlett Publishers. He is also co-editor of the widely used *Handbook of Health Administration and Policy*, published by Marcel-Dekker. Dr. Johnson has also served as editor of the *Journal of Healthcare Man-agement*, published by the American College of Health-care Executives; editor of the *Journal of Management Practice*; and founding editor of the *Carolina Health Services and Policy Review*. He is a contributing editor for the *Journal of Health and Human Services Administration*. He has served on the Board of Directors for the Association of University Programs in Health Administration and the Scientific Advisory Board of the National Diabetes Trust Foundation. Dr. Johnson has worked in over 20 countries, including Tanzania, Zimbabwe, South Africa, Nepal, China, Belize, and Mexico and has lectured at Oxford University (England), University of Dublin (Ireland), Beijing University (China), and University of Colima (Mexico). He also works on projects with the WHO and the ProWorld Service Corps-Belize and is active in the Organization Development Institute. He completed his PhD in 1987 at the Askew School of Public Policy and Administration at Florida State University and his MPA in health administration at Auburn University Montgomery.

Carleen H. Stoskopf, ScD, MS, is the Director of the Graduate School of Public Health at San Diego State University, after serving in an academic appointment at the University of South Carolina, Arnold School of Public Health for 19 years, advancing chair of the Department of Health Services Policy and Management. Dr. Stoskopf has served as a Fellow of the Accrediting Commission on Education for Health Services Administration. Dr. Stoskopf's areas of teaching include financing and reimbursement in healthcare systems and decision making. At the University of South Carolina, she was Director of Doctoral Programs and developed two additional doctoral programs in Asia, specifically Taiwan and South Korea. Prior to entering her career in academia, Dr. Stoskopf served in the U.S. Navy as an Environmental Health Officer with the Third Marine Aircraft Wing at El Toro, California and as Chief of the Preventive Medicine Service at the Naval Regional Medical Center in Okinawa, Japan. She was honorably discharged as a Lieutenant, USN in 1982. She also is also a Registered Sanitarian with the State of California.

International health has been an area of interest, and Dr. Stoskopf has worked for a variety of agencies in countries such as Haiti, Kenya, South Africa, the United Arab Emirates, People's Republic of China, the Republic of China, Republic of South Korea, the Republic of Georgia, Kazakhstan, Ukraine, and Russia. Dr. Stoskopf's activities have ranged from lecturing, providing healthcare management training for U.S. AID, healthcare management curriculum reviews, public health assessments, HIV/AIDS research, and hospital management consultation. Dr. Stoskopf has been an active researcher, conducting studies on access, utilization, and outcomes. Specific areas of research include disparities in vulnerable populations such as persons living with HIV/AIDS, those persons living with a mental illness, those living in poverty, older persons, and blacks living in the southern United States. Dr. Stoskopf has received funding from the National Institutes of Health, the U.S. Centers for Disease Control, the Health Resources and Services Administration, as well as a number of state and local agencies and foundations. Dr. Stoskopf has authored over 45 peer-reviewed journal articles. She completed her ScD in 1989 at Johns Hopkins Bloomberg School of Public Health and her MS in environmental health from the University of Minnesota School of Public Health.

Global Health and Health Systems

CHAPTER 1

Introduction to Health Systems

Carleen H. Stoskopf and
James A. Johnson

INTRODUCTION

A health system as described by the World Health Organization (WHO) is the sum total of all the organizations, institutions, and resources whose primary purpose is to improve health. A health system needs staff, funds, information, supplies, transport, communications, and overall guidance and direction. Furthermore, it needs to provide services that are responsive and financially fair, while treating people decently.[1]

Within this definition, there are several concepts that need to be understood before one embarks on the task of studying health systems. First and foremost, an agreed-on definition of health is paramount. Health is too often seen as a concept that applies only to physical well-being or the absence of disease; however, the most widely accepted definition of health is the one first published by the WHO in 1947. It states, "Health is a state of complete physical, mental, and social well being and not merely the absence of disease and infirmity."[2] This comprehensive concept of health is the one used in this book and serves to inform discussions on health systems.

The other key word that needs to be explored here is the word "system." The human body is a system comprised of many physiological subsystems that are interconnected in a holistic way. The subsystems, including respiratory, circulatory, neurological, endocrine, and musculoskeletal systems, communicate and are interdependent. They work together for the purposes of survival, adaptation, growth, and development. They also interact with the environment and respond to feedback from within and outside the system. In many ways, the interconnectivity of the various subsystems and its extension as a whole into the environment form the building blocks of larger systems such as family, community, and nation. Thus, a natural (biological) system such as a human being is also a participant in and creator of larger social systems. The human-created systems have many of the same attributes of biological systems. Additionally, it can be said that these larger systems are characterized by

- A structure that is defined by its parts and processes.
- Generalizations of reality.
- A tendency to function in the same way. This involves the inputs (material, human resources, finances, etc.) and outputs (products and services)

that are then processed, causing them to change in some way.

- The various parts of a system, which have functional as well as structural relationships between each other.

Human-created systems can be small, as in the three-person family, or quite large, as in a nation state such as India with a billion people. The most widely dispersed human-created systems are organizations. As with the other examples described previously, organizations share the same attributes and adapt accordingly to their environments. In fact, organizations are complex human systems that have evolved over time and continue to do so.[3] The natural emergence of human-created systems, such as organizations and communities, probably grew out of instinct for survival. In the hostile world of

early humankind, food, shelter, and safety needs usually required cooperative efforts. In turn, cooperative efforts typically require some form of organization.[4] This is no less true in the case of providing health. In order to meet the criteria of health as a state of complete physical, mental, and social well-being, individuals, communities, organizations, and nation states have worked together to form elaborate and diverse health systems throughout the world.

As with any system, a health system has inputs. These include financial, material, and human resources that differentiate one health system from another. The data in Table 1-1 clearly demonstrate some of these differences.

One of the major "inputs" into any healthcare system is patients. Patients present with a variety of symptoms/diseases/injuries; however, they also come with a myriad of characteristics such as personality, life

TABLE 1-1 Select Health System Financial Input Data (in U.S. dollars)

Total global expenditure for health	**$4.1 trillion plus**
Total global expenditure for health per person per year	**$639**
Country with highest total spending per person per year on health	**United States ($6,103)**
Country with lowest total spending per person per year on health	**Burundi ($2.90)**
Country with highest government spending per person per year on health	**Norway ($4,508)**
Country with lowest government spending per person per year on health	**Burundi ($0.70)**
Country with highest annual out-of-pocket household spending on health	**Switzerland ($1,787)**
Country with lowest annual out-of-pocket household spending on health	**Solomon Islands ($1.00)**
Average amount spent per person per year on health in countries belonging to the Organisation for Economic Co-operation and Development	**$2,716**
Percentage of the world's population living in Organisation for Economic Co-operation and Development countries	**18%**
Annual spending by the municipal government of New York City on health for its 8.2 million residents	**$429 million**
Annual spending by the government of Bénin on health for its 8.2 million citizens	**$86 million**
WHO estimate of minimum spending per person per year needed to provide basic, life-saving services	**$35 to $50**
Number of countries where total health spending is lower than $50 per person per year	**64**
Number of countries where health spending is lower than $20 per person per year	**30**

Author created using 2004 WHO data.

experiences, knowledge, attitudes, cultural norms, education level, income level, intellect, prejudice, religious and other belief systems, emotions, biological strengths and weaknesses, and genetic makeup. In addition, patients may or may not be plugged into society's infrastructure, such as having access to transportation, childcare, or health insurance. The complexity these many factors create cannot be overlooked by healthcare systems nor should they be overlooked by health policy makers. It has been well established that income is perhaps one of the best predictors of health. The income gradient within a population is highly associated with health status of individuals or groups in that population, and the per capita incomes and the gross domestic product (GDP) of nations are also highly correlated with the health status of that country's population. Taken from this perspective, health policy makes us also be concerned with poverty and lifting populations out of poverty through social policies designed to improve education, housing, infrastructure, job creation, and the environment.

Health systems arise within a social, cultural, political, and economic context. As with all human constructed systems, there is considerable diversity in size, scope, and form. As a result, health systems have structure, processes, and outcomes that vary considerably. Table 1-2 shows some of the variation along these three dimensions for a select group of countries. As you can

TABLE 1-2 Financial and Healthcare Resources for Selected Countries

	GDP per Capita, 2002–2006 Estimates in U.S. Dollars	GNP 2005 per Capita, in U.S. Dollars	Number of Persons per Physician, 2004	Number of Persons per Hospital Bed, 2004	Nurses per 1,000 Persons, 2001–2004	Infant Mortality Rate per 1,000 Live Births, 2004
Argentina	15,200	4,470	213	244	0.8	14.4
Australia	33,300	26,900	369	251	9.1	4.7
Belize	8,400	3,500	1,348	406	1.26	6.3
Brazil	8,800	3,460	485	371	3.84	29.6
Cambodia	2,700	380	6,169	1,405	0.61	68.8
Canada	35,600	32,600	476	274	9.95	4.8
China	7,700	1,740	673	425	1.05	25.3
Egypt	4,200	1,250	448	414	1.98	32.6
France	31,100	34,810	296	132	7.24	3.6
Germany	31,900	34,580	270	155	9.72	4.1
Ghana	2,700	380	21,086	1,089	0.74	57.7
India	3,800	620	1,853	1,139	0.8	57.9
Indonesia	3,900	1,140	9,871	1,697	0.57	36.8
Japan	33,100	36,460	472	78	7.79	2.7
Jordan	5,100	2,140	448	577	2.94	22
Kenya	1,200	530	6,623	485	1.18	61.5
Mexico	10,700	7,310	734	1,346	0.9	12.5
Nigeria	1,500	560	3,069	1,747	1.03	98.8
Panama	8,200	4,630	715	408	2.77	16.7

(continues)

TABLE 1-2   Financial and Healthcare Resources for Selected Countries   (continued)

	GDP per Capita, 2002–2006 Estimates in U.S. Dollars	GNP 2005 per Capita, in U.S. Dollars	Number of Persons per Physician, 2004	Number of Persons per Hospital Bed, 2004	Nurses per 1,000 Persons, 2001–2004	Infant Mortality Rate per 1,000 Live Births, 2004
Peru	6,600	2,610	651	643	0.67	31.9
Portugal	19,800	14,350	310	268	4.36	3.8
Russia	12,200	4,460	211	91	8.05	11.5
St. Lucia	4,800	4,310	1,740	562	2.28	14
Senegal	1,800	710	17,533	2,500	0.25	62.7
South Africa	13,300	4,960	1,438	290	4.08	53.6
South Korea	24,500	15,830	606	151	1.75	7.3
Turkey	9,000	4,710	718	414	1.70	23.6
U.K.	31,800	37,600	492	257	12.12	5.1
U.S.	44,000	43,740	334	301	9.37	6.4

Adapted from Global Health Facts (http://globalhealthfacts.org) and Encyclopedia Britannica Online Academic Edition, World Data, 2007.

see, financial and human resource inputs do interrelate with health outcomes.

BUILDING BLOCKS OF HEALTH SYSTEMS

Even though every health system is unique in its given social and cultural environment, it has common elements that are necessary to function. These building blocks not only help us to understanding health systems better but also provide opportunities for system improvement. The WHO, the World Bank, and various governments around the world have a common understanding of these key elements. Some would describe them as critical success factors that are essential to a health system's survival (Table 1-3).

One widely accepted way of measuring the building blocks or the overall functioning of a health system is through the lens of cost, quality, and access. The cost, quality, access triangle is shown in Figure 1-1.

In the era of rapid globalization and change, it is becoming increasingly prudent to add a fourth dimen-sion, innovation. This results in a cost, quality, access, innovation diamond as shown in Figure 1-2.

HEALTH SYSTEMS WITHIN LARGER SOCIAL SYSTEMS

Ron Andersen proposed a model in the 1960s that sought to identify some of the factors that influence whether a patient even accesses healthcare services. His model identifies three main components: predisposing factors, enabling factors, and need factors. Predisposing factors included family characteristics, social structure, and health beliefs. Enabling factors included family resources and community resources. The "need" factors included illness and the response to illness. This work was expanded into the "Behavioral Model for Vulnerable Populations." This model is presented in Figure 1-3. Understanding the characteristics of the population a health system serves is key to designing the system processes, providing adequate and appropriate resources, and having clear expectations for the right outcomes.

TABLE 1-3   Health Systems Building Blocks (Critical Success Factors)

Service Delivery	Medical Technology
Good health services are those that deliver effective, safe, quality personal and non-personal health interventions to those who need them, when and where needed, with minimum waste of resources.	A well-functioning health system ensures equitable access to essential medical products, drugs, vaccines, and technologies of assured quality, safety, efficacy, and cost-effectiveness, and their scientifically sound and cost-effective use.
Health Workforce	**Health Financing**
A well-performing health workforce is one that works in ways that are responsive, fair, and efficient to achieve the best health outcomes possible, given available resources and circumstances (i.e., there are sufficient staff, fairly distributed; they are competent, responsive, and productive).	A good health financing system raises adequate funds for health, in ways that ensure people can use needed services and are protected from financial catastrophe or impoverishment associated with having to pay for them. It provides incentives for providers and users to be efficient.
Health Information	**Leadership and Governance**
A well-functioning health information system is one that ensures the production, analysis, dissemination, and use of reliable and timely information on health determinants, health system performance, and health status.	Leadership and governance involves ensuring that strategic policy frameworks exist and are combined with effective oversight, coalition building, regulation, attention to system design, and accountability.

Author created from WHO framework.

The notion that one's social circumstances, or socio-economic status, can influence one's health was a notion coming into its own. In recent decades, social science researchers have laid the groundwork for further exploration for this relationship. It is thought that social circumstances lead to disease in individuals and populations via three pathways: behavioral, material, and psychological. The premise is that social circumstances such as socioeconomic status based on income and education influences behaviors. For example, smoking is a behavior more often found in persons with low socioeconomic status. Smoking then has a direct impact on health status as the incidences of lung cancer, emphysema, asthma, and other respiratory illnesses are higher among smokers. Other behaviors that are believed to be associated with lower socioeconomic status are under study and include such behaviors as drinking, risky sexual behavior, drug use, and violence.

A second pathway is material circumstances associated with deprivation. Persons living with a substantially lower income are unable to provide for the most basic needs, such as adequate food, shelter, and safety. As a result, some segments of the population suffer from malnutrition, inadequate home heating and warm clothing, and environmental exposures and are more exposed to community violence. These factors in turn result in lower health status through increased exposure to infectious diseases due to overcrowding, malnutrition, limited

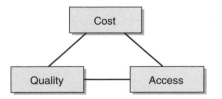

FIGURE 1-1   The Cost, Quality, Access Triangle

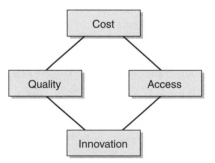

FIGURE 1-2   The Cost, Quality, Access, Innovation Diamond

Select World Health Trends and Health Systems Implications

Population Aging

A demographic revolution is under way throughout the world. Today, there are around 600 million people in the world aged 60 years and older. This total will double by 2025, and by 2050, it will reach 2 billion, the vast majority of whom will be in the developing world. Such accelerated global population aging will increase economic and social demands on all countries.

Although the consequences of population aging in the areas of health and income security are already at the center of discussions by policy makers and planners in the developed world, the speed and impact of population aging in the less developed regions are yet to be fully appreciated. By 2025, in countries such as Brazil, China, and Thailand, the proportion of older people will be above 15% of the population, whereas in Colombia, Indonesia, and Kenya, the absolute numbers will increase by up to 400% over the next 25 years—up to eight times higher than the increases in already aged societies in western Europe where population aging occurred over a much longer period of time.

Population aging is related to two factors: a decline in the proportion of children, reflecting declines in fertility rates in the overall population, and an increase in the proportion of adults 60 years of age and older as mortality rates decline. This demographic transition will bring with it a number of major challenges for health and social policy planners.

Improving health systems and their responses to population aging makes economic sense. With old-age dependency ratios increasing in virtually all countries of the world, the economic contributions and productive roles of older people will assume greater importance. Supporting people to remain healthy and ensure a good quality of life in their later years is one of the greatest challenges for the health sector in both developed and developing countries.

The Burden of Mental Illness

A large proportion of individuals do not receive any health care for their condition because (1) the mental health infrastructure and services in most countries are grossly insufficient for the large and growing needs and (2) widely prevalent stigma and discrimination prevent them from seeking help. A policy for mental health care is lacking in 40% of countries, and 25% of those with a policy assign no budget to implement it. Even where a budget exists, it is very small: 36% of countries devote less than 1% of their total health resources to mental health care. Although community-based services are recognized to be the most effective, 65% of all psychiatric beds are still in mental hospitals—cutting into the already meager budgets while providing largely custodial care in an environment that may infringe patients' basic human rights.

Cost-effective healthcare interventions are available. Recent research clearly demonstrates that disorders such as depression, schizophrenia, alcohol problems, and epilepsy can be treated within primary health care. Such treatment is well within the reach of even low-income countries and will reduce substantially the overall burden of these disorders. Interventions rely on inexpensive medicines that are commonly available and, for the most part, free of patent restrictions and that require only basic training of health professionals.

Injuries—A Hidden Epidemic of Young Men

Injuries, both unintentional and intentional, primarily affect young adults, often resulting in severe, disabling consequences. Overall, injuries accounted for over 14% of adult disease burden in the world in 2002. In parts of the Americas, Eastern Europe, and the Eastern Mediterranean region, more than 30% of the entire disease burden among male adults aged 15 to 44 years is attributable to injuries.

Air Quality

Millions of families in the world exist in environmental hazards. They are exposed to harsh weather, poor ventilation, little light, and the need for constant repair. These conditions are especially oppressive for children—their bodies, their growth and development, and their dreams. We need to find the ways to strengthen links between health and environment and integrate our work to improve quality of life in the region.

Contributed by DaNita Weddle

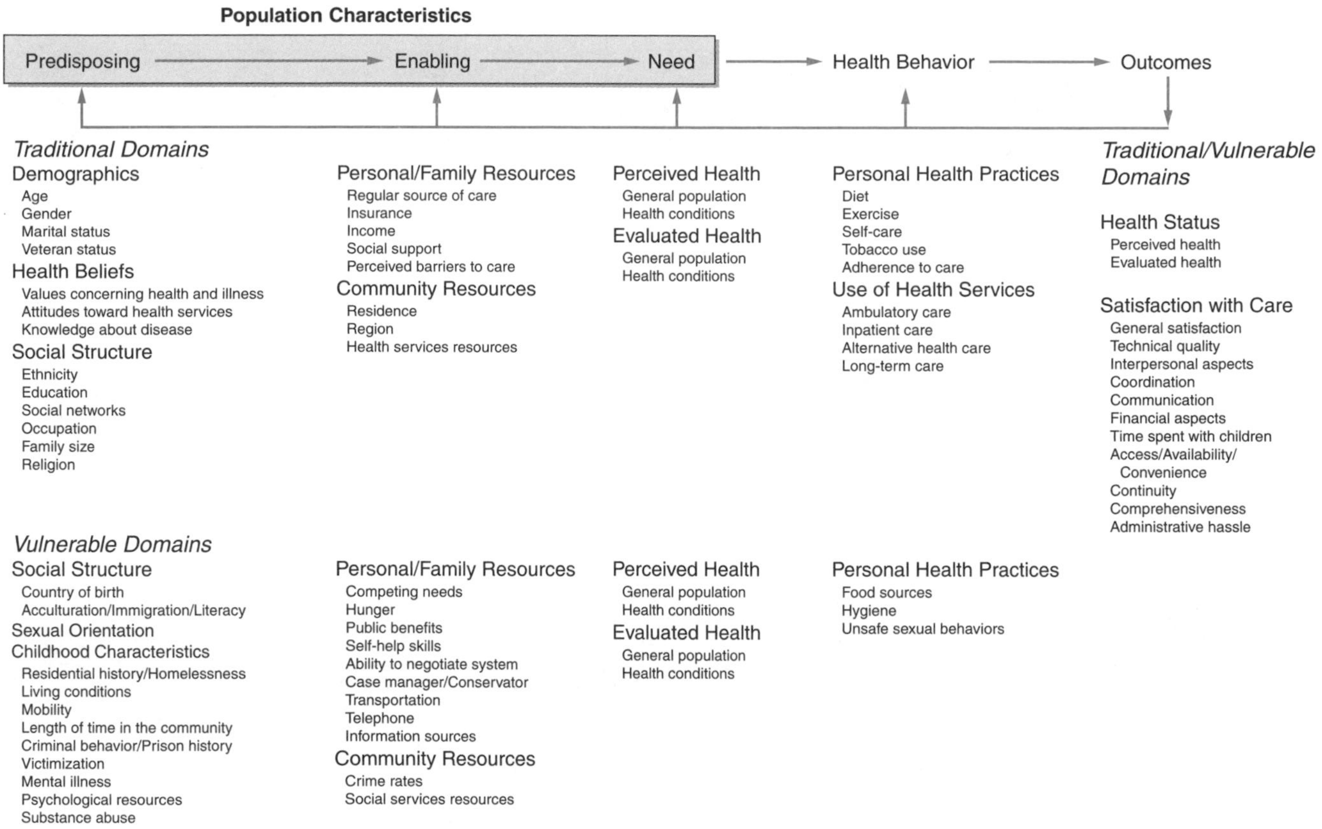

Population Characteristics

Predisposing ————————→ Enabling ————→ Need ————→ Health Behavior ————→ Outcomes

Traditional Domains

Demographics
Age
Gender
Marital status
Veteran status
Health Beliefs
Values concerning health and illness
Attitudes toward health services
Knowledge about disease
Social Structure
Ethnicity
Education
Social networks
Occupation
Family size
Religion

Personal/Family Resources
Regular source of care
Insurance
Income
Social support
Perceived barriers to care
Community Resources
Residence
Region
Health services resources

Perceived Health
General population
Health conditions
Evaluated Health
General population
Health conditions

Personal Health Practices
Diet
Exercise
Self-care
Tobacco use
Adherence to care
Use of Health Services
Ambulatory care
Inpatient care
Alternative health care
Long-term care

Traditional/Vulnerable Domains

Health Status
Perceived health
Evaluated health

Satisfaction with Care
General satisfaction
Technical quality
Interpersonal aspects
Coordination
Communication
Financial aspects
Time spent with children
Access/Availability/
  Convenience
Continuity
Comprehensiveness
Administrative hassle

Vulnerable Domains

Social Structure
Country of birth
Acculturation/Immigration/Literacy
Sexual Orientation
Childhood Characteristics
Residential history/Homelessness
Living conditions
Mobility
Length of time in the community
Criminal behavior/Prison history
Victimization
Mental illness
Psychological resources
Substance abuse

Personal/Family Resources
Competing needs
Hunger
Public benefits
Self-help skills
Ability to negotiate system
Case manager/Conservator
Transportation
Telephone
Information sources
Community Resources
Crime rates
Social services resources

Perceived Health
General population
Health conditions
Evaluated Health
General population
Health conditions

Personal Health Practices
Food sources
Hygiene
Unsafe sexual behaviors

FIGURE 1-3   The Behavioral Model for Vulnerable Populations

Gelberg L, Andersen RM, Leake BD. The Behavioral Model for Vulnerable Populations: Application to Medical Care Use and Outcomes for Homeless People. *Health Services Research*. 2000;34(6):1278.

access to appropriate medical care, exposure to pollutants both in the community and in substandard housing, and an increased risk of being a victim of violence.

The third pathway, the psychosocial pathway, is more complex. This pathway requires a connection between social structure and health. Extensive research has resulted in establishing mechanisms that make the connection between social structures, stress, and biology, or the "psychobiological stress response."

Although stress can be an important factor in survival in a "fight or flight" scenario, if prolonged stress occurs and the body no longer can return to homeostasis quickly, long-term effects on health can occur, including cardiovascular disease, cancer, infection, and cognitive decline.

A number of social determinants and social conditions have been studied to ascertain whether there is an association between these factors and health status of both individuals and populations. Table 1-4 summarizes some of the major findings in the literature.

CONCLUSION

As health systems continue to evolve in every country in the world, we will see many variations. Some will follow predictable pathways that reflect local government structure, and others will form uniquely according to cultural and social forces. All systems, regardless of locale, will be challenged by changes in economics and pressures to provide services based on measures of cost, quality, and access. As indicated in the last section of this chapter, health systems do not exist in a vacuum because they are profoundly influenced by a range of social determinants of health. The determinants shape demand on services and the range of options that need to be provided within the system. They also influence the kinds of medical practitioners needed, as well as appropriate levels of education. Finally, in the context of growing populations and diverse demands, health systems will need to find ways to adapt to globalization and meet the push for greater sustainability.

TABLE 1-4 A Summary of Some of the Social Determinants of Health Status in the Literature

Social Determinant	Mediating Factor(s)	Health Status > Increased < Decreased	Reference
Unemployment		< Health status	5–7
Employment		> Health status	8
Unemployment	Financial stress	< Health status	9, 10
Unemployment	Psychological stress	< Health status	11–13
Unemployment	Health-damaging behavior	< Health status	14–16
Poor work environment		Ill health Poor health status	17, 18
Psychosocial work environment	Job demand/control (low efficacy)	< Health status	19, 20
Psychosocial work environment	Effort–reward imbalance (low self-esteem)	< Health status	21
Psychosocial work environment		Social gradient of ill health	22–29
Transportation	Traffic-related accidents	< Health status	30
Transportation	Air pollution	> Respiratory illnesses	31
Transportation	Noise	< Health status	32
Social support		> Health status < Health status	33, 34
Social support	Moderating effects	> Health status	35–38
Inadequate nutrition		< Health status	39, 40
Proper nutrition		> Health status	41
Poor nutrition		> Obesity	42, 43
Poverty		< Health status > Mortality	44–46
Poverty	Material deprivation	< Health status	47–50
Poverty	Social deprivation	< Health status	51–53
Poverty	Unemployment	< Health status	54
Poverty	Inequity	< Health status	51, 55, 56
Poverty	Social exclusion	< Health status	57
Poverty	Minorities and/or refugees	< Health status	20, 58–60
Poverty	Homelessness	< Health status < Mental health status	61–63

(continues)

TABLE 1-4 A Summary of Some of the Social Determinants of Health Status in the Literature (continued)

Social Determinant	Mediating Factor(s)	Health Status > Increased < Decreased	Reference
Ethnic groupings		< Health status > Health status > Mortality < Mortality	64–71
Ethnicity	Income	> Health status < Health status	72
Ethnicity	Maternal education	> Health status < Health status	64
Ethnicity	Education level	> Health status < Health status	73–75
Ethnicity	Experience of racial harassment and discrimination	< Health status	76–78
Neighborhood environment		> Health status < Health status	79–81
Neighborhood environment	Physical environment	> Health status < Health status	82–86
Neighborhood environment	Social environment	> Health status < Health status	87–89
Neighborhood environment	Amenities	> Health status < Health status	90, 91
Sexual behavior		< Health status > Health status	92, 93
Sexual behavior	Increased rate of partner change	< Health status	94
Sexual behavior	Increased variation in sexual behavior	< Health status	92
Sexual behavior	Demography	> Health status < Health status	95, 96
Sexual behavior	Social disruption (war)	< Health status	97

Social Determinants of Health: Birth and Infancy as an Example

Research has shown that early life circumstance is one of the more important predictors of health status. In the 1970s, it was established that malnutrition in a pregnant woman has a direct impact on the health and well-being of her fetus and hence its susceptibility to low birth weight. Further research has demonstrated that undernutrition for a fetus results in long-term changes in physiology, metabolism, and structure. Research has shown that poor nutrition, smoking, alcohol consumption, atmospheric pollution, and infections associated with a pregnant mother are also associated with low birth weight. Low birth weight in turn is related to poor growth in children and is eventually associated with poor adult health. The accumulation of risk occurs when both poor growth and poor socioeconomic status interact to create a lifetime of poor social and health status or when adverse circumstances and health in early life, coupled with a negative health event at an older age, result in poor adult health.

Some studies have found that although poor growth in early childhood is associated with poor health in adulthood, mitigating circumstances can overcome some of these effects. Improvement in social conditions can result in better health and performance later in life. When parents improve their social condition, and attain higher levels of education, their low birth weight children have less of an association with poor health and other types of attainment as adults and achieve higher levels of cognitive development. These results may be due to improved nutrition or parental stimulation.

The phenomenon of "social accumulation" is also important in understanding the complexity of inputs into the health system. Social accumulation is due to the fact that both disadvantage and advantage tend to accumulate throughout a lifetime and can even be transgenerational. For example, a mother of lower social economic status is more likely to have a low birth weight baby, who in turn is more likely to be exposed to more environmental hazards, have poorer nutrition and less education, attain less in school, and emerge as an adult with poorer health status and the same disadvantages as those that he or she experienced in childhood. This disadvantage is then experienced by their children. The same is true for those who are advantaged. It is further found that when a person crosses social economic boundaries, his or her health status changes in accordance with the direction of change.

REFERENCES

1. Marmot M. Social determinants of health inequalities. *Lancet.* 2005;365:1099–1104.

2. Krieger N. Theories for social epidemiology in the 21st century: an ecosocial perspective. *International Journal of Epidemiology.* 2001;30:668–677.

3. Andersen RM. *Families' Use of Health Services: A Behavioral Model of Predisposing, Enabling, and Need Components.* Purdue, IN: Purdue University; 1968.

4. Gelberg L, Andersen RM, Leake BD. The behavioral model for vulnerable populations: application to medical care use and outcomes for homeless people. *Health Services Research.* 2000;34(6):1273–1302.

5. Korpi W. Accumulating disadvantage: longitudinal analyses of unemployment and physical health in representative samples of the Swedish population. *European Sociological Review.* 2001;17(3):255–274.

6. Warr P. Reported behaviour changes after job loss. *British Journal of Social Psychology.* 1984;23(3):271–275.

7. Montgomery SM, Cook DG, Barley MJ, Wadsworth ME. Unemployment predates symptoms of depression and anxiety resulting in medical consultation in young men. *International Journal of Epidemiology.* 1999;28(1):95–100.

8. Jenkins R, Lewis G, Bebbington P, Brugha T, Farrell M, Gill B. The National Psychiatric Morbidity Surveys of Great Britain: initial findings from the household survey. *Psychological Medicine.* 1997;27(4):775–789.

9. Heady P, Smyth M. *Living Standards During Unemployment.* London: HMSO; 1989.

10. Kressler RC, Turner JB, House JS. Intervening processes in the relationship between unemployment and health. *Psychological Medicine.* 1987;17(4):949–961.

11. Isaksson K. Unemployment, mental health and the psychological functions of work in male and welfare clients in Stockholm. *Scandinavian Social Medicine.* 1989;17(2):165–169.

12. Jahoda M. The impact of unemployment in the 1930s and the 1970s. *Bulletin of British Psychological Medicine.* 1979;32:309–314.

13. Fryer D. Monmouthshire and Marienthal: sociographies of two unemployed communities. In Fryer D, Ullah P, eds. *Unemployed People.* New York: Open University Press; 1987.

14. Cook DG, Cummins RO, Bartley MJ, Shaper AG. Health of unemployed middle-aged men in Great Britain. *Lancet.* 1982;1(8284):1290–1294.

15. Power C, Estaugh V. Employment and drinking in early adulthood. *British Journal of Addiction.* 1990;85:487–494.

16. Morris JK, Cook DG, Shaper AG. Non-employment and changes in smoking, drinking, and body weight. *British Medical Journal.* 1992;304(6826):536–541.

17. Schilling RSF. Health protection and promotion at work. *British Journal of Industrial Medicine.* 1989;6:683–688.

18. Morris JN, Heady JA, Raffle PAB, Roberts CG, Parks JW. Coronary heart disease and physical activity of work. *Lancet.* 1953;II:1053–1057.

19. Karasek R, Theorell T. *Healthy Work: Stress, Productivity, and the Reconstruction of Working Life.* New York: Basic Books; 1990.

20. Marmot MG, Shipley MJ, Rose G. Inequalities in death: specific explanations of a general pattern. *Lancet.* 1984;323: 1003–1006.

21. Siegrist J. Adverse health effects of high-effort/low-effort reward conditions. *Journal of Occupational Health and Psychology.* 1996;1:27–41.

22. Kohn M, Schooler C. Occupational experience and psychological functioning: an assessment of reciprocal effects. *American Sociological Review.* 1973;38:97–118.

23. Gardell B. Alienation and mental health in the modern industrial environment. In Levi L, ed. *Society, Stress and Disease: The Psychosocial Environment and Psychomatic Disease.* London: Oxford University Press; 1971.

24. Karasek RA. Job demands, job decision latitude and mental strain; implications for job design. *Administrative Science Quarterly.* 1979;24:285–308.

25. Belkic KL, Landsbergis PA, Schnall PL, Baker D. Is job strain a major source of cardiovascular disease risk? *Scandinavian Journal of Work Environment Health.* 2004;30(2): 85–128.

26. Hemingway H, Marmot M. Psychosocial factors in the primary and secondary prevention of coronary heart disease: a systematic review. In Yusuf S, Cairns J, Camm J, Fallen E, Gersch B, eds. *Evidence Based Cardiology.* London: BMJ Publishing Group; 1998.

27. Schnall P, Belkic K, Pickering TG. Assessment of the cardiovascular system as the workplace. *Occupational Medicine.* 2002;15(1):189–212.

28. Kuper H, Singh-Manoux, A, Siegrist J, Marmot M. When reciprocity fails: effort–reward imbalance in relation to coronary heart disease and health functioning within the Whitehall II Study. *Occupational and Environmental Medicine.* 2002;59(11):777–784.

29. Marmot MG, Davey Smith G, et al. Health inequities among British civil servants: the Whitehall II Study. *Lancet.* 1991;337:1387–1393.

30. Peden M, et al., eds. *The World Report on Road Traffic Injury Prevention.* Geneva: World Health Organization; 2004.

31. Schwartz J. Health effects of air pollution from traffic: ozone and particulate matter. In Fletcher T, McMichael AJ, eds. *Health at the Crossroads: Transport Policy and Urban Health.* London: John Wiley and Sons; 1997.

32. Stansfeld SA, Haines MM, Burr M, Berry B, Lercher P. A review of environmental noise and mental health. *Noise and Health.* 2000;2:1–8.

33. Pahl R. Some special comments on the relationship between social support and well-being. *Leisure Studies.* 2003; 22:1–12.

34. Cohen S, Syme SL, eds. *Social Support and Health.* London: Academic Press; 1985.

35. Cobb S. Social support as a moderator of life stress. *Psychosomatic Medicine.* 1976;38:300–313.

36. Cornman JC, Goldman N, Glei DA, Weinstein M, Chang MC. Social ties and perceived support: two dimensions of social relationships and health among the elderly in Taiwan. *Journal of Aging Health.* 2003;15:616–644.

37. Coyne JC, Downey G. Social factors and psychopathology: stress, social support, and coping processes. *Annual Review of Psychology.* 1991;42:401–405.

38. Fuhrer R, Stansfeld SA, Hudry-Chemali J, Shipley MJ. Gender social relations and mental health: prospective findings from an occupational cohort (Whitehall II Study). *Social Science Medicine.* 1999;48:77–87.

39. Brunner EJ, Rayner M, Thorogood M, et al. Making public health nutrition relevant to evidence-based action. *Public Health Nutrition.* 2001;4:1297–1299. Retrieved from http://www.nutritionreviews.org.

40. Nelson M. Nutrition and health inequalities. In Gordon D, et al., eds. *Inequalities in Health: Studies in Poverty, Inequality and Social Exclusion.* University of Bristol: Policy Press; 1999.

41. De Irala-Estevez J, Groth M, Johansson L, Oltersdorf U, Prattala R, Martinez-Gonzalez MA. A systematic review of social-economic differences in food habit in Europe: consumption of fruit and vegetables. *European Journal of Clinical Nutrition.* 2000;54:706–714.

42. Martinez JA, Kearney JM, Kafatos A, Paquet S, Martinez-Gonzalez MA. Variables independently associated with self-reported obesity in the European union. *Public Health Nutrition.* 1999;2(1a):125–133.

43. Pan-American Health Organization. *Obesity and Poverty: A New Public Health Challenge.* PAHO Sc. Publ. no. 576, Washington; 2000.

44. Kunst AE, Guerts JJM, van der Berg J. International variation in socioeconomic inequalities in self reported health. *Journal of Epidemiology and Community Health.* 1995;49:117–123.

45. MackenbackJP, Huisman M, Andersen O, et al. Inequities in lung cancer mortality by the educational level in 10 European populations. *European Journal of Cancer.* 2004;40:126–135.

46. Davey Smith G, Dorling D, Shaw M. *Poverty, Inequality and Health in Britain: 1800–2000: A Reader.* Bristol: The Policy Press; 2001.

47. Ineichen B. *Homes and Health: How Housing and Health Interact.* London: Chapman and Hall; 1993.

48. Davey Smith G, Blane D, Bartley M. Explanations for socioeconomic differences in mortality: evidence from Britain and elsewhere. *European Journal of Public Health.* 1994; 4(2):131–144.

49. Shaw M, Dorling D, Gordon D, Davey Smith G. *The Widening Gap: Health Inequalities and Policy in Britain.* Bristol: The Policy Press; 1999.

50. Shaw M. Housing and public health. *Annual Reviews in Public Health.* 2004;25:397–418.

51. Davey Smith G, Dorling D, Mitchell R, Shaw M. Health inequalities in Britain: continuing increases up to the end of the 20th century. *Journal of Epidemiology and Community Health.* 2002;56:434–435.

52. Blackburn C. *Poverty and Health: Working with Families.* Buckingham: Open University Press; 1991.

53. Graham H. Cigarette smoking: a light on gender and class inequality in Britain? *Journal of Social Policy.* 1995:24(4): 509–527.

54. Bartley M, Plewis I. Accumulated labour market disadvantage and limiting long-term illness: data from the 1971–1991 Office for National Statistics' Longitudinal Study. *International Journal of Epidemiology.* 2002;31:336–341.

55. McLoone P, Boddy FA. Deprivation and mortality in Scotland; 1981 and 1991. *British Medical Journal.* 1994;309: 1465–1470.

56. Phillimore P, Beattie A, Townsend P. Widening inequality of health in northern England; 1981–1991. *British Medical Journal.* 1994;308:1125–1128.

57. White P. Urban life and social stress. In De Pinder, ed. *The New Europe: Economy, Society and Environment.* Chichester: Wiley; 1998.

58. Corvalan CF, Driscoll TR, Harrison JE. Role of migrant factors in work-related fatalities in Australia. *Scandinavian Journal of Work Environment Health.* 1994;20(5):364–370.

59. Trovato F. Violent and accidental mortality among four immigrant groups in Canada. *Social Biology.* 1992;39(1):82–101.

60. Nazroo J. The racialization of ethnic inequalities in health. In Dorling D, Simpson S. *Statistics in Society.* London: Arnold; 1998.

61. Darbyshire JH. Tuberculosis: old reasons for a new increase? *British Medical Journal.* 1995;310:954–955.

62. Gill B, Meltzer H, Hinds K, Petticrew M. *Psychiatric Morbidity Among Homeless People. OPCS Surveys of Psychiatric Morbidity in Great Britain.* London: HMSO; 1996.

63. Folsom D, Jeste DV. Schizophrenia in homeless persons: a systematic review of the literature. *Acta Psychiatry in Scandinavia.* 2002;105:404–413.

64. Pamuk E, MaKuc D, Heck K, Reuben C, Lochner K. *Socioeconomic Status and Health Chartbook, Health, United States, 1998.* Hyattsville, MD: National Center for Health Statistics; 1998.

65. Williams DR, Neighbors HW. Racism, discrimination and hypertension: evidence and needed research. *Ethnicity and Disease.* 2001;11:800–816.

66. Harding S, Maxwell R. Differences in the mortality of migrants. In Drever F, Whitehead M, eds. *Health Inequalities: Decennial Supplement Series DS no. 15.* London: The Stationery Office; 1997.

67. Sorlie PD, Backlund E, Keller J. U.S. mortality by economic, demographic and social characteristics: The National Longitudinal Mortality Study. *American Journal of Public Health.* 1995;85:949–956.

68. Erens B, Primatesta P, Prior G. *Health Survey for England 1999: The Health of Minority Ethnic Groups.* London: The Stationery Office; 2001.

69. Sidiropoulos E, Jeffery A, Mackay S, Forgey H, Chipps C, Corrigan T. *South Africa Survey 1996/1997.* Johannesburg, South Africa: South African Institute of Race Relations; 1997.

70. Pan American Health Organization. *Equity in Health: From an Ethnic Perspective.* Washington, DC: Pan American Health Organization; 2001.

71. McLennan W, Madden R. *The Health and Welfare of Australia's Aboriginal and Torres Strait Islander Peoples.* Commonwealth of Australia: Australian Bureau of Statistics; 1999.

72. Nazroo JY. *The Health of Britain's Ethnic Minorities: Findings from a National Survey.* London: Policy Studies Institute; 1997.

73. Jaynes GD, Williams RM. *A Common Destiny: Blacks and American Society.* Washington DC: National Academy Press; 1989.

74. Orfield G. The growth of segregation: African Americans, Latinos, and unequal education. In Orfield G, Eaton ES, eds. *Dismantling Desegregation: The Quiet Reversal of Brown v. Board of Education.* New York: The New Press; 1996.

75. Wilson WJ. *The Truly Disadvantaged.* Chicago: University of Chicago Press; 1987.

76. Virdee S. *Racial Violence and Harassment.* London: Policy Studies Institute; 1995.

77. Krieger N, Sidney S. Racial discrimination and blood pressure: The CARDIA Study of Young Black and White Adults. *American Journal of Public Health.* 1996;86(10):1370–1378.

78. Chahal K, Julienne L. *We Can't All Be White! Racist Victimization in the UK.* London: YPS; 1999.

79. Humphreys K, Carr-Hill R. Area variation in health outcomes: artifact or ecology. *International Journal of Epidemiology.* 1991;20:251–258.

80. Martikainen P, Kauppinen TM, Valkonen T. Effects of the characteristics of neighborhoods and the characteristics of people on cause specific mortality: a register-based follow-up study of 252,000 men. *Journal of Epidemiology and Community Health.* 2003;57:210–217.

81. Wiggins RD, Barley M, Gleave S, Joshi H, Lynch K. Limiting long-term illness: a question of where you live or who you are? A multilevel analysis of the 1971–1991 ONS Longitudinal Study. *Risk Decision and Policy.* 1998;3:181–198.

82. Cummins S, Staffor DM, Macintyre S, Marmot M, Ellaway A. Neighborhood environment and its association with self-rated health: evidence from Scotland and England. *Journal of Epidemiology and Community Health.* 2005;59: 207–213.

83. Weich S, Blanchard M, Prince M, Burton E, Erens B, Sproston K. Mental health and the built environment: cross-sectional survey of individual and contextual risk factors for depression. *British Journal of Psychiatry.* 2002;180: 428–433.

84. Schwartz J. Air pollution and daily mortality: a review and meta analysis. *Environmental Research.* 1994;64:36–52.

85. Maheswaran R, Elliott P. Stroke mortality associated with living near main roads in England and Wales. *Stroke.* 2003;34:2776–2780.

86. Blane D, Mitchell R, Barley M. The 'Inverse Housing Law' and respiratory health. *Journal of Epidemiology and Community Health.* 2000;54:745–749.

87. Buka SL, Brennan RT, Rich-Edwards JW, Raudenbush SW, Earls D. Neighborhood support and the birth weight of urban infants. *American Journal of Epidemiology.* 2003;3(157): 1–8.

88. Wen M, Browning CR, Cagney KA. Poverty, affluence, and income inequality: neighborhood economic structure and its implications for health. *Social Science and Medicine.* 2003;57:843–860.

89. Lochner KA, Kawachi I, Brennan RT, Buka SL. Social capital and neighborhood mortality rates in Chicago. *Social Science and Medicine.* 2003;56:1797–1805.

90. Boreham R, Stafford M, Taylor R. *Health Survey for England 2000: Social Capital and Health.* London: The Stationery Office; 2002.

91. Yen IH, Kaplan GA. Poverty area residence and changes in depression and perceived health status: evidence from the Alameda County Study. *International Journal of Epidemiology.* 1999;28:90–94.

92. Rothenberg RB, Long DM, Sterk CE, et al. The Atlanta Urban Network Study: a blueprint for endemic transmission. *AIDS.* 2000;14:2191–2200.

93. Buve A, Carael M, Hayes RJ, et al. The multicenter study on factors determining differences in rate of spread of HIV in Sub-Saharan Africa: summary and conclusions. *AIDS.* 2001;15(Suppl 4):S127–S131.

94. Fenton KA, Mercer CH, Johnson AM, et al. Reported STD clinic attendance and sexually transmitted infections in Britain: prevalence, risk, factors, and proportionate population burden. *Journal of Infectious Diseases.* 2005;191: 5127–5138.

95. Fenton KA, Mercer CH, McManus S, et al. Sexual behavior in Britain: ethnic variations in high-risk sexual behavior and STI acquisition risk. *Lancet.* 2005;359:1246–1255.

96. Johnson AM, Wadsworth J, Wellings K, Field J. *Sexual Attitudes and Lifestyles.* Oxford: Blackwell Scientific Press; 1994.

97. Adler MW. The terrible peril: a historical perspective on the venereal diseases. *British Medical Journal.* 1980;281;206–211.

CHAPTER 2

Global Health and Disease

Carleen H. Stoskopf and
James A. Johnson

INTRODUCTION

In the development and management of a country's healthcare system, an essential component is an understanding of the environment or national context in terms of (1) the social and cultural beliefs and behaviors; (2) the physical environment such as exposures to environmental hazards, levels of sanitation, and food and water supply safety; (3) the political climate, including legal issues that impact the provision of health care, the design for financing health care, and the distribution of health resources; (4) economic development including poverty levels, distribution of wealth, types of industry, and agriculture; (5) other social structures such as the education system; and finally, (6) the types of diseases that are present in the population (morbidity) and rates of mortality. Assessment of the population's health needs in light of the national profile should drive how medical resources are distributed and health services are provided. Healthcare systems are called on to do disease prevention, primary treatment, secondary treatment, and tertiary treatment. Integration of the healthcare system with the public health system is essential for effective intervention in the cycles of disease that plague many populations.

Public health systems can provide a variety of nonmedical services such as sanitation improvements, environmental hazard control, vector control, health promotion, and community interventions to improve health and well-being. The public health systems are also responsible for the surveillance of disease in populations. The activity of disease surveillance is vitally important to healthcare systems that are often called on to decide how few and precious resources are to be deployed. Understanding the disease profile of a population and the burden of disease that exists in that population is essential to planning and implementation of health programs. For example, in the case of malaria, healthcare providers must rapidly identify and treat specific types of malaria to prevent further transmission. The public health system must work to eliminate vectors through destruction of breeding sites and use of safe and effective pesticides. Equally important is the role of health educators who work with the community to change behavior by encouraging use of bed nets at night. Simultaneously, researchers must continue the search for a safe and cost-effective vaccination. No campaign to eliminate or substantially reduce malaria will be successful without all of these components; therefore, it is incumbent on healthcare systems to understand the populations they serve and to work with their communities through public health efforts and other social institutions to effect change.

BURDEN OF DISEASE

Disease is measured in many ways. In public health, the term *prevalence* is used to measure the number of individuals with a disease in a specific population at a discrete point in time. *Incidence* is the number of new cases of a disease in a population over a specified period of time.[1] A vast amount of data is available on the incidence and prevalence of diseases (morbidity data) by country, states, regions, and cities and by population demographics such as age and gender. Disease severity is commonly measured by disease-specific mortality for that disease, which is the number of people who die of that disease in the population as a whole over a specified period of time. To communicate the magnitude of a disease in different populations, it can also be reported as a case fatality rate, that is, the rate of death over a specific period of time for a particular disease reported per 1,000 or 100,000 people with the disease. Mortality rates are often reported based on age groups or other demographic variables.[1] A list of commonly used health indicators can be found in Table 2-1.[2]

The burden of disease is expressed by statistics that attempt to determine the impact of disease on a population through measuring disability and healthy life years lost. The World Health Organization (WHO) initiated the Global Burden of Disease Study in 1992 that continues to the present. The study selected disability-adjusted life years for its measurement.[3,4] Other measures include quality-adjusted life years,

TABLE 2-1   Commonly Used Population Health Indicators

Indicator*	Definition**
Crude birth rate	Number of births per 1,000 people in a population during a specific period of time
Crude death rate per 1,000 people	Number of deaths per 1,000 people in a population during a specific period of time
Specific death rate per 1,000 people (age, gender, cause)	Deaths by age, gender, or per 1,000 people in a population during a specific period of time
Infant mortality rate per 1,000 live births	Deaths under 1 year of age per 1,000 live births in a population
Neonatal mortality rate per 1,000 live births	Deaths < 28 days of age per 1,000 live births in a population
Maternal mortality rate per 100,000 women	Deaths from maternal causes per 100,000 women of childbearing age
Proportionate mortality	Percentage of deaths that can be attributed to a particular disease, calculated out of all deaths within that population
Incidence rate	New cases for a condition per 1,000 people in a population during a specific period of time
Prevalence (point in time)	Number of cases of a condition at a specific point per 1,000 people in a population
Disease-specific mortality rate	Number of deaths from a specific condition in a defined population group per 1,000 people during a specified period of time
Case fatality rate	Number of deaths from a specific condition per 1,000 people suffering from that condition

* All indicators are per year. ** All definitions are per a defined population.
Data are from Basch PF. *Textbook of International Health*, 2nd ed. New York: Oxford University Press; 1999, pp. 80, 81.

health expectancies, and healthy life years.[1] Implicit in these measures is the idea that one can apply cost–benefit analyses in terms of the cost to a population to prevent and treat diseases versus the cost that population pays for years lived with disability and/or early mortality from those same diseases. Healthcare providers who avail themselves of these types of measures as applied to their populations can make better decisions in appropriating scarce resources. National health policy makers can use the economic data applied to loss of healthy life years to understand better the impact of diseases upon their nation's population and therefore its productivity as measured in gross domestic product. An understanding of the burden of disease results in better decision making in terms of allocation of resources for

specific programs for prevention, treatment, eradication, and control of specific diseases that severely impact their populations and ultimately the economic viability of the country. A good example of this is the burden that malaria places on populations where it is endemic.

The collection of health statistics is difficult and complicated, even in countries with well-developed health systems like the United States. Collection of these statistics requires standardized definitions of diseases, consistent standards for diagnosis of these diseases, and a well-defined population at risk for these diseases. For developing countries struggling to provide the most basic healthcare needs of their communities, the collection of useful statistics can be a daunting but nevertheless vital task.

TABLE 2-2 Major Causes of Death per 100,000 Population, 2002, by Selected Countries

	Causes of Death							
	Infectious Disease	Cardiovascular Disease	Respiratory Disease	Cancer	Diabetes	Accidents	Suicides	Death by Violence
Argentina	41	245.5	73	157.6	25.4	33.8	10.2	8.8
Australia	9.2	241.7	39.6	186.6	16.3	27.9	11.3	1.5
Belize	52.6	173	25.8	78.8	22.3	51.5	2.3	12
Brazil	48.8	224.8	50.1	100.8	30.4	40.1	5	32.6
Cambodia	518.1	158.1	38.6	72.4	20.3	40.2	4.2	17.1
Canada	10.7	245.1	43.4	208.1	23	27.8	11.8	1.5
China	39	230.5	110	133.5	9.6	52.3	20.9	3
Egypt	57	297.1	36.2	54.9	12.7	27.2	1.5	1.2
France	13	257.5	42.5	238.3	19	52.1	15.9	0.7
Germany	14.3	470.6	38.3	264.2	25.3	24.5	13.9	0.7
Ghana	419.3	158.9	38.5	61.5	11.1	69.5	4	9.2
India	197.3	267.7	58.1	71	14.9	76.2	17.4	5.5
Indonesia	122	215.9	50.5	86.6	21.3	50.6	11.3	9.4
Japan	16.5	244.4	38	241.7	10.1	32.5	24.6	0.6
Jordan	44.1	137.2	15.3	61.6	5.1	51.1	17.2	2.9
Kenya	725	135.9	33.5	53.1	9.2	52.2	5.9	14.9
Mexico	20.8	103.2	25	58.4	54.8	37.3	3.9	10.2
Nigeria	883.6	166.7	42.5	65.1	11.7	80.6	4.9	23.1
Panama	40.8	128.9	22.2	79.4	26.6	30.4	5	9.7

(continues)

TABLE 2-2   Major Causes of Death per 100,000 Population, 2002, by Selected Countries (continued)

	Causes of Death							
	Infectious Disease	Cardiovascular Disease	Respiratory Disease	Cancer	Diabetes	Accidents	Suicides	Death by Violence
Peru	87.3	113.3	27.4	112	14.7	54.8	1.8	3.6
Portugal	30	391.1	59.1	228.9	33.9	32.3	6.7	1.4
Russia	36.5	993.8	43	211.5	8.1	158.8	41	32.9
St. Lucia	26	231	20.6	93.6	59.3	33.7	5.4	7.6
Senegal	385	118.8	30.5	51.4	9.3	81.4	4.4	11
South Africa	898.5	199.1	44.7	85.5	27.9	53	10.5	43.2
South Korea	16.8	159.7	37.2	161.7	31.6	47	18.2	1.8
Turkey	38.8	336.7	39.8	68.6	7.1	28.9	6.7	3.4
U.K.	8.2	387.7	72	256.1	11.7	23.5	8.5	1.1
U.S.	22.1	317	62.7	191.9	26.4	36.6	10.3	5.4

Data are from WHO, Estimated Deaths per 100,000 Population by Cause and Member State, 2002 (http://who.int/healthinfo/statistics).

NONCOMMUNICABLE/CHRONIC DISEASES

During the first decade of the 21st century, we are also facing a growing prevalence of noncommunicable or chronic disease. Diseases such as heart disease, stroke, cancer, chronic respiratory disease, mental illness, and diabetes have reached epidemic status in low- and middle-income countries, as well as in high-income countries.[5] In fact, of approximately 60 million deaths worldwide each year, over half are the result of chronic disease. Cardiovascular disease is now the leading cause of death in the world and is the number one cause of death in all regions except sub-Saharan Africa, where the combination of HIV/AIDS and malaria are the culprits. Communicable or infectious diseases (discussed more later) are caused by a pathogen or infectious agent spread from person to person or from animal to person, whereas noncommunicable diseases are in many ways the opposite, as they do not spread from person to person by an infectious agent. Chronic diseases also tend to last a long time and can be disabling or cause death if not treated. The WHO says the worldwide threat is growing. They predict that deaths from infectious diseases will decline by about 3% over the next 10 years, whereas deaths caused by chronic diseases are projected to increase by 17%. This means of the 64 mil-

lion deaths projected in 2015, 41 million will die of a chronic disease.[5] To understand chronic disease fully, one must use the multicausation model,[6] as illustrated in Figure 2-1.

As demonstrated in the diagram, chronic disease relates to lifestyle and the environment in which a person lives. The WHO asserts there are common, modifiable risk factors that underlie the major chronic diseases. These risk factors explain the vast majority of chronic disease deaths at all ages, in women and men, and in all parts of the world.[7] They include the following:

- Unhealthy diet
- Physical activity
- Tobacco use

These causes are expressed through the intermediate risk factors of high blood pressure, high glucose levels, abnormal blood lipids, and obesity. Each year at least

- 5 million people die as a result of tobacco use.
- 3 million die as a result of being overweight or obesity.
- 4.5 million die as a result of raised total cholesterol levels.
- 7 million die as a result of raised blood pressure.

Of course, there are many more risk factors for chronic disease. Harmful alcohol use is a significant contributor

TABLE 2-3 Selected Demographics

	Birth Rate per 1,000 Population, 2005	Death Rate per 1,000 Population, 2005	Total Fertility Rate, 2005	Life Expectancy at Birth, 2005, Male/Female
Argentina	18.4	8	2.19	72.4/80.1
Australia	12.7	6.6	—	78.1/83
Belize	29.3	5.7	3.68	66.5/70.4
Brazil	18.1	6.1	1.93	67.7/75.9
Cambodia	26.9	9.1	3.44	57/60.9
Canada	10.5	7.3	1.61	76.7/83.6
China	12.4	6.5	1.72	70.4/73.7
Egypt	25.5	6.4	2.88	68.8/73.2
France	12.8	8.7	1.94	76.7/83.8
Germany	8.4	10.1	1.36	75.8/82
Ghana	31.8	10.1	4.2	57.4/58.9
India	22.8	8.4	2.8	63.3/64.8
Indonesia	21.1	6.3	2.5	66.8/71.8
Japan	8.4	8.5	1.25	78.6/85.6
Jordan	28.1	3.2	3.7	70.6/72.4
Kenya	40.1	14.7	4.96	48.9/47.1
Mexico	18.8	4.5	2.45	72.7/77.6
Nigeria	40.7	17.2	5.5	46.2/47
Panama	22	5.3	2.7	72.7/77.9
Peru	20.9	6.3	2.56	67.8/71.4
Portugal	10.4	9.7	1.5	74.4/81
Russia	10.5	15.9	1.27	59.9/73.3
St. Lucia	20.5	5.2	2.3	69.8/77.2
Senegal	39.2	11.4	5.26	54.6/57.3
South Africa	18.5	21.3	2.73	49.0/52.5
South Korea	9.8	5.1	1.08	71.7/79.3
Taiwan	9.1	6.1	1.18	73.6/79.4
Turkey	18.9	6.2	2.19	68.9/73.8
U.K.	12	9.7	1.79	75.9/81
U.S.	14	8.2	2.07	74.8/80.1

Data are from Encyclopedia Britannica Online Academic Edition, World Data, 2007.

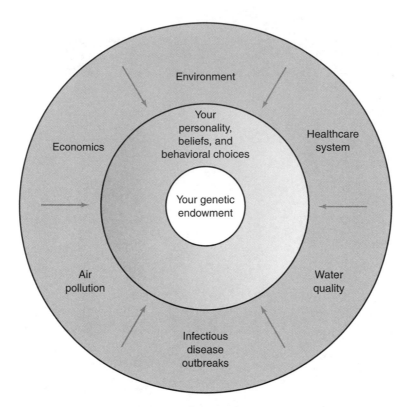

FIGURE 2-1 Multicausation Disease Model

From McKenzie JF, Pinger RR, Kotecki JE. *An Introduction to Community Health*, Sixth Edition. Sudbury, MA: Jones and Bartlett Publishers; 2008.

to injury, disability, liver cirrhosis, pancreatitis, and various cancers. Other risk factors for chronic disease include infectious agents that can lead to cervical cancer (i.e., human papilloma virus) and liver cancer (i.e., hepatitis). There are also many environmental factors such as air pollution, water pollution, and radiation that contribute to a range of chronic diseases. Finally, we cannot underestimate the impact of psychosocial and genetic factors.

The top 10 leading causes of death worldwide are as follows:

1. Heart disease
2. Cerebrovascular disease
3. Respiratory infections
4. HIV/AIDS
5. Chronic pulmonary disease
6. Perinatal conditions
7. Diarrheal disease
8. Tuberculosis
9. Malaria
10. Respiratory tract cancers

The various infectious diseases on this list are discussed in a later section of this chapter. Several of the chronic diseases along with diabetes, cancer, and mental illness will be discussed here.

Cardiovascular Disease

Cardiovascular disease or coronary heart disease is the number one killer, accounting for approximately 20 million deaths worldwide. This represents nearly 60% of all deaths in Europe and Central Asia and approximately 30% of all deaths in East Asia and the Pacific, but only 10% of deaths in sub-Saharan Africa. Cardiovascular disease includes three common conditions: ischemic heart disease, stroke (cerebrovascular disease), and congestive heart failure. As described by the Mayo Clinic, cardiovascular disease is a broad term that is used to describe a range of diseases that affect the heart or blood vessels. The various diseases that fall under the umbrella of cardiovascular disease include coronary artery disease, heart attack, heart failure, high blood pressure, and stroke.

EXHIBIT 2-1 Chronic Disease Worldwide

Prevalence of diabetes worldwide

	2000	2030
World	171,000,000	366,000,000

7.4 Million: the number of people who died from cancer worldwide in 2004. Today, cancer causes one death in every eight. If current trends continue, this could rise to one death in every 6.6 by 2015.

13 Years: the deficit in average life expectancy for men in Eastern Europe compared with those living elsewhere in Europe in 2005. Almost half of this excess mortality is due to cardiovascular diseases with a further 20% due to injuries.

150 Million: the number of people globally experiencing financial catastrophe due to the costs of chronic disease care and disability.

Data are from World Health Statistics 2008.

Although cardiovascular disease can refer to many different types of heart or blood vessel problems, it is used most often to describe damage caused to the heart or blood vessels by atherosclerosis. Over time, too much pressure in the arteries can make the walls thick and stiff—sometimes restricting blood flow to organs and tissues; however, some forms of cardiovascular disease are not caused by atherosclerosis. Those forms include diseases such as congenital heart disease, heart valve diseases, heart infections, or disease of the heart muscle called cardiomyopathy.

The cardiovascular system consists of your heart and all the blood vessels throughout your body. Diseases ranging from aneurysms to valve disease are types of cardiovascular disease. A person may be born with some types of cardiovascular disease (congenital) or acquire others later on, usually from unhealthy habits, such as smoking.

Coronary Artery Disease

This is a common form of cardiovascular disease. Coronary artery diseases are diseases of the arteries that supply the heart muscle with blood. Sometimes known as CAD, coronary artery disease is the leading cause of heart attacks. It generally means that blood flow through the coronary arteries has become obstructed, reducing blood flow to the heart muscle. The most common cause of such obstructions is a condition called atherosclerosis, a largely preventable type of vascular disease. Coronary artery disease and the resulting reduced blood flow to the heart muscle can lead to other heart problems, such as chest pain (angina) and heart attack (myocardial infarction).

Heart Attack

A heart attack is an injury to the heart muscle caused by a loss of blood supply. The medical term for heart attack is myocardial infarction. A heart attack usually occurs when a blood clot blocks the flow of blood through a coronary artery—a blood vessel that feeds blood to a part of the heart muscle. Interrupted blood flow to your heart can damage or destroy a part of the heart muscle.

Congenital Heart Disease

Congenital heart disease refers to a form of heart disease that develops before birth (congenital). Congenital heart disease is a broad term and includes a wide range of diseases and conditions. These diseases can affect the formation of the heart muscle or its chambers or valves. Some congenital heart defects may be apparent at birth, whereas others may not be detected until later in life.

Aneurysm

An aneurysm is a bulge or weakness in a blood vessel (artery or vein) wall. Aneurysms usually get bigger over time. Because of that, they have the potential to rupture and cause life-threatening bleeding. Aneurysms can occur in arteries in any location in the body. The most common sites include the abdominal aorta and the arteries at the base of the brain.

Heart Failure

Heart failure, often called congestive heart failure, is a condition in which the heart cannot pump enough blood to meet the needs of the body's organs and tissues. It does not mean that your heart has failed and cannot pump blood at all. With this less effective pumping, vital organs do not get enough blood, causing such signs and symptoms as shortness of breath, fluid retention, and fatigue. "Congestive" heart failure is technically reserved for situations in which heart failure has led to fluid buildup in the body. Not all heart failure is congestive, but the terms are often used interchangeably. Heart failure may develop suddenly or over many years. It may occur as a result of other cardiovascular conditions that have damaged or weakened the heart, such as coronary artery disease or cardiomyopathy.

High Blood Pressure

High blood pressure (hypertension) is the excessive force of blood pumping through your blood vessels. It is perhaps the most common form of cardiovascular disease in the Western world, affecting about one in four Americans. Although potentially life-threatening, it is one of the most preventable and treatable types of cardiovascular disease. High blood pressure also causes many other types of cardiovascular disease, such as stroke and heart failure.

Stroke

A stroke occurs when blood flow to the brain is interrupted (ischemic stroke) or when a blood vessel in the brain ruptures (hemorrhagic stroke). Both can cause the death of brain cells in the affected areas. Stroke is also considered a neurological disorder because of the many complications it causes. Other forms of cardiovascular disease, such as high blood pressure, increase your risk of stroke.

Arrhythmias

Heart rhythm problems (arrhythmias) occur when the electrical impulses in your heart that coordinate your heartbeats do not function properly, causing your heart to beat too fast, too slow, or irregularly. Other forms of cardiovascular disease can cause arrhythmias.

Cancer

The WHO says that dramatic increases in risk factors such as tobacco use and obesity are contributing to a worldwide rise in cancer rates, particularly in low- and middle-income countries, where more than 70% of all cancer deaths occur. Worldwide, 7.6 million people died of cancer in 2005, and 84 million people will die in the next 10 years if action is not taken, the WHO estimates.

Preventable risk factors include many environmental carcinogens. In addition, 40% of cancer incidences can be prevented by a healthy diet, physical activity, and avoiding tobacco. Cancer refers to any one of a large number of diseases characterized by the development of abnormal cells that divide uncontrollably and have the ability to infiltrate and destroy normal body tissue. Cancer also has the ability to spread throughout your body. Cancer is a leading cause of death worldwide, but survival rates are improving for many types of cancer thanks to improvements in cancer screening and cancer treatment. Cancer is caused by damage (mutations) to the DNA within cells. DNA contains a set of instructions for your cells, telling them how to grow and divide. Normal cells often develop mutations in their DNA, but they have the ability to repair most of these mutations. If they cannot make the repairs, the cells often die; however, certain mutations are not repaired, causing the cells to grow and become cancerous. Mutations also cause cancer cells to live beyond their normal cell life span. This causes the cancerous cells to accumulate. In some cancers, accumulating cells form a tumor, but not all cancers form tumors. For example, leukemia is a cancer that involves blood, bone marrow, the lymphatic system and the spleen, but does not form a single mass or tumor.

Genetic makeup, forces within the body, lifestyle choices, and the environment can all set the stage for cancer or help complete the process once it has started. For instance, if you have inherited a genetic mutation that predisposes you to cancer, you may be more likely than other people to develop cancer when exposed to a certain cancer-causing substance. The genetic mutation begins the cancer process, and the cancer-causing substance could play a role in further cancer development. Likewise, smokers who work with asbestos are more likely to develop lung cancer than are smokers who do not work with asbestos. That is because tobacco smoke and asbestos both play roles in cancer development.

Factors known to increase the risk of cancer include the following:

- Age: Cancer can take decades to develop. That is why most people diagnosed with cancer are 55 or older. Although it is more common in older adults, cancer is not exclusively an adult disease— cancer can be diagnosed at any age.
- Lifestyle: Certain lifestyle choices are known to increase your risk of cancer. Smoking, drinking more than one drink a day (for women) or two

drinks a day (for men), excessive exposure to the sun or frequent blistering sunburns, and having unsafe sex can contribute to cancer.
- Family history: Only about 10% of cancers are due to an inherited condition. If cancer is common in your family, it is possible that mutations are being passed from one generation to the next.
- Health conditions: Some chronic health conditions, such as ulcerative colitis, can markedly increase the risk of developing certain cancers.
- Environment: The environment may contain harmful chemicals that can increase the risk of cancer. Even if people do not smoke, they might inhale secondhand smoke or other indoor pollutants. Chemicals in the home or workplace, such as asbestos and benzene, also are associated with an increased risk of cancer.
- Globalization: Globalized markets and urbanization are leading to rising consumption of tobacco; processed foods high in fats, sugars, and salt; declining consumption of fruit and vegetables; and more sedentary activity levels. As a consequence the incidence of cancer and other chronic diseases is increasing.

The WHO has proposed a global goal of reducing death rates for all chronic diseases by 2% a year from 2006 to 2015. Achievement of this goal would avert over 8 million of the projected 84 million deaths caused by cancer in the next decade.

Diabetes

The International Diabetes Federation estimates that more than 245 million people around the world have diabetes. This total is expected to rise to 380 million within 20 years. Each year a further 7 million people develop diabetes.

Diabetes is a disease in which the body does not produce or properly use insulin. Insulin is a hormone that is needed to convert sugar, starches, and other food into energy needed for daily life. The cause of diabetes continues to be a mystery, although both genetics and environmental factors such as obesity and lack of exercise appear to play roles.

There are 23.6 million children and adults in the United States, or 7.8% of the population, who have diabetes. Although an estimated 17.9 million have been diagnosed with diabetes, unfortunately, 5.7 million people (or nearly one quarter) are unaware that they have the disease.

Type 1 Diabetes

This results from the body's failure to produce insulin, the hormone that "unlocks" the cells of the body, allowing glucose to enter and fuel them. It is estimated that 5% to 10% of people diagnosed with diabetes have type 1 diabetes.

Type 2 Diabetes

This results from insulin resistance (a condition in which the body fails to properly use insulin), combined with relative insulin deficiency. Most people worldwide who are diagnosed with diabetes have type 2 diabetes.

Gestational Diabetes

Immediately after pregnancy, 5% to 10% of women who had gestational diabetes are found to have diabetes, usually type 2.

Prediabetes

Prediabetes is a condition that occurs when a person's blood glucose levels are higher than normal but not high enough for a diagnosis of type 2 diabetes. There are 57 million Americans who have prediabetes. This number is even higher in Mexico, India, China, and the Middle East.

The International Diabetes Federation anticipates the following:

- By 2025, the number of people with diabetes is expected to rise to 380 million worldwide, with 80% living in the developing world.
- Each year, another 7 million people develop diabetes, while 3.8 million die of diabetes-linked causes.
- In many countries in Asia, the Middle East, and the Caribbean, diabetes already affects 15% to 20% of the adult population.
- India now has the largest number of diabetics (almost 41 million) in the world, followed by China (nearly 40 million), the United States (23.6 million), and Russia (9.6 million).
- Diabetes increasingly affects the young or middle aged, with more than half of diabetics in developing countries between the ages of 40 and 59 years.

Mental Illness

Neuropsychiatric conditions account for 14% of the global burden of disease. Within noncommunicable diseases, they account for 28% of the disability-adjusted life years and thereby more than cardiovascular disease or cancer. The most important contributions to this number are depression, alcohol abuse, schizophrenia, and dementia. Up to 30% of all people worldwide have a mental disorder, and although interventions for the treatment of mental disorders are available, the proportion of those people with mental disorders who would need treatment but who do not receive mental health care is very high. This so-called treatment gap is estimated to reach about 76% to 85% for low- and middle-income countries and still 35% to 50% for high-income countries.

Mental illnesses are medical conditions that disrupt a person's thinking, feeling, mood, ability to relate to others, and daily functioning. Just as diabetes is a disorder of the pancreas, mental illnesses are medical conditions that often result in a diminished capacity for coping with the ordinary demands of life.

Mental illnesses can affect persons of any age, race, religion, or income. Mental illnesses are not the result of personal weakness, lack of character, or poor upbringing. Mental illnesses are treatable. Most people diagnosed with a serious mental illness can experience relief from their symptoms by actively participating in an individual treatment plan.

In addition to medication treatment, psychosocial treatment such as cognitive behavioral therapy, interpersonal therapy, peer support groups, and other community services can also be components of a treatment plan and assist with recovery. The availability of transportation, diet, exercise, sleep, friends, and meaningful paid or volunteer activities contribute to overall health and wellness, including mental illness recovery.

Here are some important facts about mental illness and recovery:

- The World Health Organization has reported that four of the 10 leading causes of disability in the United States and other developed countries are mental disorders. By 2020, major depressive illness will be the leading cause of disability in the world for women and children.
- Mental illnesses usually strike individuals in the prime of their lives, often during adolescence and young adulthood. All ages are susceptible, but the young and the old are especially vulnerable.
- Without treatment the consequences of mental illness for the individual and society are staggering: unnecessary disability, unemployment, substance abuse, homelessness, inappropriate incarceration, suicide, and wasted lives. The economic cost of untreated mental illness is more than 100 billion dollars each year in the United States.
- The best treatments for serious mental illnesses today are highly effective. Between 70% and 90% of individuals have significant reduction of symptoms and improved quality of life with a combination of pharmacological and psychosocial treatments and supports.
- With appropriate effective medication and a wide range of services tailored to their needs, most people who live with serious mental illnesses can significantly reduce the impact of their illness and find a satisfying measure of achievement and independence. A key concept is to develop expertise in developing strategies to manage the illness process.
- Early identification and treatment is of vital importance. By ensuring access to the treatment and recovery supports that are proven effective, recovery is accelerated, and the further harm related to the course of illness is minimized.
- Stigma erodes confidence that mental disorders are real, treatable health conditions. Nearly all cultures of the world have allowed stigma and a now unwarranted sense of hopelessness to erect attitudinal, structural, and financial barriers to effective treatment and recovery.

INFECTIOUS DISEASE

Infectious diseases are those illnesses that are spread from person to person. They may be spread in a variety of ways. Some require an intermediary host such as those diseases that are vector borne (malaria, yellow fever, Lyme disease) or those diseases that require a zoological host (schistosomiasis). Others are spread through direct contact (impetigo, gonorrhea, syphilis, HIV, Ebola), contact with infected surfaces or fomites (*Staphylococcus aureus* infection, rhinoviruses), ingestion of contaminated water (cholera or giardiasis), infection via the blood, (hepatitis B and C or HIV), ingestion of fecal material (hepatitis A, *E. coli*), or intake via the respiratory system (tuberculosis, severe acute respiratory syndrome [SARS]). Many of these diseases are spread in more than one way.

Infectious diseases have seen a major comeback in the last four decades. In the 1970s, many public health and medical professionals believed that the age of infectious disease was over because of successful vaccination development, a reduction of potential disease vectors through pesticide use, vast increases in basic public health sanitation, and identification and knowledge about infectious disease life cycles and modes of transmission. Most health professionals living in industrialized nations thought little of infectious diseases and turned their attention to chronic disease and its management. Within this environment of complacency appeared a newly recognized pathogen, the human immunodeficiency virus (HIV).

The report of a new sexually transmitted disease whose infection led to almost certain death was a concept that shocked everyone from professionals in the medical community to the average person on the street. How could this occur? The emergence of HIV was quickly followed by other infectious diseases, including Ebola virus, SARS, and Avian flu. In addition, some infectious diseases began to spread away from their place of origin, such as the West Nile, which had migrated from Africa to North America. To contribute to this situation further, the role of commercial airline traffic in spreading disease throughout the world changed from being a theoretical concern to a public health reality. As Ebola outbreaks in Africa appeared on our television screens, we were stunned to learn that this disease jumped from other primates to humans. Now we nervously watch for new cases of Avian flu for the same reason. HIV in Africa reminds us of those historical plague epidemics that changed the basic population structure of societies as vast numbers of people died within short time periods. Those old infectious diseases that we thought were under control suddenly started to reappear or grow in prevalence. Malaria, for instance, is on the rise, and some species have now developed resistance to treatment. A virulent new form of tuberculosis has appeared that is also resistant to treatment. Nature seems to thwart us at each turn. Those in the business of providing healthcare services and those who conduct disease surveillance must very seriously assess the burden of infectious diseases on the populations they serve and be prepared to address them through prevention, early detection, and treatment.

As we progress through the early 21st century, developed countries are becoming increasingly aware of the health problems and needs of developing countries. This is not just because the developed countries are concerned that diseases endemic to developing countries may pose a hazard for their own citizens, but also out of a sense of justice. Because of real-time communication through technology such as the Internet, an increase in international travel to developing countries, and demographic changes such as immigration, people from all over the world are more aware of the conditions under which many people live.

As our global awareness has increased, so has our sense of interconnectedness, justice, and responsibility to those beyond our borders. This has motivated governments, private organizations, and international organizations to try and come to the aid of those people and nations with large burdens of illness. Unfortunately, special interests, politics, international corruption, and incompetence have thwarted many of those well-meaning efforts. Conditions in developing countries often contribute to the disease burden caused by infectious diseases. These conditions include poor sanitation, lack of potable water, little or no access to healthcare services, low levels of education, and most importantly, undernutrition. Recent studies have shown that undernutrition is a leading contributor to childhood deaths by infectious disease. Of the estimated 10 million children who die each year, the majority die from preventable causes: pneumonia and diarrhea, followed by malaria, AIDS, and measles.[8]

It is essential for healthcare delivery systems to provide effective interventions for infectious diseases, including both prevention and treatment. This is particularly true in developing countries. These systems must also work to collect and provide timely and accurate health statistics for both the planning and monitoring of the use and provision of health services by the populations they serve. It is further incumbent on healthcare services to work with their communities to reach out with interventions to those in the populations who cannot or will not access services.[8]

Vector-Borne Diseases

Of great concern to epidemiologists worldwide is the resurgence of vector-borne diseases. This resurgence is due to a number of factors, including resistance to pesticides, resistance to drugs used for treatment, the shifting of health policy from prevention to emergency response, genetic changes in pathogens, climate change, deforestation, and changes in agricultural practices.[6]

Vector-borne diseases are those that require a blood-sucking agent (arthropod) to transmit the pathogen between vertebrate hosts. They can be grouped according to three types of pathogens: (1) parasitic, (2) bacterial, and (3) arboviral diseases. Until World War II, vector-borne diseases were the number one cause of morbidity around the world. As of the early 1990s, it had become clear that vector-borne diseases contribute significantly to the burden of disease in most areas of the developing world. Table 2-4 provides a summary of three categories of vector-borne diseases that caused epidemics in the 1990s and the geographic distribution of those outbreaks.

Malaria

The vector-borne disease of greatest concern worldwide is malaria. Malaria is caused by a protozoan parasite that invades the red blood cells of humans. It is spread by mosquitoes in the genus *Anopheles* that after biting one infected person goes on to a bite someone else, thus transmitting the disease. Common symptoms include malaise, febrile episodes with cerebral damage, hypoglycemia, respiratory distress, anemia, chronic debilitation, malnutrition, and neurological syndromes. Malaria in endemic areas presents itself in two basic forms. For those under the age of 5 years, and travelers without previous exposure, the parasitemia results in acute symptoms and can eventually lead to death. In Africa, 75% of the deaths from malaria are among children.[8] Persons who live in endemic areas and who have survived early childhood episodes of malaria often develop a level of immunity. In this case, malaria may present itself with mild symptoms, including general malaise, general debilitation, and periods of low fever. Frequently, adults with malaria may be completely asymptomatic. Untreated mild or asymptomatic cases preserve a reservoir of parasites for transmission to others via mosquito vectors as the symptoms may be so mild that adults do not seek treatment.

Treatment of malaria has become complicated over time, as some of the species of malaria (*Plasmodium malariae, P. falciparum, P. vivax, P. malariae,* and *P. ovale*) have developed resistance to some drugs. As of now, there are no vaccines for malaria.[8] Long-term chemoprophylaxis with malaria-preventing drugs is not a viable option, as it can result in further resistance and poses other risks and side effects to the individual. The current recommendation is to provide targeted groups (pregnant women and small children) in endemic areas with intermittent therapeutic doses of malaria treatment.[1] Public health programs to eliminate mosquito breeding sites and to educate people in the use of bed nets are other options to weaken the chain of infection.

Of all the vector-borne diseases, malaria is believed to cause the greatest morbidity burden around the world. A worldwide campaign started in 1955 and operating through the mid-1960s resulted in a substantial reduction in malaria in areas where it was endemic.[8] As efforts abated, a resurgence of malaria occurred. This was primarily caused by the ban of DDT and the discontinuation of programs to reduce mosquito breeding areas resulting in a decrease in vector control. Additionally, strains of malaria became resistant to treatment, leaving a reservoir of pathogens in the blood of its victims for a lifetime. Perhaps most importantly, as many sub-Saharan countries earned independence in the 1950s and 1960s, the ensuing political instability, escalation of foreign debt, and decrease in international aid resulted in the collapse of the public health and healthcare systems in many countries. The result of these multifaceted factors is that malaria has returned with a vengeance. Not until 1998 were efforts once again renewed to reduce its levels by introducing the Roll Back Malaria program. The Roll Back Malaria program is a partnership between WHO, UNICEF, UNDP, and the World Bank with the goal of reducing the number of cases of malaria by one half by the year 2010. This program has had limited success in great part because of lack of adequate funding.[9] Recently renewed efforts to bring the disease under control have been funded by new organizations such as the Bill and Melinda Gates Foundation, and the Global Fund, which also pledges to decrease mortality from HIV/AIDS and tuberculosis.

The population at risk of malaria increased significantly during the 20th century. The at-risk population grew from 0.9 to 3 billion people from 1900 to 2002 with 48% of the world's population currently at risk.[10] Ninety percent of all cases occur in Africa, resulting in more than 1 million deaths per year on that continent. The geographical distribution of malaria is not expected to substantially change between now and 2010, but 400 million new births will occur in those regions where malaria is already endemic. Martens and Hall report that migration of populations caused by urban relocation and the flight of refugees increases the distribution of malaria regionally into areas that were previously malaria free. This type of population migration results from crises such as environmental changes, economic necessity, war and conflict, and natural disasters, all of which result in populations moving to neighboring areas to escape these conditions. Often this results in people moving into city shanty towns without any services such as water, electricity, or sanitation. These conditions are more likely to exist in areas where poverty is common and where malaria is endemic.[11]

Because of the debilitating nature of malaria, the disease has a major impact on the economies of the regions and countries where it is endemic, reducing productivity, lowering rates of economic growth, impeding

TABLE 2-4 Geographic Distribution of Vector-Borne Disease Outbreaks in the 1990s by Type of Pathogen

	Parasitic Disease	Bacterial Disease	Arboviral Disease
North America	Malaria	Tularemia Tick-Borne Relapsing Fever Lyme Disease Ehrlichiosis	Encephalitis: Eastern Equine, LaCrosse, Venezuelan Equine, St. Louis Dengue
South America	Malaria	Plague	Venezuelan Equine Encephalitis Dengue Oropouche Yellow Fever
Europe	None	Lyme Disease Tularemia	Sindbis Tick-Borne Encephalitis Crimean-Congo Hemorrhagic Fever Dengue
Africa	Malaria Leishmaniasis African Trypanosomiasis	Louse-Borne Typhus Plague	Rift Valley Fever Kyasanur Forest Disease Dengue Yellow Fever Crimean-Congo Hemorrhagic Fever
Asia	Malaria Leishmaniasis	Plague	Chikungunya Dengue Japanese Encephalitis California Encephalitis Sindbis Crimean-Congo Hemorrhagic Fever Tick-Borne Encephalitis
Australia	None	None	Dengue Japanese Encephalitis Ross River Barman Forest Murray Valley Encephalitis

Data are from Gubler GJ. Resurgent vector-borne diseases as a global health problem. *Emerging Infectious Diseases* 1998;4(3):442–450.

development, and discouraging savings and investment.[12] Control of malaria mostly has a clear association with economic development, although up until now malarial control has mostly occurred outside of Africa. After an area becomes malaria free, the growth in the economy over the next 5 years is significantly higher than neighboring countries for which malaria remains

a significant problem. A study of the association between malaria and economic growth looked at the years between 1965 and 1990 and found that in areas with a high incidence and prevalence of malaria, the economy grew 1.3% less per person per year, but a reduction in malaria by 10% is associated with a 0.3% increase in gross domestic product growth.[13]

Water-Borne Diseases

Water-borne diseases generally invade the gastrointestinal system, although some parasitic forms found in water can enter the body through the skin (schistosomiasis). Of particular importance are those infections that are caused by viruses (rotaviruses), bacteria (*Vibrio cholerae*, *Escherichia coli*), and parasites (*Entamoeba histolytica*). These infections result in diarrhea that can often be life-threatening because of a loss of fluids and salts. Chronic diarrheal infections can lead to poor absorption of nutrients, malnutrition, malaise, stunted growth, and chronic disability. The impact of water-borne diseases on children in developing countries can be devastating and is the second most cause of death among children worldwide.

Diarrheal Disease

Nearly 2 million children die annually from diarrhea worldwide. This statistic represents 17% of the total deaths of children under the age of 5 years, excluding neonatal causes.[14] Deaths by diarrheal illness can be prevented by promoting exclusive breastfeeding of infants for the first 6 months of life.[15] UNICEF estimates that 13% of all under-five deaths in developing countries could be prevented by exclusive breastfeeding, making it the most powerful means of preventing child mortality. An additional 6% of deaths under the age of 5 years could be avoided by the use of properly timed and administrated complementary feeding during the introduction of solid foods up until and including the time during which the child is weaned. Mortality from diarrheal diseases can also be prevented through the use of oral rehydration therapy (ORT). It is estimated that the lives of 50 million children have been saved by the use of ORT over the last 25 years and that ORT therapy is a significant factor in the reduction of yearly mortality from diarrheal diseases from over 5 million per year in the 1980s to just under 2 million a year now.[16]

There are many causes for diarrheal illness, but one of the most common causes in children is the rotavirus. Five percent of all deaths in children under the age of 5 years are caused by this specific virus. In diarrheal episodes seen in outpatient clinics in developing countries, up to 35% of them are caused by rotavirus.[17] As a cause of death, the rotavirus is estimated to cause 440,000 deaths per year, 2 million hospitalizations per year, and over 110 million visits to clinics.[18–20] A specific vaccine for rotavirus is available and has been determined to be highly effective. Vaccination programs for rotavirus infection, however, face the numerous challenges other vaccinations face in developing countries, many of which are underfunded, poorly organized, and have limited access to needed supplies.

The chain of infection for nearly all diarrheal illness is through fecal contamination of water or food, although more commonly water, and the level of sanitation present in most developing countries remains a major obstacle to relieving this burden. Today, nearly 1.1 billion people do not have access to a clean and sustainable water source,[21] and 84% of those people who live in rural areas. In these areas, the lack of potable water for cleaning and preparing food, hand washing, and bathing, not to mention drinking, results in a continuous cycle of diarrheal diseases. This problem is compounded by the fact that 2.6 billion people in the world have no access to a sanitary toilet facility and must defecate in uncontrolled areas. This contributes to the problem in many ways, as uncovered excrement can contaminate food and water supplies, and an inability to wash your hands properly can facilitate the spread of pathogens from person to person. In developed countries, the 20th century saw the development of clean water sources for the bulk of their populations, as well as municipal wastewater disposal. This single achievement is cited as one of the major reasons developed countries saw a substantial drop in infectious diseases in the early part of the 20th century.[22]

Cholera

Cholera is caused by the bacteria, *Vibrio cholerae*, and is one of three diseases that is required to be reported to the WHO (Merson et al, 2006).[1] In 1992, the WHO organized the Global Task Force on Cholera Control to reduce the number of outbreaks and to address the social and economic conditions that lead to periodic epidemics.[23] Cholera can be prevented by maintaining a clean water supply and through the treatment and management of sewage. Cholera is endemic to parts of India and Bangladesh, but periodic outbreaks occur in South America and Africa as well.

Respiratory Infections

Respiratory infections are generally categorized as upper or lower respiratory infections. Those of the upper respiratory tract include the common cold, viral and group A streptococcal pharyngitis, and middle-ear infections. Upper respiratory infections are found worldwide and in all populations regardless of socioeconomic status and general living conditions. Generally, when indicated, treatment of upper respiratory infections is successful, and as a result, they do not contribute to mortality. Many of these types of infections require only supportive care.

Lower respiratory infections, however, can often be very serious and lead to death, especially among children.[24] Lower respiratory infections are caused by viruses and bacteria, often simultaneously. The most common viral causes of lower respiratory infection are influenza, parainfluenza, syncytial virus, and adenovirus. Bacterial causes include *Streptococcus pneumoniae*, *Haemophilus influenzae*, and *Staphylococcus aureus*. It is estimated that over 2 million children die from pneumonia and other lower respiratory infections each year, making it the number one killer of children less than 5 years old. Worldwide, the proportionate mortality of children under the age of 5 years from pneumonia is 19%, not including neonatal deaths with pneumonia-related etiology. Most of these deaths are in poorer countries; however, children who live in poverty in industrialized countries are at greater risk of dying from pneumonia than those not living in poverty.[25] Children from low-income groups are exposed to a number of risk factors, including indoor air pollution, cigarette smoke, poor housing and nutrition, and limited access to health care for proper diagnosis and treatment.

Tuberculosis

Tuberculosis is caused by *Mycobacteria tuberculosis* and is considered a problem for every low-income country in the world. It is estimated that nearly one third of the world's population is infected.[1] The immune systems of healthy people successfully keep this organism in check, even while the bacteria remain alive in their systems; however, with a compromised immune system, often associated with circumstances such as poverty, poor nutrition, and stress, the infection may become active and create a clinical case. In such circumstances, the immune system can no longer protect the body from the organism. Other conditions in developing countries that contribute to the transmission of tuberculosis are close living conditions due to overcrowding and lack of healthcare services that can successfully identify and treat new cases of tuberculosis. Even in developed countries, the public health systems must be vigilant for new cases of tuberculosis, especially among those with impaired immune systems.

The treatment recommended for tuberculosis is a multiple drug therapy. Success in limiting the spread of tuberculosis is dependent on rapid detection and treatment of active cases in this manner. Some industri-alized countries have historically treated asymptomatic infected individuals with daily doses of one drug, isoniazid, for up to 1 year, but this approach has led to some drug resistance. In developing countries, the strategy for treatment has been a "directly observed short-course therapy," which has proved to be more effective in circumstances where constraining factors would otherwise result in noncompliance with a daily regimen.[26] Also, in many low-income countries, infants are given a BCG (bacilli Calmette-Guerin) vaccination. This has been successful in reducing meningitis but has had limited success in treating pulmonary tuberculosis. Currently, the biggest concern in controlling tuberculosis is antimicrobial drug resistance.

New concerns for tuberculosis have emerged as persons living with HIV have become increasingly at risk for contracting tuberculosis because of the compromised nature of their immune systems. In sub-Saharan Africa, it is estimated that 60% of tuberculosis patients are also living with HIV/AIDS.[27] Coupled with drug-resistant strains, public health professionals are working to better understand these co-morbidities.

Sexually Transmitted Diseases

Until the advent of HIV in the early 1980s, little time or interest was spent on sexually transmitted infections (STIs), especially from a global perspective. Given the nature of HIV with its high mortality rate and extensive co-morbidities, HIV infection and STIs have taken on a life of their own in the collective minds of governments. Rates of more common STIs such as syphilis and gonorrhea are often predictors of previously undetected HIV infections. Because of this relationship, surveillance of STIs is an important part of public health, as is disease prevention through education, provision of barrier prophylaxis, family planning, and treatment.

STI control has many obstacles. STIs are often asymptomatic. There are few treatments that are easy to administer in a single dose, and worldwide, there is a dearth of easy and inexpensive laboratory tests available for detection.[1] In addition, social and cultural practices often aid in the transmission process. This includes practices of polygamy, attitudes toward sexual conquests among young men, the wide use of sex workers around the world, beliefs regarding the use of condoms, taboos surrounding the teaching of sex education and family planning, and limited access to health care for women.

The primary etiologic agents of STIs are bacteria and viruses. Tracking of STIs is complicated by the fact that some can also be transmitted by blood products, including syphilis, gonorrhea, HIV/AIDS, and hepatitis B, whereas others like *Chlamydia trachomatis* can be transmitted through physical contact of mother to her newborn child (see Table 2-5).

Recently, the link between Human papilloma virus and some types of cervical cancer has been established. The availability of a vaccination for this virus has brought this issue to the forefront of public health. The vaccination holds out hope to reduce the incidence of some types of cervical cancer, but at the same time, it comes with problems of cost, distribution in poor countries, and ethical issues surrounding the use of this vaccine in girls as young as 11 years old. Professionals believe that in order for the vaccination to be successful it must be administered early when the chance of being sexually active is real. Even for developed countries, the $360 cost of the three injections in the series is considerable. Given that the total mortality for cervical cancer worldwide is 238,805, the decision of whether to vaccinate against HPV highlights the difficult dilemma faced by healthcare providers when deciding how to allocate funds. In contrast, the measles vaccination, which costs under $1 for a full series, is still underused in many countries around the world. Measles is responsible for over 700,000 deaths annually, all of which could be prevented by properly administered vaccinations. In the United States in 2002, 3,952 women died of cervical cancer; however, mortality from cervical cancer is rare for women who have regular screening tests, or Pap smears. Health insurance companies are reluctant to pay for any immunizations, especially those that are tied to conditions that are the result of behavioral choices. It has been left to public health agencies to provide immunization programs for HPV, and this has been controversial in many parts of the world.

HIV/AIDS

When HIV emerged in the early 1980s, the developed world was not prepared for a new infectious disease. Many healthcare professionals were surprised; however, the onset of this epidemic inspired efforts worldwide to confront not only HIV, but to put a renewed emphasis on all infectious diseases and their identification, control, and treatment. In addition, the emergence of HIV and its rapid spread around the world, as well as its dif-

TABLE 2-5   Principle Sexually Transmitted Diseases of Interest to Global Public Health

Etiological Agent	Disease	Transmission to Newborns	Transmission Through Blood Products
Bacteria			
Treponema pallidum	Syphilis	Yes	Yes
Neisseria gonorrhea	Gonorrhea, pelvic inflammatory disease	Yes	Yes
Chlamydia trachomatis	Cervicitis, urethritis, lymphogranuloma venereum, pelvic inflammatory disease	Yes	No
Viruses			
Human immunodeficiency virus	AIDS	Yes	Yes
Herpes simplex	Genital herpes	Yes	No
Human papilloma virus (HPV)	Genital warts, cervical dysplasia, cervical carcinoma	Unknown	No
Hepatitis B virus	Acute and chronic hepatitis, cirrhosis, hepatocellular carcinoma	Yes	Yes

Adapted from Merson MH, Black RE, Mills AJ. *International Health: Diseases, Programs, Systems, and Policies*, 2nd ed. Sudbury, MA: Jones and Bartlett Publishers, 2006.

fusion to different types of populations through sexual contacts, have served to identify the potential for rapid changes in disease patterns. Factors contributing to these changes include globalization, cultural and social contexts, resource availability, and the increasing ease of international transportation.

By the end of 2006, it was estimated that the prevalence of people living with HIV/AIDS worldwide was 38.6 million, 95% of whom live in developing countries where resources are scarce. In 2005 alone, over 4 million people were infected and nearly 3 million died. Since its identification in 1981, more than 25 million people have died of AIDS. Each year has seen an increase in incidence, prevalence, and mortality from HIV. Table 2-6 provides estimates by regions of those living with HIV/AIDS.

HIV can be spread through different channels, but its transmission is primarily sexual and therefore is most often found in people aged 15 to 49 years. Although the epidemic started primarily with men having sex with men, with some transmission by injectable drugs, the predominant mode of transmission today is heterosexual. In those areas of the world with predominantly heterosexual transmission, the epidemic has grown the fastest. In areas such as sub-Saharan Africa, the prevalence rate exceeds 20%. HIV is spreading rapidly in other areas of the world as well, such as in Eastern Europe and Asia. Transmission in these areas is often due to the sex trade and drug injection. The countries experiencing the most new cases of HIV are India, China (People's Republic), and Russia. Although much attention has been focused on sub-Saharan Africa, other areas of the world have been slow to acknowledge their problems with HIV. Only recently has China begun a program to deal with its HIV/AIDS problem, committing $100 million in 2005 and more than $185 million in 2007.[28]

Because HIV can also be transmitted to newborns during pregnancy, childbirth, and breastfeeding, identification, treatment, and control of HIV must be part of family planning efforts.[29] In 2006, an estimated 2.3 million children were living with HIV/AIDS, 90% of them in sub-Saharan Africa. Each day there are 1,500 new infections in children under the age of 15.[30] HIV in children is preventable but reliant on access to and the effectiveness of healthcare systems.

The economic cost of HIV/AIDS is catastrophic for many countries, especially in sub-Saharan Africa. Because HIV in these countries is being transmitted heterosexually, it is decimating families, with adults in their prime years as the predominant victims. The loss of these young adults has robbed many countries of their professionals and laborers, as well as the generation on whom the society typically must depend to care not only for the children but for the older persons as well. One of the most disastrous results of this trend is that

TABLE 2-6 Estimates of the Number of Persons Living with HIV/AIDS, 2004

Region	Number (Range)
North America	1.0 million (540,000–1.6 million)
Caribbean	440,000 (270,000–780,000)
Latin America (including Mexico)	1.7 million (1.3–2.2 million)
Western Europe	610,000 (480,000–760,000)
North Africa and Middle East	540,000 (230,000–1.5 million)
Sub-Saharan Africa	25.4 million (23.4–28.4 million)
Eastern Europe and Central Asia	1.4 million (920,000–2.1 million)
East Asia	1.1 million (560,000–1.8 million)
South and Southeast Asia	7.1 million (4.4–10.6 million)
Oceania	35,000 (25,000–48,000)
Global Total	39.4 million (35.9–44.3 million)

Adapted from Merson MH, Black RE, Mills AJ. *International Public Health: Diseases, Programs, Systems, and Policies*, 2nd ed. Sudbury, MA: Jones and Bartlett Publishers, 2006.

there is an entire generation of African children who are growing up as orphans. These children lack access to healthcare services and opportunities for education, not to mention the nurturing and love that they would receive if their parents were alive. It has fallen to the grandparents in many families to raise these children in their old age. Like older persons around the world, these grandparents typically have less income, less access to transportation, and less access to healthcare services than younger people do. Many of them are experiencing illness and disability as a result of natural aging. These older people are deprived of the time in their lives when they would normally expect their children to be caring for them.

In Ethiopia, Kenya, and Zimbabwe, costs for treatment and care of HIV/AIDS patients consumed more than a third, more than half, and nearly two thirds, respectively, of the healthcare budgets of these three countries in 2007.[31] Many middle-income countries have found meeting the financial challenges of HIV/AIDS difficult as well. In more developed nations, treatments have become more readily available, and people are living longer, while the cost for treatment continues to climb. As the world grapples with the epidemic in developing countries, such as those in sub-Saharan Africa, the cost of HIV/AIDS treatment will continue to increase. To bring the epidemic under control in poor and developing countries, it will take considerable financial assistance from the world's wealthier nations. In 2005, the members of the G8 (Canada, France, Germany, Italy, Japan, Russia, the United Kingdom, and the United States) as well as the European Union committed to working with the United Nations to provide programs to prevent HIV transmission, identify current cases in a timely manner, and provide treatment and care to those who are infected.

A number of programs are attempting to bring relief. The Global Fund to Fight AIDS, tuberculosis, and malaria, the U.S. President's Emergency Plan for AIDS Relief, and the World Bank are among many groups that are actively working to prevent and treat HIV. The WHO is playing the major role in coordination of these international efforts, but it is the healthcare systems in local areas that must play the central role in preventing and treating persons living with HIV. The WHO has as its goal universal access to HIV prevention, treatment, care, and support by the year 2010. To meet this goal, the WHO HIV/AIDS Program faces a number of serious challenges: (1) improving HIV testing and counseling; (2) preventing those living with HIV from passing it on to others either through sexual transmission or drug injection; (3) preventing transmission in healthcare settings through safe blood supplies and hygienic practices; (4) improving perinatal care to prevent transmission from infected mothers to their children; (5) reducing vulnerability of populations through laws and policies; (6) ensuring access to treatment and care for HIV and AIDS; (7) working with healthcare systems so that they have the resources and reach to provide these services; (8) developing sustainable financing; (9) monitoring the activities for preventing, diagnosing, and treating those living with HIV/AIDS; and (10) ensuring healthcare systems' response.

IMMUNIZATION AND OTHER INTERVENTION PROGRAMS

Ninety percent of worldwide child deaths come from 42 countries. Fifty-six percent of those deaths are from five infectious diseases: diarrhea, pneumonia, malaria, HIV/AIDS, and measles. With proper interventions, a vast majority of these deaths can be avoided. There are both "preventive interventions" and "treatment interventions" that have been identified in science-based literature as having a significant effect on childhood mortality caused by infectious diseases (Table 2-7).[32] The potential for dramatic reduction in childhood mortality only serves to remind us that healthcare systems must reach out and implement these measures.

One of the major functions of primary healthcare systems is to provide immunizations to the populations they serve. UNICEF's supply division provides vaccines and the necessary equipment for most developing countries of the world. Through a combined effort of many international health agencies, vaccines can be provided at a cost substantially below the market value in many developed countries. One major indicator of child health programs is the rate of immunization of children from measles. Every region of the world improved its rates of measles vaccine coverage between 1985 and 2005.[33] Because of these global efforts, mortality from measles dropped by 68% from 2000 to 2006.[34] Measles is one of the most contagious diseases known to human beings but is completely preventable with properly implemented vaccinations. Despite recent progress, an estimated 242,000 people, mostly children, still died from measles in 2006. Recent research into the role of political and organizational factors in immunization coverage in developing countries found that these national-level determinants can be predictors of immunization rates.[35] Tables 2-8 and 2-9 show the estimated cost to provide

TABLE 2-7 Effective Interventions for Five Childhood (< 5 years of age) Infectious Diseases and the Estimated Reduction in Associated Deaths

Infectious Disease	Intervention	Number of Deaths per 1,000 in Children < 5 Years in 2000 (%)	Estimated Number of Deaths per 1,000 Prevented in Children < 5 Years (%)
Diarrhea	Preventive: breastfeeding; complementary feeding; water sanitation and hygiene; zinc; vitamin A. Treatment: oral rehydration therapy; antibiotics for dysentery; zinc.	2,135 (22%)	1,886 (88% reduction)
Pneumonia	Preventive: breastfeeding; complementary feeding; Hib vaccine; zinc. Treatment: antibiotics for pneumonia.	2,055 (21%)	1,328 (65% reduction)
Malaria	Preventive: insecticide-treated materials; complementary feeding. Treatment: antimalarials.	915 (9%)	829 (91% reduction)
HIV/AIDS	Preventive: nevirapine and replacement feeding. Treatment: none.	312 (3%)	150 (48% reduction)
Measles	Preventive: complementary feeding; measles vaccine. Treatment: vitamin A.	103 (1%)	103 (100% reduction)

Data are from Jones G, Steketee RW, Black RE, et al. How many child deaths can we prevent this year? *The Lancet.* 2003;362:65–71.

basic childhood immunizations and the immunization coverage rate for selected countries.

EMERGING INFECTIOUS DISEASES

The threat of newly emerging and re-emerging infectious diseases is of great importance to public health professionals globally. Since 1981, we have experienced a spate of new diseases that have mutated from animal illnesses, including HIV/AIDS whose origin is in primates; the Ebola virus, which spread from monkeys; SARS, which resulted from a genetic mutation leading to a more virulent form of an existing virus; and Avian influenza, which has spread from domestic and wild bird populations. During the same time period, West Nile virus has greatly increased its geographic distribution. Diseases such as *Staphylococcus aureus*, *Mycobacteria tuberculosis*, and some strains of malaria have become resistant to the standard drug treatments that were previously effective in treating them. Between 1973 and 1995, 28 new or modified infectious agents and diseases that could infect humans were recognized.[36] Counted among those are HIV/AIDS (1983), rotavirus (1973), Ebola virus (1977), *Legionella pneumophila* (bacteria for Legionnaires' disease in 1977), *Helicobacter Pylori* (cause of peptic ulcer disease in 1983), hepatitis C (1989), *Vibrio cholerare* 0139 (new strain of cholera associated with epidemics in 1992), and *Staphylococcus aureus* (new toxin-producing strain associated with toxic shock syndrome in 1981).[36]

Many conditions lead to the emergence of new infectious diseases and the re-emergence of others. Population growth can impact the emergence of new diseases through crowding, people living in close proximity to animals, populations expanding into new ecosystems, and population migration. Changes in climate and weather patterns can result in altered disease life cycles

TABLE 2-8   Estimated Costs for Providing Childhood Immunizations in Developing Countries in U.S. Dollars for 2005*

	U.S. Dollars per Dose**	U.S. Dollars for Syringes***	Total U.S. Dollars	Number of Doses to Complete Immunization Series	Total Estimated Cost in U.S. Dollars
BCG (tuberculosis)	0.096	0.08	0.176	1	0.176
DTP (diphtheria, tetanus toxoid, pertussis)	0.134	0.065	0.199	3	0.597
Hep B Hepatitis B	0.27	0.065	0.335	3	1.005
Hib (*Haemophilus influenzae* type B for meningitis)	Not available	Not available			
MCV (measles-containing vaccine, not an MMR)	0.18	0.065	0.245	2	0.66
Oral polio virus	0.15	0.065	0.215	3	0.645
TT2+ (PAB) (second and third doses of tetanus toxoid assuming the child is protected at birth due to pregnant mother vaccination)	0.075	0.065	0.14	2	0.28
Total Cost (Less Hib)					3.36

* Costs were calculated based on data from the UNICEF Supply Division that provides a general estimate of costs for budgeting and planning.
** Some vaccines come in several different ways, and this table represents the most common.
*** We have estimated the syringe requirements based on UNICEF Supply Division recommendations of what is needed to administer a dose. None of these costs reflect other required resources such as those needed for skin disinfection, refrigeration, healthcare personnel, and in some cases transportation.

through adaptations of vectors and their habitats. Globalization, particularly as it relates to travel and transportation, can contribute to diseases emerging where they have not previously been found. Re-emergence of infectious diseases that were previously considered under control may be the result of organisms developing resistance to overused antibiotics or through genetic mutations that are known to occur on a regular basis among viruses. As these biological agents emerge, human populations are without immunity and are at considerable risk for infection and disease. In the worst case scenario, one can liken the introduction of a new or mutated virulent virus to the smallpox and measles epidemics that ravaged Native American populations in the 1800s. Add to this poorly functioning healthcare systems with limited resources and underfunded public health programs for surveillance, education, and control, and the stage is set for potential pandemics.[37] Table 2-10 outlines several major diseases that have had a major impact worldwide.

TABLE 2-9   National Immunization Coverage Rates for Selected Countries, 2005*

	2005 National Immunization Coverage Rates							
	BCG	**DTP1**	**DTP3***	**HEPB3**	**HIB3****	**MCV**	**POL3**	**TT2**
Argentina	99	90	92	87	92	99	92	n/a
Australia	n/a	97	92	94	94	94	92	n/a
Belize	96	97	96	97	96	95	96	n/a
Brazil	99	96	96	92	96	99	98	n/a
Cambodia	87	85	82	n/a	n/a	79	82	53
Canada	n/a	97	94	n/a	83	94	89	n/a
China	86	95	87	84	n/a	86	87	n/a
Egypt	98	98	98	98	n/a	98	98	80
France	84	98	98	29	87	87	98	n/a
Germany	n/a	96	90	84	92	93	94	n/a
India	75	81	59	8	n/a	58	58	80
Indonesia	82	88	70	70	n/a	72	70	70
Japan	n/a	99	99	n/a	n/a	99	97	n/a
Kenya	85	85	76	76	76	69	70	72
Korea	94	83	79	92	n/a	96	97	n/a
Mexico	99	99	98	98	98	96	98	n/a
Nigeria	48	43	25	n/a	n/a	35	39	51
Panama	99	95	85	85	85	99	86	n/a
Peru	93	94	84	84	84	80	80	n/a
Russia	97	98	98	97	n/a	99	98	n/a
Senegal	92	97	84	84	18	74	84	85
South Africa	97	98	94	94	94	82	94	n/a
Taiwan	n/a	n/a	n/a	n/a	n/a	n/a	n/a	n/a
Turkey	89	92	90	85	n/a	91	90	47
United Kingdom	n/a	97	91	n/a	91	82	91	n/a
United States	n/a	99	96	92	94	93	92	n/a

* These immunization completion rates are based on the WHO/UNICEF Joint Reporting Form and the form can be found at the following websites: http://www.childinfo.org/arease/immunization/ and http://www.who.int/immunization_monitoring/data/en/.

** Statistics are reported on the third dose of DTP, as are HIB and Hep B, to measure the completeness of this immunization schedule.

Data are from UNICEF/WHO. *Immunization Summary: The 2007 Edition.* New York and Geneva, Switzerland, 2007.

TABLE 2-10 Examples of Emerging Infectious Disease

Disease (Agent)	Source of Emergence or Re-emergence	Comments	Prevention
West Nile Virus[38,39]	Emergence in North America from Africa. First recognized in Uganda in 1937 and emerged in New York in 1999 with a 59-patient outbreak.	Transmitted by mosquito bites; birds serve as intermediary hosts; there is no specific treatment; no vaccination; severe cases in one in 150.	Reduce exposure to night-biting mosquitoes.
SARS[1,40]	Emerged in south China in 2002 from animal reservoirs. SARS-associated coronavirus (SARS-CoV).	Spread person to person by respiratory droplets; severe pneumonia symptoms; high fatality rates.	Identification; isolation of patients; quarantine exposed persons; restrictions on air travel.
Ebola Hemorrhagic Fever Virus[41,42]	Emergence in Africa (Zaire) in 1976; probably caused by contact with an animal, most likely a primate. The virus is from the Filoviridae family of RNA viruses.	Transmitted directly from person to person through blood and secretions. Fatality rates are from 44% to 88% in humans.	Early diagnosis; hemorrhagic fever isolation procedures; barrier nursing techniques; equipment sterilization; avoidance of contact with blood and secretions of patients.
Avian Influenza[43,44]	First human-to-human cases in Thailand of H5N1 subtype of A viruses in 2004; Vietnam 2005; Azerbaijan 2006; Indonesia 2006; Vietnam 2006.	Virus is found in healthy wild birds; can infect domestic birds (chickens, ducks, and turkeys) with 90% fatality in flocks; can spread person to person in small family groups; 50% fatality rate.	Early diagnosis. Concern for future virus mutation; person-to-person spread could become commonplace, like other influenza A strains (H1N1, H1N2, H3N2); H5N1 is resistant to two antiviral drugs (amantadine and rimantadine).
MRSA[45–47] Methicillin Resistant *Staphylococcus aureau.* VISA/VRSA Vancomycin-Intermediate/ Resistant *Staphylococcus aureus*	Resistance to methicillin, oxacillin, penicillin, and amoxicillin. Resistant to vancomycin.	Person to person contact, contact with contaminated surfaces, and contact with healthcare personnel who can carry the infection from one patient to the next; 20% fatality rate of invasive infection.	Early identification; good sanitation in healthcare settings, including personnel and surgical suites; possible community reservoirs in health clubs that cause skin infections.
Multidrug-Resistant Tuberculosis[46,48] Extensively Resistant Tuberculosis	Resistant to isoniazid and rifampicin. Also resistant to fluoroquinolone and at least three infectables: amikacin, kanamycin, or capreomycin.	Person to person through the air; persons with HIV are particularly susceptible.	Early identification and treatment of active tuberculosis cases; completion of treatment is especially important.

CONCLUSION

Strategies to identify and control emerging and re-emerging infectious diseases include constant disease surveillance on a worldwide basis. This strategy relies on countries being open with information on disease outbreaks and sharing information with global health agencies such as the WHO and the U.S. Centers for Disease Control. Further control can result if laboratories share information quickly as new or unusual levels of diseases are identified. The use of emergency response teams to areas where there are outbreaks so that diseases can be contained improves the prospects of limiting further spread of disease. The enforcement of travel restrictions when appropriate can help to limit contact with infectious diseases, as can quarantine techniques if required. Many of these methods require a high level of international cooperation and coordination. There have been times in the recent past when disease outbreaks, such as Avian flu in humans and SARS, were quickly identified, and international infectious disease specialists were used in response to these outbreaks in a timely manner and were successful. Other control practices are funded immunization programs, community education, and early identification by primary healthcare providers. Perhaps the most important strategy to limit infectious disease is through reduction of poverty coupled with good infrastructure such as building water and wastewater systems.

REFERENCES

1. Merson MH, Black RE, Mills AJ. *International Public Health: Diseases, Programs, Systems, and Policies.* 2nd ed. Sudbury, MA: Jones and Bartlett Publishers; 2006.

2. Basch PF. *Textbook of International Health.* New York: Oxford University Press; 1999.

3. Lopez AD, Murray CCHL. The global burden of disease, 1990–2020. *Nature Medicine.* 1998;4:1241–1243.

4. Murry CJL. Quantifying the burden of disease: the technical basis for disability adjusted life years. *Bulletin of the World Health Organization.* 1994;72:429–445.

5. Skolnick R.S. *Essentials of Global Health.* Sudbury, MA: Jones and Bartlett; 2008.

6. McKenzie JF, Pinger RR, Kotecki JE. *An Introduction to Community Health.* Sudbury, MA: Jones and Bartlett; 2005.

7. World Health Organization. *Preventing Chronic Diseases: A Vital Investment.* Geneva, Switzerland: WHO; 2005.

8. Moorthy VS, Good MF, Hill AV. Malaria vaccine development. *The Lancet.* 2004;363(9403):150–156.

9. Sachs JD. A new global effort to control malaria. *Science.* 2002;298:122–124.

10. Yamey G. Roll back malaria: a failing global health campaign. *British Medical Journal.* (serial online). 2004;328:1086–1087. Retrieved March 23, 2008, from http://www.bmj.com/cgi/content/full/328/7448/1086.

11. Hay SI, Guerra CA, Tatem AJ, Noor AM, Snow RW. The global distribution and population at risk of malaria: past, present, and future. *The Lancet Infectious Diseases.* 2004;4:327–336.

12. Martens P, Hall L. Malaria and the move: human population movement and malaria transmission. *Emerging Infectious Diseases.* 2000;6:103–109.

13. Sachs J, Malaney P. The economic and social burden of malaria. *Nature.* 2002;415:680–685.

14. Gallup JL, Sachs JD. The economic burden of malaria. *American Journal of Tropic Medicine and Hygiene.* 2001;64 (1, 2):85–96.

15. Bryce J, Pinto-Boschi C, Shibuya K, Black RE. WHO estimates of the causes of death in children. *The Lancet.* 2005; 365:1147–1152.

16. UNICEF. *Progress for Children: A World Fit for Children Statistical Review,* 6th ed. New York: UNICEF Division of Communication; 2007. Retrieved March 21, 2008, from http://childinfo.org/areas/childmortality/Progress_for_Children.pdf.

17. Fontaine O, Garner P, Bhan MK. Oral rehydration therapy: the simple solution for saving lives. *British Medical Journal.* 2007;334(Suppl 1):s14.

18. Parashar UD, Hummelman EG, Bresee JS, Miller MA, Glass RI. Global illness and deaths caused by rotavirus disease in children. *Emerging Infectious Diseases.* 2003;9(3):565–572.

19. Bern C, Martines J, de Zoysa I, Glass RI. The magnitude of the global problem of diarrhoeal disease: a ten year update. *Bulletin of the World Health Organization.* 1992;70:705–714.

20. Kosek M, Bern C, Guerrant RL. The global burden of diarrhoeal disease, as estimated from studies published between 1992 and 2000. *Bulletin of the World Health Organization.* 2003;81(3):197–204.

21. World Health Organization and UNICEF. *Meeting the MDG Drinking Water and Sanitation Target: The Urban and Rural Challenge of the Decade.* Geneva, Switzerland: WHO Press; 2006. Retrieved March 25, 2008, from http://www.childinfo.org/areas/water/pdfs/jmp06final.pdf.

22. Epidemiology Program Office, Office of the Director, CDC. Achievements in public health, 1900–1999: changes in the public health system. *JAMA* (online). 2000;283:735–738.

23. WHO. www.who.int/cholera/en/index.html.

24. Graham NM. The epidemiology of acute respiratory infections in children and adults: a global perspective. *Epidemiologic Reviews.* 1990;12:149–178.

25. Murray CJL, Lopez AD. Global and regional cause-of-death patterns 1990. *Bulletin of the World Health Organization.* 1994;72(3):447–480.

26. Dye C, Garnett GP, Sleeman K, Williams BG. Prospects for worldwide tuberculosis control under the WHO DOTS strategy. *The Lancet.* 1998;352:1886–1891.

27. Williams BG, Dye C. Antiretroviral drugs for tuberculosis control in the era of HIV/AIDS. *Science.* 2003;301:1535–1537.

28. Gill B, Okie S. China and HIV: a window of opportunity. *The New England Journal of Medicine.* 2007;356(18):1801–1806.

29. World Health Organization. Glion Consultation on Strengthening the Linkages between Reproductive Health and HIV/AIDS in Women and Children. United Nations Family Planning Agency; 2006, WHO/HIV/2006.02.

30. WHO HIV/AIDS Program. Taking Stock: HIV in Children; 2006, WHO/HIV/2006.04.

31. Gayle HD, Hill GL. Global impact of human immunodeficiency virus and AIDS. *Clinical Microbiology Reviews.* 2001;14(2):327–335.

32. Jones G, Steketee RW, Black RE, Bhutta ZA, Morris SS, Bellagio Child Survival Study Group. How many child deaths can we prevent this year? *The Lancet.* 2003;362:65–71.

33. United Nations Children's Fund (UNICEF). Immunization Summary: The 2007 Edition. New York: UNICEF Strategic Information Section; 2007.

34. World Health Organization. Measles Fact Sheet, WHO Web site; 2007. Retrieved March 25, 2008, from http://www.who.int/mediacentre/factsheets/fs286/en/.

35. Gauri V, Khaleghian R. Immunization in developing countries: its political and organizational determinants. *World Development.* 2002;30(12):2109–2132.

36. National Institute of Allergy and Infectious Disease. Emerging Infectious Diseases Research: NIAID Meets the Challenge. Dateline: NIAID, 1997. Retrieved from http://www.niaid.nih.gov/publications/dateline/0907/introsto.htm.

37. Racaniell VR. Emerging infectious diseases. *Journal of Clinical Investigation.* 2004;113(6):796–798.

38. Huhn GD, Sejvar JJ, Montgomery SP. West Nile virus in the United States: a update on an emerging infectious disease. *American Family Physician.* 2003;68(4):653–670.

39. Centers for Disease Control. West Nile virus activity—United States, January 1–December 1, 2005. *Morbidity and Mortality Weekly Report.* 2005;54(49):1253–1256.

40. Centers for Disease Control. Severe Acute Respiratory Syndrome (SARS). Fact Sheet: Basic Information About SARS. Retrieved from http://www.cdc.gov/ncidod/sara/factsheet.html.

41. Centers for Disease Control. Ebola Hemorrhagic Fever Information Packet; 2002, Special Pathogens Branch, Division of Viral and Rickettsial Diseases, National Center for Infectious Diseases.

42. Centers for Disease Control. Ebola Hemorrhagic Fever: Known Cases and Outbreaks of Ebola Hemorrhagic Fever, in Chronological Order. Retrieved from www.cdc.gov.

43. Centers for Disease Control. Key Facts About Avian Influenza (Bird Flu) and Avian Influenza A (HN1) Virus; 2007. Retrieved from http://www.cdc.gov/flu/avian/gen-info/facts.html.

44. Centers for Disease Control. Avian Influenza: Current H5N1 Situation; 2008. Retrieved from http://www.cdc.gov/flu/avian/outbreaks/current.html.

45. Centers for Disease Control. Healthcare-Associated Methicillin Resistant Staphylococcus aureus (HA-MRSA). November 16, 2007. Retrieved from http://www.cdc.gov/ncidod/dhqp/ar_mrsa.html.

46. Centers for Disease Control. Invasive MRSA. Retrieved October 17, 2007, from http://www.cdc.gov/ncidod/dhqp/ar_mrsa_Invasiv_FS.html.

47. Centers for Disease Control. VISA/VRSA: Vancomycin-Intermediate/Resistant *Staphylococcus aureus,* 2004. Retrieved from http://www.cdc.gov/ncidod/dhqp/ar_fisavrsa.html.

48. Centers for Disease Control. Multidrug-Resistant Tuberculosis (MDR TB) Fact Sheet. Retrieved January 22, 2008, from http://www.cdc.gov/tb/pubs/tbfactsheets/mdrtb.html.

Global Health: Systems, Policy, and Economics

Walter J. Jones

INTRODUCTION

The Worldwide Challenge of Health Policy Making in the 21st Century

Health care is one part of society that has always been subject to varying degrees of public scrutiny and regulation and thus health policy making in one guise or another. Because medicine originated thousands of years ago within such important social institutions as religion, no society has considered its organization and practice to be without a necessary social dimension that needed to be monitored.[1] Governments, or other social/community organizations, have intervened in health care because the nation's society has viewed it to be at least partly a social service, not an economic good. Government intervention often takes place because of market imperfections or failure or because of political imperatives that override the prerogatives of the healthcare market.[1–4]

As is discussed later, the biggest policy-making challenges faced by nations around the world are broadly similar and represent efforts to manage a medical/scientific revolution that has positively transformed the life prospects of humanity. Using almost any metric of performance, there is no area of human endeavor that has been more successful in the last 150 years than health care. In that very success lie the worldwide problems we now face. As physician and social theorist William Schwartz noted (pp. 2–3, emphasis added)[5]

> Even the prospect of dependable and sustained progress against disease—let alone the achievement of a medical utopia—emerged only after World War II. . . . [At the end of] the hundred year span beginning with the 1950s and ending in the year 2050, it seems conceivable that most of today's debilitating and fatal diseases will be preventable or curable. . . . That is the utopian vision for medicine that now, for the first time, appears to have a scientific foundation. *The critical question is at what price—economically, politically, and ethically—that vision will be realized.*

All nations now have problems controlling costs, providing effective access to care, ensuring a reasonable level of quality of care, controlling the introduction and use of technology, and validly measuring individual and community health outcomes; however, at the same time, nations are attempting to address these common health system aspects while possessing widely varying national cultures, governmental structures, economies, political systems, and population/subpopulation health statuses and lifestyles.[6] Not surprisingly, then, what U.S. policy makers are considering with respect to health systems reform differs considerably from that contemplated by their counterparts in nations such as the United Kingdom, Brazil, Russia, and China.[7,8]

It is argued here that despite these differences the general range of policy-making issues and options faced by nations can be productively analyzed and compared by using well-defined models of what can be called *micro* and *macro* health policy making. To consider health policy-making issues and activities around the world, we must first understand *how to think* about health policy making.

HOW TO THINK ABOUT HEALTH POLICY MAKING—MICRO AND MACRO MODELS

In the most fundamental way, health policy making (like any other area of policy making) is a *political* process. There may be varying technical and clinical issues at stake in any given action, and the particular actors in the policy process may differ markedly. Most policy making (whether it is taking place within a democratic or nondemocratic framework) usually involves both governmental and nongovernmental individuals and organizations. Nevertheless, all policy activities are critically determined by the interactions of individuals and interest groups within the society over the distribution of its resources. It is, at bottom, *politics*—in the words of Harold Lasswell, "who gets what, when, how."[9]

As suggested at the beginning, health policy making, like economics, can be usefully analyzed using both a "micro" and a "macro" framework. In some ways, these policy frameworks are analogous to microeconomics (the study of economic interactions at the level of individual producers and consumers) and macroeconomics (the analysis of economic activity at the sector, regional, national, and international levels). For the purposes of policy analysis, they are interrelated and should both be used if the dynamics, substance, and outcomes of health policy making are to be fully understood.

Micro Policy Making—The Policy Marketplace Model

The marketplace model of policy making is outlined most completely in the work on health legislative policy making done by Feldstein.[10] As the term indicates, it is adapted from economic theory, with suppliers and demanders, as in the economic marketplace. The policy marketplace model has the following characteristics:

• Like its economic counterpart, the policy marketplace model assumes that individuals and groups are constantly interacting to satisfy their needs. All policy actors are both suppliers and demanders because they must *exchange* some commodity in the marketplace to "purchase" the other goods that they want. For example, politicians supply favorable policies. In democratic states, these usually include financial subsidies, regulations, and additional health-related services for constituency groups such as senior citizens, hospitals, and medical schools. In exchange, the politicians receive political support, which could include financial contributions, votes, and other desirable commodities.[10] In dictatorships such as Zimbabwe, the exchanged goods could also include such items as access to basic health services, in exchange for support from armed groups, including the nation's military and police forces, used to suppress the mass public.[11]

• As in the economic marketplace, the policy marketplace around the world features disparities in power.[12] Individuals and groups that can supply more can demand more in exchange. In the United States, physicians, senior citizens, hospitals, pharmaceutical and insurance companies, and academic health centers are among the "haves," as they are politically organized, particularly through interest groups and professional associations such as the American Hospital Association, the American Medical Association, and the American Association of Retired Persons. Members of these groups receive relatively generous government services and legal protections. On the other hand, politically unorganized groups in nations as diverse as the United States and India are often less educated, politically powerful, and geographically well situated and as a consequence receive substandard or no medical services.[13,14]

- In the policy marketplace, the currency used in exchanges can be money, but it can also include superior leadership, more effective organization, access to and greater articulation through communications media, and greater group member "intensity," or a willingness to exert great efforts in order to advance the interests of the group.[15,16] The latter is evident in U.S. health policy making with disease-specific and "victim" groups, such as family members of the mentally ill, and people with HIV/AIDS,[17–19] as well as in the post–World War II development of the Japanese health insurance system.[20] Money matters, but power in the policy marketplace involves much more than money.

- To gain control over their relevant areas of the marketplace, nongovernmental groups will attempt to forge enduring alliances with governmental agencies. For example, disease-specific groups in the United States lobby for more federal government funding for research via the National Institutes of Health in their area of disease. In the distinctive policy marketplaces of the United States, Canada, the United Kingdom, and France, pharmaceutical companies attempt to influence regulation by interacting differently with the relevant national health policy makers.[21] More politically powerful groups will be more successful at this than the "have nots." Often, these groups will engage in their activities via enduring "iron triangles" or more transient "issue networks" of power and influence.[22] As a result, it *cannot* be assumed that government in any given policy system will protect "the little guy." Indeed, more often than not, governmental regulations *reinforce* power disparities in health policy making.[10]

Macro Policy Making—The Policy Systems Model

In contrast to the marketplace of micro policy making, the "macro" level of policy making can be best conceived of as the continual evolution of a complex system. Systems theory was developed in the disciplines of engineering and ecology. It was first applied to political systems by Easton[23] and has been modified for use to describe health policy making by Longest.[13] As applied to policy systems, it has the following characteristics:

- *Complexity*, with numerous influences interacting to produce a system that is continually in flux while generally attaining some level of equilibrium or stability. Individuals, social groups, and organizations are all actors in the policy process.

- *Interrelatedness*, with most significant activities connected to one another by feedback loops and both direct and indirect impacts. All policy actions create reactions within the system, some perhaps modifying the system itself.

- *Cyclical processes*. With complexity and interrelatedness, the policy process does not have a definite beginning or end but continues on as long as organized society continues to exist. There are no permanent policy successes or failures.

As noted, the systems model is cyclical, and thus, strictly speaking, there is no start or finish—just a continual cycle in which any beginning is arbitrary. In Longest's model, the policy process has the following stages:

1. *Recognition of inputs.* There are numerous elements of feedback from previous policy decisions (health outcomes, budgets, programs, elections, and so forth). These include support and opposition to current policies and demands for modifications of these policies. These inputs are recognized by policy actors (including elected officials, interest group leaders, and regulators) and lead to the reactive efforts by policy actors to engage in further policy activities.

2. *Policy formulation.* Significant policy actors attempt to develop new policies to address these new inputs. In advanced nations, these efforts usually center on formal policy-making structures, such as executive, legislative, judicial, and regulatory institutions. Executive orders are issued. Legislation passes through Congress or a similar assembly. Lawyers bring cases for consideration before judicial bodies, or regulatory agencies take up issues brought before them. As with the other stages of policy making, the actions of policy formulation cannot be separated from politics and political considerations. As suggested in a study of health policy making in advanced, industrial democracies,[24] there is no such thing as apolitical policy formulation.

3. *Policy outputs.* Efforts at formulation can result in a variety of policy outputs. The most obvious and conventional include statutory laws and regulatory directives (passed by legislatures but subsequently

implemented by regulatory agencies). These actions can also contain subsidy and taxation provisions, thus redistributing wealth from other areas of society to another. One output can in fact be a *non-decision*—a phenomenon first described by Crenson[25] and defined as a decision to do nothing that itself creates a political and policy impacts, such as when the U.S. Congress blocked President Bill Clinton's Health Security Act in 1994 without ever holding any formal hearings or votes.[26,27]

Many policy outputs also intentionally provide some element of *political symbolism*. As described by Edelman,[28] symbolic politics is virtually inseparable from policy making, as it provides both policy makers and the mass public with threatening and/or reassuring images that emotionally "condense" often complex arguments into easily accessible reactions. Often these symbols include evocative legislative titles, such as the Medicare Modernization Act of 2003, which not only added a prescription drug benefit for seniors in the United States, but also multibillion dollar subsidies for the U.S. health insurance and pharmaceuticals industries. Who could oppose "modernization"? As Edelman notes, symbols can often be used in policy making to distract the public from policy details that powerful and focused interest groups have worked out for their own benefit (if not the general public's).[28]

4. *Implementation.* Any policy output that is not a nondecision has to be implemented to have a social impact, and that implementation can be highly variable.[29,30] Government agencies must often work through nongovernmental elements of society to implement policies, and the values and political skills and preferences of leaders in these organizations often determine whether (and, if so, how) a new governmental policy is realized through implementation.[1] Because of the vagaries of implementation, the actual impacts of policies are often unanticipated.[31,32]

5. *Outcomes.* Policies create individual, group, and social impacts. In health policy, the most obvious outcome may involve changes in individual, group, and social health resource consumption and health status. Usually, however, health policies have non-health outcomes that may be equally important politically. There are always "winners" and "losers." Some individuals and groups get more resources—others pay. Some have their needs attended to; others are neglected. Policy outcomes may also have profound long-range impacts that were unantici-

pated, such as the creation of new ethical issues (e.g., in the case of new technological development resulting from the Human Genome Project), and the need for explicit resource rationing (when government research funding leads to useful but costly new medical technologies and procedures).[5,33]

6. *Feedback and subsequent modification.* As in previous policy cycles, outputs and outcomes create the reactions in society mentioned earlier and related further efforts at policy development. The policy agenda is refreshed, and the cycle continues on. Often the "success" of a previous cycle (e.g., the enaction of Medicare and Medicaid to address the lack of healthcare access for seniors and some categories of the "poor") leads to the challenges faced in a subsequent cycle (e.g., how to cope with the unsustainable healthcare demands and cost inflation triggered by events such as the introduction of large government health insurance programs such as Medicare and Medicaid).[34,35] Health policy making does result in great benefits for individuals and society, but it also seems like "one damn thing after another" when viewed in terms of day-to-day activities.

THE CONVERGENCE OF POLICY PROBLEMS, AND POSSIBLE RESPONSES

Since the rise of modern medicine in the 19th and 20th centuries,[36] national variations in health organization, practice, and policies have been gradually affected by a growing convergence due to technological change and social globalization.[37] Recent international surveys of health systems changes emphasize that nations are all coping with some of the same major problems, including cost-containment, access barriers to large population subgroups, the impact of rapidly developing new technologies, ensuring a reasonably high-quality standard for care, and measuring health outcomes.[6]

Cost Containment

All nations face the problem that the cost of providing modern health care with currently accepted standards and technologies is outrunning their abilities to generate the wealth to pay for it. Nations that do not have true healthcare "systems," such as the United States, may be racing toward the cliff of runaway healthcare costs faster than most European nations, which have historically possessed national structures for healthcare organization and delivery.[38] All nations, however, are being forced to confront the issue of allocating scarce healthcare resources. By 2020, it is estimated that healthcare spending will *triple* in real dollars, to $10 trillion, taking 21% of U.S. gross domestic product (GDP) and 16% of GDP in other Organisation for Economic Co-operation and Development nations—essentially, the economically advanced nations in North America, Europe, Asia, and Australia.[6]

The need for cost containment entails consideration of the *cost-effectiveness* of health technologies and procedures.[39] Frequently, the most cost-effective technology is not the most recently developed, particularly in areas where it appears healthcare research and development are approaching or have reached the "flat of the curve" (Dranove, 2000, Ch. 2). Cost containment requirements also includes the imperative to sometimes say "no," even when the added consumption of health resources might benefit individual and/or population health in some way.[40] The removal of "waste" in health services delivery is certainly desirable, but the ultimate challenge in cost containment is controlling and limiting the application of potentially useful health services. As the PWC (PriceWaterhouseCoopers) world leaders' survey suggests, this will require a "quest for common ground" so as to provide "basic health benefits within the context of societal priorities."[6]

Access to Care

Whether they are economically advanced and wealthy or relatively poor and less developed, all nations have at least some subpopulations that are relatively disadvantaged in their access to necessary health services. It is often difficult to address these needs, as they usually require the expenditure of additional resources (clearly limited, as noted earlier). In addition, the redistribution of national resources to "have-not" groups is often administratively and technically difficult (e.g., it is hard to reach vast rural populations in nations such as China), and politically divisive (politically active and articulate "have" groups in all nations usually want to keep their share of national wealth rather than having much of it taken away and given to others).[10]

Often, poorer citizens in nations such as Bolivia, Vietnam, and Moldova have to rely on under-the-table payments (often constituting bribery) to get even the most essential healthcare services from underpaid and overworked providers.[41] In extreme situations of political instability and repression, healthcare institutions can break down entirely, as was the case in Zimbabwe in early 2008. The health service, once resilient, is falling apart. Especially in the rural areas, people are dying fast. HIV or AIDS has hit nearly a fifth of the population. Life expectancy has dived from the highest in sub-Saharan Africa to 36 years, one of the lowest. Surgical operations in the biggest hospital have had to be stopped because basic equipment is defunct and drugs have run out. Three quarters of the doctors have emigrated, along with more than half of the nurses, physiotherapists, and social workers. Patients seeking operations and treatment must buy medicine themselves.[42]

At the same time, wider access to basic health services would save hundreds of millions of people worldwide from death and disability and serve as a powerful tool in antipoverty efforts.[43,44] The case for greater access to health care is therefore both sensible from the standpoint of national interests[45] and a global moral imperative.[46] When the wealthiest nations in the world help the poorest and sickest people in the world, they wind up doing well for themselves by doing good for others. (Indeed, if this was not the case, the outlook for the poorest and the sickest would be even worse than it is now.)

Impact of New Technologies

Health technologies have continuously and rapidly evolved in the last century, usually becoming more complex and costly. These technologies, in areas as varied as assistive technologies, pharmaceuticals, and surgical techniques, often provide major health benefits to their recipients[47]; however, all nations, facing cost-containment difficulties, have to balance the use of limited resources with these new technologies against older but cheaper services (often in the realm of primary care) that may help larger numbers of people, but less dramatically or visibly. This leads to both economic and ethical conflict, as such decision making inevitably does involve "playing God," often with life and death consequences.[48] All nations *do* have to decide who lives and who dies, at least at some level.

Quality of Care Considerations

As healthcare technologies become more complex, the issue of quality assurance looms larger. Health professionals often cannot monitor technologies through simple observation—detailed technologies are required to provide constant readings.[1] In addition, there have been breakthroughs in data collection and analysis during the last 2 decades, particularly with respect to the development of computerized data entry and aggregation (often via Internet-based means). For the first time in history, it is possible to aggregate large numbers of patient encounters and detect variations in care quality, along with their consequences, such as medical errors. Studies in the United States, the United Kingdom, Canada, and Australia constitute the first steps in defining and understanding the level of medical errors;[49–52] however, as noted in the PWC report, "No one really knows how many errors or adverse events occur because of gaps in reporting processes and differences in definition."[52]

The revolution in health information technology means that nations can consciously guide healthcare quality assurance and improvement, with enormous benefits accruing to both patients and providers. Of course, to benefit from these technologies, nations must also develop the necessary data collection systems, along with the trained professionals to administer and use them. As with other aspects of health technologies, this can pose major challenges for less economically developed nations, such as India.[53]

Measuring Health Outcomes

In the long run, the greatest potential benefit from new health information technologies is that they increase the likelihood that health status and outcomes can be measured and related back to health services used, as well as individual and community lifestyles and practices. The "health outcomes movement" has the potential to make health services delivery much more cost-effective, along with reducing medical errors and clarifying what aspects of health care and behavior are more or less important.[54]

An important part of this is showing to what extent health services and new technologies *cannot* substitute for improved individual and community health lifestyles. For example, whatever funding the nation of China puts into its health system for treatment of lung cancers, it is clear that it cannot substitute for a concerted effort to reduce the rapid increase in national tobacco consumption, which will result in the deaths of tens of millions over the next few decades.[55] The *Healthy People 2010* report notes that 70% of all premature deaths in the United States are due to individual behaviors and environmental factors.[56]

Unfortunately, as discussed later here, it is also true that nations differ in their abilities to afford and apply the systems needed for effective health outcomes research, as well the subsequent system reforms driven by research results, with poorer nations being especially hampered.

Internationally, there is a growing general consensus over the existence of the above-mentioned healthcare system problems. Within each country, there has also been some debate (if only at the upper policy-making level) over how the nation should respond to these challenges. China, a rapidly developing but still low-income nation that has never really had a structured national health system, is discussing how one might be set up and how the costs might be borne.[40] Developed nations with existing national health systems, such as Australia and Japan, are talking about to what extent (and if so, how) private sector components should be introduced and integrated to improve provider responsiveness to consumer demands.[57,58]

The United States is unique internationally in that it is a very wealthy nation with a lavishly funded healthcare sector but lacks an effective structure to direct spending and system restructuring. Thus, although the U.S. system can produce some of the best high-technology health care in the world, and leads in research and development spending, it wastes money on an epic scale and suffers from glaring disparities in health insurance coverage and access to care.[52] With the highest proportion of GDP devoted to health care of any nation, and cost inflation generally recognized as unsustainable, health reform has resurfaced on the policy agenda. Reform proposals have been put forth both by political liberals (such as the introduction of a "single payer" system like that in Canada or enhanced employer coverage within existing insurance structures) and conservatives (the increased use of individual healthcare purchasing through health savings accounts.[60,61]

In the international study done by PriceWaterhouseCoopers,[6] three clear findings emerge:

• *No* nation's study respondents are confident that their nation's healthcare system can be sustained, given current trends. Cost inflation is outrunning available resources everywhere, with nations such as the United States and France looking at possible system-wide breakdowns in the next 10 to 20 years. Entirely government-run and mixed public/private sector systems alike face financial ruin in coming decades, while developing nations' efforts to construct effective basic healthcare systems are threatened by enormous budgetary and taxation burdens.[6]
• The most important attribute of reformed national healthcare systems in coming years will be *sustainability*. "To be sustainable, health executives will need information, metrics and transparency

to support decision making. . . . Transparency enables a comparative focus on access as well as the cost and quality of care."[6]

- Increasingly, with ever-growing global communication between national health policy makers, it appears that *convergence* will characterize policy reform efforts. In the words of the PWC study, "Global convergence, as best practices are shared, and industry-wide convergence, as the barriers among pharmaceuticals, providers, clinicians, biotech and payers melt away. Sustainability requires an understanding of the blended nature of health. It requires leadership to integrate and balance the need of individual sectors for their own sustainability while creating an overall model that will support itself beyond 2020."[6]

If sustainability is the key objective for health policy makers around the world, what aspects of reform do they have to focus on to get there? Like most others who have considered the issue, the PWC analysts believe that there are some critical factors. The PWC list includes these:

1. *A quest for common ground.* Essentially, this is an effort to develop a national political consensus over the public/private sector division of healthcare responsibilities, along with a social agreement over some basic level of guaranteed access to basic health services for all citizens.
2. *A digital backbone.* This is the use of nationwide integrated clinical and administrative information systems to increase the efficiency of the healthcare system, as well as to provide data that can be utilized for program evaluation and outcomes research efforts.
3. *Incentive realignment.* This feature centers on the nation's citizens who are healthcare recipients and contends that a sustainable national system must "ensure and manage access to care while supporting accountability and responsibility for healthcare decisions."[6]
4. *Quality and safety standardization.* This feature focuses on provider accountability and responsibility, suggesting that there need to be transparent quality and safety standards so that consumer trust can be established and maintained in the nation's healthcare services.
5. *Strategic resource deployment.* This is more vaguely defined in the PWC study, as it suggests the need for resource allocation that "appropriately satisfies competing demands on systems" to balance cost

containment and access requirements without being able to provide any real definition of what might constitute "appropriate satisfaction."[6] This indicates the contingent nature of this feature, as it will most clearly be determined by the political balance of power within each society.

6. *Climate of innovation.* This feature suggests that nations need to embrace innovation in both technology and processes in order to improve the functioning of the healthcare system.
7. *Adaptable delivery roles and structures.* The PWC report calls for patient-centered care that is maximized in varying circumstances by the adoption of variable care practices and clinical roles.

Surveying the current state of national health systems around the world, what can be concluded with respect to the progress being made in policy making in these areas?

Two of the previously mentioned sustainability features are primarily technological in nature and can be assessed fairly easily. Some nations have moved materially toward a true "digital backbone" (number 2, mentioned previously), but only a few. The Netherlands has pioneered in using health information systems to improve healthcare quality within a constrained national budget.[62] Canada anticipates having electronic medical records for half of its population by 2010, and the United Kingdom plans to have an integrated electronic health record system for all providers by 2014.[63] These nations, however, already have truly integrated national health systems: The Netherlands has a national employer-based system, and the United Kingdom has a National Health Service, whereas Canada has a "single-payer" system administered by its provinces.[60] There may be significant problems with national health systems, but it *is* easier to implement uniform technical and structural reforms within them. In all of these nations, the policy marketplace has been dominated by forces (particularly the government and organized labor, along with general public opinion) in favor of national health care. As is discussed later, if that decision is made (or not made), choices concerning structure, including of information systems, are significantly affected.

In contrast, the United States is very wealthy and spends an enormous amount on health care but lacks such a national governing structure. In the policy marketplace, there is no overriding national ideological consensus in favor of a national health system, and industry groups tend to further system fragmentation through their own interests in controlling market share. Consequently, the U.S. health care has failed to produce a viable health information system through market mechanisms.[64] Smaller providers in the United States, particularly home health agencies and skilled nursing facilities, have clearly lagged behind larger private and public sector health systems in adopting health information technologies.[65]

In recent years, the need for national health information integration has become so evident that it has united conservatives like Newt Gingrich and liberals like Hillary Clinton in support of national policy initiatives.[66] A conservative Republican President, George W. Bush, followed through on this call by supporting the establishment by 2015 of a National Health Information Infrastructure, which will be a "comprehensive knowledge-based network of interoperable systems of clinical, public health and personal health information."[67] In the case of the United States, the policy marketplace is shifting to support national restructuring because of growing concerns by payers (that a lack of a national information infrastructure is very cost-ineffective) and patients/consumers (primarily due to desires for increased quality improvement and safety and easier personal access to care information).

Because they usually lack the funds and technical expertise, most poor and less developed nations are far from attaining the "digital backbone" sustainability goal put forth by PWC. For example, in Mexico, the Ministry of Health is responsible for overall health system functioning; however, provider funding is very fragmented (much of it coming from patient self-payment), and there is essentially no functioning national information system. The nation's healthcare problems are so great and government funding so limited that it will be many years before the system will be sufficiently coherent to permit a "digital backbone."[68] For these nations, sustained economic growth will be necessary to generate the required capital for health systems upgrades.

Some of the same conclusions are reached in a global examination of quality and safety standardization (number 4). In Europe and Canada, physicians have taken a leadership role in forwarding these causes. In the U.S. policy marketplace, the prominence of patient advocacy groups has provided a different avenue to advance demands for quality and safety assurance.[6] The Institute of Medicine has provided a reasonably clear blueprint as to how the United States can cross the "quality chasm."[69] Generally, in economically advanced nations, there are important and increasingly influential groups that are effectively demanding higher quality standards, although there are still debates about the extent to which

these standards should be dictated by the government, as opposed to the private sector.[70,71]

As with the "digital backbone," less economically advanced nations generally do not yet have the funds or organizational structure to provide system-wide quality and safety standards, whatever the political preferences might be. A study of practice quality in Indonesia, Tanzania, India, Paraguay, and Mexico suggests substantial variation within each country and different factors leading to each country's pattern of variation. As the study authors conclude, "Questions relating to practice quality [in low-income countries] remain unanswered in the literature, because the quality of health care in low income countries is difficult to measure."[72] Until data collection and database development related to the quality of care are improved in these nations, they will not have the necessary inputs to even begin developing and monitoring system-wide quality standards.

The same thing can be said for safety standards. Many poorer nations do not have well-established and effective regulatory structures for overseeing medical safety. China has been particularly visible with respect to safety problems. It is the largest supplier of pharmaceutical ingredients in the world, and there have been major problems reported with some medical products, most recently heparin.[73] China's chief food safety "watchdog" has said that almost 20% of products made for consumption in China were found to be substandard.[74] It appears that neither government nor voluntary private sector safety guidelines and agreements are effective in China, where there is high turnover in manufacturers and their executives.[75] The severity of the problem (and, to a significant degree, the nature of government in China) can be gauged by the fact that China executed its former State Food and Drug Administration head, Zheng Xiaoyu, in July 2007 for approving untested medicines in exchange for cash bribes.[74] These ongoing problems resulted in the United States and China signing a Memorandum of Agreement on December 11, 2007, to establish a bilateral mechanism to ensure the safety of drugs, excipients, and medical devices exported from China to the United States.[76]

Beyond the previously described two factors, it should be noted that the others listed in the PWC report ("a quest for common ground," "incentive realignment," "strategic resource deployment," "climate of innovation," and "adaptable delivery roles and structures") are fundamentally *political* in nature. Their definition within each nation depends on ideological decisions that in turn will come from widely varying political systems and structures. These varying decisions made by each will reflect *tradeoffs* between multiple valued objectives. Thus, to understand the nature of what nations will be doing in health care in the coming decades, we must understand the nature of tradeoffs and how these tradeoffs relate to national systems of ideology and ethics in health and nonhealth areas.

THE NATURE OF NATIONAL HEALTH TRADEOFFS, IDEOLOGY, AND ETHICS

In policy making, "tradeoffs" come from the inescapable fact that all policy decisions involve the use of finite resources, and to use them in one area means that they may not be available to be deployed in alternative areas. As the great economist Arthur Okun suggested, "Tradeoffs are the central study of the economist. 'You can't have your cake and eat it too' is a good candidate for the fundamental theorem of economic analysis."[3] "Resources" in policy analysis, however, can also be intangible and involve such value-laden tradeoffs as individual choice versus government dictation or political equity versus economic efficiency. That means that tradeoffs must involve ideology and ethics as well as economics.

The importance of tradeoffs in health policy making—and differing decisions on tradeoffs—has been widely recognized, both within and among nations. Dervaux, Leleu, and Valdmanis conducted an expanded Data Envelopment Analysis of World Health Organization (WHO) and individual national rankings of five health objectives: life expectancy, health distribution, health system responsiveness, responsiveness distribution, and financial contribution fairness. The authors agreed with the WHO Commission for Macroeconomics and Health that any global perspective on health policy priorities needs to be complemented by individual national health policy priority analyses and choices.[77]

When it comes to tradeoffs between economic efficiency and political equity, some researchers have attempted to provide tools that contain explicit criteria. Focusing on developing nations, James et al. suggest that more explicit analysis can aid efforts to attain social justice. "Expenditures on health in many developing countries are being disproportionately spent on health services that have a low overall health impact, and that disproportionately benefit the rich. Without explicit consideration of priority setting, this situation is likely to remain unchanged: resource allocation is too often dictated by historical patterns, and maintains vested interests."[78]

In their work, the researchers list and explain a number of efficiency and equity criteria to guide priorities, including cost-effectiveness, horizontal equity, and vertical equity. They point out that "prioritizing interventions solely on the basis of efficiency [cost-effectiveness] criteria is unlikely to optimize the welfare of society, because of peoples' concerns for equity and the potential tradeoffs between efficiency and equity."[78]

Particularly in wealthy nations with expensive healthcare systems, policy makers and clinicians are following the researchers and starting to develop guidelines for tradeoffs in healthcare decision making. New York State health officials have now developed protocols for the allocation of ventilators in the event of an H5N1 influenza pandemic. The lead author of their study, Dr. Tia Powell, calls for the public to confront such triage issues so that such decisions reflect community views as well as ethical and clinical standards. "It's not really a technical solution. . . . It's values. And the people are the experts on that."[79] Another example of this is in cancer treatment. In late 2008, the American Society for Clinical Oncology will release guidelines for physician—patient discussions of cancer treatment that explicitly take the cost of treatment alternatives into account in choosing a therapy. Dr. Leonard Saltz of Memorial Sloan-Kettering Cancer Center has called for the inclusion of treatment costs to guidelines. He argues that "if there is a need to spend it [large amounts of money], let's talk about it. If we can do it just as well less expensively, I think doctors should know that and be able to make a decision."[80]

There are clear political obstacles to explicit tradeoff analysis in health policy making. The public in most nations does not have a clear understanding of the inescapability of tradeoffs, especially if they suspect that they entail rationing of popular services.[81] As some have observed, all Americans ask for is cheap, fast, and high-quality health care, but they do not understand that they can never get it with more than two out of those three characteristics in a real-world health care of limited resources and potentially unlimited demands. Research on public response to possible cost–quality tradeoffs in clinical decisions indicates that reactions are unpredictable and not necessarily clinically or economically logical.[82] On the other hand, their findings suggest that a significant portion of the public (at least in the United States) *would* be willing to accept cost–quality tradeoffs *if* they are provided with clear information on the cost-effectiveness of specific treatments.

At the global level, it is just as difficult to analyze tradeoffs. In research conducted for the WHO Advisory Committee on Health Research, Schunemann et al. reviewed available literature on "determining which outcomes are important for the development of guidelines" and found "limited relevant research evidence." The authors offered the general recommendation that methods to examine tradeoffs and their impact on outcomes should employ "systematic and transparent methods involving key stakeholders, including consumers and people from different cultures, to help ensure that all important outcomes are considered."[83] Of course, this recommendation only addresses procedural issues and does not touch on the substance of *which* choices should be made, and the division and debate over the *substance* of health reform is the primary challenge facing both national publics and their policy makers.

As noted earlier, there is a *convergence* of opinion (at least, at the policy elite level) that current national health systems are unsustainable because of growing cost, access, and quality problems. In the ongoing global discussion over tradeoffs and possible health systems reforms, it is equally clear that there is no current consensus—only a *diversity* of ethical perspectives and ideological positions.

One thing is clear: National deliberations over health reform policy making cannot take place without recognizing that there are ethical and ideological disagreements at the heart of the debates. Unfortunately, all too often, policy makers do engage in *de facto* social experiments without ethical review and debate, both among themselves and with their nation's citizens.[84] In an analysis of the role of justice and solidarity in priority setting in health care, two ethicists point out that

> The outcomes of decisions on in- or exclusion of health care services in a benefit package need not necessarily be the same in the various countries. This is not only caused by local, regional or national differences in approach or different ideas about health, disease and quality of life, but also by different normative judgments. Concrete decisions in different countries can be based on different models of distributive justice, and the weight given to these normative considerations can be different. Also humanitarian considerations have an influence on health care package decisions.[85]

Globally, one major reason for this is that many nations do not have the ideologies or institutions of inclusive social participation and modern economics that provide the foundation for a balanced debate over tradeoffs in health systems reform. Daniels contends that "in a political process, where reforms are implemented by democratically controlled agencies, the analogy to informed consent is democratic oversight of the reform process. Unfortunately, this analogy is problematic wherever democratic control of institutions is weak . . . and wherever powerful external agencies offer large incentives and are not themselves held accountable for the reforms they impose."[84]

Scholars have developed a variety of perspectives related to this. The economist Hernando de Soto has contended that many poor nations, particularly in the "post-communist" world, have not developed the social habits of the rule of law that permit widely accepted policies for resource use. Absent these, decisions on resource allocation in all areas of society, including health care, are made largely on the basis of "might makes right." The less powerful are largely disenfranchised and simply attempt to evade the rule of the powerful (usually through governments) by the use of black markets.[86] According to the social philosopher John Rawls, "One may think of a public conception of justice as constituting the fundamental charter of a well-ordered human association."[2] In societies with volatile political and social systems in transition (including nations experiencing rapid economic and social growth, such as China and India), the principles of justice and popular participation are not well-established or widely shared, which means that health policy making may be essentially the imposition of the will of political elites. In the long run, such policy making may contribute to rather than reduce social and political instability.

Justice has both individual and social components. Ethical health policy making implies an acceptance of *individual autonomy*—the belief that individuals have the right to their own beliefs and values and to related decisions and choices with respect to the use of health services. Some of the most politically charged policy debates occur when the principle of autonomy clashes with social/communal welfare principles of treatment, as in the case of Terri Schiavo in the United States.[87] "Whose Life Is It, Anyway?" a noted play and movie, considered the dilemma of which set of priorities should prevail over life and death decisions—the individual whose life is at question, or a society which has to put forth and defend laws regulating medical treatment.

In health policy making, the social component is reflected primarily in the debate over *distributive justice*, or the "fairness" in the distribution of health benefits and burdens in society.[13] In most nations, the question of "fairness" is debated endlessly by the various participants in the policy marketplace. The economist Thomas Rice, criticizing the United States for its unique status as the only economically advanced nation without some system of national health insurance, articulates the *egalitarian* view of justice, where equal access to health services (at least, to an essential minimum package of services) for all citizens, regardless of income or class, is of central importance. He has made the ethical case for U.S. adoption of national health insurance as follows:

> The case for a national health insurance program that guarantees universal coverage is very strong. Universal coverage is consistent with prevailing notions of fairness; people should not be penalized for circumstances—such as their socio-demographic background or their current state of health—over which they may have very little control. . . . In addition, unlike other characteristics, good health is instrumental in allowing people to have the capabilities to achieve their personal goals. Consequently, financial barriers to obtaining care are doubly unfair because they not only result in poorer health, but they also frustrate people's ability to attain the other things that they value. Furthermore, most people would appear to be endowed with a communitarian spirit in which they draw pride in being part of a society in which the well-being of others is an important part of their own welfare. It is thus no surprise that nearly every developed nation is committed to providing health insurance to its population, regardless of the individual's ability to pay.[4]

In most Western nations (particularly in the United States), there is also a *libertarian* perspective of fairness that would argue that Rice's preferences are decidedly *unfair*. Libertarians (who adhere to a mix of beliefs found both on the political "left" and "right") tend to believe that individual freedom is the most important social value. "Fairness" means that individuals have the "freedom to choose" to do what they wish with their own resources and that the best set of policies rests on the belief in a minimal state, enforcing basic laws and regulatory "rules of the game," but not attempting to dictate economic outcomes or engage in large-scale redistribution of wealth.[88,89] In contrast to Rice, libertarian health economists prescribe individual choice and responsibility as the best way to "reform" U.S. health care. As one libertarian argues,[90]

> Although no country with a national health care system is contemplating abandoning universal coverage,

the broad and growing trend is to move away from centralized government control and to introduce more market-oriented features. The answer then to America's health care problems lies not in heading down the road to national health care but in learning from the experiences of other countries, which demonstrate the failure of centralized command and control and the benefits of increasing consumer incentives and choice.

Health policy making is certainly a matter of data collection and analysis, of research and forecasting, of power struggles within national policy marketplaces. Like other aspects of public policy, it is also an "inescapably moral enterprise." Because of that, health policy making and analysis will be sterile and ultimate ineffective if the policy makers and analysts do not realize—whether they want to or not—that "policy and ethics both ask the same question: 'what is the good, and how do we achieve (create, protect, cultivate) it?'"[91]

HEALTH POLICY MAKING AROUND THE WORLD—UNCERTAIN TIMES AND FUTURES

It is not at all clear how the nations of the world, with greatly differing political, economic, healthcare, and social systems, are going to meet the health systems challenges of the next 20 years. Most wealthy countries, with aging populations, are going to hit the financial wall, with unpredictable consequences. In the United States, any reasonably balanced investigation of the numbers—rising demand for more (and often more technologically intensive) health care, an aging population, declining employer-based insurance, increasing number of uninsured individuals, and above all, a healthcare cost inflation rate that outruns economic growth by a significant margin—will reveal that, sometime between the years 2015 and 2025, when the "baby boomers" will retire and expect to get all of the health care they want and "deserve" from Medicare and Medicaid (the primary government vehicle for long-term care spending), the numbers for financing the U.S. healthcare system as currently structured will not add up or balance. Something will have to give.

In the absence of reform and the establishment of a true national healthcare system, the supply/demand imbalance will lead to *de facto* rationing, with insured individuals waiting longer and longer and paying more and more to get ever more limited care. Uninsured individuals will fall completely through the cracks, as the *ad hoc* public and charity healthcare system will come apart at the seams. This is a profoundly depressing vision for anyone who believes that access to some effective level of basic health care should be a "right" that all citizens possess.

U.S. reformers who want to avoid these dire straits and advocate major national healthcare reform, including a mandated universal access system, will experience major political problems in getting any proposal enacted. Most efforts to enact national health reform (most notoriously, the 1993 Health Security Act proposed by President Clinton) are sold to the public as giving everyone the right to speedy access to comprehensive health services, with only modest costs. As was seen in 1993–1994, the largely insured public reacted badly when they found out that they would actually have to adjust their own healthcare arrangements and pay out themselves to provide insurance for those fellow citizens who were going without. They expressed their reaction through a very responsive political system: *no thanks.*

Looking back on it now, however, it is clear that the unwillingness of Americans to consent to the Clinton health reforms did not address the larger problem of what to do with a healthcare system with unsustainable cost inflation. The problems of cost containment and access in the United States have continued to mount. There is no question of maintaining the current "system"—it is visibly coming apart before our eyes. *Something* major will happen, one way or the other, in the next 10 to 20 years. Either we shape the future healthcare system now, or we will inherit the disorder of our old healthcare system as it collapses in the near future.

Any examination of the experiences of those nations that do have comprehensive national health systems, such as the National Health Service in the United Kingdom, shows that national health insurance means national health rationing, like it or not, with real consequences for patient health and well-being.[59] In any event, European nations, with rapidly aging populations and relatively expansive social expectations for public health and welfare spending, will have their own political conflicts; however, with structured healthcare systems, they would appear to have the potential to develop some political consensus over providing health care within tighter financial limits.

The situation in many developing nations will be incomparably more difficult. It is hard to see how most African nations, with their unstable political systems and desperately poor populations, could afford to even approach "advanced nation" healthcare provision anytime in the foreseeable future. Some of the Asian "tigers," like South Korea, Singapore, and Taiwan, have already reached very high economic development levels and thus can afford modern health care at the level seen in Europe and the United States. China and India, however, even assuming that they continue their extremely high rates of economic growth (10% to 12% a year for China; 8% to 9% for India), will continue to face the prospect of rapidly growing (and potentially politically explosive) social inequities, with growing numbers of relatively well-off urban populations, and *hundreds of millions* of very poor and medically underserved (or just plain unserved) people in their rural hinterlands. It is not clear how these inequities can be effectively addressed, given the other enormous demands in China and India for resources in social areas such as education, housing, and infrastructure.

Thus, the world approaches what will undoubtedly be a turbulent period, with national healthcare systems everywhere requiring major overhauls of one form or another. There is no past template that nations can employ to respond to this challenge; however, it is very important to remember that any response to escalating healthcare costs must recognize that health care has never been, and can never be, treated as a purely market good. There is clearly a role for competition and economic incentives in providing and selecting health care. At the same time, any long-range response that brings healthcare supply and demand into a sustainable balance—by regulatory fiat or by market competition—will have to recognize that, as citizens, community members, and human beings, we must all care enough about each other to ensure that *none* of us lacks the essential healthcare services that we *can* afford to provide.

CONCLUSION

To end on a note of optimism, it is important that we do not lose sight of the ongoing achievements of modern health care, which have transformed the lives of citizens in wealthy nations and are now doing the same for a majority of the poor in the rest of the world. A renewed sense of economic limits in health care need not be in opposition to this worldwide trend. In fact, it is almost certainly a requirement for its continuation. Here it is appropriate to conclude with another quotation from the scholar and visionary cited at the beginning of this chapter, Dr. William Schwartz:

Where does all this leave us as we try to sort out the challenges that face us at the beginning of a new century? We are enticed by visions of triumph over disease but disturbed by the near-term prospect of denying useful care to some patients. . . . The next 25 years will be especially challenging and possibly divisive ones, but it is important that we not lose sight of the utopian visions that are emerging. The possibility of mastery over a broad range of illnesses is no longer the sole property of philosophers and science fiction authors. Our challenge will be to tackle the ethical and social issues that accompany medical progress with the same rigor that we apply to the scientific challenges themselves. Above all, we must ensure that in the sacrifices required to realize our visions, especially in the critical area of health care rationing, we do not compromise fairness and equity, without which the conquest of disease would be a hollow victory.[5]

REFERENCES

1. Porter R. *The Cambridge History of Medicine*. Cambridge, UK: Cambridge University Press; 2006.
2. Rawls J. *A Theory of Justice*. Cambridge, MA: Harvard University Press; 1971.
3. Okun A. *Equality and Inefficiency: The Big Tradeoff*. Washington, DC: The Brookings Institution; 1975.
4. Rice T. *The Economics of Health Reconsidered*. Chicago: Health Administration Press; 1998.
5. Schwartz WB. *Life Without Disease: The Pursuit of Medical Utopia*. Berkeley, CA: University of California Press; 1998.
6. PriceWaterhouseCoopers. *HealthCast 2020: Creating a Sustainable Future*. Washington, DC: Health Research Institute, PWC; 2005.
7. Anderson OW. *The Health Services Continuum in Democratic States*. Ann Arbor, MI: Health Administration Press; 1989.
8. Capital Health and the Global Strategy Initiative. *Crisis Response: Global Health Care Strategy in the 21st Century*. Report on Symposia, Washington, DC, and Paris, France; 2004.
9. Lasswell H. *Politics: Who Gets What, When, How*. New York: World Publishing Company; 1951.
10. Feldstein PJ. *The Politics of Health Legislation: An Economic Perspective*. Chicago: Health Administration Press; 2006.
11. Gande C. Zimbabwean government triples army officer pay ahead of elections. *VOA News.Com*, February 21, 2008. Retrieved February 24, 2008, from http://www.voanews.com/english/Africa/Zimbabwe/2008-02-21-voa45.cfm.
12. Blank RH, Burau V. *Comparative Health Policy*. New York: Palgrave Macmillan; 2004.
13. Longest BB. *Health Policymaking in the United States*. Chicago: Health Administration Press; 2006.
14. Das J, Hammer J. Location, location, location: Residence, wealth and the quality of medical care in Delhi, India. *Health Affairs*. Web Exclusive, March 27, 2007:w338–w351.
15. Retrieved February 25, 2008, from http://content.health affairs.org/cgi/reprint/26/3/w338?.
15. Olson M. *The Logic of Collective Action*. Cambridge, MA: Harvard University Press; 1965.
16. James C, Carrin G, Savedoff W, Hanvoravongchai P. Clarifying efficiency-equity tradeoffs through explicit criteria, with a focus on developing countries. *Health Care Analysis*. 2005;13(1):33–51.
17. Denenberg R. The community: Mobilizing and accessing resources and services. In Cohen FL, Durham JD, eds. *Women, Children and HIV/AIDS*. New York: Springer Publishing Company; 1993.
18. Foreman C. Grassroots victim organizations: Mobilizing for personal and public health. In Cigler AJ, Loomis BA, eds. *Interest Group Politics*, 4th ed. Washington, DC: Congressional Quarterly Press; 1995.
19. Koyanagi C, Bevalacqua JJ. Managed care in public mental health systems. In Hackey RB, Rochefort DA, eds. *The New Politics of State Health Policy*. Lawrence, KS: University Press of Kansas; 2000, pp. 186–206.
20. Steslicke WE. Development of health insurance policy in Japan. *J Health Polit Policy Law*. 1982;7(1):197–226.
21. Wiktorowicz ME. Emergent patterns in the regulation of pharmaceuticals: institutions and interests in the United States, Canada, Britain and France. *J Health Polit Policy Law*. 2003;28(4):615–658.
22. Weissert CS, Weissert WG. *Governing Health*, 2nd ed. Baltimore, MD: Johns Hopkins University Press; 2002.
23. Easton D. *A Systems Analysis of Political Life*. Chicago: University of Chicago Press; 1979.
24. Wilsford D. States facing interests: struggles over health policy in advanced, industrial democracies. *J Health Polit Policy Law*. 1995;20(3):571–613.
25. Crenson MA. *The Unpolitics of Air Pollution*. Baltimore, MD: Johns Hopkins University Press; 1971.
26. Yankelovich D. The debate that wasn't: the public and the Clinton plan. *Health Affairs*. 1995;14(1):7–23.
27. Skocpol T. The rise and the resounding demise of the Clinton plan. *Health Affairs*. 1995;14(1):66–85.
28. Edelman M. *The Symbolic Uses of Politics*. Urbana, IL: University of Illinois Press; 1964.
29. Brown LD. Getting there: the political context for implementing health care reform. In Brecher C, ed. *Implementation Issues and National Health Care Reform*. Washington, DC: Josiah Macy, Jr. Foundation; 1992, pp. 13–46.
30. Thompson FJ. The evolving challenge of health policy implementation. In Litman TJ, Robins LS, eds. *Health Politics and Policy*, 3rd ed. New York: Delmar Publishers; February 25, 2008, pp. 155–175.
31. Pressman JL, Wildavsky A. *Implementation*. Berkeley, CA: University of California Press; 1973.
32. Sparer MS, Brown LD. States and the health care crisis: limits and lessons of laboratory federalism. In Rich RF, White WD, eds. *Health Policy, Federalism and the American States*. Washington, DC: Urban Institute Press; 1996, pp. 181–202.
33. Wenk E. *Margins for Survival: Overcoming Political Limits in Steering Technology*. New York: Pergamon Press; 1979.

34. Moon M. *Medicare Now and in the Future*, 2nd ed. Washington, DC: Urban Institute Press; 1996.

35. Oberlander J. *The Political Life of Medicare*. Chicago: University of Chicago Press; 2003.

36. Torrens PR. Historical evolution and overview of health services in the United States. In Williams SJ, Torrens PR, eds. *Introduction to Health Services*, 5th ed. New York: Delmar Publishers; 1999, Chapter 1.

37. Friedman TL. *The World is Flat*. New York: Farrer, Straus and Giroux; 2005.

38. Davis K, Anderson GF, Rowland D, Steinberg EP. *Health Care Cost Containment*. Baltimore, MD: Johns Hopkins University Press; 1990.

39. Gold MR, Siegel JE, Russell LB, Weinstein MC. *Cost-Effectiveness in Health and Medicine*. New York: Oxford University Press; 1996.

40. Anonymous. Health care in China: losing patients. *Economist*. 2008;386(8568):58.

41. Lewis M. Informal payments and the financing of health care in developing and transition countries. *Health Affairs*. 2007;26(4):984–997.

42. Anonymous. Coming to a crunch. *Economist*. 2008:386 (8572):51–53.

43. World Bank. *Global Monitoring Report 2005, Millennium Development Goals: From Consensus to Momentum*. Washington, DC: World Bank; 2005.

44. Sachs JD. *The End of Poverty*. New York: Penguin Press; 2006.

45. Brower J, Chalk C. *The Global Threat of New and Reemerging Infectious Diseases*. Santa Monica, CA: RAND Corporation; 2003.

46. Roychoudhuri O. The end of poverty: an interview with Jeffrey Sachs. *Mother Jones*, May 6, 2005. Retrieved January 28, 2008, from http://www.motherjones.com/news/qa/2005/05/jeffrey_sachs.html.

47. Newman PJ, Weinstein MC. The diffusion of new technology: costs and benefits to health care. In Gelijns AC, Halm EA, eds. *The Changing Economics of Medical Technology*. Washington, DC: National Academy Press; 1991, pp. 21–34.

48. Ubel PA. *Pricing Life: Why it's Time for Health Care Rationing*. Cambridge, MA: MIT Press; 2001.

49. Wilson RM, Runciman WB, Gibberd RW, Harrison BT, Newby L, Hamilton JD. The Quality in Australian Health Care Study. *Med J Aust*. 1995;163:458–471.

50. Kohn L, Corrigan JM, Donaldson MS, eds. *To Err is Human: Building a Safer Health System*. Washington, DC: National Academy Press; 2000.

51. Vincent C, Neale G, Woloshynowych M. Adverse events in British hospitals: preliminary retrospective record review. *British Medical Journal*. 2001;322(7285):517–519.

52. Baker GR, Norton PG, Flintoft V, et al. The Canadian Adverse Events Study: the incidence of adverse events among hospital patients in Canada. *CMAJ*. 2004;170(11):1678–1686.

53. Anonymous. India's fake doctors: quackdown. *Economist*. 2008;386(8568):58–59.

54. U.S. Department of Health and Human Services. Outcomes research fact sheet, 2008. Retrieved January 22, 2008, from http://www.ahrq.gov/clinic/outfact.htm.

55. BBC News. China's cigarette threat. November 19, 2007. Retrieved January 8, 2008, from http://news.bbc.co.uk/1/hi/health/216998.stm.

56. Healthy People 2010. A systematic approach to health improvement. Retrieved January 11, 2008, from http://www.healthypeople.gov/Document/html/uih/uih/_2.htm#deter.

57. Hall J. Incremental change in the Australian health care system. *Health Affairs*. 1999;18(2):95–110.

58. Ikegami N, Campbell JC. Health care reform in Japan: the virtues of muddling through. *Health Affairs*. 1999;18(3): 56–75.

59. Aaron HJ, Schwartz WB. *Can We Say No?* Washington, DC: Brookings Institution Press; 2005.

60. White J. *Competing Solutions: American Health Care Proposals and International Experience*. Washington, DC: Brookings Institution; 1995.

61. Cogan JF, Hubbard RG, Kessler DP. *Healthy, Wealthy, and Wise*. Washington, DC: American Enterprise Institute Press; 2005.

62. Grol R. *Quality Development in Health Care in the Netherlands*. Commonwealth Fund report, Commission on a High Performance Health System, Pub. 910, March, 2006. Retrieved February 16, 2008, from http://www.commonwealthfund.org/sur/doc/Grol-quality.

63. Anderson GF, Frogner KK, Johns RA, Reinhardt UE. Health spending and use of information technology in OECD countries. *Health Affairs*. 2006;25(3):819–831.

64. Kleinke JD. Dot-gov: market failure and the creation of a national health information technology system. *Health Affairs*. 2005;24(5):1246–1262.

65. Kaushal R, Bastes DW, Poon EG. Functional gaps in attaining a national health information network. *Health Affairs*. 2005;24(5):1281–1289.

66. Donald B. Newt Gingrich pushing "wired" hospitals. *Associated Press*, June 22, 2004.

67. U.S. Department of Health and Human Services. FAQs about NHII. Retrieved January 29, 2008, from http://aspe.hhs.gov/sp/NHII/FAQ.html.

68. Barraza-Llorens M, Bertozzi S, Gonzalez-Pier E, Gutierrez JP. Addressing inequity in health and health care in Mexico. *Health Affairs*. 2002;21(3):47–56.

69. Institute of Medicine. *Crossing the Quality Chasm*. Washington, DC: National Academy Press; 2001.

70. Schoenbaum SC, Audet AJ, Davis K. Obtaining greater value from health care: the roles of the U.S. government. *Health Affairs*. 2003;22(6):183–190.

71. Perrone M. Concerns over blockbuster drugs Vytorin, Avandia prompt investigation of FDA review process. *San Diego Union-Tribune*, March 4, 2008. Retrieved March 14, 2008, from http://www.signonsandiego.com/news/business/20080304-1111-drugapproval-investigation.html.

72. Das J, Gertler PJ. Variations in practice quality in five low-income countries: a conceptual overview. *Health Affairs*. 2007;w296–w309. Retrieved January 30, 2008, from http://content.healthaffairs.org/cgi/reprint/26/3/w296?.

73. Harris G, Bogdanich W. Drug tied to China had contaminant, F.D.A. says. *New York Times*. Retrieved March 10,

2008, from http://www.nytimes.com/2008/03/06/health/06 heparin.html?.

74. Associated Press. China executes former FDA chief amid product safety crisis. *Canadian Broadcasting Corporation News*, July 10, 2007. Retrieved January 10, 2008, from http://www.cbc.ca/world/story/2007/07/10/china-tainted-products.html.

75. *Consumer Reports*. More disturbing news about contaminated imports. Retrieved January 10, 2008, from http://blogs.consumerreports.org/safety/drugs/_medical_safety/.

76. U.S. Department of Health and Human Services. New agreement will enhance the safety of drugs and medical devices imported from the People's Republic of China. Press release, December 11, 2007. Retrieved January 9, 2008, from http://www.hhs.gov/news/facts/drugsmedical.html.

77. Dervaux B, Leleu H, Valdmanis V. Estimating tradeoffs among health care system's objectives. *Health Serv & Outcomes Res Method*. 2004;5:39–58.

78. James M, Hoff T, Davis J, Graham R. Leveraging the power of the media to combat HIV/AIDS. *Health Affairs*. 2004;24(3):854–857.

79. Dean C. Guidelines for epidemics: Who gets a ventilator? *New York Times*, March 25, 2008. Retrieved March 25, 2008, from http://www.nytimes.com/2008/03/25/health/25vent.html?.

80. Neergaard L. Weighing costs in choosing cancer care. *Washington Post*, March 25, 2008. Retrieved March 25, 2008, from http://www.washingtonpost.com/wp-dyn/content/article/2008/03/24/.

81. Baily MA. "Rationing" and American health policy. *J Health Polit Policy Law*. 1984;9(3):489–501.

82. Beach MC, Asch DA, Jepson C, et al. Public response to cost-quality tradeoffs in clinical decisions. *Med Decision Making*. 2003;23:369–378.

83. Schunemann HJ, Oxman AD, Fretheim A. Improving the use of research evidence in guideline development: determining which outcomes are important. *Health Policy Res and Sys*. Retrieved March 1, 2008, from http://www.health-policy-systems.com/content/4/1/18.

84. Daniels N. Toward ethical review of health system transformations. *Am J Public Health*. 2006;96(3):447–451.

85. Hoedemaekers R, Dekkers W. Justice and solidarity in priority setting in health care. *Health Care Analysis*. 2003;11(4):325–343.

86. De Soto H. *The Mystery of Capital*. New York: Basic Books; 2003.

87. Goodnough A, Hulse C. Despite Congress, woman's feeding tube is removed. *New York Times*. March 19, 2005, p. A1.

88. Friedman M, Friedman R. *Free to Choose: A Personal Statement*. Orlando, FL: Harvest Books; 1990.

89. Nozick R. *Anarchy, State and Utopia*. New York: Basic Books, Inc.; 1974.

90. Tanner MD. The grass is not always greener: a look at national health care systems around the world. The Cato Institute, Policy Analysis No. 613, March 18, 2008. Retrieved March 20, 2008, from http://www.cato.org/pub_display.php?pub_id=9272.

91. Kenny N, Giacomini M. Wanted: A new ethics field for health policy analysis. *Health Care Analysis*. 2005;13(4):247–260.

Health Systems by Country

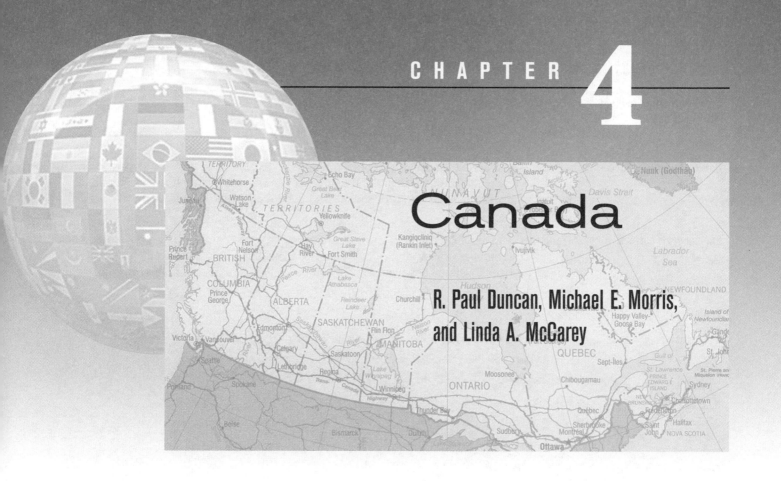

CHAPTER 4

Canada

R. Paul Duncan, Michael E. Morris, and Linda A. McCarey

COUNTRY DESCRIPTION

TABLE 4-1   Canada

Nationality	Noun: Canadian(s)
	Adjective: Canadian
Ethnic groups	British Isles origin 28%, French origin 23%, other European 15%, Amerindian 2%, other, mostly Asian, African, Arab 6%, mixed background 26%
Religions	Roman Catholic 42.6%, Protestant 23.3% (including United Church 9.5%, Anglican 6.8%, Baptist 2.4%, Lutheran 2%), other Christian 4.4%, Muslim 1.9%, other and unspecified 11.8%, none 16% (2001 census)
Language	English (official) 59.3%, French (official) 23.2%, other 17.5%
Literacy	Definition: age 15 and over can read and write
	Total population: 99%
	Male: 99%
	Female: 99% (2003 est.)
Government type	Constitutional monarchy that is also a parliamentary democracy and a federation
Date of independence	1 July, 1867 (union of British North American colonies); 11 December, 1931 (recognized by the United Kingdom)

(continues)

TABLE 4-1   Canada

Gross Domestic Product (GDP) per capita	$38,200 (2007 est.)
Unemployment rate	5.9% (November 2007 est.)
Natural hazards	Continuous permafrost in north is a serious obstacle to development; cyclonic storms form east of the Rocky Mountains, a result of the mixing of air masses from the Arctic, Pacific, and North American interior, and produce most of the country's rain and snow east of the mountains
Environment: current issues	Air pollution and resulting acid rain severely affecting lakes and damaging forests; metal smelting, coal-burning utilities, and vehicle emissions impacting on agricultural and forest productivity; ocean waters becoming contaminated due to agricultural, industrial, mining, and forestry activities
Population	33,212,696
Age structure	0–14 years: 16.3% (male 2,780,491/female 2,644,276) 15–64 years: 68.8% (male 11,547,354/female 11,300,639) 65 years and over: 14.9% (male 2,150,991/female 2,788,945) (2008 est.)
Median age	Total: 40.1 years Male: 39 years Female: 41.2 years (2008 est.)
Population growth rate	0.83% (2008 est.)
Birth rate	10.29 births/1,000 population (2008 est.)
Death rate	7.61 deaths/1,000 population (2008 est.)
Net migration rate	5.62 migrant(s)/1,000 population (2008 est.)
Gender ratio	At birth: 1.06 male(s)/female Under 15 years: 1.05 male(s)/female 15–64 years: 1.02 male(s)/female 65 years and over: 0.77 male(s)/female Total population: 0.98 male(s)/female (2008 est.)
Infant mortality rate	Total: 5.08 deaths/1,000 live births Male: 5.4 deaths/1,000 live births Female: 4.75 deaths/1,000 live births (2008 est.)
Life expectancy at birth	Total population: 81.16 years Male: 78.65 years Female: 83.81 years (2008 est.)
Total fertility rate	1.57 children born per woman (2008 est.)
HIV/AIDS adults prevalence rate	0.3% (2003 est.)
Number of people living with HIV/AIDS	56,000 (2003 est.)
HIV/AIDS deaths	1500 (2003 est.)

Central Intelligence Agency. The World Fact Book (website), 2008. Retrieved November 18, 2008, from https://www.cia.gov/library/publications/the-world-factbook.

History

Archeological records indicate that Canada was among the first lands of North America to be inhabited by humans. Aboriginal peoples settled the area roughly 10,000 years ago. At the time of the voyage of Columbus, there had been a highly developed and flourishing society in Canada for over a thousand years.[1]

It is now widely held by historians that the Norse, led by Leifur Eiriksson, were the first Europeans to set foot on Canadian soil, around the year 1000 AD. Eiriksson's and the subsequent Norse ventures to North America were short lived and yielded little lasting sway over the development of Canadian society.[2,3]

In contrast, a new and different era of European arrivals was initiated in 1497 with the voyage of Englishman John Cabot, the first post-Columbian explorer to land upon the shores of Canada. Although the English conducted the earliest exploration of the region, it was not until 1605 that the French founded the first large-scale permanent European colony. For the ensuing century and a half, rivalries between the colonial powers of France and England were to be the hallmark of the Canadian experience.[2,4]

The Treaty of Paris, 1763, represents a critical turning point in Canadian history. With the English victory in the Seven Years' War, the dual colonial structure of Canada was at an end. In its place arose an English hegemony over the Canadian colonies that would be sustained for the next century.[2,4]

Although the direct power of the French colonial presence ceased, the social and cultural influence was to endure, particularly in the region of Quebec. At the close of the American Revolution, there was a significant migration of English loyalists from the lower 13 colonies into the southeastern regions of Canada. As implied by the term *loyalist*, these new residents were staunchly supportive of the British Empire and were committed Anglophiles. As a result of the cultural divergence between these new immigrants and the existing French-Canadian peoples, the area was divided and two separate colonies were formed. One colony reflected the French heritage of Canada and the other the English. These two regions would eventually become what are now the Provinces of Quebec and Ontario. The multicultural origins and heritage of Canada continues into the 21st century to be a characteristic trait of the nation and a pivotal element in many policy areas.[2,5]

During the period of English colonial rule, the colonies that comprised what is now Canada operated as semiautonomous entities under the leadership of their respective lieutenant governors. The high degree of independence of action enjoyed by the Canadian colonies under English rule served to ingrain an ethos of local reliance.[4] This identity as independent colonies and a focus on local self-reliance laid the foundations for the structure of strong provinces that emerged with formation of the Canadian nation state in the last half of the 19th century.[2,4]

With its inauguration on July 1, 1867, the British North America Act established the Dominion of Canada. The foundations of a nation were thus laid with the unification of the Canadian colonies as a single entity.[4] Under the terms of confederation, the provinces were granted authority over broad areas of governance, and thus, they represented a powerful force within the new nation. From the outset, the issue of balancing the delegation of authority between the national government and the provinces became contentious.

The period of Dominion, 1867 to 1982, represented a slow transition toward a progressively greater degree of autonomy from England. During this era, Canada underwent three pivotal events that were to influence greatly the complexion of the contemporary nation state: the westward expansion of the nation, the Great Depression, and World War II.[4,6]

During the last half of the 19th century and the early years of the 20th, Canada began to expand westward extending the nation fully across the North American continent. As the newly formed provinces were added to the dominion, a stronger and more prosperous nation state grew. This expansion also served to reinforce the Canadian ethic of communal action as the challenges of inhabiting the vast rural territory made local and regional coordination essential for successful settlement.[4]

Canadians suffered greatly during the Depression. The enormity of the economic disaster overwhelmed the resources of individuals and local governments. Because of the scale of the crisis, Canadians began to focus more on communal action and an expanded role for the state in the lives of their citizens. As a result, many of Canada's social welfare programs at the provincial and national level can trace their origins to this time period.[7] This era also provided the catalyst for the evolution of the modern Canadian healthcare system.[8]

World War II had three primary effects on Canadian society. First, it served to galvanize further the national identity of Canada both among its own citizenry and in the international community.[4] A second influence of the war was the substantial increase in population that came in the wake of the Allied victory. This rise was fueled both by a spike in birth rates and through a wave of immigration from around the world.[9] The third significant result of World War II was the shift in taxation power between the various levels of the Canadian government that occurred as a result of the war fighting efforts. During the war years, the federal government was ceded considerable new powers by provincial governments to assess and collect taxes. This expansion of the federal tax base became a pivotal issue in future years, particularly in regard to the financing of health and social services.[8]

With the patriation of the British North America Act in 1982, Canada formally became a fully independent nation. It is recognized as a world leader in peacekeeping and an influential actor in the international economy. The nation has experienced and responded to numerous short-term challenges over the past 2.5 decades, and it has continued to deal with issues of a more fundamental nature. Two of the more prominent long-standing areas of contention that merit mention are constitutional matters related to power sharing under the federal structure of the nation and conflicts arising from the dual ethnic heritage of the nation,

particularly the issue of greater autonomy for the province of Quebec. Both issues are germane to health and health care.

Size and Geography

Canada is geographically the second largest nation in the world and the largest on the North American continent, covering 9.9 million square kilometers (3.8 million square miles; Figure 4-1). Spanning the width of the continent, Canada has a vast and varied environment ranging from its coastal regions to the arid plains of the interior and north to the polar cap.[9]

Although some population centers are spread across the nation's land mass, roughly two thirds of the population resides along the southern border. The population density of Canada is 3.5 persons per kilometer, but this figure is misleading because nearly 80% of the population resides in urban areas that are relatively dense. In metropolitan areas, the population concentration is 245 persons per kilometer, or roughly comparable with that of England. The rural areas in the west and north are very sparsely populated.[9]

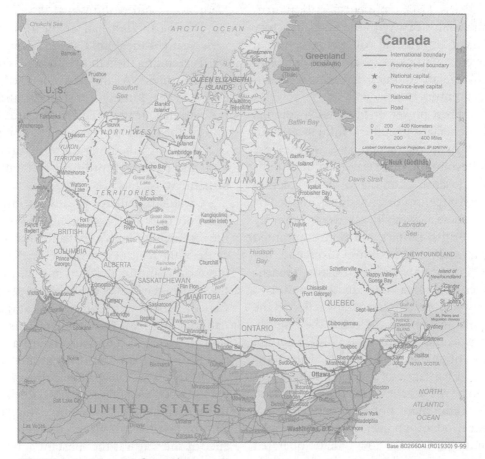

FIGURE 4-1   Map of Canada

Government or Political System

It is often said that the essence of the Canadian perspective on government and society is captured in one brief phrase from the Constitution Act of 1867, "Peace, Order and Good Government." In these few words, often noted in counterpoint to the United States' "life, liberty, and the pursuit of happiness," are conveyed the Canadian dedication to the practical application in government of communally held values and collective action. Equality represents the foundation on which the civil union in Canada is constructed, and this core value is infused throughout government policy actions and debates at the federal, provincial/territorial, and local levels, particularly in respect to health policy.[10]

As established under the British North America Act 1867 and subsequently patriated on April 17, 1982, the governmental structure of Canada is a constitutional monarchy. Under this system, Queen Elizabeth II of Great Britain and the United Kingdom rules as monarch of Canada but does not govern. The functional government of Canada is an English-style parliamentary democracy with a federal structure. The federal system of rule that exists in Canada delegates governing authority between the national and provincial governments; thus, the provincial governments are sovereign entities in their own right and not merely extensions of the national government.[10]

The national government, based in the city of Ottawa, is led by the Prime Minister, the elected leader of the political party that garnered the largest number of parliamentary seats in the previous parliamentary elections. Parliament is a bicameral body consisting of the 105 members of the Senate who are appointed by the Queen's representative, the Governor General, and the House of Commons, whose 308 members are elected by popular vote of the citizenry.[11] Among the varied levels of government in Canada, taxation authority is broadest for the national government, which holds constitutional authority to levy personal/corporate income taxes, value-added taxes on goods and services, and the exclusive power to impose excise taxes and duties on imported goods.[12]

The 10 provincial and 3 territorial governments are headed by their respective premiers, who are elected by the predominant party in the provincial assemblies. In all 13 jurisdictions, the legislatures are unicameral assemblies. The breadth of taxation authority is roughly equivalent to that of the national government with the exception of excise taxes and duties, which are solely the purview of Ottawa.[12]

Political parities emerged in Canada during the 1830s and were in essence a colonial reflection of the British two-party system, composed of the Liberal party and the Conservative party. This approach to a political system continued in Canada until the time of World War I, when conflicts over the draft ignited a rift within Canadian parties and forever changed the nation's political landscape. By 1921, the Progressive party had established a tradition of a multiparty system within Canada.[13] Over the following decades, three to five substantial political parties have existed in Canada, and minor or regional parties have played pivotal roles in many elements of Canadian governance, particularly in relationship to the development of national health insurance.[14,15]

Macroeconomics

Canada, a member of the Group of 8 (G8), is recognized as one of the leading market-based economies in the world. Government estimates based on data through November 2007 place the total gross domestic product (GDP) for the year at $1.23 trillion,[16,17] a per capita GDP of $37,272 based on 2007 population estimates.

Other indicators of the health of the economy include the rate of inflation and the unemployment rate. Overall inflationary pressures within the market as measured by the consumer price index remained controlled at 2.5% with the core consumer price index measured at 2.0%, a level safely within the target range of the Bank of Canada. Unemployment rates in 2007 rested at a 33-year low of 5.9%.[17,18]

Since the turn of the 20th century, the Canadian economy has evolved from its predominately natural resource–driven origins to encompass a richly diverse array of market sectors. The service sector is the largest element of the Canadian economy, comprising roughly 70% of GDP in the year 2006, up from 49% in the years immediately after World War II.[19] Manufacturing accounted for less than 15% of GDP in 2006.[18]

Key industries include trade, healthcare and social services, finance and insurance, machinery and auto manufacturing, production of natural gas and oil, mining, and agriculture. As is true with the population of Canada, all sectors of the economy with the exclusion of the gas, oil, and mining sectors are heavily concentrated along the southern border. Agricultural production is primarily found in the central and western provinces. The financial and insurance industries are disproportionately headquartered in the provinces of Ontario and Quebec.

Canada has a highly developed economic infrastructure with a national system of roads and highways covering 1.4 million kilometers. An extensive rail system exists providing 72,093 kilometers of track covering all areas of Canada. Air travel is available throughout the country from a system of 10 international airports located in the major metropolitan cities and 300 smaller terminals spread across the nation. Extensive maritime port facilities are located on both the Atlantic and Pacific coasts as well as along the Great Lakes, which border Canada's primary trade partner, the United States. In 2004, 452.3 million tons of goods were transported through these ports, representing 48% of Canada's exports.[20]

Public schools administered by the local and provincial government are provided at no direct cost to students throughout the nation for elementary and secondary education.[21] In 2006, education spending at all levels of government totaled over $45 billion.[22] Attendance is mandatory for children under certain ages, although the age varies by jurisdiction. Private schools are also allowed under the educational system.[21] Canada possesses a world-class postsecondary educational system. Universities in Canada not only educate Canadians but also attract students from Europe, the United States, and around the world.[23]

Demographics

As of October 1, 2007, Canada's population slightly exceeded 33 million people.[24] As is true for most industrialized nations, the population of Canada is aging. In 1985, the average age was 31.0 years, but by 2005, the average age rose to 38.5 years. It is striking that in 1964 42.4% of Canadians were under the age of 20; by 2005, that value fell to 24.3%. Persons over age 65 represented 13.1% of the population in 2005, up from 12.6% in 2001.[25] Comparing by racial and ethnic characteristics, only the Aboriginal peoples present a significantly younger demographic distribution, with an average age of 27 years. Nearly half of the Aboriginal population in 2006 was younger than 24 years of age. Aboriginal peoples, persons who are of Inuit, Métis, or First Nation heritage, represented 3.8% of the population in 2006.[26]

Data from the 2006 census indicate that 6 of 10 Canadians had some level of education beyond secondary schooling. Persons holding university degrees accounted for 27.9% of the population, whereas persons having less than a secondary education represented slightly over 15% of Canadians. A high school diploma was the highest level of educational attainment for just under 24% of the population.[27]

The median after-tax income of individuals was $21,400 in 2005. For families of two or more the median was $56,000 in after-tax earnings.[28] Income distributions across families as measured by the Gini coefficient indicate that from the late 1970s to 2005 there was a slight widening in the income gap between Canadians. The coefficient for income inequality increased from .29 to .31 during this period.[28,29] Comparing these figures with other industrialized nations, Canada has a more equitable distribution of income than the United States and the United Kingdom, but a slightly less evenly distributed income base than the central European and Scandinavian nations.[28,29]

Followers of various denominations of the Christian faith comprise the majority (76.6%) of Canadians. Roman Catholics represent the most prevalent group (43.2%), whereas Protestants account for 29.2% of the population. Other Christian faiths account for an additional 4.2%. Canadians reporting no religion represent 16.2% of the population. Muslims are the most prominent non-Christian religion, representing 2.0% of Canadians. Adherents of the Jewish, Buddhist, Sikh, and Hindu faiths each account for approximately 1.0% of the population. The remaining 1.2% of the population represents a variety of religious beliefs.[30]

Patterns of morbidity and mortality in Canada have changed greatly since the turn of the 20th century. As in every other Western industrialized nation, the predominance of infectious disease processes has been supplanted by chronic and lifestyle-related pathologies.[14] Cardiovascular disease is the leading cause of mortality in the nation, accounting for 32% of deaths among men and 34% of deaths among women in 2003.[31] It has been found that 80% of adult Canadians have at least 1 modifiable risk factor for cardiovascular disease, and 11% have 3 or more.[31] Hypertension, a significant risk factor for cardiovascular disease, was found in 14.9% of the adult population in 2005, with 14.1% of men and 15.7% of women being diagnosed with the condition.[32]

Diabetes, another known risk factor for cardiovascular disease, has steadily been rising in the Canadian population. Among the overall population, the prevalence of diabetes was 5.5% in 2005, with men (5.8%) being slightly more likely than women (5.2%) to be diagnosed with the condition.[33] The prevalence of diabetes is significantly higher among certain subpopulations, such as the First Nations, where the overall rate in 2005 was 14.5% with 12.9% of men and 16.0% of women suffering from the disease.[32] Diabetes is also significantly more common among older persons, who comprise 48% of all diabetics in Canada.[31]

Obesity has repeatedly been linked in the medical literature to cardiovascular disease, diabetes, and hypertension. In 2005, 32.5% of Canadians were reported to be overweight, with 14.9% being considered obese.[32] The trend toward greater levels of obesity is clearly demonstrated among adolescents where in the period between 1970 and 2004 the rate of overweight among 12- to 17-year-olds increased from 14% to 29%. The rate of increase in obesity among this age group is even more striking as it rose from 3% in 1970 to 9% in 2004.[31] The observation that physical activity helps to moderate obesity is demonstrated by the fact that 27% of sedentary Canadian men were found to be obese, compared with 19% of active men.[31] A hopeful sign for the future is found in that the levels of physical activity among the population in Canada appear to be rising. In 2005, 51.6% of Canadians reported being either active or moderately active as compared with 43.0% in the year 2000.[32]

Cancer continues to be among the leading causes of mortality in the country. Estimates for 2006 indicate that 153,100 cases of cancer were diagnosed, and 70,400 people died from the disease. Breast cancer and prostate cancer were, respectively, the most common form of cancer for women and men. Lung cancer remains the most common cancer-related cause of death in both genders, with 64 deaths per 100,000 men and 34 deaths per 100,000 women reported in the year 2000.[31] The rate of lung cancer death among men has been falling since 1988, but among women, it has been increasing, reflecting changes in the historical trend of smoking patterns.[31]

BRIEF HISTORY OF THE HEALTHCARE SYSTEM

Historical and sociocultural factors play a fundamental role in the evolution of a nation's health system.[34] In order to understand better the structures and performance of the current Canadian healthcare system, some context is valuable. As will become clear, the steps leading toward Canada's contemporary healthcare financing and delivery system do not dramatically differ from those observed in most of the western democracies.

Pre-World War II

From the earliest era of European influence and continuing until the beginning of the 20th century, healthcare in Canada was focused on the relationship between a physician and a patient. Independent physicians and surgeons provided services to patients predominantly in either the physician's offices or the patient's homes. The fiscal dimension of this type of care would be characterized as a private mercantile exchange. Hospitals, until the late 19th century, were viewed as places to be avoided as the level of care was sadly lacking. Socially, hospitals were stigmatized through their association with the poor.[14]

Through the 19th century, government's role in health care was limited. Some support was given for the establishment of facilities to care for the poor, but for the most part, this service was provided by religious orders. It should be noted that Canada's first hospital opened in Quebec in the year 1639 and that hospitals proliferated much more rapidly in Canada than in other areas of North America.[14]

Other areas of governmental involvement in health care before the 20th century came primarily in the fields of sanitation, quarantine during times of epidemics, and medical licensure. Infectious disease was the primary pathological process of concern during this period. As late as 1849, a single cholera outbreak was responsible for the deaths of 2% of the population of Quebec. Although there are records of some limited licensing activities in Quebec during the 18th century, it was not until well into the 19th century that any concerted effort was made in Canada to standardize certification procedures for physicians.[14]

Throughout the 19th century and into the turn of the 20th century, the status of the physician began to ascend within Canadian society. Advances in medical knowledge allowed the provision of more effective care. As occurred in the United States and Western Europe, this resulted in improved social and financial standing for physicians. Changes in the setting of medical education and patient care also began to take shape. As early as 1819, with the opening of Montreal General Hospital, the care of patients and the education of physicians began to shift to the hospital setting. This trend was further intensified throughout the 19th and into the 20th centuries by the rapid advance of medical technology and clinical knowledge.[14]

As Canada emerged from the First World War, infectious disease remained the predominant challenge. Public hygiene, the Spanish Influenza, and other population health issues catalyzed the development of the public health infrastructure under the direction of the provincial governments. In 1919, the federal government began to provide a coordinating hand to the provincial public health efforts and created the national hygiene grants program to fund these efforts. The first school of public health was opened in Canada in 1920, to provide the trained workforce needed to pursue the aims of infectious disease control.[14]

During this same time frame, changes also occurred in terms of the financing and delivery of clinical health services. Beginning in 1916, rural regions of Saskatchewan developed the Municipal Doctor Plans in order to recruit and retain physicians in these remote areas.[35] Instead of patients paying for their services, local governments paid the physicians a salary, thus guaranteeing their income.[8]

The concept of communal resource pooling again rose in Saskatchewan in 1920 when Union Hospital Districts were formed among adjacent rural towns in order to fund the construction and operation of hospitals. These collective actions, though limited to the rural areas of Canada, were viewed by some as the seeds of what would become the nation's modern healthcare system.[35]

The Great Depression of the 1930s served to galvanize the transformation of Canadian health care by fostering a new environment that embraced an active role for government. As economic hardships befell the nation, patients began to have difficulties in paying physicians and hospitals for their services. This was particularly true in the province of Saskatchewan where the impact of the depression was especially severe in an economy based on the production of commodities such as wheat. In 1928, Saskatchewan had the fourth leading per capita income in Canada; by 1933, the province was the poorest in the nation.[4] Physicians and hospitals were financially strained by the economic downturn and more open to government intervention in health care. The extent to which this position took hold is demonstrated by the Saskatchewan Medical Association openly endorsing a public health insurance program in 1933; however, the momentum for change was slowed as the economy improved and Canada entered the Second World War.[8]

With the provincial election of 1944, the process of reorganizing health care reemerged. The Cooperative Commonwealth Federation (CCF) party came to power in Saskatchewan under the banner of progressive reformation of government and its role in society. A socialist leaning party, the CCF, vigorously promoted the agenda of "socialized health services."[35]

Since World War II

At the close of World War II, the national environment seemed ripe for the establishment of a national health insurance program. A bill was drafted in Ottawa for such a program, but because of a conflict over the allocation of taxation powers between the federal and provincial governments, the bill failed to pass.[8] From this debate, it became clear that the provinces were divided in their opinions based on their level of prosperity. The wealthier provinces, especially Ontario, wanted to trim the federal government's power to levy taxes, which had been expanded during the war. The poorer provinces, such as Saskatchewan, were in favor of keeping tax policies in place as they were, in exchange for federal cash transfers to support social programs at the provincial level.[8]

In the wake of this stalemate at the federal level, the provincial governments once more provided the impetus for change. In 1946, Saskatchewan's government, led by the CCF, implemented the Hospital Services Plan. This program provided payment for all hospital-based services rendered in the province. Initially reimbursement was based on a per diem system, but this was soon recognized as contributing to an unwarranted increase in utilization. Subsequently, a prospective global budget was developed where the hospital was paid a flat monthly rate for the care of all patients treated at the facility. The rate was based on an estimated 90% occupancy rate for the hospital.[35] This method became a hallmark of hospital service financing throughout Canada.

For 10 years healthcare reform continued to be relegated to the provincial level, but in 1957, the federal government, under the leadership of the Liberal party, enacted the National Hospital and Diagnostic Services Act. This program established a 50–50 funding scheme, where the federal government would match dollar-for-dollar provincial expenditures for providing hospital services to their residents. These matching funds were contingent on the provinces meeting certain requirements on the scope of services and universal coverage. Other provinces soon adopted Saskatchewan's Hospital Services Plan as the template for hospital payment plans developed under the new federal legislation. By 1961, all 10 provinces were participating in the federal match program, providing near-universal coverage for hospital services. The experience of the Hospital Diagnostic and Services Act served to establish the constitutionality of a federal role in health care, which under the British North America Act was ostensibly a provincial matter.[35,36] The resulting program of insurance for medical care (both diagnostic and therapeutic) was popular and perceived as a success by the federal government, the provincial governments, and the vast majority of Canadians.

In 1962, Saskatchewan once more took the national lead in Canada's healthcare and health policy conversation, enacting the Medical Care Insurance Act. Under the provisions of this legislation, universal coverage was provided in the province for services provided by physicians. In response, physicians declared a strike in July 1962. For 23 days, physicians refused to treat patients in the province. The settlement reached allowed for the continuation of universal health insurance within the province administered under government control, but in exchange, physicians were to be allowed to balance bill patients for any charged amounts above the government fee schedule. Initially, 12% of physicians took advantage of this balance billing procedure, but because of market pressures, by 1974, only 2% continued the practice.[35] Other provinces soon began to consider programs comparable to that enacted in Saskatchewan.

The federal government once more capitalized on the innovations of the provinces, and in 1966, the Medical Care Act was passed by the national parliament. This act established universal coverage for physician services under provincially administered programs. Financing of the plan was a mixed model similar to that of the Hospital Act, with the federal government matching provincial expenditures at roughly a 50% rate for physician services.[37] This part of the system was quickly labeled "Medicare" (sometimes causing terminology confusion when Canada–U.S. comparisons are pursued).

As was the case for the Hospital Act, provinces had considerable latitude in developing their health plans under the Medical Care Act. Many of the provinces adopted a more rigid stance than Saskatchewan had in terms of dealing with physician balance billing. While the practice continued to exist in principle, physicians who wanted to pursue balance billing were required to "opt out" of the government sponsored plan. The physician could either accept the government fee schedule rate as payment in full for all services rendered to patients, or they could practice outside of the insurance program entirely, receiving no payments from the government. Given the consistent stream of revenue the government program offered, few physicians were willing to "opt out."[35] The Medical Care Act had the effect of creating near-universal coverage for office and clinic-based physician care and all closely related diagnostic services.

After enactment of the two federal programs, the Hospital Act and the Medical Care Act, utilization and costs were observed to rise across the country. In response, the Federal-Provincial Fiscal Arrangements and Established Programs Financing Act was passed in 1977 to provide a stronger incentive for the provinces to control escalating costs of health care by exposing them to a greater degree of the risk for such cost increases in their programs. Under the terms of the legislation, the original 50–50 expenditure matching formula for both of the jointly financed programs was revised in order to reduce the federal fiscal obligations. Through a system of block grant transfers, the federal government's contributions were reduced to a figure in 1977 that equaled roughly 25% of provincial hospital and physician expenditures.[36] Block grants effectively severed any direct connection between the costs of health care provided and the amount of the federal government's contributions to support the care.[35,38]

The Canada Health Act of 1984 served to integrate the three previously enacted pieces of federal legislation into one national framework for health insurance. This unified system of insurance/financing has come to be known as Medicare, adopting the common name previously used to denote insurance provided under the 1962 Medical Care Act. Provisions of the Act stipulated that the provinces would continue to devise and administer the health insurance system under guidelines set out by Ottawa, known as the five principles (Table 4-2), which outline the framework within which provinces develop their own unique health insurance systems. One notable change brought about by the Canada Health Act was the virtual end of balance billing by physicians. One component of the act provided that the amount of match funds provided to the provinces would be reduced by the estimated amount of revenue collected by physicians through balance billing their patients. As a result, every province in Canada passed legislation restricting the practice of balance billing.[35]

During the 1990s, stress within the economy in part triggered by a mounting national debt represented a key policy issue. In response to escalating levels of debt, Ottawa imposed significant reductions in federal expenditures. These cuts were successful at the federal level in reining in both the growth in spending and the debt. In every year since the mid-1990s, Ottawa has recorded an annual surplus; however, these fiscal decisions, made almost entirely at the federal level, had the effect of imposing real dollar cuts in federal financial support for jointly funded federal/provincial programs, including Medicare.[40]

Since 1996, the Canada Health and Social Transfer and its successor, the Canadian Health Transfer block grant system, have been the primary method used to provide federal financial support for health programs including Medicare. In its first year, this system reduced federal cash transfers to the provinces by $2.5 to 7.0 billion, depending on the estimate. Block grants ostensibly allow for great flexibility at the level of government

TABLE 4-2   Five Principles of the Canada Health Act

Public Administration	The plan must be administered and operated on a nonprofit basis by a public authority.
Comprehensiveness	Province/territorial health insurance plans must cover all medically necessary health services provided by hospitals and physicians. They must also cover hospital-based dental surgeries.
Universality	All insured residents must be entitled to all the insured health services provided by the provincial/territorial healthcare plan on equal terms.
Portability	Residents moving from one province/territory to another are entitled to continued coverage under their original health insurance plan until any waiting periods required by the new jurisdiction are met. The waiting periods may not exceed 3 months.
Accessibility	Insured persons must have uniform and reasonable access to hospital, physician, and surgical–dental services where and as these services are available in that location.

Information adapted from the *Canada Health Act Annual Report 2006–07*, pp. 4–5.[39]

enacting programs. Given the climate of budgetary restraint that has been consistent in Ottawa over the past decade, many at the provincial level see the Canada Health and Social Transfer system as simply a method to reduce federal support for provincially administered programs like Medicare. This has served to create tension within the federal structure of Canada, as the provinces felt excluded from the initial decision process for the creation of the Canada Health and Social Transfer system and also continue to feel that the financing arrangements place a disproportionately heavy burden on them to operate the Medicare program with insufficient resources.[38,41,42]

DESCRIPTION OF THE CURRENT HEALTHCARE SYSTEM

The contemporary healthcare system in Canada is characterized by a system of mixed sources of funding, delivery, and administration of services. The sources vary depending on the nature of the services being rendered and the person being treated. Hospital and physician services for approximately 97% of Canadians are covered under Medicare, the jointly funded federal/provincial health insurance system whose emergence was described in the previous section and that will be the focus of the remainder of this chapter.[43,44]

Health services for persons of First Nation and Inuit descent are solely the purview of the federal government and are handled outside of the Medicare framework. Similarly, healthcare services for veterans, members of the armed forces, and members of the Royal Canadian Mounted Police fall under the sole auspices of the federal government.[44] Together, these segments of the population totaled roughly 1 million persons in 2007 (the remaining 3% of the population).

For both the joint programs and the federal-only programs, a number of services, including portions of dental care, residential care, and pharmaceutical costs, are not covered. They are funded outside of the national health insurance plans either directly by the individual or through private sector insurance.[43]

In recent years, the Canadian health system has begun to face the repercussions of the policy decisions made in the 1980s and 1990s. With decreased financial support for the Medicare program, particularly from the federal level, investment in the maintenance and expansion of the healthcare infrastructure declined, creating a number of problems. At the core of these issues is a concern over physical access to healthcare services. Waiting times for services, particularly technologically complex or procedure-oriented services, have repeatedly been presented by critics as a problem point for the healthcare system. Concern over a lack of infrastructure such as computed tomography (CT) and magnetic resonance imaging (MRI) scanning machinery as well as a shortage of physicians and other healthcare professionals has garnered considerable attention both in the public eye and among policy circles.

The delivery of health care in Canada involves both public and private transactions. Physicians and residential care facilities are by and large nongovernmental entities. The hospital sector is substantially composed of facilities operated by local and provincial governments. In addition, not-for-profit private sector hospitals, particularly religiously affiliated institutions, constitute a smaller yet highly significant source of hospital-based care.[43,44]

The governmental component must be seen in context. As noted, a long history of geographic dispersion and independent local action created a federal structure characterized by strong provincial governments, not to mention a comparable interest in local (municipal) autonomy where appropriate. This tradition, coupled with well-documented innovation by provincial governments in the healthcare arena, contributed to both the development of the observed structure and their considerable latitude of action.[45] The provinces have adopted a wide variety of approaches for their health insurance plans; thus, it is frequently argued that Canada has (at least) 13 healthcare systems, not one.

The observed variations among provinces encompass many elements of both medical care and the healthcare system. The generosity of coverage (e.g., the inclusion of outpatient pharmaceuticals) is one example of this variation. There are also differences in the structure of the system. In British Columbia and Alberta, premiums are charged to individuals to augment tax revenues for coverage under Medicare. Although premiums are assessed, the law does not provide for the withholding of services in response to nonpayment of premiums. A greater number and more significant set of difference exist between the province of Quebec and the remaining 12 provinces and territories.

Although the healthcare system in Quebec has always had distinct elements, the divergence has become more pronounced in recent years. In 1999, Quebec declined to sign the Social Union Framework Agreement and thus distanced itself from some elements of Ottawa's influence.[38] More than any of the other jurisdictions, the healthcare system in Quebec is based on an integrated health and social services model with an increased concentration on the coordination of primary care and public health services.[46] Medical licensure requirements are uniform and fully transferable across all of the provinces and territories of Canada except Quebec, which administers its own system for licensing physicians.[35]

Facilities

Canada operates an extensive physical infrastructure for health care. Primary care services are provided in a variety of settings. Private physician offices constitute by far the most common venue for the delivery of primary care.[47] Primary health services are also delivered in ambulatory care clinics and in community health centers.[44]

In another example of this recurring theme, Community Health Centers emerged as a result of provincial innovation, in this instance taking place in Quebec. The concept spread to Ontario and then across the nation, although growth has slowed in the last ten years.[47] Although Community Health Centers provide a significant amount of care, they continue to represent a much smaller provider source when compared with private physician practices. For example, even in Quebec, there were 170 community health centers known as *centre local de services communautaires* in 2002. Together, these centers provided about 15% of primary care visits in the province.[48]

There were 746 hospitals operating 115,120 beds in Canada during the year 2003. Of these hospitals, 12 were private for-profit facilities operating 814 beds, and 6 were owned by the federal government and maintained 266 beds. The remainder were operated either by local or provincial governments or by private sector not-for-profit entities. Non-federal public hospitals represent the overwhelming majority of these facilities.[49]

The number of acute-care hospital beds in Canada has declined significantly since reaching a peak of 179,256 beds in 1989. During the period between 1986 and 1995, the number of hospitals decreased from 1,224 to 978. The number of public hospitals decreased from 1,053 to 901 during this interval. The number of private hospitals declined by almost two thirds (from 59 to 22) during the same period. A significant portion of these closures was among smaller hospitals, particularly those located in rural areas. Saskatchewan, for instance, witnessed the closure of 52 of its rural hospitals during the early 1990s.[50,51]

In summary, these closures reduced the number of acute-care beds from 178,137 in 1986 to 156,547 by 1995.[52] Some of this decline in the number of hospitals and beds reflected the transition of a number of hospitals to residential care facilities and also the reclassification within other facilities of a portion of their acute-care beds for long-term care use.[49] In the mid 1990s, 14,000 beds were reclassified for residential care use in the provinces of Alberta and Quebec alone.[49] In 2005, Canada had 290 acute-care hospital beds per 100,000 population, down from 400 per 100,000 persons in 1990. This mirrors the trend among other Organisation for Economic Co-operation and Development (OECD) nations, where the average rate of acute-care beds dropped from 510 per 100,000 people to 390 beds per 100,000 residents.[53]

In 2006, there were 4,921 residential care facilities licensed to operate in Canada serving 235,916 residents. Of these, 53.7% or 2,086 were designated for the care of the older population; 1,915 were mental health institutions; and the remaining 290 facilities were dedicated to an array of different specialties, including care of the physically disabled and delinquent youths. The distribution of facilities equates to 206,170 beds or 81.7% of the total for the care of the older population, 36,992 for mental health patients, and 9,163 beds for the assortment of other type institutions.[54]

Long-term care facilities in Canada are distributed somewhat differently than hospitals in terms of their ownership, with the private for-profit sector representing a far more substantial component of the mix. In 2006, 15.1% of residential care facilities were owned by governmental entities; 43.5% were run by private sector not-for-profit organizations, and the remaining 41.4% were private sector for-profit institutions. When looking solely at homes dedicated to the care of the aged, for-profit institutions represent an even greater portion of the total, comprising 53.7% of residential facilities for older persons. Private for-profit facilities are on average somewhat smaller in size than their not-for-profit and government-run competitors; thus, they account for only about 48.8% of all beds in older care facilities.[54]

Recent studies indicate that there are notable differences between the for-profit facilities and those operated under other modes of ownership. For-profit older person care facilities have lower staff-to-patient ratios than other institutions. The number of paid hours per bed, a measure of the level of staffing of long-term care facilities, was found to be 1,154 per bed among for-profit homes compared with 1,598 for not-for-profit and 1,892 for government homes. Correspondingly, for-profit homes have lower expenses per bed than do facilities operated under other forms of ownership.[54]

Public health in Canada is for the most part a distinct entity from the delivery of medical care. The focus of public health activities in Canada is not on supporting the delivery of healthcare services as it is in many nations, but rather on population health issues such as community health assessment, disease surveillance, health promotion, disease and injury prevention, and health protection. In Quebec, the boundary between population health and individual medical care is somewhat more blurred, as the system relies on a higher degree of integration of health services.[46]

Under the Canadian system, public health departments are the purview of provincial and local governments. The roles between the two levels of government vary from province to province, with Ontario being the most reliant on local government funding and administration. In recent years, reports by the Krever Commission and the Auditor General of Canada have raised concerns over the existing funding and infrastructure for the support of public health functions.[46]

The federal government's role has traditionally been limited in the area of public health. Implementing processes of the Quarantine Act and various pieces of health protection legislation have for the most part constituted the core of the Public Health Agency of Canada's functional role in the past. Since the outbreak in 2003 of severe acute respiratory syndrome, a restructuring of public health efforts at the federal level has been undertaken. A more active role for Ottawa appears to be taking form, more in line with the position the Centers for Disease Control holds in the United States.[46]

Workforce

Human resources are a critical element of any healthcare system. For the past 20 years, Canada has focused considerable attention on this area, particularly since the 1990s, when it was perceived that the numbers of physicians and nurses were declining. The First Ministers Accord of 2003 designated healthcare human resources planning a high-priority item in the Canadian health policy sphere. Beyond its inherent importance in the delivery of care for patients, health care is among the nation's largest sources of employment, with over 1,000,000 people directly working in this sector, representing 6% of the workforce. It is estimated that in 2007, 38.8% of healthcare costs were directly attributable to human resource costs.[55]

As of 2007, there were 65,794 physicians practicing in Canada,[56] a ratio of roughly 220 physicians per 100,000 persons in the population.[57] This is comparable to that of the United States—240 per 100,000 persons—and the United Kingdom—240 per 100,000 persons—but is below the OECD average of 300 physicians per 100,000 persons.[53]

Slightly more than half, 51.6%, of practicing Canadian physicians in 2007 were in the primary care specialties of general medicine and family practice. Medical specialists other than surgeons accounted for 35.5% of physicians, whereas surgeons were 12.9% of doctors. The remaining fraction of physicians is classified as medical scientists. The percentage of primary care physicians in the workforce is notably higher than the 36% observed in the United States but lower than the 56% found in Australia.[58]

Of physicians, 75.8%[56] were educated in one of the 17 accredited Canadian medical schools.[59] The remaining 24.2% were trained in other countries, most notably the United Kingdom, South Africa, and India.[55] Physicians are required to hold the Medical Doctor (MD) degree. To practice in Canada, foreign medical school graduates must first pass the Medical Council of Canada's Qualifying Examinations Parts I and II. This is followed by fulfilling a required residency in a Canadian medical program and completing any pertinent examinations required by the provincial or territorial medical board.[55]

Demographically, the population of Canadian physicians has been changing in recent years. From 2001 to 2006, the percentage of female physicians rose from 30.2% to 33.3% of the workforce. It is estimated that by 2015 women will account for approximately 40.0% of practicing physicians. Among medical students and physicians under age 34, women already outnumber men.[55]

The profile of the physician population is also changing in terms of age. From 2001 to 2005, the percentage of physicians under age 40 decreased 10%. Likewise the proportion of doctors over 50 years of age increased 19%.[57] In 1995, the average age of physicians in Canada was approximately 42.6 years; by 2005 that average rose to roughly 46.3 years.[55]

The change in the demographics of the physician cohort presents a challenge for the future, as research indicates that both female physicians and older physicians on average work fewer hours per week and see fewer patients than their younger male counterparts. Physicians who are women reportedly work 21% fewer hours than do male physicians. Similarly, physicians of both genders over 55 years of age steadily decrease the number of hours worked.[55] Because these changes are occurring in parallel with population aging and increasing demands for physician services, the effect is likely to be compounded.

A 2002 study conducted by the Canadian Institute for Health Information determined that in the period between 1993 and 2000 the "real" physician-to-population ratio decreased 5.1%. The "real" physician ratio was determined by adjusting the proportion of physicians per population unit by modifiers, which reflect the changing pattern of patients' demand for medical services and the changing composition of the physician workforce over the time period. The findings indicate that there has been a functional decrease in the number of physicians in Canada. It is further hypothesized that perhaps another component to the perception of a physician gap is that the expectations of the Canadian population, which rose in recent years, are in conflict with the actual capacity of the current supply of physicians.[60]

In 2005, there were 251,675 registered nurses (RN) in Canada, or 780 RNs for every 100,000 persons.[61] In addition, there were 201 licensed practical nurses (LPN) per 100,000 persons in the population.[55] The overall ratio of roughly 981 practicing nurses per 100,000 population places Canada roughly on par with Germany's 970 nurses per 100,000 persons. This is well above the 890 per 100,000 person average for OECD nations.[53]

Between 1990 and 2005, the number of practicing nurses dropped 7%.[53] Coupled with the aging of the nursing workforce, this decline raises considerable concern for the future. In 2005, nurses who were over the age of 55 represented 20% of the workforce. Nurses over 50 years of age outnumbered nurses under 35 by a 2-to-1 ratio.[57] As was seen with their physician counterparts, the nursing workforce is growing older at the same time as the general population ages and demands greater access to healthcare services.

The educational requirements for entry-level positions for registered nurses are currently undergoing a transition in Canada. The Atlantic Provinces were the first to institute the new policy requiring a 4-year baccalaureate degree for nursing licensure. Alberta is scheduled to enact this policy in 2009. Previously, nurses could be licensed through 2- and 3-year diploma programs.[55] When fully enacted across the nation, there will be an increased lag time in bringing newly trained nurses in to practice. This may produce a short-term exacerbation of the existing nursing shortage. As with physicians, foreign nursing graduates fill a considerable portion of nursing positions in Canada. In 2006, over 20,000 foreign-trained nurses were practicing in the Canadian healthcare system, the vast majority coming from the Philippines and the United Kingdom (Table 4-3).[55]

Technology and Equipment

Canada's healthcare system possesses a considerable infrastructure of advanced medical imaging and diagnostic equipment. The CT scan machine was introduced in Canada in 1973. In 2006, there were 378 machines located throughout the country. This represents 11.4 CT scan machines per million persons in the population.[62] The United Kingdom in 2005 reported 7.5 per million persons and the United States 32.2 per million population. The OECD average for 2005 was 20.6 CT scan machines per million people.[53] Between 1990 and 2006, 180 new CT scan units were installed, representing a 91% increase. Utilization of CT scans in

TABLE 4-3   Number of Health Professionals per
100,000 Canadians, 2005

Health Profession	Number per 100,000 Population
Optometrists	12
Chiropractors	22
Respiratory therapists	24
Dietitians	25
Psychologists	46
Physiotherapists	49
Dentists	58
Occupational therapists	35
Pharmacists	91
Social workers	92
Physicians (excluding residents)	190
Registered nurses	780
Licensed practical nurses	201
Nurse practitioners	4

From CIHI 2007 report Canada's Health Care Providers,
2007.

2006 was at the rate of 98 scans per 1,000 persons in the population.[62]

MRI technology was first introduced in Canada in 1982. There were 196 MRI machines in Canada in 2006, reflecting a per-million population rate of 5.9 machines.[62] This total is similar to the 5.4 per-million rate observed in the United Kingdom but is much lower than the 26.6 MRI machines per million persons found in the United States. The OECD average is 9.8 MRI machines per million persons in the population.[53] In the period between 1990 and 2006, 177 new MRI units were installed in Canada, representing a 932% increase. Utilization totals for 2006 reflect a rate of 30 MRI scans per 1,000 Canadians.[62]

Since 2000, there has been a considerable growth in freestanding private sector imaging facilities offering CT and MRI scans. In 2000, there were 2 CT machines in freestanding clinics. That number rose to 18 by 2006, which represented 5% of CT machines in the country. Similarly, there were 2 MRI machines located in freestanding clinics in 1998; by 2006, there were 32, which represented 16% of the nation's scanners. Interestingly, the funding for these freestanding facilities is different than for hospital-based machines. For hospitals, the primary source of revenue is the government's health insurance plan; for the freestanding facilities, the primary sources of revenue are private insurance and out-of-pocket payment.[62]

Imaging capacity (whether public or private, hospital based, or freestanding) is largely an urban phenomenon. In centers like Toronto, Montreal, Vancouver, and other large urban settings, the availability of such technology is comparable, if slightly lower in some cases, to other industrialized nations. Access to advanced imaging technology in the more sparsely populated areas such as the Northwest Territories as well as Newfoundland and Labrador is considerably more limited (Table 4-4).[53,62]

EVALUATION OF THE HEALTH SYSTEM

Cost

Overall spending on the healthcare system in 2007 is estimated to be $160.1 billion or approximately $4,867 per Canadian. This is an increase of 6.4% over 2006 expenditures. Expenditures vary by province within a 10% range about the mean. Quebec had the lowest per capita

TABLE 4-4   Medical Imaging Technology per
1,000,000 Canadians, 2005

Imaging Technology	Number per 1,000,000 Population
CT scanners	11.4
MRI scanners	5.9
Mammographs*	21.3
Nuclear medicine scanners	21.8
Catheterization labs	3.4
Angiography suites	5.2
PET scanners**	15
PET/CT scanners**	12
SPECT/CT scanners**	3

Primary source: CIHI report Medical Imaging
Technologies in Canada, 2006.

* Source: OECD report. Health at a Glance, 2007 OECD
Indicators.

** The figures reported as "per population" actually reflect
the total number of machines.

spending at $4,371, and Alberta had the highest at $5,390 per person. Expenditures in the territories are considerably higher with Nunavut being the highest at $10,903 per capita. This is primarily due to the small populations and vast geography of the territories. The pattern of relationships for both provincial and territorial spending has been consistent over the recent past.[40]

Trends in overall healthcare expenditures have varied significantly since 1975. In the period from 1975 until 1991, healthcare costs in Canada rose at a rate of 3.8% per year. As the effect of budget cuts during the 1990s took hold, spending on health decreased dramatically. Over the period from 1991 to 1997, healthcare expenditures rose at 0.8% per year, a value less than the overall rate of inflation in the economy, thus representing real dollar cuts in resources. As budgetary restraints were loosened the late 1990s and early 2000s, the rate of spending began to increase once more. Between 1996 and 2005, the rate of increase in spending rose to 5% per year.[40]

As a percentage of economic output, healthcare expenditures in 2007 represented 10.6% of the nation's GDP. By province, Prince Edward Island had the highest spending in relation to GDP, estimated at 14.4%. Alberta spent 7.3% of GDP on health care. Among the territories the range varied from Nunavut, which spent 26.8% of GDP in 2007, to the Northwest Territories, which is estimated to have spent 7.9%.[40]

Growth in healthcare expenditures as a percentage of GDP displays a trend quite similar to overall spending. In 1975, spending on health care represented 7% of GDP. During recession periods such as that experienced in Canada during the early-1980s, the rate of healthcare spending as a percentage of GDP rose sharply from 6.8% in 1979 to 8.3% in 1983. This reflected the steady rise in healthcare costs as national production slipped. A similar effect was witnessed with the recession in the early 1990s, and for the first time, healthcare expenditures as a percentage of GDP reached 10% in 1992. The effects of government spending cuts lowered health expenditures during the mid-1990s, and as the economy began to expand during the postrecession period, the percentage of GDP consumed by health care dropped to 8.9% in 1997. Between the years 1998 and 2005, healthcare spending expanded somewhat faster than the rate of the overall economy, reaching 10.3% of GDP in 2005.[40]

Financing of the Canadian healthcare system is achieved through the convergence of multiple streams of funding. The three primary sources of financing are the Medicare system, out-of-pocket payments by individuals, and private insurance. Since 1997, the division of spending on health care has been relatively set with the public sector contributing roughly 70% of funding and the remaining 30% coming from the private sector either in the form of out-of-pocket payments or private insurance for services not covered under Medicare.[63] In 2007, the overall per capita spending of $4,867 consisted of $3,435 from public sources and $1,432 in private sector funds. Among private sector funding, there has been a significant shift in recent years on the mix between out-of-pocket payment and that covered by private health insurance. In 1988, 29.2% of private sector spending was contributed by private insurance; by 2005, that percentage had risen to 40.9%.[40,44]

In 2005, hospital costs represented the single largest expense item, constituting 28.6% of healthcare spending. Pharmaceuticals were the second largest cost item, consuming 16.5% of every healthcare dollar, followed by physician services, which contributed 13.1% of the costs of health care. The pattern of spending since 1975 has shifted dramatically with the percentage of spending attributable to hospitals falling while that consumed by pharmaceutical costs has risen sharply.[40]

Medicare spending represents the majority of healthcare spending in Canada. Funding for Medicare is derived from tax revenues collected at both the federal and provincial levels. Federal support is delivered through Canada Health Transfer block grants to the provinces.[44,63,64] Block grants are comprised of two components: The first element is actual cash transfers, and the second is tax point transfers, which allow the provinces greater "tax room" to levy their own income tax.[65] The actual percentage of expenditures under Medicare that the federal government pays compared with the provinces has varied considerably over time. In 1980, the federal government contributed 30.6% of public funds allocated to health care; this figure dropped to 21.5% by 1996.[66]

The mechanism of funding Medicare has created a degree of tension between the federal and provincial governments. Under the Constitution Act of 1867, the provinces officially hold authority over health care and most other social welfare issues[12]; however, in practical application, the federal government holds considerable influence in these ostensibly provincial-level policy matters through the power derived from financial transfers of tax revenues.[38]

Payment systems for healthcare services vary by provider type and the nature of the service being rendered. Hospitals, regardless of ownership status, are paid through the provincial government based on a global budget for the year. Physician services in the majority of cases are handled on a fee-for-service basis. The fee schedule is negotiated annually between the provincial government and the province's medical association.[44,66] Physicians may also be paid under a blended system of fee-for-service and incentive-based payments. This is particularly common with those working in large group practices and community health centers. Some physicians are salaried employees.[44]

Pharmaceuticals are paid for under a mixed method that varies considerably by province. Quebec has a comprehensive prescription drug plan that is financed through tax revenues and covers the cost of most outpatient drugs. In the majority of Canadian provinces, some portion of outpatient drug costs are supplemented by the government at least for specific segments of the population such as low-income persons and older persons. For the remainder of the population, the bulk of outpatient prescription drug costs are paid for either through private insurance or out-of-pocket payments. This issue is complicated by the fact that provincial laws prohibit the marketing of insurance products for services covered under public health insurance.[44]

The reimbursement structure for long-term care is primarily made through a per diem system. Payments for this care represent a blend of funding streams from both the public and private sector. The public sector paid 72% of the costs for residential care in 2006. The remaining 28% was paid primarily through out-of-pocket expenses, although there is a limited market for private sector long-term care insurance.[57]

Quality

The quality of a healthcare system can be measured in numerous dimensions. Three areas that can be used are population health measures, system efficiency measures, and patient perceptions or satisfaction measures. Several clinical measures are routinely used for the comparative assessment of healthcare systems. These include infant mortality rates, life expectancy, and immunization rates. Efficiency measures in this case refer to wait times for procedures or services.

The overall infant mortality rate in Canada in 2005 was 5.4 infant deaths per 1,000 live births. This rate has remained virtually unchanged since 2002. The rates differed by gender with deaths among male infants occurring at a rate of 5.9 per 1,000 live births, whereas among female infants, the rate was 5.0 deaths per 1,000 live births.[67] This is close to the OECD national average of 5.4 infant deaths per 1,000 live births in 2005. Infant

mortality rates are higher in the United States, 6.8 deaths per 1,000 live births, and lower in the United Kingdom at 5.1 infant deaths per 1,000 live births.[53] The overall rates do not fully relate the picture as the infant mortality rate is significantly higher in some subpopulations. Residents of rural Nunavut Territory had an infant mortality rate in 2003 of 14.9, which is almost three times the national average that year.[31] Similarly, members of the First Nations have been found to have infant mortality rates upwards of three times that of the nation as a whole. Disparities also exist in infant mortality rates between people in the top quartile of income and those in the bottom quartile.[68]

Life expectancy at birth has been rising among Canadians. In 2005, the overall life expectancy was 80.4 years. Men had an expected longevity of 78.0 years compared with women who lived on average 82.7 years. Each of these longevity markers is significantly above the OECD averages and surpasses those of both the United Kingdom and the United States. Disparities in life expectancy do, however, continue to exist within certain subpopulations. Men of Aboriginal heritage live on average 7 years less than the national average. Likewise, Aboriginal women live an average of 5 years less than the Canadian average.[68]

Another significant reflection of the performance of a healthcare system is the longevity of persons after reaching the age of 65 years. Overall, Canadians can expect to live 19.6 years after reaching 65 years of age. For men, that figure is slightly less at 17.9 years, and for women, the expected additional life span is 21.1 years.[67] The expected life years remaining at age 65 years for Canadians surpass the average rate observed among OECD nations for both men and women.[53]

Immunization rates in Canada are high across the population. In 2004, the first dose of measles, mumps, and rubella vaccination was administered to 94% of children before their second birthday. The second measles, mumps, and rubella inoculation was delivered to 78% of children before the recommended age of 7 years. Other internationally recommended childhood vaccination rates are also high. It is estimated that 94% of Canadian children receive the recommended three doses of vaccine against diphtheria, pertussis, tetanus, polio, and hemophilus influenza type B by the age of 2 years.[31]

Waiting time for appointments is an issue that ha garnered considerable attention in the Canadian healthcare system. A 2005 survey indicated that Canadians waited longer to see a physician than did their counterparts in the United States, the United Kingdom, Germany, and Australia. Less than 23% of Canadians were able to see a physician on the same day that they attempted to obtain an appointment compared with more than 30% in the United States, more than 45% in the United Kingdom, and greater than 50% in both Germany and Australia.[55] Among Canadians, 36% reported that it took more than 6 days to see a physician regarding a health condition. When attempting to see a specialist, the median wait time for Canadians was 4 weeks, but 13% took more than 3 months to obtain an appointment. Similarly, wait times for diagnostic testing such CT scans and MRIs averaged 3 weeks.[55] Wait times are a significant issue with Canadians, although only about one fifth of the population considers the current circumstances "unacceptable."

Overall, Canadians are quite well satisfied with their healthcare system. In 2005, 84.4% of Canadians rated their satisfaction with health services as "very satisfied" or "somewhat satisfied." These results have been stable since the year 2000.[32] Modest variations across subpopulations have been observed. For example, males are generally more pleased with the system than are females, with 85.1% of men rating healthcare services positively versus 83.8% for women. For the most part, Canadians are satisfied with their system and are in some studies noted to be proud of its fundamental attributes, especially the degree of equity it achieves. It is a subtle but important point that can easily be lost in cross-national comparisons; Canadians are particularly proud of the perceived fairness of their system. Changes or advances that are not experienced in an equitable manner would not be viewed as improvements.

Access

Universal coverage is one of the five core principles of the Canadian healthcare system. All residents of Canada not specifically designated as being covered under another federal health insurance program are entitled to coverage for hospital and physician services under the national health insurance plan, Medicare. The cornerstone of the Canadian philosophy of health care is equality among persons.[41] Since the introduction of Medicare, it has been an expressed intent that a two-tiered system of healthcare not only be avoided but actively prevented from developing in Canada. It is felt that need, not financial position, should be the basis on which the allocation of healthcare resources is decided. Although disparities in health care do exist in Canada, they are based on processes that are not rooted in strictly defined financial access to physician and hospital services.[44]

Health insurance coverage reduces substantially, but does not eliminate all financial barriers to obtaining care. Other expenses (e.g., transportation to the site of care and the costs of uncovered services) are also impediments. The influence of such costs is disproportionately felt by persons with lower incomes, creating differential impacts on access to care.

Beyond financial issues, access to care can also be constrained by geographic, social, cultural, psychological, and other attributes of both the potential recipient of care and the potential provider of services. In Canada, the wide expanses of rural areas and the resulting travel times are a significant barrier to access. Similarly, harsh winter weather and language issues have been cited as impeding access to care. For the most part, the Canadian population views access to care in much the same way that it views other elements of the system, strongly emphasizing questions of equity and fairness.

Virtually all Canadians are covered by one of the variety of health insurance programs sponsored by some level of government; however, a small number of people do remain uninsured. The few people who fall into this category are primarily recent immigrants and refugees to Canada.[69]

CURRENT AND EMERGING ISSUES AND CHALLENGES

Canada will face several healthcare challenges as the 21st century proceeds. Among the more prominent issue domains facing the Canadian system are the financial sustainability of the system as currently deployed, questions about access to care (generally focused on system capacity), concerns about outpatient pharmaceuticals, debates of the appropriate role of the private sector, and continuing conversations about the importance of equity in assessing system performance.

In recent years, there has been considerable discussion regarding the sustainability of the Canadian healthcare system.[70,71] If considering solely the financial capacity of the nation as a whole to shoulder the rising costs of health care, international comparisons of health expenditures as a percentage of GDP indicate that Canada is operating well within a supportable range.[53,70–72] Annual federal budget surpluses also indicate that the nation remains in a solid position to sustain the healthcare system[18] and to manage any unexpected events in the relatively near term.

The 2002 Commission on the Future of Health Care in Canada, commonly referred to as the Romanow Commission, considered this topic and determined that the real issue was not the actual financial burden, but rather the willingness of the Canadian people and their governments to accept and bear the expense of universal health care. In respect to this, the commission found that Canadians were resolved to the preservation of their healthcare system in the face of increased costs of health care as long as the system was responsive to the needs and expectation of the people.[70] From this perspective, the financial sustainability of the system is intimately tied to its performance in terms of meeting the requirements of the Canadian people. The terminology is noteworthy—needs, requirements, and expectations are not the same as demand in the sense that the latter term is employed in orthodox economic terminology. It thus seems clear that the central element of Canadian health policy conversations in the coming years will be access to care.[70,73]

Problems with access to care in the Canadian context do not refer to the same financial access (insurance coverage) issues that exist in the United States and in many other nations. Rather, the focal concerns in Canada are primarily questions of availability (including distance, travel times, wait times, and the like, coupled with social, psychological, demographic, and similar elements of use and access, all noted by Andersen[74] and many other analysts of healthcare utilization).[75] In recent years, this part of the access conversation has focused heavily on waiting times, and a general perception that waiting times can and should be reduced by increasing the available supply of service capacity.

It is reasonably well-documented that waiting times for a significant number of services and procedures are longer in Canada than in comparable nations.[76] This international comparison, however, is less significant than the emerging perception among a substantial number of Canadians that some wait times, especially for appointments with primary care doctors, specialty referrals, some imaging procedures, and a relatively specific list of surgical interventions, are simply too long.[77]

In general, wait times for services can be attributed to both supply and demand factors, and given the evolving circumstances of the Canadian healthcare sector, it would seem likely that wait times will actually lengthen without some alteration in the status quo. Changes in the supply of and demand for health care caused by the shifting demographics of both the general population and the healthcare professions represent one of the most significant factors related to access of care that Canadians will have to face in the coming years. As the population continues to age, greater demands will be placed on the healthcare system. The human resources necessary to meet the evolving needs of the population must be identified, trained, and placed. This will be a particular challenge as the physician workforce transitions into a cohort that is older and more evenly distributed in terms of gender. Both older physicians and female physicians on average work fewer hours than their younger male colleagues.[55] This presents a situation in which either the number of physicians per population must be increased or steps must be taken to increase the productivity of the existing physician supply or provide for a comparable set of services from other professionals. One such step that is currently taking form in Canada is the integration of nurse practitioners to the healthcare setting. While in 2000 only seven jurisdictions in Canada permitted the licensure of nurse practitioners, in 2007, only one does not have licensing statutes in place.[55]

The overall supply of physicians is not the only concern related to this provider group. Access to primary care physicians continues to be an issue in many areas of Canada. Although physicians practicing in the primary care fields of family medicine and general practice comprise more than 51% of Canadian physicians, it has been observed that getting appointments with them can be difficult.[55] Efforts to increase the availability and accessibility of primary care practitioners in order to meet the demands of the Canadian people will certainly be a significant policy focus of the next decade.[70]

As a result of budget cuts in the 1980s and 1990s, the infrastructure for providing many technologically advanced services has not expanded a rate that aligns with the growth in demand for these services.[62] This gap in the available supply of physical infrastructure has compounded issues arising from decline in the real number of physicians practicing in Canada. Similarly, the construction of new hospital capacity, additional long-term care beds, assisted-living facilities, and other capital-intensive projects lagged over the same period.

From a relatively narrow policy perspective, achieving an increased supply of capacity requires four things. First, there must be a clear specification of the target—the numbers of doctors, nurses, beds, scanners, or whatever that is perceived to be the "right" or optimal numbers given the population. Such a target must be determined in a manner that reflects the best available data and technical analyses of the needs for service that are manifested in any particular population, as well as the wishes of that population. Second, there must be a reasonable level of agreement as to the target. Third, the investment capacity necessary to produce that amount of service must be available, in competition with other societal needs that have their own constituencies, and fourth, there must be sufficient time allocated for the investment decisions to reach fruition. It takes several years to train professional healthcare personnel. It is entirely possible for several years to pass between the moment at which it is determined that a particular community needs a new full-service hospital and the moment at which the first patient is treated in that new setting.

In the 4 decades since Canada's Medicare program was introduced in the 1960s, there have been considerable changes in the manner in which medical services are provided. Forty years ago, hospital costs were overwhelmingly the "big-ticket" component of total costs. Physician services were a somewhat distant second. Long-term care was a far distant third, and pharmaceuticals were just barely part of the picture. Today, outpatient pharmaceuticals constitute the second leading cost item among national health expenditures,[40] and many of the most expensive drugs (especially some agents for the treatment of cancer) are not included in that estimate because they are delivered only in inpatient settings as a part of hospital care. Under the federal legislation that enacted Medicare, outpatient drugs are not a required item of the provincial plans. Many provinces do offer coverage for certain segments of the population but the scope varies greatly by province, ranging from a low of 9% of the population receiving either direct coverage or premium supplements in Manitoba to 43% in Quebec. Over 75% of Canadians have some form of prescription drug coverage, primarily private sector insurance. On average, persons under the age of 65 years pay greater than 35% of the costs of prescription drugs out of pocket.[78]

In a nation where there is virtually universal insurance coverage for major medical expenses arising from hospitalization and physician services, 25% of the population having no coverage for the second leading source of medical expenditures represents a significant issue. This issue is compounded by the wide variation in the degree of coverage provided under both public and private sector drug plans. Addressing the financial eq-

uity issue in outpatient pharmaceuticals is likely to be a pressing issue in the coming years.

In a different vein, outpatient drugs also present another challenge for the Canadian healthcare system, the issue of cross-border sales to citizens of the United States. Because of the regulation of prices for patented medicines in Canada, the consumer costs are lower for some brand named medications than in the United States. As a result, at least since the 1990s, there has been a growing business in the sale of prescription drugs to Americans both in traditional over-the-counter sales and through internet pharmacies. Some estimates place the total upward of $1.2 billion in annual sales. If accurate, this would account for roughly 10% of Canadian retail pharmaceutical sales.[79]

There has been a growing concern in recent years over the potential of this cross-border industry to jeopardize drug availability in Canada or to prompt U.S. drug manufacturers to either withhold sale of medications to Canada or to greatly increase their wholesale prices. There is some anecdotal evidence to support the proposition of localized drug shortages in Canada, perhaps attributable to international resale of pharmaceuticals.[79] The recent passage of prescription drug coverage for Medicare participants in the United States may serve to decrease the total demand for medications from Canada. In the years to come, this friction point in Canadian/U.S. relations will need to be addressed.

There has also been some movement in Canada toward developing private health insurance products to support the financing of services that are also covered under Medicare. In a widely reported 2005 decision, the Canadian Supreme Court struck down Quebec's statute prohibiting the sale of insurance products that would provide payment for any services covered under the provincial Medicare plan.[80] Technically, this decision is germane only to Quebec, but other similar cases are under consideration in courts across Canada. In response to this judicial direction, some political forces are being marshaled to accomplish whatever constitutional change is necessary to effectively overturn the court's ruling.

At the core of the Supreme Court's ruling is that the government has a responsibility to provide the services covered under Medicare in a timely fashion so as to prevent undue pain and risk of death. If the government fails to meet these obligations, the statutory prohibition of persons going outside the public system to obtain care is unconstitutional under the laws of Quebec.[81] Although the long-term consequences of the movement toward privatization and the Supreme Court's decision are not clear at present, this certainly will be a central element in the future health policy debate in Canada.

Beyond these questions of supply, the changing composition of medical care, and some unique relationship issues that arise because of proximity to the United States, Canada faces an ongoing, perhaps perpetual, review and reconsideration of a fundamental philosophical question. Since the inception of publicly financed health insurance in Canada, the nation's healthcare and health policy conversations have included a delicate balancing act among three core values: (1) a respect for and commitment to communal action; (2) a faith in the abilities and power of free market economics, competition, and the private sector; and (3) a belief that the distribution of services, perhaps especially health services, should be achieved in a manner that is equitable, fair, and just. Balancing these three core values led to the development of a system that uses a community orientation for financing and making major capital decisions; leaves the individual medical care transaction in the private realm of the patient, the family, and the provider; and expects everyone to play the same game, on the same field, by the same rules. This conversation can perhaps be best understood by returning to the question of waiting times.

In 1978, Canadians were the most satisfied nation in the world in regard to their healthcare system. By 2001, a significant majority of Canadians felt "fundamental changes" needed to be made.[82] Much of this continuing conversation has been focused on waiting lists and a public perception that waiting lists for care in Canada were creating a migration of patients to the United States to receive healthcare services. Some estimates placed the expenditures outside Canadian borders in the range of $1 billion a year.

It is clear that some degree of this phenomenon is witnessed. In fact, a few Canadian provinces have standing agreements with providers in the United States to handle overflow demand for certain services at their facilities. Indeed, some such agreements are reciprocal. Canadian hospitals located near the international border are part of emergency surge plans and offer other capacity management support to their U.S. colleagues. There is no question that a quantity of cross-national service delivery occurs. Some is contractually sanctioned. Some reflects the capacity of wealthy individuals to obtain whatever care they seek in whatever setting they prefer, at whatever time meets their priorities, presuming that they have the resources necessary to implement those decisions. Despite the publicity, when taken together, all such instances sum to a relatively infrequent phenomenon. A 2002 study of the issue indicates that the majority of healthcare expenditures by or on behalf of

Canadians in the United States are the result of incidental occurrences while traveling on vacation or business and are not due to some form of medical tourism.[83]

The question of waiting times will continue to be a central part of Canada's healthcare conversation. In part, this derives from the simple fact of proximity to the United States and the perception (on both sides of the border) that care can be obtained more quickly in the United States. For an individual patient, that fact may be all the discussion that is required. Of course, at the societal level, there is no consensus as to the optimal waiting time, especially for diagnosis or therapeutic procedures that are relatively elective and not urgently time sensitive. Most thoughtful analysts recognize that establishing the quantity and distribution of capacity necessary to obtain a zero or near-zero waiting time for most people most of the time would require that same expensive capacity to sit idle for extensive periods. Such idle time is unacceptably wasteful and consumes resources that are extracted from other components of the system.

Of course, the Canadian conversation about waiting times has been influenced by activities emanating from the United States, including academic assessments, news stories, advocacy positions, mass media portrayals, and other devices. It is not unreasonable to consider whether the issues of waiting time in Canada would be viewed in the same way if there was no ongoing and sometimes rancorous health policy conversation in the United States about universal coverage and closely related questions.

Until quite recently, most Canadians appeared to view waiting times as a necessary constraint deriving from communitarian needs for fiscal responsibility and system solvency. As long as there was a perception that the wait times were within reasonable bounds of medical prudence and were fairly and equitably distributed, they were of only modest concerns. The cliché was that Canadians did not care if they had to wait in line, as long as they knew the line was moving at a reasonable pace and that everyone was in the same line together. At least some portion of the current discussion reflects new questions about the absolute duration of the wait and nagging concerns about cross-border health care in which some people are unfairly buying shorter wait times—in the vernacular, "jumping to the head of the line."

Concern about waiting times has given rise to renewed consideration of whether Canadians would, in general, prefer that the system continue under its current form, guided by the five principles of the Canada Health Act, or be modified to embrace a greater degree of privatization in the organization and financing of health services. Although there are and have always been some advocates who argue for a greater private role in Canadian health care, the momentum behind the current discussion can be traced to a perception of increased difficulties in obtaining services that began during the 1990s.[84]

At the crux of this privatization agenda is the view that the current system is failing to meet the needs of the population in terms of timely health services and that the rigors of market opportunities and constraints might be valuable in providing more services. Given the historical commitments of the nation to free market principles, it should certainly be no surprise that this proposition would be considered. It is seen by many as an obvious way to bolster the infrastructure for the delivery of high technology services, which are perceived as being in short supply.[81] Such proposals, however, are quickly extended to a discussion about whether any newly developed "private" capacity would be universally accessible or would such resources be available only to some subset of the population who are willing and able to use the new services by virtue of their private economic circumstances. If so, the private capacity would violate the "just, fair, and equitable principle" that is a hallmark of the Canada Health Act.[41] In reply, proponents of market initiatives contend that new, private capacity, even if it is available only to some, would "free up" public capacity and hence make access better for all.

CONCLUSION

During the 1980s and 1990s, Canada made political and fiscal decisions that curtailed the development of the nation's physical healthcare infrastructure and perhaps its supply of healthcare personnel. The consequences of these decisions are particularly evident in the areas of diagnostic technology and complex procedures. Waiting times for these services continue to range beyond those of comparable nations. Privatization initiatives have taken place for these services, including an increase in the number of private imaging service delivery sites (freestanding CT and MRI clinics). For proponents of some privatization, there is considerable hope that the approach taken to imaging might be extended to include such services as complex procedural interventions and appointments with specialists. For those opposed to any privatization that is not universally accessible, the same outcome is viewed with concern.[41]

Canadians still overwhelmingly support their healthcare system, and this support is indicated by favorable satisfaction rates. Their satisfaction with the system includes giving it very high marks for fairness and its achievement of community obligations, but concerns over individual access to certain areas of care are pervasive. Canadians are an affluent, well-educated population. Their needs and expectations in terms of health care reflect that status and are compounded by geographic, economic, and cultural proximity to the United States. To preserve the essential features of their healthcare system will require that the nation confront and meaningfully address the needs and expectations experienced at both the individual and community levels.[70]

REFERENCES

1. Dickason O. *Canada's First Nations: A History of Founding Peoples from Earliest Times*, 3rd ed. Toronto, Ontario: Oxford University Press; 2002.

2. Bumsted J. *The Peoples of Canada: A Pre-Confederation History*, 2nd ed. Toronto, Ontario: Oxford University Press; 2003.

3. Brune N. A History of Canada Online. Retrieved February 15, 2008, from http://canadachannel.ca/2/2Avikings.php.

4. Morton D. *A Short History of Canada*, 6th ed. Toronto, Ontario: McClelland & Stewart Ltd.; 2006.

5. Brune, N. A History of Canada Online. Retrieved February 15, 2008, from http://canadachannel.ca/3/3Cfirstsett.php.

6. Bumsted J. *The Peoples of Canada: A Post-Confederation History*, 3rd cd. Toronto, Ontario: Oxford University Press; 2007.

7. Horn M. The Great Depression of the 1930s in Canada. The Canadian Historical Association. 1984; Publication No. 39. Retrieved March 5, 2008, from http://www.collectionscanada.gc.ca/obj/002013/f2/H39_en.pdf?PHPSESSID=k742p197m5r7satns5bhmac820.

8. Ostry A. The roots of North America's first comprehensive public health insurance system. *Hygiea Internationalis*. 2001;2(1):25–44. Retrieved February 22, 2008, from http://www.ep.liu.se/ej/hygiea/ra/007/paper.pdf.

9. Statistics Canada. Portrait of the Canadian Population in 2006, 2006 Census, 2007. Retrieved February 15, 2008, from http://www12.statcan.ca/english/census06/analysis/popdwell/highlights.cfm.

10. Government of Canada. Canadians and Their Government: A Resource Guide, 2004. Retrieved February 25, 2008, from http://www.canadianheritage.gc.ca/special/gouv-gov/section1/infobox1_e.cfm.

11. Elections Canada. The Electoral System of Canada, 2008. Retrieved February 23, 2008, from http://www.elections.ca/content.asp?section=gen&document=part1&dir=ces&lang=e&anchot=3&textonly=false#3.

12. Government of Canada. The Structure of the Canadian Government, 2007. Retrieved February 25, 2008, from http://canada.gc.ca/howgoc/glance_e.html.

13. Underhill FH. Canadian Political Parties. The Canadian Historical Association, 1974, Publication No. 8. Retrieved

March 5, 2008, from http://www.collectionscanada.gc.ca/obj/002013/f2/H8_en.pdf?PHPSESSID=r30rln1chcotmhgrlluk70igr2.

14. Bernier J. Disease, Medicine, and Society in Canada: A Historical Overview. The Canadian Historical Association, 2003, Publication No. 63. Retrieved February 17, 2008, from http://www.collectionscanada.gc.ca/obj/002013/f2/H63_en.pdf?PHPSESSID=fdo50f7sm2uk4f27om114bq1o0.

15. Maioni A. Parting at the Crossroads: The Development of Health Insurance in Canada and the United States, 1940–1965. *Comparative Politics.* 1997;29(4):411–431.

16. Statistics Canada. Business, Consumer and Property Services, 2007. Retrieved February 15, 2008, from http://www41.statcan.ca/2007/0163_000_e.htm.

17. Ministry of Finance, Canada. The Economy in Brief, January 2008. Retrieved February 25, 2008, from http://www.fin.gc.ca/ECONBR/pdf/ecbr08-01e.pdf.

18. Ministry of Finance, Canada. Strong Leadership. A Better Canada: Economic Statement, 2007. Retrieved March 7, 2008, from http://www.fin.gc.ca/ec2007/pdf/Economic-Statement2007_E.pdf.

19. Statistics Canada. Gross Domestic Product by Industry, 2007, Catalog No.15-001-X. Retrieved February 14, 2008, from http://www.statcan.ca/english/freepub/15-001-XIE/200711/part1.htm.

20. Statistics Canada. Transportation, 2007. Retrieved March 21, 2008, from http://www41.statcan.ca/2007/4006/ceb4006/ceb4006_000_e.htm.

21. Council of Ministers of Education, Canada. The Development of Education, Report of Canada by the Council of Ministers of Education, Canada, 1996. Retrieved April 3, 2008, from http://www.ibe.unesco.org/countries/countryDossier/natrep96.pdf.

22. Statistics Canada. School Boards Revenue and Expenditures by Province and Territory, 2007. Retrieved April 3, 2008, from http://www40.statcan.ca/l01.cst01/govt43a.htm?sdi=education.

23. Statistics Canada. University Enrollments by Program Level and Instructional Program, 2008. Retrieved April 3, 2008, from http://www40.statcan.ca/l01/cst01/educ54a.htm?sdi=education.

24. Statistics Canada. Quarterly Demographic Estimates January to March 2007, Preliminary, 2007, Catalog No. 91-002-XIE. Retrieved February 27, 2008, from http://www.statcan.ca/english/free/91-002-XIE/91-002-XIE2007003.pdf.

25. Statistics Canada. Annual Demographic Statistics 2005, 2006, Catalog No. 91-213-XIB. Retrieved March 3, 2008, from http://www.statcan.ca/english.freepub.91-213-XIB/0000591-213-XIB.pdf.

26. Statistics Canada. Aboriginal Peoples in Canada 2006: Inuit, Métis, and First Nations, 2006 Census, 2007, Catalog No. 97-558-XIE. Retrieved April 1, 2008, from http://www12.statcan.ca/english/census06/analysis/aboriginal/pdf/97-558-XIE2006001.pdf.

27. Statistics Canada. Educational Portrait of Canada, 2006 Census, 2008, Catalog No. 97-560-X. Retrieved April 2, 2008, from http://www12.statcan.ca/english/census06/analysis/education/pdf/97-560-XIE2006001.pdf.

28. Statistics Canada. Income in Canada 2005, 2007, Catalog No. 75-202-XIE. Retrieved March 9, 2008, from http://www.statcan.ca/english/freepub/75-202-XIE/75-202-XIE2005000.pdf.

29. Statistics Canada. Income Inequality and Low Income in Canada: An International Perspective, Catalog No. 11F0019 MIE- No. 240, 2005. Retrieved March 28, 2008, from http://www.statcan.ca/english/research/11F0019MIE/11F0019MIE2005240.pdf.

30. Statistics Canada. 2001 Census: Analysis Series, Religions in Canada, 2003, Catalog No. 96F0030XIE2001015. Retrieved March 7, 2008, from http://www12.statcan.ca/english/census01/Products/Analytic/companion/rel/pdf/96F0030XIE2001015.pdf.

31. Pan American Health Organization. Health in the Americas 2007, volume II: The Countries, 2008. Retrieved February 16, 2008, from http://www.paho.org/hia/archivosvol2/paisesing/Canada%20English.pdf.

32. Health Canada. Healthy Canadians: A Federal Report on Comparable Health Indicators 2006, 2006. Retrieved February 15, 2008, from http://www.hc-sc.gc.ca/hcs-sss/alt_formats/hpb-dgps/pdf/pubs/2006-fed-comp-indicat/2006-fed-comp-indicat_e.pdf.

33. Public Health Agency, Canada. Diabetes in Canada: Highlights from the National Diabetes Surveillance System 2004–2005, 2008. Retrieved May 24, 2008, from http://www.phac-aspc.gc.ca/publicat/2008/dicndss-dacsnsd-04-05/pdf/dicndss-04-05-eng.pdf.

34. Starr P. *The Social Transformation of American Medicine.* New York: Basic Books; 1982.

35. Roemer M. *National Health Systems of the World Volume I: The Countries.* New York: Oxford University Press; 1991.

36. Vayda E. The Canadian health care system: an overview. *Journal of Public Health Policy.* 1986;7(2):205–210.

37. Iglehart J. Revisiting the Canadian health care system. *The New England Journal of Medicine.* 2000;342:2007–2012.

38. Rocher F, Smith M. Federalism and Health Care: The Impact of Political-Institutional Dynamics on the Canadian Health Care System. Commission on the Future of Health Care in Canada, Discussion Paper No. 18. 2002. Retrieved February 22, 2008, from http://www.arts.ualberta.ca/~spatten/POLS%20322%20THREE%20(Rocher%20and%20Smith).pdf.

39. Health Canada. Canada Health Act Annual Report 2006–2007, 2007. Retrieved March 3, 2008, from http://www.hc-sc.gc.ca/hcs-sss/alt_formats/hpb-dgps/pdf/pubs/chaar-ralcs-0607/chaar-ralcs-0607_e.pdf.

40. Canadian Institute for Health Information. National Health Expenditure Trends 1975–2007, 2007. Retrieved February 15, 2008, from http://secure.cihi.ca/cihiweb/Products/NHET_1975_2007_e.pdf.

41. Premont M. The Canada Health Act and the Future of Health Care Systems in Canada, 2002, Commission on the Future of Health Care in Canada, Discussion Paper No. 4. Retrieved February 25, 2008, from http://www.hcsc.gc.ca/english/pdf/romanow/pdfs/4_Premont_1E.pdf.

42. Marmor T, Maioni A. One Issue, Two Voices Health Care in Crisis: The Drive for Health Reform in Canada and the

United States, 2008, Woodrow Wilson International Center for Scholars. Issue No. 9. Retrieved April 20, 2008, from http://www.wilsoncenter.org/topics/Pubs/CI_OneIssue_9 .pdf.

43. Health Canada. Canada's Health Care System at a Glance, 2002. Retrieved February 15, 2008, from http://www.hc-sc.gc .ca/ahc-asc/media/nr-cp/2002/2002_care-soinsbk5_e.html.

44. Health Canada. Canada's Health Care System, 2005. Retrieved February 16, 2008, from http://www.hc-sc.gc.ca/ hcs-sss/alt_formats/hpb-dgps/pdf/pubs/2005-hcs-sss/ 2005-hcs-sss_e.pdf.

45. Kohn R, Radius S. Two Roads to Health Care: U.S. and Canadian Policies 1945–1975. *Medical Care.* 1974;12(3): 189–201.

46. Canadian Institutes of Health Research. The Future of Public Health in Canada: Developing a Public Health System for the 21st Century, 2003. Retrieved March 7, 2008, from http://www.cihr-irsc.gc.ca/e/pdf_19572.htm.

47. Hutchinson B, Abelson J, Lavis J. Primary care in Canada: so much innovation, so little change. *Health Affairs.* 2001; 20(3):116–131.

48. Haggerty J, Pineault R, Beaulieu M, et al. Room for improvement patients experiences of primary care in Quebec before major reforms. *Canadian Family Physician.* 2007;53: 1056–1063.

49. Canadian Institute for Health Information. Hospital Trends in Canada—Results of a Project to Create a Historical Series of Statistical and Financial Data for Canadian Hospitals over Twenty-Seven Years, 2005. Retrieved April 9, 2008, from http://secure.cihi.ca/cihiweb/products/Hospital_Trends_ in_Canada_e.pdf.

50. Barer M, Morgan S, Evans R. Strangulation or rationalization? Costs and access in Canadian hospitals. *Longwoods Review.* 2003;4:10–419.

51. Liu L, Hader J, Brossart B, White R, Lewis S. Impact of rural hospital closures in Saskatchewan, Canada. *Social Science & Medicine.* 2001;52:1793–1804.

52. Tully P, Saint-Pierre E. Downsizing Canada's hospitals, 1986/87 to 1994/95. *Health Reports.* 1997;8(4):33–39.

53. Organization for Economic Cooperation and Development. Health at a Glance 2007: OECD Indicators, 2007. Retrieved February 26, 2008, from http://miranda.sourceoecd .org/vl=2775237/cl=14/nw=1/rpsv/health2007/g1-3-03.htm.

54. Statistics Canada. Residential Care Facilities 2005/2006, 2007, Catalog No. 83-237-X. Retrieved April 7, 2008, from http://www.statcan.ca/english/freepub/83-237-XIE/83- 237-XIE2008001.pdf.

55. Canadian Institute for Health Information Canada's Health Care Providers, 2007, 2007. Retrieved March 3, 2008, from http://secure.cihi.ca/cihiweb/products/HCProviders_07_EN _final.pdf.

56. Canadian Medical Association. Results of the National Physicians Survey, 2007. Retrieved April 11, 2008, from http://www.nationalphysiciansurvey.ca/nps/2007_Survey/ 2007results-e.asp.

57. Canadian Institute for Health Information. Health Care in Canada 2007, 2007. Retrieved March 1, 2008, from http://secure.cihi.ca/cihiweb/products/hcic2007_e.pdf.

58. Bindman A, Forrest C, Britt H, Crampton P, Majeed A. Diagnostic score of and exposure to primary care physicians in Australia, New Zealand and the United States: cross sectional analysis of results from three national surveys. *British Medical Journal.* May 15, 2007. Retrieved April 2, 2008, from http://www.bmj.com/cgi/rapidpdf/bmj.39203.658970.55v1.

59. Association of American Medical Colleges. List of Accredited Medical Schools in the United States and Canada, 2007. Retrieved March 27, 2008, from http://services.aamc.org/ memberlistings/index.cfm?fuseaction=home.search&search _type=MS&wildcard_criteria=&state_criteria=CNT%3AC anada&image=Search.

60. Chan B. From Perceived Surplus to Perceived Shortage: What Happened to Canada's Physician Workforce in the 1990s, 2002. Retrieved February 15, 2008, from http://secure.cihi .ca/cihiweb/products/chanjun02.pdf.

61. Canadian Nurses Association. 2005 Workforce Profile of Registered Nurses in Canada, 2006. Retrieved April 4, 2008, from http://www.cna-nurses.ca/CNA/documents/pdf/ publications/Nurse_Practitioner_Workforce_Update_ 2006_e.pdf.

62. Canadian Institute for Health Information. Medical Imaging Technologies in Canada, 2006–Supply, Utilization and Sources of Operating Funds, 2006. Retrieved April 4, 2008, from http://secure.cihi.ca/cihiweb/en/downloads/ mit_analysis_in_brief_e.pdf.

63. Canadian Institute for Health Information. Exploring the 70-30 Split: How Canada's Health Care System is Financed, 2005. Retrieved March 28, 2008, from http://secure.cihi.ca/ cihiweb/Products/FundsRep_EN.pdf.

64. Ministry of Finance, Canada. A Brief History of the Health and Social Transfers, 2008. Retrieved March 3, 2008, from http://www.fin.gc.ca/FEDPROV/hise.html.

65. Ministry of Finance, Canada. Tax Point Transfers, 2008. Retrieved April 29, 2008, from http://www.fin.gc.ca/transfers/ taxpoint/taxpoint_e.html.

66. Naylor C. Health care in Canada: incrementalism under fiscal duress. *Health Affairs.* 1999;18(3):9–26.

67. Statistics Canada. Deaths 2005, Report No. 84F0211X, 2008. Retrieved April 9, 2008, from http://www.statcan.ca/english/ freepub/84F0211XIE/2005000/tablesectionlist.htm.

68. Public Health Agency, Canada. Reducing Health Disparities—Roles of the Health Sector: Discussion Paper, 2005. Retrieved April 3, 2008, from http://www.phac-aspc .gc.ca/ph-sp/disparities/pdf06/disparities_discussion_paper _e.pdf.

69. Caulford P, Vali Y. Providing health care to medically uninsured immigrants and refugees. *Canadian Medical Association Journal.* 2006;174(9):1253–1254.

70. Romanow R. Commission on the Future of Health Care in Canada—Final Report, 2002. Retrieved February 15, 2008, from http://www.hc-sc.gc.ca/english/care/romanow/index1 .html.

71. Dhalla I. Canada's health care system and the sustainability paradox. *Canadian Medical Association Journal.* 2007; 177(1):51–53.

72. Evans R. Economic Myths and Political Realities: The Inequality Agenda and the Sustainability of Medicare, 2007.

Retrieved April 9, 2008, from http://www.chspr.ubc.ca/files/publications/2007/chspr07-13w.pdf.

73. Stolberg H. The Canadian health care system: past, present, and future. *Journal of the American College of Radiology.* 2004;1(9):659–670.

74. Andersen R. Revisiting the behavioral model and access to medical care: does it matter? *Journal of Health and Social Behavior.* 1995;36(1):1–10.

75. Baxter N. Equal for whom? addressing disparities in the Canadian medical system must become a national priority. *Canadian Medical Association Journal.* 2007;177(12):1522–1523.

76. Health Council of Canada. Fixing the Foundation: An Update on Primary Care and Home Care Renewal in Canada, 2008. Retrieved April 14, 2008, from http://www.healthcouncilcanada.ca/docs/rpts/2008/phc/HCC_PHC_Main_web_E.pdf.

77. Soroka S. A Report of the Health Council of Canada: Canadian Perceptions of the Health Care System. Health Council of Canada, 2007. Retrieved April 9, 2008, from http://www.healthcouncilcanada.ca/docs/rpts/2007/Public%20Perceptions%20-%20English%20Final_Feb-07.pdf.

78. Demers V, Melo M, Jackevicius C, et al. Comparison of provincial prescription drug plans and the impact on patient's annual drug expenditures. *Canadian Medical Association Journal.* 2008;178(4):405–409.

79. Voelker R. Northern Rxposure U.S. Canada clash on cross-border medication sales. *Journal of the American Medical Association.* 2003;290(22):2921–2925.

80. Ouellet R. The Chaoulli decision: a debate in which physicians must be heard. *Canadian Medical Association Journal.* 2005;173(8):896.

81. Steinbrook R. Private health care in Canada. *New England Journal of Medicine.* 2006;354(16):1661–1664.

82. Tuohy C. The cost of constraint and prospects for health care reform in Canada. *Health Affairs.* 2002;21(3):32–46.

83. Katz S, Cardiff K, Pascali M, Barer M, Evans R. Phantoms in the snow: Canadians' use of health care services in the United States. *Health Affairs.* 2002;21(3):19–31.

84. Kenny N, Chafe R. Pushing right against the evidence: turbulent times for Canadian health care. *Hastings Center Report.* 2007;September–October:24–26.

CHAPTER 5

United Kingdom

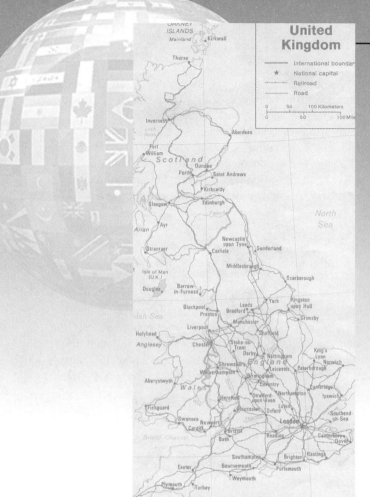

John E. Lopes, Jr., M. Nicholas Coppola, and Lisa Riste

COUNTRY DESCRIPTION

TABLE 5-1 United Kingdom

Nationality	Noun: Briton(s), British (collective plural) Adjective: British
Ethnic groups	White 92.1% (of which English 83.6%, Scottish 8.6%, Welsh 4.9%, Northern Irish 2.9%), black 2%, Indian 1.8%, Pakistani 1.3%, mixed 1.2%, other 1.6% (2001 census)
Religions	Christian (Anglican, Roman Catholic, Presbyterian, Methodist) 71.6%, Muslim 2.7%, Hindu 1%, other 1.6%, unspecified or none 23.1% (2001 census)
Language	English, Welsh (about 26% of the population of Wales), Scottish form of Gaelic (about 60,000 in Scotland)
Literacy	Definition: age 15 and over has completed 5 or more years of schooling Total population: 99% Male: 99% Female: 99% (2003 est.)

(continues)

TABLE 5-1   United Kingdom (continued)

Government type	Constitutional monarchy
Date of independence	England has existed as a unified entity since the 10th century; the union between England and Wales, begun in 1284 with the Statute of Rhuddlan, was not formalized until 1536 with an Act of Union; in another Act of Union in 1707, England and Scotland agreed to permanently join as Great Britain; the legislative union of Great Britain and Ireland was implemented in 1801, with the adoption of the name the United Kingdom of Great Britain and Ireland; the Anglo-Irish treaty of 1921 formalized a partition of Ireland; six northern Irish counties remained part of the United Kingdom as Northern Ireland and the current name of the country, the United Kingdom of Great Britain and Northern Ireland, was adopted in 1927.
Gross Domestic Product (GDP) per capita	$35,300 (2007 est.)
Unemployment rate	5.4% (2007 est.)
Natural hazards	Winter windstorms; floods
Environment: current issues	Continues to reduce greenhouse gas emissions (has met Kyoto Protocol target of a 12.5% reduction from 1990 levels and intends to meet the legally binding target and move toward a domestic goal of a 20% cut in emissions by 2010); by 2005, the government reduced the amount of industrial and commercial waste disposed of in landfill sites to 85% of 1998 levels and recycled or composted at least 25% of household waste, increasing to 33% by 2015
Population	60,943,912 (July 2008 est.)
Age structure	0–14 years: 16.9% (male 5,287,590/female 5,036,881) 15–64 years: 67.1% (male 20,698,645/female 20,185,040) 65 years and over: 16% (male 4,186,561/female 5,549,195) (2008 est.)
Median age	Total: 39.9 years Male: 38.8 years Female: 41 years (2008 est.)
Population growth rate	0.276% (2008 est.)
Birth rate	10.65 births/1,000 population (2008 est.)
Death rate	10.05 deaths/1,000 population (2008 est.)
Net migration rate	2.17 migrant(s)/1,000 population (2008 est.)
Gender ratio	At birth: 1.05 male(s)/female Under 15 years: 1.05 male(s)/female 15–64 years: 1.03 male(s)/female 65 years and over: 0.75 male(s)/female Total population: 0.98 male(s)/female (2008 est.)
Infant mortality rate	Total: 4.93 deaths/1,000 live births Male: 5.49 deaths/1,000 live births Female: 4.34 deaths/1,000 live births (2008 est.)
Life expectancy at birth	Total population: 78.85 years Male: 76.37 years Female: 81.46 years (2008 est.)

(continues)

TABLE 5-1 United Kingdom (continued)

Total fertility rate	1.66 children born/woman (2008 est.)
HIV/AIDS adult prevalence rate	0.2% (2001 est.)
Number of people living with HIV/AIDS	51,000 (2001 est.)
HIV/AIDS deaths	Less than 500 (2003 est.)

Central Intelligence Agency. The World Fact Book, 2008. Retrieved November 18, 2008, from https://www.cia.gov/library/publications/the-world-factbook.

History

The United Kingdom is a sovereign country that is composed of the four constituent countries of England, Scotland, Wales, and Northern Ireland. It is also commonly referred to as Great Britain (or Britain) and Northern Ireland. At previous points in history, it may have been common parlance to refer to England as Britain and vice versa, as England was the dominant country to the subjugated other three. Today this is not the case. England, Scotland, Wales, and Northern Ireland have a more equal share in the governance of the United Kingdom itself.

According to the CIA World Fact Book, which has been collecting geographical, political, and demographic information on all of the countries of the world and making it publically available on the web for over a decade, the first half of the 20th century saw the United Kingdom's fitness as a world power seriously depleted between two World Wars, followed by the Irish republic's withdrawal from the union.[1] The second half of the century witnessed the slow dismantling of the British Empire and the United Kingdom rebuilding itself into a modern and prosperous European nation.

As one of five permanent members of the United Nations Security Council, a founding member of North Atlantic Treaty Organization, and of the Commonwealth, the United Kingdom pursues a global approach to foreign policy. The United Kingdom is currently considering its degree of integration with continental Europe. A member of the EU, the United Kingdom chose to remain outside the Economic and Monetary Union for the time being.

Constitutional reform is also a significant issue in the United Kingdom. The Scottish Parliament, the National Assembly for Wales, and the Northern Ireland Assembly were established in 1999, but the latter was suspended until May 2007 because of wrangling over the peace process.[1]

The United Kingdom has played a huge role in shaping the democratic political structure of many Western societies. A country steeped in tradition and institutionalism, the United Kingdom has no common set of governing documents similar to the United States' Declaration of Independence, Constitution, and Bill of Rights. With its history and tradition, it is one of the very few countries in the world without a written constitution. Rather, the English system of government traces many of its roots back to the Magna Carta of 1215, which outlined and protected certain individual rights. These rights were later validated and augmented through various Acts of Parliament from constituent countries over the next 800 years. The result is a highly evolved democratic country in respect to certain individual freedoms while maintaining certain expectancy from the government for what Americans might call socialized practices. Among one of the British-perceived entitlements borne from 800 years of parliamentary enactments and expectations of the people is free and universal health care for all citizens paid for by the people through taxes but delivered by the government.

Size and Geography

The United Kingdom is 241,590 square kilometers in size (Figure 5-1). This equates to about the size of the American State of Oregon.[2] England is 130,000 km², Scotland is 77,000 km², Wales is 21,000 km², and Northern Ireland is 13,000 km² in size. The square kilometers of the United Kingdom are represented by a land composition composed of arable, 25%; pastures, 46%; forests, 10%; and other geographic features, 19%. Natural resources include an abundance of coal, petroleum, natural gas, tin, limestone, iron ore, and salt.

FIGURE 5-1   Map of the United Kingdom

As an island nation, the United Kingdom is located at the northwest corner of Europe. The climate is very temperate, as the weather is based off the capture of the warm Gulf Stream from the Caribbean. Despite the United Kingdom's relative northern proximity on the globe, the warm Gulf Stream contributes to the United Kingdom's relatively moderate, albeit boggy, climate. A national average high temperature is approximately 17°C, with an annual low of 3°C. Approximately 50% of days are overcast; however, the abundance of low mountains, hills, and plains continues the "quaint" feel of resonance when visiting the country.

Population Centers (Urban Versus Rural)

Approximately 61 million people inhabit the United Kingdom, with just over 7 million people living in London, the largest city of the United Kingdom. London is the only U.K. city inhabited by more than 1 million people. As of the writing of this paper, Birmingham has slightly fewer than 1 million people, but is expected to exceed that ceiling in 3 or 4 years. Other large cities in the United Kingdom are Leeds, Glasgow, Sheffield,

Bradford, Liverpool, and Manchester—each reporting populations around a half million. Britain is culturally split between urban and rural areas.[3]

The smallest populated area in the United Kingdom is St. David's with 2,000 inhabitants, followed by Wells with approximately 14,000. Of the approximately 70 inhabited cities or towns in the United Kingdom, more than two thirds are inhabited by fewer than 30,000 people, with the smallest rural towns capturing less than approximately 12,000 people. This dispersion and self-selection of individuals in urban and rural areas are unique cultural phenomena found primarily in European nations.[3] The concept of "suburbs," for example, people living outside major cities, but not in rural areas, is a concept foreign to the United Kingdom.

Government or Political System

The United Kingdom's current government is a constitutional monarchy. It is divided into 96 political counties. The head of the executive branch consists of the chief of state, or Queen, who has her position by birthright; however, the Queen has no real governing role. The head of government is, however, the popular parliamentary-supported Prime Minister, who subsequently appoints cabinet members to help run the government. The legislative branch is a bicameral parliament comprised of the House of Lords (approximately 500 members) and the House of Commons (659 seats). The judicial branch consists of the House of Lords, appointed by the monarch for life. There are no elections for the House of Lords. Members of the House of Commons are elected to 5-year terms by popular vote. In contrast, the executive branch for the United States consists of the elected President, whereas the legislative branch includes members of the United States Congress who are also elected. The British legal system is based on century-old principals of Common Law that served as the model for the U.S. legal system.[1,4] There are two main political parties in Britain; they are the Conservative and the Labour Parties. The Conservative Party, or "Tories," is similar to Republicans, whereas the Labour party may be analogous to American Democrats. There are several smaller political parties as well, including Liberal Democrats, Scottish Nationalist Party, Democratic Unionist Party, Sinn Fein, Social Democratic, and Independent.[1,4]

Macroeconomics

The United Kingdom has enjoyed one of the most prosperous periods of sustained growth in all of Europe, having a relatively steady rise in maturity and enterprise development for over 150 years. For its relatively small size in geography and scarcity of resources for its land mass, the United Kingdom has the fifth largest economy in the world when factors of market exchange rate and purchasing power are used as measures. Similar to many democratic societies, the United Kingdom owns few industrial manufacturing entities. In light of this, the International Monetary Fund suggests that the United Kingdom has the seventh highest gross domestic product (GDP) per capita in Europe[5]; however, the report finds that "challenges remain including improving education and skills levels, increasing labor force participation and progression, enhancing productivity growth and maintaining tax competitiveness."

In 2007, the U.K.'s GDP was $1.7 trillion (USD).[1] The real GDP growth rate was 3% with a real GDP per capita of $22,800 (USD). The inflation rate in the United Kingdom was 2.4%, and the unemployment rate was 7.5% for the same time period. Total revenues for the United Kingdom amount to $388.9 billion with expenditures of $447.6 billion. Comparing those numbers with the United States with $1,258 trillion in revenues and $1,461 trillion in expenditures, total liquid assets in the United Kingdom are a prime source of motivation to contain other sociable spending.[6]

According to Mangelsdorff, Smetana, and Love,[6] the United Kingdom is recognized as a world leader in finance and trading. It supports several commodities exchange markets to include the London Stock Exchange, the London Metal Exchange, and the London International Financial Futures and Options Exchange. Furthermore, the United Kingdom has abundant oil reserves and exports British petroleum to the United States on a regular basis.

Major Industries, Ports and Airports, Infrastructure, and Transportation Development

As previously mentioned, for a relatively small island nation, the United Kingdom has prospered industrially since decommissioning many of its state-run industries in the latter part of the 20th century. The United Kingdom has approximately 31 million people actively employed in the labor and working sector when including military personnel. This is a relatively small number when juxtaposing this figure to the American work and labor force of approximately 146 million. Within that group, 25% are in manufacturing and construction, 9.1% are employed in the government, 1.9% work in the field of energy, and 1.2% are in agriculture. Within that workforce, the unemployment rate is 9.3%, nearly double the U.S. rate at 5.6%.

Regardless, the British are a hearty working people whose major industrial and manufacturing areas and plants are colocated with Britain's major cities and populated areas. According to the U.K. EU Presidency,[7] major industries in this island nation include aerospace (third largest in the world), steel (fourth largest), automotive, financial services, tourism, electric power equipment, automation equipment, railroad equipment, shipbuilding, agriculture (cereals, oilseed, potatoes, vegetables, livestock, fish), mining and quarrying, manufacture of chemicals and chemical products, and man-made fibers. Known for fine whiskey, 80% of all of Britain's fine produced alcohol is exported. Britain is also covered by nearly 17,000 km of railways, 380,000 km of highways, and 3,500 km of waterways. The county also boasts over 200 ships, 480 airports, and 11 heliports.

A highly educated population, British engineers are renowned the world over for their prowess in colossal and magnificent man-made objects like the *Channel*

Tunnel, which connects Britain and France through a nearly 25-mile underground railway. Furthermore, the United Kingdom has a highly efficient telecommunications network that is ranked 11th in the world as of 2005. Finally, the automobile industry of the United Kingdom has a worldwide reputation and boasts some of the most favorable quality in production records over time than any other automobile manufacturer. Today many manufacturers are relocating their main plant works in Eastern Europe or in the East.

Income Distribution

According to the Office for National Statistics,[8] the wealthiest 1% of Britons own approximately 20% of the durable goods in the country, with only 7% of British citizens sharing in the combined total wealth of the country. Of Britain's elite one percentile, these same individuals are suggested to own approximately 6% of half of the total world's wealth.

According to Banks, Dilnot, and Low,[9] the saying that the rich are getting richer and the poor are getting poorer might be a good metaphor to explain the transitional aspect of wealth in the United Kingdom. Although mean and median incomes seem to rise with years of earning, more than twice the number of retired households possess more wealth than working persons. This remains true until the age of 70, when the incomes of retired persons over that age begin to drop. It is estimated that the original income, gross income, disposable income, and posttax income have all decreased per household from 1993 to 2005. It is as yet unclear as to how changes in pension funding brought about largely by poor investment practices by private companies will affect those due to retire. Final salary schemes that pay an agreed proportion of salary on retirement initially set a 1/60th salary per year employed and now pay 1/80th, and few final salary schemes take on new members.

Demographics

Age Distribution of the Population

According to the 2008 CIA World Fact Book, the United Kingdom's estimated population as of July 2007 was 60,776,238.[1] Persons at birth to 14 years of age comprise 17.2% of the population (male 5,349,053 and female 5,095,837). Persons 15 to 64 years comprise 67% of the population (male 20,605,031/female 20,104,313), and persons 65 years and over comprise 15.8% (male 4,123,464/female 5,498,540). The total medial age is approximately 40 years, with males being 39 years and females being 41 years. Migration accounts for a very small amount of the population, less than 0.2% per thousand. The population is primarily employed in service-type occupations, with 87% of its labor force in the services and manufacturing industries, with 65.3% of its women employed. The population has a very low annual growth rate of about 0.3%, reflecting a birth rate of 13.4/1,000, a death rate of 10.8/1,000, and an immigration rate of 0.17/1,000. The nation's relatively high death rate is due to its fairly older population: just 19% of the population is aged 15 or below, whereas 16% are over the age of 65 years. Almost the entire adult population is literate.

The population density is 263 persons per square kilometer. Of that density, 90% are urban, with the remaining 10% being rural.[10] The ethnicity of that population is 95% British or of Irish descent. About 5% are immigrants or the descendants of those immigrants. Comprising the whole of the United Kingdom are Britain with a population of 48.7 million, Scotland with 5.1 million, Wales with 2.9 million, and Northern Ireland with 1.6 million inhabitants. Of that population, males represent 28.6 million and females 29.8. In age, the United Kingdom is represented by 20.7% under 16 years, 61.1% between 16 and retirement age, 18.2% above retirement age, with 6.8% over 75 years of age, compared with 24%, 64%, 6.7%, and 4%, respectively, in the United States.[11] The majority of British people are white, as they are mostly of Anglo-Saxon decent. Racial characteristics include white 92.1% (of which English 83.6%, Scottish 8.6%, Welsh 4.9%, Northern Irish 2.9%), black 2%, Indian 1.8%, Pakistani 1.3%, mixed 1.2%, other 1.6%.[1]

Education Levels of Population

The United Kingdom has an extremely high literacy rate of 99% for similar democratic and industrialized nations per aggregated population density. For example, the literacy rate in the United States is 97%.[1] Britian's high outcome is achieved through a state funded and assisted education policy that mandates that all persons age 5 through 16 attend school. Approximately 20% of British citizens elect to move on to postsecondary or further education (age 16 to 18). Approximately half of British students enter into higher education. Students who wish to pursue specialized and advanced academic training must first take A-level (Advanced Level) exams, which may be equivalent to the U.S. SAT tests. Education is provided by the government via Local Education Authorities, although an increasing proportion of parents choose to pay for their children's education at independent fee-paying schools. The leadership of the United Kingdom is aware that an educated population is more apt to adjust habits to practice a healthier lifestyle.

Major Religious Groups and Their Distribution

The United Kingdom is predominantly Christian: about three quarters Protestant and one quarter Roman Catholic.[1] There are also about 1 million Muslims and 700,000 Sikh and Hindu, reflecting recent immigration from the former British Empire; however, the Islamic faith is on the rise and is the second most predominant religion after Christian faiths are combined. The nation has approximately half a million Hindu, followed by over 300,000 Sikhs, and roughly a quarter million Jewish persons. A study of British spirituality suggests that 9 of 10 persons believe in God.[3] A breakdown is as follows: Christian (Anglican, Roman Catholic, Presbyterian, Methodist) 71.6%, Muslim 2.7%, Hindu 1%, other 1.6%, unspecified or none 23.1%.[1]

BRIEF HISTORY OF THE HEALTHCARE SYSTEM

Pre-World War II

The National Health Service (NHS) of the United Kingdom was established by act of Parliament in 1946.[12] This action followed years of study and consideration by the government. The greatest changes in health care would be the nationalization of the hospital system, payment for care by the government, and universal coverage for all residents of the United Kingdom. By 1948, all of the pieces were in place for implementation, and on July 5, 1948, the NHS was born.

Before the establishment of the NHS, health services were provided by a system structurally not much different from today. Hospital services were provided by a combination of private "voluntary" hospitals, tax-supported public hospitals, and in rural areas and smaller communities, "cottage" hospitals.[13] Specialty care was provided by hospital-based outpatient departments; primary care was delivered by community-based general practitioners (GPs).

Hospitals were established to provide medical care for the sick poor. The wealthier classes were generally attended at home by their physicians. In order to provide this care, altruistic individuals might organize into charitable groups to raise the necessary funding for a hospital or perhaps individually endow an established facility or the development of a hospital. Providing care free of charge initially, financial constraints generally led these hospitals to ask patients to "voluntarily" pay what they could toward the provision of care.

In the hospitals, appointed physician and surgeon staff managed patient care. These physicians and surgeons provided general care for all conditions that were admitted. These staff appointments were few in number and were particularly prized. It was the goal of many resident medical officers to achieve an appointment to the attending staff. These staff positions did not pay well, if at all, and attending physicians supported themselves with fees from private patients and from medical students and resident medical officers who paid the attending physician or surgeon for their training. In smaller cities, the hospital might be staffed with resident medical officers (trainees) overseen by local GPs and with regular visitations by out of town specialists. The voluntary hospitals saw themselves as providers of care for the acutely ill who would benefit from a short stay and treatment or surgery, and in many cases, patients with chronic illness and infectious diseases were turned away.

Public hospitals generally developed separately from the voluntary hospitals as infirmaries associated with workhouses.[13] Initially intended for the able-bodied who were temporarily without work, the workhouses more and more became the final destination for the chronically ill, older, and mentally ill. In many instances, the number of infirmary beds quickly came to outnumber the beds available for the indigent. These infirmaries were also facilities to which the voluntary hospitals would refer or transfer the infected and chronically ill. In the early 20th century, local county governments took over the operation of the workhouses and infirmaries with some financial support from the central government and the rest made up by local taxes. Under the new arrangements, the counties could separate the hospital section of these institutions and assign them to public health committees for operation. Many local general hospitals in operation today began their existence as workhouse infirmaries, some with the original buildings still in use.

Cottage hospitals were small rural facilities, generally established and attended by a local GP. A number of these hospitals are still in operation. Advantages to the cottage hospital are care close to home and a medical staff familiar with the health histories of the patients.

Visiting consultants from the local general hospital or teaching hospital held specialty outpatient clinics.

General practice before the NHS was provided by apothecaries and physicians who were trained in the teaching hospitals and returned to their communities to establish a practice or who failed to receive an appointment to a hospital staff position. Apothecaries traced their lineage to herb merchants who compounded and sold medicinal preparations.[14] In the Rose decision of 1704, the House of Lords decided that apothecaries could both prescribe and dispense for the treatment of illness, establishing apothecaries as the forefathers of the modern GP. In 1815, the society was given statutory authority to administer examinations and license doctors in England and Wales. In addition to seeing patients in surgery, GPs also visited patients in their home and attended deliveries at the request of midwives.

Before the establishment of the NHS, health care was paid for mostly out of pocket by those who could afford to. Voluntary and public hospitals provided inpatient and some outpatient care free for the poor or for whatever the patient could afford to pay toward their care. Beginning in the 19th century, trade union, fraternal societies, and other groups established provident dispensaries, providing free medical care to their members and sometimes their families.[12] In most cases, primary care and prescriptions were paid for by the society; inpatient care was generally not covered, as services were generally free at the local charitable or public hospital. Some societies also provided coverage for worker families for an additional fee. In the mid- to late-19th century, worker participation in these programs became compulsory. These provident societies collected a regular contribution from their members (essentially the forerunner of the prepaid health plan).

Government payment for health services was established in the United Kingdom when David Lloyd George introduced the "Liberal Welfare Reforms" during the period from 1906 to 1914. One of the provisions was the 1911 National Health Insurance Act.[12] This act provided payment for workers' medical care, funded by employee, employer, and government contributions. Eligibility for care was subject to income limits. As with the provident society, payment through the National Insurance act covered payment for GP services and drugs; hospital services were still provided by public and private hospitals for free. Dental and other services were not covered. It was after the 1911 Act that GPs generally chose to be paid under capitation arrangements with local insurance committees.

Post-World War II

Emergence of the Modern Healthcare System

Each country in the United Kingdom (England, Wales, Scotland, and Northern Ireland) has a cabinet-level Secretary or Minister for Health who makes political decisions on health care in general and the NHS in particular. Some policies are generated from the central government in London and then implemented via the United Kingdom Department of Health (DH), the Scottish Executive Health Department, the Department of Health and Social Services in Wales, and the Department of Health, Social Services, and Public Safety in Northern Ireland. There are some differences in the structure and delivery of services in each of the four countries, but they are all based on the English system; thus, this chapter concentrates on the English NHS.

The Ministry of Health (now renamed the DH) was established in 1919 combining the medical and public health functions of central government.[15] The current structure of the DH was established in 1988 when the Department of Health and Social Security was divided by the Parliament into the Department of Social Security and the Department of Health. Led by the Secretary of State for Health (Health Secretary), the department's main purpose is the improvement of the health and well-being of everyone in England. The Health Secretary, a member of Parliament, is appointed by and serves at the pleasure of the Prime Minister. The department is responsible for the strategic planning for the NHS and social care in England, making sure that funds are spent effectively, monitoring the quality of health and social care services, and developing new policies in consultation with stakeholders and other government departments.

The senior civil servant of the DH is the Permanent Under-Secretary of State for Health (Permanent Secretary) responsible for the day-to-day operation of the department.[16] The Permanent Secretary is also the chief accounting officer for the department and is responsible to the Parliament for how the department spends it appropriations. The Permanent Secretary chairs the Departmental Board. The Departmental Board is made up of department ministers and nondepartmental members and is responsible for setting departmental standards, establishing the framework for management of the department, assurance and management of risk, and advising on the general budgeting in support of accomplishing the department's strategic objectives.

The DH has seven key strategic objectives:

1. Improve and protect the health of the people of England—with special attention to the needs of disadvantaged groups and areas
2. Enhance the quality and safety of services for patients and users, giving them faster access to services and more choice and control
3. Deliver a better experience for patients and users, including those with long-term conditions
4. Improve the capacity, capability, and efficiency of the health and social care systems
5. Ensure system reform, service modernization, IT investment, and new staff contracts, and deliver improved value for money and higher quality
6. Improve the service provided as a Department of State to, and on behalf of, ministers and the public, nationally and internationally
7. Become more capable and efficient in the department, and cement the DH's reputation as an organization that is both a good place to do business and a good place to work

Under the Health Secretary are Ministers of State and Parliamentary Under-Secretaries of State who support the Health Secretary in his or her work.[17] They are responsible for particular areas of the department's policies. Each DH minister and undersecretary is supported by a private office and works with other ministers, senior government officials, and key stakeholder groups to develop policies that help implement the strategic objectives of the DH. Private offices are run by civil servants who ensure that policy development is consistent with the objectives, accompany ministers when they have business before Parliament, draft speeches, and manage the minister's appointments. Responsibilities of the individual DH ministries are listed in Table 5-2. The Health Secretary, ministers, and undersecretaries are political appointees and are drawn from members of the House of Commons or the House of Lords.

The Health Secretary is also advised by the chief professional officers (CPO). All of the CPOs are senior civil servants.[18] The CPOs support the department by offering expertise in a particular health or social care discipline. The chief medical officer and the chief nursing officer serve on the department board. Currently, there are six CPOs representing medicine, nursing, dentistry, allied health professionals, pharmacists, and healthcare science and research.

The chief executive of the NHS, a civil servant, leads the NHS and serves as a member of the department board.[19] The NHS operates under guidance from the DH. The government publishes policy, generally after consultation with stakeholders, outlining in broad strokes the direction in which the healthcare system should move. The latest document is titled "Our health, Our care, Our say" and aims to move the NHS closer to the patients through the implementation of practice-based commissioning, changes in GP registration systems, movement of some services out of the hospital and into the community, and increasing the ability of the independent sector to provide services to NHS patients.[20]

Also advising the department and representing the NHS are the national clinical directors.[21] These are clinical specialists within various fields of medicine and social care who advocate on behalf of specific national service frameworks (NSF). NSFs are long-term strategies for improving specific areas of care. NSFs set measurable goals within set time frames, establish national standards for care and pinpoint key interventions for a defined service or care group, outline strategies to support implementation, and develop programs to ensure progress and compliance with timetables. The clinical directors are listed in Table 5-3.

In addition to the NHS, the DH works with three types of "arm's length bodies."[22] Arm's length bodies (ALB) are separate national organizations, supported by the DH, that perform executive functions. Executive agencies, part of and accountable to the department, have the responsibility for particular business areas. Special health authorities provide a service to the public; they are nominally independent but can be subject to ministerial direction like other NHS bodies. Nondepartmental public bodies have a role in the process of national government but are not part of government departments. Table 5-4 lists some of these arm's length bodies. Functions of the ALBs can be divided into four categories: regulation, standards, public welfare, and central services to the NHS. Examples of the responsibilities of the ALBs include fraud and abuse prevention, blood collection and processing, organ transplant oversight, development of clinical care guidelines, and monitoring fertility treatment and embryologic research.

Performance of the NHS is evaluated by the Healthcare Commission. The commission is an independent executive agency that performs annual reviews of every NHS trust in England. The commission is also responsible for reviewing the performance of independent healthcare organizations as well. The commission publishes annual ratings of the various healthcare

TABLE 5-2   Responsibilities of the Ministers for Health

Minister of State for Health Services	Minister of State for Public Health
Finance: • Spending review • NHS financial management • NHS estates, capital, private finance initiatives, and local improvement finance trusts Policy and strategy: • Provider policy • Payment by results • Professional regulation • Connecting for Health • Urgent care and emergency care • Primary care • Departmental management	Public Health: • Regional public health groups • World Health Organization • Children's public health Health improvement national programs: • Tobacco and smoking • Alcohol • Drugs and drug treatment • Obesity • Rural health • Health inequalities • Food standards agency Health protection: • Emergency preparedness • Immunization • Research and development • Medicines and health care products Regulatory Agency: • National Institute for Clinical Excellence
Parliamentary Under Secretary of State for Health Services	**Parliamentary Under Secretary of State for Care Services**
Health care quality Patient safety National clinical directors and programs Dentistry Optical Chronic diseases and long term conditions Allied health professionals Workforce	Social care, local government and care partnerships • Policy and innovation • Finance • Workforce • Inspection • Older people • Learning and physical disabilities • Disabled children Mental health Prison and offender health Careers Audiology End-of-life care

From http://www.dh.gov.uk/en/Aboutus/MinistersandDepartmentLeaders/index.htm.

providers (awarding one, two, or three stars) for public information. The commission also investigates complaints that are not satisfactorily addressed at the trust level. In 2008, the Healthcare Commission and two other arm's-length regulatory bodies, the Commission for Social Care Inspection and the Mental Health Act Commission, merged into the Commission for Healthcare Audit and Inspection. Figure 5-2 outlines how the NHS is structured and delivers health care in England.

TABLE 5-3 National Clinical Directors

National Director for Emergency Access and Clinical Director for Service Reconfiguration	National Director for Mental Health
National Director for Health and Work	National Director for Heart Disease and Stroke
National Clinical Director for Primary Care	National Director of Pandemic Influenza Preparedness
National Director for Widening Participation in Learning	National Director for Learning Disabilities and Valuing People
National Clinical Director for Kidney Services	Co-National Director for Learning Disabilities
National Clinical Director for Cancer	National Director for Equality and Human Rights
National Director for Children, Young People, and Maternity Services	National Director for Older People's Services and Neurologic Conditions

From http://www.dh.gov.uk/en/Aboutus/MinistersandDepartmentLeaders/Nationalclinicaldirectors/index.htm.

TABLE 5-4 Arm's Length Bodies

Executive Agencies
Medicines and Healthcare Products Regulatory Agency
NHS Purchasing and Supply Agency
Special Health Authorities
Health Protection Agency
Information Centre for Health and Social Care
Mental Health Act Commission
National Institute for Health and Clinical Excellence
National Patient Safety Agency
National Treatment Agency for Substance Misuse
NHS Appointments Commission
NHS Blood and Transplant
NHS Direct
NHS Institute for Innovation and Improvement
NHS Professionals
NHS Litigation Authority
Postgraduate Medical Education and Training Board
Nondepartmental Public Bodies
Commission for Patient and Public Involvement in Health
Council for Healthcare Regulatory Excellence
Commission for Social Care Inspection
General Social Care Council
Healthcare Commission
Human Fertilisation and Embryology Authority
Monitor—Independent Regulator of Foundation Trusts
Human Tissue Authority

From http://www.dh.gov.uk/en/Aboutus/OrganisationsthatworkwithDH/Armslengthbodies/Categorisationofarms lengthbodies/index.htm

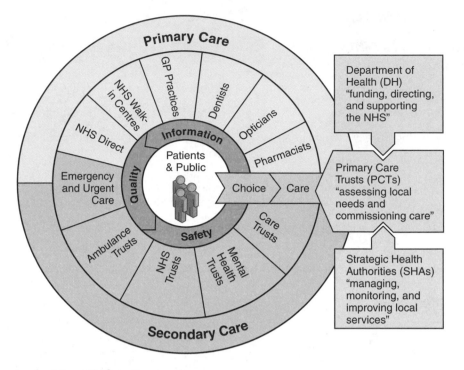

FIGURE 5-2 Structure of the NHS in England

"About the NHS: How the NHS works" from http://www.nhs.uk/aboutnhs/HowtheNHSworks/Pages/aboutthenhs.aspx, accessed February 25, 2008.

Authorities and trusts are the two types of organizations that deliver the services of the NHS at the local level.[23] Strategic Health Authorities (SHA) are the regional headquarters of the NHS. SHAs do not deliver care directly but provide guidance, support, and leadership in a defined geographic region. SHAs are accountable to the population in their regions and the DH for delivery of services and meeting targets set by the DH strategic plan. SHAs have three main tasks:

- Develop a strategic framework for the health and social care community, which clarifies priorities for action in the short, medium, and long term
- Manage and improve performance, establish performance agreements with all local NHS organizations, and work to redesign care processes with a very strong focus on patient pathways
- Build capacity and capability in terms of people, facilities, and buildings within and across organizations

The 10 SHAs in England are listed in Table 5-5.

Within each SHA are various types of trusts. The types of trusts and their responsibilities are listed in Table 5-6.

SHAs also work with local government, educational institutions, and charitable and voluntary organizations to deliver care.

In Scotland, Wales, and Northern Ireland, the functions of the SHAs and primary care trusts (PCTs) are performed by NHS boards, local health boards, and health and social care trusts, respectively.

In October 2002, the government unveiled the National Program for Information Technology, a program with responsibility for procurement, development, and implementation of a nationwide health information network.[24] In April 2005, the program was relocated to a new agency called Connecting for Health. The goal of

TABLE 5-5 Strategic Health Authorities

East Midlands SHA	South Central SHA
East of England SHA	South East Coast SHA
London SHA	South West SHA
North East SHA	West Midlands SHA
North West SHA	Yorkshire and The Humber SHA

From http://www.nhs.uk/aboutnhs/howtheNHSworks/authoritiesandtrusts/Pages/Authoritiesandtrusts.aspx.

TABLE 5-6 Types of Trusts in the NHS

Acute trusts: manage hospitals and related services. Acute trusts employ the bulk of the NHS workforce including medical, nursing, and allied health staff. Some acute trusts are regional or national centers of excellence for specialized care. Acute teaching trusts are affiliated with medical schools. Acute trusts contract with primary care trusts to provide secondary care services. As of 2009, there were 82 acute trusts.	Foundation trusts: a hospital management structure that has much more financial and operational freedom than other NHS trusts. Foundation trusts are paid based on a national tariff rate for procedures. In 2009, it was the government's plan for all acute trusts to convert to foundation trust status. There were 88 foundation trusts at that time.
Ambulance trusts: as of 2009, there were 13 ambulance services providing emergency response and transport in England.	Care trusts: these are organizations that provide health, social care, and mental health services. These trusts are cooperative organizations set up between the NHS and local authorities and provide a closer relationship between mental health and social care. There were 11 care trusts in 2009.
Mental health trusts: these provide health and social care services for people with mental health problems. Services are provided in both the community and hospital settings. As of 2009, there were 64 mental health trusts.	Primary care trusts: these control 80% of the NHS budget and commission primary and secondary care services for a defined population, usually within a geographic region. They are locally controlled organizations that are responsible for ensuring that there are enough services for the population in their region and contracting for hospital, dental, optical, and mental health services. As of 2009, there were 149 primary care trusts each serving an average population of 350,000.

From http://www.nhs.uk/aboutnhs/howtheNHSworks/authoritiesandtrusts/Pages/Authoritiesandtrusts.aspx.

the program is to improve patient care by increasing efficiency and effectiveness of clinicians and other NHS staff. Major program initiatives include the following:

- Creating an NHS Care Records Service (CRS) to improve the sharing of patients' records across the NHS with their consent
- Making it easier and faster for GPs and other primary care staff to choose and book hospital appointments for patients
- Providing a system for the electronic transmission of prescriptions
- Ensuring that the IT infrastructure can meet NHS needs now and in the future

The NHS CRS will eventually develop a consolidated electronic healthcare record for all patients within the NHS. The electronic health record will be maintained and available locally. A second part of the CRS is the summary care record, which will be available to NHS staff anywhere in the country. Initially, the summary record will provide basic demographic information, current medications, and allergies. Patients will have control of what information is disclosed by the CRS.

Choose and Book is a national electronic referral service rolled out in 2004. Choose and Book's aim is to increase patient choice of specialty or hospital provider and streamline the appointment process by allowing the GP to make the appointment for the patient from the GP surgery. Choose and Book provides the GP and patient with a list of hospitals and clinics that are able to provide the desired service; if the patient knows when and where they would like to be seen, the GP can book the appointment and provide the patient with confirmation of the time and date before the patient leaves the surgery. If the patient needs time to consider the options, the appointment may be booked at a later time. In reality few appointments are made this way, and the majority occur when the GP telephones to alert the hospital/service provider that the patient requires an appointment. This then autogenerates a letter to the patient asking them to call back for a brief telephone consultation at a specific time during which their appointment is made.

The electronic prescription service provides a centralized electronic prescription distribution service. A GP generates an electronic prescription, which is sent to the electronic prescription service, where it can then be accessed by a dispenser who then fills the prescription. Plans are to eventually allow practices to send prescriptions directly to pharmacists designated by the patient.

As part of the conditions of the General Medical Services (GMS) 2 contract, the NHS became responsible for providing IT services for GP practices. In 2004, all of the legacy systems in GP surgeries became the property of the PCTs, who then became responsible for maintenance and upgrades. Under Connecting for Health, GP Systems of Choice (GPSoC) is responsible for assisting practices and PCTs with selection, implementation, and maintenance of new IT systems. The GPSoC provides a set of standards that service and equipment providers must meet in order to have their products considered for purchase. Through the standard-setting system, providers of IT services will be encouraged to upgrade their products to conform to the increased level of service required by Connecting for Health.

GPSoC provide central funding for annual software licenses, costs of upgrading systems, and partial funding of infrastructure upgrades. The PCT is responsible for paying for infrastructure upgrades, an annual GPSoC support charge, user training, and additional services from the supplier. GPs may be responsible for some IT charges based on specific requirements of the practice.

DESCRIPTION OF THE HEALTHCARE SYSTEM

Facilities

Healthcare services are delivered from approximately 3,000 GP surgeries and almost 750 hospitals across the United Kingdom. This is divided into 360 district general, teaching, and specialty hospitals and about 390 local community hospitals. Community hospitals are generally located in rural areas and staffed by GPs, with specialty services provided by visiting consultants. Teaching hospitals are associated with medical schools and provide clinical experiences for medical students and postgraduate education for physicians and surgeons. District general hospitals are staffed by specialists and also provide postgraduate education opportunities. Hospitals are managed by acute or foundation trusts and provide all secondary care services in the NHS. Acute and foundation trusts also manage a number of smaller facilities, many of which are smaller hospital facilities without inpatient beds, that provide specialized care such as geriatrics and outpatient surgical and therapy services on a day-case basis. Secondary care trusts also provide access

to sexually transmitted disease treatment and surveillance through genitourinary medicine clinics. Public health services are provided by consultant public health physicians employed by primary care trusts.

There are approximately 190 private hospitals providing care in the United Kingdom. In addition, 93 NHS hospitals have dedicated private facilities on premises.

There are over 17,500 nursing and care homes across the United Kingdom. Care homes provide basic domiciliary care; nursing homes are more appropriate when more skilled care is required.

Primary Care

Primary care is community-based health services that represent the first, and sometimes the only, contact between the patient and the NHS. These services include those provided by GPs, practice and district nurses, health visitors, community midwives, allied health professionals (physiotherapists and occupational therapists), pharmacists, dentists, and optometrists.[25]

District nursing in the NHS is the equivalent of U.S. home health nursing. District nurses visit patients in their homes and provide wound care and chronic disease monitoring services. Community midwives provide services for pregnant women, including home birth options and domiciliary in–out (domino) births, where the woman labors at home, goes to hospital for delivery and immediate aftercare, and then is discharged home in under 6 hours. In addition, antenatal care is also provided usually via either GP or maternity clinics. Health visitors are specially trained nurses who provide care for newborn babies, infants, and children. Health visitors provide developmental screening and immunization services for preschool-age children. Once children reach school age, this care is taken over by school nursing teams along with the child's GP.

PCTs are the organizations tasked with ensuring the delivery of healthcare services to their designated populations and have the three main functions:

- Engaging with its local population to improve health and well-being
- Commissioning a comprehensive and equitable range of high-quality, responsive, and efficient services, within allocated resources, across all service sectors
- Directly providing high-quality responsive and efficient services where this gives best value

PCTs are led by a chief executive officer, hired by a board of governors appointed from the local service population. The chief executive is advised on clinical matters by a professional executive council made up of representatives from the medical, nursing, and allied health community.

The current model for commissioning care is via a format called "Practice-Based Commissioning."[26] This program was implemented in 2005 and provides GP practices with increased control over how money is spent in providing care for their patients. Each GP practice is given an "indicative" budget based on previous expenditures adjusted for inflation. Although there will be no actual money changing hands, each practice is expected to maintain a balanced budget, although overruns will be covered by the PCT. Practices may choose to arrange for community-based specialty services for their patients with long-term conditions or increased access to diagnostic services.

GPs are community based, many of them operating out of converted residences. The NHS implemented a capitol development plan aimed at replacing or refurbishing some 3,000 GP premises by 2004.[27] The NHS also committed to the development of 500 one-stop primary care centers that would house GP practices as well as mental health, community nursing, dental, and chiropodist services among others.

Secondary Care

Secondary care is delivered by a number of organizations providing specialty medical care and surgery, trans-portation, and mental health services.[28] NHS trusts manage hospitals. Hospitals provide emergency and elective care not available from a patient's GP. Hospital outpatient departments provide specialty consultation on referral from GPs. Hospitals also operate emergency assessment units to evaluate urgent problems on referral from GPs. Most hospital trusts are responsible for a number of facilities; however, not all facilities called hospitals operate inpatient services. Cost constraints and service realignments resulted in consolidation of services into larger facilities with the smaller facilities operating mainly as outpatient facilities, providing consultation, ancillary, and day surgery services. NHS trusts are allowed to reserve 5% of their beds to provide care for the private patients of their consultants. Some NHS trusts are regional or national centers for specialty services such as orthopedics, women's health, pediatrics, or cancer care. The OECD reports that there were 3.6 acute-care hospital beds per thousand population in 2004; an estimated 190,000 total acute beds (Figure 5-3).[29]

NHS foundation trusts are a new organizational and operational structure introduced in 2004.[30] Foundation trusts are established as independent public benefit corporations. This status frees the trusts from central government control and SHA management. Flexibility in management allows the foundation trust to

- Access capital on the basis of affordability instead of the current system of centrally controlled allocations

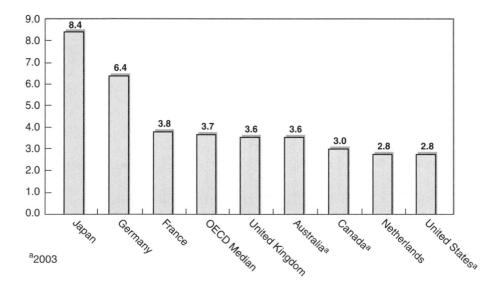

a2003

FIGURE 5-3   Number of Hospital Beds per 1,000 Population, 2004

Cylus, J. & Anderson, GF. *Multinational Comparisons of Health Systems Data, 2006.* Johns Hopkins University, May 2007. From the Commonwealth Fund. Calculated from OECD Health Data 2006.

- Invest surpluses in developing new services for local people
- Tailor new governance arrangement to the individual circumstances of their community

Foundation trusts are reimbursed for their services based on a "national tariff" or fee schedule, with payments following the patient. Freedom from central government also comes with a price; foundation trusts must operate under a balanced budget and cannot expect the government to cover any shortfalls. Foundation trusts are required to provide care under the core principles of the NHS: free care, based on need and not ability to pay. Clinical activity for private patients is strictly limited. Oversight is provided by monitor–independent regulator of NHS foundation trusts.

In an attempt to address the long waiting time for some elective procedures, the government authorized the NHS to contract with the independent sector for certain services.[30] Treatment centers are dedicated facilities that offer elective procedures such as hernia repair, cataract extraction, hip replacement, and endoscopy. These centers are operated by independent (for-profit) sector providers under contract to NHS trusts or PCTs. Treatment centers may be mobile units providing diagnostics or cataract surgery or fixed facilities separate from or colocated on NHS trust campuses. They may be staffed totally by NHS clinical and support personnel,

totally by the private contractor, or by a mix of personnel. Treatment centers are paid using the same national tariff scale as foundation trusts.

Physician and surgeon employment by NHS trusts is governed by a national consultant contract agreed on in 2003. The contract requires that a full-time consultant work a set schedule of 10 programmed activities. These are 4-hour blocks of time during which the consultant provides patient services, in either the outpatient department, operating theater, or hospital ward. There may be adjustments to this schedule based on on-call time and emergency work arising from on-call status and time spent teaching. As with GPs, locum coverage must be arranged in the absence of the consultant either by additional hours by a colleague or a locum tenens specialist. The trust is responsible for the cost of the coverage. The contract allows consultants to offer "private professional services" or private practice outside their NHS contract, as long as it does not interfere with their normal NHS duties.

Nursing home services are provided by the private sector and are regulated by the government. Care is usually paid for privately subject to asset limitations. State support for nursing home care is provided on a sliding-scale basis. Patients below the asset threshold have their care paid for by the government. Figure 5-4 shows the number of nursing home beds as compared with OECD averages. As part of the NSF for older people, the

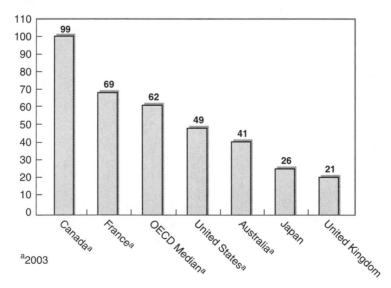

FIGURE 5-4   Number of Nursing Home Beds per 1,000 Population Over 65, 2004

Cylus, J. & Anderson, GF. *Multinational Comparisons of Health Systems Data, 2006.* Johns Hopkins University, May 2007. From the Commonwealth Fund. Calculated from OECD Health Data 2006.

DH proposed increasing the availability of services and facilities to deliver on these goals:

- Early intervention for old age conditions
- Streaming to specialist care in crisis situations
- Early transfer to the community for rehabilitation in intermediate care
- Multidisciplinary assessment prior to care home placement
- Partnership working across health and social care

In support of these goals, the DH increased investment in the intermediate care infrastructure, including stand-alone facilities for rehabilitation and support for increased home care services.

Public Versus Private Components

Private medical insurance is available through a number of companies, including BUPA, Axa PPP, Universal Provident, and Norwich Union.[31] Many firms and trade unions offer private medical insurance as a benefit to their employees or members. Private insurers handle over £2 billion in claims annually.[32] Insurance plans

may offer very comprehensive coverage to very specific coverage (accident, sport injury, international health, children, and older persons). Package products, which offer a fixed set of benefits, may cover costs for outpatient and inpatient care and for day surgery. Coverage may also include complementary and alternative treatments, home nursing care, and cash payments if off work. Choice-of-cover plans allow the purchaser or employee to select from a menu of benefits a plan that fits their special situation. Special cover plans address specific needs of the consumer and include health insurance for children, coverage for convalescent care, members of the military, and private hospital treatment. Figure 5-5 describes the differences in the level of private versus public funding for OECD countries.

A number of private hospital companies provide access to evaluation, diagnostic, and treatment facilities. Many NHS consultants will lease office space in private hospitals and see patients on private referral from GPs or on self-referral. Depending on the benefits available under the patient's plan the visit may include anything from a simple consultation visit up to complex surgical procedures and aftercare.

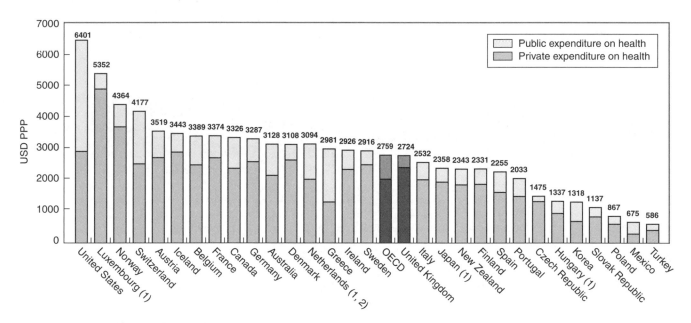

FIGURE 5-5 Healthcare Expenditure per Capita by Source of Funding, in 2005

1. 2004.

2. Public and private expenditures are 2006 expenditures.

Data are expressed in US dollars adjusted for purchasing power parities (PPPs), which provide a means of comparing spending between countries on a common base. PPPs are the rates of currency conversion that equalize the cost of a given "basket" of goods and services in different countries.

Source: *OECO Health Data 2007*, July 2007.

TABLE 5-7   Numbers of General-, Acute-, and Intermediate-Care Beds in England, 1999 to 2006

Year	Number of General and Acute Beds	Change in the Number of General and Acute Beds Since 1999/2000	Number of Immediate-Care Beds	Change in the Number of Immediate-Care Beds Since 1999/2000
1999/2000	135,080	—	4,242	—
2000/1	135,794	714	n/a	—
2001/2	136,583	1,503	7,021	2,779
2002/3	136,679	1,599	7,493	3,251
2003/4	137,247	2,167	8,697	4,455
2004/5	136,184	1,104	8,928	4,686
2005/6	133,033	−2,047	9,771	5,529

The figures for intermediate-care beds are quarter 2 figures. From Department of Health 2006d.

Workforce

The NHS is the single largest employer in England with some 1.3 million employees.[33] This number includes professional and support staff. As part of the NHS plan offered in 2000, the government committed to increasing the number of professional staff employed by the NHS. For the most part, the plan has been successful in increasing the number of GPs, nurses, consultants, and other staff in the NHS[34] (Table 5-7). Table 5-8, Table 5-9, and Figure 5-6 demonstrate the distribution of the United Kingdom health workforce.

Medical Education

Medical education in the United Kingdom is conducted at medical schools affiliated with higher education institutions.[35] The typical undergraduate curriculum offers

TABLE 5-8   Comparison of NHS Plan Growth Targets with Actual Workforce Growth

Staff Groups	NHS Plan Target for Numbers of New Staff 1999–2004	Actual New Staff 1999–2004[a]	Variance from NHS Plan Target	Percentage Increase in New Staff 1999–2006
Consultants[b,c]	7,500	7,329	2% under target	41
GP[d,e]	2,000	3,056	53% over target	16
Nurses[f,g]	20,000	67,878	239% over target	21
Allied Health Professionals[h]	6,500	11,039	70% over target	27

[a] Head count.

[b] The number of consultants includes Directors of Public Health.

[c] The NHS target for consultants was achieved in 2005, both in terms of head count and full-time equivalent.

[d] The number of GPs excluded retainers and registrars.

[e] In 2005, the target for GPs was also achieved in and full-time equivalent terms.

[f] The number of nurses includes practice nurses.

[g] The target for nurses was achieved in terms of both head count and full-time equivalent.

[h] The target for allied health professionals was achieved in terms of both head count and full-time equivalent.

From King's Fund analysis; Information Centre, 2007C.

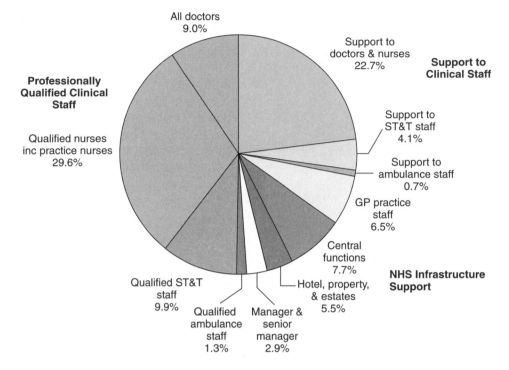

FIGURE 5-6 All NHS Hospital and Community Health Services Staff and General Practice Staff

The Information Center, UK Department of Health. *NHS Hospital and Community Health Services Non-Medical Staff in England: 1995–2005.* Copyright © 2006 The Information Centre. All rights reserved.

TABLE 5-9 NHS England Hospital and Community Health Service and General Practice Workforce (2005)

Total	1,366,038
Professionally qualified clinical staff	**679,157**
All doctors	122,987
All doctors excluding retainers[a]	122,345
Consultants (includes directors of public health)	31,993
Registrars	18,006
Other doctors in training	26,305
Hospital practitioners and clinical assistants (nondental specialties)[b]	3,587
Other medical and dental staff	10,739
GMPs excluding retainers[a]	35,302
GMPs excluding retainers and registrars	32,738
Contracted and salaried GPs	29,340
Other practitioners[c]	3,398
GP registrars	2,564
GP retainers	642

(continues)

TABLE 5-9   NHS England Hospital and Community Health Service and General Practice Workforce (2005) (continued)

Total	1,366,038
All qualified nurses (including practice nurses)	404,161
Qualified nurses, midwives, and health visitor staff	301,257
Practice nurses[d]	22,904
Total qualified scientific, therapeutic and technical staff	134,534
Qualified allied health professionals[e]	61,082
Other qualified ST&T staff	73,452
Qualified ambulance staff	18,117
Support to clinical staff	**376,219**
Support to doctors and nursing staff	310,441
Support to ST&T staff	55,715
Support to ambulance staff	10,063
NHS infrastructure support	**220,387**
Central functions	105,562
Hotel, property, and estates	74,431
Manager and senior manager	39,391
Other nonmedical staff and those with unknown classification	435
Practice staff other than nurses[f]	89,190

[a] GP retainers were first collected in 1999 and have been omitted for comparability purposes.

[b] Most of these doctors also work as GPs. To avoid double counting they are excluded in the all doctors total.

[c] Other practitioners include GMS Other (previously included GMS assistants, GMS salaried doctors, GMS flexible career scheme GPs and GMS returners), and PMS others (previously included PMS other, PMS salaried doctors).

[d] Practice nurse head count information was estimated in 1999. Underlying figures for 2000 suggest the practice nurse figure may be an overestimate.

[e] Qualified allied health professionals are qualified staff from chiropody, dietetics, occupational therapy, orthoptics/optics, physiotherapy, radiography, and art/music/drama therapy occupational codes.

[f] Includes direct patient care, administration, and clerical and other.

Data as of 30 September 2008.

Sources: The Information Centre General and Personal Medical Services; Medical and Dental Workforce Census; Nonmedical Workforce Census. © 2006 The Information Centre. All rights reserved.

the Bachelor of Medicine/Bachelor of Chirurgy or Surgery (MBChB or MBBS) degrees. The program is 5 years in length. The first 2 years provide a foundation of basic science knowledge and skills required prior to beginning clinical experience in years 3 to 5.

After graduation from medical school, each new graduate must complete a 2-year foundation program at a teaching hospital. These programs are designed to provide a predefined, competency-based experience. The first year of the placement has the aim of preparing doc-tors for full registration by the General Medical Council and for the second year of the program. Under current European regulations, full registration as a doctor in the European Union can only be granted on completion of 5,500 hours or 6 years of theoretical and practical instruction supervised by a university. The second year builds on skills and knowledge gained in the first year through a series of rotations that provide a spectrum of practical clinical experience, enabling the trainee to enter specialist or general practice training.

Specialty training is regulated by the Postgraduate Medical Education and Training Board (PMETB). The PMETB is a nongovernmental body accountable to Parliament that operates on an integrated four-nations basis. The role of the PMETB includes certifying doctors for the GP and specialist registers; prospective approval of all training posts that lead to the award of a Certificate of Completion of Training (CCT); approving specialist training curricula and assessment developed by the medical Royal Colleges; quality assurance and evaluation of the management of postgraduate training; and setting criteria for selection into specialist training; and providing policy development for the sector.

The actual training is implemented by postgraduate deaneries. Postgraduate deans work with the royal colleges/faculties, NHS trusts, PCTs, and GP practices to deliver postgraduate training to PMETB standards. The postgraduate deans are accountable to strategic health authorities in England, the Welsh ministers, NHS Education for Scotland, and the DH, Social Services, and Public Safety in Northern Ireland. After a doctor is accepted into a program leading to the award of a CCT, he or she will be able to continue in specialty training to the award of a CCT so long as the trainee passes all necessary assessments at each stage of progression.

Technology and Equipment

NHS trusts are also responsible for providing access to ancillary services such as diagnostics. Laboratory testing and diagnostic radiology services are available to GPs under commission by the PCT. In 2005, the number of MRI scanners was 5.4 per million population (estimated 330 total scanners) and the number of CT scanners was 7.5 per million (estimated 460 total scanners).[32] Both numbers are significantly below the OECD average. The government, however, increased the budget for diagnostic equipment and is replacing aging scanners and purchasing new ones. The majority of MRI and CT scanners currently operational in the NHS have been purchased since 2000.[34] As a means to enhance access and reduce waiting times, the NHS contracted with private sector mobile scanner services to provide diagnostic imaging for NHS clients.

EVALUATION OF THE HEALTH SYSTEM

Cost

Funding for health care in the United Kingdom is a mixture of public and private sources. The NHS, which covers all legal residents, is funded via central taxation and fees on certain services. Each resident of the United Kingdom pays a payroll tax to National Insurance, with a contribution from employers. Funds are also appropriated from general tax revenues. Fees for services are assessed on prescriptions (subject to certain exemptions), dental services, and optician services. Otherwise, care is free at the point of service.

The NHS Plan, launched in 2000, increased spending on the NHS.[27] The increased spending aimed to redress pay inequities, invest in new infrastructure, improve access to services, and reduce waiting times for both outpatient and inpatient care. Spending increased from £55 million in 2002/2003 to almost £90 million in 2007/2008. This represents an increase of 7.1% per year,[36] which is scheduled to reduce to 4% per year by 2010/2011 representing projected expenditure of £110 million. The current Labor government projects an increase in health spending to 7.8% of GDP, in line with average spending of other states in the Organisation for Economic Co-operation and Development. In spite of the almost doubling of health spending in the first decade of the 21st century, the United Kingdom still spends significantly less per capita than most countries in the OECD (Figures 5-7, 5-8, and 5-9).

In 2004, the government introduced a number of new primary care contracting arrangements.[37] The aims of these arrangements were to increase the range and quality of services available to the patient and deliver them closer to home.

The GMS contract is the standard contract between GPs and PCTs. In 2004, a new contract was implemented that changed the way GPs were paid and the services they were expected to provide. The new contract also changed the way GPs operated their practices. Under the new contract (called GMS 2), the practice, not the individual GP, is paid a global sum based on patient list size, adjusted for geographic location. Lists are updated quarterly and payments are made quarterly. Out of this global sum, the practice is expected to pay all expenses for staff, facilities, and supplies.

For the basic payment, the practice is expected to provide "essential" services. Essential services covered the management of acute illness and injury, general management of patients who are terminally ill, and management of chronic diseases. The practice is also expected to provide what are categorized as "additional" services. These include cervical cancer screening, contraceptive services, vaccinations and immunizations, child health surveillance, maternity services (excluding intrapartum care), and minor surgery procedures. If the

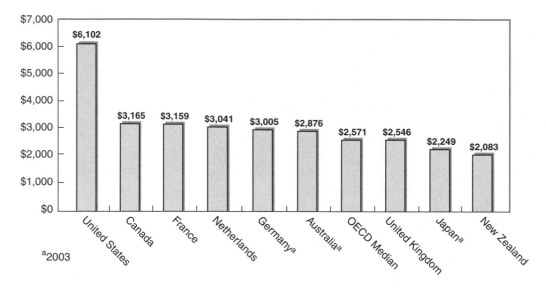

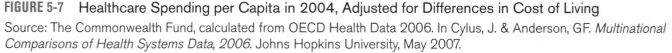

FIGURE 5-7 Healthcare Spending per Capita in 2004, Adjusted for Differences in Cost of Living

Source: The Commonwealth Fund, calculated from OECD Health Data 2006. In Cylus, J. & Anderson, GF. *Multinational Comparisons of Health Systems Data, 2006.* Johns Hopkins University, May 2007.

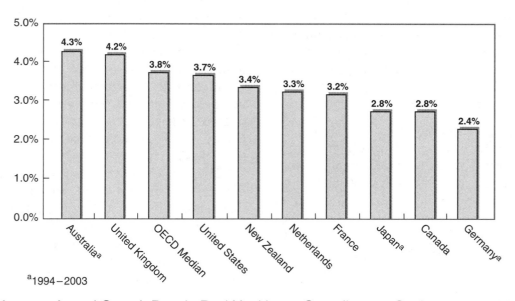

FIGURE 5-8 Average Annual Growth Rate in Real Healthcare Spending per Capita, 1994–2004

Source: The Commonwealth Fund, calculated from OECD Health Data 2006. In Cylus, J. & Anderson, GF. *Multinational Comparisons of Health Systems Data, 2006.* Johns Hopkins University, May 2007.

practice wishes to opt out of providing additional services, a portion of the global sum is withheld, allowing the PCT to contract for these services. Finally, the practice may provide "enhanced" services. Enhanced services include more specialized services such as intrapartum care, intrauterine device insertion, monitoring of anticoagulant therapy, and monitoring drug and alcohol abuse treatment. Practices are paid an an-

nual retainer, based on the contract, for the provision of enhanced services. Enhanced services were written into the GMS contract to reduce demands on the secondary care system.

The GMS 2 contract also relieved the GP from having to provide 24-hour coverage for his or her patients. In exchange for a portion of the practices global sum payment (6% in 2005), the GP could have the PCT

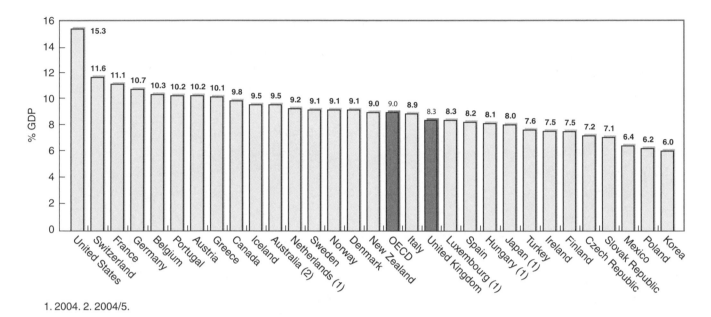

1. 2004. 2. 2004/5.

FIGURE 5-9   Percentage of Gross Domestic Product Spent on Health Care in 2005
Source: *OECD Health Data 2007*. July 2007.

provide for out-of-hours coverage. The GP is then only responsible for being available for 10 "sessions" per week to provide care (in-hours care). A session is essentially a 3- or 4-hour block during which the GP would schedule appointments. The GP generally schedules morning and evening sessions. The workday usually starts at 9:00 AM and ends at 7:00 PM. Morning hours generally run from 9:00 AM to noon and evening hours from 3:00 to 6:30 PM. During the period between sessions, the GP may attend meetings or make house calls. Each GP surgery sets geographic boundaries within the PCT from which it will accept patients, generally based on the ease of making house calls. If the GP is not available all 10 sessions, he or she must arrange for coverage by a locum tenens doctor during the absence. In response to open consultations conducted in 2005 and 2006, the government is now requiring PCTs to arrange for more opening hours from GPs to address the express needs of the patients, including late evening and weekend hours.

The GMS 2 contract introduced payment for results to primary care. The contract introduced a quality and outcomes framework (QOF) based on the best available evidence as determined by a joint committee of the British Medical Association and the NHS Confederation. Within the framework are domains, with each domain being divided into areas described by key indicators. The indicators are the measure against which the practice is rated. The domains and areas are listed in Table 5-10.

The clinical indicators were divided into three types: structure, process, and outcome. Each practice is able to score up to 1,050 points within the QOF divided into 550 points for the clinical domain, 184 points for organization, 36 points for additional services, 100 points for patient experience, 100 points for holistic care payments, and 30 points for quality practice payments. An access bonus of 50 points is also awarded. The practice decides how many points it aspires to and submits this to the PCT. The practice receives quarterly payment based on the aspiration with the payment adjusted at the end of the fiscal year based on actual performance.

Primary medical service (PMS) is a second form of contracting arrangement. In contrast to GMS, PMS is a truly local arrangement between the practice and PCT. Under PMS, the practice does not have to be the traditional GP surgery but could include a nurse-led service with salaried GP, or other primary care professionals. PMS was introduced to provide greater freedom for practices to address the specific needs of their patients. PMS also allowed the option of GPs being salaried rather than practice owners so they would benefit from a more assured income and enhancing the ability for practices to recruit providers into underdoctored areas. More than 40% of GPs in England operate under PMS contracts.

Alternative provider medical service allows PCTs to enter into agreements with any individual or organization who meets the provider conditions under the rules. This includes the independent sector, voluntary sectors,

TABLE 5-10 Quality and Outcome Framework: Domains and Areas

Clinical domain:	Organizational domain:
Coronary heart disease	Records and information
Stroke and transient ischemic attacks	Communicating with patients
Hypertension	Education and training
Hypothyroidism	Medicine management
Diabetes	Clinical and practice management
Mental health	
Chronic obstructive disease	
Asthma	
Epilepsy	
Cancer	
Additional services:	**Patient experience:**
Cervical screening	Patient survey
Child health surveillance	Consultation length
Maternity services	
Contraceptive services	

From United Kingdom NHS 2007. Retrieved from http://www.dh.gov.uk/en/Healthcare/Primarycare/Primarycare contracting/QOF/index.htm.

not-for-profit organizations, NHS trusts, and other PCTs. These agreements give the PCT the flexibility to provide services that are not available in their area, provide services GPs opt not to provide, and improve access and responsiveness to the specific needs of their population.

Primary care trust medical service gives PCTs the ability to directly employ staff to provide a full range of services or services in special situations. Under primary care trust medical service, PCTs might employ GPs to provide out-of-hours coverage for any practices that opt out of that service under GMS 2. PCTs could also hire a GP to provide services in practices where the doctor retires or relocates until a permanent replacement is found.

Quality

All British citizens have access to free universal health care. As a result, according to Mangelsdorff, Smetana, and Love,[6] the United Kingdom's human poverty index ranking is 15, rating it relatively high in the national stage for healthy persons. Approximately 95% of the United Kingdom's population was immunized against measles. The United Kingdom reports that 100 percent

of its population has access to potable water and excretal disposal. The United Kingdom does not produce any tobacco, but is one of the world's largest importers of unmanufactured tobacco.[11]

Infant Mortality, Mortality Rates by Age Groups, Life Expectancy by Age Groups

The death rate in the United Kingdom is 10.1 per 1,000, compared with 8.3 per 1,000 for the United States.[1] The United Kingdom recorded a total of 750,700 live births and 627,600 deaths, with an infant mortality rate of 6.2% for this statistical year (2008).[3]

Heart disease results in the highest levels of mortality; the non–age-adjusted rate is 188.6 of 1,000 die every year due to this illness. Various forms of cancer follow closely behind at 162 deaths per thousand.[11]

Average life expectancy at birth is 78 years, up 2 years in the last 10. Infant mortality is 5.0 deaths per 1,000 live births and is down from 7.2 from a decade ago.[1] Since 1948, life expectancy has increased by 7.6 years for men and 7.8 years for women, or about one and a half years per decade. Over the same period, infant mortality declined by more than 80%. Life expectancy and in-

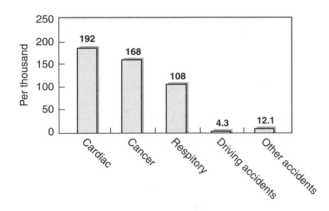

FIGURE 5-10 Causes of Mortality per Thousand Population in Millions

Data from *OECD Health Data 2007*. July 2007.

fant mortality rates today are similar to other nations in Western Europe and slightly better than in the United States.[1,11]

Injuries and deaths in the United Kingdom due to motor vehicle accidents totaled 3,897 in 2003. Male suicide rates were 3.34 per 1,000, whereas female suicide rates were somewhat lower at 0.922 per 1,000 according to the World Health Organization.

Two-Tiered Healthcare Systems (by Income)

Contributions to the National Health Insurance system are from "taxes" applied to individuals earning £62 per week or more. Their weekly contribution is £1.42 plus 10% of their weekly earnings between £62 and £465.

The total population per doctor is about 1,900 individuals. There are 3,000 persons per dentist.[3] The numbers of physicians in practice average 26,000 and 15,900 dentists. In 1994, 456 million prescriptions were filled in United Kingdom.[3] Immunizations are close to the U.S. rates. For the total population, diphtheria coverage is 92%, polio 94%, and measles 95%. The totals found for tetanus suggested an immunization rate of 100% as compared with 70% in the United States. The ratio for doctors per thousand population in the United Kingdom is 1.4. Nurse-to-physician ratio is 2:1, and there are 3.6 hospital beds per thousand individuals. These numbers compare closely with United States figures with 5.3, 2.8, and with a little greater disparity with numbers of beds at 2.38 per thousand.[3] Secondary health care is the responsibility of 170 hospital trusts. There is particular emphasis in keeping long-term patients in the home. To contain costs, the preferred mode for provid-

ing long-term care is in the home with nursing visits from home health agencies. The United Kingdom has one of the world's largest home healthcare systems with nurses being a regular part of many families' lives.

Other Health Statistics (Immunization Rates, Days Waiting for Elective Procedures, Patient Satisfaction Measures, Etc.)

In a socialized health service, the waiting periods are of concern for the consumers of health care. Comparing waiting periods to access care, 570,000 patients waited up to 3 months to see their provider. Those patients waiting 1 year to 18 months numbered 4,600. The United Kingdom spent $58.6 billion opposed to $817 billion in the United States for medical care in 1994. A comparison shows 6.9% and 12.8% gross domestic product were spent in the United Kingdom and United States, respectively.[6] There is a current program to ensure that all patients who are referred for procedures have their treatment started within 18 weeks of their referral.

Access

Health care in the United Kingdom is dominated by the NHS, which provides most medical care without charge. This comprehensive healthcare plan was started in 1948. The program itself is extremely popular with the British people. The right to receive free medical care is seen as among the most important aspects of citizenship. Private, voluntary health insurance also exists in the country. It was promoted as a means of saving taxpayer money. Presently, about 10% of Britons are covered by private insurance, and 8% of the United Kingdom's health care is paid for through the private system. The chief benefit of having private insurance is a reduction in the waiting time for elective surgery. The NHS provides hospital-, family-, community-, and social-based healthcare services. Its stated mission is to improve Britons' mental and physical health through health prevention and promotion and diagnosis and treatment. The service also provides care for long-term illnesses and disabilities. Overall responsibility for the NHS resides with the Secretary of State for Health, who is supported by the staff of the DH. Operational responsibility lies with the NHS Executive, whose headquarters in the DH is supplemented by 14 regional offices. With a £40 billion budget and about 1 million employees, the NHS is one of the world's largest employers. The NHS provides three basic levels of care: primary care through family doctors and practices that operate in partnership with social service departments, secondary care through hospitals and ambulance services, and tertiary care through specialist hospitals. Among the service's employees are 30,000 general practitioners, 45,000 physician specialists, 15,000 dentists, and 10,000 pharmacists. NHS also employs midwives, "health visitors" (who make house calls upon families with infants and small children), community health nurses, physical therapists, opticians, and other healthcare professionals.[11]

CURRENT AND EMERGING ISSUES AND CHALLENGES

As social wealth has increased over the last several decades, a move toward fee-for-service medical care has emerged. Primarily used by the retired population for specialty care services and the few for-profit hospitals in the country, Britons are increasingly accepting the concept of pay-as-you-go health care for services not readily available through the national health system or services with protracted or inconvenient wait times. One example of this was end-stage renal disease. Once classified as a terminal illness, those who could afford treatment for the ailment were able to seek pay-for-service care and receive treatment. In response, the NHS later moved toward treating end-stage renal disease as a covered illness; however, as the cost of treatment even in the United Kingdom is becoming increasingly more complex and costly, the NHS is struggling with complicated policies and plans to discern covered versus noncovered services.

Another new emphasis is in cooperative partnerships with private sector medical care entities. Although the NHS is not being replaced in any way, shape, or form, there is a recognition by the government that certain economies of scales and cost-efficiencies can be achieved through horizontal integration within the community rather than the NHS building munificent monuments unto itself. In a similar way to what President Nixon tried to do by enacting the HMO Act of 1973 to help stem the rising government costs associated with Medicaid and Medicare, the United Kingdom is increasingly looking to provide beneficial legislation that will increase access while decreasing the sole source of burden of care away from the government.

In addition to public needs and cultural movements perceiving different demands for services covered, Brits are increasingly less likely to be tolerant of protracted waiting times. The NHS is working toward leveraging technology to increase access to care as well as augmenting ambulatory care access as a stand-alone priority.[11]

An American invention—utilization management—is likewise seeing some attention overseas. Utilization management seeks to emphasize teamwork along the continuum of care and provide care providers an opportunity to partner with one another rather than provide care inside the proverbial box of the solo physician and independent-care facility. Patients overseas are seeing increasing satisfaction with utilization management (UM) techniques and the United Kingdom has seen a return on investment by this initiative.[11]

A continued trend on the horizon for the United Kingdom is to convert district health authorities into quasi cooperatives that can act in the best interests of both the government and the community by enlisting the support of prime vendors for durable and expendable goods, as well as the delivery of services in colloquial areas. In this manner, the local districts can better decentralize some aspects of the NHS so that colloquial priorities and best practices can be maintained on a more cost- and quality-efficient standard.[10]

Sustainability of the Health System

The NHS in the United Kingdom is facing many of the challenges that the American system of Medicaid and Medicare have faced since their inception over 40 years ago. Like American Medicaid and Medicare programs, the cost of continued, regular, and recuring care to the British public was grossly underestimated. Without the benefit of American paradigms such as experience ratings and co-payments, moral hazard principals have injected themselves into the economic behavior of patient-seeking motivation. Costs for the NHS have exceeded budgeted tax revenues, similar to what happened with American Medicare and Medicaid programs. Unfortunately, for the NHS, free universal health care has become a very popular program with enough inertia to maintain its integrity despite challenges in sustained revenues to meet cost of inflation indices. Increased taxes are one of the only sustainable mechanisms for maintaining the healthcare system, as are opportunity cost shifts from other aspects of Britain's profitable industries.

A familiar and global problem facing the British National Health System is the graying of the British population. Life expectancy has grown by almost 2 years for both women and men over the last decade, creating not only more individuals to treat within the NHS but also higher severity of medical needs often requiring more costly treatment plans. Cancer and cardiac illness and disease remain the main focal points of mortality in the British system.

REFERENCES

1. CIA World Fact Book 2008. Retrieved February 28, 2008, from https://www.cia.gov/library/publications/the-world-factbook/index.html.

2. Reddy M, ed. *Statistical Abstract of the World*, 2nd ed. Detroit: Gale Research; 1996.

3. Office for National Statistics website, 2008. Retrieved February 24, 2008, from http://www.statistics.gov.uk/.

4. Manglesdorff AD. *International Health and Demographics.* Paper presented at Executive Healthcare Resource Management course, 2007 April; Brooks City Base, TX.

5. OECD Economic Survey of the United Kingdom. Retrieved February 25, 2008, from http://www.oecd.org/document/17/0,3343,fr_2649_201185_39352401_1_1_1_1,00.html.

6. Mangelsdorff AD, Smetana WR, Love WR. *Comparative Health of the UK (1997–2007).* Available at White Paper Collections, Army-Baylor Graduate Program in Health & Business Administration, Academy of Health Science, Medical Education and Training Center, Fort Sam Houston, TX.

7. About the UK. Retrieved February 28, 2008, from http://www.i-uk.com/servlet/Front?pagename=Open Market/Xcelerate/ShowPage&c=Page&cid=1115141709899.

8. Share of the Wealth. Retrieved February 25, 2008, from http://www.statistics.gov.uk/cci/nugget.asp?id=2.

9. Banks J, Dilnot AW, Low H. The Distribution of Wealth in the UK. Retrieved February 25, 2008, from http://www.ifs.org.uk/publications.php?publication_id=512.

10. Manglesdorff AD, Metcalf D. *Comparative Health of the UK (1996–2007).* Available at White Paper Collections, Army-Baylor Graduate Program in Health & Business Administration, Academy of Health Science, Medical Education and Training Center, Fort Sam Houston, TX.

11. Manglesdorff AD, Hutson V, Tidwell T. *Comparative Health of the UK (2000).* Available at White Paper Collections, Army-Baylor Graduate Program in Health & Business Administration, Academy of Health Science, Medical Education and Training Center, Fort Sam Houston, TX.

12. Roemer MI. *National Health Systems of the World: Volume I the Countries.* Oxford: Oxford Press; 1991.

13. Rivett G. The Development of the London Hospital System 1823–1892. Retrieved December 15, 2007, from http://www.nhshistory.net/Londonshospitals.htm.

14. Origins & History. Retrieved December 16, 2007, from http://www.apothecaries.org/index.php?page=6.

15. History of the Department: Department of Health—About Us. Retrieved December 15, 2007, from http://www.dh.gov.uk/en/Aboutus/HowDHworks/DH_074813.

16. The Health and Social Care System. Retrieved December 15, 2007, from http://www.dh.gov.uk/en/Aboutus/HowDHworks/DH_074669.

17. Ministers and Department Leaders. Retrieved December 15, 2007, from http://www.dh.gov.uk/en/Aboutus/MinistersandDepartmentLeaders/index.htm.

18. Chief Professional Officers. Retrieved December 15, 2007, from http://www.dh.gov.uk/en/Aboutus/Chiefprofessionalofficers/index.htm.

19. About the NHS—How the NHS works. Retrieved December 16, 2007, from http://www.nhs.uk/aboutnhs/HowtheNHSworks/Pages/aboutthenhs.aspx.

20. Department of Health. Our Health, Our Care, Our Say: a New Direction for Community Services. Retrieved December 12, 2007, from http://www.dh.gov.uk/en/PublicationsandstatisticsPublications/PublicationsPolicyAndGuidance/DH_4127453.

21. National Clinical Directors. Retrieved December 15, 2007, from http://www.dh.gov.uk/en/Aboutus/MinistersandDepartmentLeaders/Nationalclinicaldirectors/index.htm.

22. Organisations That Work with DH. Retrieved December 15, 2007, from http://www.dh.gov.uk/en/OrganisationsthatworkwithDH/index.htm.

23. NHS Authorities and Trusts. Retrieved December 16, 2007, from http://www.nhs.uk/aboutnhs/HowtheNHSworks/authoritiesandtrusts/Pages/authoritiesandtrusts.aspx.

24. Connecting for Health. Retrieved December 16, 2007, from http://connectingforhealth.nhs.uk.

25. Delivering Primary Care. Retrieved December 15, 2007, from http://www.dh.gov.uk/en/Aboutus/HowDHworks/DH_074639.

26. Practice-Based Commissioning. Retrieved December 15, 2007, from http://www.dh.gov.uk/en/Managingyourorganisation/Commissioning/Practicebasedcommissioning/index.htm.

27. Department of Health. The NHS Plan: A Plan for Investment, a Plan for Reform. Retrieved December 11, 2007, from http://www.dh.gov.uk/en/Publicationsandstatistics/Publications/PublicationsPolicyAndGuidance/DH_4002960.

28. Delivering Secondary Care. Retrieved December 15, 2007, from http://www.dh.gov.uk/en/Aboutus/HowDHworks/DH_074637.

29. Cylus J, Anderson GF. Multinational Comparisons of Health Systems Data, 2006. Retrieved December 13, 2007, from http://www.commonwealthfund.org/publications/publications_show.htm?doc_id=482648.

30. Secondary Care. Retrieved December 16, 2007, from http://www.dh.gov.uk/en/Healthcare/Secondarycare/index.htm.

31. The Gateway to Private Healthcare in the UK. Retrieved January 15, 2008, from http://www.privatehealth.co.uk.

32. OECD Health Data Update, 2007. Retrieved December 15, 2007, from http://www.oecd.org/document/30/0,3343,3n_2649_37407_12968734_1_1_1_37407,00.htm.

33. Workforce. Retrieved December 15, 2007, from http://www.ic.nhs.uk/statistics-and-data-collections/workforce.

34. Wanless D, Appleby J, Harrison A, Patel D. Our Future Health Secured? A Review of NHS Funding and Performance. Retrieved December 15, 2007, from http://www.kingsfund.org.uk/publications/kings_fund_publications/our_future.html.

35. College: FAQ—How Is a Physician Trained? Retrieved January 12, 2008, from http://www/rcplondon.ac.uk/college/faq_training.asp.

36. Appleby J, ed. Funding Health Care: 2008 and Beyond. Retrieved December 15, 2007, from http://www.kingsfund.org.uk/publications/kings_fund_publications/funding_health.html.

37. Primary Care Contracting. Retrieved December 16, 2007, from http://www.dh.gov.uk/en/Healthcare/Primarycare/Primarycarecontracting/index.htm.

CHAPTER 6

Ireland

Linda F. Dennard, Joan Buckley,
Carol Linehan, and Patricia Gunn

COUNTRY DESCRIPTION

TABLE 6-1   Ireland

Nationality	Noun: Irishman (men), Irishwoman (women), Irish (collective plural)
	Adjective: Irish
Ethnic groups	Celtic, English
Religions	Roman Catholic 88.4%, Church of Ireland 3%, other Christian 1.6%, other 1.5%, unspecified 2%, none 3.5% (2002 census)
Language	English (official) is the language generally used, Irish (Gaelic or Gaeilge; official) spoken mainly in areas located along the western seaboard
Literacy	Definition: age 15 and over can read and write
	Total population: 99%
	Male: 99%
	Female: 99% (2003 est.)

(continues)

TABLE 6-1   Ireland (continued)

Government type	Republic, parliamentary democracy
Date of independence	6 December 1921 (from United Kingdom by treaty)
Gross Domestic Product (GDP) per capita	$45,600 (2007 est.)
Unemployment rate	5% (2007 est.)
Natural hazards	n/a
Environment: current issues	Water pollution, especially of lakes, from agricultural runoff
Population	4,156,119 (July 2008 est.)
Age structure	0–14 years: 20.9% (male 448,333/female 418,476) 15–64 years: 67.3% (male 1,400,222/female 1,398,194) 65 years and over: 11.8% (male 218,459/female 272,435) (2008 est.)
Median age	Total: 34.6 years Male: 33.9 years Female: 35.4 years (2008 est.)
Population growth rate	1.133% (2008 est.)
Birth rate	14.33 births/1,000 population (2008 est.)
Death rate	7.77 deaths/1,000 population (2008 est.)
Net migration rate	4.76 migrant(s)/1,000 population (2008 est.)
Gender ratio	At birth: 1.07 male(s)/female Under 15 years: 1.07 male(s)/female 15–64 years: 1 male(s)/female 65 years and over: 0.8 male(s)/female Total population: 0.99 male(s)/female (2008 est.)
Infant mortality rate	Total: 5.14 deaths/1,000 live births Male: 5.63 deaths/1,000 live births Female: 4.61 deaths/1,000 live births (2008 est.)
Life expectancy at birth	Total population: 78.07 years Male: 75.44 years Female: 80.88 years (2008 est.)
Total fertility rate	1.85 children born/woman (2008 est.)
HIV/AIDS adult prevalence rate	0.1% (2001 est.)
Number of people living with HIV/AIDS	2,800 (2001 est.)
HIV/AIDS deaths	Less than 100 (2003 est.)

Central Intelligence Agency. The World Fact Book, 2008. Retrieved November 18, 2008, from https://www.cia.gov/library/publications/the-world-factbook.

History

Among the first countries to join the European Union in 1973, the Republic of Ireland has emerged in recent years as an economic force on the European scene. The farthest west of the European countries, Ireland dug itself out from under three separate waves of invasion over a thousand years and overcame the devastation of famine, poverty, civil war, and the limits of political isolation to become one of the wealthiest countries on the planet by the end of the 20th century.[1]

After years of attempted home rule and land reform, independence from Britain was secured by a contested treaty in 1922, which divided the country between the "Free State" in the south and Northern Ireland, where much of the colonization by Scottish and English Protestants had taken root. At the core of the much-publicized violence in Northern Ireland, particularly during the "troubles" of the 1970s, were deep divisions, not merely between Catholics and Protestants, but more between those who favored the continued existence of the Northern state and those who still hoped for a unified Ireland.[2] These conflicts have been ameliorated in recent years by a decommissioning of arms by paramilitary groups and other factors, including a demilitarization of the North by the British and improved economic growth in both states.[3] The first constitution of the Free State was approved in 1937. By 1948, the state had become the Republic of Ireland, although it is commonly referred to as simply "Ireland."

The people of the Republic of Ireland are largely of Celtic origin, although along the eastern borders families can trace their linage to early Norse invaders and in the west to the Normans, who took on the Irish culture more readily than the Vikings. Catholicsim is still the primary religion, having "rewritten" Celtic mythology with biblical themes in the 8th century, although the control the Church once had on politics is not as profound as it was before the Republic emerged from isolation in the late 1950s.[4]

Eamon De Valera, the first taoiseach (prime minister) of the Free State of Ireland, was opposed to the treaty that divided the country. As he led the new nation toward becoming a republic in 1948, De Valera favored isolationist policies that kept "Ireland for the Irish" in response to centuries of subordination to other countries. He also supported groups like the Gaelic Athletic Association and the Gaelic League that regulated Irish culture, producing standards for what was the "real Irish" in everything from hurling (the national sport) to dance, music, art, and religion. Of particular impor-

tance to these early nationalists was saving the Irish language—a form of Gaelic. Irish is still taught in schools and spoken in the Republic, especially in the Gaeltacht on the western coast. It is also enjoying somewhat of a revival because of the increasing numbers of Irish-language primary schools; however, English is the primary language, especially in urban areas. During the years after the revolution, women were confined to traditional roles as part of this early movement. One of the marked changes in Irish culture in recent years has been the rapid migration of women to the workforce and into key positions in business and government.[5] Data produced by the Irish Central Statistics Office (CSO) in 2007 show just under 2 million persons aged 15 years and over as employed. Of that, males at work constitute 1.2 million and females 850,000.[1]

Isolation, however, was keeping Ireland poor and threatened to produce another famine when the country did not become as self-sufficient as De Valera had hoped. In the late 1950s, Séan Lemass, the taoiseach at the time, reversed the isolationist policies and began reaching out to the world, encouraging involvement with the new European market and actively soliciting investment from the United States and other countries. As an early member of the European Union, Ireland benefited from heavy investment in economic infrastructure by the EU as well. By the late 1970s, the effects of this turnaround were beginning to be felt in the Irish economy, and a short 20 years later, the economy was booming as the Celtic Tiger was born.[1]

Size and Geography

The area occupied by the Republic of Ireland is slightly larger than the U.S. state of West Virginia. The Irish Republic is bounded on the north by the North Channel, which separates it from Scotland; on the northeast by Northern Ireland; and on the east and southeast by the Irish Sea and St. George's Channel, which separate it from England and Wales. To the west, from north to south, the coast is washed by the Atlantic Ocean. The Irish coastline is 3,000 miles long and indented by numerous peninsulas. The coast is accentuated by mountains along much of its perimeter. Ireland's capital city, Dublin, is located on the Irish Sea coast.

Ten percent of the terrain is arable. Meadows and pastures comprise 77% of the terrain. Another 11% is in use for rough grazing. Inland waterways comprise the final 2%. The climate is a temperate maritime climate (Figure 6-1).[6]

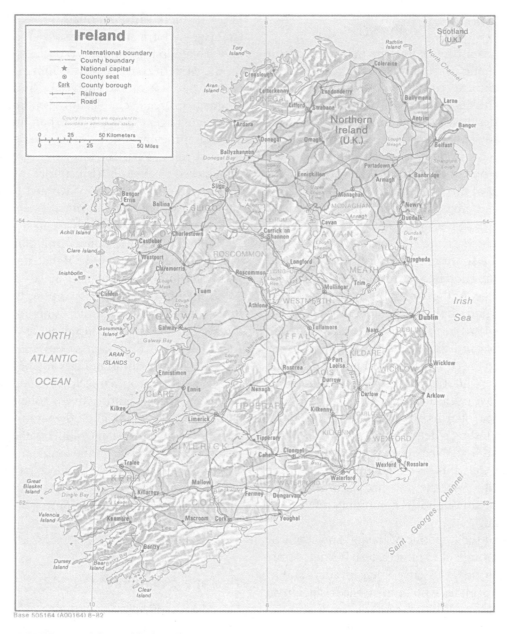

FIGURE 6-1   Map of Ireland

Government or Political System

As a parliamentary democracy, Ireland has two houses. The Oireachtas (Parliament) is composed of Dáil Éireann (the House of Representatives) and Seanad Éireann (the Senate). The Irish Constitution was enacted into law in 1937 and defines the powers and functions of the Oireachtas, the President, and the government. The constitution has been modified since. After a robust public debate, for example, the constitution was amended to allow a transfer of certain sovereign powers to the European Union. Member states are bound by the treaties they sign and therefore are also bound by the policies and directives of the European Union.

The taoiseach (the Prime Minister) heads the government or the executive branch with the support of the tánaiste (Deputy Prime Minister). The taoiseach is elected by the Dáil as the leader of the political party, or coalition of parties, that wins the most seats in the national elections, which are conducted every 5 years unless called earlier. Executive power is vested in a cabinet whose ministers are nominated by the taoiseach and approved by the Dáil.

Dáil

The 166 members of the Dáil are known as TD (Teachta Dála), all of whom are directly elected by the people. General elections take place at least once every 5 years, and the most recent was in May 2007. Since 1922, Ireland has used an electoral system based on proportional representation through the single transferable vote. This system is used to elect members to the Dáil, local councils, and the European Parliament. Electors indicate their most favored candidate by putting a "1" beside the candidate's name on the ballot paper and can then go on to indicate their second, third, and lower preferences. Under the Constitution, there must be at least one TD for every 20,000 to 30,000 people, and at present, there are 166 members from 42 constituencies. These are revised at least once every 12 years but are normally revised after a census of population, which takes place every 5 years. Alongside their main role as members of Dáil Éireann, TDs are also often members of health boards, community groups, and vocational education committees. Deputies usually divide their time between their constituency and attendance at meetings of Dáil Éireann and its specialist committees. Dáil Éireann has its own committee system that offers advice on a wide range of legislative, social, economic, and financial issues. These committees also process legislation and examine government expenditure. Deputies also serve in international bodies such as the Council of Europe, the British–Irish Inter-parliamentary Body, and other parliamentary associations; conduct research on issues; and influence policy at the national and international levels.

Seanad has 60 members—11 are nominated by the taoiseach, and the remainder is elected from a number of vocational panels and by graduates of Irish universities. Seanad can initiate or revise legislation, but the Dáil has the power to reject these proposals or amendments. In theory, Seanad Éireann does not recognize party affiliations; however, voting trends tend to follow party lines. Seanad Éireann's main authority lies in revising legislation sent to it by the Dáil; however, in recent years, the government has tended to make greater use of Seanad Éireann to initiate legislation. Under the constitution, it has the authority to both initiate and revise legislation; however, only the Dáil can initiate financial legislation. Seanad, however, can make recommendations but not amendments to such bills.

The president, who serves as head of state in a largely ceremonial role, is elected directly by the people for a 7-year term and can be re-elected only once. The president does not have an executive or policy role. She or he does have absolute discretion to refuse the dissolution of the Dáil when the taoiseach has ceased to retain a majority in the house. The president can also refer a bill to the Supreme Court for a judgment on its constitutionality. Presidential candidates need the nominations of 20 members or ex-members of the Oireachtas or nomination by the councils of four administrative counties. Sitting presidents can nominate themselves, but may only serve for two terms. Where there is more than one candidate, the people elect the president by direct vote.

Government Departments

Currently, there are 15 government departments, each headed by a minister. The Department of Foreign Affairs, for example, has responsibility for Ireland's engagement with the global Millenium Development Goals (especially through its development wing—Irish Aid), although many other departments impact on the Millenium Development Goals, especially the Department of Agriculture, the Department of Enterprise and Trade, the Department of the Environment, and the Department of Finance. Healthcare policy is regulated by the Department of Health and Children. Health matters are primarily the responsibility of the minister of health, who heads the Department of Health and Children, but aspects of wider social policy that impact on public health also fall under the remit of the Department of Social and Family Affairs.

Political Parties

Six main political parties are active in Ireland. Irish politics, however, remain dominated by the two political parties that grew out of Ireland's bitter 1922–1923 civil war. Fianna Fáil has been the largest party in the Dáil since 1932. It is part of the Union for Europe group in the European Parliament. Fianna Fáil was formed by those who opposed the 1921 treaty that partitioned the island. Although treaty opponents lost the civil war, Fianna Fáil soon became Ireland's largest political party. Fine Gael, the second largest party, is part of the European People's Party. Fine Gael was formed by those forces in favor of the 1921 treaty that partitioned the island. The much smaller Labour Party is a member of the Party of European Socialists in the European Parliament. The

Progressive Democrats were established in 1985 to create a liberal party in the European mold and are currently an extremely small political party. The Green Party is associated with Green Parties in over 30 other countries. Sinn Féin is an Irish republican party that has only begun contesting elections in the Republic in recent years.

The European Parliament

Additionally, members of European Parliament are elected (usually at the same time as national elections) to serve as Ireland's representatives in the European Parliament. Under the terms of the various treaties with the EU of which Ireland is a partner as a member, the importance of the members of European Parliament in both international and national politics is increasing.[7]

Macroeconomics

Poverty and emigration plagued Ireland until the early 1990s; however, these phenomena virtually disappeared over the next decade as the new economy of the "Celtic Tiger" gathered momentum. Over the past decade, the Irish government has implemented a series of national economic programs designed to curb inflation, ease tax burdens, reduce government spending as a percentage of gross domestic product (GDP), increase labor force skills, and promote foreign investment. The republic joined in launching the Euro currency system in January 1999 along with 10 other EU countries.[8] In January 2003, Ireland marked the 30th anniversary of its EU membership. EU membership was a decisive milestone in opening Ireland to a global economy and reducing its economic dependence on the UK. Since accession, per-capita GDP in Ireland has increased from almost 60% of the EU average in 1973 to well over 100% today, and the proportion of exports to non-UK destinations has increased from 45% to over 80%.[9]

Ireland's economy is now one of the world's most globalized, with extensive external trade and investment links. Indeed, a sustained expansion of exports has been a critical factor in Ireland's economic success. Since 1960, the value of exports has increased over 40 times in real terms and, on average, contributes about one half of Ireland's annual economic growth performance. Since the mid-1990s, Ireland's rate of export growth has outpaced world trade growth by a factor of three, and Ireland's annual rate of real export growth in goods and services has consistently ranked in the top 5 of the 30-member Organisation and Economic Co-operation and Development (OECD).[10]

Unprecedented economic growth began in the early 1990s. Between 1990 and 1995, the economy grew at an annual average growth rate of 4.8%, and between 1995 and 2000, it averaged 9.5%. Growth rates have since been maintained in the 4% to 5% range, a level almost five times higher than the old 15-member EU average. The growth in the Irish economy is reflected in annual increases in national GDP, which in 2005 reached €160 billion. On a per-capita basis (population of 4.3 million), this is equivalent to €38,000 per person, the second highest in the EU after Luxembourg. Measured on the basis of purchasing power, Ireland's level of economic activity or GDP per inhabitant is now almost 40% above the average for the current 25 members of the EU.[11] By 2005, Ireland had the second highest per capita at 38.9% above the EU 25 average; however, based on gross national income, Ireland was in fifth place at 18.6% above the EU 25 average. Ireland also has consistently topped the OECD economic growth tables, often by a substantial margin. For the 5-year period (2001 to 2005 OGCD), Ireland's average GDP growth rate of 5.3% was again the highest.[11]

The growth that began in the 1990s continues now. In 2005, for example, the economy grew by 4.7% in GDP terms and by 5.4% in GNP terms. Led by the construction sector, employment increased by 4.6%, and total employment at the end of 2005 stood at 1.98 million. The unemployment rate currently stands at 4.4%, the third lowest in the EU 25, the average rate of which is 8.2%. The unemployment rate for people under age 25 at 9% is the third lowest in the EU 25, which has an average of 17.7%. The employment rate in Ireland rose from 56.1% in 1997 to 68.1% in 2006. Participation rates for women increased by over 14 percentage points in that period, whereas the rate for men rose by around 10 percentage points.

Productivity in Ireland, measured as GDP per person employed, was the second highest in the EU 27 in 2005. The employment rate of persons aged 55 to 64 at 51.7% was higher than the EU 27 average of 42.3% in 2005; however, only 37.4% of women in Ireland in this age group were in employment compared with 65.7% of men. The unemployment rate in Ireland increased from a low of 3.6% in 2001 to 4.3% in 2006. Ireland had the third lowest unemployment rate in the EU 27 in 2006 at just over half of the EU 27 average of 7.9%. The long-term unemployment rate in Ireland was 1.4% in 2005, which was lower than the EU27 average of 4%.[9]

2008 and Beyond

With a shaky world economy emerging in the first quarter of 2008, it is perhaps no surprise that Ireland anticipates a slowdown of the Celtic Tiger phenomenon. Economic growth for the year was forecast to be at the lowest rate since 1993 according to the Economic and Social Research Institute (ESRI). Before 1993, the growth rate was 2.3%. The ESRI predicted that economic growth would fall from 5.4% expected in 2007 to less than 4% in 2008. In a separate report, Davy Stockbrokers forecast that the GNP would expand by only 3% compared with 7.4% in 2006.[12] The resilience of the Irish economy will be tested by the economic downturn. Four macroeconomic challenges have been identified by the ERSI study reports:

- Maintaining a high potential growth rate
- Restoring competitiveness
- Managing potential risks to macroeconomic and financial stability from the housing market
- Adjusting to shocks originating outside the Euro area

Impact of an Economic Downturn on Health Care

A possible slowing of the economy may have contributed to a proposed hiring freeze in early 2008 on the number of medical staff hired by the public health system. Reports of the freeze were denied in May 2008 by the health service.[13] This downturn plus health cost overruns will have implications for planned growth in the healthcare system in coming years. ESRI predicted that the current government deficit would be increased by €1 billion in 2008; however, a surplus in overall government finances should remain at between 0.8% and 1.7% of GDP, according to forecasts.[12]

Demographics

Since the 1970s, Ireland's population has been increasing, displaying a turnaround for the country that experienced population decline and high levels of emigration for decades. The population now stands at just over 4.3 million, its highest level in 130 years. The current 2.5% annual rate of population increase is the highest in the EU, driven in part by high levels of immigration especially among Eastern and Central Europeans, from countries which are new members of the European Union. Along with increased numbers of women in the labor force, a population increase has helped boost the labor supply to its highest level ever, at over 2 million people.

During the 1990s, Ireland's labor force expanded at five times the EU rate. The increasing numbers of immigrants to Ireland add pressure on public healthcare services according to the Central Statistics Office April 2007 report[9]; however, 2007 immigration was more balanced by emigration than in previous years. The total number of immigrants to Ireland in the year ending April 2007 was 109,000, up almost 2,000 from the previous year and substantially higher than for any other year since 1987. Of these, about 48% were nationals of the new EU accession states, 10 of which joined in 2004 and 2 that joined in 2007, according to the CSO report. About 1 in 10 immigrants were under the age of 15 years, and more than half were aged 25 to 44 years.

On the other hand, the estimated number of emigrants from Ireland to other countries was 42,200 in the same period—also considerably higher than in recent years. As a result, net migration has fallen from the record high of 71,800 in the year ending April 2006 to 67,300 in 2007. The natural increase in population through live births for 2007 was 38,800—double the number in 1994. The combined effect of the natural population increase and the net migration increase was an increase in population in Ireland of 106,100, or 2.5%. The population in April 2007 was estimated at 4.34 million, according to CSO statistics.[9]

Currently, Ireland has a younger population than the rest of Europe, with over 40% of the population under the age of 25. Additionally, 20.8% of the population is between the ages of 0 and 14 years, with about 442,664 males and 413,556 females. About 67.6% of the population is between the ages of 15 and 64, with 1,387,803 male and 1,385,355 females. Finally, 11.7% of the population is over the age of 65 with 212,783 males and 266,962 females. The national median age is 34.3 years, with 33.5 years for males and 35.1 years for females. The proportion of the population over 65 is the lowest in Europe, as is the overall dependency ratio (the proportion of the population aged under 15 and over 65). Within the EU 15 group, Ireland had the proportionally largest economically active age group (16 to 64), which bodes well for the future labor force. According to UN projections, by 2010 the people under age 25 will comprise 32.8% of the Irish population compared with the projected average for all of Europe of 27.9%. By 2020, these proportions are respectively projected at 31.8% and 26.3%; however, statistics from the CSO indicate that there was growth across all age groups in 2007 except the 10- to 19-year-olds—a factor that may be attributed to the influx of immigrants. In 30 years, roughly 20% of the population will be over 65 years, and 40% will be over 50. Ireland has a birth rate of 14.4 births per 1,000 and a death rate of 7.79 deaths per 1,000 population. CSO figures for 2002 suggest an average life expectancy of 75.1 for men and 80.3 for women.[9]

Religion

Roman Catholics comprise 88.4% of the population. Three percent of the population are members of the Church of Ireland, and 1.6% are other Christians. Additionally, 1.5% are other religions, including Muslim. About 2% of the population did not specify a religion in the 2002 census, and 3.5% of the population reported no religion;[14] however, there has been a marked decrease in religious observance in Ireland in the last 20 years. Although the majority of people still report themselves as Catholic, the society has become noticeably more secular.[14]

Poverty Rates

Between 1994 and 2001, consistent poverty levels were reduced from 14.5% to around 5% in 2001, a figure that had increased slightly by 2006. In 2001, 192,000 people (5% of the population) lived in consistent poverty. In 2001, more than 862,000 people (almost 22% of the population) lived on less than €164 per single person per week. A further 6% of the population lived without basic necessities and on weekly incomes of less than €172 per adult. In 2006, according to a report from the CSO,[15] 6% of men and 7.5% of women were in consistent poverty with unemployed people being the most vulnerable. According to the CSO study, those at risk for poverty, after taking into account pensions and social transfer payments, numbered 20%, a drop of 2% from previous years. The effect of pensions and transfers on reducing risk of poverty, however, was lower in comparison to other EU countries, a fact that has prompted a call for more social safety nets.[15]

Literacy and Education

The literacy rate in the Republic of Ireland is around 99% according to the CSO. The Irish education system is largely state funded, and considerable emphasis has always been placed on education in national policy. The high education standards are a key factor in the economic promotion of the country internationally. One third of the workforce aged 25 to 64 years has a third-level (university) qualification. That is compared to 12.3% among the 18-to-24 aged group in 2006. Among those who dropped out, the unemployment rate was around 19% compared with a rate of 8.2% among all others aged 18 to 24 years. Male early school leavers are more likely to be unemployed than their female counterparts. The incidence of early school leaving is also more concentrated in areas of lower socioeconomic profile.[16]

General Health of the Population

According to the Irish Department of Health and Children, 48% of Irish people rate their own health to be "excellent" or "good." Another 15% rate their health as "fair" or "poor." Those responding to the department's survey felt that their health would improve if these factors were addressed: stress, personal willpower, weight, and money.[21] Furthermore, according to findings of the World Health Organization (WHO) in 2004,[17] 86% of the Irish population report their health to be good or very good, the highest such average in Europe. Infant mortality rates were comparable to other European countries. The main causes of 84% of all deaths in Ireland are noncommunicable conditions. Cardiovascular diseases accounted for 39% of deaths; cancers resulted in 27% of the deaths, respiratory diseases 14%, and intentional and unintentional injury 6%. Compared with European averages, more men died from injuries and more women died from cancers.

According to the 2004 WHO report, tobacco use in Ireland is 12% higher than the European average. In 2004, the incidence of lung cancer in women was 47% higher than the average for all women in Europe. For Irish men, however, the estimated incidence was below the average. The numbers of smokers is decreasing, the report says. Between 1994 and 2002, smoking became less prevalent among men and women generally, decreasing among 15-year-old boys and increasing slightly for 15-year-old girls. A nationwide public smoking ban authorized in 2004 is expected to further lower statistics.

Since 1980, pure alcohol consumption has increased according to the WHO report, whereas the European trend is toward decreased drinking. In 2001, Ireland's level was the third highest in Europe, whereas perhaps surprisingly, the incidence of chronic liver disease and cirrhosis as an indicator of harmful drinking is considerably *below* European averages. Increases have been seen in other health areas. From 1996 to 2002, for example, the rate of newly diagnosed HIV infections in Ireland increased by a factor of 3.4. Between 1999 and 2002, the rate almost doubled. In 2002, 62% of new infections were attributed to heterosexual contact, and over four fifths of those were among immigrants. Obesity is on the rise in Ireland as more reliance on cars and fast food in a busy economy changes eating patterns among both adults and young people. About 10% of 15-year-old Irish boys are preobese, and about 1% are obese, according to the 2004 report. About 11% of 15-year-old Irish girls were preobese, and 2% were obese—a rate that is among the highest in the European area.[18]

BRIEF HISTORY OF THE HEALTHCARE SYSTEM

Pre-World War II

As in other countries, including the United States, the Irish healthcare system began as a response to the poor. The first hospitals, funded by philanthropists, were started in Ireland in the early 18th century. Catholic religious orders were responsible for much of the early growth of hospitals and medical services. By the mid-19th century, however, the British had institutionalized and politicized health care through the punitive workhouse system. Infirmaries, dispensaries, and medical staff provided minimal care in these houses of last resort for the Irish poor. In the colonialist mind-set of the British at the time, helping the Irish too much would discourage them from working harder.[19]

After the revolution, the Free State government converted the dreaded workhouses into county homes for the poor in need of both shelter and medical care. Health services in the poorly funded new state, however, were not a financial priority, and hospital health care was delivered through the local network of county and city hospitals until 1970 through the Hospital Sweepstakes lottery; however, the early state conducted a vigorous campaign to eradicate tuberculosis in the late 1940s. There were also some developments aimed at improving general public health such as the provision of free milk to children and pregnant women in the early 1930s.[20]

Since World War II

Incrementalism

As the first Prime Minister of Ireland (taoiseach), Eamon De Valera, shepherded the Irish Free State into the era of the modern Republic, national government began to take a more active part in the delivery of health care. The new government published "An Outline of Proposals for the Improvement of Health Services" and established the first Department of Health in 1947 with the intent

of providing free health care at the point of use. A system of universal health care was proposed in a second paper, "Social Security," in 1949, setting a course for a welfare state and a universal, national health service; however, the Roman Catholic Church, which retained a significant role in government policy process throughout much of the 20th century, was strongly opposed to the plans for state-sponsored universal health care. Along with the Department of Finance and the medical community, the Church successfully defeated both the healthcare proposal and a social insurance proposal. The finance department argued that the new state could not afford a welfare state on par with Britain and Northern Ireland. Health care was then subject to incremental changes based on existing service delivery rather than on more visionary planning.[21]

One of the first such incremental measures was the 1953 Health Act. Among the most notable features of the act was that it provided funding to voluntary (nonprofit) agencies for health and related services. Health was broadly defined to include many social services. "Section 65 Funding" became the largest source of funding for voluntary and community organizations in Ireland. Indeed, by 2001, Section 65 Funding to voluntary and community groups was €486 million. The name was changed to Section 39 grants under the Health Act of 2004. Applications for these grants were rerouted through 32 local health offices (LHOs). Voluntary and community organizations, however, were not given a role in decision making by the 2004 act as a way to mediate the effect of local politics on the administration of health care.[22]

Over time, an incremental approach to healthcare planning resulted in a patchwork of services, no clear channels for accountability, and an inconsistent pattern of healthcare delivery. Furthermore, there was confusion among users, in particular, as to who was eligible for care. The Health Care Act of 1970, for example, organized the country into eight regional health boards with similar governing structures. Each board had three programs areas (hospital services, special or psychiatric hospitals, and community care), each under a manager with broad authority. The health boards were made up of local authority councilors, representatives of the senior medical professions, and citizens nominated by the Minister for Health. Each board met once a month. There were frequent differences in the availability of services and facilities between health board regions. The Eastern Health Board was subdivided in the 1990s into three smaller boards (northern, southwestern, and east coast), increasing the number of regional boards to

11. Additionally, 40 semistate agencies concerned with health care co-evolved, each with specialized functions ranging from giving healthcare advice and health promotion to health regulation.[23]

In 2004, the Oireachtas (Parliament) approved a major reorganization in the administration of healthcare, which sought to separate the management of healthcare services from the more political nature of the evolving system and to clarify responsibility for the delivery of quality health care. This followed a number of major reports issued by the Health Service Reform Program concerning the health service, including one entitled "Quality and Fairness," which surveyed current practice and benchmarked international healthcare standards.[24] A further factor that influenced the decision to reorganize the health service was the European Union Working Time Directive, which laid down specific guidelines for acceptable working hours for all categories of health professionals.[25]

The Department of Health and Children, accountable to the Minister of Health and Children and the government, is now responsible only for policy, whereas management of public health services falls to the new Health Service Executive Agency (HSE) administered by an executive board; however, as the healthcare system makes the transition, these two roles have been difficult to separate. The executive agency operates four regional health offices (RHOs) and 32 LHOs in addition to a number of local healthcare centers. Additionally, the HSE publishes an annual service plan outlining service delivery plans for the coming year and has budgetary and financial responsibility for the health system. More significantly, the reorganization shifted health services from a decentralized "federal" system to a centralized system—one controlled more by management principles and conceivably less subject to local political pressures. Delivery of primary, community, and continuing care is coordinated by the 32 LHOs and the local healthcare centers around the country in addition to many privately operated medical general practitioners who mainly deal with a mix of public and private patients.[26]

The function of each of the four regional administrative HSEs is to provide or arrange for the provision of health, community care, and personal social services to people in its areas, according to Brendan Drumm, the HSE board's first CEO. Professor Drumm maintains that his stated priority is the quality of patient care. "For patients and front-line staff the changes should mean more integration, consistency and accountability," Professor Drumm maintains.[27]

Health Service Executive Administrative Areas

Each HSE is organized into nine administrative "directorates." The critical ones for service users are as follows:

> *Primary, Continuing, and Community Care*: responsible for general practitioner (GP, primary care physician) and community-based health and personal social services, including services for older people, children, disability, and other related services.
>
> *National Hospitals Office*: responsible for public hospitals and ambulances.
>
> *National Shared Services Center*: responsible for centralized administration of procurement, human resources, and finance.
>
> *Population Health*: responsible for providing immunizations and infection control by working with LHOs.[26]

The 2004 act also consolidated responsibility for hospitals within the National Hospitals Office. In a further effort to integrate services, the 2004 act also gives authority to four regional RHOs for overseeing and coordinating regional and local medical services. According to the HSE, the RHOs do not run services in the manner of the older health regions. Rather, they provide a "discussion and feedback structure" for the public and local politicians for monitoring patient experiences for the HSE. Ten new hospital "networks," based on the old regional health board structure, also now exist, as well as the 32 LHOs, which report to the HSE directorate of primary, community, and continuing care. The system of accountability also requires interactions among the various national and regional administrative and policy structures.

DESCRIPTION OF THE CURRENT HEALTHCARE SYSTEM

Facilities

Health Service Executive Hospitals

These hospitals are owned and funded by the national HSE. Most major cities and towns have a general hospital providing a full range of services, including treatment and diagnosis for inpatients, day patient care, and accident and emergency facilities (A&E). Rural areas are served by a regional hospital providing basic medical care, but often without an A&E unit. Psychiatric, orthopedic, maternity (such as the National Maternity Hospital), a Skin and Cancer Hospital, an Eye and Ear

Hospital as well as children's hospitals also exist. For admission to a specialist hospital, a doctor's referral is required. Day hospitals offer outpatient care such as physiotherapy and at a lower cost than inpatient care. In recent years, the Minister of Health and Children has struggled with reports in the media of "scandals" in which older patients and acute-care patients spent long hours or even days on trolleys (gurneys) in hospital hallways because of a shortage of beds in rooms. In response to this situation, plans are being made to care for geriatric patients in special departments, allowing for an increase in the number of beds available for acute patients. An increase in usage of hospitals, especially by geriatric patients, is attributed in part to the change in the pattern of social relationships in Ireland, in which older persons are less likely to be cared for by the extended family, but it also involves an increased awareness of healthcare services and the need for treatment.[28]

Voluntary Public Hospitals

Voluntary hospitals are owned by private organizations, often religious groups; however, they are still heavily subsidized by the government. Indeed, with the 2004 reorganization, the HSE assumed regulation of voluntary hospitals. Ireland has 22 voluntary hospitals—18 in County Dublin, 1 in County Galway, 2 in Cork, and 1 in Limerick. Each accepts both private and semiprivate patients; however, voluntary hospitals must make a distinction with patients between public and private beds. Consultants (doctors) often work in both voluntary and public hospitals. Although public and private would seem to overlap in practice, in the regulatory environment, they are considered quite separate in terms of financial and service accountability.[29]

Private Hospitals

The 16 private hospitals in Ireland receive no government funding. Six private hospitals are located in County Dublin, with two each in County Cork and County Galway. Patients in a private bed, whether in a public or private hospital, must pay room and treatment costs. Patients selecting private care generally have private healthcare insurance.[30] Currently in Ireland, there is a significant debate about the proposed colocation of public and private hospitals on campuses owned by the health authority. Proponents argue that it would enable private patients to move from public hospitals to private facilities on the same site, thereby freeing up significant capacity for public patients. Opponents, however,

argue that the move would enhance existing inequalities in the health service and would fundamentally undermine the espoused commitment by Drumm and others to a fair and equal healthcare system.[31]

Workforce

A report produced by the skills and labor market research unit with the IRISH FAS in 2005 refers to OECD figures that indicate the ratio of GPs employed per thousand of the population in Ireland is the second lowest in the EU. The EU average is approximately one GP per thousand of the population. The Irish ratio is less than half the EU average of 0.47 per thousand. There are almost 2,500 GPs in Ireland, although not all are in full-time practice. Approximately 10% of these deal with only private patients—all others deal with a mix of public and private patients. Currently, there are about 8,000 medical and dental personnel in Ireland, representing an increase of about 9% since the end of 2005. The nursing population numbers 37,500, which also is an increase of slightly less than 7% since 2005. The numbers of other healthcare specialists such as speech and language therapists have also increased since 2005 to 15,500, an increase of about 10%.[32]

Technology and Equipment

In 2008, the Irish government authorized a €490 million budget for Internet technology to improve access to timely health information. The money is also budgeted to develop electronic patient records to improve coordination of inpatient and outpatient records and for sustaining patient history. At Cork University Hospital, the island's largest acute-care hospital and principal teaching hospital, uses its new Internet capabilities to provide hospitalwide clinical order entry and reporting of patients' diagnostic records at point of care. The Cork facility qualifies as a level 1 trauma center. The information management expenditure is in compliance with the 2004 mandate for ensuring optimal use, efficiency, effectiveness, and quality of health information within a confidential healthcare system.[33]

The initiation of centralized web portals for healthcare information in Ireland has been listed among the best practices in European countries by the Center for Administrative Innovation in the Euro-Mediterranean Region. Such technology would bring Ireland in line with the developing practices of the European Union in providing access to health information and services through interconnecting websites.[34]

Pharmaceutical Regulation

Ireland, in common with the rest of the EU, restricts advertising of prescription pharmaceuticals. Only over-the-counter drugs may be promoted directly to consumers with the usual restrictions as to honesty and accuracy. Promotion of prescription drug pharmaceuticals is restricted to those with prescribing powers, and the promotional methods allowed are increasingly regulated. On the other hand, the European Union Commission is considering relaxing the ban on the promotion of prescription drugs directly to consumers and allowing informative advertising on the basis that it will allow consumers to have more informed discussions with prescribers. Opponents to the proposed relaxing of the ban argue that the benefits to multinational pharmaceutical manufacturers will far outweigh the benefits to consumers.[35]

EVALUATION OF THE HEALTH SYSTEM

Cost

An average of € 2,223 per person was spent on noncapital public expenditures on health care in Ireland in 2004, representing an increase of over 80% from 1995 levels. About 70% of the funding for health care is public money coming from tax revenues. The remaining 30% in financed by private insurance and user fees, according to Department of Health and Children statistics in 2008.[15] Noncapital expenditure on health care in Ireland as a proportion of gross national income (GNI is equal to the GNP plus European subsidies less EU taxes) decreased from 6.2% in 1955 to 5.6% in 1998 but increased again to 7.6% by 2004. Public noncapital expenditures include services, administration, community health and welfare expenditures, and services for the disabled (Table 6-2). Ireland's expenditure on public and private health was 7.1% of the GDP in 2004 (Table 6-3). The largest employer in Ireland, the HSE directly employs more than 65,000 staff members, and an additional 35,000 receive funding from the HSE. The annual budget of €15 billion exceeds that of any other public sector organization in Ireland.

Quality

In a 2006 survey administered by HSE, over 79% of patients reported being satisfied with the service that they received during their hospital stay, and nearly 86% said they had "complete trust" in their GP. The Health Infor-

mation and Quality Authority directed by the HSE monitors quality control in the system. The Health Information and Quality Authority collaborates with numerous groups, including patients, clients, health professionals, academic institutions, and international health monitoring agencies.[36]

Health services are provided at three levels, according to the HSE.

- Primary care, which is usually provided by a general practitioner or a social worker at the local level. A primary role of the GP is to ensure the availability of preventive services.
- Secondary care, which is care or treatment provided by a specialist.
- Tertiary care, which is acute care provided by a specialist available only at a few specialized hospitals.

Although recently criticized by a government-sponsored research report for not meeting its assigned goals (see Current and Emerging Issues and Challenges later here), the HSE has articulated six "transformation" priorities for the Irish healthcare system, to be accomplished by 2010: (1) develop integrated services across all stages of the care "journey"; (2) configure primary, community, and continuing care services so they deliver optimal and cost effective results; (3) configure hospital services to deliver optimal and cost-effective results; (4) implement a model for the prevention and management of chronic illness; (5) implement standards based on performance measurement and management throughout HSE; and (6) ensure all staff engage in transforming health and social care in Ireland.[36]

Innovations

An innovation in the system designed to increase preventive intervention has involved strengthening the role of the directorate for primary community and continuing care by installing approximately 500 primary care teams nationwide in the coming years. Each multidisciplinary team will provide care to defined populations of about 7,000 each. The goals are to allow for quicker and more efficient response in acute-care cases and also to improve diagnosis of community illness by providing diagnostic facilities at the local level. It is also expected that this will reduce "clogging" by redistributing health care among specific populations.[36] This innovation, however, is proving slow to introduce because of the current nature of primary care provision and the

TABLE 6-2 Public Health Expenditure, 1997 to 2006 (€m)

	1997	1998	1999	2000	2001	2002	2003	2004	2005	2006 (estimate)	% Change 1997–2006	% Change 2005–2006
Total Public Noncapital Expenditure on Health	3,504	3,886	4,647	5,423	6,802	7,933	8,853	9,653	10,578	11,742	235.1	11.0
Net Public Noncapital Expenditure on Health	3,443	3,819	4,574	5,359	6,739	7,867	8,783	9,561	10,502	11,646	238.3	10.9
Total Public Capital Expenditure on Health	167	187	231	294	374	507	514	509	516	595	256.3	15.3
Total Public Expenditure	3,671	4,073	4,878	5,717	7,176	8,440	9,367	10,162	11,094	12,337	236.1	11.2

Net noncapital expenditure excludes national lottery funding and treatment benefits (funded from the vote of Department of Social and Family Affairs).

Figures for 2006 are estimated.

Data are from Non-Capital Expenditure, "Estimated Non-Capital Health Expenditure 1990 to 2006 Categorised by Programme and Service." Retrieved from www.dohc.ie.

TABLE 6-3 Capital Public Health Expenditure by Program, 1997–2005 (€000)

Program	1997	1998	1999	2000	2001	2002	2003	2004	2005	% Change 1997–2005	% Change 2004–2005
Acute Hospitals	99,046	116,900	127,800	165,372	208,038	327,190	396,032	390,603	277,964	180.6	−28.8
Community Health	34,510	21,787	36,125	39,531	55,371	74,033	25,754	24,018	115,671	235.2	381.6
Mental Health	3,158	3,639	4,150	15,916	17,891	33,975	8,258	2,702	25,759	715.7	853.3
Disability Services	16,303	21,045	22,439	47,069	57,658	38,613	40,257	19,728	32,335	98.3	63.9
Miscellaneous	2,760	5,083	13,752	7,861	8,227	4,633	3,811	3,997	5,781	109.5	44.6
ICT	11,184	18,512	26,427	18,195	26,436	28,669	40,074	67,431	58,400	422.2	−13.4
Total Capital Expenditure	166,961	186,966	230,693	293,944	373,621	507,113	514,186	508,479	515,910	209.0	1.5

From Revised Estimates for Public Services

limited prior experience of shared decision making among participants in the process.

The National Expert Advisory Group (EAG) also has been established by the HSE. Led by clinicians from a wide range of disciplines, the advisory group will be involved in planning and delivering services. Each EAG will focus on a specific area of health care. The first four EAGs are mental health, diabetes, children, and older people. It is hoped that these measures will improve the consistency as well as the quality of services in Ireland.

Quality control is also manifested in the planned interactions of the multiple operational arms of service delivery, according to HSE. For example, the LHOs are often the first contact that a member of the public makes in the system. Each of the 32 offices is administered by a local health manager who is directed to collaborate with hospital managers in their geographic area to ensure that patients' needs are met. Also, the LHOs work in tandem with the population health directorate by providing immunizations and infection control at the local level.

Access

By authority of the 2004 Health Act, the HSE is legally required to provide hospital services for everyone. Other services, such as home health care, *may* be provided. For example, the Department of Health and Children states that even though an individual may be "eligible" for a variety of services, there does not exist an "entitlement" to them. The Health Act requires HSE to provide free services to eligible recipients. The legislation, however, does allow for changes to be made in this provision. Users sometimes pay office fees as a contribution toward the cost of medical services, but this does not necessarily mean that services can be denied if the fee is not paid.

Eligibility for healthcare services is based on residency and means, rather than on payment of tax or pay-related social insurance. If an individual lives in Ireland and plans to continue living there at least 1 year, he or she is considered to be "ordinarily" a citizen and therefore eligible for a range of health services that is free and/or subsidized in certain cases. For purposes of eligibility, the Irish population is designated as either Category I (medical care holders) or Category 2 (nonmedical card holders). Those with medical cards are eligible for a full range of health benefits without charge. European Union citizens, residing in Ireland but insured in another EU country, automatically receive a medical card, as do pensioners and those working in Ireland legally. In other cases, eligibility for a medical card is dependent on income standards. The upper income limit is adjusted each January and varies with age, family status, and other factors. Generally, however, medical card eligibility is for those with incomes from around €6,500 to €12,000 annually, which is about 36% of the population.[37]

A medical card entitles the bearer to free health care funded from general taxation, which includes the following:

- GP services
- Prescribed drugs and medicine
- Public hospital services
- Dental services
- Optical services
- Aural services
- Maternity and infant care services
- A wide range of community care and personal social services

In contrast, nonmedical card users include everyone else who is eligible for public health care. They are required to pay up to €86 per month of prescription costs while the government pays the rest. Inpatient treatment for nonmedical card users requires a co-payment of €40 per day with a maximum of €400. Maternity care and public outpatient services are free; however, charges apply to inpatient accommodation and visits to the A&E—usually €65 if not referred by a GP. Category 2 users also may be eligible for some community care and personal social services. Additionally, general health services may be available for free to persons on the basis of need or health status rather than on whether they have a medical card.

- Those suffering from certain illness qualify for free prescribed drugs.
- Child health services are available to all children, though very often those with private health insurance use their insurance or pay privately to access private services for children where there are significant waiting lists. There are state-funded inoculation, general health, and dental programs available to children in the primary school system free of charge.
- Health promotion is aimed at the entire population.

Private Insurance

Category 2 individuals are encouraged to purchase voluntary private insurance. The key features of private medical insurance in Ireland are as follows:

- The policyholder retains the right to use the public system.
- There is no reduction in tax/social insurance contributions.
- The state provides tax relief on the full premium.
- The private insurance market is heavily regulated.
- There is community rating, ensuring that younger and older policyholders pay the same for similar health coverage throughout their lives as a means of regulating the affordability of health insurance into old age; however, those enrolling over age 35 years may be charged additional fees on enrollment. Also, new enrollees may not be immediately eligible for certain benefits such as enhanced maternity benefits.
- There is open enrollment, which entitles all persons of all ages, whatever their current health status, to obtain health insurance.
- The lifetime coverage ensures that individuals do not lose their health insurance in the course of their lifetime.
- Risk equalization transfers funds from insurance companies that have a disproportionate share of young health subscribers to companies that have a disproportionate share of older people who are more susceptible to disease.

The cost of the most popular private medical insurance coverage in Ireland is about €583 annually per adult and about €212 per child. Private healthcare insurance is often favored by those who can afford it, as the time spent on waiting lists especially for surgery can extend beyond one year. Since 1990, the number of privately insured has doubled. The proportion of the number of privately insured Irish compared with the entire population in the Republic is a less than one half.[38]

CURRENT AND EMERGING ISSUES AND CHALLENGES

Changing demographics produced by an increase in immigration in recent years, an increase in income among Irish workers as a result of the robust economy, lifestyle changes brought on by increasing wealth, a shift in traditional patterns of family relationships, and policy directives from the European Union are among the variables affecting Irish healthcare policy in the 21st century. For example, the Economic and Social Research Institute of Dublin reports this:

With high level of economic growth, more people have been buying private health insurance such that about half the population is now privately insured. At the same time the numbers with eligibility for health services without charge have decreased, while those from lower socioeconomic groups continue to have higher levels of utilization. Equity issues arise, however, with regard to access to public hospitals as the rate of growth in admissions for private patients outstrips that for public patients. While all statements of national strategy consistently put forward equity and efficiency as objectives for health system development, the achievement of these objectives remains an ambition rather than a reality. Private patients continue to have better access to public hospitals than public patients.[12]

Yet, the report goes on to say that the National Treatment Purchase Fund (NTPF) implemented in 2005 to purchase treatment in private facilities for public patients on waiting lists raises both efficiency and equity questions as the treatment of private patients in public hospitals is heavily subsidized while, at the same time, the state pays full costs for the treatment of public patients in private facilities.[23]

An increase in national wealth has allowed heavy development in terms of technology and information development, but the system has moved awkwardly toward efficiency as it struggles to transcend past patterns of healthcare delivery and the difficult politics associated with it. Free health care has also often meant "free" to wait. With the initiation of the National Treatment Purchase Fund, however, wait times are being significantly reduced. For example, the waiting time for 70% of the children needing heart operations in 1997 was over a year. In 2007, by comparison, no child waited a year. In 1997, 75% of adults waited over a year for heart treatment. By 2007, on the average, the wait time had been reduced to a few months. Figures released by the Department of Health and Children in October 2007 showed general reductions in wait times for most services. The number of adults waiting for more than 3 months was 19,083, and the number of children was 2,320—a total of 21,403. For the most common procedures, adults and children now wait an average of 2 to 5 months compared with 2 to 5 years before the NTPF.[39]

A continuing problem is the availability of beds for patients coming to A&E departments. During the flu season especially, emergency rooms are overcrowded with patients on gurneys who may lie in the hallways for several days.[28] The government's response has been to seek the expansion of nursing home care, moving older persons from acute hospitals and therefore freeing beds. According to government reports, the ministry is also committed to providing 3,000 new beds by 2011. Waiting lists and long waiting times in A&E departments have also been a problem, one also addressed by the NTPF, which initiated a patient treatment register for better triage.[40]

The majority of patients now registered with NTPF are receiving services in private facilities, with a small number still traveling to the United Kingdom for treatment. The success rate is enough to encourage the government to say that the problem of long waiting lists is by and large solved; however, a question still remains regarding the increasing number of private patients being allowed access to public hospitals to be treated at subsidized rates while service for public waiting-list patients must be purchased at full cost from the private sector in Ireland and the United Kingdom.[40]

An additional challenge is an anticipated shortage of nurses. Nurses make up about 36% of the Irish health staff. One reason for the expected shortage is that the nursing degree has changed from a 3-year program to a 4-year bachelor of science. No new nurses, therefore, will be completing their program for a period of a year. This means that 1,500 fewer nurses will be available to the system. Many hospitals are responding to this shortage by recruiting nurses from the Philippines, South Africa, England, and Australia.[41]

Furthermore, despite increased wealth, health inequality is still an issue. Identified health inequalities include higher death rates in the lowest economic class due to cancer, stroke, and accidents. Perinatal mortality is three times higher in poorer families than in richer ones, whereas women among the unemployed are more than twice as likely to give birth to low-weight babies compared with professional women. The National Health and Lifestyles Survey found that those living in poverty are more likely to smoke cigarettes, drink alcohol excessively, exercise less, and have poorer nutrition than upper socioeconomic classes. The nomadic Irish ethnic group known as Travellers and homeless individuals appear to be most affected by health disparities.[42]

New health challenges have presented themselves in recent years as well. For example, a growing reliance on cars and fast food by an Irish population busy keeping up with the economic boom has produced a sharp rise in obesity and obesity-related problems.[28] Adding to the challenges ahead for the HSE are changes looming in European Community healthcare policy proposed by the Lisbon Treaty in 2007, which has yet to be ratified by the Irish people. Health has become a central policy issue for the EU that is developing an overarching system of integrating health policies with themes, including fostering good health in an aging population, protecting citizens from health risks, and the development of dynamic health systems, new models of health, and advanced technology. Although the EU does not intend to duplicate services already offered by member states, it can be expected that the new policies will ultimately impact how the HSE does business.[43]

Finally, a continuing problem for the HSE is associated with a transition from a decentralized system of care to one that is both bureaucratic and centralized. The HSE was under fire in 2008 for cost overruns, and in April, the trade union impact voted overwhelmingly to strike at the end of May if demands were not met. Some 28,000 healthcare workers would be involved in a strike action. Union members claimed that HSE had done little to address more than politically expedient goals related to waiting lists and had ignored promised improvements in primary care, disability, and mental health services as well as care for older people. The largest bone of contention, however, was a second freeze on recruitment of nurses and consultants put into effect by HSE in January 2008 because of cost overruns. In a system already facing healthcare worker shortages, a hiring freeze was untenable to union members.[44] The complaints of the union seemed supported in a report also issued in the spring of 2008 that sharply criticized the HSE for not putting more effort into longer range goals or meeting promised objectives. The report, commissioned by the government, was researched and prepared by the OECD as part of the government's efforts to assess progress in meeting economic goals in the country. The report also indicated that there needed to be a better clarification of roles between the HSE and the health ministry and a general improvement in communication among the various levels of bureaucracy.[45]

The need of the Irish people for efficient and affordable health care has grown in importance as a national policy issue at a similar rate to that of economic growth. As the Celtic Tiger has taken Ireland from "third-world" status in the mid-20th century to being among the wealthiest nations in the world by the first decade of the 21st century, state-of-the-art healthcare, accessible to the full population, is a realizable vision. Indeed, it is a matter of pride among new generations of healthcare providers and managers that Ireland could be a world leader in the provision of innovative health care that results in a steady state of health for residents.

The "transformation" of the Irish health system is being led by the new class of managers who rightfully are concerned about securing a closer link between government policy and implementation and avoiding the classic pitfall of Irish local politics—that in which health care access has sometimes been a commodity for political patronage rather than accessible to all. Put in perspective, the Health Care Act of 2004 is a challenging piece of legislation; however, it would seem that the Irish have everything they need in terms of resources, expertise, and political will to meet that challenge. Yet, there are already signs of conflict among policy makers and HSE executives as constituents lobby for more visible outcomes from the huge financial outlays for health care and the new healthcare bureaucracy. Public debate in Ireland, however, is seldom confined to the brief space of time when a policy is devised and passed in Parliament. Rather, it is an ongoing process by which citizens reconcile themselves with change.

If there is a cautionary note, beyond the obvious need to set aside surpluses for economic downturns, it is to recognize that the bureaucracy and its efficiency still cannot replace the importance of the experience of the patient in the health process or the need to ensure that individuals are actively engaged in their own health maintenance. That is, there needs to be a healthy relationship between policy makers, those accountable to their constituencies, and healthcare executives responsible for translating those policies in healthcare delivery; however, the relationship needs to be more collaborative than adversarial. If the end goal is indeed quality health care accessible to all residents, there must be an open engagement of criticism and a realistic response rather than merely a chance to blame the other guy.

In truth, the new Irish healthcare system is not simpler to understand than the previous complex and decentralized system of health boards. Indeed, the layering effects of so many new administrative units may, in the long run, may make accountability more difficult rather than more precise. Worse, it may be more discouraging for individuals who, like Americans, could come to discover that maneuvering among specialist and facilities and playing their role in some new efficiency measure put forth by health administrators is often more stressful than their illness.

REFERENCES

1. Sweeney P. *The Celtic Tiger: Ireland's Continuing Economic Miracle*. Dublin, Ireland: Oak Tree Press; 2002.
2. McKittrick D, Mallie E. *Endgame in Ireland*. Ireland: Coronet Books; 2003.
3. Cronin M. *A History of Ireland*. Hampshire, England: Palgrave Macmillan; 2003.
4. McHahon J. *Grand Opportunity: The Gaelic revival and Irish society, 1893–1910*. Syracuse, NY: Syracuse University Press; 2008.
5. Hartford J. *The Opening of University Education to Women in Ireland*. Dublin, Ireland: Irish University Press; 2008.
6. Ireland: Location, size and extent. Encyclopedia of the Nations. Retrieved from http://www.nationsenclyclopedia.com/Europe/Ireland.
7. Collins N, Cradden T. *Irish Politics Today*, 4th ed. Manchester University Press; 2008.
8. Enterprise Ireland. Ireland Economic Profile. Retrieved April 18, 2008, from http://www.enterpirse_Ireland.ie.
9. Central Statistics Office Ireland. Measuring Ireland's Progress. Retrieved April 18, 2008, from http://www.cso.ie.
10. Central Statistics Office Ireland. Measuring Ireland's Progress. Retrieved April 18, 2008, from http://www.cso.ie, 53, 76.
11. Central Statistics Office Ireland. Measuring Ireland's Progress. Retrieved April 18, 2008, from http://www.cso.ie, 89.
12. Economic and Social Research Institute Ireland. Irish Health. Retrieved April 20, 2008, from http://www.ESRI.ie.
13. Irishhealth.com. Hiring Freeze Denied. Retrieved May 31, 2008, from http://www.irishhealth.com/index/html.
14. Church & Theology in the Contemporary World. Conference Proceedings Feb. 11–12, 2002. Retrieved May 31, 2008, from http://www.bu.edu/sth/ctpi/2002.pdf.
15. Ireland Department of Health and Children. Health Statistics. Retrieved March 30, 2008, from www.dohe.ie.
16. Enterprise Ireland. April 22, 2008.
17. World Health Organization. Highlights on Health Ireland 2004. Retrieved March 30, 2008, from http://www.euro.who.int.eprise/main/WHO/Progs/CHHIRE/sum/2004 1125_2.
18. Harvey B. Evolution of health services and health policy in Ireland. Dublin: Combat Poverty Agency, 2007. Retrieved April 19, 2008, from http://cpa.ie/publications?EvolutionofHealthServices_2007.pdf.
19. Citizens Information Board. Health Services—How They Are Organized, Dublin: April 8, 2008. Retrieved April 19, 2008, from http://www.citizensinformation.ie/categories/health/health-service-agencies.
20. Harvey B. Evolution of Health Services and Health Policy in Ireland. Dublin: Combat Poverty Agency, 2007. Retrieved April 19, 2008, from http://cpa.ie/publications?EvolutionofHealthServices_2007.pdf.
21. IrishHealth.com. Retrieved May 31, 2008.
22. CIB. Hospital Services—Introduction. Dublin, 2008. Retrieved April 19, 2008, from http://www.citizensinformation.ie/categories/health/health-service-agencies.
23. Hunter N. Health Reform Gets More Confusing. IrishHealth.com, 2005. Retrieved April 21, 2008, from http://www.irishhealth.com/index/html?level=4&id8283&var=print.

24. Health Service Reform Program. Quality & fairness: a health service for you. *HSRP*, Dublin: 2003. Retrieved May 1, 2008, from http://www.healthreform.ie/publications/reprints.html.

25. Sheddon T. Pressure mounts over European working time directives. *British Medical Journal.* 2004;328:911.

26. Health Service Executive. An introduction to HSE. Retrieved April 21, 2008, from www.hse.ie.

27. Drumm B. Professor Drumm talks to Irish health. Retrieved May 31, 2008, from http://www.irishhealth.com/index/html/level=4&id=8798.

28. IrishHealth.Com. Bed shortage core of hospital crisis. *Irishhealth.com 2007*. Retrieved April 15, 2008, from http://www.healthreform.ie/publications/reprints.html.

29. Wiley MM. The Irish health system: developments in strategy, structure, funding and delivery since 1980. *Health Economics.* 2005;14:S169–S186.

30. Millar M, McKevett D. Accountability and performance measurement: an assessment of the Irish health care system. *International Review of Administrative Sciences.* 2000;66:285.

31. Organisation for Economic Co-operation and Development. Health working papers: private health insurance in Ireland, *OECD*, Dublin: 2008. Retrieved May 21, 2008, from http://oecd.org/dataoecd/55/29/29157620.pdf.

32. FÁS (Irish Training & Employment Authority). Jobseekers report, *FÁS*, Ireland: 2006. Retrieved April 18, 2008, from http://www.fas.ie.

33. HealthNews. Ireland moves forward on eHealth. *HealthNews*, January 24, 2008. Retrieved March 20, 2008, from http://www.healthnewsdirect.com/?p=243.

34. Centre for Administrative Innovation in the Euro-Mediterranean Region. Best practices in the European countries: The Republic of Ireland, *CAIMED*. Italy, 2007. Retrieved March 23, 2008, from http://www.caimed.org.

35. Permanand G. *European Pharmaceutical Regulation: The Politics of Policy Making.* Manchester, UK: Manchester University Press; 2006, pp. 1–14.

36. Health Executive Service. Transformation Program 2007–2010. HSE, Dublin: 2006. Retrieved April 26, 2008, from http://www.hse.ie.

37. Department of Health and Children. Health Information and Quality Authority (HIQA), DOHE, 2006, Dublin. Retrieved April 26, 2008, from http://www.dohe.ie.

38. Health Service Executive. The Law on Entitlement to Public Health Services, Dublin, 2005. Retrieved April 26, 2008, from http://www.hse.ie.

39. Department of Health and Children. Health Strategy: Quality and Fairness—a Health System for You. *Business 2000 Case Study*. Dublin: Woodgrange Technologies Ltd. 2005. Retrieved April 19, 2008, form http://business2000.ie/cases/cases_6th/case28.htm.

40. National Treatment Purchase Fund. Annual report of national treatment purchase plan: treating people faster. *NTPF* Dublin, 2006, 1–3. Retrieved from www.ntpf.ie/news/ntpf%20ann.Report%202006.pdf.

41. O'Halloran D. Ireland's understaffed medical sector. *IrishJobs.ie Workwise*, 21 August 2006. Retrieved April 24, 2008, from http://www.irishjobs.ie?ForumWW/WWIndividualArticle.aspx?ForumTYPEID=1936.

42. Economic & Social Research Institute. National Health and Lifestyle Survey. *ESRI*, April 28, 2008. Retrieved May 29, 2008, from www.esri.ie/news_events/latest_press_releases/national_health_andlifes/index.xml.

43. Economist. The EU treaty: what Lisbon contains: small print of a notably complicated document. *The Economist*, October 25, 2007. Retrieved April 24, 2008, from www.economist.com/world/Europe/displaystory.cfm?story_id+10024471.

44. Taylor C, Logue P. Health care workers vote for industrial action. *The Irish Times*. April 29, 2008. Retrieved April 30, 2008, from Ireland.com.

45. OECD Health Working Papers.

CHAPTER 7

Portugal

Clara E. Dismuke and Pedro Pita Barros

COUNTRY DESCRIPTION

TABLE 7-1   Portugal

Nationality	Noun: Portuguese (singular and plural) Adjective: Portuguese
Ethnic groups	Homogeneous Mediterranean stock; citizens of black African descent who immigrated to mainland during decolonization number less than 100,000; since 1990, East Europeans have entered Portugal
Religions	Roman Catholic 84.5%, other Christian 2.2%, other 0.3%, unknown 9%, none 3.9% (2001 census)
Language	Portuguese (official), Mirandese (official—but locally used)
Literacy	Definition: age 15 and over can read and write Total population: 93.3% Male: 95.5% Female: 91.3% (2003 est.)

(continues)

TABLE 7-1   Portugal (continued)

Government type	Republic; parliamentary democracy
Date of independence	1143 (Kingdom of Portugal recognized); October 5, 1910 (republic proclaimed)
Gross Domestic Product (GDP) per capita	$21,800 (2007 est.)
Unemployment rate	8% (2007 est.)
Natural hazards	Azores subject to severe earthquakes
Environment: current issues	Soil erosion; air pollution caused by industrial and vehicle emissions; water pollution, especially in coastal areas
Population	10,676,910 (July 2008 est.)
Age structure	0–14 years: 16.4% (male 912,995/female 835,715) 15–64 years: 66.2% (male 3,514,905/female 3,555,097) 65 years and over: 17.4% (male 764,443/female 1,093,755) (2008 est.)
Median age	Total: 39.1 years Male: 37 years Female: 41.3 years (2008 est.)
Population growth rate	0.305% (2008 est.)
Birth rate	10.45 births/1,000 population (2008 est.)
Death rate	10.62 deaths/1,000 population (2008 est.)
Net migration rate	3.23 migrant(s)/1,000 population (2008 est.)
Gender ratio	At birth: 1.07 male(s)/female Under 15 years: 1.09 male(s)/female 15–64 years: 0.99 male(s)/female 65 years and over: 0.7 male(s)/female Total population: 0.95 male(s)/female (2008 est.)
Infant mortality rate	Total: 4.85 deaths/1,000 live births Male: 5.31 deaths/1,000 live births Female: 4.36 deaths/1,000 live births (2008 est.)
Life expectancy at birth	Total population: 78.04 years Male: 74.78 years Female: 81.53 years (2008 est.)
Total fertility rate	1.49 children born/woman (2008 est.)
HIV/AIDS adult prevalence rate	0.4% (2001 est.)
Number of people living with HIV/AIDS	22,000 (2001 est.)
HIV/AIDS deaths	Fewer than 1,000 (2003 est.)

Central Intelligence Agency. The World Fact Book, 2008. Retrieved November 18, 2008, from https://www.cia.gov/library/publications/the-world-factbook.

History

Portugal is a European country with origins going back to the early middle ages. In the 15th and 16th centuries, it gained the status of a world power during Europe's "Age of Discovery," as it acquired a vast empire, including possessions in South America, Africa, and Asia. In the next 2 centuries, Portugal gradually lost much of its wealth and status, as the Dutch, English, and French took an increasing share of the spice and slave trades, the economic basis of its empire. Portugal's military decline began with two battles in Morocco in 1578 and Spain's abortive attempt in 1588 to conquer England, with whom Portugal has the oldest diplomatic alliance (Treaty of Windsor signed in 1386). The country was further weakened by the destruction of much of its capital city in a 1755 earthquake, occupation during the Napoleanic Wars, and the loss of its largest colony, Brazil, in 1822.

In 1910, there was a revolution that deposed the monarchy; however, the republic that emerged was not capable of resolving the country's problems. Amid corruption, repression of the Church, and the near bankruptcy of the state, a military coup in 1926 installed a dictatorship that remained until another coup in 1974. When the 48-year Salazar-Caetano dictatorship ended in a nonviolent revolution, the African Colonies of Portugal (Angola, Mozambique, Guinea-Bissau, Cape Verde, and São Tomé and Principe) became independent countries after 13 years of war. Portugal also returned Macao to China in 1999, which had been under its sovereignty since 1887.

Portugal has been a constitutional democratic republic since 1974 and is a founding member of the North Atlantic Treaty Organization, the Organisation for Economic Co-operation and Development (OECD), and the European Free Trade Area and entered the European Union (EU) in 1986. It was one of the initial members of the Euro zone within the EU.

Size and Geography

The Portuguese mainland consists of 91,900 squared kilometers, with 832 kilometers of coastline on the Atlantic Ocean and 1,215 kilometers of the Iberian Peninsula on a border with Spain as shown in Figure 7-1. The continent is divided into two distinct geographical areas by the Tagus River. The northern and central regions are rich in rivers, valleys, forests, and mountains, whereas the south is much flatter, drier, and less populated.

The climate is varied. The southern region (Algarve) often experiences very high temperatures in midsummer, whereas the north is much cooler, often receiving a great deal of rain and even snow in the mountains. This variation contributes to a wide range of natural flora, including species typical of both Western Europe and the Mediterranean.

Government or Political System

The President is elected directly by means of universal suffrage through national elections. The Parliament is made up of 230 members who are elected according to a system of proportional representation and the highest average method (Hondt method). The Prime Minister is appointed by the President on the basis of the parliamentary election results and after consultation with all political parties. The President also appoints the other members of government on the recommendation of the Prime Minister. The Prime Minister is the leader of the executive branch of government and is generally recognized as performing the day-to-day management of the country, whereas the President has important authority such as dissolving the existing government and veto power.

Macroeconomics

After experiencing its second technical recession in less than 3 years, the Portuguese economy began recovering in the first half of 2005 because of private consumption and exports. Stronger growth in Europe stimulated an increase in exports and gross domestic product (GDP) growth in 2006. The expansion became more broadly based in 2007, with investment growing as well with gross fixed capital formation going from 1.6% in 2006 to 2.5% in 2007. It is expected that growth will strengthen even more in 2009 because of increases in domestic demand. There is still a large negative output gap that should drive inflation down in 2009. It is also expected that wage increases will be moderate because of relatively high (7.9% in 2007) unemployment rates. Portugal has made a significant impact on its budget deficit with the general government financial balance by increasing the retirement age to 67 years and reducing other government expenditures and entitlement programs, including expenditures in health care services. The Organisation for Co-operation and Economic Development recommends that the government maintain its momentum in structural reforms in order to provide a basis for growth in the long run. They also recommend that Portugal continue to enhance human capital and increase competition in the domestic market in order to

FIGURE 7-1 Map of Portugal

Demographics

As of 2005, the total population was estimated to be approximately 10.57 million, representing a 5.26% increase since the mid-1990s.[2] The density of the population is 114.78 per square kilometer, which is similar to France. There has been significant legal and illegal immigration from Brazil and Eastern Europe to accompany the traditional immigration from the former African colonies. As of 2005, the legal immigrant population represented 2.61% of the resident Portuguese population, with a majority (52%) living in Lisbon, the capital. Because approximately 78% of immigrants are in the working age groups (15 to 64 years), they are having a significant impact on the economy.

Urbanization of the population has been dramatic, climbing from 25.9% of the population living in urban areas in 1970 to 55.1% of the population living in urban areas in 2004.[2] This is still below the average for the EU, which is approximately 70%.[3] The two main metropolitan areas are greater Lisbon (2.013 million in 2005) and Oporto (1.276 million in 2005). The rapid growth of suburban neighborhoods without sufficient expansion of public transportation networks is causing significant traffic problems for city centers.[4]

The median age of the population has been rising steadily from 31 in 1986 to 40 in 2005. The dependency ratio (relationship of those under 15 and over 65 years to the remaining population that composes the workforce) fell from 0.57 in 1980 to 0.49 in 2004. It is expected that the Portuguese population will continue to grow slightly but then decline after 2010. The increase in the percentage of the population over 65 years and decline in the population under 15 years is expected to result in a "double-aging" effect.[4] Females make up a little over half of the population (51.7% in 2004). The fertility rate has declined significantly over time from 2.76

help boost productivity and growth over the long term (OECD Economic Outlook 82 database).[1]

in 1970 to 1.42 in 2004. Females in Portugal also have one of the highest labor market participation rates in Europe.[5]

Using 60% of the national median equalized income as the poverty threshold, it has been estimated that 24% of the population lives in monetary poverty. These households are largely made up of single individuals over the age of 65 years and single parents with children under the age of 16 years. Geographically, it is the northern region (above 40%) and the autonomous regions of Madeira and the Azores with the highest levels of poverty. Rurality is also important, with more than 50% of individuals in rural areas considered to be living in poverty. These individuals tend to receive the bulk of their income from social transfers so that government assistance apparently has not been sufficient in pushing people above the poverty threshold.[6] Approximately 84% of the population consider themselves to be Roman Catholic, although only 19% attend Mass regularly. Women and individuals in rural areas adhere more to regular attendance.

BRIEF HISTORY OF THE HEALTHCARE SYSTEM

Pre–World War II

Portugal's healthcare system is characterized as a National Health Service (NHS), which was created in 1979 after the political reforms in 1974. Before the 18th century, health care was provided only for the poor by religious charity hospitals known as *Misericórdias*. During the 18th century, the government established a small number of teaching and public hospitals to supplement the provision of charity hospital care. In 1860, municipal doctors were appointed to provide healthcare services to the poor, and they were salaried. Public health provision began in 1901 with the establishment of a network of physicians known as medical officers who were given responsibility for public health.

Since World War II

In 1945, a law was passed to provide public maternity and child welfare services, as well as national programs for tuberculosis, leprosy, and mental health. The first social security law was passed in 1946, which changed the funding and provision of healthcare services to the Bismark model whereby employed individuals and their employers were obliged to pay into social security and sickness funds to pay for their healthcare services as well

as their dependents. Initially, this model covered only industrial workers, and then other sectors of the workforce were added in subsequent years until 1971. In that year, the right to health care by all Portuguese citizens was formally recognized, which provided the basis for policies implemented after the 1974 revolution and the establishment of the formal NHS in 1979.[7]

DESCRIPTION OF THE CURRENT HEALTHCARE SYSTEM

Portugal has an NHS system, overseen by the Ministry of Health, through a public institute created in 2007, Administração Central do Sistema de Saúde, IP; however, 16% of Portuguese citizens are also covered by a health subsystem through their employer (e.g., government employees), 10% being covered also by voluntary private health insurance, and a little less than 2% being covered by all three systems.[8] In 2005, 72.3% of healthcare expenditures were estimated to be paid for by the government.[1] There is a mix of public and private healthcare provision with a high number of physician providers operating in both systems. Many physicians, especially specialists, may work in a public facility part of the time and see patients under the NHS umbrella and then work in a private clinic where they can bill the patients privately via private health insurance, subsystem coverage, or out-of-pocket payments. Patients are also expected to provide public providers with information regarding their coverage via subsystems or private insurance so that public providers may bill for care otherwise provided to patients under NHS budgets. Figure 7-2 shows the relationship between various providers and funding bodies.

The Ministry of Health is responsible for developing health policy and overseeing and evaluating its implementation and functioning. The Minister of Health is a cabinet position that reports directly to the Prime Minister. The ministry contains a number of bodies that it administers directly and others that it regulates indirectly. The organization of the Ministry is shown in Figure 7-3.

The Ministry of Health also works closely with the Ministries of Finance, Labor, and Social Solidarity, and Science and Higher Education. The Ministry of Finance must approve the creation of new posts in the NHS whether hospital based or not. It also presents an NHS budget to be included in the general government budget annually and is approved by Parliament. The Ministry of Labor and Social Solidarity is responsible

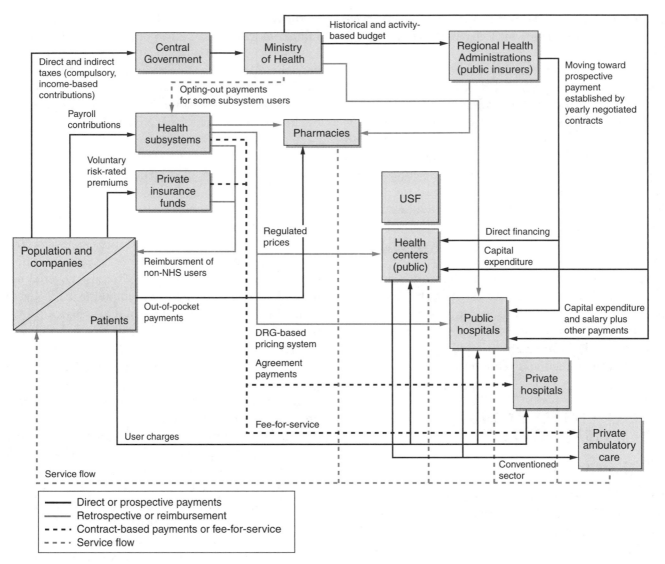

FIGURE 7-2 Health Care System in Portugal

Data from the WHO Europe Regional Office Report 2007.

for social benefits (pensions, unemployment, disability) for employees in the NHS. It also works with the Ministry of Health to address coordination between health care, long-term care, and social care services for individuals with disabilities and older persons. The Ministry of Science and Higher Education is responsible for providing undergraduate medical education and funding for basic medical research. Specialty training is a joint responsibility between the Ministry and the Portuguese Medical Association, Ordem dos Médicos.

Regional Health Authorities (RHAs) were created in 1993 with the goal to decentralize decision making in the NHS. The RHAs were to be given financial responsibility by administering a budget for a defined patient population, but in practice, the authority of the RHAs for this purpose has been limited to the area of primary

care since hospital budgets continue to be set and hospital administration appointed centrally.[4]

Facilities

Portugal had a higher number of beds per 1,000 population in 2005 (3.0) relative to the United States (2.7) but lower than the United Kingdom (3.1) and France (3.7).[1] As of 2004, Portugal had 171 hospitals, 89 public and 82 private. About half of the private hospitals are for-profit entities. Between 1970 and 1980, there was a sharp decline in hospitals owned by the charity, *Misericórdias*, which currently operates mostly rehabilitation, long-term care, and residential care facilities for older persons and the disabled. There was a significant decrease in the total number of hospitals in Portugal from 634 in

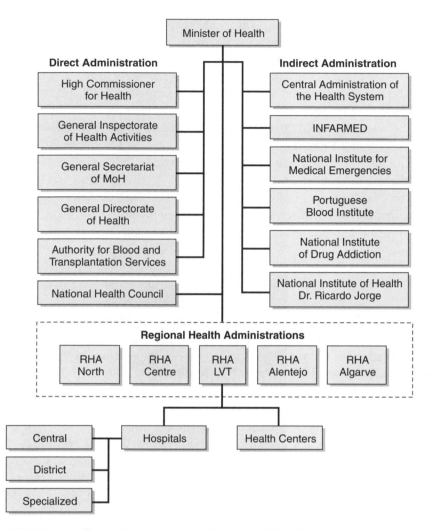

FIGURE 7-3 Organization of the Ministry of Health in Portugal
Data from the WHO Europe Regional Office Report 2007.

1970 to 171 in 2004.[4] In 2004, there were 22,007 acute-care beds, 1,000 in psychiatric hospitals, and 851 in long-term care hospitals.[9]

Secondary and tertiary care is mainly provided in hospitals. Hospitals in Portugal are classified according to the type and range of services they provide. Central hospitals provide highly specialized services with advanced technology and specialist human resources. Specialty hospitals provide different types of specialty services, such as cancer hospitals and maternity hospitals. District hospitals are located in the main administrative districts and provide a smaller range of specialty services than central hospitals. District Level One hospitals only provide internal medicine, surgery, and one or two other basic specialties. Since the mid-1990s, there have been major improvements in existing hospitals, and seven new hospitals were built.

Primary care is mostly provided through a large network of primary care centers (PCCs). The first point of contact within the NHS is the general practitioner (GP) or family doctor in a PCC. Each PCC covers an average of 28,000 people, but coverage can range from 5,000 to 100,000 people. It is estimated that about 750,000 people (about 7.5% of the total population) may lack formal enrollment in a PCC.

Capital investments in the Portuguese NHS are funded by the Ministry of Health and other special programs. The 2007 budget planned an expenditure of approximately €40 million (U.S. $61,974,962). Investments were below the budgeted amounts in 2004 and 2005 with about 45% co-financed by the EU.

One of the government's objectives is to improve the NHS's capacity to provide services while increasing the value for the money. Private entities are being encouraged to build, maintain, and operate new facilities under a similar model used in the United Kingdom, known as Public Private Partnerships (PPPs). This transfers the financial risk from the government to the private sector. Although the intention is to extend this capacity to all types of healthcare facilities, the initial priority is for hospitals. Between 2003 and 2006, four hospital projects were started under PPPs. The formal procedures of selecting the partner take a long time. Seven PPPs are planned for the near future, including both replacement of existing facilities and building of new hospital facilities. The first two PPP projects started operations in April 2007, one a rehabilitation hospital, and the NHS call center.

Workforce

There has been a consistent increase in the number of practicing physicians (per thousand individuals) in Portugal since 1990, which followed a significant jump from 0.95 in 1970 to 2.83 in 1990. By 2005, the number of physicians was 3.4 per 1,000, which is slightly above the EU average of 3.2.[3] Portugal's physician ratio is similar to France (3.4) and above both the United Kingdom (2.4) and the United States (2.4). Future relative ratios may change because in 2005 there were 20.8 medical school graduates per 1,000 practicing physicians, which is higher than France (17.5 in 2004) but lower than the United Kingdom (35.8) and the United States (26.5 in 2004).[1]

According to the Portuguese Medical Association (Ordem dos Médicos), the number of foreign trained physicians is about 10% of the total of practicing physicians. There was an increase from 2,987 in 2003 to 3,564 in 2007. Most are of European origin (largely from Spain), followed by Brazil (485), and 456 from other Portuguese-speaking African countries; however, the greatest increase has been from non-EU countries, with an increase from 57 in 2003 to 210 by the end of 2006. There is also an emigration of Portuguese students to foreign medical schools, with about 600 leaving Portugal in 2006.[4]

The number of certified nurses (per 1,000 individuals) experienced a considerable climb between 1970 (0.97) and 1980 (2.24); however, by 2005, nursing resources in Portugal were much lower (4.6 per thousand) than the EU average (7.0 per thousand).[3] This is also lower relative to France (7.7), the United Kingdom (9.1), and the United States (7.9); however, this problem may be alleviated in the future, as nursing graduates per 1,000 practicing nurses in 2005 was higher at 52.4 relative to France (44.6) and the United Kingdom (38.5).[1]

In 2005, the Ministry of Health was the second largest employer in the public sector, with 142,777 employees. Between 1990 and 2004, the number of workers in the NHS increased 30.6%.[1] According to the Portuguese Medical Association (Ordem dos Médicos), there were 34,225 medical doctors on the Portuguese mainland in 2004, and 23,389 of these were employed by the NHS in hospitals and PCCs. GPs and family doctors comprised 29.5% (lower than the EU average), whereas hospital-based specialists made up 42.5% of physicians, and public health medical doctors accounted for 2% of total practicing physicians.[10] Approximately 74% of nurses work in central and district hospitals, whereas about 20% work in primary care and 3% in psychiatric care services. The PCCs employ about 30,000 people (25% of physicians and 20% of nurses). There is an average of 80 health professionals per PCC, although this can range from 1 physician to 200 healthcare professionals in a PCC. In 2004, there were 6,437 GPs in PCCs and 700 specialists.[11]

Geographically, the ratio of physician to 1,000 individuals ranges from 0.689 in the North to 0.750 in the interior Alentejo region, as shown in Figures 7-4 and 7-5.

Hospital-based physicians ranged from 0.967 in Alentejo to 1.884 in Lisbon. Alentejo's higher physician ratio is due to non–hospital-based physicians. The ratio of GPs ranged from 0.041 in the southern coastal Algarve region to 0.078 in Lisbon, with hospital-based GPs ranging from 0.235 in Alentejo to 0.546 in Lisbon. Alentejo also has the highest ratio of nurses at 1.111 per 1,000, and Lisbon has the lowest ratio at 0.605 per 1,000; however, Lisbon has the highest ratio of hospital-based nurses at 3.151 per 1,000, and the lowest ratio is in the North at 2.869.[10]

A number of things have affected and will affect future human resources in health care. Most NHS staff members are civil servants, and all new posts have to be approved by the Ministry of Finance; however, an increasing number of staff are being hired under individual contracts without the same rights as those under the traditional civil status rules. In 1977, a clause was established to limit the number of places in medical and nursing schools. The extreme shortage of nurses, imbalance of primary care and specialist physicians, and retirement of a significant number of physicians led to two resolutions. The first in 1998 outlined potential solutions: (1) founding of health sciences departments in existing

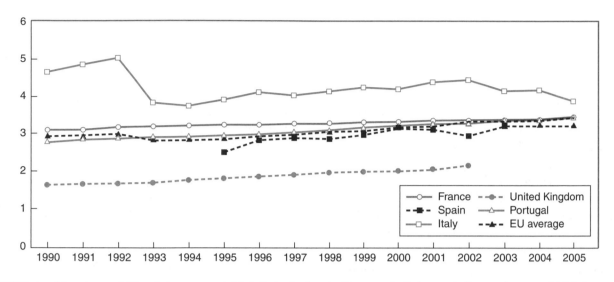

FIGURE 7-4 Number of Physicians per 1000 Population in Portugal, Selected Countries, and EU Average, 1990 to 2005

Data from the WHO Europe Regional Office Report 2007.

universities, (2) creation of new graduate programs in medicine in the northern region of the country, (3) improvement of existing conditions for the current graduates in medicine and dentistry, (4) reorganization of the nursing and technological public schools network, (5) a gradual increase in the number of student admissions, and (6) creation of various partnerships between the Ministry of Health and the Ministry of Science and Graduate Education.

The result of the 1998 resolution was the creation of two new medical schools (Minho in the North and Beira Interior in Alentejo) and several private institutions offering degrees in nursing and paramedic training.[4]

The second resolution, in December 2001, presented a detailed needs assessment taking into account EU averages as well as regional imbalances within Portugal. The chronic understaffing of nurses in primary and long-term care was also addressed and set the European

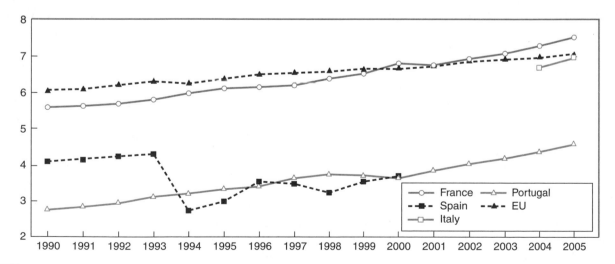

FIGURE 7-5 Number of Nurses per 1000 Population in Portugal, Selected Countries, and EU Average, 1990 to 2005

Data from the WHO Europe Regional Office Report 2007.

averages as the target for NHS staffing levels by the year 2010.

Although there is a shortage of GPs, there is also a shortage of internship opportunities so that there was a decrease of 1.1% in the number of physicians working for the NHS between 2004 and 2006. This problem has caused the NHS to actively recruit foreign physicians, especially from neighboring Spain.

Medical training in Portugal currently takes place in seven medical schools. The five oldest schools follow the same 5-year curriculum. The two newest schools are developing innovative programs that include problem-oriented lectures, promotion of training closer to communities, and less hospital-focused, more interdisciplinary integration. After graduation, all graduates must do an 18-month internship with 6 months in general practice and 6 months in public health training and a year in hospital-based training. After the completion of 18 months, students are conferred physician status and are allowed to practice general medicine without supervision; however, for those who wish to have a career in the NHS, they must have further specialization training. The duration of training for the different specialties is 4 to 6 years for hospital specialties, 3 years for general practice/family medicine, and 4 years for public health medicine (which includes a 1-year postgraduate public health course).

To become a nursing student, individuals must have completed 12 years of schooling. The course lasts 4 years so that there are no nursing auxiliaries or other types of nursing programs in Portugal. After 4 years, nurses can specialize by pursuing postgraduate training in midwifery, pediatrics, psychiatric, and community nursing.[4]

Dental professionals in Portugal have increased at a steady rate since the early 1990s, and there were 0.58 per 1,000 individuals in 2005, very close to the average for the EU (0.6). Several private dental schools have opened since the mid-1990s to supplement the existing public schools of dental medicine. The course of dentistry was changed from 6 years to 10 semesters. Most dentists work in the private sector because there is little dental coverage in the NHS.[3]

The ratio of pharmacists per thousand individuals (0.9) has increased in recent decades and is currently slightly above the EU average of 0.7. The distribution of pharmacies on the continent is highly regulated.[12] The Ministry of Health decides whether there is a need for a new pharmacy in a residential area. There must be proof of at least 4,000 new clients and no other pharmacy within 200 meters of the proposed site. Established

pharmacies thus have substantial monopoly power in the limited market area in which they operate. Since December 2006, there has been the possibility of a limited service within hospitals for dispensing pharmaceuticals (only those with no co-insurance payment) to outpatients. Similarly, health centers are only allowed to dispense vaccinations that do not have any co-insurance payment. Other vaccines have to be purchased in private pharmacies.[4]

The rules for ownership and opening of a pharmacy were changed in 2007. Previously restricted to pharmacists, ownership is now basically open to others; however, no individual entrepreneur or company can hold more than four pharmacies, and distance and population density criteria are still in place for new locations.

Recently, regulations allowing for Internet sales and home delivery of pharmaceutical products have been enacted by the government. Only pharmacies operating a physical facility can sell through the internet. Home delivery can only be performed by companies that already have experience in delivering pharmaceutical products to retail outlets (pharmacies and over-the-counter sales points).

Technology and Equipment

A separate central investment plan determines capital outlays within the NHS. Most of the investment is provided internally by the Portuguese state budget through the Central Administration's Investment and Development Plan. A list of all equipment was made in 1998,[13] but this has not been updated. Portugal does not have a tradition of health technology assessment. Most big-ticket technologies (about 67%) are located in the private sector. Hospitals contract with the private institutions for use of the technology.

National and regional ratios for major medical technologies for diagnostic imaging, including computerized tomography and magnetic resonance imaging, were calculated in 1998 by the Ministry of Health. Since then, growth of diagnostic technology services has been strong, especially in the Lisbon area. At the end of 2005, there were four positron emission tomography scanners on the continent.[14] In 2005, Portugal had fewer magnetic resonance imaging units per million people than the United Kingdom (5.4), France (4.7) and the United States (26.6); however, Portugal had a higher number of computerized tomography scanners with 26.2 per thousand, as compared with France (9.8) and the United Kingdom (7.5).[1]

EVALUATION OF THE HEALTHCARE SYSTEM

Cost

General Expenditures and Financing

The NHS is mainly financed out of general tax revenues, especially indirect taxes that account for approximately 60% of total tax revenue. Income tax comprises about 39% of tax revenue. A budget for the NHS is set annually by the government. Generally actual expenditures exceed the budget by a wide margin requiring a supplementary budget be approved. In addition to government money, the NHS gets revenue from hospital charges for special services such as private rooms, payments from beneficiaries from subsystems, private insurance, renting of space and equipment, investment income, donations, fines, and some flat-rate admission charges. These revenues account for approximately 13.4% of the overall public hospital budget. Out-of-pocket payments in Portugal are among the highest in Europe. Twenty-three percent of all healthcare costs in 2004 were out of pocket.[4] It has been shown that the theoretically progressive, redistributive income tax system in Portugal is in fact slightly regressive due to the high out-of-pocket spending on health care, as well as high indirect taxes.[15] Indirect taxes on goods and services accounted for 35.2% of total government revenue, whereas taxes on income and profits represented 23.8% of total government revenue in 2006. Households in the highest income brackets get a higher percentage of tax refunds (27%) than the lowest (6%). The burden of health expenditures thus falls relatively more on low-income households.[4,16] Total healthcare expenditures in Portugal rose steadily from 3% in 1970 to 10.2% of the GDP in 2005, above the EU average (9%). Portugal currently spends more than France and the United Kingdom and less than the United States at 15.3% of GDP.[1] Portugal has not been able to contain costs as successfully as other European countries. One reason may be due to the political reluctance to impose strict cost-control measures after it was assumed that investment was needed to build up new facilities and promote the expansion of NHS coverage.[17] Another contributing factor may be the government's willingness to reinforce budgets that have been underfunded when hospitals overspend. Between 1997 and 2006, there were five government budget reinforcements or debt regularization exceptional measures. This practice may have undermined the credibility of budgets as a management tool as hospitals' debts to suppli-

ers, especially pharmaceutical companies, climbed as both parties understood that budgets were not rigid.[4] The years 2005 to 2007 proved to be somewhat different, as overall public budgets for health care remained under tight control.

Hospitals

Since 2003 hospital reimbursement has evolved to a contract-based approach. In that same year, about half the hospitals were given corporate-like status (public companies similar to the hospital trusts in the United Kingdom). This approach has now been extended to public hospitals whereby contracts are set for 1 year and stipulate the overall payment and expected production level of the hospitals by broadly defined lines of activity.[4]

Hospital budgets are calculated and allocated by the Ministry of Health through the Administração Central do Sistema de Saúde, which is the management and financing arm of the ministry. Currently public hospitals are allocated global budgets based on contracts. These contracts are based partially on the previous year's funding adjusted for inflation and a diagnosis-related group (DRG) case mix similar to the DRG system traditionally used to reimburse hospitals under Medicare in the United States. The need to collect information for DRG grouping of each inpatient stay has led to vastly improved information systems in hospitals.

Budget setting is also adjusted for hospital peer groupings whereby a small set of benchmark hospitals is determined, and the likelihood that a particular hospital should be in the same group with other hospitals is calculated (e.g., a medium-sized hospital may have a probability of 30% of being like a small benchmark hospital and a 70% chance of being like a large benchmark hospital). This method was developed by Vertrees and Manton.[18] Nonadjusted hospital outpatient volume is also taken into consideration, and an attempt to adjust for ambulatory surgery classifications is under way.[4]

Health Centers

Health centers do not yet have financial or administrative autonomy. The Ministry of Health allocates funds to the RHA, which then funds the activities of the health centers. The health centers receive a small budget for rent, utilities, and so forth based on historical costs, and all other patient care costs are paid directly by the subregional coordination level. An experiment conducted in the Lisbon and Vale do Tejo RHA in 2000 to allocate global budgets to health centers based on historical costs, activity-adjusted weighted production units, and number of residents was not replicated further. Another proposal in 2003 to allow private management of PCCs also was not successful; however, in 2006, a new policy was implemented to allow multidisciplinary teams to be reimbursed partially based on the dimension of the list of patients, house calls, number of working hours, and annual contracting for specific surveillance activities for high-risk patients. These incentives appear to have the potential to at least reduce the costs of visits and prescribed medications.[19]

Physician Payment

All NHS physicians are salaried government employees. The fixed salary is established according to professional category and tenure without any adjustment for productivity. Physicians are classified as full-time but not exclusive (35 hours per week), extended full-time with exclusive NHS employment (42 hours per week with no private practice allowed), and part-time (this is not allowed for physician administrators). There are no data on the distribution by categories and no incentives currently for physicians to locate in rural areas or the interior of the country. Since 2002, individual labor contracts have been allowed for new physicians, but it is not known how many physicians have opted for these contracts. In 2006, NHS physician salaries ranged from €1769.00 (US$2,741) per month for interns to €5,013.50 (US$7,768) per month for the highest paid specialists. It is permitted to pay physicians for overtime, particularly to staff emergency departments.

A new scheme for paying GPs in PCCs was introduced in 1998/1999 to reimburse these physicians based on capitation and professional performance. It is estimated that about 12% of these physicians enrolled. This agreement has a basic salary component base adjusted for the population profile, a fee-for-service payment for some services such as home visits and minor surgery, and a provision for preventive care and services to pregnant women and postnatal care. Some problems were encountered with the design, and it was restructured in 2006 in legislation known as Family Health Units, where incentives are based on performance of the teams as well as the physicians.[19] It is estimated that about half of physicians also engage in private practice where prices have been traditionally set by the Portuguese Medical Association (Ordem dos Médicos). This was challenged by the Competition Authority, and the Medical Association changed it.

Nurses

Nurses are also classified as state employees in the NHS and are paid based on a civil service pay scale based on the professional category and time of service, and unrelated to productivity. They can be classified as full-time (35 hours per week), part-time (20 to 24 hours per week), or extended full-time (42 hours per week). The number of extended full-time nurses is capped at the institution at 30% of total nursing staff. There is a shortage of nursing personnel in Portugal as in the United States and many other countries.

Dentists

Except for a very few dentists and stomotologists working in the NHS, dentists work in private practice and are reimbursed either by patients directly or via their subsystems or private insurance. Dentists determine their own fees and are required to post a list of fees publicly for the menu of services they provide.

Pharmacists working in an NHS institution (mostly hospitals) are paid by the institution directly. Those in retail pharmacies are reimbursed on a combination of NHS per prescription and out-of-pocket, subsystem, or private insurance from patients. Their reimbursement for prescribed drugs from any source is capped. Prices and co-insurance are listed on the drug packaging for the different categories of patients and payers. Pharmacists are reimbursed via the National Association of Pharmacies, which collects monies owed from the RHA for primary care prescriptions.

One of the perverse incentives of this scheme is the benefits from dispensing more expensive drugs. Over-the-counter drugs yield the highest profits, as these fees are free to be set by the pharmacy. Ownership of pharmacies has been strictly regulated, making them monopolies in the markets in which they operate. There is proposed legislation to change the laws regulating pharmacy ownership, which may encourage more competition in the future.

Other Healthcare Personnel

Healthcare technicians and other personnel working in the NHS are paid salaries directly by their institutions and are not performance based. Private sector personnel are paid on contracts and fee-for-service regardless of payers, NHS, subsystem, private insurance, or out-of-pocket by the patient.

Management Boards

Management of NHS institutions is appointed and paid by the Ministry of Health. Managers receive a fixed salary, which is unrelated to the performance of their institution. There is presently a debate to change this in the future especially as institutions are converted to public company status.[4] Legislation enacted in February 2008 created a framework to evaluate the performance of management boards of NHS hospitals, and a pilot evaluation was carried out during 2008.

Pharmaceuticals

Portugal's pharmaceutical expenditure (excluding hospitals) was approximately 21.9% of total expenditures, which is much higher than France (16.4%) and the United States (12.4%). In 1995, a new policy was introduced to allow prescriptions issued in the private sector to be reimbursed by the NHS, as well as those in the public sector, to reduce duplication. Since 1993, all pharmaceuticals must be approved by the National Institute of Pharmacy and Medicinal Products (INFARMED) in order to be reimbursed by the NHS. INFARMED requires a demonstration of effectiveness (issued guidelines in 1999), as well as efficacy. Approximately 100 products have been removed from the approved NHS list since 1999.[4]

INFARMED also sets the co-payments on pharmaceuticals based on age, income, and illness of the individual. There have been three categories of NHS co-insurance since 1992. Pensioners with a maximum annual income of up to 14 times the national minimum monthly wage are eligible for a lower level of co-insurance payments.

Pharmaceuticals needed by individuals considered vulnerable populations are fully covered under the NHS (e.g., drugs to treat diabetics, epilepsy, Parkinson's, neoplasms, and immunomodulators). The NHS percentages are lower for generics than for brand-name drugs for pensioners, which may limit incentives to switch from brand names to lower cost generics in this group of undoubtedly heavy users of pharmaceuticals.

The percentages of pharmaceuticals reimbursed by the NHS are shown in Table 7-2.

Hospitals are subject to pharmaceutical formularies, but physicians are not restricted to formularies for prescribing. A number of policies have been established to attempt to control pharmaceutical costs. A budget cap was introduced in 1997 by voluntary agreement between the government and the pharmaceutical industry

TABLE 7-2 NHS Co-Insurance (Percentage Paid by the NHS)

Category	Regular Individual Brand or Generic	Eligible Pensioner Brand Drugs	Eligible Pensioner Generic Drugs
A	95%	100%	100%
B	69%	84%	79%
C	37%	52%	47%
D	20%	35%	30%

From Portugal NHS 2007.

whereby the industry agreed to pay back to the NHS 64.3% if the industry revenue exceeded 4% above 1996 levels; however, if revenue exceeded 11% more than 1996, the industry did not have to share that portion above 11% with the NHS. This actually created a perverse incentive to exceed the limit even further so that by the middle of the first year of implementation, growth in pharmaceutical expenditures had attained 16% growth over 1996.

Because all pharmaceuticals distributed through private pharmacies are prepackaged (unlike the United States where unidose is common), the dimensions of prepackaged medicines were extensively revised in 2001 and 2002. Smaller packages were created for short-term and intensive medicines and larger ones for pharmaceuticals used by patients with chronic illnesses.

Since 1991, the prices of pharmaceuticals in Portugal have been negotiated between the government and pharmaceutical companies based on reference pricing. Pharmaceuticals with generic substitutes are grouped according to their active ingredients, and a reference price is set for the group based on the average, or lower priced, pharmaceutical in the group. The reference price for a particular drug was then set at the highest price of the generics. For brand names under patent protection, the government expected a significant discount based on the experience of the drug in other countries. The system has been adjusted periodically and can be adjusted every 3 months.[20] In March 2007, the government passed a new ruling on establishing maximums, rather than fixed prices, for medicines. According to the new ruling, pharmaceutical products sold in Portugal cannot have a higher price than the average of four reference countries' prices (Spain, France, Italy, and Greece). Under the old regulation, the price in the Portuguese market could not be higher than the minimum price on the same product in three countries (Spain, France, and Italy).

Generics

Perhaps the most important cost-reducing initiative has been to increase the use of generics. Accompanying various public information campaigns in 2000, the price of generics were lowered 20% to 35% below the original price (until 2007). The reimbursement rate by the NHS was also increased by 10% to stimulate demand by patients for generics. A law was passed in 2001 requiring physicians to prescribe using the international common designation, or generic name, but allowing them to add the brand name as well. In 2002, pharmacists were allowed to substitute a generic for a brand name prescribed by the physician if the physician signed to authorize such a substitution. By February 2007, generics represented about 17% of all reimbursed pharmaceuticals.[21]

Capital

Capital investments in the NHS are funded by the Ministry of Health and some by special programs. The government budget for 2007 was estimated to spend about 40 million euros (U.S. $62,010,162) on the national health program. Investments under PIDDAC were about 138 million euros (U.S. $213,916,858) in 2004 and 92 million euros (U.S. $142,624,327) in 2005, below the budgeted amounts and included a significant component (about 45%) of co-financing from the EU.

Quality

As of 2005, Portugal has a higher overall life expectancy at birth (78.2) than the United States (77.8 in 2004), but lower than France (80.3) and the United Kingdom (79.0). Females have an even higher life expectancy (81.4) than the United Kingdom (81.1), but males in Portugal have a lower life expectancy at birth (74.9) than the United States with 75.2 in 2004.[1] A recent study by Nolte and McKee[20] compared Portugal, along with other OECD countries, on one important measure of overall health system performance, "amenable mortality." Amenable mortality is death that can be averted by the presence of effective health care.

Portugal has performed extremely well in the area of infant mortality, with rates decreasing sharply over the last 2 decades from 17 to 5 per 1,000 between 1985 and 2002. This is the most important reason for the sustainable increase in life expectancy. In 2005, Portugal had a lower infant mortality rate (3.6 per 1,000) than the United Kingdom (5.1) and the United States (6.8 per 1,000) in 2004.[1] Improvements in health have also been the result of increases in child preventive care, use of new technologies, and changes in nutritional habits.[22] The readmission rate in 30 days (indicating premature discharge) fell from 9.0% in 2004 to 8.5% in 2006. Evidence about patient satisfaction is mixed, with lower socioeconomic groups being more satisfied, and a greater satisfaction with services provided in the private sector.[23,24]

Human resources in Portugal have historically been characterized by a higher emphasis on specialist care and a scarcity of nurses relative to other countries. Recent policies have sought to correct this imbalance, especially to improve the ratios of GPs to specialists and nurses to physicians. Consults have increased faster than emergency department episodes, which represents an improvement in resource allocation. Another important measure, waiting lists, indicates that the number of patients on waiting lists decreased from 241,425 in 2005 to 225,409 in 2006. The median waiting time for interventions dropped from 8.6 months in 2005 to 6.9 months in 2006.[4]

Access

All Portuguese residents have access to health care provided by the NHS. The NHS is universal and almost free (according to the Portuguese constitution), although co-payments have been increasing over time, and co-insurance is higher for pharmaceutical products. In addition, approximately a quarter of the population has additional coverage through a subsystem or private insurance plan.

Residents of Portugal have certain stated rights and obligations according to a patient charter (Carta dos Direitos e Deveres dos Doentes) from 1997: (1) the right of the patient to be informed of his or her health status, and to a second opinion; (2) the right of the patient to accept or refuse any procedure, either for treatment, research, or teaching purposes; (3) the right of the patient to the privacy of his or her own records and access to the clinical data regarding his or her treatment and clinical history; (4) the patient's responsibility to look after his or her own health status and to provide all necessary information to healthcare personnel in order to be provided with the most appropriate treatment; (5) the patient's obligations to follow all the healthcare delivery system's rules; and (6) the patient's duty to actively avoid any unnecessary expense under the NHS. There have not yet been any studies assessing the effectiveness of the charter's implementation.[25]

Patients are also entitled to payment by the NHS for care provided outside of Portugal with previous medical approval from a NHS physician. Recently, the Ministry of Health increased cooperation with Spain to allow births to women living close to the border that occur in Spain to be reimbursed by the Portuguese NHS. EU regulations state that all citizens have the right to be treated in other countries for emergencies. A Portuguese resident must go through a long and complicated process to get an authorization for services not provided in Portugal. It is then the hospital, where the certifying physicians are based, that is responsible for reimbursing the care out of their budgets.

The NHS mostly provides direct acute hospital care, general practice, and mother and child care services. Theoretically, there are no services excluded from the NHS except dental service. Specialist and dental consultations, diagnostic services, renal dialysis, and physiotherapy treatments are more commonly provided in the private sector. Diagnostic services, renal dialysis, and physiotherapy treatments are usually done based on contractual agreements and reimbursed by the NHS. Most dental consults and many specialist consults in private ambulatory settings are paid for out of pocket. In 2006, about 92% of dental visits and 60% of specialty consults occurred in the private sector. In the public sector, the family physician does act as a gatekeeper to access to specialized care provided in the hospitals. In 2005, Portugal was below the EU average of 6.8 visits per year per person, with only 3.8 visits per year per person. The range of services provided by the PCCs are (1) general medical care for the adult population, (2) pediatric care, (3) women's health, (4) family planning and perinatal care, (5) first aid, (6) certification of incapacity to work, (7) home visits, and (8) preventive services including immunization and screening for breast and cervical cancer and other preventable diseases.

Patients must register with a GP and can choose among the available clinicians within a geographical area. GPs work with a system of patient lists containing an average of 1,500 patients per GP. Individuals are free to change their GP if they request in writing and explain their reasons to the RHA board. It is estimated that 750,000 Portuguese citizens are without a GP.

Portugal has one of the highest poverty rates in the EU. Poorer and geographically isolated people have less access to healthcare services because more services are concentrated in the more populated and urban areas.

The 2006 Spring Report found that 25% of first consults occurred in hospitals and 20.7% in PCCs. A higher proportion of first consultations is seen as an indicator of better access.

Mental Health

Mental health services have change substantially since 1963. The current provision of mental health services is organized around certain principles: The referral model is that of community care. Local mental health services are the basis of the system, in conjunction with PCCs and hospitals. When local mental health services cannot be provided, they are organized regionally. The mental health teams are multidisciplinary and serve a population of approximately 80,000. Ambulatory services are based in PCCs, and inpatient admissions and emergencies are treated in hospitals. Care for children and adolescents is provided by specific teams at the local level. Social rehabilitation is carried out in conjunction with the state health sector, social security, and employment departments. Psychiatric hospitals support the local health teams, provide specialized inpatient care, and provide residential services for patients without any family or social support systems.[4]

Dental Care

Because of the lack of dental professionals in the NHS, the government has increased financing for oral care projects aimed at school populations. Funding increased from 3 million euros (U.S. $4,652,136) in 2004 to 5 million euros (U.S. $7,753,503) in 2007. This investment appears to have increased the percentage of children without tooth decay from 33% in 2000 to 51% in 2006.[4]

Complementary and Alternative Medicine

It is estimated that as many as 2 million people regularly seek alternative modes of medicine approved by the World Health Organization, such as acupuncture, homeopathy, osteopathy, naturopathy, phitotherapy, and quiropraxy. The Ministry of Health began a project in 2006 to regulate these six areas. Portugal would be the first European country with an extensive regulation of this area.[4]

CURRENT AND EMERGING ISSUES AND CHALLENGES

At the beginning of the 21st century, the healthcare system in Portugal continues to face many problems. There are not enough public ambulatory services, resulting in high use of hospital emergency departments. There are long waiting lists for surgical procedures. The evidence is mixed regarding satisfaction of consumers and professionals with public services (particularly with waiting lists and emergency departments). Health expenditures are increasing, and control is difficult. Demand is increasing for health care from vulnerable groups. Because of traffic accidents and lifestyle-related diseases, reducing mortality further presents challenges.

According to Oliveira and Pinto,[21] disagreements between the two major political parties slow reform. The Social Democrats see the private sector as competing with the public sector, whereas the Socialists see it as a complementary sector. Social Democrats want centralized contracting, and Socialists want decentralized contracting. The Social Democrats want a fast pace in change, and the Socialists want slow change with negotiations among stakeholders.

This raises the important question as to whether meeting the budget (done for the first time in 2006) is a new trend or a short-lived phenomenon. Given the government deficit targets set by the EU for Portugal, this trend would be extremely good news. It may be that the recent reforms of private management of public health institutions, flexible labor contracts, generic drug promotion, increased numbers of GPs and nurses relative to specialists, and hospital payment based on performance have put Portugal on the path to a much more efficient system. It remains to be seen what the effect on health outcomes will be.

REFERENCES

1. OECD. *OECD health data* [online database]. Available in Paris; Organisation for Economic Co-operation and Development; 2007. Accessed April 28, 2008, from http://www.oecd.org.
2. INE. *Estimativas de População Residente, Portugal, NUTS II, NUTS IIIe Municípios [Estimates for the population living in Portugal by geographical unit].* Lisbon: National Statistics Institute; 2007.
3. WHO Regional Office for Europe. *European Health for All.* database [offline database]. Copenhagen: WHO Regional Office for Europe; 2007.
4. Barros PP, Simões JA. Portugal: health system review. In Allin S, Mossialos E, eds. *Health Systems in Transition.* Geneva: World Health Organization; 2007.
5. Cardoso AR. Women at work and economic development: who's pushing what? *Review of Radical Political Economics.* 1996;28:1–34.
6. Rodrigues A, Marques FB, Ferreira PL, Raposo PL. *Estudo do Sector das Farmácias em Portugal [Study on the Pharmacy Sector in Portugal].* Coimbra: Centre for the Study and Research in Health of the University of Coimbra (Report to the Ordem dos Farmacêuticos); 2007.
7. Simões J. *Retrato Politico Da Saúde—Dependência do Percurso Einovação em Saúde: Da Ideologia ao Desempenho [Political Portrait of Health—Path Dependency and Innovation in Health: From Ideology to Performance].* Coimbra: Livraria Almedina; 2004.
8. Portuguese National Institute of Health. *4th National Health Survey—2005/2006.* Lisbon: National Institute of Health, Dr. Ricardo Jorge; 2007.
9. Oliveira M. *Deinstitutionalization of Mental Health Care in Portugal: Barriers and Opportunities.* Report prepared for the European Mental Health Economics Network II; 2006.
10. General Directorate of Health. *National Health Plan Indicators* [in Portuguese]. Lisbon: General Directorate of Health, 2005. Retrieved April 28, 2008, from http://www.acs.min-saude.pt/acs/resources/metaspns/main.html.
11. IGIF. *Estatísticas do Movimento Assistencial [Health Care Deliverystatistics].* Lisbon: Institute for Financial Management and Informatics; 2005.
12. Portuguese Ministry of Health. *Response from Portugal to the Commission Consultation on Community Action on Health Services.* Lisbon, Ministry of Health; 2007. Retrieved April 28, 2008, from http://ec.europa.eu/health/ph_overview/co_operation/mobility/docs/health_services_co276.pdf.
13. Wagstaff A, et al. Equity in the finance of health care; some further international comparisons. *Journal of Health Economics.* 1999;18:263–290.
14. Simões JA, Barros PP, Pereira J, eds. *A Sustentabilidade Financeira do Serviço Nacional de Saúde.* Lisboa: Ministério da Saúde; 2008.
15. Dixon A, Mossialos E. Has the Portuguese NHS achieved its objectives of equity and efficiency? *International Social Security Review.* 2000;53(4):49–78.
16. Vertrees JC, Manton KG. A multivariate approach for classifying hospitals and computing blended payment rates. *Medical Care.* 1986;24:283–300.
17. Gouveia M, Silva S, Oliveira P, Pinto LM. *Análise dos Custos dos Centros de Saúde e do Regime Remuneratório Experimental [Analysis on the Costs of Primary Care Centres and Experimental Remuneratory Regime].* Lisbon: Unidade de Missão dos Cuidados de Saúde Primários (Report to the Primary Care Task Force); 2006. Retrieved April 28, 2008, from http://www.min-saude.pt/portal/conteudos/a+saude+em+portugal/publicacoes/estudos/cahsa.htm).
18. Portela C, Pinto M. *Contribuição do Sistema de Preços de Referência Para a Concorrência no Mercado Farmacêutico em*

Portugal [Reference Pricing as a Competition Trigger on the Portuguese Pharmaceutical Market]. Speech.

19. INFARMED. *Mercado de Medicamentos Genéricos [The Market for Generics]*. Lisbon: National Pharmacy and Medicines Institute; 2007.

20. Nolte E, McKee M. Measuring the health of nations: updating an earlier analysis. *Health Affairs*. 2008;27(1):58–71.

21. Oliveira M, Pinto C. Health care reform in Portugal: an evaluation of the NHS experience. *Health Economics*. 2005;14:S203–S220.

22. OPSS (Portuguese Health System Observatory). *Um Ano de Governação em Saúde: Sentidos e Significados [A Year of Government in Health: Directions and Interpretation]*. Coimbra: Centre for the Study and Research in Health of the University of Coimbra; 2006. Retrieved April 28, 2008, from http://www.observaport.org/NR/rdonlyres/ebkvphcy 4nxyspcp3whgfag73gynjmrmg7dqpshwvh22y4plc2hwy7yr x7dw6axt2ssimbhwgxxczp/RP_2006.pdf.

23. MoH and Ministry of Labour and Social Solidarity. *Health Care and Long-Term Care*. Brussels, European Commission Preliminary report, Social Protection Committee, European Commission. 2006. Retrieved April 28, 2008, from http://ec.europa.eu/employment_social/social_protection/ docs/hc_ltc2005_pt_en.pdf.

24. Santana P. Ageing in Portugal: regional inequities in health and health care. *Social Science and Medicine*. 2000;50: 1025–1036.

25. Barros PP. Challenges ahead for Portugal: the health sector. *The Portuguese Economy*. Lisbon: Fundação Calouste Gulbenkian, in press.

CHAPTER 8

Germany

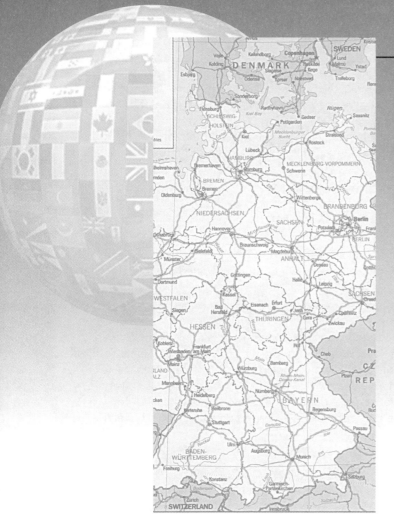

Katherine H. Leith, Astrid Knott,
Alexander G. Mayer, and
Jörg Westermann

COUNTRY DESCRIPTION

TABLE 8-1 Germany

Nationality	Noun: German(s)
	Adjective: German
Ethnic groups	German 91.5%, Turkish 2.4%, other 6.1% (made up largely of Greek, Italian, Polish, Russian, Serbo-Croatian, and Spanish)
Religions	Protestant 34%, Roman Catholic 34%, Muslim 3.7%, unaffiliated or other 28.3%
Language	German
Literacy	Definition: age 15 and over can read and write
	Total population: 99%
	Male: 99%
	Female: 99% (2003 est.)
Government type	Federal republic

(continues)

TABLE 8-1 Germany (continued)

Date of independence	January 18, 1871 (German Empire unification); divided into four zones of occupation (United Kingdom, United States, USSR, and later France) in 1945 after World War II; Federal Republic of Germany (FRG or West Germany) proclaimed May 23, 1949 and included the former British, American, and French zones; German Democratic Republic (GDR or East Germany) proclaimed October 7, 1949, and included the former USSR zone; unification of West Germany and East Germany took place October 3, 1990; all four powers formally relinquished rights March 15, 1991
Gross Domestic Product (GDP) per capita	$34,400 (2007 est.)
Unemployment rate	9.1% This is the International Labor Organization's estimated rate for international comparisons; Germany's Federal Employment Office estimated a seasonally adjusted rate of 10.8% (2007 est.)
Natural hazards	Flooding
Environment: current issues	Emissions from coal-burning utilities and industries contribute to air pollution; acid rain, resulting from sulfur dioxide emissions, is damaging forests; pollution in the Baltic Sea from raw sewage and industrial effluents from rivers in eastern Germany; hazardous waste disposal; government established a mechanism for ending the use of nuclear power over the next 15 years; government working to meet EU commitment to identify nature preservation areas in line with the European Union's Flora, Fauna, and Habitat directive
Population	82,369,548
Age structure	0–14 years: 13.8% (male 5,826,066/female 5,524,568) 15–64 years: 66.2% (male 27,763,917/female 26,739,934) 65 years and over: 20% (male 6,892,743/female 9,622,320) (2008 est.)
Median age	Total: 43.4 years Male: 42.2 years Female: 44.7 years (2008 est.)
Population growth rate	−0.044% (2008 est.)
Birth rate	8.18 births/1,000 population (2008 est.)
Death rate	10.8 deaths/1,000 population (2008 est.)
Net migration rate	2.19 migrant(s)/1,000 population (2008 est.)
Gender ratio	At birth: 1.06 male(s)/female Under 15 years: 1.05 male(s)/female 15–64 years: 1.04 male(s)/female 65 years and over: 0.72 male(s)/female Total population: 0.97 male(s)/female (2008 est.)
Infant mortality rate	Total: 4.03 deaths/1,000 live births Male: 4.46 deaths/1,000 live births Female: 3.58 deaths/1,000 live births (2008 est.)

(continues)

TABLE 8-1   Germany (continued)

Life expectancy at birth	Total population: 79.1 years Male: 76.11 years Female: 82.26 years (2008 est.)
Total fertility rate	1.41 children born/woman (2008 est.)
HIV/AIDS adult prevalence rate	0.1% (2003 est.)
Number of people living with HIV/AIDS	43,000 (2001 est.)
HIV/AIDS deaths	Less than 1,000 (2003 est.)

Central Intelligence Agency. The World Fact Book, 2008. Retrieved November 18, 2008, from https://www.cia.gov/library/publications/the-world-factbook.

History

The origin of what is known today as the Federal Republic of Germany lies not in the ancient Germanic forests, but in the Holy Roman Empire, which covered the entire midsection of the European continent. By the year 1400, several areas of this empire, including North Italy, Savoy, Burgundy, and the Swiss Confederations, were only nominally included and, along with Lorraine and Brabant, were considered "*Teutsche Lande*" (German Country).[1]

As a result of the Napoleonic war, the German Empire was replaced by the Confederation of the Rhine. Prussia and Austria remained outside the Confederation. At the Vienna Congress in 1815, the German Confederation, a loose conglomerate of states in Germany, including Prussia and Austria, was founded. After the Prussian-Austrian war in 1867, the German Confederation was re-formed into the North German Confederation, without Austria and Bavaria.[1]

In 1862, Otto von Bismarck became Prime Minister (*Ministerpräsident*) of Prussia. He ardently pursued German unity not through "speeches and majority decisions" (*Reden und Majoritätsbeschlüsse*) but through "blood and iron" (*Blut und Eisen*).[2] The foundation for the second German Empire was laid on January 18, 1871, when Wilhelm I was crowned Emperor of the new constitutional monarchy, in the Room of Mirrors in the Palace of Versailles in Paris.[2] Only 5 years later, in 1876, the German Empire was created "from above" with the merger of the German states, Austria not included. Under the chancellorship of Otto von Bismarck, Germany transitioned into a socially advanced state, with the stepwise introduction of a federal system of social insurance. Although the German political leadership loathed social democracy and sought to weaken social democratic movements by passing anti-socialist laws, Bismarck himself explained the motivation for his political actions by saying that "without social democracy, even the small gains we have made in social reform up until now would not yet exist."[2] After this time, Germany played a central role in World War I and World War II. It experienced the rise and fall of Adolf Hitler and a rebuilding of its war-torn economy (more is discussed about this period in the history of the healthcare system later here). East and West Germany, which were divided by World War I, were reunified in the 1980s, and Germany has since become a leader in the formation and advancement of the European Union (EU).

Size and Geography

The *Bundesrepublik Deutschland* (Federal Republic of Germany) is located in Central Europe and is bordered by the Netherlands, Belgium, Luxembourg, and France to the West, Switzerland and Austria to the South, the Czech Republic and Poland to the East, and Denmark to the North. The territory of Germany covers about 357,092.90 km^2 (approximately 137,846 square miles), which makes it slightly smaller than the state of Montana.[3] The longest distance from north to south is 876 km; from west to east, it is 640 km.[4] With a current population of 82 million inhabitants, it is the largest country by population in the EU and the second largest in Europe after Russia.[3] At 596 inhabitants per square mile, the population density in Germany is four times as high as in the United States[5]; however, the population is not evenly distributed. More than three quarters of inhabitants (76%) live in cities: 13% in small cities/towns, 28% in large cities, and 35% in medium-sized cities.[4]

The largest proportion of Germany's total surface area is used for agriculture (53.0%). A much smaller surface area (12.8%) is dedicated to settlement areas and transportation uses. Forests make up 29.8%, water surfaces 2.3%, and wasteland and other surfaces together 2.1% of the total surface area.[6]

Government or Political System

As its name implies, Germany is a federal republic that is comprised of 16 states (*Bundesländer*; see Figure 8-1 and Table 8-1). Each of the states has a constitution that must be consistent with the republican, democratic, and social principles embodied in the constitution, known as the Basic Law (*Grundgesetz*). The constitutionally defined bodies that have primarily legislative functions are the lower and upper chambers of parliament, namely the Federal Assembly (*Bundestag*) and the Federal Council (*Bundesrat*).[4] The national capital of Germany is Berlin. The head of state is the President (*Bundespräsident*), whereas the Chancellor (*Bundeskanzler*) is the head of government. The President has mostly representative duties. The second highest official in the German order of precedence is the President of the *Bundestag* and the third highest official is the Chancellor, who is also the head of government.[7]

The *Bundestag* (Federal Assembly, lower house of parliament) and the *Bundesrat* (Federal Council, upper house of parliament) are the legislative organs of the German government. Federals law are passed by the *Bundestag* with a simple majority. They only become effective if the upper house of parliament does not veto

FIGURE 8-1   Map of Germany

them or if, when required by law, the Federal Council, the *Bundesrat*, concurs. Amendments to the Basic Law require a two-thirds majority in both chambers of parliament.[4] The federal states have their own constitution, laws, and parliaments. They are represented in the *Bundesrat* and, through this medium, participate in federal lawmaking. The jurisdictions of the Federal Constitutional Court are constitutional issues and the integrity of the Basic Law.

The most important characteristics of German foreign policy are its Western political orientation as well as its integration in Europe. Germany has been instrumental in developing European organizations. The country has been a member of the Council of Europe since 1950, and it signed the Treaties of Rome in 1957, which formed the basis for today's EU. In 1955, Germany joined the North Atlantic Treaty Organisation and thereby laid the foundation for its Western political affiliation. Together with France, Germany plays a leading role in the EU, and it attempts to create a common, effective system of European foreign and security policy.

In addition to its membership in North Atlantic Treaty Organisation, Germany is also a member of the United Nations, the Organisation for Economic Development and Co-operation (OECD), the Organization for Security and Cooperation in Europe, and the Group of Eight (G8).

Macroeconomics

Major Industries and Where They Are Located

Because Germany is comparatively poor in raw materials, the country's economy focuses on industrial manufacturing and the service sector. Although only 2% to 3% of the population is employed in agriculture, over 40% of the total land area is used for agrarian purposes. With an estimated gross domestic product (GDP) of $2.833 trillion in 2007, Germany is the world's third largest economy.[3,8] The German economy is heavily export oriented; therefore, the country has been called the export champion of the world. The United States is Germany's second largest trading partner, after France. In 2006, 8.7% of German exports went to the United States.[3] Principal exports are automobiles, commercial vehicles, electrotechnical devices, machine tools, and chemical products.

Infrastructure and Transportation

The first paved roads were constructed during Roman times. The first large highways were built in the 18th century. With the invention of the automobile, the impor-

tance of road construction increased dramatically. The "AVUS" roadway in Berlin was the first motorway in the world when it was completed in 1921. During the economic recovery of the 1950s, road transport replaced railways as the most important means of transportation. Today, Germany has one of the most dense road grids in the world. The federal highway grid has more than 12,500 kilometers of highways (*Autobahn*) and more than 40,000 kilometers of federal roads (*Bundesstraßen*). The German railway system had approximately 36,000 kilometers of tracks in 2003, down from 40,981 in 1990.[9] The network is used by 27,196 passenger and 4,674 freight trains each day.[10] Germany has approximately 430 airports and airfields, the highest density of takeoff and landing strips in the world. The most important German airport is Frankfurt/Main, which is the hub for Lufthansa, the major German airline.[11] Because of its focus on foreign trade, Germany is heavily dependent on maritime trade. Although a number of modern seaports exist in Germany, a large portion of German trade is shipped overseas through ports in neighboring countries, especially the Netherlands. The three highest-volume German harbors are Hamburg, Wilhelmshaven, and Bremen (combined with Bremerhaven). The most important Baltic Sea port is Lübeck. In addition to seaports, Germany also has a highly developed network of inland waterways. The network is comprised of 6,636 km of inland waterways.[9]

Demographics

Age Distribution of the Population

Like most industrialized countries in the 21st century, the Federal Republic of Germany is characterized by low birth rates and an aging population. Although birth rates in the two formerly divided Germanys were similar up until the 1960s, they developed quite differently after the mid-1970s. In the former West Germany, the (Federal Republic of Germany), it fell to its lowest mark by the mid-1980s, when less than 1.3 children were born to each woman. Since then, it has risen again slightly, and it has oscillated moderately around 1.4 children per woman. In contrast, in the former East Germany (the German Democratic Republic), spurred by government policy, the birth rate rose to 1.94 children per woman in the 1980s and has declined somewhat since then. Since the reunification, the decline has accelerated dramatically; the overall birth rate has fallen from 1.52 children to 0.77 children per woman.[12] Concurrent with the declining birth rate, life expectancy has been increasing, and consequently, the age distribution in Germany has been shifting upward. By 2050, male life expectancy at birth is expected to reach 83.5 years, whereas female life expectancy is believed to reach 88.0 years—an increase of 7.6 and 6.5 years, respectively, from 2003 to 2004. Today, Germany has more people ages 65 or older than people ages 15 years and younger.[12]

Education Levels of Population

In Germany, the 16 federal states are responsible for the organization of the educational system. Superordinate control, up to a certain degree, is provided via the nationwide Conferences of Ministers of Education (*Kultusministerkonferenzen*). Pupils are required to attend school for 9 years to obtain a general education. Subsequently, they may choose to start vocational training or to continue their schooling to prepare them for higher education. Most federal states have a three-pronged school system beyond primary education: *Hauptschule* (lowest-level secondary school; up to 9th or 10th grade), *Realschule* (lower-level secondary school), and *Gymnasium* (equivalent to the American high school). Only a high school diploma from a *Gymnasium* affords pupils an opportunity to continue their studies at a traditional university. The general qualification required for university entrance is 12 or 13 years of schooling, depending on the state. Students graduating from a *Hauptschule* usually continue on with vocational training. This form of training is typically a combination of practical skills training or work at a business or factory with theoretical instruction at a vocational school (*Berufsschule*). It usually lasts for 2 to 3 years. Institutions of higher education are divided into universities (103) and universities of applied sciences (176).[3] The latter are practice-oriented professional schools.

Religion

Freedom of religion is guaranteed in Germany as a fundamental right. The area that today is Germany has been Christianized since the early Middle Ages; therefore, the majority of German citizens belong to a Christian denomination. Other religious groups are Muslims (3.3 million) and Jews (165,000).[13] In 2005, only 4% of Protestants and 14% of Catholics attended Sunday services.[14] A third of the population is nondenominational or nonreligious.[15]

Distribution of Major Morbidity in the Country

The most frequent causes of death in Germany are cardiovascular diseases (46.78%), followed by cancer (24.95%), illnesses of the respiratory system (6.37%), illnesses of the digestive system (4.97%), suicide (1.32%), fall injuries (0.85%), and traffic accidents (0.84%).[14]

BRIEF HISTORY OF THE HEALTHCARE SYSTEM

The story of the German healthcare system is one of political compromise and of successful implementation of communitarian values. The system has remained relatively intact over time, even in the face of governmental change and recent reforms.[13,15] Today, Germany's healthcare system is one of universal healthcare coverage that offers protection to about 90% of the country's residents via a number of sickness funds (*Krankenkassen*) that can be classified as company-, trade-, or profession-based insurance plans.[16] It is also the world's oldest social insurance health system.[17] Access to high-quality comprehensive healthcare services is stipulated under Germany's statutory health insurance (*Gesetzliche Krankenversicherung* [GKV]). The GKV provides an organizational framework for the delivery of public health care that has shaped the roles of payers, insurance or sickness funds, and providers, physicians, and hospitals since major reforms in the system took place in the 1880s.[18] First adopted on June 15, 1883 as the Health Insurance Act (*Krankenversicherungsgesetz*) of 1883, the system was designed as mandatory health insurance applied only to low-income blue-collar workers and certain government employees but has since gradually been expanded to cover virtually the entire population.

As shown in Table 8-2, the German healthcare system has several key strengths and weaknesses: Although access to services is available to almost all German citizens and although care is virtually free, generous benefits and an ability to select providers freely have led to overconsummption and rising healthcare costs. Traditionally, fees for the system have been paid almost entirely through the labor market. They are equally paid by employers and employees.[19] Although the German government has continued to subsidize costs for the unemployed and to partially reimburse costs for low-income workers, it neither finances nor pays for the provision of healthcare services, nor does it run the system per se.[20] Rather, the German government serves primarily a regulatory role, much like the Health Care Financing Administration in the United States.[20] Among other things, it regulates drug prices, sets guidelines for private health insurances, and stipulates the rules

TABLE 8-2 Strengths and Weaknesses of the German Healthcare System

Strengths	Weaknesses
Ability to provide comprehensive, uniform, and universal coverage	Overconsumption of healthcare resources because of generous benefits packages
Ability to cover almost every German citizen	Cost shifting of escalating healthcare costs on employers and employees
Access to virtually cost-free outpatient, inpatient, and preventive care	Unresolved, ongoing tension between the forces of centralization and decentralization
Right to select freely a healthcare provider of choice or any physician within a given geographical area	Division of inpatient and outpatient care, leading to underutilization of outpatient care and significant inefficiencies
A simplified claims process	A dual financing system in which hospitals finance operational costs and state governments finance capital costs
An extremely patient-oriented healthcare system	

Data are from Swami B. The German health care system. In Thai KV, Wimberley ET, McManus SM, eds. *Handbook of International Health Care Systems.* New York: Marcel Dekker, Inc.; 2002, pp. 333–358.

under which employers are to provide coverage to their employees.

Pre-World War II

The core component of the German healthcare system is the sickness fund, whose precursor can be traced to the Middle Ages when guilds, trade associations, industries, and mutual societies established private relief funds to help pay for health care, funerals, and other related expenses.[4,20,21] By the end of the 17th century, five distinct types of relief funds had emerged in different regions across Germany: relief funds for journeymen, relief funds for craftsmen modeled after the mutual support systems of the guilds, factory relief funds founded by socially oriented entrepreneurs, relief funds founded by local authorities for workers or tradespeople, and community relief funds for people who could not otherwise find insurance.[19] By 1848, the German government had granted local municipalities the authority to recognize these voluntary funds and to make participation in them compulsory; for example, in Prussia—the largest of the German states—health insurance became compulsory for miners, and local communities could oblige employers and their employees to pay financial contributions toward health insurance.[4] In 1854, local authority was further expanded, allowing local com-

munities to require that all uninsured local residents create insurance funds for mutual support.[17,22]

The cornerstone for the foundation of the modern system was laid in 1876, with the establishment of the ministry of health (*Reichsgesundheitsamt*).[19] That same year, a formal law on relief funds (*Hilfskassengesetz*) was passed, stipulating that workers were to receive public financial support in case of illness or death. An imperial message (*Kaiserliche Botschaft*), delivered on November 17, 1881, by King Wilhelm I to parliament, recognized the importance of "material" (i.e., financial) protection (*materielle Absicherung*) for all German citizens and announced pending laws regarding accidents, illness, disability, and retirement.[2,4] It clearly announced the duty of the German government to ensure the welfare of the population and cleared the way for the creation of the modern German healthcare system. The subsequent evolution of that system can be best described according to four major periods in recent German history: introduction of mandatory national health insurance and competing interests of the medical profession from 1883 to 1933, Hitler's Third Reich and World War II from 1933 to 1945, the postwar period between 1945 and 1989 during which Germany was split into two separate German states, and the fall of the Berlin Wall and subsequent reunification of the Federal Republic of Germany since 1989.[4]

National Health Insurance Act of 1883 and the Medical Profession

The German healthcare system, as it exists in its modern form today, is unanimously credited to Otto von Bismarck, the first German chancellor (*Bundeskanzler*), who began implementing his "Bismarck System" in the early 1880s with a series of social policies. Bismarck, known as the "Iron Chancellor" (*Eiserne Kanzler*), had recently overseen the unification of Germany, thereby establishing the German Empire under the rule of the Prussian King Wilhelm I. Shortly thereafter, Bismarck introduced legislation that resulted in the now famous Health Insurance Act of 1883, making Germany the first country in Europe to offer compulsory social health insurance. The act was only one component of Bismarck's conservative social legislation (*Sozialgesetzgebung*) with the goal to maintain the old social order.[21,23] At the time, Germany's blue-collar workers were very poor with very little public support, and Bismarck sought to "buy" their loyalty in exchange for economic security and material benefits. Indeed, his motivations were not purely altruistic; rather, they reflected his "Sugarbread and Whip" approach to politics (*Politik von Zuckerbrot und Peitsche*) in his attempt to separate the working class from the increasingly popular Social Democratic Party (*Sozialdemokratische Partei*).[2] Largely because of his role in introducing social reform and despite his otherwise impeccable right-wing, nationalist credentials, Bismarck would later be called a socialist. In his own speech to Congress (*Reichstag*) during the 1881 debates, Bismarck remarked, "Call it socialism or whatever you like. It is the same to me."[24]

By 1885, the Health Insurance Act covered only 26% of blue-collar workers (or 10% of the population); however, coverage through various sickness funds was subsequently expanded several more times to eventually include almost the entire German population.[15] By 2003, of the 90% of the population who were covered through a sickness fund, coverage was mandatory for about 77%, whereas the rest could choose to enroll voluntarily. An additional 10% of individuals opted for private health insurance, frequently offering them additional benefits. About 2% had coverage through a governmental scheme, and only 0.2% had no third-party coverage at all.[4,25]

In his quest to mollify the working class and to weaken socialism, Bismarck continued his creation of a remarkably advanced German welfare state by following the Health Insurance Act of 1883 with laws that provided assistance for work-related accidents (*Unfal-*lversicherung) in 1884, for old age and disability (*Alters- und Invaliditätsversicherung*) in 1889, and for unemployment (*Arbeitslosenversicherung*) in 1927.[2,4] At the time, this system—known as the Bismarck System—was the most advanced in the world and, to a degree, still exists in Germany today. The law for accident insurance included a mandate that employers must insure their employees against invalidity; it also set up professional societies (*Berufsgenossenschaften*) and disability pension (*Erwerbsunfähigkeitsrente*), the latter of which was to be paid for by employer contributions and federal subsidies.

The success of the newly created healthcare system is evidenced by the longevity of the policies and programs first developed and implemented under Bismarck. Even more remarkably, Bismarck was able to advance his political and social agendas with no input from individual physicians or medical organizations; in fact, the medical profession took scarcely any notice, and the new system was not even debated in professional journals until after it had already been adopted.[4,21] Bismarck was quite clever in introducing his system while avoiding the impression of making radical changes to the existing structure; nevertheless, the National Insurance Act of 1883 did not clearly define the relationship between sickness funds and physicians nor did it address the qualification of healthcare professionals, leaving full authority to determine these matters to the funds.[4,15] By the 1890s, physicians had grown increasingly frustrated; they began to seek autonomy and to exert influence through several strikes and lobbying. In 1900, they formed a professional association, the Hartmann Union (*Hartmannbund*), and by 1910, 75% of all German physicians were members. Finally, in 1913, and with intervention by the German government, sickness funds and physicians forged the Berlin Agreement, which significantly changed the relationship between physicians and sickness funds and established regular procedures for negotiating in conflicts that is, albeit in modified form, still in practice today.[15,21]

Hitler's Third Reich and World War II

The rise of Hitler and the coming of the Third Reich marked the beginning of another phase in the German healthcare system.[15] On January 30, 1933, Adolf Hitler was sworn in as Chancellor and soon thereafter began his stepwise process toward systematic seizure of power and toward the absolute rule of the Hitler regime. At the time, Germany was beset by widespread unemployment, and Germans felt a general sense of insecurity and intimidation. Hitler immediately set out to adopt a system of totalitarian control, to create a permanent state of emergency (*Ausnahmezustand*), and to implement "forcible-coordination" (*Gleichschaltung*), the synchronization and tight, centralized coordination—by means of an invasive police force—of all aspects of government, society, and commerce.[2,26] In 1934, the Hitler regime appointed a director for the sickness funds and one for other insurance programs; both reported directly to the regime.[15] In fact, between 1933 and 1935, the funds, community health services, other nongovernmental organizations dealing with welfare or health education, and health-related professional organizations came under centralized leadership in accordance with Hitler's leader principle (*Führerprinzip*).

One of Hitler's goals, perhaps even his ultimate purpose, was to create a German "master race" (*Herrenrasse*) of racially and ethnically pure Germans. One of the intended consequences was to expel German citizens of Jewish decent and other stigmatized minorities from membership in the sickness funds and to deny them access to healthcare services. Increasingly, but especially with the onset of World War II in 1939, public funds for social care, welfare, and health education were diverted toward satisfying the political targets of racial hygiene, eugenics, and social control.[4] The notion of racial hygiene in particular became the basis for many health-related and other laws. For example, it allowed the misuse of private health information to perform compulsory sterilizations of over 400,000 men and women, primarily those with mental handicaps, because they were deemed likely to have "defective" children.[27]

Despite the strongly centralized, totalitarian rule under the Hitler regime, several improvements in social and health insurance coverage were made between 1933 and 1945, simply because they served the political agenda of the regime's leader, Adolf Hitler. In 1941, public health insurance coverage was expanded to include pensioners. In 1942, accident insurance was expanded to include all workers, regardless of occupation. Sick care was no longer limited, and a 12-week, fully paid, job-protected maternity leave was offered.[15] A much more sinister development was the trend among the majority of German physicians—the profession with the highest membership in Hitler's National-Socialist Party—to welcome systematic exclusion of their Jewish colleagues from the practice of medicine.[4] Swayed by Hitler's push for racial hygiene, Germany's medical community held the belief that curing patients was worthwhile; however, "healing" the nation was eminently more important. A majority of physicians willingly prescribed to and promoted the ideas of racial hygiene; to a large degree, the medical profession was not politicized but politics became medicalized.[28]

Since World War II

Two German States

At the end of World War II and after the surrender of Hitler's army on May 8, 1945, the four main Allied Forces (including the "Big Three" United States, Great Britain, and the Soviet Union, along with France) took control of Germany, and the country was divided into two separate states. The Western Federal Republic of Germany (*Bundesrepublik Deutschland*) represented the global bloc in the west, under American, British, and French control, whereas the Eastern German Democratic Republic (*Deutsche Demokratische Republik*) represented the global bloc in the east, under Russian control. In the years immediately after World War II, health care in Germany was characterized by ad hoc public health interventions aimed at controlling and/or preventing outbreaks of epidemics and at distributing meager and often inadequate resources for health care.[4]

While under Allied control and then after the end of the war on March 20, 1948, the healthcare systems in the two German states developed in a very different fashion, resulting in two different German health systems. East Germany gradually moved toward a national socialist, state-financed health system, with the option to purchase private health insurance for additional treatment. This system was one of strong, centralized state control; it provided ambulatory care and treatment by company physicians at reasonable, controlled costs. Essential health care was provided at the expense of technological and pharmaceutical development.[29] In West Germany, the pre–World War II system was re-established. As before, it was supervised by the government but was not government run. Now it further developed into a highly decentralized corporate system in the face of modest parliamentary control. Political authority extended to benefits, eligibility, compulsory membership, covered risks (physical, emotional, mental, curative, and preventive), income maintenance during temporary illness, employer–employee contributions to the GKV, and other central issues. Healthcare coverage was expanded considerably, codified by social law (*Sozialgesetzbuch*) and by the GKV. More than 1,000 autonomous statutory sickness funds arose, which led to the broadest coverage within the free market system.[29,30]

On May 23, 1949, the new constitution (*Grundgesetz* [or GG]) was promulgated for the recently formed

Federal Republic of Germany. In it, Germany was established as a "democratic and social federal state" (GG, Article 20), where "social" rights were defined by legislation. This legislation, with the exception of certain prescribed areas, came under the purview of state parliaments. Before reunification, the Federal Republic of Germany consisted of 11 states (*Länder*); each *Land* has its own elected parliament (*Landtag*). All states continue to have ministries of social security, and most have health ministries.[31] State legislation was subordinate to federal law only in the areas of epidemics, university education in medicine, food and drug control, social security, and since 1972, financing of hospitals.[32] In 1951, employee contributions for health insurance were reduced, whereas employer contributions were raised. Previously, the share of employees toward health insurance was two thirds, and that of employers was one third; now shares were split evenly between both.[4,20]

The Fall of the Berlin Wall and a Reunified Germany

Twenty-eight years after construction began on the Berlin Wall on August 13, 1961, to demarcate formally the German Democratic Republic from the Federal Republic of Germany, German citizens from both states began scaling it and tearing it down on November 9, 1989. Eleven months later, on October 3, 1990, the two Germanys were officially reunited. With the signing of the Treaty of Reunification (*Vereinigungsvertrag*), 17 million East German citizens now became fully integrated into the system of the Federal Republic of Germany and thereby the political, economic, and social responsibility of the West German government. Although the public was quite critical of political and economic structures, it regarded social welfare and health care much more positively.[4] Consequently, there were no fundamental changes to the structure of the West German healthcare system as it had been conceived by Otto von Bismarck in 1883, whereas the former East German system underwent significant growth and adaptation.[33] Despite only minor compromises being made to the way in which health care was to be financed and delivered, East Germany's national health insurance system was quickly transformed to adopt the pluralist system of West Germany.[4,34]

Until the early 1990s, the number of sickness funds rose steadily to over 1,200; however, by 2004, they had decreased again to fewer than 300, largely as result of mergers.[34] About 60% of health expenditures were derived from compulsory and voluntary contributions to statutory health insurance. About 21% were derived from general taxation. About 7% were derived from private insurance, and about 11% were represented by unreimbursed, out-of-pocket expenditure. By 2004, 75% of Germany's healthcare system was government funded, whereas 23% was privately funded.[35] In comparison with the United States, the German system has managed to provide health care relatively economically. In 2003, about 10.8% of Germany's GDP went into medical care, or $2,983 per capita, compared with 15.2% of the GDP and $6,711 per capita in the United States.[36,37] Even so, the German healthcare system is one of the most expensive in Europe; only Switzerland, Luxembourg, and Norway spend more.[38]

The extraordinary task of uniting and combining two formerly separate and distinct health care systems brought about unprecedented healthcare reforms in the late 20th century, which continue in the 21st century. Over the course of a little more than a decade, the Health Care Reform Act (1989), the Health Care Structure Act (1992), the Health Insurance Contribution Rate Exoneration Act (1996), the First and Second Statutory Health Insurance Restructuring Acts (1997), the Act to Strengthen Solidarity in Statutory Health Insurance (1998), and the Reform Act of Statutory Health Insurance 2000 (1999) were passed.[4,33] By the mid-1990s, healthcare benefits provided through the GKV were extensive and included, among other benefits, ambulatory care (care provided by office-based physicians), choice of office-based physicians, hospital care, full pay to mothers (from 6 weeks before to 8 weeks after childbirth), extensive home help, health checkups, sick leave to care for relatives, rehabilitation and physical therapy, medical appliances (such as artificial limbs), drugs, and stays of up to one month in health spas every few years.

Some recent reforms in the German healthcare system occurred in 2007. By 2004, there was considerable pressure to adopt a major reform, including a move to integrating inpatient and ambulatory care, which traditionally have been completely separate from one another in Germany.[39] The system was facing a deficit for the last few years, amounting to $1.50 billion in the first quarter of 2006 and potentially reaching $8.75 billion by the end of the year. Thus, healthcare reforms had become inevitable. That year, the German Minister, Ulla Schmidt, announced her plan for comprehensive and innovative healthcare reform; a list of key elements are shown in Exhibit 8-1.[40] Starting in 2009, employers and employees pay the sickness funds premiums as a uniform percentage of gross wages or of income across all sickness funds. Sickness funds will then immediately

EXHIBIT 8-1   German Health Reform 2007

The reform law requires everybody to have health insurance, either public or private. If someone is uninsured and does not join or pay premiums as of July 1, 2007, and becomes ill, he or she is not entitled to more than basic medical attention for acute injury or major pain and then is required to pay the owed premiums retroactively together with a penalty fee.

The changed law has provisions for some new benefits for members of the government scheme:

1. Members will be able to choose between different tariffs that allow for some co-payments or bonus payments in return for a reduction of premium. This is new, and each *Krankenkasse* can offer these to a select group of members only.
2. Members will often be able to choose to be invoiced by doctors, dentists, and hospitals (*Kostenerstattung*) instead of receiving the services by simply showing their membership card (*Sachleistungsprinzip*). This is a major change and means that medical practitioners will be able to invoice a government scheme member as if the

patient were privately insured as long as this has been agreed on with the *Krankenkasse* in advance. The logic behind this measure is to allow customers to benefit from extra coverage, over and above that which the *Krankenkassen* would normally allow and either pay for the difference themselves or to use private supplemental tariffs to fill the gap.

3. Benefits for recommended vaccinations, parent/child respite care, rehabilitation, geriatrics, and palliative medicine will become obligatory and must be provided by each *Krankenkasse*.
4. Home nursing care will be extended and will also become part of the long-term care system.
5. Integrated medical facilities such as local medical centers, until now almost nonexistent in Germany, will be supported and encouraged in order to save money and to improve the quality of diagnosis and therapy.

From German Ministry of Health, 2007.

TABLE 8-3   Average Life Expectancy in Germany

			2002/2004	2003/2005	2004/2006
Age 0	Men	Years	75.89	76.21	76.64
	Women	Years	81.55	81.78	82.08
Age 20	Men	Years	56.55	56.85	57.24
	Women	Years	62.07	62.28	62.56
Age 40	Men	Years	37.37	37.63	37.98
	Women	Years	42.46	42.66	42.92
Age 60	Men	Years	20.05	20.27	20.58
	Women	Years	24.08	24.25	24.49
Age 65	Men	Years	16.26	16.47	16.77
	Women	Years	19.77	19.94	20.18
Age 80	Men	Years	7.24	7.35	7.51
	Women	Years	8.64	8.72	8.87
Deceased During First Year of Life Per 1,000 Live Births			2004	2005	2006
			4.1	3.9	3.8

Source: German Ministry of Health Statistics, 2006.

pass those premiums to a central national fund (*Gesundheitsfonds*). Additionally, effective January 1, 2009, every German is required to have health insurance coverage for the basic benefit package.[39]

In large part because of the seemingly never-ending reforms, attitudes about the social welfare system have been undergoing a pronounced revision among German citizens since the reunification. Shortly after the reunification, 16% of East Germans rated West German social security better than their own; 65% thought the old East German system was better. A short 5 years later, only 3% preferred the Western system, whereas 92% favored the East German one. Similarly, 65% of East Germans in 1990 thought that the healthcare system in West Germany was better than in the East; in 1995; 57% said the East German system was better.[41]

DESCRIPTION OF THE CURRENT HEALTHCARE SYSTEM

The modern German healthcare system has achieved a high degree of equity and justice, despite its fragmented federal organization: No single group is in a position to dictate the terms of service delivery, reimbursement, remuneration, quality of care, or any other important concerns. Access to health care is regarded as a right of all German citizens. That right reflects universality of coverage, comprehensive benefits, the principle of the healthy paying for the sick, and a redistributive element in the financing of health care. The structure of the German health insurance system is rooted in several assumptions about the nature of German society. First, it has been assumed that most Germans will have stable, long-standing connections to jobs, either through their own employment or through the employment of a spouse or parent. Second, it has been assumed that wage income would grow as quickly as the healthcare costs of the covered population; however, recent changes in German society have made these assumptions about the organizational structure of German healthcare system less valid.[19]

What does remain as two integral features of the system are the fundamental principles of solidarity and subsidiarity.[15,23] Both principles have been endorsed by the left, central, and right parties across the political spectrum and are secured in Germany's Basic Law of 1949.[15] Solidarity refers to a shared commitment among members of society toward respect and mutual care; sub-

sidiarity refers to their common understanding that social action should be transferred to the most appropriate level, with particular emphasis on the local and communal levels.[42] Both principles closely relate to the concept of generalized reciprocity or the willingness to give to someone without expecting that person to return the benefit directly, but rather expecting that somehow, in some way, the benefit will be returned eventually.[43] In the context of health care, it is the agreement among insured persons to share health risks and to assess contributions commensurate with one's ability to pay, while discharging government from any functions which could be solved better, or at least equally as well, via private efforts and responsibility.[42] In Germany, the belief in generalized reciprocity ultimately provides the conceptual basis for the evolution of the modern health insurance system.[22]

Facilities

The current situation in the German healthcare system is marked by several recently implemented reform efforts. A central goal of such reforms by the German government has been to induce more competition in the healthcare marketplace, which in turn will lead to more efficiency. As one result, the number of general hospitals has been in a steady decline for years and in 2006 was reported as 2,104.[42] About 28% of those hospitals are owned privately, about 38% are owned by not-for-profit organizations, and about 34% are owned by local, state, or federal government.[42] The German healthcare system also consists of 1,255 prevention and rehabilitation hospitals and clinics. Approximately 57% of those institutions are owned privately, and about 25% are run by not-for-profit organizations; 18% are owned by the local, state, or federal government.[42]

Increased competition can be seen among pharmacies as well, especially as it is now legal for individuals to own up to four pharmacies in Germany as a result of a change in the law that took effect January 1, 2004; however, the increased competition has not led to a consolidation of pharmacies as of yet. The number of pharmacies is still high at 21,570 in 2007.[43]

Workforce

The German healthcare system is marked by a high number of healthcare personnel. According to the OECD, Germany had 3.4 practicing physicians per 1,000 population in 2005, which is up from 3.0 in 1990.[44] The OECD average was 3.0 physicians per 1,000 population. Approximately 136,200 physicians work in private practice. Hospitals employ about 148,300. An additional 9,900 physicians can be found within government settings and 16,900 in other settings such as industry. About 13% of all practicing physicians are working in general medicine, and another 13% are working in internal medicine. The number of practicing nurses per capita was reported to be relatively high in 2005 at 9.7 nurses per 1,000 population compared with an average across OECD countries of 8.6 practicing nurses per 1,000 population.[44] The number of dentists per 100,000 inhabitants was reported at 78.9 in 2005.[45]

The reduction of the average length of stays in German hospitals has led to a reduction of the number of hospital beds per capita. In 2005, Germany reported 6.4 hospital beds per 1,000 population in acute care. The average across OECD in 2005 was 3.9 acute-care hospital beds per 1,000 population.[44]

Technology and Equipment

The past decade has shown a rapid growth in the availability of diagnostic technologies such as computed tomography scanners and magnetic resonance imaging (MRI) units in Germany. The number of MRIs, for example, increased in Germany from about 1 per million population in 1992 to 7.1 in 2005, which is still significantly below the OECD average of 9.8 MRI units per million population. The number of computed tomography scanners was 20.6 per million population on average across the OECD compared with 15.4 in Germany.[44]

EVALUATION OF THE HEALTHCARE SYSTEM

Cost

As is true for most of the Westernized countries, German citizens continue to pay relatively little out-of-pocket for their health care. With the GDP at $32,860 per capita, 11.3% of all medical expenses nationwide are borne by households, while the rest is assumed by social health insurance or by the government.[46] Since the beginning of the new millennium, Germans must pay more than ever before for their health care. In a deeply unpopular reform, those enrolled in the statutory insurance plan have been required to pay €10 per quarter since January 2004 to see a general practitioner. They also have to contribute toward the cost of prescription drugs, wound dressings, and bandages, and they must

now assume 15% of the cost of other items and 20% of the cost of supports, as well as a share of the cost of inpatient preventive treatment and rehabilitation, outpatient rehabilitation, inpatient hospital care (at €9 per day), and dentures.[47]

Sickness fund membership is compulsory for employees whose gross income does not exceed a certain level (a little less than €40,000 annually in the western parts of the country and around €32,000 annually in the parts in the former GDR) and is voluntary for those above that level. Through Chapter 3 of the Social Code Book V, the following types of benefits are currently legally included in the basic benefit package, usually in generic terms:

- Prevention of disease
- Screening for disease
- Treatment of disease (ambulatory medical care, dental care, drugs, nonphysician care, medical devices, inpatient/hospital care, nursing care at home, and certain areas of rehabilitative care)
- Transportation

In addition to these benefits in kind, sickness funds have to give cash benefits to sick insured after the first 6 weeks of sickness; during the first 6 weeks, employers are responsible for sick pay. Although employers have to pay 100% of income, sickness funds pay 80% for up to 78 weeks per period of illness.[4]

Total Healthcare Spending and Health Dollars Spent per Capita

Overall, healthcare expenditures have been steadily on the rise in Germany since the passage of the National Health Insurance Act in 1883. In 1985, they accounted for 8.8% of the GDP; by 1995, they had risen to 10.1%, and by 2005, they had reached 10.7%—1.7 percentage points higher than the average 9.0% for OECD countries.[37] By the latter part of the 20th century, dramatic cost increases for physicians and hospital care had taken place. Between 1970 and 1990, payments by sickness funds for members rose by five times, from $518 to $2,350. Similarly, hospital cost rose dramatically from 3% to 25% of total healthcare expenditures.[48] Similar to overall healthcare expenditures, per capita expenditures have also been on the rise in Germany. In 1970, per capita healthcare spending was $663, accounting for 4.48% of the per capita GDP. By 2002, per capita healthcare spending had risen to $2,066, accounting for almost double, 8.5%.[49]

Use of Third-Party Payer Distribution

At first glance, healthcare financing in Germany appears to be a rather straightforward process because almost all German citizens belong either to a statutory sickness fund, while the remainder belong to a private insurance plan; therefore, one could assume that there exist only two types of payers.[20] Although it is true that statutory sickness funds represent the most important type of payer in Germany's healthcare system, there are a number of different payers in the German healthcare system.

Public Health Infrastructure

Much like the German education system, the German public health system is decentralized to the states and localities, although the federal government holds legislative authority. As in the United States, the system is responsible for protecting public health, including water systems, sewer systems, other forms of environmental protection, food safety, and health promotion. The environmental protection measures have been quite successful in cleaning up major rivers and other forms of water pollution. Similarly, air quality has also markedly improved over the past 35 years.[48]

Public health promotion efforts have received considerably less attention. From 1989 to 1996, health promotion measures were actually offered as a type of benefit by sickness funds directly to their members. This benefit was abandoned under the Second Social Health Insurance Restructuring Act; however, it has been partly reintroduced through the Reform Act 2000. Although the Social Code Book regulates preventive services and screening in considerable detail (e.g., concerning diseases to be screened for and intervals between screening), it leaves further regulations to the Federal Committee of Physicians and Sickness Funds. This committee has considerable latitude in defining the benefits catalogue for curative, diagnostic, and therapeutic procedures.[4]

Quality

Infant Mortality

In 2006, Germany recorded 683,000 live births, down from 747,000 in 2000.[50] Infant mortality was 3.8 per 1,000 live births in 2006, and maternal mortality was 9 per 100,000 live births in 2000.[51,52] The German infant mortality rate is lower than the EU average but is on par with other long-standing EU members, such as France and Spain, and higher than in Scandinavian countries. Mortality for children under 5 years old was 5 per 1,000 live births in 2004, well below the average for the World Health Organization European Region and below the rates for the United States (8 per 1,000 live births).[51,53] The main causes of deaths among children under 5 years of age in Germany are neonatal causes, injuries, pneumonia, and other causes.[51]

Two-Tiered Healthcare Systems (by Income)

For employees with monthly gross incomes of €400, insurance in the statutory health insurance system is mandatory.[54] Since February 2, 2007, employees are eligible to leave the statutory health insurance (SHI) system and become privately insured if they earned more than the income threshold for 3 consecutive calendar years and are also earning more than the threshold in the current year. For 2008, the income threshold is €48,150.[54] By comparison, the per capita gross national product in 2005 was $34,870.[55] Historically, younger people earning above the income thresholds had an incentive to leave the statutory health insurance and become privately insured because they were offered lower premiums because of their young age, good health status, and lack of dependents. Private health insurance offers benefits not available to those insured in the statutory health insurance system, such as single occupancy rooms during inpatient stays and treatment by senior physicians.

The perception has long been that privately insured patients get preferential treatment because of higher reimbursement to physicians by private health insurance. One recent study showed disparate wait times for elective treatment according to insurance type, with those in the SHI waiting approximately three times longer for appointments for selected tests than the privately insured.[56] An international comparative survey of sick adults found those with private health insurance receiving more health services than those with statutory insurance. They were more likely to see specialists, be admitted, and have nonemergency surgery.[57] Those patients also had shorter wait times and reported more duplicative testing. The latter raises concerns about the potential of overtreatment for private health insurance patients.[57]

Other Health Statistics

Immunization rates for children are generally high and improving. For measles, for instance, Germany has achieved high vaccination rates: 94% for the first dose and 77% for the second dose[50]; however, measles outbreaks continued to be a problem.[58,59] In 2006, Germany reported 2,307 cases of measles, up from 778 in 2005.[50]

These outbreaks were attributed to local variations in immunization coverage and suboptimal coverage for the second dose of measles vaccine.[59,60] However, Germany met the goal of the European Region of the World Health Organization, eliminating indigenous measles from the region by 2007.[61]

Influenza vaccination rates have been increasing in Germany as in the rest of Europe. In 2006, 32.5% of the eligible population was immunized against influenza.[62] A study of vaccination rates in five European countries between 2002 and 2005 found Germany to have the highest immunization rate.[63]

An international comparison of health systems found relatively few sick patients (4%) in Germany rating their health care as excellent compared with those in the United Kingdom, the United States, New Zealand, Australia, and Canada; however, if those ranking their care as excellent or good were added together, Germans rated their care similar to patients in the other countries.[57] In an international comparison of adult healthcare experiences in seven developed countries by the Commonwealth Fund, Germans seemed unhappy with their current system: Only 20% said that the health system needed only minor changes, whereas 16% of U.S. respondents felt that way about their health system; 51% thought the health system needed major changes compared with 48% in the United States (not a significant difference). Twenty-seven percent said the system should be totally rebuilt compared with 34% in the United States.[64] Approximately a quarter of respondents (24%) were very confident that they will get high-quality, safe care compared with 35% in the United States.[64]

Access problems in Germany related to cost are lower than in the United States: 12% did not visit a physician when sick (United States, 25%); 8% skipped a medical test, treatment, or follow-up recommended by a physician (United States, 23%); 11% did not fill a prescription or skipped doses (United States, 23%); and 21% answered "Yes" to at least one of these compared with 37% in the United States.[64]

In comparison to the other countries, Germany ranked high for access related to timeliness of care. In the Commonwealth comparison, 55% said that they could get a same-day appointment when sick (United States, 30%); 50% of people in Germany thought it was somewhat or very difficult to get care on nights or weekends without going to the emergency room compared with 55% in the United Kingdom and 67% in the United States.[64] Waiting times for elective surgery are not a problem in Germany. In the Commonwealth study, more Germans (72%) than U.S. patients (62%) who had elec-

tive surgery in 2007–2008 reported waiting less than a month. The percentages reporting waiting more than 6 months were not significantly different (Germany 3% and United States 4%).[64]

In 2004, Germany established a federal commissioner for patient issues in the health system. The position is currently held by a political appointee; the commissioner is charged with ensuring that patient issues are considered at different levels in the health system.[65] An analysis of the public inquiries received by the commissioner reveals that most complainants are older. Health insurance, especially medications, was a major topic as were concerns over communication with healthcare providers. Older complainants were more likely to mention anxiety, uncertainty, and feelings of injustice, and the personal financial burden of health services featured prominently.[65]

Quality reporting is in its infancy in Germany. Since 2005, all German acute-care hospitals are required to publish hospital quality reports biennially.[66] The target audience for these reports is patients. The reports cover specialty services available, number of beds, staff qualifications, outpatient services available, technology, and additional services, the 30 most common diagnoses, the 30 most common surgeries performed, and the documentation rate by external quality control (number of procedures monitored and documented by external quality control) for the hospital in question.[67] Currently, the usefulness of the reports is limited as less than a fifth of people are aware of the reports[68]; however, hospitals are increasingly discovering the potential of the reports, as marketing materials and the reports are getting more comprehensive.

In addition, hospitals participate in external quality control for acute care. Hospitals report their data in certain predetermined areas of care to the Federal Agency for Quality Control (*Bundesgeschäftsstelle Qualitätssicherung*), which compiles an annual report.[69] The results are discussed at regularly convened nationwide conferences on quality control and are incorporated into the day-to-day running of hospitals.[70]

Comprehensiveness of the System

The statutory health insurance covers a wide variety of services including preventive care for children and adults, prevention-oriented dental care, vaccinations, physician and dental visits, medications and other remedies including hearing aids and wheelchairs, inpatient treatment, partial or full payment of prevention and rehabilitation, sick pay, home care, and maternity benefits.[54] The statutory health insurance provides sick pay after 6 weeks and 70% of the gross wages but not more than 90% of the last net wages.[54] The insured are also entitled to up to 10 days of sick pay per year for each dependent child under 12 years old.[54] The Law to Strengthen the Competition in the Statutory Health Insurance (*Gesetz zur Stärkung des Wettbewerbs in der gesetzlichen Krankenversicherung*) took effect in 2007 and changed the mandated standard insurance benefits that are provided by statutory health insurance; they now include medical rehabilitation and vaccinations among other benefits.[70]

Health reforms over the last decade have increased individual financial responsibility within the SHI. SHI patients have to pay out of pocket for so-called individual healthcare services, which are not covered by the SHI but are increasingly promoted by physician practices. Patients pay a quarterly €10 practice charge (*Praxisgebühr*). In the SHI, co-payments for prescription medications are 10% of the price of the medication, at least €5 but not more than €10. Children are exempt from these co-pays.[71] Over-the-counter drugs are not covered anymore after the SHI Modernization Law (*GKV-Modernisierungsgesetz*) took effect in 2004.[71] After a deductible of 2% of annual gross income is reached, the insured will be exempt from further co-payments for medications, inpatient care, and rehabilitation.[54]

Access

Equity/Universality

Insurance coverage is essentially universal, with the majority of the population either mandatory or voluntarily insured in the statutory health insurance and approximately 10% of the population insured privately. Even though the number of uninsured is very low compared with the United States, it has been increasing over the last decade. It increased from 145,000 (0.2% of the population) in April 1999 to 211,000 (0.3%) people during the first quarter of 2007.[72] As a result of the 2007 healthcare reform efforts, 115,000 people gained health insurance who either were never insured before or who had lost their insurance coverage.[73]

Even in a society with near-universal coverage, however, insurance health status and mortality vary with social status. Important factors in this correlation are higher illness incidence, disparities in education and material resources, and higher psychosocial burden experienced by those at the lower end.[74] In a national study of heart and circulatory diseases, males in the lowest so-cial stratum had a 50% higher risk of dying than those in the highest stratum. Females showed a similarly significant effect, but the effect was not linear.[74] Men in the lowest quintile of the population on average die 10 years younger than those in the top quintile; for women, the difference is 5 years.[75]

Life expectancy of the privately insured is higher than that of the general population; a privately insured female at birth has a life expectancy of 87.02 years and a male of 83.37 years in 2008.[76] The population average was 82 years for females and 76 years for males in 2005.[51]

In a national survey, self-reported health status among sick adults—that is, those with poor health status, a chronic condition or disability, and/or an inpatient stay—was related to income, education, and insurance type (private vs. statutory), but not related to gender, age, location of residence, location of birth, and out-of-pocket costs.[57]

The old and the new federal states (*alte/neue Bundesländer*) differ on a number of health-related measures. This may partly be due to the legacy of the past, the migration of a large number of people from the East to the West since the fall of the Berlin wall, resulting in a rapid aging of the population in large parts of the East, and less per capita income in the East. A large national survey found worse self-reported health status among sick adults in the new federal states compared with those in the old federal states, as well as worse preventive care for patients with diabetes.[57] A higher proportion of those in the new states (36%) felt that the health system should be totally rebuilt than those in the old states (29%).[57] These patients had lower out-of-pocket costs than comparable patients in the United States and Australia, but higher costs than in those in the United Kingdom, Canada, and New Zealand. German patients had paid on average $238 out-of-pocket in the prior 12 months compared with $609 for U.S. patients.[57]

Uninsured Populations

The uninsured in Germany are mainly self-employed who find themselves unable to afford the premiums after the failure of their business venture, self-employed who take the risk of not buying coverage, privately insured persons who find themselves unable to continue to afford private coverage because of declining income or rising premiums, and the long-term unemployed who lost unemployment benefits (*Arbeitslosengeld II*) after introduction of the Hartz IV employment market reforms and therefore lose their entitlement for health insurance coverage.[73] Low-income employees, divorced persons, alien residents, university students, and those who did not graduate from school are also at risk.[77]

CURRENT AND EMERGING ISSUES AND CHALLENGES

Cost Containment

Rooted in the Bismarck System of Social Health Insurance, the German healthcare system has always put more emphasis on free access and high numbers of providers and technological equipment than on cost-effectiveness or cost containment per se.[78] By the year 2000, the German government had become extremely concerned with the ever-rising cost of health care and undertook efforts to curb spending. In November 1999, the *Bundestag* (lower house of parliament) passed the "Reform 2000" bill, which was drafted to place severe limits on spending by physicians, dentists, and pharmacists and to impose heavy penalties on doctors who exceeded their budgets. The bill was rejected by the *Bundesrat* (upper house of parliament) only a month later.[20] The era of cost containment actually started much earlier, with the introduction of the Cost Containment Act of 1977. Since then, sickness funds and healthcare providers have been required to pursue a goal of contribution stability (i.e., holding increases in contributions level with the rate of rise in contributory income).[78] Additionally, a series of cost-containment acts employing various tools have been used, including the following:

- Budgets for sectors or individual providers
- Reference-price setting for pharmaceuticals
- Restrictions on high-cost technology equipment and number of ambulatory care physicians per geographic planning region
- Increased co-payments (both in terms of level and number of services)
- The exclusion of young people from certain dental benefits during 1997 and 1998

These acts led to a moderation of healthcare cost increases and to stabilized expenditures by the sickness funds as a proportion of the GDP per capita.[78] Additional cost containment measures were initiated in 1992 and considerably expanded in 1993. Providers and patients alike were issued a call for shared sacrifice; nevertheless, physician expenditures have continued to exceed

growth in worker wages by 2.1%, and hospital, pharmaceutical, and dental costs have also continued to be above estimates.[48]

Integration of East and West Germany

At the time of reunification of the two formerly separate German countries, the East German healthcare system could not have been more different from the West German system. It was a state-run system, with physicians as salaried state employees making an average of $10,000 annually. In contrast, physicians in the West were making an average of $100,000 annually.[20] Although the two systems roughly matched each other in numbers of physicians and hospital beds per capita, the characteristics and quality of each system were quite different as well.[48] The major challenge of reunification of the two countries, and of the two healthcare systems, can be summed up in one word: modernization. Many of the facilities in the former East were old, substandard structures in great disrepair or even obsolete. In a similar vein, health insurance coverage was provided primarily through company-based funds, in large part caused by the fact that many East German citizens were employees of state-run enterprises.[20] Shortly after the reunification, the West German government set out to bring the Eastern system more in line with its Western counterpart and to reflect better the Western (i.e., modern) image. Rather than to consider the strengths and weaknesses of both systems and pursue a more strategic merger emphasizing the former, the Western system was rapidly introduced into the East, even eliminating resources that had proven to be cost-effective, such as the policlinics with a defined referral system.[79] Making a successful transition from two very different systems to create a new and improved system has taken some time and will likely take more.

The Aging Population

The aging of the population and concomitant increasing prevalence of chronic diseases will put significant pressure on the political and healthcare system in Germany. According to a prediction by the federal statistical agency, there will only be 74 million inhabitants by 2050, a 31% decline of the population under 20 years of age (to 15.4% of the total population) and a 40% increase in the number of inhabitants 60 and over (to 38.9%).[12] For each 100 persons in the 20-to-60 age group, there will be 33.7 persons under age 20 and 85.1 persons age 60 and over.[12]

A parliamentary commission described the anticipated picture as follows: A decreasing population will lead to decreasing population density with great regional variations. The shift in the age structure of the population is going to be greater than anticipated until recently, and although immigration may soften the impact, it cannot reverse that shift, the average age of the population is going to increase considerably.[80] This trend is not limited to Germany but can be found in most developed countries and has effects beyond the healthcare system.

Germany is rated by the EU to be at medium risk with regard to the sustainability of its public finances because of a number of factors—aging of the population prominent among them, due to reforms of the pension system[81]; however, great challenges remain, not just for the healthcare system but also for German politics. The idea of solidarity in financing and providing access to health irrespective of means to pay—which are fundamental to the German healthcare system—will be severely tested.

REFERENCES

1. Schulze H. *Kleine Deutsche Geschichte*. München: C. H. Beck; 1996.

2. Jesse E. *Deutsche Geschichte: Vom Kaiserreich bis heute. Politik, Wirtschaft & Wissenschaft, Kunst & Kultur, Gesellschaft & Sport, Weltgeschichte*. München, Germany: Trautwein Lexikon Verlag; 2004.

3. Central Intelligence Agency. The World Factbook: Germany, April 15. Retrieved April 28, 2008, from https://www.cia.gov/library/publications/the-world-factbook/geos/gm.html.

4. R Busse, A Riesberg. *Health Care Systems in Transition—Germany: European Observatory on Health Care Systems*. Copenhague: WHO Regional Office for Europe; 2000.

5. German Embassy Washington DC. Questions & Answers about Germany, 2008. Retrieved April 30, 2008, from http://www.germany.info/relaunch/info/facts/facts/questions_en/landandpeople/population2.html

6. Statistisches Bundesamt. Bodenfläche nach Nutzungsarten, August 31. Retrieved April 30, 2008, from http://www.destatis.de/jetspeed/portal/cms/Sites/destatis/Internet/DE/Content/Statistiken/Umwelt/Umweltoekonomische Gesamtrechnungen/Flaechennutzung/Tabellen/Content75/Bodenflaeche,templateId=renderPrint.psml.

7. Bundesministerium des Inneren. Protokollarische Rangfragen. Retrieved April 30, 2008, from http://www.bund.de/nn_168112/Microsites/Protokoll/Rang-und-Titulierung/Protokollarische-Rangfragen/Protokollarische-Rangfragen knoten.html.

8. Bundesagentur für Außenwirtschaft. VR China bald drittgrößte Volkswirtschaft August 7. Retrieved April 30, 2008, from http://www.bfai.de/DE/Content/bfai-online news/2007/013/medien/s4-drittgroesste-volkswirtschaft.html.

9. European Commission. *Panorama of Transport*. Luxembourg, Germany: Office of Official Publications of the European Union; 2007.

10. Deutsche Bahn. Der DB-Konzern auf einen Blick, April 17. Retrieved May 1, 2008, from http://www.db.de/site/bahn/de/unternehmen/konzern/basisinformation/zahlen__fakten/aufeinenblick.html.

11. Arbeitsgemeinschaft Deutscher Verkehrsflughäfen. Pressemitteilung NR. 3/2008. Verkehrswachstum an den internationalen Verkehrsflughäfen in Deutschland steigt 2007 auf sechs Prozent, February 12. Retrieved May 1, 2008, from http://adv-net.org/download/presse/kumulierte_Werte_07.pdf.

12. Statistisches Bundesamt. Bevölkerung Deutschlands bis 2050. 11. koordinierte Bevölkerungsvorausberechnung (Presseexemplar), December. Retrieved April 30, 2008, from https://www-ec.destatis.de/csp/shop/sfg/bpm.html.cms.cBroker.cls?cmspath=struktur,vollanzeige.csp&ID=1020576.

13. Presse-und Informationsamt der Bundesregierung. Deutschland auf einen Blick. Retrieved May 1, 2008, from http://www.deutschland.de/aufeinenblick/uebersicht.php.

14. *Statistisches Jahrbuch*. Wiesbaden: Statistisches Bundesamt (Federal Statistical Office); 2007.

15. Forschungsgruppe für Weltanschauungen in Deutschland (fowid). Religionszugehörigkeit, Deutschland, Bevölkerung, 1950, 1961, 1970, 1987, 1990, 2003, 2004, 2005, November 21. Retrieved April 28, 2008, from http://fowid.de/file admin/datenarchiv/Religionszugehoerigkeit_Bevoelkerung_1950-2005.pdf.

16. Altenstetter C. International perspectives forum: Insights from health care in Germany. *J Am Public Health Assoc.* 2003;93(1):38–44.

17. Altenstetter C. From solidarity to market competition? Values, structures, and strategy in German health policy. In Powell FD, Wessen AF, eds. *Health Care Systems in Transition: An International Perspective*. Thousand Oaks, CA: Sage; 1999, pp. 47–112.

18. Solsten E, ed. *Germany: A Country Study*. Washington, DC: GPO for the Library of Congress; 1995.

19. Amelung V, Glied S, Topan A. Health care and the labor market: learning from the German experience. *Journal of Health Politics, Policy, and Law.* 2003;28(4):693–714.

20. Swami B. The German health care system. In Thai KV, Wimberley ET, McManus SM, eds. *Handbook of International Health Care Systems*. New York: Marcel Dekker, Inc.; 2002, pp. 333–358.

21. Starr P. *The Social Transformation of American Medicine: The Rise of a Sovereign Profession and the Making of a Cast Industry*. New York: Basic Books; 1982.

22. Herder-Dornreich P. *Ökonomische Theorie des Gesundheitswesens*. Baden-Baden, Germany: Nomos; 1994.

23. Kamke K. The German health care system and health care reform. *Health Policy.* 1998;43(2):171–194.

24. Brief history. Retrieved March 30, 2008, from www.social security.gov/history.ottob.html.

25. Funding health care: options for Europe. Copenhagen, Sweden: European Observatory on Health Care Systems, WHO Regional Office for Europe; 2002. Policy Brief No. 4.

26. Evans R. *The Third Reich in Power, 1933–1939*. New York: The Penguin Press; 2006.

27. Naas GE, Kretschmer R. Trauma nursing in the German health care system. *Int J Trauma Nurs.* 2007;8(1):9–14.

28. Ernst E. Commentary: the Third Reich—German physicians between resistance and participation. *Int J Epidemiol.* 2001;30:37–42.

29. Arabin B, Raum E, Mohnhaupt A, Schwartz FW. Two types of health care systems and their influence on the introduction of perinatal care: an epidemiological twin model in Berlin from 1950 to 1990. *Matern Child Health J.* 1999;3(2): 81–91.

30. Wahner-Roedler DL, Knuth P, Juchems RH. The German health care system. *Mayo Clin Proc.* 1997;72:1061–1068.

31. Green DG, Irvine B. *Health care in France and Germany: Lessons for the UK*. Lancing, UK: Hartington Fine Arts; 2001.

32. Kirchenberger S. Health care technology in Germany. In Banta D, Battista R, Gelband H, Johnson E, eds. *Health Care Technology and Its Assessment in Eight Countries*. Washington, DC: United States Congress; 1995, pp. 137–170.

33. Hurst JW. Reform of health care in Germany—reunification of Germany brings about health care reform, especially in Eastern Germany. *Health Care Finance Rev.* 1991;12(3): 76–83.

34. *Health Care Systems in Transition: HiT Summary*. European Observatory on Health Systems and Policies. Portugal 2004.

35. World Health Organization. Life expectancy at birth (years), 2005. Retrieved April 12, 2008, from http://www .who.int/whosis/database/country/compare.cfm?country= DEU&indicator=LEX0Male,LEX0Female&language= english.

36. Health care spending in the United States and OECD countries, 2007. www.kff.org/insurance/snapshot/chcm010307 oth.cfm.

37. OECD health data 2006. Organisation for Economic Co-operation and Development, 2006. Retrieved April 3, 2008, from www.oecd.org/dataoecd/46/36/38979632.xls.

38. Anderson R. Health care IT in Europe and North America, 2005. www.cl.cam.ac.uk/~rja14/Papers/nao-report-final.doc.

39. Cheng TM, Reinhardt UE. Shepherding major health systems reform: a conversation with German health minister Ulla Schmidt. *Health Aff* (*Millwood*). 2008;27(3):204–213.

40. Bundesministerium für Gesundheit. Welcome to Solidarity! Information on the 2007 Health Reform, March. Retrieved April 13, 2008, from http://www.bmg.bund.de/cln_040/ nn_600148/EN/Health/2007-health-reform,templateId= raw,property=publicationFile.pdf/2007-health-reform.pdf.

41. Dornberg J. Five years after reunification: easterners discover themselves, German Life, 1995, December 1995/ January 1996. www.germanlife.com/Archives/1995/9512_ 01.html.

42. Schweigert FJ. Solidarity and subsidiarity: Complementary principles of community development. *Journal of Social Philosophy.* 2002;33(1):33–44.

43. Putnam RD. Making democracy work: civic traditions in modern Italy. Princeton, NJ: Princeton University Press; 1993.

44. Organisation for Economic Co-operation and Development, OECD Health Data 2007. Retrieved May 1, 2008, from http://www.oecd.org/dataoecd/45/55/38979836.pdf.

45. World Health Organization Regional Office for Europe. European Health for all database. Retrieved April 27, 2008, from http://data.euro.who.int/hfadb/.

46. WHO Statistical Information System: Core health indicators, 2006. Retrieved March 22, 2008, from www.who .int/whosis/database/core/core_select.cfm.

47. Health care in Germany: National Coalition in Health Care, April 14, 2008, 2005.

48. Lassey ML, Lassey WR, Jinks MJ. *Health Care Systems Around the World: Characteristics, Issues, Reforms*. Upper Saddle River, NJ: Prentice-Hall; 1997.

49. Hagist C, Kotlikoff LJ. *Who's Going Broke? Comparing Healthcare Costs in Ten OECD Countries*. Cambridge, MA: National Bureau of Economic Research; 2005. Paper #11833.

50. World Health Organization. Immunization Profile— Germany, December 20. April 9, 2008, from http://www .who.int/vaccines/globalsummary/immunization/country profileresult.cfm?C='deu'.

51. World Health Organization. Mortality Country Fact Sheet 2006: Germany. Retrieved April 12, 2008, from http://www .who.int/whosis/mort/profiles/mort_euro_deu_germany .pdf.

52. Eurostat. Infant mortality (per 1000 live births). Retrieved April 12, 2008, from http://epp.eurostat.ec.europa.eu/ portal/page?_pageid=1996,39140985&_dad=portal&_ schema=PORTAL&screen=detailref&language=en& product=Yearlies_new_population&root=Yearlies_new_ population/C/C1/C14/cba13072.

53. World Health Organization. Mortality Country Fact Sheet 2006: United States of America. Retrieved April 12, 2008, from http://www.who.int/whosis/mort/profiles/mort_amro_ usa_unitedstatesofamerica.pdf.

54. Bundesministerium für Gesundheit. Informationen zur gesetzlichen Krankenversicherung. Retrieved April 13, 2008, from http://www.bmg.bund.de/cln_041/nn_666724/ DE/Themenschwerpunkte/Gesundheit/Gesetzliche Krankenversicherung/gesetzliche-krankenversicherung node,param=.html__nnn=true.

55. *Statistisches Bundesamt. Statistisches Jahrbuch 2007*. Wiesbaden: Statistisches Bundesamt, 2007.

56. Lungen M, Stollenwerk B, Messner P, Lauterbach KW, Gerber A. Waiting times for elective treatments according to insurance status: a randomized empirical study in Germany. *Int J Equity Health.* 2008;7:1.

57. Sawicki PT. [Quality of health care in Germany: a six-country comparison]. *Med Klin* (*Munich*). 2005;100(11):755–768.

58. Wichmann O, Hellenbrand W, Sagebiel D, et al. Large measles outbreak at a German public school, 2006. *Pediatr Infect Dis J.* 2007;26(9):782–786.

59. Siedler A, Tischer A, Mankertz A, Santibanez S. Two outbreaks of measles in Germany 2005. *Euro Surveill.* 2006; 11(4):131–134.

60. Heininger U, Loos K, Lorenz I, Rascher W. Compliance with recommended immunizations in adolescents. *Eur J Pediatr.* 2006;165(10):671–676.

61. World Health Organization, Regional Office for Europe Copenhagen. *Health21: The health for all policy framework for the WHO European Region (European Health for All Series; No. 6) 1999.*

62. Holm MV, Blank PR, Szucs TD. Trends in influenza vaccination coverage rates in Germany over five seasons from 2001 to 2006. *BMC Infect Dis.* 2007;7:144.

63. Muller D, Szucs TD. Influenza vaccination coverage rates in 5 European countries: a population-based cross-sectional analysis of the seasons 02/03, 03/04 and 04/05. *Infection.* 2007;35(5):308–319.

64. Schoen C, Osborn R, Doty MM, Bishop M, Peugh J, Murukutla N. Toward higher-performance health systems: adults' health care experiences in seven countries, 2007. *Health Aff (Millwood).* 2007;26(6):w717–734.

65. Schneider N, Dierks ML, Seidel G, Schwartz FW. The federal government commissioner for patient issues in Germany: initial analysis of the user inquiries. *BMC Health Serv Res.* 2007;7:24.

66. Geraedts M, Schwartze D, Molzahn T. Hospital quality reports in Germany: patient and physician opinion of the reported quality indicators. *BMC Health Serv Res.* 2007;7:157.

67. Redaktionsbüro Gesundheit. Qualitätsberichte der Krankenhäuser: Ausdruck einer neuen Transparenz-Kultur. Retrieved April 23, 2008, from http://www.die-gesundheitsreform.de/gesundheitssystem/themen_az/gesundheit_kompakt/pdf/gesundheit_kompakt_qualitaetsberichte_kranken haeuser.pdf?param=d.

68. Geraedts M. *Qualitätsberichte deutscher Krankenhäuser und Qualitätsvergleiche von Einrichtungen des Gesundheitswesens aus Versichertensicht, 2006.*

69. Gemeinsamer Bundesausschuss. Gemeinsamer Bundesausschuss führt Verfahren zur Datenvalidierung in der externen stationären Qualitätssicherung ein, December 21. April 26, 2008, from http://www.g-ba.de/informationen/aktuell/pressemitteilungen/131/.

70. Gesetz zur Stärkung des Wettbewerbs in der gesetzlichen Krankenversicherung (GKV-Wettbewerbsstärkungsgesetz—GKV-WSG) vom 26. März 2007. Bundesgesetzblatt. Vol. 2007. Bonn, 2007.

71. Bundesministerium für Gesundheit. Start des Pharmadialogs der Bundesregierung: Bilanz der Auswirkung des GKV-Modernisierungsgesetzes auf die Arzneimittelversorgung, November 24. Retrieved April 26, 2008, from http://www.bmg.bund.de/nn_600184/DE/Presse/Pressemit teilungen/Archiv/Presse-BMGS-1-2004/PM-24-11-2004 6288,param=.html.

72. Statistisches Bundesamt Deutschland. 1. Quartal 2007: Mehr als 200 000 Menschen waren nicht krankenversichert, February 7. Retrieved April 13, 2008, from http://www .destatis.de/jetspeed/portal/cms/Sites/destatis/Internet/DE/ Presse/pm/2008/02/PD08__045__122.psml.

73. Bundesministerium für Gesundheit. Ein Jahr Gesundheitsreform: Über 100.000 Rückkehrer in die Krankenversicherung. Retrieved April 1, 2008, from http://www.bmg.bund .de/cln_041/nn_600110/DE/Home/Neueste-Nachrichten/1 Jahr-Gesundheitsreform.html.

74. Weyers S, Lehmann F, Meyer-Nurnberger M, et al. [Strategies for action to tackle health inequalities in Germany]. *Bundesgesundheitsblatt Gesundheitsforschung Gesundheitsschutz.* 2007;50(4):484–491.

75. Rosenbrock R. [Health and justice in Germany]. *Gesundheitswesen.* 2007;69(12):647–652.

76. *Verband der privaten Krankenversicherung e. V. Zahlenbericht der privaten Krankenversicherung 2006/2007.* Köln: PKV. 2007.

77. Greß S, Walendzik A, Wasem J. Persons without health insurance in Germany: who are they and what can be done? Paper presented at Annual Meeting of the European Public Health Association (EUPHA), November 16–18, 2006, Montreux, Switzerland.

78. Busse R. Germany. In Wieners WW, ed. *Global Health Care Markets: A Comprehensive Guide to Regions, Trends, and Opportunities Shaping the International Health Arena.* San Francisco: Jossey-Bass; 2001, pp. 139–152.

79. Arabin B, Raum E, Mohnhaupt A, Schwartz FW. Two types of health care systema and their influence on the introduction of perinatal care: an epidemiological twin model in Berlin between 1950 and 1990. *Maternal and Child Health Journal.* 1999;3(2):81–91.

80. Deutscher Bundestag. *Schlussbericht der Enquête-Kommission "Demographischer Wandel-Herausforderungen unserer älter werdenden Gesellschaft an den Einzelnen und die Politik" (Drucksache 14/8800).* Berlin: Deutscher Bundestag, March 28, 2002, Drucksache 14/8800.

81. European Commission. Die langfristige Tragfähigkeit der öffentlichen Finanzen in der EU, April 12. Retrieved April 30, 2008, from http://europa.eu/scadplus/leg/de/lvb/l25091 .htm.

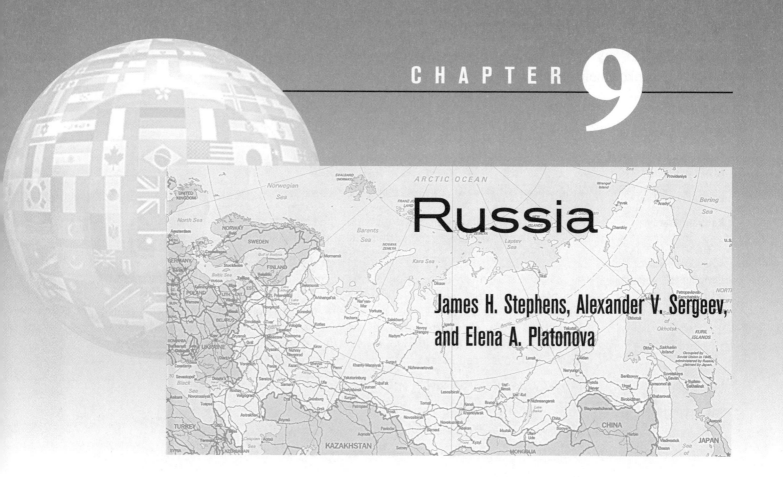

CHAPTER 9

Russia

James H. Stephens, Alexander V. Sergeev, and Elena A. Platonova

COUNTRY DESCRIPTION

TABLE 9-1 Russia

Nationality	Noun: Russian(s)
	Adjective: Russian
Ethnic groups	Russian 79.8%, Tatar 3.8%, Ukrainian 2%, Bashkir 1.2%, Chuvash 1.1%, other or unspecified 12.1% (2002 census)
Religions	Russian Orthodox 15% to 20%, Muslim 10% to 15%, other Christian 2% (2006 est.) Estimates are of practicing worshipers; Russia has large populations of nonpracticing believers and nonbelievers, a legacy of over 7 decades of Soviet rule
Language	Russian, many minority languages
Literacy	Definition: age 15 and over can read and write
	Total population: 99.4%
	Male: 99.7%
	Female: 99.2% (2002 census)

(continues)

TABLE 9-1   Russia   (continued)

Government type	Federation
Date of independence	August 24, 1991 (from Soviet Union)
Gross Domestic Product (GDP) per capita	$14,600 (2007 est.)
Unemployment rate	5.9% (2007 est.)
Natural hazards	Permafrost over much of Siberia is a major impediment to development; volcanic activity in the Kuril Islands; volcanoes and earthquakes on the Kamchatka Peninsula; spring floods and summer/autumn forest fires throughout Siberia and parts of European Russia
Environment: current issues	Air pollution from heavy industry, emissions of coal-fired electric plants, and transportation in major cities; industrial, municipal, and agricultural pollution of inland waterways and seacoasts; deforestation; soil erosion; soil contamination from improper application of agricultural chemicals; scattered areas of sometimes intense radioactive contamination; groundwater contamination from toxic waste; urban solid waste management; abandoned stocks of obsolete pesticides
Population	140,702,094 (July 2008 est.)
Age structure	0–14 years: 14.6% (male 10,577,858/female 10,033,254) 15–64 years: 71.2% (male 48,187,807/female 52,045,102) 65 years and over: 14.1% (male 6,162,400/female 13,695,673) (2008 est.)
Median age	Total: 38.3 years Male: 35.1 years Female: 41.4 years (2008 est.)
Population growth rate	−0.474% (2008 est.)
Birth rate	11.03 births/1,000 population (2008 est.)
Death rate	16.06 deaths/1,000 population (2008 est.)
Net migration rate	0.28 migrant(s)/1,000 population (2008 est.)
Gender ratio	At birth: 1.06 male(s)/female Under 15 years: 1.05 male(s)/female 15–64 years: 0.93 male(s)/female 65 years and over: 0.45 male(s)/female Total population: 0.86 male(s)/female (2008 est.)
Infant mortality rate	Total: 10.81 deaths/1,000 live births Male: 12.34 deaths/1,000 live births Female: 9.18 deaths/1,000 live births (2008 est.)
Life expectancy at birth	Total population: 65.94 years Male: 59.19 years Female: 73.1 years (2008 est.)
Total fertility rate	1.4 children born/woman (2008 est.)
HIV/AIDS adult prevalence rate	1.1% (2001 est.)

(continues)

TABLE 9-1 Russia (continued)

Number of people living with HIV/AIDS	860,000 (2001 est.)
HIV/AIDS deaths	9,000 (2001 est.)

Central Intelligence Agency. The World Fact Book, 2008. November 18, 2008, https://www.cia.gov/library/publications/the-world-factbook.

History

Modern Russians are descendants of the Slavic tribes that settled in the contemporary Western part of the Russian Federation (RF) where the state of "Kievan Rus" was established by the 9th century. In the 18th century, the Russian Empire was proclaimed under Tzar Peter the Great (Peter I) who conducted "Westernalization" reforms. After abolishment of serfdom in 1861, the process of industrialization and urbanization began. The Revolution of 1905 resulted in some constitutional reforms. The Romanov Tzar dynasty was overthrown during the February Revolution of 1917, and the Bolsheviks led by Vladimir Lenin seized power during the October Revolution of 1917. In 1922, the Union of Soviet Socialist Republics (the USSR) was formed with the Russian Soviet Federated Socialist Republic constituting the largest republic. Major industrialization and communist reforms in agriculture (collectivization) were under way in the 1920s to 1930s. The Soviet Union's war with Nazi Germany (the Great Patriotic War of 1941–1945) was a major theater of World War II. After the death of Joseph Stalin, some liberalization reforms were initiated by Nikita Khruschev. Later, under Leonid Brezhnev, a period of economic stagnation emerged, followed by major economical and political reforms, *perestroika* (restructuring) and *glasnost* (openness), under Mikhail Gorbachev. After the failed coup of August 1991 organized by Gorbachev's opponents, the USSR was abolished. In 1991, the official name of the Russian state was changed from the Russian Soviet Federated Socialist Republic to the RF.

FIGURE 9-1 Map of Russia

Size and Geography

Geographically, the Russian Federation (RF) is the world's largest country; the RF covers an area of 17,075,200 square kilometers (6,592,800 square miles), which is over one eighth of the earth's land area (Figure 9-1). The RF is located in two continents, Europe and Asia. Eight percent of the country's land is arable. The country's land border is 12,430 miles, and its coastline is 23,400 miles. The exclave region of the RF, Kaliningrad Oblast, borders Lithuania and Poland. The capital of the country is Moscow. As of November 2007, the population of the RF is 142.0 million[1]; it ranks as the ninth largest in the world. There are more than 180 ethnic groups in the RF[2]; the largest ones (each comprising more than 1% of the total population) are Russian (80%), Tatar (3.8%), Ukrainian (2.0%), Bashkir (1.2%), and Chuvash (1.1%). The official state language of the RF is Russian.

The average population density is about 8.4 people per square kilometer (about 3.2 people per square mile), whereas in the European part of the country, it is 25 people per square kilometer (9.7 people per square mile). The urban population constitutes 73.1% of the population. There are 1,095 cities in the RF. Eleven cities have a population of over 1,000,000 people, and 167 cities have populations over 100,000.

The RF is comprised of 84 federal subjects (constituent units): 47 oblasts (regions), 21 republics, 8 krais (territories), 5 autonomous okrugs (districts), 1 autonomous oblast (region), and 2 federal cities (Moscow and Saint Petersburg).

Government or Political System

The RF is a federative state with a republican form of government. There are three branches of power: executive, legislative, and judicial. The President, the Federal Assembly (parliament), and the government (ministries) and the courts exercise state power in the RF. The head of the state is the President. The President is elected by universal and direct suffrage for a 4-year term; the maximum number of consecutive presidential terms of office is two. The President appoints the Prime Minister, with the State Duma approval.

The Federal Assembly (parliament) consists of two chambers: the State Duma and the Federation Council (the upper chamber). The Federation Council consists of elected representatives of federal subjects (two representatives from each subject). The State Duma proposes and adopts laws; the Federation Council approves them.

The Constitutional Court and the Supreme Court constitute the judiciary. The Constitutional Court rules on cases of compliance of laws and presidential decrees with the Constitution. The Constitutional Court consists of 19 judges. The Constitutional Court judges are nominated by the President and are appointed by the Federation Council.[3] The Supreme Court is the highest appellate court in civil law, administrative law, and criminal law cases. The lower courts are supervised by the Supreme Court.

There are 15 political parties in the RF that are registered by the Central Election Commission of the RF. To be registered, a political party must have at least 50,000 members and have regional branches in more than half of the federal subjects of the RF, according to the federal law "On Political Parties."

Macroeconomics

The structure of the Russian economy is characterized by a significant prevalence of large companies, and a relatively high proportion of them are extraction industries and heavy industry.[4] The major industries are machinery, ferrous and nonferrous metallurgy (the Ural Economic Region, Siberia, and the Far East Economic Region), chemicals and petrochemicals (the Central Economic Region, the North West Economic Region, and the Volga Economic Region), forestry, timber processing, paper and pulp (the North and Far East parts of the country), light industry (mostly the textile industry), and the food industry. The economic regions are not constituent units of the RF. The gas reserves of the RF are the world's largest, and its oil reserves are the seventh largest in the world.[5] The fuel and energy sector accounts for about 50% of RF exports.[6]

For the last 15 years, the economic policy of the RF has been oriented on economic stabilization, liberalization of prices, and integration into the global economy.[7,8] Since 1993, labor moved from sectors with low productivity (agriculture) to high-productivy sectors (manufacturing and service).[9]

The Russian currency is the ruble—1 ruble = 100 kopeks. As of January 2008, the exchange rate was approximately 24.5 rubles for one U.S. dollar. In 2007, the RF ranked the eighth in the world, with a gross domestic product (GDP) of 1.224 U.S. trillion dollars, whereas in 2006, the country ranked the 11th in the world with a GDP of 26,883.9 billion rubles (987 billion U.S. dollars).[10] GDP growth has remained strong, with growth rates of 7.3% in 2003, 7.2% in 2004, 6.4% in 2005, 6.7%

in 2006, and 7.9% in the first half of 2007.[9,11] As a percentage of GDP, the breakdown in 2004 was industry at 27.9%, agriculture at 5.0%, construction at 7.2%, other production of goods at 0.8%, transportation and communications at 8.6%, trade at 21.9%, other market services at 17.9%, and nonmarket services at 10.6%.[12] The Russian economy has experienced an investment boom, but major investment activities are concentrated in the nontradable sectors and extraction industries. Although foreign investment substantially increased in the first half of 2007, foreign investment is concentrated in nontradable sectors and extracting industries.[9]

In recent years, annual inflation in the RF has been 10% and as high as 28.9% in January 2000.[9,13] The average monthly U.S. dollar salary in 2007 was USD 520.[9] In the first 9 months of 2007, the average unemployment rate had decreased to 6.3% as compared with 7.3% in the corresponding period of 2006.[9]

There are a total of 933,000 kilometers (about 587,000 miles) of automobile roads, including 755,000 kilometers (469,000 miles) of concrete or macadam roads and 128,000 kilometers (80,000 miles) of railroads in the RF.[14] The total length of the oil and gas pipelines is 224,000 kilometers (139,000 miles), and the total length of internal waterways is 102,000 kilometers (63,000 miles).[14] The major ports are Arkhangelsk, Vladivostok, Kaliningrad, Murmansk, Novorossiysk, Nakhodka, Magadan, Saint Petersburg, Tuapse, Astrakhan, Volgograd, Kazan, Krasnoyarsk, Moscow, Nizhniy Novgorod, Rostov, Samara, and Khabarovsk. The major airports are Sheremetyevo (Moscow), Domodedovo (Moscow), Vnukovo (Moscow), Pulkovo (Saint Petersburg), Tolmachevo (Novosibirsk), Koljtsovo (Yekaterinburg), Adler (Sochi), Pashkovskiy (Krasnodar), Yemelyanovo (Krasnoyarsk) and Kurumoch (Samara).

The Constitution of the RF (Article 43) guarantees the right to education for everyone. The legal regulations for the education system are laid down in the federal law "On Education." Ethnic minorities have the right to be educated at school in their native languages. The learning of the state language, Russian, is a compulsory component of a secondary school curriculum.[15] The report of the European Observatory on Health Systems and Policies states that the quality of education in the RF is high.[8]

Educational system of the RF consists of (1) preliminary education (kindergarten for children 3 to 6 years old), (2) compulsory incomplete secondary education (school grades 1–9), (3) complete secondary education (school grades 10–11, equivalent to high school

in the U.S. educational system), (4) higher education programs at universities (also known as institutes and academies) leading to a bachelor's degree (4 years), a specialist diploma (one additional 1 year beyond the bachelor's degree), or a master's degree (an additional 2 years beyond the bachelor's degree). After students finish their incomplete secondary education, students may enroll in either complete general secondary education programs at secondary schools or in complete vocational secondary education at vocational schools (equivalent to community colleges in the U.S. educational system). Higher medical education programs are 6 years of study for MD and 5 years for DDM. They are taught at medical institutes, medical academies, or medical universities (all these institutions are equivalent to medical schools in the United States). Professional preparation for nurses, physician assistants, and midwives is conducted in medical colleges (secondary medical education programs).

Postgraduate academic programs (*aspirantura*) are 3 to 4 years long, and they lead to a PhD (*Kandidat Nauk*) degree and require students to conduct original research, publish at least three original research articles based on their research results, pass candidate exams, and successfully defend their dissertation. Those who have obtained a master, specialist, or medical degree (MD or DDM) are eligible for enrollment in PhD programs. Bachelor degree holders and graduates of secondary medical education programs (nurses, physician assistants, and midwives) are not eligible for enrollment in PhD programs. The Russian *Kandidat Nauk* degree is equivalent to a PhD degree in the United States and Western Europe.[16] Those PhD degree holders who have achieved outstanding scientific results can be awarded another academic doctoral degree, which has no equivalent in other countries.[16]

Demographics

The age distribution of the population in 2006 is presented in Table 9-2.

According to the RF Census 2002, only 0.6% of the population 15 years old and older is illiterate. The RF has more academic graduates than any other country in Europe. Over 20% of the population aged 25 to 59 has graduate or postgraduate degrees; over 81% of the population aged 25 to 54 has educational attainment of at least a complete secondary education (equivalent to high school diploma in the U.S. educational system). In recent years, the demand for commercially oriented

TABLE 9-2 Age Distribution of the Population, 2006 (Federal State Statistics Service)

Years	Thousand Persons	Percentage of Total	Females per 1,000 Males of a Given Age
Total population	142,754	100	1,158
0–4	7,037	4.9	949
5–9	6,418	4.5	954
10–14	7,790	5.5	957
15–19	11,825	8.3	964
20–24	12,405	8.7	978
25–29	11,049	7.7	1,002
30–34	10,295	7.2	1,013
35–39	9,417	6.6	1,033
40–44	10,949	7.7	1,074
45–49	12,054	8.4	1,121
50–54	10,645	7.5	1,202
55–59	8,590	6.0	1,284
60–64	4,407	3.1	1,480
65–69	7,609	5.3	1,674
70 and over	12,264	8.6	2,452

From *Federal State Statistics Service, 2006*. Retrieved January 21, 2008, from http://www.gks.ru/free_doc/2007/b07 _12/05-02.htm.

education has emerged, resulting in an expansion of private institutions of higher education offering graduate degrees in law, business, and economics. As of 2006, there were 6,133,100 students enrolled in 660 state institutions of higher education, and 1,176,800 students were enrolled in 430 private institutions of higher education in the RF.[17]

The Gini Index (ranges from 0 indicating absolute equality of income distribution to 1.0 representing absolute inequality) for the RF is 0.456.[18] In terms of absolute poverty, 7.5% of the country's population reported living on no more than 2.15 U.S. dollars per day.[18] Orthodoxy (Russian Orthodox Church) constitutes the largest religious group (practiced by approximately 75% of Census respondents). The second largest group is Muslims (about 8%). Other religious groups constitute less than 2%.[19]

In the RF, the top five conditions contributing to the total disability-adjusted life years are cardiovascular disease, unintentional injuries, neuropsychiatric conditions, intentional injuries, and malignant neoplasms for males and cardiovascular disease, neuropsychiatric conditions, unintentional injuries, malignant neoplasms, and digestive diseases for females. The top three risk factors for males are alcohol consumption, smoking, and high blood pressure. For females, the risk factors are high blood pressure, high serum cholesterol, and obesity (high body mass index).[18]

BRIEF HISTORY OF THE HEALTHCARE SYSTEM

Since 1991, the main focus of the healthcare system in the RF has been a transition from an integrated, hierarchical model of healthcare delivery to a more decentralized and insurance-based structure of public health care. Before the 1990s, the Soviet healthcare system was wholly financed from general government revenues.[20] The Soviet Union's total expenditures for medical care in 1960 were approximately 6.6% of the GDP. It dropped to 6% in 1970 and 5% by 1980. In principle, healthcare services were provided free to all citizens, and all health personnel were state employees. Socialized healthcare practices led to overutilization of hospital beds. Interestingly, the system's priority was on the control of epidemics and infectious disease, which contributed to a large public health network with the goal of isolating infected patients. Needless to say, the Soviet System tended to underestimate the importance of primary care and placed enormous emphasis on specialists and hospital care. Despite such weaknesses, the previous integrated model successfully dealt with infectious diseases such as tuberculosis, typhoid fever, and typhus; however, during the 1960s and 1970s, life expectancy and other health indicators stalled and even reversed. By 1991, many of the strengths of the old integrated state system had eroded as a result of underinvestment in general and declining funding for prevention. Despite a doubling in the number of hospital beds and doctors per capita between 1950 and 1980, the quality of care was in decline by the early 1980s.[21]

Facing such a declining situation, Russian authorities decided to make the transition to an insurance-based system. The goal was to maintain the established idea of a citizen's right to health care free of charge while restructuring the system to make it more efficient and responsive to people's needs. In 1991, the RF created a Federal Fund for Mandatory Medical insurance (*Federal'niy Fond Obayazatel'nogo Meditsinskogo Strakhovamiya-FFOMS*), as well as territorial funds in each constituent region. It was the intent of the mandatory medical insurance (*obyazatel'noe meditsinskoe strakhovanie—OMS*) system to enable patients to choose among competing insurance companies who would function as buyers of medical services; therefore, OMS funds would be directed to healthcare providers through insurance companies and give incentives both for quality patient care and efficiency.

Anna Korotkova, head of healthcare quality research for the Russian Ministry of Health's Public Research Institute in Moscow, stated that inadequate health insurance funding is only part of the problem; recent research suggests that patients are hospitalized too long and too often for the wrong reasons. Korotkova further stated, "Of course, we need more money for health care. But throwing more money at this won't solve the real problem if we don't also act to change clinical practice."[22]

Despite the original plan of shifting to an insurance-based system, federal and regional budgets still administer about 60% of public healthcare expenditures.[23] The remaining healthcare expectations are channeled through the OMS system. In 2001, the OMS system received a unified social tax equal to 3.6% of payroll, 3.4% to regional OMS funds, and 0.2% to the FFOMS. This left the system as a whole underfinanced. Interregional disparities could be managed only through various regional support programs operating under the federal budget; however, such transfers went to regional budgets, not regional OMS funds. Many regions decided not to transfer the funds to OMS but to use them for other purposes. It is also the responsibility of regional governments to pay the health insurance of people who are not employed, including children, pensioners, and the disabled.[24]

Russian President Vladimir Putin provided a boost to the healthcare system with the release of a report condemning inefficient healthcare delivery and mismanagement of the federal insurance fund. The report from the Kremlin's government concluded that because Russia's health insurance fund receives only a fifth of the funds needed to sustain the system adequately, patients are denied "equal access to free medical services guaranteed by the state." Sergei Shishkin, senior researcher at Moscow's Institute for the Economy in Transition stated, "The Putin government is increasingly serious about overhauling health funding, which currently relies on an eclectic and inefficient mix of funds from government budgets and health insurance."[31] Although the Russian constitution still guarantees universal access to medical care, healthcare quality has declined since the Soviet collapse.

The largest proportion of household spending on health care is payment for prescriptions. Russia's attempt to control rising prescription costs was through a combination of cost sharing and regulations. Typically, drugs are provided to hospital patients free, but outpatients may have to pay for most of their prescriptions. Such a situation provides incentives for unnecessary hospitalization. In practice, it is estimated that about 80% of inpatients pay a portion of the prescriptions. Generally, hospitals have to buy drugs on commercial contracts from their budgets, which are limited. Combined with poorly enforced controls on wholesale and retail markups, drugs are often not available for hospital patients unless they can pay. It is believed that a significant proportion of drugs needed by Russians are not available.[8] Drugs account for 30% of total healthcare spending. The high share of spending on drugs might also reflect an cultural expectation left over from the Soviet period that any consultation with a physician will result in a prescription.[8,25,26]

The Russian healthcare system still relies too much on specialist treatment and hospitalization. Hospital inpatient stays are common and too long. Although there has been some success in changing this practice method, progress has been slow. Starodubov reports that the share of healthcare expenditures devoted to inpatient services fell by only two percentage points over the preceding decade, and Russians still spend about twice as much on inpatient care as on outpatient services. Approximately 30% of Russian physicians work in outpatient care settings, where 60% of them are specialists. It has been the history of Russia that primary care has been the least prestigious and least paid field of medicine. The reputation of primary care physicians is low among the profession and the population. Recent substantial salary increases for primary care physicians and nurses in policlinics slowed the workforce flow away from primary health care and helped to fill understaffed positions in policlinics.

DESCRIPTION OF THE CURRENT HEALTHCARE SYSTEM

Facilities

Russian laws passed in 1991 and 1993 reduced the government's responsibilities for all but a few dozen hospitals, recognized as top national centers. The responsibilities were turned over to local government, while establishing a mandatory medical insurance system.[19] There is little private provision of health care except in large Russian cities like Moscow and St. Petersburg, although even there, they are used by only a small elite group. Even the elite hospitals, such as Moscow's 200-bed Hematology Science Center, suffer from dire financial conditions.[22]

For most citizens of the RF, health care is provided by facilities managed by their regional/district administration. Most of these facilities have a service area of 15,000 to 50,000 people. A central district hospital is responsible for the administration of all facilities in the district with specialized facilities accountable to the regional health administration. The few tertiary-level facilities are owned by the federal Ministry of Health. These facilities receive part of their funding from regional and federal budgets, in addition to funding from the federal health insurance fund.[27] Facilities are generally not well maintained, and equipment tends to be seriously outdated. In rural areas, physicians' access to the Internet is limited.

Workforce

The healthcare industry of the RF employs 7% of the working population, totaling 4.5 million people in 2000. According to RosStat, the National Committee on Statistics, medical facilities employ 3,563,000 people. Rehabilitation facilities employ 300,000 people, and social care employs 372,000 people.[28]

There were 680,000 physicians in 1990, with a ratio of 4.07 per 1,000 population. Of these, 154,000 were specialists in internal medicine, 89,000 surgeons, 69,500 pediatricians, 55,000 dentists, and 41,000 obstetrician/gynecologists. Only 1,500 physicians have been trained in modern family medicine or general practice.[29] Males tend to focus on the highest profile areas, such as surgery, urology, gynecology, and other specialties, that earn significantly higher incomes, whereas females generally are in the first-level district facilities. The former Soviet system's medical education was rigid and centralized, lacking adequate teaching faculty familiar with world educational standards and a comprehensive vision of the role of medical education in the healthcare system and society.[30] Medical schools, even the most prestigious and higher-quality schools in Moscow and St. Petersburg, were generally freestanding institutions and not affiliated with a university.[31] The collapse of the Soviet Union left Russia unprepared to operate a system of medical education at the level of Western educational standards. Various institutions from abroad are now assisting in overhauling and modernizing the system.[32]

Over the past decade, the countries from central Asia and Eastern Europe have been discarding the Russian health system. Development of a new model of general practice began in the 1980s, with pilot projects in St. Petersburg, Kemerovo, and Samara.[33] A new training curriculum was developed at the federal level, while allowing regional variations. Training centers were established, often with help from international donors. The first cohort of general practitioners was trained in 1992. The adoption of the new model based on general practice sought to strengthen primary care while tackling excessive specialization.[34] There was a political imperative to converge with western European models, which were somewhat influential, arguing that radical change would be easier than reforming the entrenched present model; however, some Russian critics argued that the transformation of specialists into generalists will be problematic and will require a major investment in training and institutional change. Others argue how the newly trained staff is often isolated, leading to two disconnected models of care with fundamental structural problems being ignored.[35] On the other hand, family practice has been implemented successfully in some places where there has been a coherent reform framework, with institutional support and consistent incentives.[36] Which model is best remains a subject of debate, although the general practice model has been universally implemented, with little testing of alternatives.

The organization of primary care in Russian cities and district levels is delivered in policlinics, whereas in rural areas, it is mostly delivered in small primary care practices staffed by *feldshers*, a form of physician assistant. Russia has four categories of policlinics: those for adults, those for mothers and children, women's health policlinics ("zhenskie konsuljtatsii"), and those for specific disorders such as tuberculosis, sexually transmitted diseases, mental disorders, and addictions. Policlinics are staffed by district physicians, each responsible for a geographically defined population of approximately 1,700 people. In addition, the clinics have "specialists" to include internal medicine, pediatrics, obstetrician/gynecologists, and otorhinolaryngology. Less often, they have general practice. There are also parallel systems serving the employees of some ministries and industries. The small private sector consists mainly of general practitioners and "outpatient specialists." Policlinic staff provides only basic treatment and little gatekeeping or follow-up, and these clinics are often bypassed, with patients seeking hospital care through formal or informal channels.[37]

The largest share of new general practitioners (75%) returned to work after training to traditional district policlinics and in outpatient facilities linked to industries (5%). Both types of facilities are mainly in urban areas; only 8% of the new general practitioners work in rural facilities, although 27% of the population is rural.[38] A few (6%) went to independent practices or private facilities. New general practitioners reported that they faced major barriers in applying what they learned, and they faced opposition from senior physicians, unreformed financial structures, and scarce equipment. Most general practitioners are paid salaries, although four regions are experimental sites that have introduced other methods. Many show enthusiasm for a shift to capitation payments and per procedure payments. Still, many comment on huge discrepancies between the average monthly income of general practitioners in state versus private primary care facilities.

A scale regulates all salaries in the public sector. A distinguishing feature of the Russian healthcare system is that physicians' one full-time effort (1.0 FTE) workday does not exceed 8 hours, and some physicians who specialize in policlinics have 6.5-hour workdays. Because of very low physician pay, this arrangement enables them to work in more than one place.[28] Some even subsidize their income by being taxicab drivers at night.

There was a significant decline in the number of nurses in the 1990s. Among nurses, 65% are general nurses, 10% midwives, and 10% nurse practitioners, and less than 5% work in specialized clinical operations. The Ministry of Health indicates that 99% of nurses in the RF are women. Most of these nurses (74.4%) work in inpatient facilities. There is a disparity in the number of nurses between rural and urban areas.

Health managers in the Russian health system are physicians. The directors of regional and federal health organizations are almost exclusively physicians. Most often, they continue their clinical practice. There is only one regular health management program for nonphysicians, comprised of 2 years of training in health management and public health; however, many new graduates are not attracted by working conditions in the government healthcare sector, as they cannot compete for positions historically held by physicians.

Implementation of primary care reform in Russia has proven difficult and slow. The scale of the task was underestimated, given the estimated need for 90,000 general practitioners. Only 2,500 have been trained so far.[39] The broad, federal legislative framework provides no detailed guidance on the roles and responsibilities of general practitioners and their relationship with specialists. General practitioners have little opportunity to use their new skills. There is also little evidence of meaningful integration into the healthcare system, with the persistent hierarchy and hospital-dominated system leading to demoralization.[37] Yet the new model seems popular with patients, as has been noted in other former communist countries.[40]

EVALUATION OF THE HEALTHCARE SYSTEM

Cost

In the Soviet Union, the majority of healthcare services were constitutionally free of charge for its citizens. In fact, the Soviet Union was the first nation that guaranteed a wide range of free medical services for the entire population.[8] The healthcare system was uniform with the government responsible for managing and financing health care at every level (republic, oblast, and local) and was funded from general revenues (state tax–financed model).[8] Despite the stated goals of comprehensiveness and equitable access for the entire population, the Soviet Union did not have sufficient resources to implement the strategy. Additionally, the existence of the "parallel" healthcare systems (e.g., Ministry of Defense, Ministry of Transportation, Ministry of Internal Affairs) increased costs for society.[41] The system was hospital dominated and policies were oriented toward expansion of medical services. For instance, budget allocations for hospitals were based on the number of beds and hospital personnel, therefore creating an incentive to fill the beds.[42] Consequently, the healthcare sector was severely underfunded, inefficient, and offered low-quality services.[8,43] At the beginning of the 1990s, the RF was the only industrialized country in which population life expectancy and other basic health indicators had significantly deteriorated.[32,44,45] There was a growing realization that Russia's healthcare system was in a deep crisis and that it had to be reformed.[42,44,46–48] Russian reformers decided to address the problem through reform of healthcare financing and mandatory health insurance.[46,48,49] The key goals of the reform were to continue providing comprehensive medical coverage for the entire population by bringing in additional funds and therefore strengthening healthcare financially. There was an effort to shift away from the previous method of central government planning, management, and financing. To improve healthcare efficiency and quality, financial incentives for health care providers, insurers, and patients were introduced.[8,33,46,48,50,51] The reforms were also intended to focus on primary health care by attracting the most competent doctors to this sector. The objective was to encourage primary care providers to treat patients on an outpatient basis in an ambulatory setting instead of giving referrals to hospitals.[8] This would reduce hospitalizations, increase efficiency, and improve the quality of medical care.[33,52,53]

The law "On Health Insurance of Citizens in the Russian Federation" was passed in 1991, and mandatory health insurance was introduced in 1993. The law stipulated that the majority of healthcare funds be raised by regional/territorial governments.[54] It requires that employers and territorial governments make contributions to one of the territorial Mandatory Health Insurance Funds (MHIF) located in the oblasts/territories of the RF. MHIFs are nonprofit, independent entities responsible for managing healthcare finance at the oblast (territory) level and accountable to the respective government. Employers are expected to contribute 3.6% of their payroll costs (with no matching employee contribution) to the MHIFs. From those funds, 3.4% is retained at the territorial level and is used mainly for the services provided by territorial and local health authorities (HAs). The remaining 0.2% is transferred to the Federal Mandatory Health Insurance Fund in Moscow for equalization purposes (to subsidize poorer territories). MHIFs would transfer the retained funds (3.4%) to private health insurance companies (in the territories where they exist) based on a weighted capitation formula. Oblast/territorial governments would cover medical expenses for the nonworking segments of the population such as children, students, retired, or unemployed, as well as individuals on disability by paying contributions to respective MHIFs. According to the law, mandatory health insurance may be supplemented with voluntary (private) insurance if patients want a higher level of healthcare services and can afford to purchase private insurance.[46] Employers may also purchase private health insurance for their employees for services not covered by mandatory health insurance.[8]

The system was thought to facilitate market mechanisms by means of introducing a third-party payer (health insurance companies) and relying on competition between healthcare insurers and healthcare providers. Private health insurance companies would have the incentive to select efficient healthcare providers who would deliver high-quality health services; insurers would have to compete for contracts with MHIFs, thus creating an incentive to improve health services quality.[55] Physicians and healthcare facilities would compete for contracts with heath insurers and have the incentive to deliver high-quality, low-cost service; patients would have freedom of choice of both healthcare providers and insurers.[8]

The law allows healthcare providers to supplement their income by redeploying some resources and selling services to private patients and contracting with enterprises for the provision of services to their employees.[56,57] Hence, there are formal/legal (through a cash register) payments for privately delivered care and extra services (so-called chargeable health services). "Chargeable" services may be provided by healthcare facilities only if they have special permission from a corresponding HA. "Chargeable" services may include some diagnostic and treatment services, as well as orthopedic and dental prostheses.[50,57]

Russia's implementation of universal health insurance, however, has been extremely challenging.[56,58] The key obstacle was the failure to get sufficient financial resources for reform implementation.[56] The relative portion of government allocations to health care has been falling steadily since the introduction of the reform.[59] In 2003, governmental contributions, both from the federal and territorial levels of government, represented approximately 50% of total funding.[8] Additionally, the proposed reform was structurally and managerially complex. A combination of old and new financial arrangements, wide variations in reform execution in different territories, poor coordination, and ill-defined responsibilities among major stakeholders in healthcare finance contributed to slow and incomplete implementation. The failure to introduce competition among insurance companies also contributed to its demise.[49] Furthermore, in some territories, the new financing mechanisms were not introduced at all, and in other territories, the new system was introduced only in some districts. In some territories, insurance companies did not exist at the time of reform implementation.[8] According to a survey of practicing managers in the mid-1990s, the reform was unfinished or defective.[48]

Current Healthcare Financing

Currently, the healthcare system in Russia is characterized by a mixed structure of formal and informal healthcare financing.[50,59] The formal funds come from two major sources: governmental (federal, territorial, and municipal) budgets and MHIFs payments in the oblasts/territories of the RF. Each year the Ministry of Health and the Ministry of Finance develop a national healthcare budget. The national budget includes federally funded core programs such as immunizations, diagnosis and treatment of diabetes and tuberculosis, and medical technologies development, among others. Federally funded programs are financed nationally through general taxation. The national budget also includes other expenditures such as direct Ministry of Health costs and maintenance of federal healthcare facilities.[8]

The second major source of financing is payments from MHIFs and territorial/local governments. MHIFs' budgets are developed primarily using the insurance premiums from employers for their workers and payments from local governments for the nonworking populations (children, unemployed, students, disabled, older

persons) in their respective oblasts/territories.[46] MHIFs finance primary and secondary care, which amounts to about two thirds of the budget. Territorial and local governments finance tertiary and specialized care.[8]

These two major funding sources are sometimes supplemented by direct contracts between companies and healthcare providers. Additionally, the healthcare system gets allocations from other state ministries. For example, the Ministry of Finance does not only transfer budget funds to the Ministry of Health but also transfers funds for social purposes directly to oblasts/territories.[46] The territories then independently decide how much of the transfers to allocate to health care, education, and other social services. Territories subsequently transfer funds to districts. The districts decide independently on how to allocate the funds.[8] The funds transferred from the Ministry of Finance are typically used for capital investments in hospitals, facility repairs, buying equipment, building special facilities such as psychiatric hospitals, maternal hospitals, and funding federal healthcare facilities.[46]

Other significant funding sources of health care are transfers from the "parallel" healthcare systems, whose finances are completely independent from the Ministry of Health,[8] and out-of-pocket payments from individuals.[59] A considerable proportion of out-of-pocket payments is paid informally/illegally ("under the table"). Some experts believe that under-the-table payments are one of the major sources of healthcare funding.[4] A comprehensive review on informal, out-of-pocket payments for health care in Russia was published by the Moscow Public Science Foundation and Independent Institute for Social Policy in 2003.[56] According to their analysis, 10% of respondents had to pay for outpatient services in 2001, and only about half of the payments were made legally (via a cash register). About 56% of payments were made directly to healthcare providers in cash, or patients had to give gifts to the providers later. The largest part of informal/illegal payments is made for hospital services. It is estimated that one third of all hospital payments are illegal.[8] A Russia Longitudinal Monitoring Survey[56] found that about 15% of all hospitalized patients had to pay for inpatient treatments in 2001. Furthermore, hospitalized individuals often have to bring their own medications, hypodermic needles, bandages, and sometimes even their own bedding. Specifically, one study found that about 12% of hospitalized patients had to buy and bring medications, needles, and bandages to the hospital.[59] A recent study of pediatric hospitals in Russia by European and Russian researchers found that although hospitalizations were officially free for admitted children, their parents often had to buy expensive medications and give them to attending physicians to treat their children because hospitals did not have the necessary medications.[60] The study found that hospital care was characterized by unnecessary use of multiple drugs, and the costs were passed onto patients and their families. Out-of-pocket expenditures for many allegedly free-of-charge healthcare services are becoming a common practice in Russia.[46,56,59,60]

Healthcare Expenditures

The exact amount of financial resources spent on health care in Russia is unknown because of incomplete reporting of financial flows.[8] Parallel systems' budgets are typically not included in the calculations of publicly funded health care. Also, territories now have more control and independence in resource allocation. Territorial healthcare budgets amount to about 45% of healthcare financing and have also significantly declined since the inception of the reform.[8] MHIF funding has been steady for years at about 15%. The role of private health insurance is still negligible in Russia but is rising. According to the World Health Organization (WHO), private health insurance contributed only 3.5% of total healthcare financing in 1999, and by 2004, it already represented 9.9%. Continuous funding shortages and cost escalation result in higher out-of-pocket payments,[61] which have increased dramatically, especially payments for pharmaceuticals.[8] In 2004, out-of-pocket expenditures on health, as a percentage of private expenditure on health, were 76.7%.[62]

Additionally, there are considerable unreported official and unofficial (illegal) out-of-pocket payments for health services. The International Monetary Fund (IMF) reported that in 2006 total governmental expenditures on health represented 4% of Russia's GDP.[63] Out-of-pocket and illegal payments bring total healthcare spending to 6.5% to 7.0% of the nation's GDP.[8] This estimation is in line with the assessment provided by the WHO in 2007.

Provider Reimbursement

According to the health insurance law, healthcare providers in Russia can be paid in a number of ways including capitation, fee-for-service, diagnosis-related groups (DRGs), global budgets, or a combination of methods. Each territory decides independently on a preferred method of payment.[57,59] Tariffs on healthcare services covered by mandatory health insurance are de-termined by territorial governments, insurance companies, and professional medical associations and are stipulated in the contracts between healthcare providers and MHIFs/insurance companies.[46] MHIFs transfer funds to competing insurance companies (in territories where they exist) using a weighted capitation formula to address the issue of different medical costs for different population groups. MHIFs make direct payments to healthcare providers in territories where insurance companies do not exist.[46]

Primary and Secondary Care Financing   Different payment methods may be used to reimburse providers, including capitation, number of visits, or payments for specific procedures that provide an incentive to treat patients in outpatient settings instead of referring them to hospitals. Healthcare providers may or may not enter into contracts with local insurance companies. Providers also receive considerable amounts of funding from the local government.[8] Local HA receives its budget from its respective government and allocates fixed budgets (on a per capita basis) to MHIFs for payment to policlinics.[46]

Hospital Financing   Budget allocations for hospitals are typically based on the number of beds and hospital staff; however, hospitals are experimenting with various payment methods.[64] Territories are using different payment methods simultaneously, such as DRGs and global budgets, among others. Sheiman[64] analyzed trends in hospital payment in Russia and found that DRG payments had increased by 8% within a few years. According to another study, new hospital payment methods in territories where they were introduced amounted to about one third of hospital revenues. The remaining two thirds comes from territorial budgets and is based on traditional payment methods that are retrospective.[8]

In territories where insurance companies are active, the insurance companies negotiate with hospitals a system of case payments (a type of DRG payment), which specify an adequate length of stay (LOS), appropriate treatments, and procedures expected for each case for a given diagnosis. Insurers typically pay hospitals on a case-by-case basis and then retrospectively bill a respective MHIF for each item reimbursed by them. Hence, insurers do not create incentives for inpatient facilities to reduce volumes and costs. The insurers' role is therefore claims processing.[8]

Healthcare Personnel Compensation   The pay system was inherited from the former Soviet Union: Healthcare professionals are employed by a respective level of government and are paid salaries.[8,57] Basic salary levels are determined centrally and upgraded annually in accordance with Ministry of Health and Ministry of Finance assessment. Healthcare personnel are also paid performance-based bonuses.[8] A recent study of general practice in Russia by British researchers found that most general practitioners are paid salaries though respondents expressed interest in switching to capitation.[65] There is not much difference between how primary care doctors and specialists are reimbursed; however, there are more opportunities for specialists and hospitalists to improve their clinical expertise and have higher workloads. Thus, they tend to have slightly higher salaries.[8] Medical doctors and nurses continue to be underpaid. In 2001, the average pay was at 61% of the national pay average[59]; however, official numbers may be quite misleading as extensive illegal payments to physicians and nurses may considerably supplement their official salaries.[8]

The private healthcare sector appears to use a variety of approaches to reimburse physicians. They often pay physicians a share of profits in addition to a basic salary. Physicians offering private consultations charge a fee for service. If they work out of a clinic, they may keep a significant amount of the fees.[8]

Public Health Financing

In the Soviet Union, a public health service was based on the Sanitary–Epidemiological system covering the entire country, which carried out traditional roles such as environmental health and epidemiological control.[42,66] Public health was traditionally oriented toward curative health services, with a bias toward inpatient care in hospitals rather then health promotion and prevention.[67,68] Consequently, public health activities were often ill-focused and underfunded.

Public health continues to be highly centralized and hierarchical.[67] Most of the activities related to disease prevention and health promotion are controlled and directly financed by the Ministry of Health. There are also other industries involved in public health financing. For instance, the Ministry of Labor and Social Development covers certain prevention activities for the working population. It provides vouchers to sanatoriums, health resources, and children's summer camps. The vouchers are then sold for a reduced price to employees and their families.[66]

The public health sector in the RF receives less attention and resources than funding of clinical care and healthcare providers.[42,45,66,69] Local public health agencies are severely understaffed, with staff levels meeting 60%

to 70% of the demand.[52] HAs and health insurance companies are managed by physicians who sometimes may underestimate prevention. Additionally, there is very limited collaboration between the curative and preventive parts of the healthcare system.[67]

Consequently, the healthcare system is not effective in addressing current health problems.[66] Compared with the rest of Europe, male life expectancy,[45,70] low birth rates, high infant mortality rates, cardiovascular diseases, alcoholism, tuberculosis, HIV/AIDS, road accidents, and suicides are the worst and are resulting in a demographic crisis.[45,52,70] The grim situation is exacerbated by the reappearance of communicable diseases that were practically eliminated (e.g., syphilis and poliomyelitis) or were effectively controlled (e.g., tuberculosis) in the former Soviet Union.[69]

Quality

According to the WHO, in 2004, the infant mortality rate (the probability of dying under the age of one) was 13 per 1,000 live births, and maternal mortality was 67 per 100,000. In 2005, Russia had the largest population in Europe and the lowest life expectancy: 59 years for males and 72 years for females.[62] A study[60] assessed quality of care in pediatric hospitals in Russia using a standard WHO assessment tool and found that the quality of care is insufficient because of the lack of modern treatment technologies, facilities, and medications. The study also found that the typical quality problems were over-hospitalization, overdiagnosis, and resultant overmedication. These conclusions are in line with Sheiman's[64] estimate that about one third of all hospitalized patients at any time could be treated on an outpatient basis. Other major quality-related issues are a lack of evidence-based approaches in clinical decision making, organization of medical care, and disincentives for efficient medicine.[60]

Consequently, many Russians are dissatisfied with the accessibility and quality of medical care, the inability to choose a physician, long lines in outpatient facilities, insufficient compassion by healthcare personnel, and insufficient protection against low-quality health care.[44] Many Russians feel that in addition to having decreased availability of health care there are no realistic guarantees of quality care.[8] According to a 2005 empirical study,[72] all respondents from different territories of Russia reported deterioration in quality of care. The respondents also thought that the most important healthcare quality problems were high costs, unavailability of medications, quality of hospital facilities, and information given to patients. In the same study, approximately

25% of respondents were convinced that quality deteriorated after the reforms were introduced. Another patient survey shows that about 74% of the population believes that either the availability of medical care had decreased or there was no change in the situation since the inception of the reform.[72]

Access

An empirical study[71] conducted in eight countries of the former Soviet Union in 2000–2001 found that access to medical care and medications seemed to be generally affordable in Russia. A 2006 study found that access to inpatient care in Russian pediatric hospitals was generally good and that the majority of pregnant women had access to healthcare.[60] Officially, high-quality, free healthcare should be available for everyone in the nation. In reality, healthcare quality varies considerably. There are elite medical institutions that are typically accessible for a limited number of well-connected individuals; for the "average" patient, access and quality of health care are notoriously poor.[22,59,61] There is a widening gap between social groups regarding healthcare access and availability. Additionally, the distribution of healthcare funds between rural and urban areas is worsening. Although large urban areas are doing relatively well, rural areas are severely underfunded and these inequities are getting worse.[8,61] Furthermore, high and continuously rising costs of health care and medications are forcing segments of the population to go without some medications and medical services.[59]

Access to health care and insurance mostly depends on the employment status of an individual and the geographic location. Although by Russian law no one can be denied urgent/hospital care, individuals must be registered in the territory of their residence to be assigned to a policlinic and have access to primary healthcare services. Consequently, marginalized and hard-to-reach groups such as migrants, temporary workers, and informal workers have inadequate or no access to primary health care.[55]

CURRENT AND EMERGING ISSUES AND CHALLENGES

For more than 15 years, since 1992, the RF has been undergoing major healthcare reforms. Their successful implementation and achievement of the intended results pose major current challenges for the Russian health system. Before 1992, the overcentralized Soviet-era health system was in place. Since 1992, the major changes from the vertically integrated and state-regulated "socialized medicine" to "market medicine" have been conducted at a fast pace with an intention to introduce into the healthcare system incentives to improve the system's efficiency and quality of care. The reforms were supposed to encourage competition between healthcare providers, to decrease the state's involvement in health services financing by developing a contribution-based system of funding, to increase individuals' responsibility for their health, to reward physicians for providing good health care, and to decrease provision of unnecessary care.[73–78] It became a challenge for many people to accept the adaptation of the field of medicine to the "free market," which was the major goal of the reforms.[53,78–82] While some healthcare professionals believed that the reforms constituted a way to a sustainable health system, others believed that the reforms were ruining rather than strengthening Russian health care.[33,83–86]

A growing demand for additional healthcare management education has been observed not only among administrators, but among practicing physicians as well.[87] Appropriate effort is needed to meet this demand. The regional authorities were provided with an unprecedented amount of decision-making authority in local governing issues, including healthcare financing and delivery. On a positive side, delegation of more real power to the local authorities made it possible to develop and implement decisions tailored to specific local needs.

Decentralization of health system regulation was supposed to make expenditures of healthcare budgets more effective; however, a lack of federal control made it possible for some local authorities to spend money on building new expensive healthcare facilities and purchasing high-tech medical equipment based on political motivations, without considering the availability of similar facilities and/or equipment already available in the geographic area. This resulted in heterogeneity of opinions expressed by major healthcare system stakeholders (including patients, healthcare professionals, hospital administrators, Mandatory Health Insurance Funds/Obligatory/Compulsory Health/Medical Insurance Funds, insurance companies, and employers) ranging from supporting the ongoing reforms to suggestions to return to the previously existing system of socialized medicine.

Both chief medical officers (CMOs), those holding the top executive positions and holding an MD degree in charge of hospitals, and directors of regional MHIFs agree that 3.6% employer payroll tax for health insurance is too low and should be increased to about 8%.[88] Although it was noted that 3.6% might not be enough, a 10.8% employers' contribution proposed in 1991 was not approved.[81]

As compared with the hospital CMOs, the regional MHIF directors tend to be stronger supporters of health-care reforms. The directors express stronger support to healthcare cost-decreasing measures, such as reduction of inpatient LOS and shifting a substantial portion of in-patient health care to an outpatient basis.[88] While the regional MHIF directors consider the mandatory health insurance system's performance as satisfactory, hospital CMOs are dissatisfied with the administrative expenses of the insurance system and tend to consider MHIFs and insurance companies as money-wasting middle-men. The CMOs are also unhappy about administrative limitations prohibiting them from shifting financial re-sources between designated hospital budget lines, such as medications, salaries, utilities, and so forth. Although many CMOs are market minded, some of them are holdovers of the Soviet-era "socialized medicine."[88]

A 33% decrease in expenditures on health care was observed from 1991 to 1998. In 1991, 100% of health-care financing was from the state budget. Compared with 1991 (100%), the level of healthcare financing dropped to 67%, of which 51% of the financing was from the state budget, and 16% was from mandatory health insurance contributions.[89] Generally, there is a broad agreement among major stakeholders that sub-stantial improvement of the health system would re-quire additional financial resources to supplement ongoing structural reforms.[80,90]

Population decline is a serious problem faced by the RF.[91,92] Male mortality in the RF is higher than in most other countries with a similar per capita income.[93]

The emergence of infectious disease, especially tu-berculosis and HIV/AIDS, poses a challenge for the Russ-ian health system. During the period from 1991 to 2000, tuberculosis rates in the country doubled, and multiple drug resistance is of special concern.[94–99] In 2001, Presi-dent Putin signed the federal law "On Prevention of the Spread of Tuberculosis in the Russian Federation." Im-plementation of the Directly Observed Treatment Short Course is a challenging task, especially for remote regions of the RF;[100,101] long-term inpatient TB treatment is still a common practice in the country.[102]

As for HIV/AIDS, the RF reports an HIV prevalence of 5% in the intravenous drug users, but it is still below 1% in pregnant urban women.[102] Activities of NGOs working in the HIV/AIDS field are focused mostly on the problem of prevention among high-risk groups

that are difficult to contact by traditional public health institutes.[102]

Noncommunicable diseases and injuries constitute the top ten causes of death in the country, accounting for about 70% of total mortality.[93] Cardiovascular dis-eases, cancer, and injuries account for about 78% of mortality among the working-age population.[93,103]

The IMF points out an excessively complicated current system of healthcare financing.[13] According to the IMF, the budget constraints for the MHIFs and the funds' incentives to monitor healthcare providers are compromised by a complicated financing system that combines federal and regional budget financing with the federal and regional health insurance funds.[13] The com-petition among insurance companies is not sufficient because most healthcare providers are operated by the local authorities, and insurers are typically chosen by employers without consideration of their performance. As a result, insurance companies bear relatively small risks, while creating an extra 3% of administrative costs by acting as middlemen.[13] The IMF report[13] emphasizes that "health care financing could be simplified and made more incentive-compatible" and points out that the Russian healthcare system can benefit from outcome-based (rather than input-based) financing and per-formance pay.

Pharmaceutical shortages are another challenge that has emerged since the 1990s because of changes in the economical relationship between the RF and Eastern European countries. Historically, the Soviet Union relied substantially on pharmaceuticals manufactured in those countries that were then communist countries. The RF did not develop its own large pharmaceutical industry. For commercial reasons, the western drug companies that began expansion into the Russian pharmaceutical market in the early 1990s prefer to sell expensive pro-prietary (brand) medications rather than lower-priced generics.[32] The IMF points out very high spending on medications and recommends progressive co-payments be put in place to control unusually high spending.[13] Overall, citizen advocacy groups and NGOs are less ac-tive in the RF as compared with the Western countries.[32]

The RF was admitted to the IMF and the World Bank of Reconstruction and Development in 1992. In 1992–199x, the country borrowed about 21 billion U.S. dollars from the IMF. During 1992–2003, a total of 58 projects with a total value of approximately 13.4 billion dollars were approved for the RF in cooperation with the World Bank. In 1993–2002, the World Bank and International Development Agency invested over 8 bil-lion dollars in the country's economy.[104] The third loan for economic restructuring (in 1998) was the biggest loan the World Bank made to the RF (1.5 billion U.S. dollars).[105] In April 2003, the World Bank approved a 150-million-dollar loan to the RF for the Tuberculosis and AIDS Control Project.[106] This loan is designated to support the Russian government's federal program "On Prevention and Control of Social Diseases," the first countrywide project on TB and HIV/AIDS in the RF.

Another recent loan from the World Bank is a 30-million-dollar loan to the RF for the Health Reform Implementation Project (2003–2008). It is expected that implementation of the project will result in a 30% increase in utilization of the outpatient and primary care system, hospital admissions will decrease by 10%, and average inpatient LOS will decrease by 10%. Another goal of the project is closure of hospitals based on a decrease in admissions and LOS, resulting in a 5% decrease in inpatient costs.[107]

REFERENCES

1. Federal State Statistics Service (RosStat). Population. Table 5.1. Resident population. 2007. Retrieved February 28, 2008, from http://www.gks.ru/free_doc/2007/b07_12/05-01.htm.

2. Russian Census 2002. Volume 4. Nationality, languages, citizenship. Retrieved December 20, 2007, from http://www.perepis2002.ru/index.html?id=17.

3. Constitutional Court of the Russian Federation, 2004. Retrieved December 20, 2007, from http://ksrf.ru/about/index.htm.

4. Saraev V. Innovatsionnaya asimmetriya [Innovation asymmetry]. Top-Manager, 2007. Retrieved January 23, 2008, from http://top-manager.ru/?a=1&rid=7.

5. International Monetary Fund. Russian Federation: selected issues No. 06/43, Washington, DC: International Monetary Fund; 2006.

6. Grinberg R. Russian fuel and energy sector: dynamics and prospects. In Broadman HG, Paas T, Welfens PJJ, eds. *Economic Liberalization and Integration Policy: Options for Eastern Europe and Russia*. Berlin: Springer-Verlag; 2006, pp. 171–184.

7. Libman A. Russia's integration into the world economy: an interjurisdictional competition view. In Broadman HG, Paas T, eds. *Economic Liberalization and Integration Policy: Options for Eastern Europe and Russia*. Berlin: Springer-Verlag; 2005, pp. 334–348.

8. Tragakes E, Lessof S. *Healthcare Systems in Transition: Russian Federation*. The European Observatory on Health Systems and Policies No. 5-3. Copenhagen, 2003. World Bank. Russian economic report No. 15. World Bank Moscow Office, November 2007.

9. Federal State Statistics Service. Main Indicators of System of National Accounts. Retrieved January 21, 2008, from http://www.gks.ru/bgd/free/b00_25/IssWWW.exe/ Stg/dvvp/i000331r.htm.

10. World Bank. *Russian economic report no. 12*. World Bank Moscow Office; April 2006.

11. International Monetary Fund. Russian Federation: statistical appendix No. 06/431. Washington, DC: International Monetary Fund; 2006.

12. International Monetary Fund. Russian Federation: selected issues No. 07/352. Washington, DC: International Monetary Fund; 2007.

13. Federal State Statistics Service (RosStat). Transport and Communication. Table 17.27. Length of transport lines, 2006. Retrieved February 28, 2008, from http://www.gks.ru/bgd/regl/b07_13/IssWWW.exe/Stg/d04/17-27.htm.

14. Schmidt G. Russian Federation. In Horner W, Dobert H, von Kopp B, Mitter W, eds. *The Education Systems of Europe*. Dordrecht, the Netherlands: Springer; 2007, pp. 646–668.

15. Federal State Statistics Service (RosStat). Education. Table 7.44. Institutions of higher education, 2006. Retrieved December 20, 2007, from http://www.gks.ru/bgd/regl/b07_13/IssWWW.exe/Stg/d02/07-44.htm.

16. UNESCO. *Handbook on Diplomas, Degrees and Other Certificates in Higher Education in Asia and the Pacific*, 2nd ed. United Nations Educational, Scientific and Cultural Organization; 2004.

17. WHO/Europe. Highlights on Health in the Russian Federation 2005. Retrieve January 10, 2008, from http://www.euro.who.int/document/E88405.pdf.

18. Russian Public Opinion Research Center. Religion in our life Press-Release No. 789. Moscow: Russian Public Opinion Research Center (VCIOM); October 16, 2007.

19. Burger E, Field M, Twigg J. From assurance to insurance in Russian health care: the problematic transition. *American Journal of Public Health*. 1998;88(5):755–758.

20. Schroeder G, Denton ME. *An Index of Consumption in the USSR in USSR: Measures of Economic Growth and Development*. Washington, DC: Joint Economic Committee; 1982.

21. Webster P. Russia hunts for funds for ailing health service. *The Lancet*. 2003;361:498.

22. Reforming healthcare. *OECD Economic Surveys*. 2006; 17:182–193, 195–214. Retrieved January 17, 2008, from ABI/INFORM Global database (Document ID: 1180723001).

23. Burger E, Field M, Twigg J. From assurance to insurance in Russian health care: the problematic transition. *American Journal of Public Health*. 1998;88(5):755–758.

24. Karnitski G. *Health Care Systems in Transition: Belarus*. Copenhagen: European Observatory on Health Care Systems; 1997.

25. Hovhannisyan SG, Tragakes S, Lessof H, Aslanian, Mkrtchayan A. *Health Care Systems in Transition: Armenia*. Copenhagen: European Observatory on Health Care Systems; 2001.

26. Chernichovsky D, Polapchik E. Genuine federalism in the Russian healthcare system: changing roles of government. *Journal of Health Politics, Policy and Law*. 1999;24(1):115–144.

27. Goskomstat. *Zdravoohranenie v Rossii*. Moscow: National Committee on Statistics; 2001.

28. Danishevski K. Russian Federation. In Rechel B, Dubois C, McKee M, eds. *The Health Care Workforce in Europe*. United Kingdom: Cromwell Press; 2006, pp. 101–114.

29. Barr DA, Schmid R. Medical education in the former Soviet Union. *Acad Med.* 1996;71(2).

30. Ryan M. *Doctors and the State in Soviet Union.* New York: St. Martin's Press; 1990.

31. Barr D, and Field M. The current state of health care in the former Soviet Union: implications for health care policy and reform. *American Journal of Public Health.* 1996;86(3): 307–312.

32. Sheiman I. New methods of financing and managing health care in the Russian Federation. *Health Policy.* 1995;32(1–3): 167–180.

33. Reamy J, Gedik G. Health human resource reform in Tajikistan: part of a master plan for change. *Cah Sociol Demogr Med.* 2001;41:327–345.

34. Sharbarova Z. Primary healths are in the NIS: history and current situation: an overview. American International Health; 2001. Retrieved December 2007 from www.aiha.com/resource/Html/zoya.htm.

35. McEuen M. The pilot process: case study on piloting complex health reforms in Kyrgzstan. Abt Associates; 2004. Retrieved December 2007 from www.phrplus.org/Pubs/Tech036_fin.pdf.

36. Rese A, Balabanova D, McKee M, Sheaff R. Implementing general practice in Russia: getting beyond the first steps. *British Medical Journal.* 2005;331:204–207.

37. Goskomstat. Population census of the Russian Federation. Moscow: Goskomstat; 2002. Retrieved December 2007 from www.perepis2002.ru/index.tml?id=11.

38. Ministry of Health. *Indicators of Health and Health Care.* Moscow: Ministry of Health; 2003.

39. Kersnik J. An evaluation of patient satisfaction with family practice care in Slovenia. *Int J Qual Health Care.* 2000;12: 143–147.

40. Vienonen M, Vohlonen I. Integrated health care in Russia: to be or not to be? *International Journal of Integrated Care.* 2001;1–7.

41. Tkachenko E, McKee M, Tsouros A. Public health in Russia: the view from the inside. *Health Policy and Planning.* 2000; 2:164–169.

42. Twigg J. Health care reform in Russia: a survey of health doctors and insurance administrators. *Social Science and Medicine.* 2002;55:2253–2265.

43. Pidde A, Krivosheev G, Kiselev A. 2003, Bringing the Russian health-care system out of its crisis. *Sociological Research.* 2002;42(4):81–96.

44. Atun R. The health crisis in Russia. *British Medical Journal.* 2005;331:1418–1419.

45. Sinuraya T. Decentralization of the health care system and territorial medical insurance coverage in Russia: friend or foe? *European Journal of Health Law.* 2000;7:15–27.

46. Danishevski K, McKee M. *The Lancet.* 2005;365: 1012–1014.

47. Twigg J. Obligatory medical insurance in Russia: the participants' perspective. *Social Science and Medicine.* 1999;49: 371–382.

48. Shishkin S. Problems with transition for tax-based system of health care finance to mandatory health insurance model in Russia. *Croatian Medical Journal.* 1999;40(2):195–201.

49. Danishevski K, Balabanova D, McKee M, Atkins S. The fragmentary federation: experiences with the decentralized health system in Russia. *Health Policy and Planning.* 2006; 21(3):183–194.

50. Chernichovsky D, Potapchik E. Health system reform under the Russian health insurance legislation. *The International Journal of Health Planning and Management.* 1997;12: 279–295.

51. Aris B. Money for health in Russia: at long last. *The Lancet.* 2005;366:1254–1255.

52. Sheiman I. The development of market approaches in Russia. *The International Journal of Health Planning and Management.* 1994;9(1):39–56.

53. Burger E, Field M, Twigg J. Health care: the problematic transition. *American Journal of Public Health.* 1998;88(5): 755–758.

54. Balabanova D, Falkingham J, McKee M. Winners and losers: expansion of insurance coverage in Russia in the 1990s. *American Journal of Public Health.* 2003;93(12):2124–2130.

55. Shishkin S, Bogatova T, Patapchik Y, Chernets V, Chirikova A, Shilova L. *Informal Out-of-Pocket Payments for Health Care in Russia.* Moscow, Russia: Moscow Public Scientific Foundation & Independent Institute for Social Policy; 2003.

56. Semenov V, Sheiman I, Rice J. The context of provider payment reforms in the Russian Federation: a challenging arena for managerial development for twenty-first century Russia. *The Journal of Health Administration Education.* 1996;14(2):15–132.

57. Twigg J. Health care reform in Russia: a survey of health doctors and insurance administrators. *Social Science and Medicine.* 2002;55:2253–2265.

58. Rimashevskaia N, Korkhova I. Poverty and health in Russia. *Sociological Research.* 2004;43:5–30.

59. Duke T, Keshishiyan E, Kuttumuratova A. Russian health system update (unpublished paper). 2006.

60. Tamburlini G. Quality of hospital care for children in Kazakhstan, Republic of Moldova, and Russia: systematic observational assessment. *The Lancet.* 2006;367:919–925.

61. Osborn A. Half of Russia's doctors face sack in healthcare reforms, *British Medical Journal.* 2004;328:1092.

62. World Health Organization, 2007. Retrieved January 2008 from http://www.who.int/whosis/database/core/core_select_process.cfm?country.

63. The International Monetary Fund. *2007, Russian Federation: Staff Report for the 2007 Article IV Consultation.* Washington, DC: International Monetary Fund; 2007.

64. Sheiman I. Paying hospitals in Russia. *Eurohealth.* 2001; 7(3):79–81.

65. Rese A, Balabanova D, Danishevski K, McKee M, Sheaff R. Implementing general practice in Russia: getting beyond the first steps. *British Medical Journal.* 2005; 331:204–207.

66. Axelsson R, Bihari-Axelsson S. Intersectoral problems in the Russian organization of public health. *Health Policy.* 2005; 73:285–293.

67. Coker R, Atun R, McKee M. Health-care system frailties and public health control of communicable diseases on the European Union's new eastern border. *The Lancet.* 2004;363: 1389–1392.

68. The World Bank. 2007. *Russian Economic Report—November 2007*. Retrieved February 2008 from www.worldbank.org.ru.

69. Titterton M. Social policy in a cold climate: health and social welfare in Russia. *Social Policy and Administration.* 2006;40(1):88–103.

70. Parfitt T. Russia's population crisis. *The Lancet.* 2005;365: 743–744.

71. Balabanova D, McKee M, Pomerleau J, Rose R, Haerpfer C. Health service utilization in the former Soviet Union: evidence from eight countries. *Health Services Research.* 2004; 39:(6II):1927–1949.

72. Rimashevskaia N. The social vector of the development in Russia. *Russian Social Science Review.* 2005;46(6):4–51.

73. Pidde A, Krivosheev G, Kiselev A. Bringing the Russian health-care system out of its crisis. *Sociological Research.* 2003;42:81–96.

74. Fotaki M. Users' perceptions of health care reforms: quality of care and patients rights in four regions in the Russian Federation. *Social Science and Medicine.* 2006;63:1637–1647.

75. Barr D, Field M. The current state of health care in the former Soviet Union: implications for health care policy and reform. *American Journal of Public Health.* 1996;86(3): 307–311.

76. Chernichovsky D, Potapchik E. Health system reform under the Russian health insurance legislation. *Int J Health Plann Manage.* 1997;12(4):279–295.

77. Fotaki M. Users' perceptions of health care reforms: quality of care and patient rights in four regions in the Russian Federation. *Soc Sci Med.* 2006;63(6):1637–1647.

78. Sheiman I. Forming the system of health insurance in the Russian Federation. *Soc Sci Med.* 1994;39(10):1425–1432.

79. Brown JV, Rusinova N L. Russian medical care in the 1990s: a user's perspective. *Soc Sci Med.* 1997;45(8):1265–1276.

80. Burger EJ, Field MG, Twigg JL. From assurance to insurance in Russian health care: the problematic transition. *Am J Public Health.* 1998;88(5):755–758.

81. Field MG. Reflections on a painful transition: from socialized to insurance medicine in Russia. *Croat Med.* 1999; 40(2):202–209.

82. Volkov V. Reform: medicine has begun undergoing treatment [in Russian]. *Moskovskiye Novosti.* 1997;(32)9.

83. Fedorov SV. Medicine should be liberated [in Russian]. *Meditsinskaya Gazeta.* 1998;(15)3.

84. Gerasimenko NV. The health care code [in Russian]. *Meditsinskiy Vestnik.* 1999;(3)3.

85. Grishin VV. Mandatory health insurance is the way to a decent health care in a civilized society [in Russian]. *Meditsinskaya Gazeta.* 1998;(46–47)3.

86. Taranov AM. Mandatory health insurance is a powerful force for the reforms [in Russian]. *Meditsinskaya Gazeta.* 1999;(46–47)3.

87. Rekhter N, Togunov IA. Needs assessment for health care management education in Russia. *J Contin Educ Health Prof.* 2006;26(4):314–326.

88. Twigg JL. Health care reform in Russia: a survey of head doctors and insurance administrators. *Soc Sci Med.* 2002; 55(12):2253–2265.

89. Vienonen MA, Vohlonen IJ. Integrated health care in Russia: to be or not to be? *Int J Integr Care.* 2001;1:e38.

90. Twigg JL. Obligatory medical insurance in Russia: the participants' perspective. *Soc Sci Med.* 1999;49(3):371–382.

91. Anderson BA. Russia faces depopulation? Dynamics of population decline. *Popul Environ.* 2002;23(5):437–464.

92. Putin VV. State-of-the-Nation Address (May 10, 2006). Russian Federation Report; 2006.

93. Marquez P, Suhrcke M, McKee M, Rocco L. Adult health in the Russian Federation: more than just a health problem. *Health Aff (Millwood).* 2007; 26(4):1040–1051.

94. Balabanova Y, Ruddy M, Hubb J, et al. Multidrug-resistant tuberculosis in Russia: clinical characteristics, analysis of second-line drug resistance and development of standardized therapy. *Eur J Clin Microbiol Infect Dis.* 2005;24(2): 136–139.

95. Drobniewski F, Balabanova Y, Nikolayevsky V, et al. Drug-resistant tuberculosis, clinical virulence, and the dominance of the Beijing strain family in Russia. *JAMA.* 2005;293(22): 2726–2731.

96. Drobniewski F, Balabanova Y, Zakamova E, Nikolayevskyy V, Fedorin I. Rates of latent tuberculosis in health care staff in Russia. *PLoS Me.* 2007;4(2):e55.

97. Ruddy M, Balabanova Y, Graham C, et al. Rates of drug resistance and risk factor analysis in civilian and prison patients with tuberculosis in Samara Region, Russia. *Thorax.* 2005;60(2):130–135.

98. Spradling P, Nemtsova E, Aptekar T, et al. Anti-tuberculosis drug resistance in community and prison patients, Orel Oblast, Russian Federation. *Int J Tuberc Lung Dis.* 2002;6(9): 757–762.

99. Yerokhin VV, Punga VV, Rybka LN. Tuberculosis in Russia and the problem of multiple drug resistance. *Ann N Y Acad Sci.* 2001;953:133–137.

100. Dimitrova B, Balabanova D, Atun R, Drobniewski F, Levicheva V, Coker R. Health service providers' perceptions of barriers to tuberculosis care in Russia. *Health Policy Plan.* 2006;21(4):265–274.

101. Marx FM, Atun RA, Jakubowiak W, McKee M, Coker RJ. Reform of tuberculosis control and DOTS within Russian public health systems: an ecological study. *Eur J Public Health.* 2007;17(1):98–103.

102. Bobrik AV. Combating HIV/AIDS, malaria, and other diseases. In Bobylev SN, Alexandrova AL, eds. *Russia in 2015: Development Goals and Policy Priorities (Human Development Report 2005 for the Russian Federation)* (pp. 94–107). Moscow: United Nations Development Programee; 2005.

103. Oganov RG, Maslennikova G. Prevention of cardiovascular diseases: real way to improvement of demographic situation in Russia [Profilaktika serdechno-sosudistykh zabolevaniy: realjniy putj uluchsheniya demografichskoy situatsii v Rossii]. *Kardiologiia* 2007;47(1):4–7.

104. The International Monetary Fund. *Russian Federation: Staff Report for the 2007 Article IV Consultation.* Washington, DC: International Monetary Fund; 2007.

105. Grinberg R. Russia and international economic structures. In Graham EM, Oding N, Welfens PJJ, eds. *Internationaliza-*

tion and Economic Policy Reforms in Transition Countries. Berlin: Springer-Verlag; 2005, pp. 121–160.

106. World Bank. *Project Appraisal Document on a Proposed Loan in the Amount of US$150 Million to the Russian Federation for a Tuberculosis and AIDS Control Project* (Report No. 21239-RU, March 10, 2003).

107. World Bank. *Project Appraisal Document on a Proposed Loan in the Amount of US$30 million to the Russian Federation for a Health Reform Implementation Project* (Report No. 23260-RU, February 20, 2003).

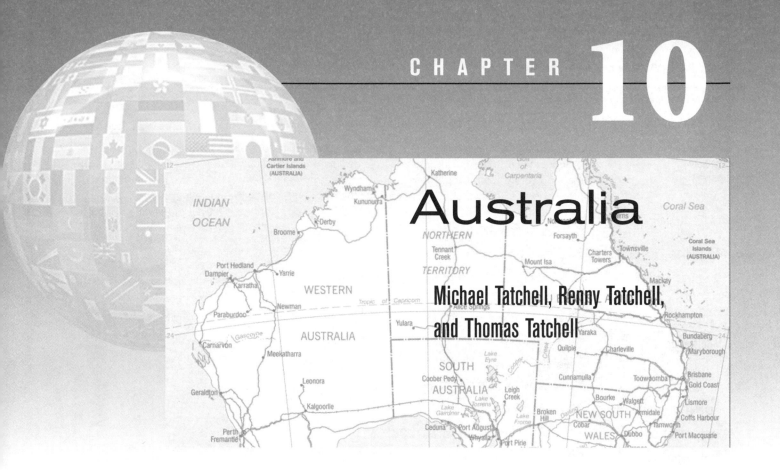

CHAPTER 10

Australia

Michael Tatchell, Renny Tatchell, and Thomas Tatchell

COUNTRY DESCRIPTION

TABLE 10-1 Australia

Nationality	Noun: Australian(s)
	Adjective: Australian
Ethnic groups	White 92%, Asian 7%, aboriginal and other 1%
Religions	Catholic 26.4%, Anglican 20.5%, other Christian 20.5% Buddhist 1.9%, Muslim 1.5%, other 1.2%, unspecified 12.7%, none 15.3% (2001 Census)
Language	English 79.1%, Chinese 2.1%, Italian 1.9%, other 11.1%, unspecified 5.8% (2001 Census)
Literacy	Definition: age 15 and over can read and write
	Total population: 99%
	Male: 99%
	Female: 99% (2003 est.)
Government type	Federal parliamentary democracy
Date of independence	January 1, 1901 (federation of UK colonies)
Gross Domestic Product (GDP) per capita	$37,500 (2007 est.)

(continues)

TABLE 10-1   Australia (continued)

Unemployment rate	4.4% (November 2007 est.)
Natural hazards	Cyclones along the coast; severe droughts; forest fires
Environment: current issues	Soil erosion from overgrazing, industrial development, urbanization, and poor farming practices; soil salinity rising because of the use of poor-quality water; desertification; clearing for agricultural purposes threatens the natural habitat of many unique animal and plant species; the Great Barrier Reef off the northeast coast, the largest coral reef in the world, is threatened by increased shipping and its popularity as a tourist site; limited natural freshwater resources
Population	20,600,856
Age structure	0–14 years: 19.1% (male 2,014,230/female 1,920,604) 15–64 years: 67.5% (male 7,005,588/female 6,895,817) 65 years and over: 13.4% (male 1,226,432/female 1,538,185) (2008 est.)
Median age	Total: 37.4 years Male: 36.6 years Female: 38.3 years (2008 est.)
Population growth rate	0.801% (2008 est.)
Birth rate	11.9 births/1,000 population (2008 est.)
Death rate	7.62 deaths/1,000 population (2008 est.)
Net migration rate	3.72 migrant(s)/1,000 population (2008 est.)
Gender ratio	At birth: 1.05 male(s)/female Under 15 years: 1.05 male(s)/female 15–64 years: 1.02 male(s)/female 65 years and over: 0.8 male(s)/female Total population: 0.99 male(s)/female (2008 est.)
Infant mortality rate	Total: 4.51 deaths/1,000 live births Male: 4.89 deaths/1,000 live births Female: 4.11 deaths/1,000 live births (2008 est.)
Life expectancy at birth	Total population: 80.73 years Male: 77.86 years Female: 83.75 years (2008 est.)
Total fertility rate	1.76 children born/woman (2008 est.)
HIV/AIDS adult prevalence rate	0.1% (2003 est.)
Number of people living with HIV/AIDS	14,000 (2003 est.)
HIV/AIDS deaths	Less than 200 (2003 est.)

Central Intelligence Agency. The World Fact Book, 2008. Retrieved November 18, 2008, from https://www.cia.gov/library/publications/the-world-factbook.

History

Australia is a vast, ancient island continent. It was first settled more than 50,000 years ago by migrating tribes making the short trip across from southeast Asia to the northern parts of the continent. These Aboriginal and Torres Strait Islander people spread across the land, including the island of Tasmania to the south, and are thought to have numbered around 350,000 at the time of first European contact in the 17th century.[1]

After a period of exploration by Dutch, French, and English explorers, the eastern parts of Australia were claimed in 1770 by Captain James Cook in the name of Great Britain. Initial settlement quickly followed. The first fleet of 11 ships carrying 700 convicts and 400 guards and officials arrived in January 1788 to establish the penal colony of New South Wales. Five more self-governing British crown colonies were then established during the early part of the 19th century. On January 1, 1901, after a countrywide referendum, the six colonies federated, and the Commonwealth of Australia was formed.

Australia's history since British settlement in 1788 has been marked by several important events. The discovery of gold in the early 1850s brought many immigrants to Australia from Britain, Ireland, Europe, North America, and China. This and subsequent gold discoveries heralded a period of considerable prosperity, population growth, and spread. Involvement in two world wars and in other major conflicts of the 20th century, notably Korea and Vietnam, cost the country dearly in lost lives and resources but helped to create national unity and identity.

A massive program of European immigration after World War II—some 2 million people arrived between 1948 and 1975—saw Australia's population grow substantially, helping to fuel a lengthy period of economic prosperity and growth. Discovery and exploitation of the country's natural and mineral resources have underpinned Australia's development and wealth and encouraged rapid development of agricultural, mining, and manufacturing industries.

Most recently, a period of prolonged drought has fueled concerns about climate change and its implications for the environment, the economy, and the nation. These matters are preoccupying Australia's leaders and will no doubt play an important part in shaping the nation's future.

Size and Geography

Australia has a land area of some 7.7 million square kilometers. This is about twice the size of the European Union and is close to the size of the United States of America (excluding Alaska). Situated in the southern hemisphere between the Indian and Pacific oceans, a large proportion of the continent (around 40%) lies within the tropics (see map in Figure 10-1). Distances are huge, some 4,000 kilometers from west (Steep Point in Western Australia) to east (Byron Bay in New South Wales) and 3,680 kilometers from north (Cape York in Queensland) to south (Wilson's Promontory in Victoria).

Beyond her continental shores, Australia also has jurisdiction over a large number of islands, most notably the island of Tasmania, but also many others such as Melville Island (off the Northern Territory), Kangaroo Island (South Australia), King and Flinders Islands (Tasmania), the Torres Strait islands (Queensland), and more distant islands such as Macquarie Island (well south of Tasmania) and Lord Howe Island (off New South Wales).

Government or Political System

Since achieving nationhood in 1901, Australia has had a federal system of government whereby power is divided between the Commonwealth Government and the governments in each of Australia's six states and two territories. The form of government reflects the country's British heritage, a constitutional monarchy with the British sovereign as Head of State (currently Queen Elizabeth II). The monarch is represented federally by the governor general and at state levels by state governors.

Separation of powers, legislative, executive, and judicial, is imbedded in the system of government. This is well described by Healy et al.[2]:

> The Parliament makes the laws, the Government implements and supervises, and the Courts interpret them. The legislative power of the Commonwealth is vested in a Federal Parliament. The executive power is vested in the Queen and is exercizable by the Governor-General as the Queen's representative. Judicial power is exercised by the High Court of Australia and the Federal Court of Australia, and other State courts exercising federal jurisdiction.

The Commonwealth Parliament, located in the nation's capital Canberra (in the Australian Capital Territory), is bicameral. Elections for the two chambers, the House of Representatives (the lower house) and the Senate (the upper house), take place every 3 years. Electorates in the 150-seat lower house are allocated by population size, and members are elected for 3 years with a preferential voting system. Electorates in the upper house are allocated equally across the states. Each state is represented by 12 senators and each territory by 2, elected for 6 years by proportional representation.

FIGURE 10-1   Map of Australia

The political party that wins the majority of seats in the lower house is empowered to form a government. Since 1944, when the Liberal Party was formed by Robert Menzies, successive commonwealth governments have been formed either by the Australian Labor Party or a coalition of the Liberal and National parties. The most recent federal election (in November 2007) saw a change in government from the John Howard–led coalition government (in power from 1996) to a labor government led by Prime Minister Kevin Rudd. Interestingly, the Labor party also holds power at present in every state and territory jurisdiction, a first since federation in 1901.

Another interesting and unusual feature of Australia's system of government is that voting is compulsory for all enrolled citizens aged 18 years and over, in each state and territory and at the federal level.

Macroeconomics

Australia's advanced, mixed economy has enjoyed 17 years of growth since the recession of 1991. Significant reforms since the 1980s, including financial deregulation,

floating the exchange rate, lowering of tariffs, and changes to the tax system, have helped to produce a diversified and internationally competitive economy with per capita gross domestic product (GDP) (A\$37,500/US\$35,388 in 2007) on par with several major European economies such as the United Kingdom, Germany, and France. During the 1990s and early 2000s, Australia's economy performed particularly well, boasting one of the OECD's fastest growing economies during that period.

An abundance of natural resources has enabled Australia to become a major exporter of agricultural products, minerals, metals, and fossil fuels. Much of Australia's economic focus is now on the economies of the Asia-Pacific region. The boom in mining exports of recent years has been fueled by China's emergence as an economic force in the world economy.

A short summary of Australia's most recent economic statistics reveals that (1) inflation has moved above 3% per annum (as of February 2008), (2) unemployment is at a historical low (4.0% as of February 2008), (3) the exchange rate (A\$ relative to US\$) is above 0.9 and appears to be rising toward parity, and

(4) bank lending rates are above 9% and rising as monetary policy is tightened in an attempt to control inflationary pressures.

As to the future, the Australian economy is entering a phase of significant international uncertainty. The U.S. economy (and the global economy) is slowing, and the fallout from the U.S. subprime financial crisis is having a substantial effect on all Australians with borrowings. In addition, inflationary pressures continue to build because of capacity constraints, full employment, and high oil prices. As a result, Australia's long run of economic growth may well be at risk. There is no doubt that economic growth will be slower over the next few years, with the greatest threat coming from rising inflation and the resultant upward pressure on interest rates.

Demographics

Australia's population passed the 21 million mark in June 2007,[3] a 1.4% increase over the previous year. Around half of this increase is due to natural increase (births less deaths) and half to net overseas migration. Since federation in 1901, the population has increased by close to 17 million people; from 1996 to 2006, the population increased by around 2.4 million.[4]

The majority of Australians are of European descent, a reflection of early settlement from the British Isles during the colonial era and to post-federation immigration from Europe. More recently, an increasing number of immigrants to Australia are from Asia and Oceania. Australia has one of the largest proportions of immigrant populations in the world. More than 23% of Australians were born overseas.[5]

The indigenous population, mainland Aborigines and Torres Strait Islanders, was 455,027 (2.3% of the total population) in 2006,[5] a significant increase from the 1971 census, which showed an indigenous population of 115,953.[6] Australia's population is highly urbanized with two thirds living in major cities around the coastal fringe. The state capitals are all coastal: Sydney, Melbourne, Brisbane, Adelaide, Perth, and Hobart. The exception is the nation's capital, Canberra, which is inland from Sydney but still within 100 km of the coast.

Although Australia has no official state religion, the 2001 census[7] provides a snapshot of the religious beliefs of the population. Results shows that 68% of Australians called themselves Christian, of which 27% identified themselves as Roman Catholic and 21% as Anglican. Followers of non-Christian religions numbered 5% and 16% were categorized as having "no religion" (which includes nontheistic beliefs such as humanism, atheism, agnosticism, and rationalism). A further 12% declined to answer this census question or did not give a clear response.

BRIEF HISTORY OF THE HEALTHCARE SYSTEM

Pre-World War II

A range of influences have shaped the complex system of health care now in place in Australia. From early beginnings as a convict settlement in the colony of New South Wales in 1788, health services in Australia have evolved into a mix of public and private delivery, based largely on British and American models and shaped inevitably by unique political, economic, and social events.

The first 100 or so years of European settlement were characterized by a somewhat haphazard mix of private medical services and government-funded hospitals for convicts, paupers, and the indigent. Support for health costs was also forthcoming from a range of benevolent and charitable organizations and friendly societies. During the 19th century, colonial governments across the country also assumed responsibility for the maintenance of public health such as sanitation and the control of infectious diseases, through the passage of comprehensive public health acts modeled on British legislation of the time.[8]

The coming of nationhood in 1901 brought with it a federal system of government under which responsibility for the provision of health services was shared between the Commonwealth Government and the governments of the six states and two territories.

Since World War II

Initially, the Commonwealth's health responsibilities were restricted to quarantine matters only, but an amendment to the Constitution in 1946 enabled the Commonwealth to make laws with respect to (among other things) "pharmaceutical, sickness and hospital benefits, medical and dental services, but not so as to authorize any form of civil conscription...." This latter clause was inserted into the amendment following pressure from the medical profession, a response no doubt to the perceived threat of a British-style National Health Service being introduced in Australia.

Prohibition of civil conscription, interpreted to mean that medical practitioners could not be compelled to work for the government, not only helped to entrench the predominant fee-for-service payment system for medical services, but also played a part in delaying the introduction of the Commonwealth-funded prescription insurance system under which all Australians have access to subsidized life-saving medicines. As a result, the Pharmaceutical Benefits Scheme (PBS) as it is known, first mooted in 1945, was not fully implemented until the Pharmaceutical Benefits Act passed through Federal Parliament in 1948. Passage of this act had not been easy. It was passed twice and overturned once; it was the subject of a national referendum, constitutional change, and fierce public debate on the powers of the Commonwealth Government.

The 1946 Constitutional amendment also enabled the Commonwealth Government to enter into funding agreements with the states for the provision of free public hospital care for patients in public wards. This arrangement, intended to protect patients from the high cost of hospital care, has remained the basis of hospital financing agreements between the commonwealth and the states ever since.

The other main features of the health system (given effect through the 1953 National Health Act) were the pensioner medical services arrangements and the medical benefits scheme. The former ensured the provision of free health services to aged and invalid pensioners through agreements with the Australian Medical Association, whereas the latter subsidized medical costs for members of nonprofit health insurance schemes.

These four pillars of Australia's health system—(1) subsidized medicines, (2) commonwealth funding for state hospitals, (3) subsidized health care for pensioners, and 4) subsidized private health insurance—remained in place largely unaltered for the next 20 years until the introduction of a national health insurance scheme known as Medibank in 1975. Not surprisingly, the move from a system funded predominantly through subsidized private insurance to one funded predominantly by government was met with strident opposition from vested interests and political opponents alike. After rejection of the necessary legislation by the opposition-controlled Senate in 1973 and 1974, dissolution of both houses of Parliament and a subsequent general election, Medibank was finally enacted in July 1974 and came into operation a year later. The major elements of the new scheme were subsidized medical services for patients and free access to public hospital care through hospital cost-sharing arrangements between the commonwealth and the state and territory governments.

From 1975, a period of conservative government ensued (the Fraser-led Liberal-National coalition), during which several changes were made to Medibank, which saw a gradual return to greater reliance on private health insurance for medical services.[9] Election of a Labor Government in 1983 then heralded the return of a universal tax-funded national health insurance scheme known as Medicare. Subsequent changes of government (in 1996 and 1983) have not materially affected these arrangements that have now enjoyed bipartisan political support and widespread public support for more than 20 years.

DESCRIPTION OF THE CURRENT HEALTHCARE SYSTEM

The Australian healthcare system is complex with numerous providers of services, funding arrangements, and regulatory mechanisms. The overall aim of the system is to provide all Australians with ready access to healthcare services at low cost or no cost at all. Service providers include medical practitioners (physicians), various health professionals, private and public hospitals, and government and nongovernment agencies. Responsibility for funding is shared between all levels of government and the nongovernment sector such as private health insurers and individual consumers.

The Commonwealth Government is responsible for funding the provision of medical services, pharmaceutical benefits, and aged residential care services, as well as public health, research, and national information management. The state and territory governments are responsible for delivery and management of a range of health services such as public hospital services, mental health programs, community support programs, and women's and children's services.

Facilities

Medicare is the centerpiece of Australia's health system. It is a universal publicly funded health insurance system that allows all Australians to access affordable high-quality health care. In place in its present form since 1984, Medicare is financed by general taxation revenue and a Medicare levy based on taxable income. Medicare provides free or subsidized treatment by medical practitioners (physicians) and grants to the states and territories to assist with the cost of running public hospitals. The commonwealth jointly funds public hospitals with the states so that these services are provided free of charge to patients. In 2003–2004, there were 1,266 acute-care hospitals throughout Australia, of which 741 were public hospitals containing a total of

TABLE 10-2 Australia's Hospitals and Available Beds, 2003–2004

| | Public Hospitals | | | |
	Public Acute	Public Psychiatric	Private Hospitals	Total
Hospitals	741	20	525	1,286
Available beds	50,915	2,560	26,589	80,064
Available beds per 1,000 population	2.6	0.1	1.3	4.0

Australian Institute of Health and Welfare. *Australia's Health 2006.* Canberra, 2006, p. 372.

50,915 beds.[10] In that same year, there were 525 private hospitals in Australia (Table 10-2), with a total of 26,589 beds.[10] There were also a small number of public psychiatric hospitals containing a total of 2,560 beds.

Workforce

In common with many other countries around the world, Australia is experiencing significant shortages of health professionals across the spectrum of occupations. This is despite significant growth in the overall health workforce in recent years. Between 2000 and 2005, the total number of persons employed in health occupations grew by 26% from 452,000 to 570,000.[11] This compares with a 10% increase in persons employed in all other occupations over the same period. Table 10-3 shows total numbers employed in selected health occupations, as well as rates per 100,000 population. Health occupations are also heavily feminized, although as the table shows, this varies markedly across the professions.

Technology and Equipment

Australia's fortunate status as a wealthy developed nation has enabled it to build and foster a health system with access to advanced and up-to-date medical and surgical technologies. Although direct measures of the stock and spread of these technologies and equipment are not available, it is possible to identify particular technologies—new pharmaceutical listings for example— and to measure their impact on health costs and (in some instances) health outcomes.

A recent study by the Productivity Commission (a Commonwealth Government Agency) into the impacts of advances in medical technology in Australia[12] concluded that (1) advances in medical technology in Australia have brought large benefits but have also been a major driver of increased health spending in recent years and that (2) overall, advances in medical technology arguably have provided value for money, particularly as people highly value improvements in the quality and length of life.

The predominance of public funding in Australia's health system brings with it various rationing and gatekeeping mechanisms aimed at controlling the cost impact of new technologies. The underlying philosophy of these mechanisms is for "evidence-based health care." New drugs and medical procedures, for example, must be assessed as cost-effective before they can be subsidized for listing on the PBS or the Medicare Benefits Schedule. Indeed, Australia was the first country in the world to require drug manufacturers seeking to have a new drug listed on the PBS to demonstrate its cost-effectiveness.

TABLE 10-3 Australia's Health Workforce, Selected Occupations, 2005

Occupation	Number	Per 100,000 Population	Proportion Female
Nurses	204,700	1006.9	90.9
General physicians	36,300	178.6	43.4
Specialist physicians	23,600	116.3	27.9
Pharmacists	14,900	73.3	57.6
Physiotherapists	14,300	70.6	59.6
Dental practitioners	8,700	42.9	23.5
Occupational therapists	7,800	38.4	83.6

Australian Institute of Health and Welfare. *Australia's Health 2006.* Canberra, 2006, pp. 316, 323.

Another feature of Australia's system is the drive to increase the diffusion and use of information technology at all levels of health care. There is high-level commitment from all levels of government to encourage the uptake of information technology to improve clinical and medical practice. Most physician practices are computerized both for clinical and administrative purposes, and plans are well advanced to introduce a national health management system that electronically stores individual medical records accessible by health providers and their patients. This network is intended to reduce errors and adverse events, duplication of services, and the incidence of inappropriate treatments. There remains considerable scope for progress in this area, which to date has been delayed by understandable concerns about patient privacy and confidentiality.

EVALUATION OF THE HEALTHCARE SYSTEM

Recent years have witnessed a growing awareness of and emphasis on health system performance in Australia. An indication of this was the establishment in 1999 of a national health performance committee. Its purpose was to develop "a national health performance framework to support benchmarking for improvement and to provide information to monitor performance."[13] The performance criteria cover a wide range of indicators, including equity, effectiveness, appropriateness, efficiency, responsiveness, accessibility, safety, continuity, capability, and sustainability. Also high on the list in any evaluation of health system performance are measures of health status and health outcomes.

Cost

Health spending in Australia totaled A$87 billion (US$82 billion) in 2005–2006 or A$4,200 (US$3,900) per person.[14] This represents 9% of Australia's GDP, which puts Australia around the average in comparison with other OECD countries, below countries such as the United States, France, Germany, and Canada, and above the United Kingdom, Spain, Turkey, and Finland. Table 10-4 shows how spending on health services in Australia has progressed in the past decade.

There has been a noticeable slowing in the rate of growth in health spending in the recent past. After adjusting for inflation, total health spending increased by 3.1% in 2005–2006, well below the annual average growth in the past decade of 5.1%. A large part of this reduction is due to a noticeable slowing in spending on medications, which increased by just 1.6% in 2005–2006 compared with the annual average growth in the past decade of 8.6%.

Australia's health services are funded predominantly from taxation sources with federal, state, and territory governments, contributing close to 70% of all health spending (see Figure 10-2). Nongovernment funding is drawn mainly from out-of-pocket payment by individuals and health insurance funds, which help to cover the cost of treatment in private hospitals and a range of other medical and ancillary health services.

The public share of health spending has varied markedly over the years reflecting the major policy changes of the federal government. The introduction of Medibank in 1975 saw the public share jump from 57% to 73%; this share then declined to 63% in the late 1970s with the gradual dismantling of Medibank by the Fraser Coalition Government. The public share of health

TABLE 10-4 Trends in Health Spending in Australia, 1996 to 2006

	1996	2001	2006
Total health expenditure, current prices			
(A$ million)	39,047	58,287	86,879
(US$ million)	38,864	55,029	82,016
Total health expenditure as a percentage of GDP	7.5	8.5	9.0
Total per capita health expenditure, current prices			
(A$)	2,146	3,023	4,226
(US$)	2,026	2,854	3,990
Public share of total health expenditure (%)	66.3	67.6	67.8

Australian Institute of Health and Welfare. *Health Expenditure Australia 2005–06.* Canberra, 2007.

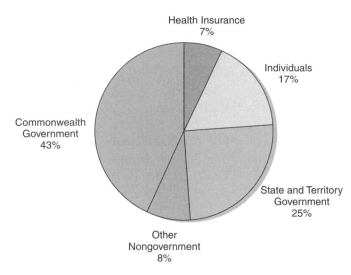

FIGURE 10-2   Source of Funds for Health, 2005–2006

Australian Institute of Health and Welfare. *Health Expenditure Australia 2005–06.* Canberra; 2007: 21.

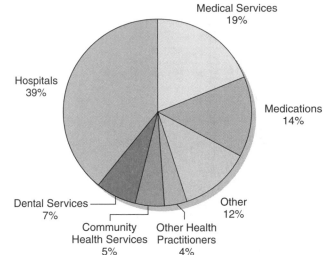

FIGURE 10-3   Uses of Funds for Health, 2005–2006

Australian Institute of Health and Welfare. *Health Expenditure Australia 2005–06.* Canberra; 2007: 50.

spending jumped to 72% after the introduction of Medicare by the Hawke Labor Government in 1984.

Figure 10-3 shows that the greatest proportion of health funding is spent on hospitals (39%), followed by medical services (19%), medications (14%), dental services (7%), community health services (5%), and other health practitioners (4%). The remaining spending is spread between research (2%), administration (3%), aids and appliances (3%), public health (2%), and patient transport services (2%).

Under Medicare, patients are entitled to access hospital care at no charge. This includes free medical and surgical care from physicians and surgeons, accommodation, meals, and other health services while in the hospital if they are admitted as public patients. Alternatively, if they choose to be admitted as private patients, then additional fees and charges are likely. In these instances, the patient can choose their own physician/surgeon. When in private hospitals, patients are charged fees for accommodation, nursing care, and other hospital care. They are also charged separately for any medical and surgical treatment. Private health insurance is available to cover such expenses if people wish to subscribe. Any premiums are additional to the Medicare levy (1.5% of income), which all Australian taxpayers are obliged to pay.

Under Medicare, the government pays a flat rate per physician consultation. A physician can choose to charge the patient either that amount or more. A patient pays any difference. Other services funded through Medicare

include services from participating optometrists and services delivered by a practice nurse on behalf of a general practitioner and for certain services from eligible dentists and allied health practitioners. Claims can be made by post or over the counter at Medicare offices, or the physician can "bulk bill" patients. In this case, physicians send accounts directly to Medicare and accept the Medicare rebate as full payment for the service. There is no cost to the patient. Nearly 7 of 10 physicians "bulk billed" the government for their patient consultations in 2004–2005.[14]

In 2004–2005, there were 236.3 million Medicare services, an average of 11.7 services per person, at a total cost of A$9.9 billion (US$9.3 billion).[14] Figure 10-4 provides a breakdown of the Medicare services provided from 2004–2005. The main services were general practitioner consultations, followed by pathology tests, diagnostic imaging, and specialist physician attendances.

As with Medicare, the PBS is also a central and unique feature of Australia's health system. Since its inception in 1948, the PBS has consistently provided reliable, timely, and affordable access to important medicines for all Australians. In so doing, the PBS has proven itself to be one of the best systems in the world. Medicines on the Australian market are not only of high quality, they are also less costly than in most other countries. Under the scheme, consumers can access more than 2,300 brands of prescription medicines that they are assured have been rigorously tested and found

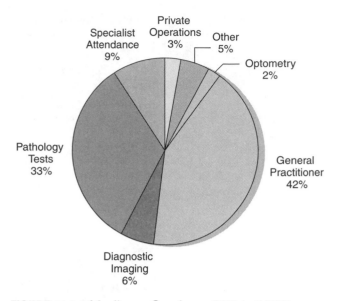

FIGURE 10-4   Medicare Services, 2004–2005

Australian Institute of Health and Welfare. *Australia's Health 2006.* Canberra; 2006: 344.

to be cost-effective. These medicines are available from a network of 5,000 independently owned community pharmacies spread across all parts of Australia.

Currently, most of the population (general consumers) pay a maximum of A$31.30 for any one prescription item. Concessional patients and pensioners pay only A$5 (US$4.71) per item. The remainder of the cost of the medicines is paid by the Commonwealth Government. In fact, the government contributes, on average, A$33.50 (US$31.60) to the cost of every prescription dispensed through the scheme (see Figure 10-5).

The cost of the scheme has risen significantly over the years. In its first year of operation, around 300,000 prescriptions for PBS medicines were dispensed, at a cost to the Commonwealth Government of 150,000 Australian dollars (US$141,527). By 1960, this had grown to 24 million prescriptions at a cost of A$44 million (US$41.5 million). In 2006–2007, the PBS covered 170 million prescriptions at a total cost (government and private) of A$6.7 billion (US$3.6 billion). That is an average of more than eight subsidized pharmaceutical benefit prescriptions per person in that year. Although the cost of the PBS scheme has increased greatly since 1989, the average number of subsidized prescriptions dispensed per capita has hardly changed; however, the average cost of each prescription has risen from A$21.49 (US$20.27) in 1996 to A$38.75 (US$36.57) in 2006 (Figure 10-5).

There are several reasons for this increasing cost. First, the number of available medicines continues to grow. In 1950, there were 139 lifesaving PBS medicines on the scheme that people could use. Today there are 593 generic drugs available in 1,469 different forms and strengths and marketed as 2,351 different brands.

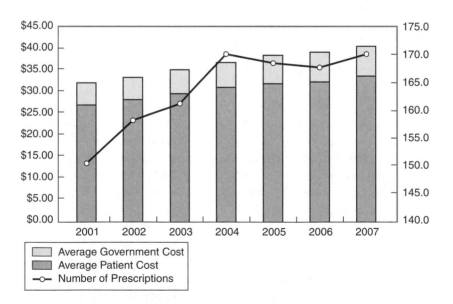

FIGURE 10-5   Average Cost of a Prescription (A$) and PBS Prescription Volume in Millions

Commonwealth Department of Health and Aging; 2007.

Second, the new generation drugs listed on the PBS are more costly and doctors tend to prescribe the newer, more potent, and more effective products. Thus, the mix of drugs being prescribed by doctors is increasing in cost. Third, Australia's population is aging, and we tend to use more medications as we get older. The number of prescriptions dispensed per person increases with age as medicines play an important role in improving the quality and longevity of people's lives. Fourth, the number of people eligible for concessional and pensioner pharmaceutical benefits is increasing, which in turn adds to the cost for the PBS.

Quality

Quality of care is but one of a number of factors, in addition to socioeconomic, environmental, behavioral, biomedical, and genetic factors, that help to determine the health and well-being of the population. Quality is difficult to define and even more difficult to measure. It can be subjective, such as an individual patient's view of the quality of a particular encounter with the health system or the wider public's view of the performance of their local hospital or ambulance service.

There is no doubt that health services in Australia have saved lives, prolonged life, improved health, and enhanced the quality of life of the population. The quality of those health services has played its part in this. "Australians generally enjoy very good health and Australia's international ranking for numerous aspects of health is high and better than a decade or so ago." This is the principle conclusion of the latest Biennial Report[11] of the Australian Institute of Health and Welfare, the tenth in this excellent series of report cards on the state of the nation's health. For 2 decades, this report has brought together a substantial body of information and statistics to provide a comprehensive picture of the health status of Australia's people, the main determinants of health, the health services provided, and the amounts spent on health. Not all of the news is good, but on balance and by international yardsticks, the health of Australians is good and improving.

In the 18 years since *Australia's Health* was first published, Australia's ranking among comparable countries has improved on most measures: (1) Australia's life expectancy at birth (83 years for females and 78 years for males) now places Australia among the top five nations in the world. (2) Marked improvements in ranking are evident for mortality rates from coronary heart disease, stroke, lung cancer, and transport accidents. (3) Rates of smoking continue to fall, moving Australia into

the "best third" of OECD countries on this measure. (4) Australia also scores well and has improved rankings on self-rated health, dental health, various mortality measures, and lower alcohol consumption.

On the downside, Australia's ranking has fallen in the past 2 decades on measures of mortality from suicide, diabetes, respiratory diseases, and infant mortality. The ranking for obesity has not changed, but Australia is among the "worst third" group of OECD countries on this measure.

Another report,[15] this time from patients' viewpoint, provides an alternative perspective on the comparative performance of Australia's health system. Undertaken by the Commonwealth Fund in 2007, this study compares patient and physician views of the performance of the health systems of a small group of countries including Australia. Australia ranks third overall among the six countries in the study, below Germany and the United Kingdom and above New Zealand, Canada, and the United States. This position varies, though, when the various performance dimensions are compared. Australia is ranked first on the "healthy lives" dimension, which includes measures of infant mortality, health life expectancy, and deaths that could have been prevented with timely and effective care. Australia also ranks second on the "equity" dimension, which measures variations in quality of health care because of gender, geographical location, and socioeconomic status.

The authors derived the rankings for each country using the results of three international surveys: (1) patient experiences of getting and using health services and their opinions of health system structure and recent reforms; (2) sicker patients' views of each healthcare system, quality of care, care coordination, medical errors, patient–physician communication, waiting times, and access problems; and (3) primary care physician experiences of providing care to patients, use of information technology, and teamwork in the provision of care. These survey data were then supplemented by health spending and health outcome measures for each of the six countries in the study.

Access

Equity of access to health services is one of the main objectives of Australia's health system and in particular is one of the underpinning principles of the universal taxpayer funded Medicare and Pharmaceutical Benefits systems. Both are funded through general taxation as well as by a 1.5% Medicare levy on income. Patients also contribute through a system of structured co-payments for prescription medicines. For physician services, patients pay any gap between the amount that the physician charges and the Medicare rebate for the service.

Access to public hospital services is available for Australian citizens who can elect to have free accommodation, medical and nursing care, as well as necessary medicines as public patients. Patients can also choose, if they wish, to be treated in a private hospital, or as a private patient in a public hospital. They are then required to meet the associated medical, surgical, and accommodation costs with the assistance of private health insurance and some assistance from Medicare.

Access to a wide range of prescription medicines is made possible through the Pharmaceutical Benefits Scheme. This scheme aims to provide "timely access to the medicines that Australians need, at a cost individuals and the community can afford."[9] As described previously here, patients are required to contribute to the cost of their medicines through a system of co-payments. In addition, a "safety net" is in place, which provides further protection for individuals and families against the financial burden associated with high use of medicines. Access to pharmaceutical services is also facilitated through a set of regulations that govern where Australia's nearly 5,000 community pharmacies are located. This is particularly important in rural and remote parts of Australia where population density is low and communities are few and far between.

CURRENT AND EMERGING ISSUES AND CHALLENGES

Australia is fortunate to have a health system that features a sophisticated infrastructure, advanced medical technologies, and highly trained health professionals, all of which have helped to deliver high levels of health across most sectors of the population. Several challenges and emerging issues are apparent in the early years of the 21st century. The final section of this chapter focuses on four of these: (1) the challenges of an aging population, (2) the sorry state of indigenous health, (3) the twin health challenges of increasing levels of obesity and diabetes, and (4) the immediate organizational and structural challenges facing the newly elected Labor government.

An Aging Population

"Demography shapes destiny" was one of the catch cries of Australia's Treasurer, Peter Costello, during the later years of the Howard Coalition government. Costello was referring to the inevitability of the aging of the population in the country, described elsewhere as "a quiet transformation, because it is gradual, but also unremitting and ultimately pervasive."[16] Falling fertility, the aging of the baby-boomer generation, declining mortality, and increased life expectancy are combining to increase the number and proportion of the population that is older, that is, those aged 65 years or more. This trend will accelerate over the next 50 years to such an extent that the number of older persons will have increased from the present 2.6 million to between 7 and 9 million in 2051 (between 26% and 28% of the population).[17] Moreover, the number of old–old (those aged 85 years and over) will increase from just under 300,000 now to between 1.6 and 2.7 million by 2051 (between 6% and 8% of the population).

The implications of an aging population for healthcare costs have been the focus of much analysis and commentary in the past decade. The government's Intergenerational Report[18] concluded that "a steadily aging population is likely to continue to place significant pressure on Commonwealth government finances" and that "Commonwealth health and aged care spending is projected to grow significantly, due to the increasing cost of new procedures and medicines, with the aging of the population also increasing demand for health spending."

The upward pressure on health costs applied by an aging population results both from the fact that older people tend to have a greater need for health services and that they use those services more often than other age groups. The other major drivers of rising health costs are the increasing cost and availability of new health technology, as well as burgeoning consumer demands and expectations. Consumers increasingly expect and demand the latest and best, whether it is the latest medical/surgical advance or the latest blockbuster drug.

Growing older is accompanied by an increasing incidence of nonfatal diseases of aging and chronic degenerative diseases. These include arthritis, diabetes, heart disease, cancer, and dementia. Such diseases can severely impact on the quality of life and independence of older people. They also bring with them markedly increased utilization of health services such as medications, doctor consultations, and hospital admissions.

Although there are many who believe an aging population is a crisis in the making, the prevailing view is not so pessimistic. Population aging is gradual. Governments, health planners, and administrators have plenty of time to develop new policy approaches to address the challenges ahead. The Productivity Commission, for example, points out[16] that future productivity growth will ensure that Australians are much richer and are better able to afford the costs associated with aging. Moreover, although people are living longer, they are generally healthier than previous generations. We should not assume that the older population of tomorrow will be an economic or social burden on society because of poor health.

Indigenous Health

One of the major challenges for the incoming Rudd Labor Government is the sorry state of health of Australia's indigenous people, often described as a national disgrace. Certainly, the new government has flagged its intentions early in its electoral term by establishing a joint Parliamentary Commission, involving both the Government and Opposition parties, to tackle as a first step the housing crisis in Aboriginal communities.

Aboriginal and Torres Strait Islander people (there are some 500,000 in Australia at present) die on average 17 years younger than other Australians.[11] Their life expectancy is equivalent to the average Australian's life expectancy 100 years ago. On almost every measure of health, the gap between indigenous and nonindigenous people in Australia is significant and alarming[11]: (1) Indigenous people have twice the rate of hospitalization for injury or poisoning, 17 times the rate for dialysis, and four times the rate for endocrine, nutritional, and metabolic diseases (which include diabetes). (2) Indigenous children are three times as likely to have ear and hearing problems. (3) Indigenous people have three times the general rate of diabetes. (4) Overall age-standardized death rates are three times as high for indigenous people. (5) Babies of indigenous mothers are twice as likely to be of low birth weight, putting them at greater risk of poor health and early death. (6) Indigenous people are more likely to be obese, to be physically inactive, to smoke, to drink to excess, and to have poor nutrition. Much of this disparity in health status is due to a range of social conditions that affect health, including the inadequate and overcrowded living conditions of many indigenous people that do not satisfy the basic requirements of shelter, safe drinking water, and adequate waste disposal.

Around $1.8 billion was spent on health services for indigenous Australians in 2001–2002, about 2.8% of all health spending.[19] This equates to around A$3,901 (US$3,679) per indigenous person, compared with A$3,308 (US$3,120) for each nonindigenous person, a difference of about 18%; however, higher spending per person does not mean that indigenous people use more health services.

In fact, health services to indigenous people are often more costly to deliver, both because of the remoteness of many indigenous communities and because many of the health services are provided in different ways. A much higher proportion of health dollars for indigenous people is spent on hospital services, and proportionately much less on primary health care, particularly Medicare and the PBS. Average Medicare and PBS spending for each indigenous Australian in 2001–2002 was around one third of such spending on other Australians. Average spending per indigenous person on dental, private hospital, and other professional health services was also much lower than for other Australians.

The Rudd Government's recently announced initiatives are yet another in a long line of attempts to tackle a problem described by the previous Minister for Health and Aging, Tony Abbott, in June 2006, as "probably the biggest and certainly the most intractable challenge we face." He went on to say, "There are no magic bullets here. It's easy to spend money, but hard to make a difference improving services to deprived people in depressed places."[12] We can but hope that this time the government's initiatives do indeed "make a difference."

Obesity and Diabetes

Two significant and related health challenges for Australia in the early years of the 21st century are obesity and diabetes. In common with many other developed nations, Australia has been experiencing an increasing prevalence of obesity in recent years. Described by the World Health Organization as a global epidemic, obesity (or excess body fat) is associated with an increased risk of type 2 diabetes, cardiovascular disease, high blood pressure, certain cancers, sleep apnea, osteoarthritis, psychological disorders, and social problems.[20]

The latest statistics[21] on the prevalence of overweight and obesity in Australia shows that (1) more than half (53%) of all adults (or 7.4 million people aged 18 years and over) are either overweight or obese, up from 44% in 1995; (2) the rate of overweight adults increased from 32% in 1995 to 35% in 2005; and (3) the rate of obesity in adults increased from 12% to 18% over the same period.

These rates of overweight and obesity are similar to those in the United States of America, Canada, and the United Kingdom and are substantially above those recorded in France and Japan.[11] Apart from the well-documented health and social consequences of obesity, the associated costs are significant and growing. A recent study by economic consultants Access Economics[22] estimates the total cost of obesity in Australia in 2005 to be close to A$21 billion (US$19.8 billion), made up of lost productivity costs (A$1.7 billion/U$S1.6 billion), health system costs (A$0.9 billion/US$0.85 billion), carer costs (A$0.8 billion/US$0.75 billion), and loss of well-being costs (A$17.2 billion/US$16.2 billion).

Policy options abound, but successful outcomes are few and far between. Imposing a tax on food products considered likely to contribute to obesity is not favored, as it targets food products consumed by obese and nonobese alike. It also cannot be assumed that higher tax on certain foods will necessarily shift consumption away from them toward healthier alternatives. Pressure on the government to impose advertising restrictions, such as bans on food advertisements for children, has also been rejected to date. Instead, there is a voluntary code of practice in place for advertising to children that aims "to not encourage or promote an inactive lifestyle combined with unhealthy eating or drinking habits."[14]

The government's preferred approach in recent times has been to fund awareness, health promotion, and prevention campaigns. These have included physician management plans, health checks, after-school exercise programs, a "Better Health Initiative," and joint partnerships involving private sector provision with public subsidies.

Diabetes "represents one of the most challenging public health problems of the 21st century." This is one of the main conclusions of the recently published Aus-Diab 2005 Study[23] that found that every year 8 of every 1,000 people in Australia develop diabetes, and every day approximately 275 adult Australians develop diabetes. In 2002, almost 1 million Australians had diabetes, and of those, around half remain undiagnosed. Untreated, people with diabetes have high blood glucose levels while their tissues lack nourishment. Diabetes can cause diseases of the eyes, kidneys, nerves, and cardiovascular system, which can lead to a reduced quality of life and premature death. Type 2 diabetes, the most common form, has increased in prevalence in Australia since the 1980s, and further increases in obesity and physically inactive lifestyles and increases in the aging of the population have the potential to continue this increase. Diabetes has been among conditions of concern to Australia's health ministers (federal, state, and territory) for some time and continues to be a focus of the Council of Australian Governments' broader commitment to reducing the prevalence of avoidable chronic diseases and their risk factors.

There is also much concern about the financial burden of diabetes, recently estimated to be as much as A$3.1 billion (US$2.9 billion),[24] comprising healthcare costs (hospitalization, ambulatory services, and pharmaceuticals), home care costs, and non-healthcare costs (mainly home support and special foods). This is a groundbreaking study that demonstrates the substantial cost impact of diabetes in Australia. "For the first time we have local data, specific to our health system and services, available to inform and guide resource allocation and to provide a baseline and benchmark for future cost of illness assessment and economic analyses of diabetes."[24]

Structural and Organizational Issues

International comparisons suggest Australia has a health system that produces high levels of health at reasonable cost (close to the OECD average). The predominantly publicly funded system provides universal access to high-quality health and hospital services, ensuring that Australians are ahead of most other comparable countries on most measures of health. Despite these successes, Australia's historical, political, and societal characteristics, in particular the complexities associated with its federal/state structure, have given rise to some fundamental and somewhat intractable fiscal and organizational problems. Five-year Health Care Agreements between the Commonwealth and state/territory governments determine the amount of federal funding to be allocated to the states and territories to help cover the costs of running public hospitals. Funding for the current agreement (from 2008 to 2013) is likely to exceed A$50 billion (US$47 billion). Tensions inevitably arise between federal and state governments concerning the adequacy and distribution of this funding. Accusations of cost shifting between different levels of government, of inefficiencies, and of overlap and duplication of services are commonplace and make for ongoing public controversy and debate.

Australia's Labor Government, led by Prime Minister Kevin Rudd, is determined to address these problems, to improve the way health care is delivered, and to make it sustainable for the future. To this end, a National Health and Hospitals Reform Commission was established in February 2008 and charged with developing "a blueprint for tackling future challenges in Australia's health system, including: (1) the rapidly increasing burden of chronic disease; (2) the aging of the population; (3) rising health costs; and (4) inefficiencies exacerbated by cost shifting and the blame game."[25]

The commission has been asked by the government to focus in particular on health financing issues, the public/private divide, workforce needs, and rural health. It remains to be seen whether the Rudd Government's plans to make a good health system better will succeed. It is an imposing task. The system is large and complex, approaching A$100 billion (US$94 billion) in cost and close to 10% of GDP. Nevertheless, currently, the political will is there at all levels of government, and the necessary structures and processes are in place to ensure that future change is more than just a pipe dream.

REFERENCES

1. Smith L. *The Aboriginal Population of Australia*. Canberra, Australia: Australian National University Press; 1980.

2. Healy J, Sharman E, Lokuge B. Australia: Health System Review. *Health Systems in Transition*. 2006;8:9.

3. Australian Bureau of Statistics. *Australian Demographic Statistics*. Canberra, Australia; 2007.

4. Australian Bureau of Statistics. *Year Book Australia 2008*. Canberra, Australia; 2008.

5. Australian Bureau of Statistics. *Census 2006*. Canberra, Australia; 2007.

6. Australian Bureau of Statistics. *Yearbook 2004*. Canberra, Australia; 2004.

7. Australian Bureau of Statistics. *Census 2001*. Canberra, Australia; 2002.

8. Sax S. *A Strife of Interests*. George Allen and Unwin; 1984.

9. Deeble JS. Unscrambling the omelet: public and private health care financing in Australia. In McLachlan G, and Maynard A, eds. *The Public-Private Mix for Health*. London: Nuffield Provincial Hospitals Trust; 1982.

10. Australian Institute of Health and Welfare. *Australia's Health 2006*. Canberra, Australia; 2006, p. 372.

11. Australian Institute of Health and Welfare. *Australia's Health 2006*. Canberra, Australia; 2006.

12. Productivity Commission. *Impacts of Advances in Medical Technology in Australia*. Melbourne, Australia; 2005.

13. Healy J, Sharman E, Lokuge B. Australia: health system review. *Health Systems in Transition*. 2006;8.

14. Australian Institute of Health and Welfare. *Health Expenditure Australia, 2005–06*. Canberra, Australia; 2007.

15. Davis K, Schoen C, Schoenbaum SC, et al. *Mirror Mirror on the Wall: An International Update on the Comparative Performance of American Health Care*. New York: The Commonwealth Fund; 2007.

16. Productivity Commission. *Economic Implications of an Ageing Australia*. Canberra, Australia; 2005.

17. Australian Bureau of Statistics. *Population Projections Australia 2004 to 2101*. Canberra, Australia; 2005.

18. Treasury. *Intergenerational Report 2007*. Canberra, Australia; 2007.

19. Australian Institute of Health and Welfare. *Expenditure on Health for Aboriginal and Torres Strait Islander Peoples 2001–02*. Canberra, Australia; 2005.

20. World Health Organisation. *Obesity: Preventing and Managing the Global Epidemic*. Report of a WHO Consultation, WHO Technical Report Series 894. Geneva, Switzerland; 2000.

21. Australian Bureau of Statistics. *Yearbook Australia 2008*. Canberra; 2008.

22. Access Economics. *The Economic Cost of Obesity*. Canberra, Australia; 2006.

23. Barr E, Magliano DJ, Zimmet PZ, et al. *The Australian Diabetes, Obesity and Lifestyle Study*. Melbourne, Australia: International Diabetes Institute; 2006.

24. Colagiuri S, Colagiuri R, Conway B, Grainger D, Davey P. *DiabCost Australia, Assessing the Burden of Type 2 Diabetes in Australia*. Canberra, Australia: Diabetes Australia; 2003.

25. Media Release. Prime Minister and Minister for Health and Ageing. *National Health and Hospitals Reform Commission*. Canberra, Australia; February 25, 2008.

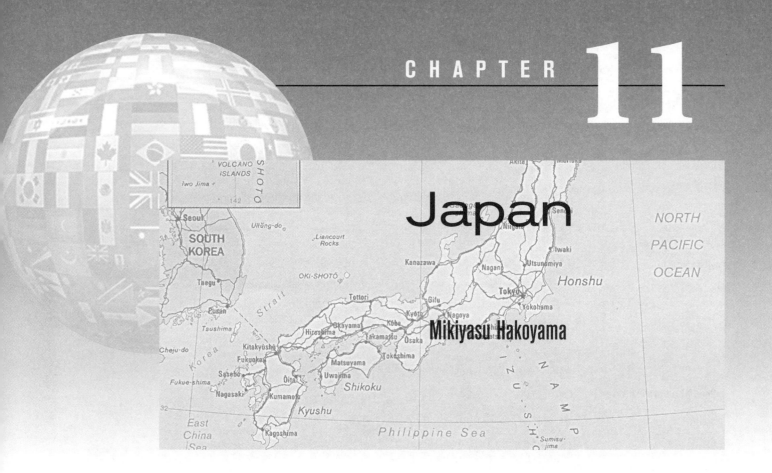

CHAPTER 11

Japan

Mikiyasu Hakoyama

COUNTRY DESCRIPTION

TABLE 11-1   Japan

Nationality	Noun: Japanese (singular and plural) Adjective: Japanese
Ethnic groups	Japanese 98.5%, Koreans 0.5%, Chinese 0.4%, other 0.6% Note: up to 230,000 Brazilians of Japanese origin migrated to Japan in the 1990s to work in industries; some have returned to Brazil (2004)
Religions	Observe both Shinto and Buddhist 84%, other 16% (including Christian 0.7%)
Language	Japanese
Literacy	Definition: age 15 and over can read and write Total population: 99% Male: 99% Female: 99% (2002)
Government type	Constitutional monarchy with a parliamentary government
Date of independence	660 BC (traditional founding by Emperor Jimmu)
Gross Domestic Product (GDP) per capita	$33,800 (2007 est.)

(continues)

TABLE 11-1 Japan (continued)

Unemployment rate	4% (2007 est.)
Natural hazards	Many dormant and some active volcanoes; about 1,500 seismic occurrences (mostly tremors) every year; tsunamis; typhoons
Environment: current issues	Air pollution from power plant emissions results in acid rain; acidification of lakes and reservoirs degrading water quality and threatening aquatic life; Japan is one of the largest consumers of fish and tropical timber, contributing to the depletion of these resources in Asia and elsewhere
Population	127,288,419 (July 2008 est.)
Age structure	0–14 years: 13.7% (male 8,926,439/female 8,460,629) 15–64 years: 64.7% (male 41,513,061/female 40,894,057) 65 years and over: 21.6% (male 11,643,845/female 15,850,388) (2008 est.)
Median age	Total: 43.8 years Male: 42.1 years Female: 45.7 years (2008 est.)
Population growth rate	−0.139% (2008 est.)
Birth rate	7.87 births/1,000 population (2008 est.)
Death rate	9.26 deaths/1,000 population (2008 est.)
Net migration rate	N/A
Gender ratio	At birth: 1.06 male(s)/female Under 15 years: 1.06 male(s)/female 15–64 years: 1.02 male(s)/female 65 years and over: 0.73 male(s)/female Total population: 0.95 male(s)/female (2008 est.)
Infant mortality rate	Total: 2.8 deaths/1,000 live births Male: 3 deaths/1,000 live births Female: 2.58 deaths/1,000 live births (2008 est.)
Life expectancy at birth	Total population: 82.07 year Male: 78.73 years Female: 85.59 years (2008 est.)
Total fertility rate	1.22 children born/woman (2008 est.)
HIV/AIDS adult prevalence rate	Less than 0.1% (2003 est.)
Number of people living with HIV/AIDS	12,000 (2003 est.)
HIV/AIDS deaths	500 (2003 est.)

Central Intelligence Agency. The World Fact Book, 2008. Retrieved November 18, 2008, from https://www.cia.gov/library/publications/the-world-factbook.

History

Archaeological evidence indicates that the current inhabitants of Japan may have been there continuously for the last 30,000 years. The first period of Japanese prehistory is from approximately 10,000 BCE to 300 BCE, which is known as the Jomon era. The name *Jomon* is derived from design patterns found on clay vessels that are created by pressing a rope. It is assumed that Jomon people lived a simple nomadic life consisting of hunting, fishing, and picking edibles. The Yayoi era began at approximately 300 BCE. During this period, residents of Japan developed a more sophisticated lifestyle. They adopted wet field or water-irrigated rice cultivation, which ensured them a steady food supply. This adoption of agriculture made it possible for the early Japanese to stop being nomadic and form permanent communities.[1]

For over 1,000 years from the Yamato era to the Azuchi-momoyama era, Japan's history has been characterized by continuous civil wars. It was not until the Edo era that began in the beginning of the 17th century that Japan became a peaceful country. It was at this time that the Dutch began to visit Japan for trading. Being afraid of strong foreign influences, especially the spread of Christianity, the Japanese government promulgated sakoku-rei (an isolationist policy) in the mid-17th century, which protected Japan from being westernized by an influx of foreign influences. This isolationist policy prohibited any interactions with foreign countries except China and the Netherlands. Trading with the Dutch was allowed only in Dejima, a man-made island in Nagasaki. This arrangement continued for nearly 230 years.[2]

It was during the Meiji era (1868–1912) that Japan passionately adopted Western technology to establish a modernized and militaristic nation. At the end of the 19th century, Japan used its military force to gain new territories successfully, including Korea and part of China. Japan's military invasions continued into the mid-20th century. This eventually led to a war against the United States with a surprise attack by Japanese aircrafts on the U.S. Pacific fleet in Pearl Harbor, Hawaii, on December 7, 1941. Japan's militaristic ambition was finally forced to end in August 1945 when the United States detonated two atomic bombs in Japan, the first on Hiroshima on August 6, 1945, and the second on Nagasaki 3 days later. The U.S. occupation that followed immediately after Japan's unconditional surrender and lasted until 1952 immensely impacted the construction of modern Japan in various areas from economy to politics. During this period of U.S. occupation, a framework for a democratic government was established. Based on a British model, Japan established a parliamentary system and an independent judiciary. The emperor was retained as a symbol of the state.[2]

The current educational system was also restructured during this period by adopting the American system of a 6-year elementary school, a 3-year junior high, and a 3-year high school.[2] The Japanese are nearly 100% literate, and their level of educational attainment is high.[2]

Size and Geography

Japan, the nation of the rising sun, lies off the coast of the Eurasian continent in the Far East, or in the western end of the Northern Pacific Ocean. The Japanese archipelago consists of four large islands and several thousand small islands and stretches 1,200 miles from northeast to southwest (Figure 11-1). The four main islands are, from the north to the south, Hokkaido, Honshu, Shikoku, and Kyushu. Honshu is the largest. It is narrow and long in shape, and the widest point is only 160 miles. Unlike many other islands and continents, Japan did not break off from the Eurasian continent. Instead, the Japanese islands were formed as a result of volcanic eruptions. Approximately 60 volcanoes remain active in Japan.[3]

The total land area of Japan is approximately 145,379 square miles, which is larger than Great Britain or Italy. Because the great majority of its land area is extremely mountainous, nearly all of the population inhabits approximately one sixth of its total land area. Japan is, therefore, more crowded than the population density per square mile indicates.[4]

Government or Political System

The foundation of Japan's current democratic government was also laid during the U.S. occupation. The present constitution was written and adopted in 1947, which provides for universal suffrage for both genders and also for an independent judicial system. The Diet consists of two houses. The upper house, or the House of Councilors, has 242 members who are elected for 6-year terms. The lower house, or the House of Representatives, has 480 members who serve 4-year terms. Terms in the lower house can be shortened, however, if opposing parties call for a re-election because of a vote of no confidence. Whenever the election takes place, the prime minister must be elected again.

A great deal of political power remains in the lower house, however, because a bill, once defeated by the upper house, can still be passed and become law if the lower house passes it for a second time with a two thirds

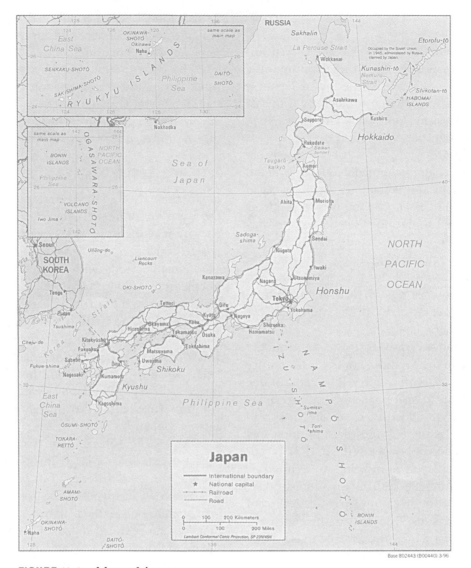

FIGURE 11-1 Map of Japan

majority.[2] The prime minister is elected by the House of Representatives from among its members; therefore, the support of the majority party becomes essential in the selection of the prime minister, who in turn appoints the members of his cabinet.[4] The cabinet members are composed of heads of ministries and other government agencies.[2]

The Japanese political world is composed of multiple parties, the majority leading party, and several minority opposition parties. The Liberal Democratic Party (LDP), which is conservative and probusiness, was the majority leading party for most of the second half of the 20th century, during which time Japan strived for and achieved its goal of becoming an economic giant. Structural change within Japanese political dynamics took place in the mid-1990s when the Japanese economy faced a serious economic crisis. With the burst of the

so-called bubble economy, the LDP was no longer able to maintain the majority; however, the LDP maintained its control by forming a coalition with other minority parties. At this time, the LDP has successfully regained its members and currently holds the majority on its own.

Macroeconomics

Japan experienced rapid and acute economic growth during the 1960s and 1970s, during which time Japan was reconstructed as a modernized nation. Japan's economy slowed in the 1980s, and the growth rate of the gross domestic product (GDP) decreased. Japan's economy suffered severely during the 1990s as a result of the abrupt ending of the bubble economy.

Japan's real GDP in recent years, when focused on change from the previous year, increased 1.4% in 2003,

2.7% in 2004, 1.9% in 2005, 2.4% in 2006, and 2.1% in 2007. These consistent figures indicate the stability of Japan's economic growth, especially when they are compared with those of the late 1990s and early 2000s when the growth rate fluctuated widely from 2.9% to −2.0%.[5] When focusing also on the changes in percentage from the previous year, Japan's total domestic demand has increased 1.7% in 2005, 1.4% in 2006, and 0.9% in 2007. The change in 2008 was projected to remain the same (0.9%) as in 2007, but the growth rate was projected to go up 1.4% in 2009.[6]

Demographics

Japan's current population is estimated to be approximately 128 million, consisting of slightly more females (3 million more) than males. The population aged 15 to 64 makes up approximately two thirds (65.5%) of the total population. The population aged 65 and over constitutes approximately 21% of the total population. This is a considerably larger percentage than that comprised of children (aged 0 to 14 years), which accounts for only 13.6% of the total population.[7] As these statistics indicate, an aging population has become a persistent concern for today's Japan.

Statistics indicate that Japan is a relatively safe society compared with many of its counterparts in the world. Rates of violent crime, theft, and drug abuse in Japan are among the lowest in the world. A statistical comparison between Japan and the United States revealed that despite the fact that Japan has one third as many police officers per capita as the United States, it has only 37 prisoners for every 100,000 people, 7% of the number of prison inmates (519) per 100,000 in the United States.[2]

Poverty

Poverty has become an urgent concern for the Japanese in recent years. According to the report by the Organisation for Economic Co-operation and Development (OECD), Japan ranked the second worst in relative poverty among OECD nations. Relative poverty is defined as earning less than one half of the median household disposable income. According to this, the proportion of the population living in relative poverty was 13.5% in 2000, the second highest among OECD members, following 13.7% within the United States.[8] One factor contributing to the high relative poverty rate in Japan is the increase in single working parents, more than half of whom were in relative poverty in 2000. Furthermore, it was revealed that the poverty rate for single parents was higher for those who worked than

for those who were not employed. This high relative poverty rate among single parents is also one of the factors that affects child poverty, measured at 14% in 2000, higher than the OECD average.[9]

Single-parent families have become a serious social concern in Japan. It is estimated that there were approximately 1,225,400 father-absent families in 2003, which is an increase of 28.3% from the previous survey conducted 5 years earlier. A great majority of these families were the result of divorce, which has drastically increased in the past decade. Although the divorce rate in Japan remains lower than that of the United States, it is now as high as that of the European Union (EU). The number of such families is still relatively small, as it accounted for only 2.7% of the nation's 45.8 million families in 2003. Nevertheless, it requires immediate attention, as the vast majority of children in these single-parent families are likely to live in poverty.[10]

Religion

The two major religions in Japan are Shinto and Buddhism. Shinto is an indigenous, shamanic religion of Japan that venerates kami (superior beings), whose spirits are believed to inhabit objects or plants temporarily. The central tenets of Shinto are thought to have originated in the Yayoi era (300 BCE to 300 CE). It was not until the 7th century, however, that these beliefs became recognized as a coherent religion called Shinto, primarily in order to differentiate these existing beliefs from those of Buddhism, the newly introduced religion.[3] Shinto is a nonexclusive religion that has no founder, doctrines, or texts. The kami, often translated as deity, are numerous and frequently applied to objects such as mountains, big trees, and large rocks, which are very dissimilar to the transcendent deities of Western religions.[4]

Since the 7th century, Buddhism has constantly been supported by the Japanese government and has come to be the major religion along with Shinto.[4] Both Shinto shrines and Buddhist temples are found throughout Japan and are visited by people on numerous occasions every year. Although approximately 90% of Japanese report that they are Buddhists, they also visit Shinto shrines.[2] Religion to Japanese, whether it is Shinto or Buddhism, is an important aspect of their traditional lifestyle and is qualitatively different from what it means to be religious for Christians, Muslims, Hindus, or Jews. Many Japanese marry and christen babics at Shinto shrines and gather for funerals at Buddhist temples. At the same time, more young people are choosing Christian churches as the place to get married. It is perhaps more accurate to conclude that most Japanese are much more secular than their American counterparts.[2]

Although it has long been debated whether Confucianism is a religion or philosophy, there is no doubt that it has profoundly influenced northeast Asian nations including Japan. Although Confucian teachings have long been influential, their influence was enhanced when Confucianism was incorporated into the nation's legal system more than 300 years ago. Teachings of Confucius are deeply integrated into Japanese life, which include emphasis on appropriate virtue and conduct in this world, such as hard work, education, obligation, and reciprocity. Japanese society is status conscious, one of the characteristics of the Confucian influence. Vertical relationships are clearly structured and superiors and subordinates owe each other certain obligations, including protection, loyalty, and good team play. Many Japanese, however, do not connect these values imbedded in Japanese culture to Confucianism.[2]

BRIEF HISTORY OF THE HEALTHCARE SYSTEM

Pre-World War II

Foreign influences on Japanese health care and medicine began in the 6th century when traditional Chinese medicine was introduced, treatment of which featured the use of acupuncture and herbal medicines. Both are still popular in Japan.[11] A thousand years after the Chinese influence, the Japanese were exposed to Western medical practices by Portuguese missionaries. This influence was minimal, however, because of the isolation policy the Tokugawa government issued in the 17th century, effectively barring the Portuguese from Japan. Besides the Chinese, only the Dutch were allowed to trade with Japan during the centuries of this isolation period. Because of this, the influence of Dutch medical care practices on the development of Japan's healthcare system has been profound.[12]

During the Meiji era that began in the late 19th century, the Japanese were willing to open themselves up to a variety of Western influences.[11] Although Japanese accepted various Western knowledge and technologies for the modernization of their nation, they expressed a particular interest in the German healthcare system, which was regarded as the best in Europe at that time.[13] The Japanese constructed its nationwide health insurance system based heavily on the German model.[11]

Japan's health insurance system improved gradually from the 1920s to the 1960s. The Health Insurance Law enacted in 1922 was designed to direct employers to provide health insurance coverage mainly for their blue-collar workers such as factory workers and miners.[14] In 1938, the Ministry of Public Health and Social Welfare was established, and the National Health Insurance Law was enacted, which required local governments to offer health insurance coverage to those who were not subject to the 1922 law, such as those engaged in fishing, farming, and forestry.[15] It is estimated, however, that as many as one third of the citizens were uninsured in 1955. It was not until 1961 when health insurance coverage was extended to every citizen.[15]

In 1931, when the population was 64.5 million, Japan had 3,710 hospitals, which, by 1940, increased to 4,732 with an approximate ratio of one doctor and two nurses to every 1,000 Japanese. These conditions worsened, however, during the early 1940s when Japan was at war, and the number of hospitals and clinics, as well as doctors, nurses, and beds per 1,000 decreased sharply. In 1945, when World War II ended, all of these conditions began to improve again.[15]

Since World War II

One of the public health issues during the U.S. occupation immediately after the end of World War II was to deal with infectious diseases such as smallpox, cholera, and diphtheria. The most feared disease was smallpox. Some 17,000 cases were reported during the first year of the occupation. Immediate measures were taken that included production and inoculation of sufficient vaccines to the total population, as a result of which the epidemic subsided. Tuberculosis was also a major threat to the Japanese during the 1930s and 1940s. It had been the leading cause of death, and in the year 1945 alone, more Japanese died from tuberculosis than by all the fire raids and bombings, including the two atomic bombs. When the U.S. occupation first took place, it was estimated that there were 1 to 2 million clinical cases of tuberculosis. The Public Health and Welfare officials, concluding that vaccination was the best approach, developed a dried BCG vaccine and successfully immunized 30 million people under 30 years old. Although immunization contributed to the drop in mortality and morbidity, it was in 1960 when streptomycin became available to treat those who were already infected that tuberculosis was no longer the number one cause of death in Japan.[15]

Another challenge in reestablishing healthcare systems after World War II was rebuilding the physical infrastructure of costly healthcare facilities. Because of successful reduction in the rates of infectious disease, hospital resources could be reallocated for other purposes. The quality of care provided by these hospitals, however, was in need of improvement. In order to cope with issues related to quality care, a model hospital was set up in each prefecture that was to serve as a benchmark for cleanliness and efficient management. A legal step was taken in 1948 to improve healthcare quality by reinspecting and classifying hospitals. Small hospitals that had fewer than 10 beds were downgraded to clinics and were limited in patient care as they lacked sufficient operating rooms and laboratory services. Although the number of doctors in Japan was adequate, their quality was questioned, as more than 60% of the 77,000 doctors were graduates of second-class medical schools that required only 4 years of medical education beyond high school. Based on the new standards established, all the medical schools were inspected, as a result of which schools not meeting the standards were closed. By the early 1950s, the quality of doctors in Japan improved significantly. The quality of nursing was also improved in a similar fashion during this period.[15] Currently all physicians, dentists, and pharmacists must attend 6 years of college beyond high school and pass the national exam to be certified. This allows Japanese to practice medicine at a younger age than their American counterparts.

The number of physicians in relation to population steadily increased, and by the end of 1992, there were approximately 220,000 physicians (1.77 physicians per 1,000 population). More than 95% of these physicians were in medical practice, about 27% of which were owners of medical care facilities such as hospitals or clinics, whereas the rest were employed in medical care facilities.[16]

DESCRIPTION OF CURRENT HEALTHCARE SYSTEM

Facilities

As of October 1, 2006, the number of healthcare facilities in operation in Japan was 174,944. Of the 174,944 facilities, 8,943 (5.1%) are hospitals (20 or more beds), 98,609 (56.4%) are clinics (19 or fewer beds), and 67,392 (38.5%) are dental clinics.[17] Whereas 88.0% (7,780) of hospitals are general hospitals, the rest are mental hospi-

tals (1,072) and tuberculosis sanatoria (1). When these hospitals are classified according to sponsorship, 5,697 (63.7%) are medical corporations, followed by 1,351 hospitals run by public (governmental) medical corporations (15.1%).[17] Of the 98,609 clinics, 87% (85,751) have no beds. As for the sponsorship of these clinics, more than one half of them (50,355) are individually owned, followed by medical corporations (32,196).[17]

The total number of beds is 1,786,649. More than 50% of beds (911,014) belong to general hospitals. There are 1,273 beds per 100,000 inhabitants. A little more than one half (717.0 beds per 100,000) are for general patients, whereas about a quarter (275.8 per 100,000) are psychiatric beds, and another quarter (274.1 per 100,000) are for long-term care.[17] Considering Japan's fast-growing older population, demand for beds, especially long-term care beds, is expected to rise.

Workforce

The number of physicians grew steadily over the past few decades. The number of physicians was 230,519 in 1994, which grew to 277,927 in 2006 (20.6% increase from 1994). The ratio of physicians to population grew as well. The number of physicians to 100,000 population was 188.4 in 1994 and reached 217.5 physicians per 100,000 population in 2006. Of these 277,927 physicians, 225,743 (82.8%) are males, and 47,929 (17.2%) are females; however, the number of female physicians is gradually increasing. The average age of physicians is 48.5 (49.8 for males and 42.5 for females).[17] The largest proportion of physicians are engaged in hospitals (44.5%), followed by those in clinics (34.3%) and those in medical school–affiliated hospitals (16.1%).[18] Because most clinics are private physician-owned operations, for many young doctors with no economic resources, their choice is limited to working for hospitals. The number of physicians per capita in Japan is lower than most other OECD countries and 50% lower than that of the OECD average. This is partially due to the governmental policies restricting the number of new entrants in medical schools.[19]

The number of dentists has grown as well. Currently, there are 97,198 dentists (as of December 31, 2006), an increase of 19.9% from the 1994 figure of 81,055. The number of dentists per 100,000 population was 64.8 in 1994, which grew to 76.1 in 2006, an increase of 17.4%. A great majority of these dentists (84.7%) are engaged in clinics, followed by those in dental school–affiliated hospitals (9.8%), and general hospitals (2.8%).

There are considerably more male dentists than female dentists (80.5% male and 19.5% female), although the proportion of female dentists is also increasing. The average age is 48.1 (49.4 for males and 42.9 for females).[17]

The number of pharmacists has also been increasing over the past decade. According to the latest information available (December 31, 2006), the number of pharmacists is 252,533, or approximately 197.6 pharmacists to 100,000 inhabitants. There were 124,390 pharmacists in 1982 and 176,871 pharmacists in 1994. The number of pharmacists more than doubled over the last 25 years. Nearly one half (49.6%) of the pharmacists are engaged in pharmacies, followed by those in hospitals and clinics (19.4%). Unlike physicians or dentists, there are more female pharmacists (60.9%) than male pharmacists (39.1%). The average age for pharmacists is 43.7 (44.8 for males and 43.0 for females), which is slightly younger than that of physicians or dentists.[17] Six years of schooling beyond high school are required to become a pharmacist.

There are 811,972 nurses and 382,149 assistant nurses currently working. The number of nurses has more than doubled since 1982, while the increase of assistant nurses has been more moderate.[18] There are 635.5 nurses, 299.1 assistant nurses, 31.5 public health nurses, and 20.2 midwives currently working per 100,000 population. Disparity is apparent in distribution of these professionals from prefecture to prefecture. For instance, the number of nurses available to 100,000 inhabitants in Kochi prefecture is twice as large as that of Saitama prefecture or Chiba prefecture, and the assistant nurses available in prefectures such as Kagoshima and Miyazaki are more than three times those of Kanagawa or Tokyo. Similar disparity is observed in the distribution of public health nurses, whereas the differences across prefectures is less obvious for midwives.[18]

Technology and Equipment

Computed tomography (CT), also called computed axial tomography scanners, magnetic resonance imaging (MRI) units, mammography, and radiation therapy equipment are major modern medical technologies.[20] CT scanners and MRI units are both used to produce cross-sectional views of the inside of the patient's scanned body, which can assist physicians in making prompt diagnoses. As shown in Table 11-2, there are 92.6 CT scanners per 1 million population in Japan, which is

TABLE 11-2 Medical Technologies in OECD Countries, Number per Million Population, 2005 (or Latest Available)

Rank	CT Scanners		MRI Units		Radiation Therapy Equipment	
1	Japan	92.6	Japan	40.1	Iceland	13.5
2	Australia	45.3	United States	26.6	Slovak Republic	9.8
3	Korea	32.2	Iceland	20.3	Switzerland	9.8
4	United States	32.2	Austria	16.3		
5	Belgium	31.6	Italy	15		
6	Austria	29.4	Finland	14.7		
7	Luxembourg	28.6	Switzerland	14.4		
10					Japan	6.8
	OECD	20.6	OECD	9.8	OECD	6.2

1. In Australia, data for MRI units, mammographs, and radiation therapy equipment relate only to those eligible for reimbursement under Medicare.
2. In Japan, data for CT scanners relate to 2002 rather than 2005 because the 2005 data are more limited in terms of coverage of institutions and type of CT scanners.

Source: Data are from OECD Health Data, 2007.

by far the highest number among the OECD countries, the average of which is 20.6. There are 40.1 MRI units per 1 million population currently available in Japan, which is far less than that of CT scanners; however, it is also the highest number among all the OECD countries. Japan has 6.8 radiation therapy equipment per 1 million population, which is slightly higher than that of the OECD average (6.2).[20] These figures suggest the possibility that Japan's health care focuses more on preventive and diagnostic aspects than therapeutic aspects; however, the smaller amount of radiation therapy equipment may be reflective of lower cancer rates in Japan.

EVALUATION OF HEALTHCARE SYSTEM

Cost

Japan is the first nation in Asia to have introduced a comprehensive social insurance program, featuring universal coverage by mandating everyone to join a health insurance coverage plan available at either a place of employment or a place of residence. It is mandatory for all companies employing five or more workers to contribute to a health insurance plan for their employees. Those not covered by their employers join the National Health Insurance (NHI) program administered by municipal governments and NHI associations.[11] Both the EHI and the NHI plans cover dependent family members in the same household. Premiums for the Employee's Health Insurance (EHI) plan are determined based on the employee's monthly income, which is adjusted periodically according to medical expenditure. The employer is required to contribute 50% of the cost. Currently, the monthly payment for the EHI plan is 8.2% of the employee's monthly income for those who are under 40 years of age and 9.45% for those aged 45 to 65. The average income over a 3-month period is calculated to determine the EHI payment. This includes every form of income such as overload pay and commuting expenses covered by the employer. As an example, if a 25-year-old employee's average income for the three-month period is 200,000 yen (approximately $1,982 based on the 04/10/08 exchange rate of 100.93 yen to the dollar), the EHI payment would be 16,400 yen ($162.5) per month (200,000 yen × 8.2%), half of which (8,200 yen = $81.25) is covered by the employer and the rest (8,200 yen) by the employee. The EHI premium is adjusted annually. Currently, approximately 60% of the nation's people (75,520,000) are covered through EHI, whereas about 40% (51,580,000) are covered through NHI.[18] Retired people who are no longer eligible for the EHI switch to NHI or become dependents of other family members, such as their adult children who are covered by EHI.

The monthly payment for the NHI plan also depends on the resident's income. Because the NHI is administered by local governments and each government uses its own system in calculating the cost, the figure varies widely depending on residence. The difference could be more than double between two neighboring cities, although it is likely to be around 5% to 10% of the resident's income. The maximum amount of premium per year per household for the NHI is 530,000 yen ($5,251). Individuals insured by the NHI are responsible for 30% of their medical expenses, whereas the NHI covers 70%; therefore, if a doctor's visit costs $100, the NHI covers $70, and the patient is responsible for $30. Individuals insured by the EHI also share 30% of the cost, an increase from 20% in 2003.[21]

A universal point system is used in determining medical care cost. For instance, the first-visit fee for outpatients is 270 points, to which extra points are added based on medical care offered (e.g., 18 points for an injection, 250 points for a 20-minute rehabilitation, 6,210 points for an appendectomy, and 6,100 points for general anesthesia). Each point is worth 10 yen (about 10 cents).[22]

The nation's health expenditure has gradually increased over the past decade, as did the ratio of the nation's health expenditure in relation to its GDP. In 1994, health expenditure accounted for 6.9% of GDP, which went up to 8.9% a decade later (2004).[22] According to the latest OECD data available, Japan's health expenditure per capita is $2,358, which ranks 19th of 30 nations. This is slightly lower than the OECD average of $2,759 and almost one third of the highest-ranked expenditure of the United States ($6,401).[20] Japan's annual average growth rate in real health expenditure per capita over the decade since 1995 is 2.6%, much lower than that of the OECD average, with a rank of 26th out of 30 nations.[21] Although health insurance premiums keep increasing and each citizen's share of the medical cost has also increased, because of universal coverage, every citizen has access to decent medical care at a reasonable cost.

Quality

Detailed licensing regulations for hospitals including the structure, the equipment, and the number of staff are provided by the Medical Service Law, which ensures the quality of health care available to citizens. All the hospitals must meet these standards before they are given permission from the prefectural governor to operate. The prefectural government sends medical inspectors periodically to ensure that all the hospitals abide by the regulations.[16]

Because the number of medical schools is limited and only so many seats are available each year, it is very competitive to become a physician in Japan. There are only 80 medical schools throughout Japan, 43 of which are national schools and 8 of which are public (e.g., prefectural) schools. Although it is not very costly to attend public medical school, it is much more costly to attend private medical school. After successfully completing 6 years of medical school education, all medical school students must pass the national medical examination administered by the Ministry of Health, Labor and Welfare before they are licensed to practice medicine.[16] Although it had been customary for new physicians to be engaged in residency training for at least 2 years in medical school hospitals or in those hospitals designated by the Ministry of Health, Labor and Welfare, this 2-year residency training was mandated in 2004.[23] This new law ought to increase confidence in the ability to practice in novice physicians, which in turn may contribute to the quality of medical care made available.

Assessment of quality of health care is by no means simple and easy, as many elements are intertwined. One way of assessing healthcare quality is to examine current health status, including outcomes such as the mortality rate and the survival rate after cardiac arrest. Life expectancy at birth for Japanese in 2005 was 82.1 years, ranked at the top of the 30 OECD nations. This is a remarkable accomplishment considering that the life expectancy in 1960 was 67.8 years, ranked one of the bottom five. Although the life expectancy at birth of Japanese women is 85.5 years, the highest in the OECD nations, that of men is 78.6 years, the third after Iceland (79.2 years) and Switzerland (78.7 years).[20] It is interesting that although life expectancy at birth for Japanese is very high, Japan's health expenditure per capita is relatively low. One conceivable explanation is that Japanese require less professional health care due to factors such as a culturally healthy diet and high health self-consciousness. It may also be because high-quality health care is provided for less cost in Japan than it is in other OECD countries.

Life expectancy at age 65 is 23.2 years for Japanese women and 18.1 years for Japanese men, both of which are ranked at the top among the OECD nations. This is nearly 8 years of gain for women and 5.6 years for men in the years since 1970. This can partially be explained by an apparent reduction in death rates due to heart disease and stroke among older people.[20]

Ischemic heart disease (IHD), often resulting in acute myocardial infarction or heart attack, is a leading cause of hospitalization and death in OECD countries, accounting for 16% of all deaths in 2004. Japan's mortality from IHD is the lowest of all the OECD countries for both genders, although this rate is higher for men than for women. Despite Japan's low mortality rate from IHD, its in-hospital fatality rate for acute myocardial infarction is close to the average for OECD countries.[20]

Stroke is one of the most prevalent causes of mortality in OECD countries, accounting for 10% of all deaths in 2004. Mortality from stroke in Japan, as shown in Table 11-3, is relatively high especially for men, the eighth highest among 27 OECD countries (women's mortality from stroke is the 19th)[20]; however, in-hospital fatality rates for stroke are the lowest of all OECD countries. This suggests that stroke victims who survive and are hospitalized generally receive excellent care.

Mortality rates for stroke in particular and cardiovascular disease in general are higher for men than women in Japan, which may explain part of the gender difference in longevity. It is conceivable that health-related behaviors such as drinking alcoholic beverages, smoking, and lack of exercise are partially accountable for this gender difference. For instance, a considerably higher number of men than women smoke in Japan (men are four times more likely to smoke than women), as well as drink alcohol.

Vaccination rates are a reliable indicator for assessing quality of care for communicable diseases. Although influenza is a common infectious disease that affects individuals of all ages, older people and those with chronic medical conditions are at higher risk for complications, including death. Effective vaccination, therefore, is a recommended way to prevent illness, hospitalization, and mortality among this at-risk population. Based on the latest OECD available data (2002–2005, depending on the nation), Japan's influenza vaccination rate in older people aged 65 and over is not very high. While 79.1% of older people in Australia and 64.6% in the United States received an influenza vaccination, only 48% of Japanese older people were vaccinated in 2005. This is much lower than the OECD average of 55.3%; however, the percentage has nearly doubled from 28% in 2004, indicating that extra effort has been put to promoting vaccination.[20]

Children are also vulnerable to communicable diseases. Appropriate vaccination is one of the most cost-effective health policy interventions. Effective vaccinations successfully eradicated polio and diphtheria across

TABLE 11-3 Stroke Mortality Rates in OECD Countries, 2004

	Country	Female	Male	Country
1	Hungary	108.6	160.8	Hungary
2	Portugal	99.6	125.9	Portugal
18	Norway	41.2	105.6	Slovak Republic
19	Japan	39.6	102.5	Poland
20	Australia	39.5	96.0	Greece
21	Spain	39.1	65.7	Japan
22	United States	38.3	43.7	Australia
25	Canada	32.3	41.4	United States
26	France	29.5	41.1	France
27	Switzerland	26.2	39.0	Canada
	OECD	54.4	33.2	Switzerland
			68.5	OECD

Data are from OECD Health Data 2007.

OECD countries. Vaccination against measles and pertussis (whooping cough) has also been promoted, and as a result, vaccination rates for both diseases are high in most OECD countries. Based on the latest data available (2003–2006, depending on the country), Japan's vaccination rate for pertussis is 93% (2004) and for measles is 94% (2004), in both cases close to the OECD average. The vaccination effort to combat measles, however, appears to be inadequate. Japan's incidence rate of measles is still 4.7 per 100,000 population (2005), much higher than the 1.22 per 100,000 OECD average. Continued promotion of vaccination against measles, therefore, is an important issue relating to quality of care.[20]

The majority of patients in Japan, both inpatient and outpatient, are satisfied with the overall hospital care they receive. Two major dissatisfactions outpatients express are long waiting times and medical expenditure. Dissatisfactions expressed by inpatients are content of meals and quality of facilities such as hospital rooms and bathrooms. Although the majority of patients feel secure regarding the medical care they receive, approximately 20% of them expressed some concerns regarding the actions of physicians and nurses, as well as examinations and therapeutic procedures.[18] These patients' views may be a reflection of less attention being paid to patients' comfort in Japan, which may in turn relate to aspects of Japanese culture encouraging hard work, while discouraging the pursuit of luxury.

TABLE 11-4 In-Hospital Case-Fatality Rates Within 30 Days After Admission for Ischemic Stroke, 2005 and Earlier Years (Where Available)

	Country	Latest Year
1	Mexico (2004–2005)	20.1
2	Korea (2004)	15.2
3	Canada (2001–2005)	13.1
	Average	10.1
21	Iceland (2004–2005)	5.8
22	United Kingdom[1] (2003–2004)	5.5
23	Japan (1999–2005)	3.3

1. 2002–2003/2003–2004

Data are from OECD Health Data 2007.

Access

One factor that influences patients' access to high-quality medical care is the supply of well-trained and geographically well-distributed health professionals such as physicians and nurses. This can be assessed by examining physician density (the number of practicing doctors per capita). Currently, there are two physicians per 1,000 inhabitants in Japan, which is way below the OECD average of 3 per 1,000 and ranks 27th of 30 OECD nations. Access to medical care in Japan also varies depending on residence as there is an apparent disparity in physician density across prefectures. Although there are 250.7 physicians per 100,000 population in Kyoto prefecture, there are only 112.1 physicians in Saitama prefecture, less than half of Kyoto.[24] Disparity in dentist density is also apparent across prefectures. Although there are 120.2 dentists per 100,000 in Tokyo, the number drops to 46.1 in Fukui.[25] Nurse shortages have become an issue for some countries, and it is expected to continue to be an issue, especially in aging countries such as Japan. The number of practicing nurses per 1,000 population in Japan is 9, which is neither impressive nor disappointing, as it is approximately the same as the OECD average of 8.9. Japan ranks 15th of 30 OECD countries.[20]

Another important element in assessing quality of care, especially in aging countries like Japan, is access to long-term care beds in hospitals and nursing homes, which are mostly used to care for older people with either chronic illness or disability. There are 27 long-term care beds per 1,000 people aged 65 and over in Japan, which is far lower than the OECD average of 41, and only one third of the rate in Switzerland. It is preferred by most OECD countries to have more long-term care beds in nursing homes where services are more care oriented than treatment oriented and also more cost saving than hospitals; however, more than one half of the long-term care beds in Japan belong to hospitals. Although the number of long-term care beds in nursing homes has increased in recent years in Japan, considering the continuously growing older population, that number is still insufficient.[20]

Access to emergency medical care in Japan varies across disciplines. Although nearly 50% of facilities specializing in internal medicine accept emergency patients during night hours, only 27.8% of those specializing in orthopedics, 16% of pediatric hospitals, and less than 14% of psychiatric care services are available for nighttime emergencies.[18]

Because medical cost is an issue for most individuals, one of the factors that influences access to healthcare services is health insurance coverage. Lack of coverage frequently discourages many people from having access to appropriate medical care in a prompt manner. Lack of coverage also restricts those in need from having access to innovative treatments, as well as preventive services such as screening and vaccination. Along with the majority of the OECD nations, 100% of Japanese have public health insurance coverage for a core set of services. The individual's share of medical cost is usually 30%.[25] One advantage of the Japanese health insurance system is that practically every clinic and hospital accepts any type of health insurance. All one has to do is to present an insurance card at the window at the time of the first visit.

The majority of hospitals are privately owned, and most clinics and small hospitals are physician-owned operations. Practically all medical facilities provide primary care services, and individuals can select any facility of their choice. Although there are people who have their own home doctor, there are many others who do not. Depending on their health conditions, many individuals select one of the clinics nearby for primary care. When the patient's health condition is diagnosed to be more serious than the clinic can manage, the physician refers the patient to a larger hospital where appropriate treatment can be provided. In large hospitals, treatment is more costly, and outpatient visits are frequently limited to the morning hours. Except for those who live in extremely isolated areas, access to medical care is not an issue in Japan. Access to high-quality care, however, may depend on each individual's attention to their local doctor's reputation for high quality.[13]

CURRENT AND EMERGING ISSUES AND CHALLENGES

Care for the Older Population

Japan is one of the world's most rapidly aging societies, with 20.0% of the population age 65 and over, the highest in all the OECD countries (the OECD average is 14.7%, and that of the United States is 12.4%). It is projected that in Japan this proportion will increase to 27.4% in 2025, whereas that of the United States will be at 18.3%. It is not only the increased proportion of the older population in Japan that requires attention but the rapid speed with which this demographic change is occurring. It is predicted that it will take 69 years for the older population (aged 65 and over) in the United States to grow from 7% to 14% of the overall population; however, for Japan, this change took place in only 24 years. This is remarkable, especially when compared with other nations such as Great Britain (46 years), Sweden (82 years), and France (114 years).[26] Furthermore, although Japan's longevity ranks the highest, its fertility rate is one of the lowest in OECD countries (27th out of 30).[20]

These trends clearly indicate the importance of health-care services for an older population in Japan. The number of older people in need of medical care has increased over the past decade. Of the 7,073,000 outpatients per day in 2005, 1,554,800 (22.0%) were 65 to 74 years old, and 1,523,100 (21.5%) were 75 years old or older. The number of inpatients per day in 2005 for those aged 65 to 74 was 298,800 (20.5%), and for those aged 75 and older, it was 638,600 (43.8%), with a total of 64.3% of inpatients being 65 years old or older.[18]

Although national medical care expenditure per capita increases gradually with age, expenditure by those aged 70 and over is much higher than for younger people. Although the expenditure is 353,900 yen ($3,506 at 100.93 yen to the dollar) per capita for those aged 60 to 64 and 443,100 yen ($4,390) for those aged 65 to 69, it is 608,200 yen ($6,026) for those aged 70 to 74 and 731,300 yen ($7,246) for those aged 75 to 79. Furthermore, much of the increase in expenditure from one age group to the next is due to an increase in hospital inpatient expenditure.[16] Because of continuously increasing medical costs, the premiums for each insured patient, as well as the patient's share of his/her medical cost, have been increasing in recent years. In order to cope with the extra medical expenditure related to nursing home care for older persons, it was mandated in 2000 that everyone aged 40 to 64 years pay an additional premium. This system was created to lighten the financial burden of those who are in need of long-term care; however, for this system to support those in need efficiently, there are many issues remaining to be dealt with, such as accessibility and sufficient number of providers.[18]

Traditionally, Japanese families formed extended families consisting of three generations. The family's eldest son was to keep living with his parents after marriage, and his wife was expected to take care of her husband's aging parents; therefore, each family was expected to be self-sufficient in caring for older people in the family; however, this type of family structure is no longer common, even in conservative rural areas. Frequently, adult children of older people are not able to live close enough to their parents to make a regular visit or to help their aging parents when needed. Many Japanese women are hesitant to marry if there is a possibility that they will have to live with their husband's parents in the future.

In order to cope with the healthcare needs of an ever-increasing older population in Japan, an innovative healthcare system must be quickly developed to ensure an adequate number of facilities and workforce, effective methods of delivering nursing care, and sufficient funds for the system to be smoothly sustained.

Antismoking Campaigns

In the arena of public health, smoking continues to be an issue in Japan. Smoking is known to be the single largest preventable cause of disease and premature death. It has been documented that smoking can lead to heart disease, stroke, lung disease, and cancer of many types. It is also reported that about 25% of all deaths from heart disease, and 75% of the world's chronic bronchitis are related to smoking. Although it is believed that smoking-related diseases kill 1 in 10 adults globally, about a third of the male adult global population smokes.

Although the number of smokers in Japan has decreased, it is still quite high for a developed country.[27] In 2003, 27.7% of adults aged 20 and older reported that they smoked daily. (Because the legal age for smoking is 20 in Japan, smokers under 20 years old were not included.) Although the number of female smokers was relatively small (11.3%), nearly one half of males (46.8%) identified themselves to be daily smokers. Of these smokers, more than 50% of males aged 20 to 59 years were daily.[28] The number of male daily smokers in Japan is, along with three other nations, Turkey, Greece, and Korea, extremely high compared with other OECD nations.[20] At this time, it is estimated that one in eight deaths is due to smoking (approximately 100,000 deaths a year).[29]

Japanese people tend to be tolerant of smoking. There are currently 500,000 cigarette vending machines on the streets of Japan. This high number may also be linked to the fact that Japan's Ministry of Finance is a major shareholder in Japan Tobacco, Inc. According to the World Health Organization, Japan's antitobacco laws are weaker than other developed nations, that is, providing fewer smoke-free public environments. Antismoking campaigns have been implemented, and the number of daily smokers has decreased; however, it is still customary to allow smoking during work hours in many offices, and many hospitals have not yet implemented no-smoking policies for their entire facilities.

Diabetes Prevention

Along with many other nations, diabetes has become one of the most important public health concerns in Japan. It is estimated that over 150 million adults are affected worldwide. Diabetes can lead to blindness, as well as renal failure. Although it is difficult to estimate accurately the number of people with diabetes, it is estimated that there are 7.4 million Japanese who are confirmed diabetics, an increase of 500,000 people over 5 years, and 8.8 million suspected diabetics, an increase of 2 million over

5 years.[30] The higher the age, the higher the risk of becoming diabetic. For Japanese men, the incidence rate greatly increases for those aged 50 years and older, whereas for women, the risk increases at 60 years old.[31] In order to improve health quality of life, as well as to lighten the financial burden of the nation, effective preventive approaches, including promotion of physical activity and proper diet, must be promptly implemented.

Breast Cancer Screening: Promoting Mammography

Considering the high prevalence of breast cancer (it is the most common cancer among women in all OECD countries), a serious approach toward prevention should be adopted throughout the world. Japanese women, along with other women in Far Eastern countries, are at a lower risk of developing breast cancer than women in Western countries. It is estimated that Japanese are five times less likely to develop breast cancer than their American counterparts.[32] Japan's breast cancer mortality rate is 10.4% and is the second lowest among all the OECD countries. It is less than half of the OECD average (22.0%).[20] Although breast cancer is the most common cancer among women in Japan compared with other OECD countries, Japan seems to be doing well in coping with breast cancer. It was estimated that there were 154,000 breast cancer patients in 2005, 50% more than colorectal cancer patients, the second most commonly treated cancer (98,000 patients).[18]

Despite the relatively low incidence of breast cancer in Japan, the 5-year relative survival rate for breast cancer patients is 83.1%. This is lower than the OECD average. Although many factors might contribute to Japan's lower 5-year survival rate, it is likely that the extremely low rate of mammography screening is one of the most significant. The effectiveness of breast cancer screening has been documented repeatedly, and early detection is likely to contribute to higher survival rates. Mammography screening is far more popular in Scandinavian countries such as Sweden, Norway, and Finland, where more than 80% of women aged 50 to 69 years are screened (98% in Norway, 87.7% in Finland, and 83.6% in Sweden). The OECD average is 54.7%. Compared with these figures, Japan's rate of 4.1% is very low and by far the lowest of all the OECD countries.[20] Public campaigns that encourage women aged 50 years and older to receive annual mammography screenings are bound to increase the rate of early breast cancer detection, which, in turn, should contribute to a higher survival rate.

Suicide Prevention

High suicide rates are an important issue in Japan. The suicide rate in Japan had been declining from the mid-1980s to the mid-1990s; however, since the later 1990s, it has begun to increase again. Although the OECD average rate decreased by 22% over the past quarter century, that of Japan increased by 7%. In Japan, there were 19.1 deaths per 100,000 population because of suicide in 2004, which is the third highest in OECD countries, following 24.2 deaths per 100,000 in Korea, and 22.6 deaths per 100,000 in Hungary. The OECD average is

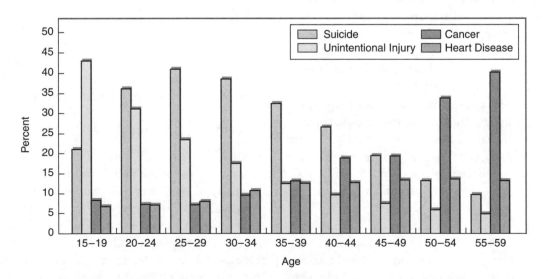

FIGURE 11-2   Cause of death, Japan, 2003 (Male)
Japanese Ministry of Health, Labor and Welfare

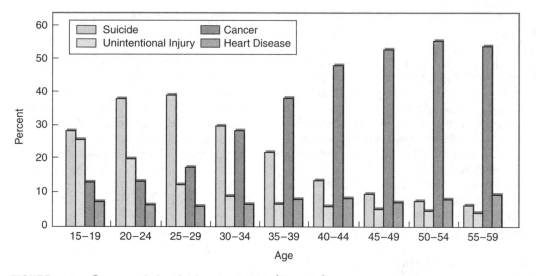

FIGURE 11-3   Cause of death, Japan, 2003 (Female)
Japanese Ministry of Health, Labor and Welfare

12.1.[17] According to the statistics by the Ministry of Health, Labor and Welfare, suicide is the leading cause of death for individuals aged 20 to 39 and the second leading cause of deaths for those aged 15 to 19 and 40 to 49.[33] Stigmas related to mental illness must be dealt with more effectively, and mental healthcare services must be made more accessible. Although more attention has been paid to mental health in recent years and campaigns are carried out that focus on mental health,[34] considering that suicide is the number one cause of death for people of varying ages, both men and women, continuous and consistent efforts are needed to enhance the mental health of the nation.

REFERENCES

1. Frederic L. *Japan: Encyclopedia*. Cambridge, MA: Harvard University Press; 2002.

2. Richie D. *Introducing Japan*. New York: Kodansha International, Limited; 1996.

3. Woolley PJ. *Geography & Japan's Strategic Choices: From Seclusion to Internationalization*. Washington, DC: Potomac Books; 2005.

4. Ellington L. *Japan: A Global Studies Handbook*. Santa Barbara, CA: ABC-CLIO, Incorporated; 2002.

5. Development of real GDP, March 12, 2008. Retrieved April 1, 2008, from http://www.esri.go.jp/index.html.

6. OECE economic outlook 82. Retrieved April 2, 2008, from http://www.oecd.org/country/0,3377,en_33873108_33873539_1_1_1_1_1,00.html.

7. Statistics Bureau. Current population estimates (as of October 1, 2006). Retrieved March 15, 2008, from http://www.stat.go.jp/english/data/jinsui/2.htm.

8. Japan ranks 2nd worst among OECD nations in relative poverty, July 20, 2005. Retrieved March 31, 2008, from http://asia.news.yahoo.com/060720/kyodo/d8ive9u80.html.

9. Economic survey of Japan 2006: Key challenges to sustaining Japan's improved economic performance. Retrieved March 31, 2008, from http://www.ceri-sciences-po.org/archive/sept06/artoecd.pdf.

10. Curtin S. Japan, land of rising poverty, February 1, 2005. Retrieved April 2, 2008, from file:///C:/Documents%20and%20Settings/hakoy1m/My%20Documents/Japan%20Healthcare/GB11Dh01.html.

11. Graig LA. *Health of Nations: An International Perspective on U.S. Health Care Reform*, 3rd ed. Washington, DC: Congressional Quarterly; 1999.

12. Iglehart JK. Japan's medical care system. *New England Journal of Medicine*. 1988;319:807–812.

13. Hashimoto M. Health services in Japan. In Raffel MW, ed. *Comparative Health Systems*. University Park, PA: The Pennsylvania State University Press; 1984.

14. Steslicke WE. Development of health insurance policy in Japan. *Journal of Health Politics, Policy and Law*. 1982;7:197–226.

15. Jones SG, Hilborne LH, Anthony RC, et al. *Securing Health: Lessons from Nation-Building Missions*. Santa Monica, CA: RAND Corp.; 2006.

16. Nakahara T. The health system of Japan. In Raffel MW, ed. *Health Care and Reform in Industrialized Countries*. University Park, PA: The Pennsylvania State University Press; 1997, pp. 105–133.

17. Statistics & Other Data. Summary of health care facilities 2006. Retrieved April 9, 2008, from http://www.mhlw.go.jp/toukei/saikin/hw/iryosd/06/index.html.

18. Health & Social Statistics. Health statistics in Japan 2007. Retrieved April 9, 2008, from http://www.mhlw.go.jp/english/database/db-hss/index.html.

19. Briefing not for OECD health data 2007: How does Japan compare. Retrieved April 10, 2008, from http://www.oecd

.org/topicdocumentlist/0,3448,en_33873108_33873539_1_
1_1_1_37407,00.html.

20. Source OECD health at a glance 2007: OECD Indicators. Retrieved April 10, 2008, from http://caliban.sourceoecd .org/vl=2309846/cl=17/nw=1/rpsv/health2007/4-7.htm.

21. Social insurance agency. Retrieved April 10, 2008, from http://www.sia.go.jp/e/index.html.

22. Health insurance. Retrieved April 10, 2008, from http://www.mhlw.go.jp/bunya/iryouhoken/index.html.

23. Medical care. Retrieved April 11, 2008, from http://www .mhlw.go.jp/english/index.html.

24. Idoshingi-kai. Retrieved April 11, 2008, from http://www .mhlw.go.jp/shingi/2006/12/s1215-10.html.

25. Summary of statistics. Retrieved April 11, 2008, from http://wwwdbtk.mhlw.go.jp/toukei/youran/index-kousei .html.

26. Seki F. The role of the government and the family in taking care of the frail elderly: a comparison of the United States and Japan. In Weisstub DN, Thomasma DC, Cauthier S, Tomossy GF, ed. *Aging: Caring for our Elders*. Boston, MA: Kluwer Academic Publishers; 2001, pp. 83–105.

27. Regional office for the Western Pacific: fact sheets—smoking statistics, May 28, 2002. Retrieved April 13, 2008, from http://www.wpro.who.int/media_centre/fact_sheets/fs_200 20528.htm.

28. Health. Retrieved April 12, 2008, from http://www-bm .mhlw.go.jp/bunya/kenkou/index.html.

29. Koseikagakushingi-kai. Retrieved April 28, 2008, from http://www.mhlw.go.jp/shingi/2002/12/s1225-7.html.

30. Health: coping with diabetes-midterm report, December 27, 2007. Retrieved April 13, 2008, from http://www.mhlw .go.jp/shingi/2007/12/s1227-13.html.

31. Survey on diabetes 2002, August 6, 2003. Retrieved April 15, 2008, from http://www.mhlw.go.jp/shingi/2003/08/s0806-4 .html.

32. Epidemiology. Retrieved April 28, 2008, from http://www .breastcancersource.com/breastcancersourceHCP/10010_ 11092__.aspx?mid=6.

33. Statistics: summary of suicide. Retrieved April 14, 2008, from http://www.mhlw.go.jp/toukei/saikin/hw/jinkou/ tokusyu/suicide04/index.html.

34. Labour standards information: mental health at work. Retrieved April 14, 2008, from http://www.mhlw.go.jp/bunya/ roudoukijun/anzeneisei12/index.html.

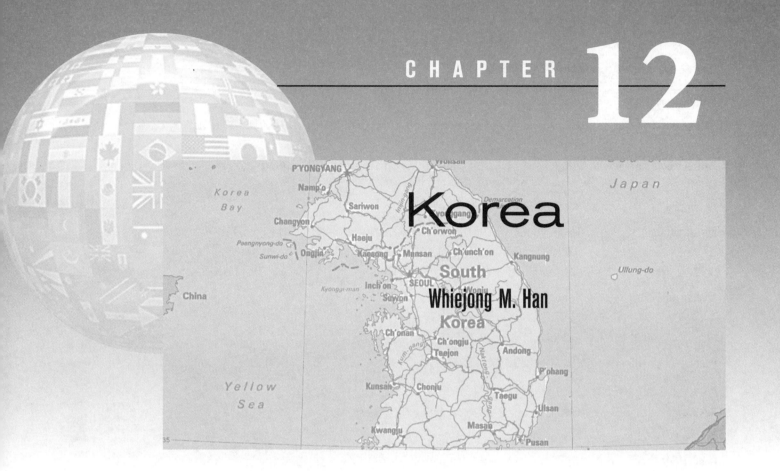

CHAPTER 12

COUNTRY DESCRIPTION

TABLE 12-1 Korea

Nationality	Noun: Korean(s) Adjective: Korean
Ethnic groups	Homogeneous (except for about 20,000 Chinese)
Religions	Christian 26.3% (Protestant 19.7%, Roman Catholic 6.6%), Buddhist 23.2%, other or unknown 1.3%, none 49.3% (1995 census)
Language	Korean, English widely taught in junior high and high school
Literacy	Definition: age 15 and over can read and write Total population: 97.9% Male: 99.2% Female: 96.6% (2002)
Government type	Republic
Date of independence	August 15, 1945 (from Japan)
Gross Domestic Product (GDP) per capita	$24,600 (2007 est.)

(continues)

TABLE 12-1   Korea (continued)

Unemployment rate	3.2% (2007 est.)
Natural hazards	Occasional typhoons bring high winds and floods; low-level seismic activity common in southwest
Environment: current issues	Air pollution in large cities; acid rain; water pollution from the discharge of sewage and industrial effluents; drift net fishing
Population	49,232,844 (July 2008 est.)
Age structure	0–14 years: 17.7% (male 4,579,018/female 4,157,631) 15–64 years: 72.3% (male 18,150,771/female 17,464,610) 65 years and over: 9.9% (male 1,997,032/female 2,883,782) (2008 est.)
Median age	Total: 36.4 years Male: 35.3 years Female: 37.4 years (2008 est.)
Population growth rate	0.371% (2008 est.)
Birth rate	9.83 births/1,000 population (2008 est.)
Death rate	6.12 deaths/1,000 population (2008 est.)
Net migration rate	Not available
Gender ratio	At birth: 1.08 male(s)/female Under 15 years: 1.1 male(s)/female 15–64 years: 1.04 male(s)/female 65 years and over: 0.69 male(s)/female Total population: 1.01 male(s)/female (2008 est.)
Infant mortality rate	Total: 5.94 deaths/1,000 live births Male: 6.33 deaths/1,000 live births Female: 5.53 deaths/1,000 live births (2008 est.)
Life expectancy at birth	Total population: 77.42 years Male: 74 years Female: 81.1 years (2008 est.)
Total fertility rate	1.29 children born/woman (2008 est.)
HIV/AIDS adult prevalence rate	Less than 0.1% (2003 est.)
Number of people living with HIV/AIDS	8,300 (2003 est.)
HIV/AIDS deaths	Less than 200 (2003 est.)

Central Intelligence Agency. The World Fact Book, 2008. Retrieved November 18, 2008, from https://www.cia.gov/library/publications/the-world-factbook.

History

Korea is located in Eastern Asia and has one of the oldest histories. Throughout the establishment and collapse of many dynasties through 5,000 years of history, Korea developed its own distinctive culture. Under the last dynasty, Joseon, before modernization, Korea became known as the "Land of Morning Calm" because the name "Joseon" in Korean means "morning calm." With Confucianism and Buddhism in its long history, Korea is also known as the country of courtesy in the East. From 1910 to 1945, Korea was under Japanese rule. During this period, many different groups inside and outside Korea fought for independence. The Provisional Government of Korea was established at that time to fight for independence. The Provisional Government declared war on Japan and provided close cooperation with Allied Powers during World War II. In 1945, Japan surrendered to the Allies, ending war in the Pacific, and withdrew from the Korean Peninsula. Soon after, however, Korea was divided into two parts along the 38th parallel, South and North Korea, because of ideological conflicts between various groups. A communist form of government came into power in North Korea (Democratic People's Republic of Korea), and the United States turned its authority over to South Korea (Republic of Korea). On Sunday morning, June 25, 1950, North Korea invaded South Korea (Korea hereafter) without declaration of war. It was the beginning of the Korean War, which lasted for about 3 years. With military support from the United Nations, the Korean War ended with an armistice on July 27, 1953.

The war destroyed the country and yielded many economic, political, and social problems. In the aftermath, the Korean government focused on rebuilding the country. Under the leadership of the third President, Jeong-Hee Park, Korea achieved dramatic economic growth. During the Park administration, the human and natural resources of the nation were effectively organized for the first time in modern history. The economy began to grow at an annual rate of 9.2%. Per capita gross domestic product (GDP) increased from a mere U.S. $87 in 1962 to U.S. $1,503 in 1980, and exports rose by 32.8% a year from U.S. $56.7 million in 1962 to U.S. $17.5 billion in 1980.[1] Continuous efforts by the Korean government after the Park administration resulted in Korea becoming one of the modern and developed countries in the world. In 1996, Korea joined the Organisation for Economic Co-operation and Development (OECD), marking its advancement into the ranks of developed nations. As of 2007, the GDP of Korea was 957 billion U.S. dollars, and the GDP per capita was $19,750.[2] In the presidential election of 2008, Mr. Myung Bak Lee, who was a former CEO of a major construction company in Korea, was elected. President Lee began his term in office in February 2008, and most Koreans believe that it will be another time of prosperity for Korea.

Size and Geography

Figure 12-1 shows the map of the Korean Peninsula. The Korean Peninsula lies in East Asia, adjacent to China and Japan. The west coast of the Korean Peninsula borders the Korean Bay to the north and the Yellow Sea to the south. The east coast faces the East Sea, and the south coast faces the South Sea. Because of the long north–south stretch and topographic character, Korea has several distinct regions with significantly different climate, although Korea is a geographically small country. The total area of the Korean Peninsula, including both South Korea (Korea) and North Korea, is approximately 223,600 km², and it includes 3,300 scattered islands. The land area of Korea, which occupies about 45% of the Korean Peninsula, is 99,720 km², with a population of 49 million as of 2007. The area of Seoul, the capital city of Korea, is 605 km². The distance between South Korea's two big major cities, Seoul and Busan, one in the very northwest and the other in the very southeast, is only 210 miles.[3]

Rapid industrialization and urbanization in the 1960s and 1970s has been accompanied by continuing migration of rural residents into the cities, particularly Seoul. The administrative divisions of Korea consist of nine providence and seven metropolitan cities. As of 2005, more than 80% of the entire population in Korea lives in metropolitan areas.[4] In recent years, however, an increasing number of people have begun moving to suburban areas.

Government or Political System

Korea has a democratic form of government based on the separation of powers. The constitution was first adopted in 1948 when the Republic was established and has been revised nine times as the country struggled to make democracy work effectively. The most recent revision of the constitution provided, among other things, for the direct election of the President for a single 5-year term and for the institution of a system of local

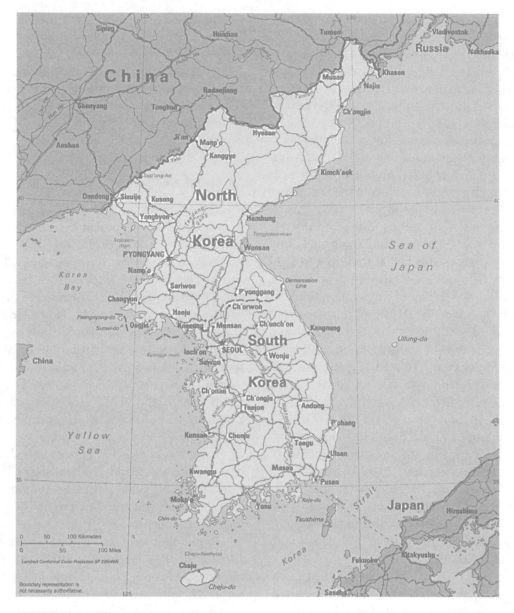

FIGURE 12-1   Map of Korea

autonomy for the first time in 30 years. These two provisions are keys to the strengthening of democratic institutions in the Republic. The revision also reinstated the right of the National Assembly to inspect all aspects of state affairs on a regular basis, as a check on the power of the executive branch. Finally, it charges the government to seek to reunify the nation.

The political system of Korea is based on a republic form of government, with the President as chief of the state and the Prime Minister as the head of government. The government consists of three branches: (1) the legislature, in the form of a unicameral National Assembly; (2) the judiciary, consisting of district and appellate courts and the Supreme Court; and (3) the executive, headed by the President. The President is also commander-in-chief of the armed forces, and the President is assisted by the Prime Minister and the State Council.

Macroeconomics

Korea has achieved exponential economic growth since the mid-20th century. Referred to as the "Miracle of the Han River," the economy of Korea grew dramatically, and it ranked 13th in the world in terms of GDP as of 2007. Over decades, Korea enjoyed an average of 5% in

GDP growth per year. As of 2007, GDP of Korea was 957 billion U.S. dollars, and the GDP per capita was $19,750,[2] which showed dramatic growth in less than 45 years. In the year 2007, the amount of exports reached U.S. $371 billion, and imports were about $351 billion U.S. dollars. Major partners in trading are China (22%), the United States (12.5%), and Japan (7.1%) for exports, whereas imports were mainly from China (17.7%), Japan (16%), and the United States (10.7%) in 2007.[5]

In 1970s and 1980s, the Korean economy emphasized heavy industry and the automotive industry. Hyundai, Samsung, LG, and POSCO are Korean-based global companies that have a strong reputation in the world. In the 1980s, the Korean economy started to divert into the service industry. Since then, service industries have grown to 57% of GDP, whereas manufacturing accounted for 37% of GDP.[5] In the 1990s, Korea entered into the information technology business, starting the information technology project with strong government support. Within a few years, Korea became a world leader in information technology.

In 1998, the Korean economy, like other Asian countries, faced financial crisis. All industries and citizens suffered from the crisis. With well-planned government strategies and financial support from the International Monetary Fund, Korea overcame the financial difficulty and bounced back in a few years. After the crisis, the government attempted financial reform to restore economic stability. The economic growth rate again reached 9% in 2000, and the unemployment rate started to decline from 6% to 3.5% by 2006.[6]

A well-developed infrastructure, such as transportation, roads, and communication, facilitated expansion of industries. Rapid improvement in transportation and road systems increased mobility. More than 100 of the airports and ports support industries' business activities. Because of the topographical characteristics of Korea, most industries locate in the northwest or southeast of country. Services and manufacturing are located in the northwest, whereas heavy industry is located in the southeast.

Koreans believe that education is a critical key to success, and thus, much energy is put into learning. Learning a second language, particularly English and Chinese, is believed to be a stepping stone for future success in a trend of globalization. For this reason, English is taught as a required subject starting in elementary school. Many people, especially in the business sectors, are voluntarily learning Chinese as well. A large number of high school and college-level students go to advanced countries, particularly to the United States, to study for years. According to U.S. statistics, 103,394 Korean students are studying in the United States as of December 2007. Korea ranked the first in terms of the number of active students in the United States from abroad, followed by India (88,051) and China (72,190).[7]

Demographics

According to the "2006 Annual Report on the Economically Active Population Survey," published by the Korean National Statistical Office (KNSO), the population in Korea was 48.3 million in 2006. Of those, 38.7 million (80%) were age 15 years and older. Almost 24 million were economically active persons. Among them 23.2 million were employed, and the labor participation rate in economic activities was 61.8%. Because of a low birth rate and aging society, however, KNSO projects that economically active persons will decrease from 2016 and the total population will start to decline in 2019.[4] By age group, the number of those less than 15 years old has steadily decreased since 1970, whereas the older population (aged 65 year and over) is increasing. Projection of population growth rates from the United Nations indicates that the growth rate in Korea will be the second to last by 2010.[8]

One problem in the population structure of Korea is population density in city areas. In 2005, almost half (48.2%) of the total population lived in the Seoul metropolitan area, including Incheon and Gyeonggi provinces. Seoul, by itself, had almost 10 million people (20.8%) living in it. Population density in Seoul is 17,213 people per km^2, and among cities with more than 10 million people, Seoul was ranked second worldwide, following Mumbai, India.[1] This unequal population distribution creates many problems, such as housing shortages, high prices of commodity, pollution, unequal education opportunity, and even the availability of medical services.

In 2007, an average of 3.27 persons was in each household in Korea. Average annual income per house is U.S. $38,600. Among the 38.7 million age 15 and over in 2006, 36.2 million people (94%) had at least a high school diploma. Of those who are employed, 75.6% were high school graduates or above.[4]

Religion

In terms of religious groups, the major religions in Korea are Christianity, Buddhism, and Confucianism. According to the Korean National Statistical Office, it is estimated that more than 40% of Koreans profess these three religions.[5] Because of influences from China in the history of Korea, Buddhism and Confucianism were dominant religion groups until the late 19th century. Still, Buddhism is one of the major religions in Korea, and it is estimated that 35% of Koreans are Buddhists.[5] With the beginning of modernization and industrialization, however, Confucianism rapidly declined, and it is estimated that only 0.2% of Koreans falls under Confucianism. Because of the influence of Buddhism and Confucianism, the morality of Koreans still gives high value to the family, relationships, respect, and cooperation.

Arriving Catholic and Protestant missionaries in Korea in the 19th century changed religious affiliation in Korea. Christianity and Catholicism spread rapidly, and a significant number of Koreans converted. Currently, it is believed more than 30% of Koreans are Christians.[5] Methodism, Presbyterianism, and Catholicism are the most popular in Korea.

BRIEF HISTORY OF THE HEALTHCARE SYSTEM

Pre-World War II

Through the long history of Korea, Koreans have used traditional Korean medicine and remedies, including acupuncture and herbal medicine. Korean traditional medicine has its focus on prevention as well as treatment of diseases. People often visit traditional medicine clinics, which typically are family inherited, to preserve their health or to cure sickness. This long-held tradition was almost destroyed when Japan annexed Korea in the early 20th century.

During the period of occupation, the Japanese prohibited Koreans from using traditional medicine. Instead, the Japanese put their own healthcare system in Korea, which included Westernized medicine.

Since World War II

National liberation in 1945 brought back these revered Korean traditional medicine practices. Since then, both Westernized medicine and traditional medicine have coexisted in Korea. After World War II, Korea experienced Western culture and medicine at an accelerating pace. Rapid development of the economy in the 1960s pushed the Korean government to consider the welfare and health of its citizens.

In 1963, the Korean government enacted the Medical Insurance Law, permitting voluntary health insurance. After this first step, however, development of a healthcare system was slow because of the government's devotion to economic expansion. Health insurance corporations, such as Busan Blue Cross Plan, offered individual policies, but they did not become a major source of health insurance coverage because of the very low participation from citizens.[9]

In 1977, the government passed a law mandating employers with more than 500 employees to provide health insurance to their employees and families. This requirement of health insurance coverage has been gradually increased over time. In 1979, all companies with 300 and more employees were required to provide health insurance. The same year, the government expanded mandatory health insurance coverage to government employees and private school teachers. It was expanded again in 1981 to companies with more than 100 workers and to the self-employed. In addition, the government started demonstration programs in some rural areas to provide health insurance coverage. These step-by-step expansions finally achieved universal coverage in 1989.[10] A year before, the Korean government mandated health insurance coverage to all residents in rural areas, and in 1989, the government mandated coverage to all residents in urban areas, no matter what their employment status. At that time, the government controlled three different medical insurance societies: (1) the medical insurance society for employees, (2) a regional medical society of the self-employed, and (3) a society for government employees and private school employees.

Since then, the Korean government implemented two major reforms, integration reform in 1998 and separation reform in 2000. In October 1998, the first integration reform integrated two medical insurance societies into one. With the establishment of the National Health Insurance Corporation (NHIC) in 2000, the second initiative of integration was implemented, where all medical insurance societies were integrated under the control of the NHIC.[11,12]

The separation reform in July 2000 was for specialization and quality improvement. Before this reform, both physicians and pharmacists could prescribe and dispense drugs for outpatient services. This resulted in overuse and misuse of drugs. The reform separated the function of prescribing and dispensing drugs between doctors and pharmacists.

In 2000, the Health Insurance Review and Assessment Service (HIRA) was established to assess effectiveness and efficiency of clinical services in order to improve quality of care. Moreover, the Hospital Service Evaluation Program was launched in 2004 to ensure high quality of services.

DESCRIPTION OF THE CURRENT HEALTHCARE SYSTEM

Facilities

In 2006, the total number of hospitals/clinics, including specialized hospitals/clinics, in Korea was 51,285. Tables 12-2 and 12-3 indicate the total number of hospitals and clinics. Total numbers have been gradually increasing over time, and the ratio of each type of facility has been steady. The ratio of clinics to the total number was 51.5%, and 25.6% of all facilities were dental hospitals/clinics in 2006. Oriental medicine hospitals/clinics, however, rapidly increased since 2002. In 2006, there were a total of 10,436 oriental medicine facilities were in Korea, and they accounted for 20.6% of all types of hospitals/clinics.[6]

In terms of specialized hospitals/clinics, long-term care hospitals were remarkably increased over the last few years. Since 2004, the number of long-term care facilities has doubled each year. This was mainly due to the increasing needs and demands of an aging society. There were no regulations for long-term care facilities, and in a hypercompetitive market, healthcare providers with financial difficulties simply diverted into long-term care as a market niche for their business.

An increase in mental hospitals is another interesting trend in Korea. Unlike other developed countries, the number of mental hospitals in Korea has steadily increased over time. Mental care in Korea is mostly provided on an inpatient basis.

Most healthcare facilities in Korea are owned and operated by the private sector. Table 12-4 provides the types and numbers of providers. All citizens have freedom in the selection of healthcare providers. Insurance beneficiaries, however, are required to receive the initial treatments from a first-level healthcare provider. All providers in Korea, except specialized hospitals, are endowed as first-level providers. When patients need to have specialized care, they can be referred to the second-level providers. This two-level provider system is not only to use the limited medical resources efficiently but also to prevent the tendency of preferring general hospitals. The first-level hospitals or clinics, therefore, play the role of gatekeeper for health services.

Korea is the only nation among the OECD countries that has an increase in inpatient beds (Figure 12-2). According to OECD Health Data published in 2007, the number of beds per 1,000 persons in Korea was 6.5, which was higher than the average of 4.1 beds among other OECD countries. Korea ranked second, after Japan (8.2 beds/1,000 persons) in terms of the number of beds per 1,000 persons. Between 1991 and 2005, the number of beds in Korea increased by 124.1%, whereas the average number of beds among OECD countries during the same period decreased by 12.7%.[13,14] All types of facilities experienced an increase in the number of beds except in oriental medicine hospitals/clinics. The growing demand and supply of dental surgeries, such as dental implants, also made the number of beds available increase in dental hospitals/clinics.[6] Table 12-5 demonstrates the number of beds in Korea, by types of institution.

Because the majority of healthcare facilities is owned and managed by the private sector, many medical services providers target mass markets. More than 44 thousand facilities (87.2%) were concentrated in urban areas

TABLE 12-2 Number of Hospitals and Clinics by Types: 2000–2006

Year	Hospital			Dental Facility		Oriental Medicine Facility	
	General Hospital	Hospital	Clinic	Hospital	Clinic	Hospital	Clinic
2000	285	581	19,472	56	10,471	136	7,279
2001	268	599	20,819	60	10,556	131	7,499
2002	284	691	23,299	80	11,120	135	8,097
2003	283	730	23,502	99	11,890	151	8,734
2004	282	763	24,491	107	11,968	154	9,196
2005	290	794	25,412	123	12,520	146	9,765
2006	295	850	26,078	134	12,808	142	10,294

Source: Ministry of Health and Welfare, Healthcare Resources Team.

TABLE 12-3   Number of Specialized Hospitals and Clinics by Types, 2000–2006

Year	Long-Term Care Hospital[a]	Tuberculosis Hospital	Mental Hospital	Midwifery	Dispensary[b]
2000	–	3	79	120	185
2001	–	2	70	100	1696
2002	–	2	75	76	169
2003	68	4	88	71	150
2004	92	3	95	67	158
2005	177	3	102	46	187
2006	363	3	107	39	172

[a] Data for 2000–2002 are not available.

[b] Dispensary belongs to clerical and industrial establishments for employees.

Source: Ministry of Health and Welfare, Healthcare Resources Team.

TABLE 12-4   Number of Medical Institutions by Types of Establishment, as of End of 2006

Classification	Hospital[a]	Clinic	Dental Facility[b]	Oriental Medicine Facility[b]
Public	74	12	6	8
School Foundation	47	24	11	35
Social Welfare Foundation	44	77	4	16
Medical Corporation	461	170	20	104
Individual	831	25,168	12,873	10,193
Others[c]	158	627	28	80

[a] Hospital includes general hospitals, hospitals, long-term care, and mental hospitals.

[b] Both dental facilities and oriental medicine facilities include hospital based and clinic based.

[c] Others include Religious Foundation, Special Juridical Corporation, Corporation Aggregate, and Military.

Source: NHIC, Statistical Yearbook 2007.

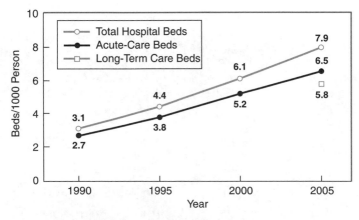

FIGURE 12-2   Total Number of Beds (per 1000 person), by Types of Facility

Data from OECD Health Data, 2007.

TABLE 12-5   Number of Beds by Types of Institutions, as of End of 2006

Year	Hospital[a]	Long-Term Care Hospital	Clinic	Dental Facility[b]	Oriental Medicine Facility[b]
2003	223,880	8,355	96,338	187	8,472
2004	238,500	10,445	91,702	184	9,585
2005	247,447	25,501	93,972	247	9,210
2006	259,747	43,336	95,224	254	8,723

[a] Hospital includes general hospitals, hospitals, and mental hospitals.
[b] Both dental and oriental medicine facilities include hospital based and clinic based.
Source: Ministry of Health and Welfare, Healthcare Resources Team.

in 2006. This unequal distribution of medical services created a problem in accessibility. Citizens living in rural areas have difficulty accessing medical services, especially specialty care. With a great safety net system, however, delivery of primary care has been done well for citizens in rural areas. Table 12-6 shows healthcare facilities by geographic locations, and Table 12-7 represents the number of safety net providers available in Korea.

Health centers, subhealth centers, and primary healthcare posts are mostly located in rural areas in Korea. As safety net providers, these government-subsidized facilities mainly provide primary care services to citizens in rural areas and to citizens who cannot afford the high cost of care in hospitals/clinics. A total of 3,442 facilities are health centers, subhealth centers, or primary healthcare post. Subhealth centers and primary healthcare posts are considered as branches of health

TABLE 12-6   Healthcare Facilities by Types and Geographic Location, 2003–2006

Year	Hospital[a]		Clinic		Dental Facility[b]		Oriental Medicine Facility[b]	
	Urban	Rural	Urban	Rural	Urban	Rural	Urban	Rural
2003	811	202	20,562	2,940	10,572	1,426	7,792	1,093
2004	891	154	22,249	2,242	11,187	904	8,442	908
2005	927	157	23,001	2,411	11,745	907	9,005	906
2006	955	190	22,464	3,614	11,577	1,365	9,146	1,290

[a] Hospital includes general hospitals and hospitals.
[b] Both dental and oriental medicine facilities include hospital based and clinic based.
Source: Ministry of Health and Welfare, Healthcare Resources Team

TABLE 12-7   Health Centers, Subhealth Centers, and Primary Health Care Posts, 2001–2006

Year	Total	Health Center	Subhealth Center	Primary Health Care Post
2001	3,401	242	1,267	1,892
2002	3,401	242	1,268	1,891
2003	3,416	246	1,271	1,899
2004	3,420	246	1,273	1,901
2005	3,433	248	1,280	1,905
2006	3,442	251	1,280	1,911

Source: Ministry of Health and Welfare, Healthcare Resources Team.

centers that supervise these facilities. These providers also act as gatekeepers. For patients who need complex care, they refer patients to a higher level of medical institution or to specialty physicians.[15]

Workforce

Tables 12-8 and 12-9 indicate the number of licensed health care professionals and qualified medical specialists, respectively. The number of licensed healthcare professionals in Korea has grown fast over the last decades. The average overall growth rate for healthcare professionals is approximately 4%. The number of nurses is the fastest area of growth, increasing an average of 5%, followed by oriental medicine doctors, who have an average growth rate of 4%. In spite of this fast-growing workforce, the number of practicing physicians per 1,000 population in Korea was 1.6 in 2005, which was the lowest among OECD countries. Similar to the ratio of practicing physicians, practicing nurses per 1,000 persons was 1.9. This ratio was also the lowest among OECD countries. The average number of practicing nurses per 1,000 persons in OECD countries was 9.0 in 2005. Like other countries, Korea faces nursing shortage. The ratio of practicing physicians to practicing nurses in 2005 was 1.2%, which ranked the lowest among OECD countries with average of 2.9%.[6,13,16]

Table 12-10 shows the number of healthcare professionals in health centers, subhealth centers, and primary healthcare posts. To increase accessibility caused

TABLE 12-8 Number of Licensed Healthcare Professionals, 2000–2006

Year	Physician (MD)	Dentist	Oriental Medicine Doctor	Pharmacist	Nurse
2000	72,503	18,039	12,108	50,623	160,295
2001	75,295	18,887	12,794	51,872	170,845
2002	78,609	19,672	13,662	53,168	181,800
2003	81,328	20,446	14,553	54,381	192,480
2004	81,998	20,772	14,421	53,492	202,012
2005	85,369	21,581	15,271	54,829	213,644
2006	88,214	22,267	15,918	55,845	223,781

Source: Ministry of Health and Welfare, License Information System of MOHW. Numbers include those living abroad.

TABLE 12-9 Number of Qualified Medical Specialists by Types of Specialty, 2000–2006

Year	Primary Care[a]	General Surgery	Orthopedics	Radiology	Others[b]
2000	18,983	4,670	3,174	1,990	17,053
2001	20,273	4,850	3,403	2,187	18,331
2002	21,433	5,010	3,660	2,369	19,573
2003	22,607	5,223	3,911	2,461	20,662
2004	22,896	5,125	4,017	2,518	21,392
2005	24,170	5,316	4,213	2,573	22,535
2006	25,198	5,441	4,389	2,618	23,545

Numbers include those living abroad.

[a] Primary care includes Internal Medicine, Pediatrics, OB/GYN, and Family Medicine.

[b] Others include all other specialties.

Source: Ministry of Health and Welfare, License Information System of the Ministry of Health and Welfare.

TABLE 12-10 Healthcare Professionals in Health Centers, Subhealth Centers, and Primary Healthcare Posts, 2003–2006

Year	Physicians[a]	Dentists[a]	Oriental Medical Doctors[a]	Nurses[b]	Public Health Workers
2003	2,186	1,018	683	8,311	1,522
2004	2,236	1,020	878	8,338	1,603
2005	2,201	1,125	864	8,431	1,494
2006	2,223	1,037	831	8,420	1,616

[a] Include both medical officers and public health doctors.

[b] Include nursing assistants.

Source: Ministry of Health and Welfare, Healthcare Resources Team

by the unequal distribution of services, the Korean government forced medical college/university graduates to serve in rural areas. By serving in rural areas as public health doctors, they can waive service in the army, which is mandatory for all Korean males. Most medical college graduates take this option as a replacement of military service.

Technology and Equipment

In terms of medical technology and equipment, Korea is one of the countries with rapid adoption of new medical technology. Table 12-11 describes the numbers of some high-technology equipment available in Korea. According to the OECD, the number of computed tomography scanners per million population in Korea increased rapidly from 12.2 in 1990 to 32.2 in 2005, which makes Korea a leading country among OECD member countries. Similarly, the number of magnetic resonance imaging machines per million population also dramatically increased, from 1.4 in 1990 to 12.1 in 2005. As of 2005, the number of lithotriptors and mammograph machines per million population in Korea was 9.1 and 28.7, respectively. Again, Korea was a leader in this medical technology for these machines among OECD member countries.[13,17]

EVALUATION OF THE HEALTHCARE SYSTEM

Cost

Over decades, Korea has experienced fast economic growth and rapid industrialization. As a result of the profoundly developing economy, Korea joined the OECD in 1996, becoming the 29th member country and the second country in Asia. Economic development has dramatically improved the health of the population, particularly with the inception of national health insurance.

The national health insurance was introduced in Korea in 1977. Through the gradual coverage of additional population groups, Korea could provide universal health coverage to all of its citizens by 1989, only 12 years after its first introduction. Since then, healthcare expenditure has increased rapidly.

Healthcare expenditure in Korea was 6% of the GDP in 2005, which was 3% lower than the OECD average. Medical spending per capita in Korea was $1,318 US dollars in the same year. It is also ranked below the OECD average of $2,759 in 2005.[13] The rate of growth in health spending was two times greater (8.7%) than the average of the OECD countries (4.3%) in 2005 as the result of increase in public spending. Public spending on health accounted for 53% of the total healthcare expenditure in 2005, which shows a dramatic increase from 30% in 1985.[13,18] Another factor affecting the rise of health spending is pharmaceutical spending. Although the growth of pharmaceutical spending has slowed, it still comprises a large part of the healthcare expenditure. Spending on pharmaceuticals in 2005 was 27.3% of total healthcare expenditure, which was higher than the OECD average of 17.2%.[19]

NHIC of Korea provides health coverage to citizens by their employment status. Two medical insurance societies for industrial workers and the self-employed are under the Korean National Health Insurance (NHI) program, which covers approximately 97% of citizens. The Medical Aid program, which is under local government control, provides health coverage to low-income and indigent people. Table 12-11 shows the enrollment of NHI and Medical Aid programs, which cover all citizens. In 2006, more than 47 million (96.2%) were insured with NHI, and the remaining 1.8 million (3.8%) were covered by Medical Aid.[6]

Financing of health care comes from three sources: the mandatory health insurance contribution (premium), government subsidies, and patients' out-of-pocket payments. The mandatory health insurance contribution is set by and includes a contribution from both the employer and employee. The contribution rate for industrial workers is based on income and their personal properties. Employers are responsible to pay 50% of the contribution of their employees. As of 2006, the contribution rate was about 4.3% of salaried income. Although this rate is one of the lowest among OECD countries, many Koreans feel that it is a heavy financial burden for them. According to a national survey, only 19% said that the contribution rate was appropriate for the offered benefits.[4,15] For the self-employed, the contribution is set by economic activity, income, and property.

Government subsidy accounts for a small portion of total financing. The government's share, however, has been increasing since 2002, to give financial relief to the NHI. The subsidy comes from tax revenue, both general taxation and cigarette tax in accordance with the Special Act for Financial Stabilization. This act was

legislated to solve the financial crisis of the NHI that has rapidly deteriorated since 1999.[10,20]

One of the distinct features of the Korean healthcare system is the domination of the private sector in healthcare delivery and even in healthcare financing. The relatively high private share (about 42%) of healthcare financing is related to substantial out-of-pocket payments.[21,22] Private providers supply the majority of healthcare services, with public providers playing a residual role. More than 90% of hospitals and clinics are privately owned. In most cases, therefore, physicians both own and manage the facilities. Physician clinics have inpatient facilities and most hospitals operate large outpatient centers, which promotes competition between hospitals and clinics. All pharmacies are owned and operated by individual pharmacists as well.

Cost sharing is controlled by one insurer, the NHIC of Korea. Insurance allowance is also controlled with strong government intervention; however, it is difficult to control the costs for services that are not covered by NHI. Since adoption of the NHI system, administration costs have been managed with strong governmental regulation. With expansion of benefit coverage and increasing demands from customers, however, it has been rapidly increasing in recent years.

The reimbursement mechanism in Korea is traditional fee-for-service, which calculates medicine,

TABLE 12-11 Covered Person of Health Insurance, by Category of Insured (Unit: 1,000 Persons, Percentage)

Classification	Total[a,b]	Health Insurance for		Indigent Group (Medical Aid)
		Industrial Workers[c]	Self-Employed	
2003	48,556 (100)	24,834 (51.1)	22,268 (45.8)	1,453 (3.1)
2004	48,900 (100)	25,979 (53.1)	21,392 (43.7)	1,528 (3.2)
2005	49,153 (100)	27,233 (55.4)	20,158 (41.0)	1,761 (3.6)
2006	49,238 (100)	28,445 (57.7)	18,964 (38.5)	1,828 (3.8)

[a] All numbers include dependents.

[b] Numbers in parentheses are proportion of enrollments.

[c] Industrial workers include government employees and private school teachers.

Source: MOHW, Health Insurance Policy Team/National Health Insurance Corporation

material, and treatment costs separately and reimburses under a predetermined fee schedule.[10] Many medical examinations and treatments are done competitively under fee-for-service. To create demand and to secure more patients, providers excessively purchase new and advanced technologies. Providers induce demand by prescribing more drugs, requiring that patients have more visits for care, and encouraging treatments which are not included in the NHI's benefit package. This results in increases in customers' out-of-pocket costs and total healthcare expenditure.

For medical services, patients are responsible for paying some portion of the medical cost as a form of either a deductible or coinsurance. Deductibles and coinsurance are predetermined by the NHIC in annual negotiations with organizations representing providers, such as the Korean Medical Association, the Korean Dental Association, and the Korean Physicians Association. Deductibles are applied only to people in medical aid programs. Depending on the patient's income level, a patient can use medical services either at no cost or for a small charge (about 1 to 2 U.S. dollars).

Coinsurance rates vary by types of services (inpatient or outpatient care) and types of healthcare facilities (clinic, hospital, and general hospital). For outpatient services in clinics, patients are responsible for 30% of the total charges. The rate is 50% for services in hospitals and 55% in general hospitals. For inpatients, the coinsurance is 20% of total medical charges.[10,15]

Other than deductibles and coinsurance, some patients pay an extra/special fee for outpatient services from certain physicians. When patients want services from certain doctors who have more experience and an exceptional reputation, those patients are required to pay this special fee on top of regular medical charges. Typically, senior medical staff in general hospitals are in this category.

To control increasing healthcare expenditures, the NHIC introduced diagnosis-related groups in 1997 as a pilot program. It was planned to apply to all providers after 3 years. Because of the strong opposition from providers, however, only a few providers voluntarily participate in this system, which is currently applied to eight selected procedures. In 2001, a Resources-Based Relative Value Scale payment system was implemented in Korea. The payments to providers increased, but without a mechanism to control the volume and expenditure.[20]

The flow of medical claims is important to understand. After providers provide medical services to insurance beneficiaries, they send medical claims to both the NHIC and the Health Insurance Review and Assessment Service (HIRA). The HIRA reviews claims submitted by providers for appropriateness of medical procedures provided and the claim costs. After the HIRA evaluates claims, the NHIC makes payments to providers in accordance with the review results.[10]

For certain chronic diseases and serious illnesses, for example, diabetes and cancer, the NHI cuts patients' out-of-pocket costs for the elderly. The benefit package of the NHI has been expanded over time.

Even with separation of dispensing authority from medical practices, antibiotics are still overused because of the practice patterns of physicians. Most primary care and preventive services, which are critical for public health, are still not included in the NHI's benefit package. Complaints from customers regarding preventive services are growing.

Overutilization, low reimbursement rates, addition of preventive services in the benefit package, and unnecessary duplication of services of medical shopping by customers are issues to be solved by the Korean government. These factors yield high administrative costs and eventually will increase in healthcare expenditure.

Quality

Rapid economic development in Korea was paralleled by unprecedented achievements in the health of the population. Dramatic improvements have been attained in life expectancy, and infant mortality rates have been steadily reduced. Mortality and morbidity patterns have changed from communicable diseases to chronic and lifestyle-related diseases. The infant mortality rate per 1,000 live births has been decreased to 5.3 in 2005 from 45.0 in 1970, whereas life expectancy at birth reached 78.5 years (males, 75.1 years; females, 81.9 years) in 2005. Both figures are about average for OECD countries, which are 75.4 and 78.6 years, respectively.[6,13]

One factor in the improvement of population health is due to a regulated healthcare system in Korea. Because the fee-for-service system in Korea is strongly regulated, healthcare providers do not compete with others in price. To secure more patients, providers compete with quality of service. Providers realize that patient-centered care, high quality with advanced medical technologies, and friendly services are essential for success in their businesses. This phenomenon in a hypercompetitive market contributes to improving continuously the quality of health services. On the other hand, indiscreet provider-induced demand in some areas yields overutilization. In addition, the areas with poor populations still have limited access and poor quality of care because of risk pooling.

For the year 2006, the major causes of mortality were cancer, cardiovascular diseases, and external causes, accounting for 62.6% of all death.[6] Accidents are the primary cause of early death, and smoking still remains a major health risk factor in Korea. For cancer, major cancer incidents in Korea in 2002 were stomach, lung, liver, colorectal, and breast cancer, which accounted for 62.7% of all cancer incidents. The 5-year relative survival rate for those major cancer incidents, however, increased in the 1998 to 2002 period than in the previous 5 years.[6,16]

According to "Report on the Social Statistics Survey," which was done by KNSO in 2006, the majority of people who used medical services responded that they were satisfied with those medical services. Table 12-12 shows the level of satisfaction for medical services by types of healthcare facilities.[6,15]

Annual Report of Cancer Incidence 2002 in Korea

For those who were dissatisfied with medical services, the reasons of dissatisfaction were high medical charges (42.3%), unsatisfactory treatment (38%), and long waiting times (35.5%).

Healthcare expenditure depends not only on price, but also on the volume of services provided. Under the fee-for-service system that strictly regulated fees, physicians have perverse incentives to increase the frequency of office visits and hospital admissions, as well as the intensity of services. The high rate of caesarean sections in Korea is one good example of provider-induced demands. Although the rate of caesarean operations has declined in recent years, it is still the highest among OECD countries.[13,16]

Obesity is one of the growing health issues in many countries. As demonstrated in Table 12-13, the prevalence of obesity among those age 20 years and older in Korea was 31.8% in 2005, which was the lowest among the OECD countries. This prevalence has increased over decades. Since the year 2001, however, the growth has slowed.[13] Interestingly, the overall increase was due to the increase of overweight in the male population, whereas the prevalence of obesity in women declined slightly during the same time.[1,6]

Access

The Korean NHI achieved a goal to cover all citizens for medical care. With freedom of choice, citizens can access medical services any time of the year and from whom they want. When NHI was introduced in Korea, it initially allowed citizens to use medical services for only 180 days per year, but by 2006, this service limitation was removed. According to OECD health data, the number of physician visits per citizen in Korea was 10.6 in 2005, exceeding the average number of visits of OECD member countries. In addition, length of stay in acute hospitals in Korea was 10.6 days as compared with the OECD average of 7.4 days. This is mainly because the Korean NHI does not have a prospective payment system that helps to contain costs. Moreover, many hospitals tend to increase capacity for the same reason. Korea is the only country among the OECD countries that has an increasing number of beds over time.[6,13,23]

Accessibility to medical care in Korea is considered high overall, but like many countries, accessibility is less in rural areas. The distribution of medical services is not even. Because most of the healthcare providers are privately owned, they tend to be concentrated in cities where there are many customers and where a lifestyle for their families can be realized. The limited availability

TABLE 12-12   Level of Satisfaction for Medical Services, by Types of Healthcare Facilities (Unit: Percentage)

Type of Facility	Very Satisfied	Moderately Satisfied	Acceptable	Moderately Dissatisfied	Very Dissatisfied
General Hospital	15.7	29.5	33.0	18.9	2.9
Hospital/Clinic	10.0	33.5	44.3	11.3	0.9
Public Health Center	26.3	35.0	30.9	6.8	1.1

Source: MOHW, Cancer Control Policy Team/Korea Central Cancer Registry.

TABLE 12-13 The Prevalence of Obesity Among Those 20 Years and Older, in Selected Years (Unit: Percentage)

Classification	1995	1998	2001	2005
Total	20.2	26.3	30.6	31.8
Men	18.2	26.0	32.4	35.2
Women	22.2	26.5	29.4	28.3

Source: MOHW, Health Investment Planning Team.

Obesity, body mass index ≥ 25.0.

of healthcare services in rural areas with small populations is a problem for Korea.

CURRENT AND EMERGING ISSUES AND CHALLENGES

Along with a rapid expansion of the economy, health care in Korea improved remarkably in a short period. Every citizen has healthcare coverage since introduction of National Health Insurance. With strong government regulation, National Health Insurance has been successful in both cost-containment and quality improvement. Some statistics, however, indicate that the growth of healthcare expenditures in Korea is fast and that it is above the average of OECD countries, although healthcare expenditures in terms of GDP in Korea still remain below the OECD average. Moreover, rapidly changing environments such as increasing demand, seeking high quality of care, and hypercompetitive healthcare markets put more burdens on the insurer (NHIC), providers, and even citizens. Growing distrust of the NHIC caused by increasing cost of care and out-of-pocket payment is one of the current issues in Korea.

Second, the number of long-term care providers is growing. Since 2003, the number of long-term care facilities has dramatically increased because of an aging society and increasing demands. There are many new long-term care facilities, and many existing healthcare providers are diverting their focus to long-term care as a market niche strategy in a hypercompetitive market. There is relatively little regulation for long-term care in Korea.

Third, the structure of the healthcare industry in Korea is changing. One distinct characteristic in Korea is that the private sector, particularly small hospitals and clinics, dominates the healthcare market. In a competitive market, those providers undergo financial difficulty because of increasing costs. To survive, many of those providers are moving toward integration in order to achieve economies of scale. Either horizontal or vertical integration activities through networking, franchising, or partnerships among providers are becoming prevalent in Korea's healthcare market.

On December 2006, the Korean government announced Service Industry Development Plans for the healthcare sector. The government proposed (1) to encourage providers to adopt practice guidelines and clinical pathways in order to improve quality of care, (2) to allow the establishment of Management Service Organizations (MSO) to provide management services for healthcare providers, (3) to give consideration to having for-profit hospitals in the healthcare market, which is still illegal in Korea, (4) to introduce private health insurance for healthcare services, and (5) to give governmental support to providers to attract customers from abroad (medical tourism).

After the government's plans were announced, several MSOs were established to provide management services to healthcare providers. Typically, hospitals/clinics in Korea are owned and managed by physicians. By contracting with MSOs, physicians at hospitals/clinics can be focused delivering care but also gain efficient management; nevertheless, private health insurance and for-profit hospitals are controversial. These proposed changes will face strong opposition from stakeholders.

Finally, for medical tourism, a few big hospitals in Korea are preparing to have patients from other countries. Because the quality of care and services are the main concern in medical tourism, those hospitals are making every effort to improve performance. One of these hospitals is now accredited by the Joint Commission International.

Like many developed countries, Korea must face the challenge of growing healthcare costs, as the portion of the GDP going to healthcare continues to increase. Because healthcare spending exceeds economic growth, there is cause for concern for the long run. This problem is not unique to Korea. The government may be considering moving to a prospective payment system or to global budgeting to control utilization. It may be that Korea must revisit their benefit package and include more preventive care services.

Continuous quality improvement will remain a challenge. The government will make every effort to improve and monitor quality of care, especially for long-term care. There is no systemized control system to monitor and evaluate long-term care services. Government should strengthen the accreditation process for long-term care facilities.

Third, an appropriate method to incentive providers to use resources effectively and efficiently should be considered. Even with strong government regulation and a relatively low reimbursement rate to providers, there is overutilization and misuse. These are resources that could better be used elsewhere in the system.

Fourth, the NIH should maintain its financial status in balance. From the beginning of the 2000s, the NIH suffered from financial difficulty with huge deficits. Consideration might be given to raising contributions rates and tight cost control. The contribution rate (premium) from citizens is relatively low when compared with other countries, even though Koreans enjoy high-quality and technology-driven medical services. Although the NHIC could face opposition from citizens, it should think of raising contribution rates gradually.

Finally, the NHI in Korea has been remarkably successful in the past. For last few years, however, the NHIC is facing not only financial burdens, but also complaints from both providers and citizens. Reestablishing trust in the NHI system and reinforcing the NIHC's accountability will be another challenge. The Korean government should improve public relations and be more responsive to the increasing demands of its citizens.

Consistent and continuous efforts to reach consensus, to contain cost, and to build social solidarity around the objectives of equity, efficiency, and quality will be the ultimate task for future growth of the Korean healthcare system.

REFERENCES

1. Korea National Statistical Office, Korean Statistical Services. Retrieved April 2, 2008, from http://www.kosis.kr.
2. International Monetary Fund. World Economic Outlook Database, April 2008. Retrieved May 4, 2008, from http://www.imf.org/external/pubs/ft/weo/2008/01/weodata/weoselgr.aspx.
3. Korean Government. About Korea: Geography. Retrieved April 14, 2008, from http://www.korea.net/korea/kor_loca.asp?code=A0101.
4. Korea National Statistical Office. *2006 Annual Report on Economically Active Population Survey*. Seoul, Korea: Korea National Statistical Office, 2007.
5. Government of the United States of America. Central Intelligence Agency, 2008. The World Factbook. Retrieved April 12, 2008, from https://www.cia.gov/library/publications/the-world-factbook/geos/ks.html.
6. Korean Government. Ministry of Health and Welfare. *Yearbook of Health and Welfare Statistics, 2007*. Seoul, Korea: Ministry of Health and Welfare; October 2007;53.
7. U.S. Department of Homeland Security, U.S. Immigration and Customs Enforcement, Student and Exchange Visitor Information System, General Summary Quarterly Review, 2008. Retrieved April 16, 2008, from http://www.ice.gov/doclib/sevis/pdf/quarterly_report_jan08.pdf.
8. United Nations. World Population Prospects: The 2004 Revision Vol. III Analytical Report. Retrieved April 24, 2008, from http://www.un.org/esa/population/publications/WPP2004/WPP2004_Vol3_Final/Chapter1.pdf.
9. Anderson GF. Universal health care coverage in Korea. *Health Affairs*. 1989;8(2):24–34.
10. Korean National Health Insurance Corporation. *National Health Insurance Program in Korea*. Seoul, Korea: National Health Insurance Corporation; 2004.
11. Kwon SM. Changing health policy process: Politics of health care reform in Korea. Retrieved April 27, 2008, from http://www.hsph.harvard.edu/takemi/RP206.pdf.
12. Lee JC. Health care reform in South Korea: Success of failure? *Am J Public Health*. 2003;93(1):48–51.
13. Organization for Economic Co-operation and Development. *OECD Health Data 2007*. Paris, France: OECD; 2007.
14. Organization for Economic Co-operation and Development. *Review of the Korean health care system*. Paris, France: OECD; 2002.
15. Korean Government. Ministry of Health and Welfare. *The White Paper on Health and Welfare 2006* [in Korean] Seoul, Korea: Ministry of Health and Welfare; July 2007.
16. Korean National Health Insurance Corporation and Health Insurance Review & Assessment Service. *2006 National Health Insurance Statistical Yearbook*. Seoul, Korea: NHIC and HIRA; December 2007.
17. Bae SI, Kim YS, Tae YH, Lee CJ. *The Current Condition and Prospect of Health Care in Korea: View from International Statistics* [in Korean]. Research Paper Series 2007-27. Korea: National Health Insurance Corporation; December 2007.

18. Center for Health Policy Research. *Lessons Learned From the South Korean Health Care System.* Tulsa, Oklahoma: Oklahoma Medical Research Foundation; February 1992.

19. OECD. Monetary and real flows in the Korean health care system. *In OECD Reviews of Health Care Systems, Korea.* Paris, France: OECD; 2003, pp. 27–44.

20. Kwon SM. Payment system reform for health care providers in Korea. *Health Policy Plan.* 2003;18(1):84–92.

21. Shin Y. Health care systems in transition II. Korea, part I: an overview of health care systems in Korea. *J Public Health Med.* 1998;20(1):41–46.

22. Yang BM. The role of health insurance in the growth of the private health sector in Korea. *Int J Health Plan Manage.* 1996;11(3):231–251.

23. Anderson GF, Poullier JP. Health spending, access, and outcomes: trends in industrialized countries. *Health Affairs.* 1999;18(3):178–192.

CHAPTER 13

India

Sudha Xirasagar and Puneet Misra

COUNTRY DESCRIPTION

TABLE 13-1 India

Nationality	Noun: Indian(s)
	Adjective: Indian
Ethnic groups	Indo-Aryan 72%, Dravidian 25%, Mongoloid and other 3% (2000)
Religions	Hindu 80.5%, Muslim 13.4%, Christian 2.3%, Sikh 1.9%, other 1.8%, unspecified 0.1% (2001 census)
Language	English enjoys associate status but is the most widely used language for national, political, and commercial communication; Hindi is the national language and primary tongue of 30% of the people; there are 21 other official languages: Assamese, Bengali, Bodo, Dogri, Gujarati, Kannada, Kashmiri, Konkani, Maithili, Malayalam, Manipuri, Marathi, Nepali, Oriya, Punjabi, Sanskrit, Santhali, Sindhi, Tamil, Telugu, and Urdu; Hindustani is a popular variant of Hindi/Urdu spoken widely throughout northern India but is not an official language
Literacy	Definition: age 15 and over can read and write
	Total population: 61%
	Male: 73.4%
	Female: 47.8% (2001 census)
Government type	Federal republic

(continues)

TABLE 13-1   India (continued)

Date of independence	August 15, 1947 (from United Kingdom)
Gross Domestic Product (GDP) per capita	$2,700 (2007 est.)
Unemployment rate	7.2% (2007 est.)
Natural hazards	Droughts; flash floods, as well as widespread and destructive flooding from monsoon rains; severe thunderstorms; earthquakes
Environment: current issues	Deforestation; soil erosion; overgrazing; desertification; air pollution from industrial effluents and vehicle emissions; water pollution from raw sewage and runoff of agricultural pesticides; tap water is not potable throughout the country; huge and growing population is overstraining natural resources
Population	1,147,995,898 (July 2008 est.)
Age structure	0–14 years: 31.5% (male 189,238,487/female 172,168,306) 15–64 years: 63.3% (male 374,157,581/female 352,868,003) 65 years and over: 5.2% (male 28,285,796/female 31,277,725) (2008 est.)
Median age	Total: 25.1 years Male: 24.7 years Female: 25.5 years (2008 est.)
Population growth rate	1.578% (2008 est.)
Birth rate	22.22 births/1,000 population (2008 est.)
Death rate	6.4 deaths/1,000 population (2008 est.)
Net migration rate	−0.05 migrant(s)/1,000 population (2008 est.)
Gender ratio	At birth: 1.12 male(s)/female Under 15 years: 1.1 male(s)/female 15–64 years: 1.06 male(s)/female 65 years and over: 0.9 male(s)/female Total population: 1.06 male(s)/female (2008 est.)
Infant mortality rate	Total: 32.31 deaths/1,000 live births Male: 36.94 deaths/1,000 live births Female: 27.12 deaths/1,000 live births (2008 est.)
Life expectancy at birth	Total population: 69.25 years Male: 66.87 years Female: 71.9 years (2008 est.)
Total fertility rate	2.76 children born/woman (2008 est.)
HIV/AIDS adult prevalence rate	0.9% (2001 est.)
Number of people living with HIV/AIDS	5.1 million (2001 est.)
HIV/AIDS deaths	310,000 (2001 est.)

Central Intelligence Agency. The World Fact Book, 2008. Retrieved November 18, 2008, from https://www.cia.gov/library/publications/the-world-factbook.

History

India is the second most populous country in the world, with 1,125 million people[1] (about 3.5 times that of the United States of America). It has 22 officially recognized languages, with 844 different dialects rooted in two ancient indigenous languages, Sanskrit and Tamil, with elements of Persian, Arabic, and English imbibed in the course of trade relations and armed conquests. English is one of two official national languages, the other being Hindi. The major religious–cultural identity is Hinduism (82%), followed by Islam (13%) and Christianity (3%).

The Indo-Gangetic valley civilization is possibly the world's oldest surviving civilization to this day, dated as a mature civilization at about the 7th millennium BC.[2] Evidence of sewage systems and public baths are found in archeological excavations dated to about 4,000 BC. The earliest Vedic treatises and scriptures transmitted in the oral tradition (that can be dated by astronomical events recorded within them) reflect a culture that relied on strong hygiene orientation, pastoral lifestyle and lactovegetarian preference, economic systems including weights and measures, and use of copper, iron, and barley.[2]

The Vedic civilization laid the foundation of Hinduism's approach of an integrated physical, mental, social, civic, and spiritual way of life, which continues to influence subtly the attitudes and lifestyles related to education, health, illness, treatment, death, and dying, until today. In addition to Hinduism, with its many philosophical schools, India birthed two other ancient religions, Buddhism founded by Buddha (1887 to 1807 BC)[2] and Jainism, and more recently, Sikhism in the 16th century. These traditions share with Hinduism core doctrines of the sacredness of all life (therefore a bias toward vegetarianism), introverted pursuit of enlightenment to gain liberation from the endless cycle of rebirth and death, self-sacrifice and self-denial to attain enlightenment, belief in rebirth and karma, and a shared heritage of yoga and Ayurveda. As a result of the shared philosophy of life, there has been fluid interchange, including intermarriage, conversions, and cross-identification, with Hinduism identifying Buddha as its 10th avatar (God taking human form). Currently, a small percentage of population identifies with these religions (2%), in contrast to the widespread prevalence of Buddhism into and beyond the Himalayas and on to Japan.

Two major spinoffs from the Vedic culture's focus on knowledge and spiritual enlightenment were yoga and Ayurveda (knowledge or science of life). The surgical branch of Ayurveda gained much momentum in the post-Buddha era because of Buddhism's focus on a practical version of spirituality and real-time compassion (in contrast to the ritual and other-worldly focus of Hinduism). Together, these two health systems prescribe a way of healthful life and healing, based on a premise that the self (and self-discipline) is the root of health and healing. Many elements of yoga and Ayurveda are intimately woven into the prescribed (and for the most part, ritually practiced), daily personal lifestyle, civic norms, and social traditions. Ayurveda, yoga, and Sidha (a south Indian system of medicine, several millennia old) continue to provide the foundation of many indigenous health and healing practices in modern India, particularly among the rural population.

The Indian subcontinent, known since ancient times for its riches, driven by trade in spices, gold, and precious stones, experienced many invasions, from Alexander of Greece, through the Islamic invasions (from the 8th century AD onward, through the Persian Moghul invasion and rule between the 15th and 19th centuries), and British rule (consolidated in 1757, lasting up to 1947). These historic events triggered much religious and cultural diversity, particularly the widespread conversions to Islam, and birth of Sikhism. Christianity entered the subcontinent through the west coast, close to the time of Jesus Christ, but has not gained much ground through the centuries.

The British colonial period marked a political milestone by initiating a crucial shift from a variegated administration pattern across the many dynastic kingdoms to adoption of system-based institutional structures and the rule of law. Other contributions also facilitated the modern nation–state form to assume political stewardship of a hitherto apolitical culture. These include modern communications such as railroads, the postal system, and the telegraph. Parallel with its modernizing effects, however, British colonialism also led to the disappearance of many local arts, crafts, economic activities, Ayurvedic and other indigenous medicinal treatises, and local medicinal traditions and knowledge.[2]

After World War II, the Indian subcontinent's nonviolent struggle for independence led to freedom from British rule on August 15, 1947, concurrent with partition into the Muslim state of Pakistan (east and west) separated by a secular, predominantly Hindu India. (In 1971, the eastern segment of Pakistan seceded to form Bangladesh.) Other neighboring nation–states, Afghanistan and Burma (Myanmar), were also created at this time. Within India, the indigenous, universal civic institution of decentralized village self-rule (Panchayati raj) was overlaid with the new nation–state identity and governance. Its new Western-educated political leaders determined that parliamentary democracy was best suited to govern India's diverse people with a multitude of caste, religious, and language identities. These identities continue to drive social and political life, including voting patterns in political elections.

For millennia, the Hindu caste system defined individuals' place in the occupational and social hierarchy. The millennia-old major castes with the allocated vocations are Brahmins (responsible for priestly, spiritual and intellectual pursuits, and asserted to be closest to final enlightenment from the cycle of rebirth), Kshatriyas (warriors), Vaishyas (businessmen), and Shudras (farmers/artisans/other labor occupations). Outside of this mainstream caste system were the untouchables or dalits (previously known as Harijans), who experienced much discrimination, often severe exploitation, and exclusion from all development and governance roles in preindependent India. The caste system became entrenched as a hereditary hierarchy sometime during the 1st millennium BC, when it was asserted that one's birth in a caste was the result of karma (deeds) in previous births. If each individual fulfilled their role dutifully, all would eventually attain spiritual enlightenment through successive rebirths into higher order castes. The caste system persists to this day, defining boundaries for marriage and cultural associations, and dietary patterns (such as meat eating permitted only for the physically laboring castes, kshatriyas, shudras, and dalits). Since 1947, the Indian Constitution, promulgated in 1950, abolished untouchability (making it a felony) and established affirmative action, reserving 22.5% of all educational and job opportunities in government and public sector industries for the dalits and tribals (forest dwelling people). Over the past 6 decades, these constitutional guarantees along with economic and educational development have enabled much upward social and economic mobility for dalits, tribals, and lower castes, significantly reducing caste-based social and economic disparities, particularly in urban areas.

Size and Geography

India is a land of 3,287,263 km^2 (approximately a third of the U.S. land area); it is bound by the Himalayan mountains to the north and northeast, with its peninsular part surrounded by oceans (the Indian Ocean, Arabian Sea, and Bay of Bengal). It has a land frontier of 15,200 km and a coastline of 7,516 km^3 (Figure 13-1). The northernmost state of Jammu and Kashmir re-

mains disputed, with Pakistan occupying a third of this state after a postindependence war.

Government or Political System

In 1950, promulgation of the Indian Constitution conferred sovereign, secular, and democratic republic status, with a multiparty, parliamentary system of democratic governance, similar to Britain.[3] Within this governance structure, its mixed economic model (public and private sector) was premised on the concept of a welfare state, with the central government assuming much of the responsibility for improving socioeconomic and health conditions through establishing large public sector industries (heavy engineering, coal, steel, power, etc., the "commanding heights of the economy") to serve as the engines of economic development and social equalization of the traditionally oppressed castes. Additionally, much infrastructure, including health and education, has been funded by the central government through successive Five Year Plans, which have ensured consistency in the pattern, as well as speed of development of the public health infrastructure across India's diverse states.

The central government has three wings: the legislature (two houses of Parliament), executive (Prime Minister and Cabinet), and the judiciary (Supreme Court to deal with constitutional law and Lok Ayukta to monitor standards of governance and related codes of conduct). The country is divided into 550 electoral districts that directly elect their representative (universal suffrage, all citizens aged over 18 years) to the Lower House or Lok Sabha (literally, People's Council), who in turn elect the Prime Minister. Elections to the Lok Sabha are held every 5 years, unless advanced by political shifts or major national crises. Multiple parties are represented, and either the majority party or a coalition assumes power and chooses the Prime Minister. The Prime Minister is the nation's chief executive, sharing responsibility and power with the cabinet. The Prime Minister selects cabinet members (Ministers) to lead the departments, based on electorate represented and political exigencies. The cabinet provides political leadership to the departments run by career civil servants.

The key lawmaking agency is the Lok Sabha, with ratification from the Upper House or Rajya Sabha (literally *governing council*). The latter is composed of indirectly elected members by state legislators and by the nation's college graduates. The President is the titular head of government, Chief of the Armed Forces, and serves a reserve executive governance function during

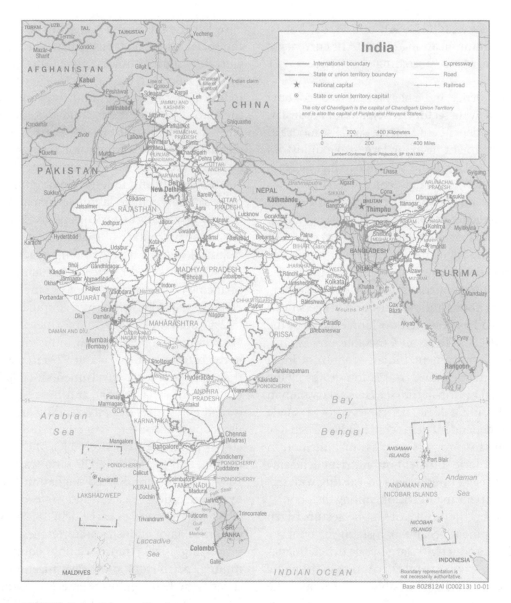

FIGURE 13-1   Map of India

national emergencies or parliamentary deadlocks. India has a semifederalist structure, divided into 28 states (mostly on linguistic bases, and few on cultural [tribal] basis) and seven union territories, further divided into 612 administrative districts.[3] Each state government is modeled along similar lines as the Central Government, with subject jurisdictions laid out under central (e.g., defense), state (e.g. education), or concurrent lists. Since independence, except for a 2-year period of national emergency declared by the Prime Minister during 1975–1977, the country has been governed under constitutionally elected governments.

States do not levy income taxes but derive revenues from sales and excise taxes. Income and other central tax revenues are shared with the states using a combination of formulas and discretionary disbursements, driven by political, natural disaster, and national interest considerations. Below the state level, local governments are governed by directly elected councils on local issues (district councils, municipalities, and over a half-million village panchayats), much hamstrung by wide and growing gaps between revenues and infrastructure/ service needs of a growing population.

Macroeconomics

The major economic sectors by contribution to gross domestic product (GDP) (2007) are agriculture, forestry, and fishing (21%); manufacturing, mining, and construction (26.1%); financial, information technology

(IT), and other services (13.5%); and trade, hotels, transport, and communication (25.1%).[4] Its currency is the rupee (exchange rate approximately 40 rupees = $1 in 2008).

Since independence, India has had a mixed economy with public and private sector participation in industry. In the early postindependent years, a socialist model of public sector investment in many large-scale industries (particularly steel, coal, oil, heavy engineering, defense, and power generation), with tight controls on foreign direct investment, served important purposes in nation building: (1) emergence of a significant, salaried, middle class (from a preindependent situation of over 90% of population starving or at the margin), (2) nominally universalized the idea of equality of castes, including the untouchables, (3) generated significant domestic purchasing power for goods and services, and (4) generated a well-educated and professional workforce fueled by the emerging middle class. To recall a metaphor by Swaminathan S. Aiyar, a prominent Indian economist, India graduated from "mass famine (starvation deaths by the tens of thousands) in British India, to mass starvation in the sixties" (chronic caloric deficiency; not a single famine in postindependent democratic India). Then one observes the onward progress to mass malnutrition in the 70s and 80s (calorie sufficient but nutrient deficient) and since then a rising middle class co-existing with significant micronutrient malnutrition among the poor.

Soon, however, the utility of public sector-driven economic development became hamstrung by poor accountability, low productivity, large-scale deficit financing, and politician–civil servant corruption in the name of bureaucratic controls, ostensibly to "regulate" the greedy and exploitative for-profit sector. Bureaucracy, corruption, and unbridled populism (the latter fueled by a multiparty democratic setup within a socially, linguistically, and religiously fragmented electorate, dominated by the poor and near poor) began to stymie economic growth. In 1991, a situation approaching bankruptcy propelled major economic liberalization reforms favoring the free market, gradual privatization, dismantling dysfunctional regulation, and the silent, unfettered rise of the IT industry.

The reforms unleashed a dramatic economic revolution, lifting millions out of poverty. In 2007, it produced an estimated total GDP of PPP $2.965 trillion (in purchasing power parity) or $3,460 per capita in 2007,[5] logging over 7% annual growth rate since 1997 (8.5% in 2007),[6] led by IT or IT-enabled services and by industrial manufacturing. On the flip side, liberalization has led to large and rapidly widening income/wealth gaps between the haves and have-nots, poised to threaten the social and civic fabric particularly in urban areas. Currently, agriculture accounts for 60% of the total estimated workforce and only 16.6% of GDP. The Gini index of distribution of family income was 0.37 (2004), the lowest 10% by household income consume/earn 3.6% of GDP, and the top 10% earn 31.1% of GDP.[7] An estimated 44.2% of population lives on less than a dollar a day (per capita).[8] Unemployment stands at 7.2% (with a significant, indeterminate number under employed).[4] The female labor participation rate is 43%, with 59% working as agricultural workers and 7% (similar to the percentage of male workers) in professional, technical, administrative, and managerial occupations.[9]

A major issue for civic infrastructure and healthcare financing is the distribution of its employed population: Among the total employed population, 27 million (5.2%) are employed in the formal sector of industry (18.5 million in public sector industries and 8.5 million in the private sector),[10] about 22% in government (central, state, and local governments), 60% in agriculture (entirely informal sector), and the rest in small or self-owned enterprises or petty vending and services. Thus, the income tax base for government revenues is limited largely to the approximately 30% of the employed population, and the tax-to-GDP ratio was 11.4% in 2006–2007, up from a prolonged stagnation at 8% to 10% for over a decade.[11] Federal and state debt combined is 58.8% of GDP and external debt 18.4% of GDP in U.S. dollars.[7] Major industries are textiles, chemicals, food processing, steel, transportation equipment, cement, mining, petroleum, and heavy machinery. In the past decade, the IT/IT industry emerged. Industrial production growth was estimated at 10% in 2007. Although IT and IT-enabled services are mostly limited to the major metropolitan cities, the remaining industries are widely distributed.

Agricultural production led by the green revolution since 1951 has made major strides, moving the country from being a net food importer at independence to a net food exporter.[10] India also became the world's leading milk producer (overtaking the United States) in 2002; nevertheless, malnutrition continues to be a widespread issue, with pulses and legumes (the major source of protein for its largely vegetarian population) declining in per capita availability from 60 g in 1951 to 36 g in 2004.[10] These numbers obscure major inequalities in actual consumption because of poor purchasing power of the lowest income decile of population.

Major shortages are faced in electricity, energy, and transportation, with seasonal shortages of water. Major infrastructure shortages are also faced in roads, sanitation, water supply, and so forth. The Census 2001 showed that 89% of households have access to drinking water (only 62% have taps within homes or nearby), and 69% of the urban population have access to piped water.[12] Of greater concern is the rapidly diminishing water resource availability per capita, expected to fall below water stress levels by 2025 (with many areas already under stress/scarcity conditions). This causes experts to predict a grave water crisis in the near future, attributable entirely to the increasing population. Deteriorating water quality further compounds the issue. Approximately 63% of the urban population and 28% of the rural population have access to sanitary water. Water and sanitation deficiencies will continue to be key challenges because of significant population with very low purchasing power. Less than 30% of the population without these facilities were prepared to pay for even community-based facilities.[12] The National Family Health Survey reported that in 2005 to 2006, 68% of households had electricity, and 46% lived in robust housing (other than thatched roofs or otherwise temporary structures).[9]

Transportation is largely road and rail based, with 65% of freight and 80% of passenger traffic transported by road[13] and the rest by rail. Inadequate road length and width[13] and poor quality are a major drag on industrial productivity. Poor connectivity in rural areas also directly hampers rapid medical attention. Road infrastructure status is considered a key infrastructural weakness (along with water, sanitation, and electricity) that will limit India's current upward spiral in development and global economic participation.[14] There are 12 major ports developed and maintained by the central government and 187 minor ports.[15]

Education is another area of serious concern, particularly for the rural and urban poor. According to the Census 2001, the literacy rate among the population aged 7 years and older was 65.5% (76% among males and 54% among females).[10] A substantial proportion of illiteracy is accounted for by older adults. During recent years, children show near-universal primary school enrollments, although dropout rates are high. Despite laws requiring primary school enrollment of age-appropriate children, a combination of economic factors, distance barriers, inadequate teachers, a lack of accountability in teacher attendance, poor infrastructure, and poor-quality schooling results in rural children receiving a poor quality education. They drop out early (particularly girls) to turn to domestic or economically productive activities such a farming and petty economic activities. Although much progress is evident in enrollment statistics from independence (42.6% of eligible children enrolled in grades 1–5 in 1951 compared with 98.2% in 2003 and 3.1% versus 62.4% for grades 6–8), females are significantly disadvantaged at higher grade levels beyond primary school.[8] Recent figures show that although literacy is higher among younger females, it is still no more than 74% among the 15- to 19-year-old group compared with 89% among males.[9] Studies show that 42% of boys and 23% of girls reported economic reasons for dropping out, and approximately 15% reported distance barriers.[16] Furthermore, there are large disparities in quality between urban and rural areas.

The previously mentioned factors have major implications for communicable diseases, maternal and child health, general population health, healthcare access, affordability, power relations among economic and health haves versus have-nots, financing mechanisms, and service delivery.

Demographics

India's population profile and vital statistics are presented in Table 13-2.[1,17,18] Population density in 2008 is about 342 per km^2 (over 10 times that of the United States), with 16.7% of the world's population living on 2.4% of the world's surface area. The dependency ratio is 62 per 100, 35.5% below 15 years old and 7.2% aged over 60 years old.[17] India's population continues to be predominantly rural (about 785 million living in 638,588 villages).[17,18] At 72.2% of total population, the current rural percentage is not much different from the 80% rural population at independence in 1947. The rural sector of population has consistently attracted strong policy and public investment emphasis from successive governments that continues today.[19] Except for the five largest cities of 6 million or more—Delhi, the capital city; Mumbai, the most densely populated city; Kolkota; Chennai; and Bangalore—India's urban population is widely distributed: 56.6% of its urban population lives in 322 cities of 100,000-plus population, and 43.4% in 4,293 towns of 1,000 to 100,000 population).[10]

Population growth, far outpacing civic and infrastructure growth, remains the chief concern, causing an ever-increasing gap between need and availability of water, sanitation, housing, health care, agricultural land, law enforcement, primary and secondary education institutions (both quality and quantity), and other basic needs of development. The current population and expected short-term growth are widely agreed to be India's "fundamental social, economic,

TABLE 13-2 India's Demographic Profile and Vital Statistics

Indicator	Current Status
Total population (2008)	1,125.6 million[1]
Crude birth rate (2006)	23.5 per 1,000[18]
Crude death rate (2006)	7.5 per 1,000[18]
Annual growth rate (2004)	1.7%[17]
Population doubling time at current growth rate	30 years[17]
Population rural (2002)	72.2%[17]
Population density per km² (2008, computed)	342
Adult literacy rate (2001)	65.38%[17]
Females 15–19 years (2005–2006)	74%[9]
Males 15–19 years (2005–2006)	89%[9]
Age appropriate school attendance (2005–2006)	
Primary	72%[9]
High school	51%
Population aged below 15 years (2003)	35.35%[17]
Population aged above 65 years (2007 est.)	7.2%[9]
Average family size (2003)	3.0
Females (15–49 years) age at marriage (2003)	20.1 years (mean)[17]
	17.2 years (median)[17]
Annual per capita GDP (2007 est., CIA government)	$2,700 (PPP)[6]
Percent below poverty line (2005–2006 est.)	27%[9]
Dependency ratio	62 per 100[17]
Infant mortality rate (2006)	57/1,000 live births[18]
Rural (2006)	62/1,000 live births[18]
Urban (2006)	39/1,000 live births[18]
Maternal mortality rate	5.4/1,000 births[5]
Life expectancy at birth (2001–2006) (CGHI)	64.1 years (male)[17]
	65.8 years (female)[17]
Total fertility rate (per woman, 2005–2006)	2.7[9]
Desired total fertility rate (women, 2005–2006)	1.9[9]
Labor force participation (2005–2006)	43% (women 15–49)[9]
	87% (men 15–49)[9]
Regular exposure to mass media (television, newspapers, radio, cinema):	
Females (2005–2006)	65%[9]
Males (2005–2006)	82%[9]

All 2005–2006 data are from the National Family Health Survey 3, 2005–2006, sampling a nationally representative sample of 109,041 households interviewing 198,744 women and men of reproductive age group.

and environmental problem[s]."[6] Population concerns have long guided India's domestic policies, with the world's first government-sponsored, voluntary, family planning program, based on education and motivation launched in 1952.[17]

Major Morbidity and Its Distribution

The major health problems can be classified into communicable diseases, environmental and sanitation-related problems, nutritional problems, and noncommunicable diseases. These issues are fueled by rapid population growth, which arose out of the rapidly falling death rates after independence caused by eradication of famines and massive reductions in communicable disease mortality (notably malaria, plague, smallpox, and diarrheal disease) and infant mortality. From a crude death rate of about 35 per 1,000 and an infant mortality rate of 160/1000 live births in the preindependence era,[20] the crude death rate fell to 15 per 1,000, and the infant mortality rate fell to 129/1,000 live births by the 1971–1981 decade and further to 7.5 and 58/1,000 in 2004, respectively[17]; therefore, despite high contraception prevalence levels (56% among currently married women),[9] early marriage of a very large youth population from the 1970s and 1980s population expansions has continued to fuel large population increases in the 1990s and will continue up to 2020. Out-of-wedlock births are very uncommon. Demographic pressures seriously undermine the impact of significant additions to public health and healthcare infrastructure achieved through massive investments, causing the percentage of population with access to health, water, and sanitation facilities to improve modestly or even stagnate in some sectors.

Despite mandatory birth and death registration, rural vital statistics have been unreliable until recently. Reliable data are available from the Sample Registration System, covering a nationally representative sample (1.1 million households in 2004).[21] Among communicable diseases, malaria is a leading cause of morbidity. In 2005, 1.8 million cases and 940 deaths were reported.[17] The malaria situation has remained stable at low-grade endemic levels, after the early dramatic reductions from an estimated 75 million cases out of 350 million population at the time of independence[16] to about 1 million cases among an expanded population of about 550 million in 1976 because of the National Malaria Eradication/Control Program.[17] Environmental sanitation infrastructure deficiencies and climatic conditions favoring mosquito propagation, as well as lack of timely case detection and treatment, permit endemic low-grade

transmission, particularly in the rainy season. Two endemic, chronic diseases with long latent periods and a low lifetime probability of disease are tuberculosis and leprosy. The tuberculosis incidence has remained stagnant since first measured in the 1960s, at 4 sputum-positive (infectious) tuberculosis cases per 1,000 population and 16 per 1,000 X-ray–positive cases, and 30% of the population is infected. An estimated 400,000 tuberculosis deaths take place every year.[17] Tuberculosis remains greatly undertreated because of the need for long-term treatment, the lack of consistency of public health services in providing free treatment, and poverty that limits access to private health care and antituberculosis drugs. Leprosy continues to cause morbidity, with 220,000 new cases in 2003–2004 (60% of the world's cases), including 15% child cases, 1.8% having deformity of grade II and above and 35% multibacillary (infectious) cases.[17] The latter figure indicates that, like tuberculosis, leprosy transmission continues, with newly infected persons carrying the potential to break down to active disease through their lifetime. Widespread implementation of multidrug therapy since 1983 under the National Leprosy Eradication Program has substantially reduced the deformity rate and number of chronic cases.

Other major public health problems are diarrheal disease, responsible for 700,000 deaths each year, mostly children under 5 years of age, predisposed by nutritional deficiencies (vitamin A, protein energy malnutrition, and anemia), and filariasis, with at least 6 million cases of acute filarial infection each year, with a cumulative number of at least 45 million having chronic residual damage.[17,4] Other communicable diseases include visceral leishmaniasis, typhoid and related enteric fevers, and intestinal parasitic infestations, which are not notifiable and therefore difficult to estimate because the majority of cases are treated in the private sector.

The population-based prevalence of HIV was assessed for the first time in 2005–2006,[9] covering 105,477 women and men in the reproductive age group (15–49 years). The test participation rate was 94.5% among 111,616 sample eligibles. This established a nationwide HIV-positive rate of 0.28% in these age groups (0.22% among women and 0.36% among men), translating to a total of 1.7 million cases nationally among adults aged 15 to 49 in 2006. As with other diseases, there is much variation across states within this overall figure. The survey also found near universal awareness of major routes of HIV transmission and prevention. Most men and women (63% and 82%, respectively) wanted HIV-AIDS to be a part of the school curriculum.[9]

Widespread nutritional deficiencies directly and indirectly impact the population's health by mediating maternal health risks and children's susceptibility to infections and succumbing to disease. Among children aged 6 months to 5 years, almost 70% are anemic (40% moderately anemic and 3% severely anemic).[9] Anemia levels have not been reduced in recent years and, in fact, have increased in the past few years, the reasons for which are not clear.[9] Among children under the age of 5 years, 48% are stunted, and 43% are underweight, with 20% of these showing wasting. Immunization coverage for the full number of doses and all recommended vaccines is at 44%, largely because of dropout after one or two doses of DPT or polio vaccine.[9] The under-5 mortality cause pattern reflects that these major health handicaps, coupled with water and sanitation infrastructure deficiencies, and the maternal health and perinatal care deficiencies, confer significant mortality risk on infants and young children.

Despite major strides in maternal health care, much remains to be done. In 2005–2006, 76% of women with a live birth in the previous 5 years received antenatal care, with only two thirds of them receiving three or more antenatal visits.[9] The contraception prevalence rate is 56%, two thirds being female terminal methods (tubal ligation).[9] The contraception rate has steadily increased and accelerated among traditional nonusers in the last few years. Fertility has been reduced significantly to 2.7 per woman, although still well above the replacement level of 2.1 per woman.[9] Of concern is the fact that contraception and its obverse (fertility) are inversely related to poverty and female education level (increasing the maternal and child mortality risk of these groups), but the good news is that reduction in family size (with increasing contraception) is expanding to subgroups with persistent high fertility in the past,[9] which bodes well for maternal and child health, as well as population control.

Infant mortality, child mortality, nutritional status, and long-term growth and educational–economic prospects for children are inversely related to maternal health and nutrition. Eighty-five percent of the total under-5 mortality is accounted for by neonatal conditions, diarrheal diseases, and pneumonia,[5] all closely linked to maternal/child nutritional status or maternal health issues. In turn, these factors are linked to low interpregnancy interval/early child bearing or deficiencies in prenatal/intrapartum/postnatal care.

The maternal mortality rate, although significantly reduced from preindependence levels, continues to be unacceptably high, at 5.4 per 1,000 live births.[5] Analysis shows that 64.3% of maternal deaths (1997–1998) are due to anemia, bleeding during pregnancy or childbirth, malposition of the fetus leading to obstructed labor, or puerperal sepsis.[22] These causes reflect two major structural weaknesses in the rural healthcare system: a lack of access to meaningful obstetric services and a blood-banking system in a timely/geographically accessible sense. As discussed later, these weaknesses are related to structural weaknesses in the secondary health service system in rural areas, as well as infrastructure and manpower distribution problems.

The previously mentioned diseases characteristic of the "age of receding pandemics" (in Omran's epidemiological transition terms)[23] are typically readily controlled by public health interventions, health education, and nutritional changes (relatively cheap public health interventions). Concurrent with these receding diseases, there are unfolding problems of noncommunicable diseases, requiring expensive secondary and tertiary care, largely cardiovascular disease, mental illness, diabetes, and cancer. Cardiovascular disease is a major silent killer, causing 25% of deaths among adults in the 30- to 50-year-old group.[24] Bronchial asthma affects an estimated 15 to 20 million (about 1.5% of population). Nationwide mental illness and cancer rates on a population basis are not available.

BRIEF HISTORY OF THE HEALTHCARE SYSTEM

Pre-World War II

Before World War II, the British set up hospitals in the major cities with British officers and troops stationed to administer the colonial functions and local administration. British India's government (under the Governor–General) had the Surgeon General oversee the development and administration of medical care facilities (largely in cities and towns) and had the Public Health Commissioner oversee public health functions largely from a colonial perspective: control of epidemics and prevention during large scale fairs and pilgrim events, sporadic water and sanitation activities, and communicable disease (malaria and gastroenteritis) research.

As for rural primary health care based on modern medicine, the first primary health centers (PHCs) were established by the Maharajah (king) of Mysore (in South India) in the 1920s, financed from the royal treasury, providing grassroots services such as sanitation education, purification of wells, physician services, and family planning advice. These PHCs may be some of the earliest publicly financed PHCs with an integrated public health and primary care orientation in the world. Generally, however, in the preindependent era, PHCs remained occasional curios in princely states with progressive kings.

Use of Traditional Medicine as Part of the Culture

Ayurveda (in north India) and Sidha (in South India) are two indigenously derived systems of medicine, well established before 1000 BC,[25] constantly incorporating new knowledge over time. Other alternative systems are Unani (Arabic medicine-based) and homeopathy. Sushruta, placed somewhere between 600 and 1000 BC, was the founder of surgery in the Ayurvedic medical system.[25] Charaka was the founder of medicine. Many texts and pharmacopeias developed through the ages were lost through the various invasions and during the British colonial period. Currently, Ayurveda and Sidha are practiced at two levels: the household level, where common knowledge, herbs, and practices, passed on by word of mouth are a part of people's routine response to prevent and treat certain illnesses; and the professional level, with formal training of 4.5 years plus a year of internship (similar to allopathic medical training). The formal system uses pharmacopeias to systematically treat diseases, particularly chronic diseases (such as rheumatoid arthritis). Many medical colleges and other government hospitals, as well as large, financially self-sustained nonprofit establishments, operate in South India and some parts of north India. It is impossible to quantify the magnitude of use because much consulting (including advice on household herbs) takes place at an informal level.

Since World War II

After independence, the Indian government integrated the functions of the Surgeon General and the Public Health Commissioner into the office of the Director General of Health Services and faced up to the extremely inadequate healthcare infrastructure and manpower. The Health Survey and Development Committee submitted to the outgoing British government[20] reported that one in every four Indians were affected by malaria—1% of the population had plague, a maternal mortality rate of 20/1,000 live births, and a crude death rate of about 35/1,000 (nearly balancing the crude birth rate of 44/1,000). Yet the hospital bed availability was 3/10,000 population; physicians were 1/10,000, and nurses were 5/100,000.[8] Importantly, although 80% of the population was rural, almost no beds were located in rural areas.[20]

In successive Five Year Plans since 1951, the government has systematically expanded the health infrastructure with an emphasis on rural PHCs, urging PHC medical officers to provide logistic and supervisory support to the public health programs that were led by district program officers. All public health programs except family planning (e.g., malaria, leprosy, and tuberculosis) are funded jointly by the central government and state governments, with family planning funded by the central government.[17] Public medical care institutions (hospitals and clinics) are funded by state governments. The district civil surgeons/chief medical officers (chiefs of all government funded curative services in each district) and medical officers at primary and community health centers (CHCs) are responsible for primary and first-level referral medical care, as well as public health programs. Each district also has a chief medical superintendent and specialists at district hospitals, who are concerned with secondary-level medical care.

In 1977, when smallpox was declared eradicated in India and malaria moved from epidemic status to low-grade endemicity, the government officially adopted family planning as its chief public health concern. It established the National Institute of Health and Family Planning and launched the Rural Health Scheme to systematically establish rural PHCs (1 for every 30,000 population).[17] Each PHC served as the ultimate implementation unit and hub for all public health programs, led by medical officers, and powered by trained health workers for malaria surveillance and control, and diarrheal disease control through chlorination of wells, providing safe delivery and maternal health services, training traditional birth attendants in hygienic delivery, health education, and under-5 children's health. This development received further impetus in the following year by the historic Alma-Ata declaration of "Health For All by 2000" in 1978, signed by 126 countries under the aegis of the World Health Organization.[26] The HFA declaration called for a population-based network of PHCs in rural and urban areas to provide "essential health care to individuals, families, and communities (preventive and essential health care), in a culturally and socially acceptable manner, at a cost that the country and community could afford."

During the following 2 decades, the Indian government systematically expanded PHCs in rural and remote tribal/hilly areas (1/20,000 tribal/hill population), with a male and a female medical officer, one male and female health worker, field supervisory staff, a basic obstetric facility (for vaginal delivery), and a basic laboratory facility with microscopy for major communicable disease detection (malaria, tuberculosis, and leprosy). Under each PHC were six subcenters, for 1/5,000 rural population (3,000 in tribal areas) with one resident female health worker and one male health worker. Both male and female health workers visit households in their care, the male health worker primarily responsible for door-to-door surveillance/presumptive treatment/compliance monitoring of malaria, filariasis, tuberculosis, and leprosy; regular chlorination of wells; and demonstration of sanitary pit latrines and environmental sanitation. The female health worker is primarily responsible for fortnightly visits of all households in her area to provide prenatal and postnatal care, motivate couples for temporary and permanent family planning methods, organize child immunization clinics, conduct surveillance for diarrheal disease and respiratory infection among children, and conduct home treatment of common ailments including intestinal parasites.

To provide inpatient and surgical referral care for medical, surgical, and obstetric patients in rural areas, government-run CHCs were established with 30 beds each, to serve the area of four PHCs, or 120,000 rural population. CHCs were located in semiurban towns, with an internist, general surgeon, and obstetrician/gynecologist, along with an anesthesiologist at selected CHCs. The next level of publicly funded curative facilities is the district level, with additional specialties, including ear-nose-throat (ENT), ophthalmology, psychiatry, and other specialties. Expansion of infrastructure was carried out with a combination of central Five Year Plan funds and multilateral/bilateral agency loans (e.g., World Bank, Overseas Development Assistance-UK). Most maintenance, including salaries and administration/supervision, was the responsibility of the state governments, with health being a state subject.

DESCRIPTION OF THE CURRENT HEALTHCARE SYSTEM

The health system is a mosaic of institutions that can be viewed through several lenses: government/private ownership, rural/urban distribution, public access/closed insurance facilities, and different medical science systems (allopathic/Indian systems of medicine).

Facilities

Government Health Facilities

In line with the welfare state approach that ruled India's politics until recently, the government health infrastructure is the most widely available, universally accessible, and well documented in number and distribution. Because of disproportionate vulnerability and poverty among the rural population, successive governments have focused more heavily on rural primary health care, leading to much of the government health infrastructure located in rural areas, particularly a multitiered primary care system.

Table 13-3 shows the present status of healthcare infrastructure in India, including primary care infrastructure and hospital bed capacity in the government and private sectors. It also shows the healthcare infrastructure classified by open-access versus closed panel facilities that cover specific employer-based population subgroups. The rural healthcare system has integrated public health and curative care at the PHC and subcenter level, both serving as the first point of contact with the healthcare system. Secondary health care provides for internal medicine, surgical, and obstetric/gynecology care at the CHC level. These facilities are constructed with central government funding and are administered/maintained by state governments under state directorates of health services. Starting with the first 725 rural PHCs during 1951–1955,[8] there are currently 23,109 PHCs, 142,655 subcenters, and 3,222 CHCs in rural areas.[27]

Although PHCs and subcenters were established based on population to center ratios, the establishment of CHCs, small 30-bed hospitals in rural areas (expected ratio of 1 for every 4 PHCs), has not been materialized. This is due to complex reasons: availability of other urban government hospitals such as district and taluk hospitals for referral cases, the need for substantial investments (equipment and consumables) going beyond just building the facility, a proliferation of small private inpatient and surgical facilities in the private sector that compete for patients, the lack of consistent piped water supply and electricity in semirural areas, the lack of critical support infrastructure such as blood banks, the need for complex management roles among government-employed physicians to plan and manage materials and manpower, and resistance of government-employed specialists caused by potential competition for their parallel private practices/private hospitals.

Above the level of CHCs are government curative facilities with specialists, taluk hospitals (subdistrict level), district hospitals, and medical college hospitals; these are administered and maintained by state governments under directors of medical services. In addition, there are municipal hospitals (mostly maternity centers). There are a total of 2,256 such urban hospitals with a combined bed capacity of 292,813 beds.[10] Combining urban and rural bed capacity in the government sector, an estimated 2,336 population is served per bed in allopathic medicine facilities in the government sector.

There are 22,550 clinics of Indian systems of medicine and homeopathy, both government and private

(mostly Ayurveda and homeopathy clinics, some Unani clinics based on Arabic-medicine rooted system, and Sidha [south Indian indigenous system] clinics). There are also 24,880 beds in 1,110 hospitals of Indian systems of medicine and homeopathy, of which 450 are medical college hospitals.[28] Apart from these professionally staffed institutions, herbal medicines and preventive practices are widely used in rural and semiurban areas, partly as an integral part of lifestyle and partly through informal consulting with local (mostly Brahmin) scholars of traditional texts.

TABLE 13-3 Primary Health Care and Secondary/Tertiary Health Infrastructure

Institutional Type	Number
Allopathic medicine/public health (government/public)[10]	
Rural primary health centers	23,109 (2004: 1/33,840 population)
Rural subcenters	142,655 (2004: 1/5,480 population)
Community health centers (inpatient and surgery)	3,080
Other rural hospitals	884
CHCs in urban locations	433
Other urban hospitals (including tertiary-care centers)	2,256
Total publicly funded rural hospital bed capacity	111,872 beds (1 bed/7,000 population)*
Total publicly funded urban hospital bed capacity	292,813 beds
Total government-funded bed capacity open to public	469,672 beds (1 bed/2,336 population in 2005)
Indian systems of medicine and homeopathy (government)[10]	
Outpatient clinics and onsite basic clinics	22,550 (2004)
Hospitals	1,110 (including 450 medical college hospitals)
Hospital beds	24,880 (at 450 medical college hospitals)
Closed-panel government-owned facilities for insured populations[29]	
Employees state insurance (for industrial workers/families)	
Covered beneficiaries	32.97 million (including family members)
Outpatient clinics and onsite basic clinics	1,427 (2005)
Hospitals	144
Hospital beds	23,760 (1 bed/1,388 covered persons)
Central Government Employees Insurance[32]	
Covered beneficiaries	4.28 million (including family members)

(continues)

TABLE 13-3   Primary Health Care and Secondary/Tertiary Health Infrastructure (continued)

Institutional Type	Number
Outpatient clinics and onsite basic clinics	432
Inpatient care (purchased from government and private hospitals)	As required (statistics not available)
Medical facilities for workers of hazardous (privately owned) industries (mica, iron ore, limestone, etc.)[32]	
Covered beneficiaries	No information
Outpatient clinics and onsite first aid clinics	275
Hospital beds	525
Indian Railways Health Service[32]	
Covered beneficiaries	5.58 million (including family members)
Outpatient clinics and onsite basic clinics	661
Hospital beds	13,504 (1 bed/413 covered lives)
Private closed panel (in-house) /contracted health care: public sector industries/undertakings[32]	
Employees (central, state, local government owned)	18.1 million
Covered beneficiaries	72 million (approximate estimate)
Outpatient clinics/hospitals/beds	No information
Closed-panel (in-house) facilities: private sector large industries	
Employees	1.034 million (computed from Central Bureau of Health Intelligence)[8]
Covered beneficiaries	4.13 beneficiaries (estimated)
Outpatient clinics and onsite basic clinics	No information
Hospitals/beds	No information
In-house facilities: armed forces personnel	
Covered beneficiaries	4.4 million (estimated from 1.1 million personnel)[9]
Outpatient clinics/hospitals/beds	No information
Private sector facilities open to public*	
Hospitals	3327
Beds	265,137(1/3,536 population)
Total bed capacity open to public (government and private)	734,809 (0.7 bed/1,000 uninsured population)

* Estimated based on Rafei (2001)[29]: Applying the figures of 1993: 66% of total hospitals and 35% of total bed capacity in the private sector.

The author computed using data from various sources, as indicated.

In addition to a publicly accessible health infrastructure, there is a large network of closed panels of hospitals and outpatient clinics for employees and their dependents in most of the formal sector of the economy. Eligible dependents include all individuals residing in an extended family household. The major covered populations within closed-panel provider networks are central government employees, armed forces, Indian Railway employees, small industries with more than 25 workers, hazardous small industries such as privately owned mines, and large industries, both public and private.

Table 13-3 also shows the availability of health facilities under health insurance or other closed-panel schemes for such defined population groups. As shown, central government employees are covered by the Central Government Health Scheme, a combination of a closed panel of outpatient clinics and purchased inpatient care from approved public and private hospitals.[10] The health system for armed forces and defense employees is also a closed system with primary, secondary, and tertiary care fully provided within the Ministry of Defense health facilities. The tripartite, mandatory Employee State Insurance Scheme, funded by the state governments, employers, and nominal employee contributions, provides comprehensive health care to employees of all private industries employing between 25 and 1,000 employees. This is also a closed system with outpatient clinics and secondary-level hospital beds with all basic specialties. They are located in major small-scale industry hubs in all states. Tertiary care is purchased from other public or private hospitals.

The Indian Railways has its own in-house network of clinics and hospitals throughout the country; it is limited to railway employees and their dependents, and for vicitims of railway accidents. Another closed-panel system covers employees of hazardous, privately owned, small industries (mainly mining); it provides outpatient care close to the mining/residential sites. Overall, approximately 55 million beneficiaries are covered with comprehensive, in-house (or purchased inpatient) services as shown in Table 13-3. Because these are unionized or otherwise assertive groups, the quality and comprehensiveness of care is quite substantial, far above the public access government facilities. There is also a large network of in-house comprehensive healthcare facilities that are mandated for any large manufacturing or mining industry with more than 1,000 employees, public or private. Based on employee numbers, large industries have to comply with regulations regarding in-house outpatient and inpatient facilities. Industries that do not opt to own facilities have to provide comprehensive healthcare coverage under a social insurance plan. Information is not available on the total beneficiaries and medical facilities for this segment of the covered population.

Table 13-3 shows that about 125 million people (a little over 10%) are covered with comprehensive care by such closed-panel systems. Because most of this population is unionized and assertive, these groups receive quite comprehensive secondary and tertiary care of a high quality, mostly free of cost at the point of service.

Medical Care Facilities in the Private Sector

Recent information on hospitals and beds in the private sector is not available. Applying the 1993 level of 66% of total hospitals and 35% of total bed capacity being in the private sector,[29] an estimated 3,327 hospitals and 265,137 beds are available.

Facilities for Older Persons

There are few institutional facilities specifically established for the care of older persons, and little information is available. It is the cultural norm that children or other relatives take care of parents until their death. Regardless of medical conditions, older persons live with their children or relatives, getting sporadic medical care.[30] For the indigent older population, there are social security funding provisions to support nongovernment organizations (NGOs) managing group homes. Recent legislation requires children to take care of older parents or face prosecution.

Workforce

Table 13-4 presents the availability of medical, paramedical, and nursing personnel, as well as rural health workers.[5,10,32] Fashioned after Britain's medical education system, physicians are trained at the first level to be general family medicine doctors through a 4.5-year academic program, followed by 1 year of clinical internship, rotations through the basic specialties in hospitals, and 3 months of rural primary care facility postings. After internship, Indian doctors are awarded a bachelor's degree in medicine and surgery and are licensed by the Indian Medical Council to practice independently as a doctor of medicine. For specialty training, there are 3-year postgraduate programs (residency and additional academic preparation), leading to an MD (medical specialties) or MS (surgical specialties) degree.

TABLE 13-4 Health Workforce Statistics

Category	Number
Doctors of allopathic medicine (2004)	645,825 (0.60/1,000)[5]
Nurses—RN/BSN (2004)	865,135 (0.80/1,000)[5]
Auxiliary nurse midwives (public health) (2004)	506,924 (0.47/1,000)[5]
General nursing midwives (hospital trained) (2003)	839,862 (0.78/1,000)[32]
Health worker/nurse-midwife supervisors (2005)	40,536[10]
Dentists (2004)	61,424 (0.06/1,000)[5]
Pharmacists (2004)	592,577[5]
Doctors of Indian Systems of Medicine* (2003)	500,400 (0.46/1,000)[30]
Doctors of Homeopathy* (2003)	217,460 (0.20/1,000)[30]

* Graduated from recognized Indian systems of medicine and homeopathy medical colleges.

Dentists undergo a 4-year program of study plus 6 months of internship to earn the Bachelor of Dental Surgery degree. The master's program in dental surgery consists of advanced training in specialized fields for an additional 2 years. Nurses can be either registered nurses (RN) or bachelor's degree holders. RNs undergo a 3.5-year program of study, including practice internships in hospitals. Nurses who earn a bachelor's degree get 4 years of training, including a clinical internship. There are masters- and doctoral-level trained individuals for academic nursing positions. Male and female health workers (the latter trained as auxiliary nurse-midwives) are trained at Rural Health and Family Welfare Training Centers located in each state. Female health workers are trained as auxiliary public health nurses/midwives. Allopathic medical, dental, nursing, and Indian Systems of Medicine teaching institutions are regulated and accredited by national councils (Medical Council, Dental Council, and Nursing Council, Central Council of Indian Medicine).

Source: The author created from various sources, as indicated.

NGOs in Health Care

There are over 10,000 NGOs working in health promotion or medical care activities in India, with most organizations pursuing health as part of a larger community-based development project in rural and tribal areas, as well as urban slums. These include the church-associated organizations (3,226 member institutions of the Catholic Health Association of India in 2008,[33] 330 member institutions of the Christian Medical Association of India[34]) and approximately 4,500 members of the secular Voluntary Health Association of India,[35] besides countless others that are not members of associations. Many church-associated hospitals are self-financed through fees and hospital charges. Most community health and development NGOs are funded by foreign aid agencies, collectively estimated to account for 0.5% of total health expenditures.[5] These NGOs have significantly impacted the most disadvantaged communities, providing health education and facilitating improved nutrition, income, water sanitation, liaison for underserved populations accessing government health care institutions, and community development. Recog-

nizing NGOs' contributions to health, India's National Health Policy—2002 calls for a 10% allocation of public health program funds for NGO involvement.[8]

Technology and Equipment

Given the overwhelming preponderance of communicable diseases, maternal and child health problems, and other primary healthcare issues since independence, successive governments have heavily focused on primary care infrastructure and personnel. With significant increases in sedentary life styles, consumption of fat with increasing prosperity, and increasing life expectancy, cardiovascular disease and cancer incidence is increasing, causing increased demand for tertiary-care services using advanced technology. Although statistics are available on hospital bed capacity, there are no data on healthcare technology. At a generic level, it can be stated that most of the population's high-tech care needs are served largely by the private sector and industrial hospitals, both public and private sector industry hospitals. The premier central government medical institutions and government medical college hospitals also have considerably advanced technology, providing "free" care to the poor and lower-middle-classes.

EVALUATION OF THE HEALTHCARE SYSTEM

Cost

Based on National Health Accounts, the estimated total per capita expenditure on health (public and private spending combined) is $91 in international dollars (PPP), or 5% of GDP, slightly higher than the World Health Organization South East Asia Region average of 4% and far lower than the global average of 8.7%.[5] Public health expenditure (all government) amounts to 0.9% of GDP, and personal health care is 4.1%.[36] India's government spending of preventive and promotive services (0.9% of GDP and 20% of total government health expenditure) is lower than neighboring countries with a similar socioeconomic status, such as China and Sri Lanka; they each spend two thirds of their public expenditures on public health services.[29] Their population health indicators mirror these differences.

Government expenditure on health amounts to 2.9% of total government expenditures[5] (central and states, with the states accounting for 80% of government expenditures[29]). Out of the total health expenditure, 17.3% is spent from government funds (central and states) and 82.7% from private and out-of-pocket sources. Of the total private expenditure on health (all spent on personal healthcare services), 93.8% is out of pocket,[5] and the rest, approximately 6%, is funded by social health insurance for employees and dependents in the formal sector of the economy.[32]

The distribution of out-of-pocket expenditures is extremely regressive. Most of the middle class, particularly those employed by private sector industry, spend a negligible proportion out of pocket because of comprehensive coverage, including prescription drugs, under various social insurance plans fully funded by their employer/government combination. The personal healthcare service share of the large section of the population employed in the informal sector of the economy (including agriculture and petty entrepreneurial occupations) is covered from two sources: approximately 0.2% of GDP spent by the government on curative services at government hospitals and PHCs (17.3% of total 5% of GDP spent on health, less public health expenditure),[29,32] supplemented by out-of-pocket payments either at private or government facilities (in-

formal payments). Despite considerable government healthcare infrastructure, particularly in rural areas, informal payments for care often required by clinical providers and paramedical staff equalize people's out-of-pocket expenditures in public and private facilities.[32] Health expenditure is the leading cause of family debt among the poor.[34] Both the rural population and urban poor face significant risk of overwhelming debt from any surgical or major medical event. Financial barriers to care are major drivers of the wide gap between life expectancy at birth (62 and 64 years for men and women) and Healthy Life Expectancy at Birth, HALE (53 and 54 years, respectively).[5] External resources (foreign aid, including charities) account for 0.5% of total health expenditures (included in the private sector numbers).[5]

There is much disparity in health services across states, rural/urban residence, and socioeconomic status. Of total government expenditure, approximately 33% is spent on public health programs (immunization, antenatal, maternal and postnatal care, contraceptives and other family-planning measures, community-based services such as spraying for malaria, and health education). Of the two thirds spent on curative care, 75% is spent on secondary and tertiary hospitals, primarily located in urban areas.[29] Thus, a tiny fraction of publicly funded curative services is available in rural areas, requiring most rural residents to travel to nearby towns for health care.

In absolute terms, the cost of medical care is very modest compared to other countries. This is because of the low average income of most of the population and provision of services by salaried physicians in government institutions or system-owned institutions for the insured population, with no incentives to induce demand. No data are available on quality indicators; however, the health indicators, including morbidity and mortality statistics, suggest that the technical quality of care may be good, although responsiveness and interpersonal aspects are very inadequate, particularly for poor and disadvantaged populations.

Quality

Population Health Outcomes, Utilization, and Disparities

Reflecting the regressive nature of health financing that disproportionately challenges poor and rural populations, rural–urban public health indicators show significant disparities.[5] The under-5 mortality rate (probability of dying before the fifth birthday) is 111.4 per 1,000 live births in rural areas compared with 65.4 in urban areas, a ratio of 1:7. By wealth quintile, the ratio is 3:1, and by educational level of the mother (no education to high school or more), it is 2.5. When under-5 child stunting for age (height deficiency) is considered, these ratios are 1:4 (48.5% and 35.7%, respectively), 2:2, and 1:8, respectively. For births attended by skilled health personnel (doctor or nurse, including nurse midwife), the ratios are 2:2 (33.5% and 73.3%), 5:1, and 3:1, respectively. For measles immunization coverage, the ratios are 1:5 (45.3% and 69.2%), 2:9, and 2:2, respectively.[5] These disparities are consistent with disparities in infrastructure/personnel, regressive health expenditure burden, and access to personal healthcare services.

Annual morbidity estimates show a little less than two episodes of illness per year, being higher in rural populations and females in the reproductive age group.[29] Of those reporting illness, approximately 10% did not seek treatment (higher proportion for rural populations, females, older persons, and never married individuals). Treatment was mostly outpatient care (93%), largely at private clinics, and inpatient care (7%), mostly at public hospitals. There is also disproportionately higher use of public facilities for catastrophic and serious illnesses such as tuberculosis, complicated pregnancy and childbirth, injury, and sexually transmitted diseases. People in hilly and economically backward areas, the dalit, castes, and tribals, rely almost fully on public facilities. Surveys show that the morbidity rate increases with increased health or development level, showing higher morbidity in the most wealthy state of Punjab, and demographically most advanced state of Kerala, compared with poorer or demographically less advanced states.[29]

Access

Apart from the dedicated health facilities (funded by employers) accessible to those employed in the formal sector and a large network of private facilities, there is a nominally large network of government healthcare facilities, funded by tax revenues. Because health care is a state subject, the infrastructure funded by the central government through revenues from income taxes and excise duties suffers considerable financial difficulties after the built facilities are turned over to the state governments for maintenance. Finances of these institutions are meager, barely meeting the mandatory salary expenditures, with little to meet equipment and recurring expenditures on drugs and consumables. No state levies state income taxes because of electoral considerations. All states depend on sales and value-added taxes (low or uncertain because much trade is informal and undocumented), as well as devolved taxes from central income and excise taxes (uncertain volume due to political and exigent situations); therefore, state health facilities tend to be chronically underfunded and have decrepit equipment, and consumables and drugs are woefully inadequate. The public, mostly the poor and underserved who access care from government hospitals, has to purchase many items of care and drugs out of pocket,[36] in addition to informal payments.[32]

Government curative services are weighted in favor of the nonpoor, with the ratio of care accessed by the poor versus the richest quintile, being 1:4.[36] Hospitalized Indians spend, on average, 58% of their total annual income, and over 40% of them borrow heavily or sell assets to cover hospital expenses. Twenty-five percent fall into poverty.[36]

In the wake of the recent economic boom, several innovations have been initiated, funded by buoyant tax revenues, to address the most refractory problems affecting the rural, poor, women, and children. The National Rural Health Mission launched in 2005[36] took a significant change of direction from earlier initiatives in allocating public moneys for services provided by private facilities to rural and poor families for maternal and child health care. Services include transportation, facilitation services by trained female volunteers in each village, and outpatient/inpatient care. It has initiated training (in a phased manner) of community-based female volunteers (Accredited Social Health Activists, ASHA, meaning hope) in each village, who are compensated based on units of services delivered to promote and facilitate maternal and child healthcare utilization at public or private facilities, which are reimbursed by the district health officers. It also recognizes and mainstreams effective local health traditions. Several state governments are underwriting comprehensive maternal and child health care for the rural and urban poor, reimbursing the private sector on a fee-for-service or DRG basis (Gujarat).

For the approximately 150 million covered population (125 million beneficiary populations shown in Table 13-3, plus state and local government employees), allocations are made from their employers' budgets, together with payroll deductions to finance care. Providers in these systems are either owned or fully funded by the insurance/industry/government. In the event of purchase of services, reimbursement is by a combination of DRG-type capped rates by procedure and retrospective fee-for-service reimbursement for nonsurgical care and tertiary-care services.

CURRENT AND EMERGING CHALLENGES AND OPPORTUNITIES

Despite significant proactive involvement of the central and state governments in health development since independence, prominent challenges remain. These are as follows: (1) Onsite availability of physicians and support personnel at PHCs and of specialists at CHCs has been consistently a challenge. (2) Informal payments, almost the norm at government facilities and parallel private practice by government doctors, have kept effective care out of reach of many poor and rural people. (3) Water and sanitation infrastructure remains a major issue that directly and indirectly impacts women and children's health. (4) The looming problems of noncommunicable diseases are barely addressed for the majority of informally employed population. (5) Innovative initiatives by the central and state governments have much potential to impact maternal and child health as well as fertility, but their impact will be moderated if bureaucracy and abuse dominate the process. (6) Booming tax collections from a rapidly growing economy have fueled innovations thus far, but in the event of an economic slowdown, the fragile reform process is likely to stall, especially because incentivizing care access is a major bulwark of recent reforms.

Opportunities

Some opportunities are noted: (1) Recent government initiatives to facilitate care access through paid local activists and to underwrite care provided by private facilities should substantially change the situation in the coming years, addressing major bottlenecks that plague rural and poor people who depended on "free" care at government health facilities; (2) recognizing the significant contribution of the NGOs, the National Health Policy 2002 document directs disease control programs to allocate at least 10% of funds for implementation of suitable aspects through the NGO sector[8] and advocates for the first time handing over public health service outlets to respected NGOs along with funds earmarked for such institutions for better management and service delivery;[8] (3) an enormous, nationwide surge of interest and practice of yoga, Ayurveda, Sidha, and other local systems, and healthful traditions/local herbal use that has much potential to reduce morbidity and extend healthy life expectancy, both in rural and urban areas, aided by massive penetration of television, internet and mobile phones in recent years; (4) there is a large stock of subspecialty beds and high-tech care services in the

private sector, providing state-of-the-art care of high quality at a fraction of the prevailing cost in the west, and the National Health Policy–2002[8] explicitly provides for fiscal incentives and the status of deemed exports (as with other exports) for providers of medical services to overseas patients; (5) the instantaneous communication now possible because of cheap Internet and mobile phones has shrunk distances and dramatically increased public officials and physicians' responsiveness to individual and public health crisis situations, and therefore, responses tend to be more timely, before severe consequences, including death, supervene; (6) a critical mass of public awareness and assertiveness has been created by decades of developmental and health activism by tens of thousands of local NGOs, and this has perhaps stimulated some of the recent innovations by government and created fertile conditions for the innovations to be effectively used by the target populations; (7) the massive upsurge in demand for education in rural areas bodes well for improved health conditions; (8) the National Rural Health Mission, launched in 2005, represents a major break from past preoccupation with supply-side interventions (mainly expanding government infrastructure and personnel postings) to a demand-side set of interventions and provides financial teeth to rural populations to access health care regardless of private or public provider, with compensated village facilitators (ASHA), to ensure that the most disadvantaged are not left behind; and (9) for the first time, mainstream Indian systems of medicine (Ayurveda, Yoga, Unani, Sidha, and Homeopathy, acronym AYUSH) are providing AYUSH medicine kits to health workers and encouraging use of AYUSH-trained medical doctors.[36]

The health status and challenges are daunting; however, many developments that have lately matured after a prolonged dormancy for decades represent an unfathomable break from traditional conceptualizations of health development in the developed countries. The current Western paradigm of illness and medical care calls for multiplicative increases in health infrastructure and investments to meet the population's healthcare needs. This predicts a gloomy outlook for India, considering the billion-plus population to be "provided" for; however, unforeseen and little studied, grassroots phenomena have the potential to generate an unprecedented dynamic of population health development without traditional healthcare investments. These include the rising popularity of health and medicine practices rooted in self-driven health behaviors and low-cost indigenous sciences (yoga, meditation, ayurveda, etc.), rise of volunteerism through NGOs, and other developments. Although the dynamic of profit- and illness-driven modern medicine flowing from specialists and pharmaceuticals/bioengineering will continue to provide value for many illnesses, its magnitude is likely to be significantly toned down by these new developments, whose implications are yet unfolding. Time will tell whether India's health culture will blend with the globally surging pill-popping culture, engaging in an endless struggle to keep up with the never-satiable demand/need for medical care or whether it will evolve a self-help, locally determined health-enhancing route to trim the need for care at source.

REFERENCES

1. Government of India. *Know India*. Population Commission, New Delhi, 2008. Retrieved March 2, 2008, from http://populationcommission.nic.in/.

2. Lakshmikantham V. *The Origin of Human Past*. Mumbai, India: Bharatiya Vidya Bhavan Press; 1988.

3. Government of India. 2008. *Know India: Profile*. Retrieved February 2008 from http://www.india.gov.in/knowindia/profile.php.

4. Government of India, Central Statistical Organization, 2008. Summary Data Real Sector 2007. Updated March 12, 2008. Ministry of Statistics and Program Implementation. Retrieved March 13, 2008, from http://mospi.gov.in/sdrsum.htm.

5. World Health Organization. *World Health Statistics 2007*. Geneva, Switzerland.

6. U.S. Department of State. Background Note: India. Bureau of South and Central Asian Affairs, 2007. Retrieved February 17, 2008, from http://www.state.gov/r/pa/ei/bgn/3454.htm.

7. Government of the United States of America, Central Intelligence Agency, 2008. The World Factbook. Retrieved March 2, 2008, from https://www.cia.gov/library/publications/the-world-factbook/geos/in.html#Econ.

8. Government of India, Ministry of Health and Family Welfare, 2002. National Health Policy 2002. Retrieved March 3, 2008, from http://mohfw.nic.in.

9. International Institute for Population Sciences and Macro International. National Family Health Survey—3, 2005–06: India: Volume I. Mumbai: IIPS, 2007. Retrieved February 19, 2008, from http://www.nfhsindia.or g/volume_1.html.

10. Government of India, Central Bureau of Health Intelligence. Health Information of India 2005. New Delhi, 2006. Retrieved February 15, 2008, from http://www.cbhidghs.nic.in/hia2005/content.asp and http://www.cbhidghs.nic.in/hia2005/9.01.htm.

11. Government of India, Ministry of Finance. Union Budget and Economic Survey 2007–08. Retrieved March 5, 2008, from http://indiabudget.nic.in/.

12. Government of India, Planning Commission. Mid term appraisal of water resources in the 10th Five Year Plan. Retrieved February 18, 2008, from http://www.india.gov.in/outerwin.htm?id=http://planningcommission.nic.in/midterm/english-pdf/chapter-06.pdf.

13. Government of India, Department of Road Transport and Highways, 2007. Annual Report 2005-06. Retrieved March 3, 2008, from http://morth.nic.in/writereaddata/sublinkimages/chapter12109984519.pdf.

14. Government of India, Ministry of Railways, Annual Report and Accounts 2006–07. Retrieved March 1, 2008, from http://www.indianrailways.gov.in/deptts/stat-eco/annualrep-0607/passenger-business.pdf.

15. Government of India, Department of Shipping, 2007. Annual Report 2005–06. Retrieved March 2, 2008, from http://shipping.gov.in/writereaddata/linkimages/Part15736133545.pdf.

16. National Council of Applied Economic Research. 2008. Annual Report 2006–07. Retrieved February 15, 2008, from http://www.ncaer.org/annualreport.html.

17. Park K. *Textbook of Preventive and Social Medicine*. Jabalpur, India: Banarasidas Bhanot Publishers; 2007, pp. 747–748.

18. Government of India, Ministry of Health and Family Welfare. Bulletin on Rural Health Statistics in India, 2007. Retrieved March 2, 2008, from http://mohfw.nic.in/Bulletin%20on%20RHS%20-%20March,%202007%20-%20PDF%20Version/Title%20Page.htm.

19. Government of India, Planning Commission. Towards Faster and More Inclusive Growth: An Approach to the 11th Five Year Plan, 2006. Retrieved March 13, 2008, from http://planningcommission.gov.in/plans/planrel/app11_16jan.pdf.

20. Government of India. *Report of the Health Survey and Development Committee*. Simla, India: Government of India Press; 1946.

21. Registrar General of India. *Sample Registration System, Statistical Report 2004*. New Delhi, India: Registrar General of India; 2005.

22. Registrar General of India. *Medical Certification of Causes of Death 1998*. New Delhi, India.

23. Omran AA. The epidemiological transition: a theory of epidemiology of population change. *Milbank Memorial Fund Quarterly*. 1971;49:509–538.

24. Government of India, Ministry of Health and Family Welfare, 2007. National Program for Prevention and Control of Diabetes, Cardiovascular Diseases and Stroke. Retrieved March 2, 2008, from http://www.mohfw.nic.in/for%20websitediabetes.htm.

25. Chari PS. Susruta and our heritage. *Indian J Plast Surg*. 2003;36:4–13.

26. World Health Organization. 1978. Health For All by 2000. Retrieved March 11, 2008, from http://www.euro.who.int/AboutWHO/Policy/20010827_1.

27. Government of India, Central Bureau of Health Intelligence. Health Information of India 2005. New Delhi, 2006. Retrieved February 15, 2008, from http://www.cbhidghs.nic.in/hia2005/8.01.htm.

28. Government of India, Central Bureau of Health Intelligence. Health Information of India 2005. New Delhi, 2006.

Retrieved February 15, 2008, from http://www.cbhidghs.nic .in/hia2005/15.01.htm.

29. Rafei UM, Sein UT. Role of private hospitals in healthcare. *Regional Health Forum.* 2001;5(1). Retrieved February 28, 2008, from http://www.searo.who.int/EN/Section1243/ Section1310/Section1343/Section1344/Section1352_5254 .htm.

30. Gumber A. Structure of the Indian Health Care Market: Implications for the Health Insurance Sector. *Regional Health Forum.* 2000;4(3). Retrieved February 28, 2008, from www.searo.who.int/EN/Section1243/Section1310/ Section1343/Section1344/Section1352_5254.htm.

31. Government of India. Ministry of Labor, Labor Bureau. New Delhi, 2007. *Pocket Book of Statistics 2006.* Retrieved March 1, 2008, from http://www.labourbureau.nic.in/ PBS2K6%20Contents.htm.

32. Government of India. *Health Information of India 2004.* Central Bureau of Health Intelligence. New Delhi, 2005. Retrieved February 12, 2008, from http://www.cbhidghs.nic .in/HII2004/chap7.asp.

33. Catholic Health Association of India. Retrieved March 11, 2008, from http://www.chai-india.org.

34. Christian Medical Association of India. Retrieved February 11, 2008, from http://www.cmai.org/index.html.

35. Voluntary Health Association of India. Retrieved February 21, 2008, from http://www.vhai.org/htm/index.asp.

36. Government of India. *National Rural Health Mission.* Ministry of Health and Family Welfare. New Delhi, 2005. Retrieved March 4, 2008, from http://www.mohfw.nic.in/ NRHM.

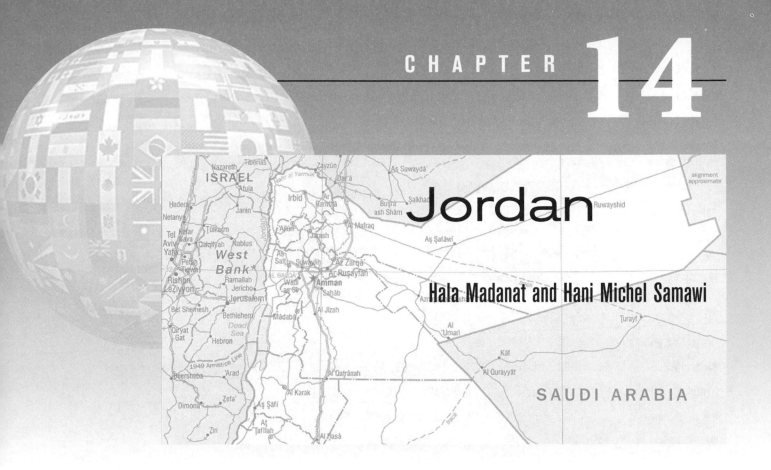

CHAPTER 14

Jordan

Hala Madanat and Hani Michel Samawi

COUNTRY DESCRIPTION

TABLE 14-1 Jordan

Nationality	Noun: Jordanian(s) Adjective: Jordanian
Ethnic groups	Arab 98%, Circassian 1%, Armenian 1%
Religions	Sunni Muslim 92%, Christian 6% (majority Greek Orthodox, but some Greek and Roman Catholics, Syrian Orthodox, Coptic Orthodox, Armenian Orthodox, and Protestant denominations), other 2% (several small Shi'a Muslim and Druze populations) (2001 est.)
Language	Arabic (official), English widely understood among upper and middle classes
Literacy	Definition: age 15 and over can read and write Total population: 89.9% Male: 95.1% Female: 84.7% (2003 est.)
Government type	Constitutional monarchy
Date of independence	May 25, 1946 (from League of Nations mandate under British administration)
Gross Domestic Product (GDP) per capita	$4,700 (2007 est.)

(continues)

TABLE 14-1   Jordan   (continued)

Unemployment rate	13.5% official rate; unofficial rate is approximately 30% (2007 est.)
Natural hazards	Droughts; periodic earthquakes
Environment: current issues	Limited natural fresh water resources; deforestation; overgrazing; soil erosion; desertification
Population	6,198,677 (July 2008 est.)
Age structure	0–14 years: 32.2% (male 1,017,233/female 976,284) 15–64 years: 63.7% (male 2,110,293/female 1,840,531) 65 years and over: 4.1% (male 122,975/female 131,361) (2008 est.)
Median age	Total: 23.9 years Male: 24.6 years Female: 23.2 years (2008 est.)
Population growth rate	2.338% (2008 est.)
Birth rate	20.13 births/1,000 population (2008 est.)
Death rate	2.72 deaths/1,000 population (2008 est.)
Net migration rate	5.97 migrant(s)/1,000 population (2008 est.)
Gender ratio	At birth: 1.06 male(s)/female Under 15 years: 1.04 male(s)/female 15–64 years: 1.15 male(s)/female 65 years and over: 0.94 male(s)/female Total population: 1.1 male(s)/female (2008 est.)
Infant mortality rate	Total: 15.57 deaths/1,000 live births Male: 18.62 deaths/1,000 live births Female: 12.34 deaths/1,000 live births (2008 est.)
Life expectancy at birth	Total population: 78.71 years Male: 76.19 years Female: 81.39 years (2008 est.)
Total fertility rate	2.47 children born/woman (2008 est.)
HIV/AIDS adult prevalence rate	Less than 0.1% (2001 est.)
Number of people living with HIV/AIDS	600 (2003 est.)
HIV/AIDS deaths	Less than 500 (2003 est.)

Central Intelligence Agency. The World Fact Book, 2008. Retrieved November 18, 2008, from https://www.cia.gov/library/publications/the-world-factbook.

History

Jordan is a small Arab country that has limited natural resources. Its history, during and after World War I, is most relevant to understanding the current state of its healthcare system; however, historically, the land, known today as Jordan, was where major highways connecting the Middle East met and crossed.[1] Thus, its location has always been of great strategic importance to trade and communications.[1]

Since the mid-7th century, Jordan has been under the control of various Arab and Islamic dynasties, the last of these being the four centuries of Ottoman rule (1516–1918).[2] The Ottoman rule was generally seen as a period of limited development and much oppression. As World War I broke, the Ottoman Empire sided with the Germans and the Arabs saw a chance for liberation of their land. Sharif Hussein, great grandfather of King Hussein (the third king of Jordan) and head of the Arab Nationalist, negotiated with the British, who promised support for a unified Arab Kingdom. Consequently, he initiated the Great Arab Revolt against the Ottoman rule; however, when the war ended, Britain and France denied Arabs their unified kingdom and had already divided the land into mandates and protectorates. The land of Jordan was now a British mandate, with Sharif Hussein's son Emir Abdullah being proclaimed ruler in 1921. That same year, he established the first centralized governmental system in Amman (the capital of Jordan).[1,2]

The years that followed were all spent establishing modern Jordan and achieving independence. In 1928, a constitution was developed that provided for a parliament; it was known as the Legislative Council, and elections were held in February 1929. In 1946, Jordan received its full independence from the British and was now known as the Hashemite Kingdom of Jordan, with King Abdullah named as the first king of the country. On the other side of the Jordan River, however, Palestine, which had been a British mandate but had been promised in the 1917 Balfour declaration as a Jewish homeland, became the state of Israel in 1948 as the British left it. This led to the first Arab-Israeli war, and over half a million displaced Palestinian refugees came to Jordan and were granted citizenship. The remainder of the Palestinian territories that were not under Israeli rule became part of the Kingdom of Jordan.[2]

In 1951, King Abdullah was assassinated in Jerusalem, and his eldest son, Crown Prince Talal, assumed the throne. King Talal abdicated the throne because of health reasons in 1952; however, during his short reign, King Talal was able to develop a new modern constitu-

tion that is still being used today. According to this constitution, King Talal's eldest son could not assume his duties as king until he had reached the age of 18 under the Muslim calendar (16 years of age). Thus, a council performed his functions until May 2, 1953, when King Hussein became the third king of Jordan.[2]

The years that followed had much political upheaval, and in 1967, Jordan and other Arab countries lost to Israel the remainder of the Palestinian territories. This led to an increase in the Palestinian refugees in Jordan, which were now estimated at over 1 million. This was followed by increased power by the Palestinian resistance groups in Jordan (known as fedayeen), and in 1970, this led to open fire between the Jordanian armed forces and the Palestinian fighters, who were expelled from Jordan in 1971.[2]

The years that followed were of much importance politically and economically. In 1973, the Arab nations were involved in another war with Israel. In 1974, King Hussein issued a royal decree dissolving the parliament, and in 1978, he replaced it with the National Consultative Council (until 1984).[3] In 1989, elections were reinstated, and the country initiated political and economic reforms. The Gulf War of 1990–1991, however, saw the return of many Jordanians working in the Gulf. This significantly decreased the income from worker remittances and further increased the population.[2]

In 1999, King Hussein died of cancer, and his eldest son King Abdullah II assumed the throne and continued his father's major economic reforms; however, the U.S.-led war in Iraq in 2003 led to influx of 750,000 Iraqi refugees into Jordan, which further strained its economy.[4]

Size and Geography

Jordan has a coastline of 16 miles (26 km). The land area is 34,318 square miles (88,884 km^2), and the water area is 127 square miles (329 km^2). Jordan's total area is 34,445 square miles (89,213 km^2). The land forms in Jordan are generally a flat desert plateau, east and west. In the west, the Great Rift Valley (high hills and mountains) separates the East and West Banks of the Jordan River. Significant bordering bodies of water include the Dead Sea, the Gulf of Aqaba, and the Sea of Galilee. The highest Point Jabal Rum reaches 5,689 ft. (1,734 m), and the lowest point is the Dead Sea at −1,338.6 ft (−408 m) below sea level[5] (Figure 14-1).

Jordan is divided into 12 governorates, including Ajlun, Al 'Aqabah, Al Balqa', Al Karak, Al Mafraq, 'Amman, At Tafilah, Az Zarqa', Irbid, Jarash, Ma'an, and

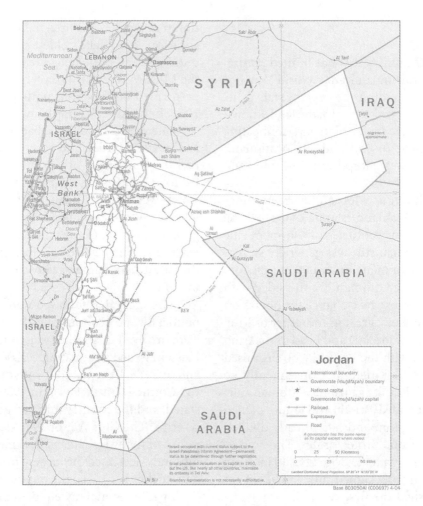

FIGURE 14-1   Map of the Hashemite Kingdom of Jordan

Madaba. Urbanization rates have increased drastically over the last 3 decades, and currently, 82.6% of the population lives in urban areas compared with 17.4% living in rural areas. More specifically, the population is concentrated in three main urban centers: Amman (38.8%), Zarqa (14.9%), and Irbid (17.8%).[6]

Government and Political System

According to its constitution, the Hashemite Kingdom of Jordan is "parliamentary with a hereditary monarchy."[7] The king is the head of state, the chief executive, and the commander-in-chief of the armed forces. The king exercises his executive authority by appointing the prime minister, who then organizes a cabinet of ministers that has to be approved by the king. The prime minister and the cabinet must then be approved by the Lower House of Parliament, the House of Deputies. If the House of Deputies votes against the prime minister,

he and his entire cabinet must resign. The Lower House can also vote any individual minister out of office. The king also appoints all of the members of the Upper House of Parliament, known as the House of Senate. The number of senators cannot exceed one half of the number of elected representatives.[7]

The cabinet is responsible before the elected House of Deputies, which along with the House of Senate constitutes the legislative branch of the government. The judicial branch, however, is an independent branch of the government.

The Constitution in Jordan specifically guarantees the rights of Jordanian citizens, including the freedoms of speech and press, association, academic freedom, organization into political parties, freedom of religion, and the right to elect parliamentary and municipal representatives.[7]

Moreover, in the Constitution, the king must approve laws before they can take effect, although his authority can be overridden by a two thirds majority vote of both houses of Parliament. He also authorizes the appointment and dismissal of judges, regional governors, and the mayor of Amman. He also approves constitutional amendments and declares war. As the commander-in-chief of the armed forces, the king ratifies treaties and agreements with the approval of the cabinet and parliament. The king is also entitled to grant special pardons and amnesties.[7]

Macroeconomics

Jordan's economical resources are based on phosphates, potash, and their fertilizer derivatives; tourism; overseas remittances; and foreign aids. These sources are its principal sources of hard currency earnings. Jordan lacks forests, coal reserves, hydroelectric power, or commercially viable oil deposits.

In the late 1980s, Jordan went through a major economic crisis. In 1988, the Jordanian dinar depreciated by 48.5%. Unemployment rates reached an unprecedented 20%, and inequality and poverty increased dramatically.[8] During the first Gulf War, Jordan dealt with major reductions in its foreign aid, especially from the United States. Its trade was also largely affected because of the restrictions imposed on export of its agricultural products to Iraq, the primary location for export of its goods, and the rest of the Gulf countries. The number of refugees and returning workers from Iraq and the Gulf region further exacerbated the problem, especially with the large number of Palestinian refugees already in the country.[8]

The 1989 economic reforms were mainly geared toward liberalization, privatization, and removal of all trade barriers. In 2000, Jordan became the 136th member of the World Trade Organization and signed a free-trade agreement with the United States that same year. Furthermore, the private sector has been working closely with the government on development issues, such as the opening of export markets and attracting foreign and private investors into the country with hope of increasing job opportunities for Jordanians and decreasing the unemployment rates.[9]

Economically, Jordan is considered a lower-middle-income country with a human development index of .773 and a Gini coefficient of .364.[10] Its per capita gross domestic product (GDP) increased from $4,300 in 2002 to $4,700 in 2007; however, there has been a decline in real per capita income, increase in poverty, and decline in living standards. It is estimated that 27% of families live under the poverty line. This is a significant increase from 19% in 1987 and 21% in 1992.[11]

In 2006, Jordan's total GDP was $14.2 billion, up from $12.7 billion in 2005. The estimated GDP growth rate was 6.4% in 2006 and 7.2% in 2005, and a growth of at least 5% is expected to continue until 2010. Moreover, in 2006, services (including finance, real estate, transport and communications, and government services) continued to dominate the economy, accounting for more than 65% of the GDP. Industry contributed about 31.7% of GDP (including manufacturing, 20% of GDP). Agriculture provided just 2.7% of GDP.[12]

Demographics

Jordan faces a unique situation in terms of its demographic transition. In 1980, the population was 2.2 million and doubled by 1999 and is expected to double again by 2035.[6] There are currently 5.6 million people in Jordan, with a median age of 20.3 years, reflecting a young population.[6] These demographic changes are due to the influx of refugees from surrounding countries, as well as the healthcare reforms that are associated with decreased infant mortality rate and continued high fertility rates. Infant mortality rates have dropped from 160 per 1,000 live births in 1950 to only about 24 per 1,000 live births in 2006.[6,8] Although fertility rates have declined from 7.8 in 1970 to about 3.7 in 2006, they still remain higher than surrounding countries. Life expectancy has also dramatically changed, increasing from 54 years in 1970 to 72 years today.

The age distribution of the population is as follows: 37.3% who are under the age of 15, 59.4% who are between the ages of 15 and 64, and only 3.3% who are 65 years of age or older. Approximately 48.5% of the population is female, and 51.5% is male. The literacy for those 15 years of age or older is 90.7%, with 53.1% of the population having less than secondary education, 28.2% with a secondary education, 8.0% with an intermediate diploma, and 10.7% of the population with at least a bachelor's degree.[6] The religious distribution is as follows: Sunni Muslim (92%), Christian (6%), and others (2%).[13]

BRIEF HISTORY OF THE HEALTHCARE SYSTEM

Pre-World War II

Jordan's healthcare system passed through two distinct phases. The first phase (1921–1946) was before Jordan was recognized as a kingdom. In 1921, Math'har Pasha Arsalan was recognized as the first health consultant to work in Jordan, and Dr. Rida Tawfiq was appointed as director of health. That same year, Jordan's first public hospital was established with 20 hospital beds. In 1923, Transjordan issued its first health law, which related to the practice of hospital medicine and was issued by the advisory council of the time. In 1924, the Italian Hospital in the city of Salt was approved by Prince Abdullah, and the city of Jerusalem established its first medical laboratory (the first laboratory to open in Amman was not until 1940). The following year, the first pharmacy opened in Transjordan, and Dr. Haleem Abu Rahmeh established the first health department, where he continued to work until 1939.[14] The first regulatory health law was decreed in Transjordan in the year 1926 and was used until 1971. About 28 male and female physicians were working in Transjordan by the year 1926, and the number increased to 39 by the end of the following year. That same year, the number of beds reached 60 in public hospitals and 99 in private hospitals.[14] By 1946, there were seven hospitals in the capital city of Amman.

Since World War II

The second phase started in 1948 until present. During this phase, the Arab-Israeli wars occurred, which added more burdens on the healthcare system because of the large influx of Palestinian refugees.[14] In 1950, however, the first ministry of health (MOH) was established and started its functions in 1951, followed by establishment of the physician union in 1954, and the central laboratory for medical tests was established in 1955.

Starting with opening of the first nursing school in 1953, health-related educational programs increased. In 1962, the Princess Mona nursing college opened, followed by the first medical school at the University of Jordan in 1970, the institute of allied health professions in Amman in 1973 and in Irbid in 1978, and the first college of pharmacy in 1980.

The first health insurance system implemented was in 1963 for armed forces personnel, and the first public health insurance system for civilians was implemented in 1965. The King Hussein Medical Center was inaugurated in 1973 and is currently the largest referral and teaching hospital in Jordan and a part of the Royal Medical Services (RMS).

DESCRIPTION OF THE CURRENT HEALTHCARE SYSTEM

Jordan is considered as having one of the most modernized healthcare infrastructures in the region.[15] The healthcare system is also more complex, as it is made of three sectors: public, private, and donors. The public sector is further divided into four groups: the MOH (see Figure 14-2 for an organizational chart of the MOH), the RMS, the smaller university-based programs, the largest of which are the Jordan University Hospital (JUH) in Amman and the King Abdullah University Hospital (KAUH) in Irbid, and medical services linked to the ministries and public institutions.[16]

The MOH is considered the "single institution financer and provider of health care services in Jordan" and is the largest component of the healthcare delivery system compared with all other parts of the public and private sectors.[15] On the other hand, the RMS services are extended to all military and security personnel, as well as all uninsured patients referred from the MOH and the private sector.[15]

The private sector includes private hospitals, private clinics, and privately owned diagnostic facilities and allied health services.[16] A SWOT analysis (strengths, weaknesses, opportunities, and threats) of the private sector in Jordan reveals a need for better collaboration between the public and private sectors, as well as better regulation of its services.[15]

The donor sector includes services provided by the United Nations Relief and Works Agency for Palestine Refugees in the Near East (UNRWA) and other clinics and medical services provided by foreign nongovernmental agencies (NGOs).[16]

Facilities

As of 2006, there were 101 hospitals in Jordan, up from 95 in 2002, with 11,049 hospital beds, of which 38.3% were in MOH hospitals, 19.2% in RMS hospitals, 8.9% in the two university-based hospitals, and 33.6% in private hospitals. Thus, there were 1.7 hospitals beds per 10,000 in the population. In addition to its hospitals, the MOH operates 58 comprehensive health centers, 370 primary health centers, 243 peripheral health centers, 406 maternal and child health centers, 12 chest disease centers, and 274 dental clinics.[16] Furthermore, the UNWRA provides care for more than 600,000 Palestinian refugees, many of whom are also covered by MOH and RMS. UNWRA currently operates 23 health and maternal and child health centers, but all inpatient services are provided through the MOH or RMS.[15] Although nursing homes exist in Jordan, the majority of the older population is cared for by family members. The health services (clinics and hospitals) are well distributed throughout the country. It is estimated that the average travel time to the nearest health center is 30 minutes.[15]

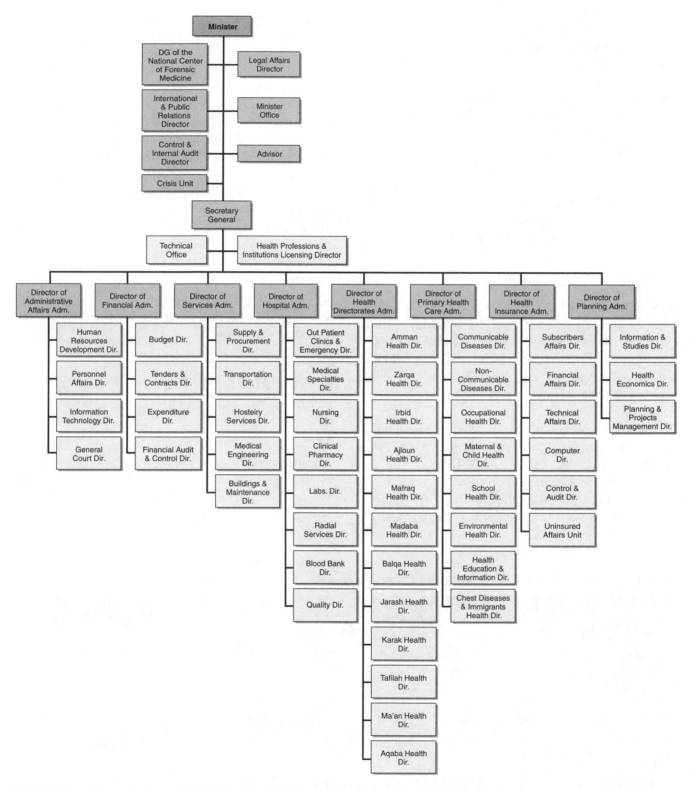

FIGURE 14-2 Organizational Chart for the Ministry of Health

Jordan Ministry of Health. Available at http://www.moh.gov.jo/MOH/En/organizational_chart.php.

Workforce

Currently, the private sector employs the majority of health professionals, with 61.8% of all physicians, 93% of all pharmacists, 71% of all dentists, and 52% of nurses working in the private sector. It is estimated that the MOH and RMS hire 25% and 8% of all practicing physicians, respectively.[15]

Jordan has a large workforce of health professionals. The rate of health professionals for 10,000 population is as follows: 24.5 physicians, 8.2 dentists, 12.0 pharmacists, 17.1 registered nurses, 3.7 associate degree nurses, 9.4 assistant nurses, and 2.8 midwives.[16] Table 14-2 shows the health professionals by sector.

Technology and Equipment

Although Jordan's healthcare infrastructure is considered modern and better than many middle-income countries in the region, it continues to lag in production of medical equipment, which is generally below international standards and limited to beds, medical dressing, plastic syringes, some optical products, and dental supplies.

In 2004, however, the MOH set a plan with public and private sectors to generate an annual $1 billion in medical tourism by the year 2010. To reach this goal and to compete with neighboring countries that also have the ambition of becoming medical hubs in the region, there is a need to continuously upgrade and improve the medical services and medical facilities and institutions, including the quality of hospital and clinic management and administration. Most of the medical equipment used is purchased from U.S. products and is exempt from custom duties.

Jordan's pharmaceutical industry is the second largest exporting industry (75% of Jordanian production is exported, and Jordanian firms are the biggest pharmaceutical exporters by trade volume in the region). There are 22 factories in the pharmaceutical sector, with five major companies dominating the export business. The sector has modern plants, established regional marketing channels, and a skilled, low-cost workforce. Recently, local production grew by 15%. Despite increasing local production, the demand for imported, patented medicines is expected to increase. U.S. pharmaceutical exports to Jordan totaled $243 million in 2005, and market opportunities for U.S. products are expected to increase.[15]

EVALUATION OF THE HEALTHCARE SYSTEM

Cost

Comparatively, Jordan spends a high percentage of its GDP on health. In 2006, 6.1% of the GDP was spent on health by the public sector alone, up from 3.5% in 2001. No data on private health expenditures were found after

TABLE 14-2 Health Personnel by Selected Category and Health Sectors in Jordan, 2007

| Category | Sector | | | | | | Total | Rate per 10,000 of Population |
	MOH	RMS	JUH	KAUH	Private	UNRWA		
Physicians	3,702	1,083	426	395	9,561	112	15,279	26.7
Dentists	533	194	72		4,061	31	4,891	8.5
Pharmacists	273	151	26	20	7,615	2	8,087	14.1
Registered Nurses	2,465	1,442	456	408	3,776	46	8,593	15.0
Associate Degree Nurses	1,413	1,190	72				2,675	4.7
Assistant Nurses	3,307	309	122	117	2,077	186	6,118	10.7
Midwives	1,111	81		19	604	34	1,849	3.2

Data are from MOH, RMS, JUH, KAH, UNRWA, and doctors, dentists, pharmacists, and nurses associations. In Jordan Ministry of Health Annual Statistical Book 2007. Retrieved from http://www.moh.gov.jo/MOH/En/publications.php.

2001; however, that year, 5.6% of the GDP was spent on health in the private sector, and an additional 0.5% of the GDP was spent on international health expenditures. Thus, total health expenditures accounted for 9.6% of the GDP in 2001.[16] The total healthcare expenditure that year was approximately JD598 million ($854 million), which translated into a per capita healthcare expenditure of JD115.4 ($165).[15]

One of the largest constraints of the healthcare system in Jordan has been the high cost of pharmaceuticals. In 2001, the pharmaceutical expenditure accounted for 30.9% of the total health expenditure translating into JD35.6 ($51) per capita, with 81.5% of these expenditures in the private health sector.[15]

Jordan's healthcare system is financed by three sources, including (1) public funding (46%), such as general taxation and premiums paid by public firms; (2) household spending (47.7%), which refers to payroll deductions for insurance or direct expenditure on private healthcare services and pharmaceuticals, and premiums paid by private companies to insure their employees; and (3) donor contributions (6.3%), which includes the UNRWA and other NGOs.

With the decline in public expenditure on health over the last 2 decades (51% in 1990 to 35% in 2001), it appears that the private sector has risen as an important source of healthcare services in Jordan. An area of concern has been the weak investment in public health and health education. In 2001, 58% of public expenditure on health was spent on secondary and tertiary health care, 27% on preventive services and primary care, 5% on administrative activities, 3% on training, and 7% on miscellaneous activities.[15] It can be assumed that if Jordan does not increase its spending on prevention efforts, a higher percentage of its GDP will eventually be spent on health.[15] According to the Health Law of Jordan, the MOH is responsible not only for providing curative services, but also preventative and surveillance programs. In addition, the MOH is in charge of supervising both the public and private health sectors, providing insurance for the citizens, and establishing and managing educational and training programs for health.[15]

Quality

According to the MOH's mortality statistics, chronic diseases are the leading cause of mortality in Jordan. There were 38.2% of deaths in 2003 that were attributed to cardiovascular diseases and 14.3% to cancers.[17] Table 14-3 presents the 2005 mortality data for the leading causes of death. One alarming fact was the 17.4% increase in the age-adjusted death rate from road-traffic accidents from the previous year.[18] Overall external causes of mortality (i.e., injuries both intentional and unintentional) surpassed cerebrovascular diseases to become the third leading cause of death.

Furthermore, the age-adjusted death rates were highest among the older age groups. Table 14-4 shows the numbers of deaths, death rates, and percentage of change in death rates by age and gender.[18] In addition, the infant mortality in 2006 was 24 per 1,000, and the under-5 mortality rate was 29 per 1,000, with life expectancy at 71.7 (70.8 for males and 72.5 for females). The total fertility rate in 2002 was 3.7 and, as expected, was higher (4.2) in rural areas compared with urban areas (3.5).[6] Although Jordan seems to have accurate mortality data, morbidity data are inadequate with almost all non-MOH clinics and health centers and most hospitals not coding diseases.[15]

Jordan, however, has achieved universal child immunization since 1988. It has been polio free since 1995, and no diphtheria cases have been reported since 1993, with a small number of pertussis and tetanus cases reported. It is estimated that 97% of children have been immunized for polio and DPT.[15]

The public sector programs are comprehensive and include access to pharmaceuticals with minimal cost to the patients. Although the uninsured are able to receive all public health services at highly subsidized prices, they have to pay full price for pharmaceuticals. On the other hand, private insurances vary widely in their comprehensiveness.

Access

Understanding the coverage provided by the healthcare system in Jordan is complicated largely because of the fact that often individuals are eligible for more than one insurance program, and many choose to pay out-of-pocket premiums to maintain private insurances. It is estimated that 48% of the population is covered through the MOH or RMS, and an additional 20% are covered through private insurance or UNRWA. The remaining 32% that are not eligible for free health care through the public sector are still able to purchase all MOH facility services at highly subsidized prices; this makes it possible for everyone to receive health care.

Although almost half of the population is covered through MOH and RMS, a higher spending (58%) occurs in the private sector, indicating that a portion of those eligible for public sector services chooses to use the private sector instead. In reviewing the equity of

TABLE 14-3   2005 Mortality Data for Top 10 Leading Causes of Death in Jordan

Rank[a]	Cause of death (Based on the *International Classification of Diseases*, 10th Revision, 1992)	Number	Percentage of Total Deaths	2005 Crude Rate	Age-Adjusted Rate	
					2005	Percent Change, 2004–2005
Not applicable	All causes	12,066	100.0	2.20	3.75	−4.3
1	Ischemic heart diseases (120–125)	1,595	13.2	0.29	0.58	−15.9
2	Malignant neoplasms (C00–C97)	1,555	12.9	0.28	0.52	−3.7
3	External causes of mortality (V01–Y89)	1,239	10.3	0.23	0.26	−3.8
4	Cerebrovascular diseases (160–169)	1,203	10.0	0.22	0.45	−8.9
5	Diabetes mellitus (E10–E14)	868	7.2	0.16	0.32	8.7
6	Hypertensive diseases (110–115)	744	6.2	0.14	0.28	23.5
7	Congenital malformations, deformations, and chromosomal abnormalities (Q00–Q99)	553	4.6	0.10	0.09	0.9
8	Heart failure (150)	375	3.1	0.07	0.13	−4.4
9	Chronic lower respiratory diseases (J40–J47)	330	2.7	0.06	0.12	30.6
10	Renal failure (N17–N19)	320	2.7	0.06	0.11	18.5
Not applicable	All other causes (residuals)	3,284	27.2	0.06		

[a] Rank based on number of deaths.

Mortality in Jordan, 2005. Retrieved from http://www.moh.gov.jo/MOH/En/publications.php.

the healthcare system, the World Health Organization (WHO) concluded the following:

> In assessing the "fairness" of the contribution/revenue base for financing the health system, one should consider whether individuals' contributions both through the general government revenue system and out-of-pocket are based on "ability to pay." The overall incidence of Jordan's general revenue structure is not progressive, since only a very limited proportion of revenues derive from progressive income taxes. In terms of individuals' contributions for services, while the Government, in effect, does potentially finance and provide subsidized care for the entire population, the structure of MOH and RMS eligibility and premiums as well as the higher payment levels required by the uninsured suggest that equity could be improved.[15]

The report also indicates, however, that the government has taken significant measures to improve equity:

(1) All government employees are eligible for the Civil Health Insurance Program (CHIP) regardless of their position; (2) children and husbands of female government employees are eligible for CHIP; (3) all children under the age of 6 years and people living in poverty pockets will have free health insurance; and (4) any citizen who wishes to enroll in CHIP can at the highly subsidized rates. The intent of those changes was to achieve coverage for all with minimal costs for the patient.[15]

In addition, the WHO report finds Jordan has a "well-developed delivery system with a significant amount of capacity," recognizing that there are differences by governorates and some groups such as the near poor and those in rural geographic areas have more difficulty accessing secondary and tertiary health services; however, the Royal Court clinics have devised a system in which these individuals can apply and be referred to the public hospitals for all needed health services and the government reimburses these hospitals for the full cost of the services.[15]

TABLE 14-4   Mortality Data by Age and Gender

Age	Both Genders	Male	Female	Both Genders	Male	Female	Both Genders	Male	Female
		Number			Rate		Percentage Change in Rate, 2004–2005		
All ages	12,066	7,066	5,000	NA	NA	NA	NA	NA	NA
Crude	NA	NA	NA	2.20	2.50	1.89	−3.5	−3.7	−3.3
Age adjusted	NA	NA	NA	3.75	4.29	3.18	−4.3	−4.5	−4.0
Under 1 year	1,386	754	632	10.51	11.18	9.81	9.6	11.9	7.1
1–4 years	480	243	237	0.85	0.84	0.86	−9.4	−20.6	5.8
5–9 years	214	123	91	0.31	0.35	0.27	−7.0	−10.3	−2.3
10–14 years	148	98	50	0.23	0.29	0.16	−11.2	3.0	−30.2
15–19 years	196	134	62	0.33	0.43	0.21	−5.6	4.0	−21.3
20–24 years	267	183	84	0.46	0.61	0.30	−6.5	−5.3	−8.8
25–29 years	256	180	76	0.52	0.70	0.33	0.9	13.5	−20.1
30–34 years	237	154	83	0.55	0.69	0.40	−11.6	−10.9	−12.8
35–39 years	317	201	116	0.91	1.11	0.70	7.2	4.0	13.4
40–44 years	352	216	136	1.36	1.62	1.08	8.5	1.5	22.0
45–49 years	379	257	122	2.07	2.74	1.37	−2.2	−1.1	−4.6
50–54 years	439	280	159	3.19	4.03	2.33	0.0	−2.9	5.7
55–59 years	662	412	250	5.43	6.89	4.03	−12.7	−7.0	−20.6
60–64 years	1,087	676	411	10.26	12.10	8.20	−7.9	−10.5	−3.2
65–69 years	1,343	808	535	17.47	20.46	14.31	−2.4	−4.4	0.8
70–74 years	1,359	764	595	26.87	30.09	23.62	−4.9	−6.6	−2.6
75–79 years	1,222	733	489	45.97	51.95	39.21	−3.2	−0.4	−7.1
80–84 years	749	390	359	51.83	60.09	45.10	−7.9	−2.6	−13.0
85 years and older	931	440	491	113.68	111.39	115.80	−6.2	−11.2	−1.3
Not stated	42	20	22	NA	NA	NA	NA	NA	NA

Mortality in Jordan, 2005. Retrieved from http://www.moh.gov.jo/MOH/En/publications.php.

CURRENT AND EMERGING ISSUES AND CHALLENGES

Noncommunicable Diseases

As Jordan has gone through both epidemiologic and demographic transitions, the expected declines in infant mortality, maternal mortality, total fertility rate, and infectious diseases have occurred, but these have given rise to an increase in noncommunicable diseases such as cardiovascular diseases and cancer.[15] These changes have occurred at a fast rate with the declines starting in the late 1970s (approximately 25 to 30 years ago) and burdened the healthcare system, which was equipped to deal with the communicable diseases but not with noncommunicable diseases, which often require more expensive diagnostics, treatments, and more training for the health professionals. It appears that Jordan's healthcare system has been able to catch up with many of those changes.[15]

It seems, however, that the current emerging health issues in Jordan are related to the increases in noncommunicable diseases. Jordan has observed dramatic increases in lifestyle-related diseases and conditions such as lung cancer, cardiovascular diseases, obesity, and diabetes.[19] For example, two studies found that the majority of women (54%) were overweight or obese, and approximately 42% fell in the normal range of body mass index.[19,20] Furthermore, in assessing the prevalence of risk factors associated with noncommunicable diseases in this population, the behavioral risk factor surveillance system found high levels of obesity, hypertension, high cholesterol, and diabetes, in addition to high percentages of undiagnosed cases. Only 15.2% had been told they had hypertension compared with 30.2% who had hypertension; 8.5% had been diagnosed with high cholesterol compared with 23.1% who had high cholesterol; 22.4% thought that they were obese compared with 34.8% who were actually obese; and only 9.0% had been told they were diabetic compared with 16.9% who were. These high levels of underdiagnoses are alarming and require that a plan is developed and put into action to increase awareness, diagnosis, and early prevention or treatment.[17]

One study on the impact of Westernization on eating styles, body image, and the nutrition transition finds that Jordanian women had high levels of overweight and obesity coupled with large levels of restrained eating, emotional eating, and disordered eating attitudes and behaviors; however, women had lower body dissatisfaction than is observed in other countries. It was argued that these women were caught between the traditional and modern societies, where the dietary patterns and eating habits were increasingly Westernized while the body esteem and body size preferences remained more traditional. Furthermore, the study highlights the importance of assessing eating disorders in the population.[20]

Another important risk factor for noncommunicable diseases is tobacco use. Studies have shown alarming rates of smoking in the general population of Jordan. It is estimated that 48% of adult males and 25% of boys ages 13 to 15 years smoke a tobacco product, whereas use for females was 10% of adult females and 14.5% of girls ages 13 to 15 years.[21] Studies have also shown a high prevalence of smoking among medical professionals and students in Amman: 22.4% for male and 9.1% for female physicians, 42% for male nurses and 13% for female nurses, and 26% for male students and 7% for female medical students.[22–24] This unhealthy behavior has been of much concern, as lung cancer has become the third leading cancer in Jordan.[25] Jordan has one of the oldest tobacco policies (1977) prohibiting smoking in public places; however, enforcement of this law remains low. Attempts to reduce consumption of all tobacco products in developing countries have been problematic. The WHO identifies the "lack of adequate financial resources, inadequate commitment among some government sources, and lack of adequate studies on the smoking hazards" as Jordan's main obstacle in tobacco prevention; understanding the factors that deter or influence tobacco consumption in this population is crucial to developing appropriate health education programs.[26]

Another cause for alarm is the number of deaths associated with road-traffic injuries. These deaths are easily preventable through the enforcement of traffic laws and improved pedestrian walkways. Jordan has committed to reducing these deaths and injuries; however, this commitment is recent, and there are currently no data available on the changes in road-traffic deaths.[18]

Environmental Factors

Jordan is considered one of the world's 10 most water-stressed countries. In addition to the lack of water resources, pollution has made the situation worse. The majority of water pollution is linked to lack of management of domestic wastewater and disposal of industrial waste, leaching from unsanitary solid waste landfills and agrochemical sources.[15]

Solid waste collection and disposal has been inefficient largely because of budgetary constraints of the MOH and the Ministry of Environment, which are both in charge of its management. This problem is further exacerbated by the lack of trained professional and low public awareness. The current design for collection of solid waste has been deemed environmentally unfriendly with severe impacts on ground water, air quality, and health. Furthermore, it is estimated that the annual use of chemicals has increased dramatically (0.7 to 1.2 million kg from 1980 to 1998), leading to increases in chemical poisoning and detrimental environmental impacts, which can be attributed to lack of oversight and legislation. The decline in air quality has also been associated with the increased emission of pollutants such as SO_2, NO_2, CO, and lead linked to large increases in number of automobiles and emissions from plants, mining, and other industries.[15]

Refugee Populations

The large influx of refugee populations since Jordan's independence has affected its healthcare system. UNWRA data indicate that over 1.9 million Palestinian refugees are registered in the country, and the UNFPA estimates the number of Iraqis currently residing in country to be 481,000.[4,27] There are differences in these two groups' health status and access to health. The UNWRA has been serving the majority (60%) of Palestinian refugees in Jordan, and their health status report for 2007 indicates that the Palestinian refugees have generally similar health status compared with the Jordanian population. Fertility rates have dropped significantly for this population, largely because of UNRWA's family planning programs that were supported by the MOH providing contraceptives.

The case of the Iraqi refugees is different because most of them have not been granted official status and thus do not have access to public services and resources. In addition, there are no data on the health status of this population. One study reports on breastfeeding among Iraqi refugees in Jordan that all women who had given birth in the last year had given birth in a hospital but that they had not received much information before or after delivery regarding the importance of breastfeeding or where to go for help regarding breastfeeding even though the majority had been encouraged in the hospital to breastfeed every 2 to 3 hours. This study highlights the lack of existing information regarding Iraqi refugees and the difficulty in providing services to these individuals through a healthcare system that is already facing large budget concerns.[28]

Health System Challenges

According to a 2002 Joint MOH/WHO report, Jordan's health system needs to deal with the following challenges:[15]

- "The demographic changes representing an increase in population and higher life expectancy.
- Considerable changes in lifestyles favoring the development of determinants and risk factors for chronic diseases, accidents, injuries, and substance abuse.
- The epidemiological transition and changes in the pattern of disease characterized by a progressive increase in the magnitude of noncommunicable diseases like cardiovascular diseases, cancer, diabetes, and mental health problems as well as accidents and health of the elderly.

- Inefficiencies observed in the provision and financing of health services.
- The lack of a rigorous appraisal (and reorientation) of the current state of human resources development in health.
- The negative impact of poverty on accessibility to quality health care particularly in view of the high proportion of uninsured people.
- The increasing demands and expectations of the public for effective and accessible health care.
- The rapid advances in technology and rising healthcare costs.
- Inadequate coordination between the public sector and the increasingly significant private sector and the lack of effective systems for monitoring and auditing clinical practice.
- The emerging environmental health issues."

Although Jordan's healthcare system has undergone major reforms over the last 3 decades, it remains to be seen whether the MOH's commitment to improving coverage, reducing noncommunicable diseases, and maintaining and improving the quality health care for its citizens is achieved.

REFERENCES

1. Salibi K. *The Modern History of Jordan.* New York: IB Tauris; 1998.
2. The King Hussein Website. Keys to the Kingdom: History. Retrieved on June 3, 2008, from http://www.kinghussein.gov.jo/history.html.
3. The Hashemite Kingdom of Jordan's Parliament. History of Parliamentary Life in Jordan. Retrieved June 3, 2008, from http://www.parliament.jo/english/history_parliamentary_life.shtm
4. United Nations Population Fund. Iraqis in Jordan. Retrieved June 3, 2008, from http://www.dos.gov.jo/sdb_pop/sdb_pop_a/index_o.htm.
5. Ministry of Tourism and Antiquities. Helpful Facts about Jordan. Retrieved June 3, 2008, from http://www.tourism.jo/Inside/AboutJordan.asp.
6. Department of Statistics. Jordan in Figures. Retrieved June 3, 2008, from http://www.dos.gov.jo/jorfig/2006/jor_f_a.htm.
7. The Hashemite Kingdom of Jordan's Parliament. The Constitution of the Hashemite Kingdom of Jordan. Retrieved on June 3, 2008, from http://www.parliament.jo/english/constitution_EN.shtm.
8. Bloom DE, Canning D, Huzarski K, Levy D, Nandakumar AK, Sevilla J. Demographic Transition and Economic Opportunity: The case of Jordan, 2001. Retrieved June 4, 2008, from www.riverpath.com/library/pdf/jordan.pdf.

9. The King Hussein Website. Foreign Affairs. Retrieved on June 4, 2008, from http://www.kinghussein.gov.jo/f_affairs3.html#The%20Economic%20Restructuring%20Program.

10. United Nations Development Programme. Jordan: The Human Development Index—Going Beyond Income. Retrieved on June 4, 2008, from http://hdrstats.undp.org/countries/country_fact_sheets/cty_fs_JOR.html.

11. Takruri H. FAO—Nutrition Country Profile: Jordan: Food and Agricultural Organization, 2003. Retrieved on June 4, 2008, from ftp://ftp.fap.org/es/esn/nutrition/ncp/jormap.pdf.

12. World Bank. Country Profiles: Jordan, Jordan Data at a Glance. Retrieved June 4, 2008, from http://web.worldbank.org/WBSITE/EXTERNAL/COUNTRIES/MENAEXT/JORDANEXTN/0,,menuPK:315156~pagePK:141132~piPK:141109~theSitePK:315130,00.html.

13. Central Intelligence Agency's World Factbook. Jordan. Retrieved on June 4, 2008, from https://www.cia.gov/library/publications/the-world-factbook/geos/jo.html.

14. Ministry of Health. Focal point of health information: Jordan. Retrieved on June 4, 2008, from http://www.moh.gov.jo:7778/MOH/En/about.php.

15. World Health Organization. Health System Profile—Jordan. Retrieved on June 5, 2008, from http://gis.emro.who.int/healthsystemobservatory/main/Forms/CountryInfo.aspx?Country=JORDAN.

16. Ministry of Health. Ministry of Health Annual Statistical Book 2006. Retrieved June 5, 2008, from http://www.moh.gov.jo/MOH/En/publications.php.

17. Zindah M, Belbeisi A, Walke H, Mokdad AH. Obesity and diabetes in Jordan: findings from the Behavioral Risk Factors Surveillance System, 2004. *Preventing Chronic Disease.* 2008;5(1):1–8.

18. Ministry of Health. Mortality in Jordan, 2005. Retrieved June 5, 2008, from http://www.moh.gov.jo/MOH/En/publications.php.

19. Demographic and Health Survey of Jordan. Nutritional Status, Prevalence of Anemia, and Micronutrient Supplementation. Retrieved June 6, 2008, from www.measuredhs.com/pubs/pdf/FR138/10Chapter10.pdf.

20. Madanat HN, Brown RB, Hawks SR. The impact of body mass index and Western advertising and media on eating style, body image, and nutrition transition among Jordanian women. *Public Health Nutrition.* 2007;10(10):1039–1046.

21. The Global Youth Tobacco Survey Collaborative Group. Differences in worldwide tobacco use by gender: findings from the Global Youth Tobacco Survey. *Journal of School Health.* 2003;73(6):207–215.

22. Merrill R, Madanat H, Kelley AT. In Press. Smoking prevalence, attitudes, and perceived smoking, and control responsibilities and practices among nurses in Amman, Jordan. *International Journal of Nursing Practice.*

23. Merrill R, Madanat H, Layton B, Madsen C, and Hanson C. smoking prevalence, attitudes, and perceived smoking prevention and control responsibilities and behaviors among physicians in Jordan. *International Quarterly of Community Health Education.* 2006–2007;26(4):397–413.

24. Merrill R, Madanat H, Cox E. In Press. Smoking prevalence and perceived effectiveness of smoking policy and counseling patients about smoking among medical students in Amman, Jordan. *Eastern Mediterranean Health Journal.*

25. Ministry of Health. Health News, 2004. Retrieved February 15, 2008, from http://www.moh.gov.jo/MOH/arabic/health_newsdetails.php?newsid=343.

26. World Health Organization. EMRO Tobacco Free Initiative—Country profile, 2000. Retrieved June 6, 2008, from http://www.emro.who.int/TFI/CountryProfile-JOR.htm.

27. United Nations Relief and Works Agency for Palestinian Refugees in the Near East. Annual Report of the Department of Health 2007. Retrieved on June 6, 2008, from http://www.un.org/unrwa/publications/pubs07.html.

28. Madanat H, Farrell H, Merrill R, Cox R. breastfeeding education, support, and barriers among Iraqi refugee women in Jordan. *International Electronic Journal of Health Education.* 2007;10:138–149.

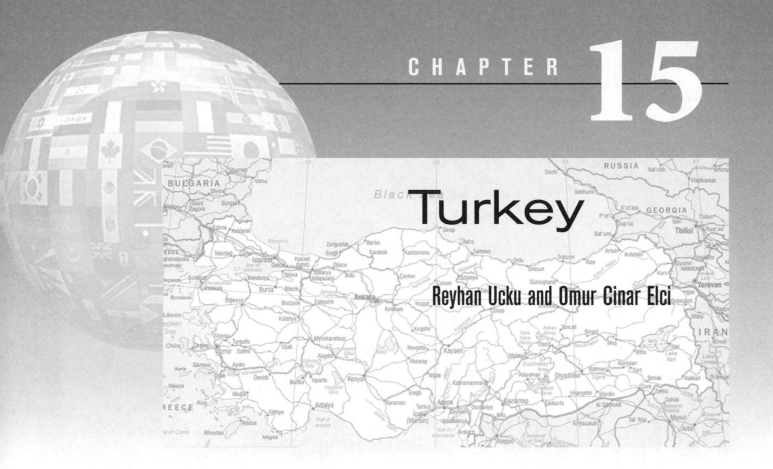

CHAPTER 15

Turkey

Reyhan Ucku and Omur Cinar Elci

COUNTRY DESCRIPTION

TABLE 15-1 Turkey

Nationality	Noun: Turk(s) Adjective: Turkish
Ethnic groups	Turkish 80%, Kurdish 20% (estimated)
Religions	Muslim 99.8% (mostly Sunni), other 0.2% (mostly Christians and Jews)
Language	Turkish (official), Kurdish, Dimli (or Zaza), Azeri, Kabardian; also a substantial Gagauz population in the European part of Turkey
Literacy	Definition: age 15 and over can read and write Total population: 87.4% Male: 95.3% Female: 79.6% (2004 est.)
Government type	Republican parliamentary democracy
Date of independence	October 29, 1923 (successor state to the Ottoman Empire)
Gross Domestic Product (GDP) per capita	$9,400 (2007 est.)

(continues)

TABLE 15-1   Turkey   (continued)

Unemployment rate	9.7% plus underemployment of 4% (2007 est.)
Natural hazards	Severe earthquakes, especially in northern Turkey, along an arc extending from the Sea of Marmara to Lake Van
Environment: current issues	Water pollution from dumping of chemicals and detergents; air pollution, particularly in urban areas; deforestation; concern for oil spills from increasing Bosporus ship traffic
Population	71,892,807 (July 2008 est.)
Age structure	0–14 years: 24.4% (male 8,937,515/female 8,608,375) 15–64 years: 68.6% (male 25,030,793/female 24,253,312) 65 years and over: 7% (male 2,307,236/female 2,755,576) (2008 est.)
Median age	Total: 29 years Male: 28.8 years Female: 29.2 years (2008 est.)
Population growth rate	1.013% (2008 est.)
Birth rate	16.15 births/1,000 population (2008 est.)
Death rate	6.02 deaths/1,000 population (2008 est.)
Net migration rate	0 migrant(s)/1,000 population (2008 est.)
Gender ratio	At birth: 1.05 male(s)/female Under 15 years: 1.04 male(s)/female 15–64 years: 1.03 male(s)/female 65 years and over: 0.84 male(s)/female Total population: 1.02 male(s)/female (2008 est.)
Infant mortality rate	Total: 36.98 deaths/1,000 live births Male: 40.44 deaths/1,000 live births Female: 33.34 deaths/1,000 live births (2008 est.)
Life expectancy at birth	Total population: 73.14 years Male: 70.67 years Female: 75.73 years (2008 est.)
Total fertility rate	1.87 children born/woman (2008 est.)
HIV/AIDS adult prevalence rate	Less than 0.1%; no country-specific models provided (2001 est.)
Number of people living with HIV/AIDS	Not available
HIV/AIDS deaths	Not available

Central Intelligence Agency. The World Fact Book, 2008. Retrieved November 18, 2008, from https://www.cia.gov/library/publications/the-world-factbook.

History

In 1922, after World War I, the Ottoman Empire collapsed, and the Anatolian peninsula was occupied by allied forces from the United Kingdom, Greece, Italy, and France. After the freedom war that was led by Kemal Ataturk, the modern Republic of Turkey was founded on October 29, 1923. Ataturk was also the first president of the country and held this post until his death in 1938. Ataturk initiated various social, cultural, political, linguistic, and economic reforms to establish the foundation of the new republic. From 1924 to 1946, there was a single-party government, which focused on the modernization and Westernization of Turkey. Ataturk's ideology was based on secularism, nationalism, and modernization. It was during the same period from 1924 to 1946 that many of these reforms took place and the new republic turned its direction toward the West. After World War II, which Turkey did not enter until the very end, Turkey was transformed from a single-party system to a multiparty system. Although this new parliamentary democracy was halted by military coups in 1960, 1971, and 1980, today Turkey is governed under a multiparty parliamentary democracy.[1]

After the 1960 and 1980 coups, the Constitution was changed, which had significant impacts on the health system in the country. In the 1961 Constitution,[2] the state had been identified as a "social welfare state," and health had been defined as a "fundamental right for every citizen." In the 1982 Constitution, however,[3] the state was entitled to organize and supervise health services. This significant transformation later led the country into today's challenges, which are discussed at the end of this chapter.

Size and Geography

The Republic of Turkey is located in the northern hemisphere, at the crossroads of Asia and Europe (Figure 15-1). The majority of its 814,578 km² land is on the Asian peninsula called Anatolia, which is surrounded by the Black Sea to the north, the Mediterranean Sea to the south, and the Aegean Sea to the west. There is also an inland sea, called the Marmara Sea, that separates Asia and Europe to the northwest. Turkey's neighbors are Greece and Bulgaria to the northwest; Georgia, Armenia, Azerbaijan, and Iran to the east; and Iraq and Syria to the southeast. There are 7 geographical regions and 81 provinces in the country. The eastern Anatolia region consists of 21% of the area and includes 16 provinces, although it has the lowest population density. The northwestern Marmara region has the highest population density, and Istanbul is the biggest city in the country. Istanbul has a unique location, as it has two sections; one

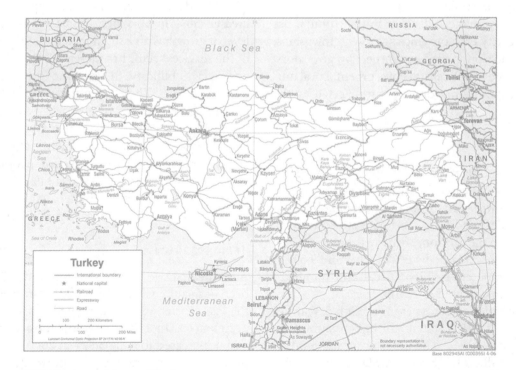

FIGURE 15-1 Map of Turkey

is on the continent of Europe, and the other is on the continent of Asia. The capital of Turkey is Ankara, which is the second largest city and is located in central Anatolia. The third largest city, Izmir, is located in the western Ege region. The other two regions are Karadeniz in the north, with 18 provinces, and Akdeniz in the south, with 9 provinces.[1,4]

Government and Political System

The government structure and the political system are described in the Constitution. As we discussed earlier, the first constitution, dated 1924, was replaced by new constitutions in 1961 and again in 1982. According to the Constitution,[3] the Republic of Turkey is a secular and democratic welfare state. The official language is Turkish, and the capital city is Ankara. There are three governing bodies in Turkey. The Turkish National Assembly is the legislator, the president and the cabinet run the government, and independent courts are responsible for justice and the implementation of law. The Turkish National Assembly consists of 550 representatives who are elected by the people every 5 years. The president is elected by the National Assembly every 7 years; each president can serve only one term. The governing cabinet includes the prime minister and other ministers. The president appoints the prime minister, who selects his cabinet members from among the members of the National Assembly. Since July 2007, the 60th Cabinet has been in session.

There are 81 provincial districts in the country. Besides the central city, each province has towns, townships, and villages. Each province is governed by governors, who are appointed by the central government. Local municipalities are run by mayors, who are elected by the people locally.

Macroeconomics

Because of the monetary policies applied during the 1990s, instability increased in Turkey's macroeconomics. Unstable growth, a high inflation rate, high public deficits, interest expenditures, and debt stock were the main problems in the economy during this period. The Turkish economy decreased by 6% in 1994 and 9.5% in the 2001 economic crisis. Tight fiscal and monetary policies were implemented after this crisis.[5]

Basic economic indicators from the 9th 5-year development plan of DPT (State Planning Organization) are shown in Table 15-2.[5] The gross domestic product (GDP) is 363.4 billion USD, 5,042 USD per capita, and 8,145 USD per capita according to the GDP based on

TABLE 15-2 Basic Economic Indicators from 9th 5-Year Development Plan of DPT

Economic Indicators	2005
GPD (billion U.S. dollars)	363.4
Per capita GPD (U.S. dollars)	5,042
Per capita GPD (U.S. dollars)	8,145
Growth (%)	7.4
Exports (billion U.S. dollars)	73.4
Imports (billion U.S. dollars)	116.5
Trade balance (billion U.S. dollars)	−32.8
Labor force participation rate (%)	48.3
Employment level (million persons)	22.1
Unemployment rate (%)	10.3

Source: IX. Five-year Development Plan, Official Journal, 2006.

purchasing power parity. The GDP growth was 7.4% in 2005, with the average of 4.4% in the period from 2001 to 2005. As far as industrial growth is concerned, the biggest growth took place in the industrial sector (5.1%) during this period, 4.3% in the services sector, and 1.1% in the agricultural sector. The proportion of basic sectors in GDP is as follows: agriculture 10.7%, industry 26.6%, and service 62.7%. The agricultural sector has decreased 50% in 10 years. Industry has kept the same level of growth with a slight increase, and the proportion of the services sector has increased. Deficit in trade balance is 32.8 billion USD, and the imports coverage by exports is 63%. The 2007 inflation rate, based on the Consumer Price Index, is 8.4%, whereas it is 8.2% based on the Producer Price Index.[5,6]

The unregistered employment ratio is very high among the 22.1 million employed people; in sectors other than agriculture, this ratio is 34%. Unemployment, at 10.3%, is an important problem, especially among the younger age group, where this figure is twice as high.

Demographics

After the first two censuses in 1927 and 1935, there have been *de facto* censuses every 5 years until 2000. In 2007, the last census was implemented based on household occupancies. In 1927, the population was 13,648,278, and it increased to 67,803,927 in 2000. Until the 1960s, pronatalist demographic policies were in practice, and in 1960, the demographic growth rate reached its peak of 28.5 per 1,000. In 1965, the Demographic Planning Law initiated antenatalist policies, which decreased the demographic growth rate to 18.3 per 1,000 in 2000 and to 12.4 per 1,000 in 2006. In the 2007 census, the population was 70,586,256, of which 71% were living in the urban areas. Turkey still has a relatively young population: 0- to 14-year-old children constitute 26% of the population, whereas elderly persons age 65 years and over constitute 7% of the population. The dependent population is 50%. Women are 49.9% of the total population, while they comprise 57% of the 65-and-over age group.[7-8]

According to a 2006 poverty survey,[9] 18% of the population is below the poverty line; this figure is higher in rural areas (almost one third) and lower (9%) in urban areas. Poverty, however, increases to 34% among the illiterate population and 43% among the members of crowded (over seven people) households. There is a significant economic disparity in the country. The overall income of the richest 20% is 7.3 times higher than the poorest 20% of the people. The indicator of this disparity, the Gini index, for Turkey is 0.40.[5]

According to the recent health and demography survey in 2003,[10] the infant mortality rate was 28.7 per 1,000 live births, and the under 5-year-old child mortality rate was 37 per 1,000. With the 2006 estimations, the infant mortality rate was 22.6 per 1,000. These figures are higher among rural populations and in the Eastern part of the country. Overall, the total fertility is 2.23 births per women, which has decreased to 2.18 with the 2006 estimations. Life expectancy is 71.5 years overall, with 69.1 years expected for men and 74.0 years expected for women.[11]

BRIEF HISTORY OF THE HEALTHCARE SYSTEM

The history of the healthcare system in Turkey can be summarized in two periods: (1) the period after the foundation of the Turkish Republic from 1923 to 1960 and (2) the period beginning with the socialization of health services in 1961 to the present.

1923–1960

Before the foundation of the Turkish Republic, the Health Directorate in the Ministry of Interior Affairs was responsible for health services. At the provincial level, there were district health officers, whose responsibility was to provide preventive and curative health services.

In 1920, before the Republic was founded, the Ministry of Health (MoH) was established. After the foundation of the Republic, in 1923, a new era began in which efforts were made to improve the health status of the population. At the beginning of this era, there were not only a shortage of health facilities and health manpower, but also an inequality in distribution. The population was nearly 13 million in 1923. Although 78% of the population was living in rural areas, there were no accessible health services in the villages. The most important health problems were communicable diseases, mainly malaria, syphilis, trachoma, and tuberculosis. There were only 554 physicians, and the number of population per physician was 22,500. The same shortage existed for hospital beds; there were approximately five beds per 10,000 population. The infant mortality rate was very high, with 250 infant deaths per 1,000 live births. The MoH budget was 2.21% of the general budget.[8,12-14]

In this period, providing health services was accepted as one of the main responsibilities of the government. Government health policy was aimed at the promotion of health and prevention of disease, increasing the population, and the struggle against communicable diseases. Dr. Refik Saydam, who was the Republic's first MoH, was assigned to carry out these objectives. In his nearly 13 years as minister, the objectives of the health policy were improving health organization; expanding health and social services to rural areas; increasing physician, midwife, and health technician numbers; struggling against malaria, tuberculosis, leprosy, trachoma, and syphilis; establishing a model hospital and maternal and children hospitals; enacting laws related to health; and founding the Hygiene Institute and School.[8]

During this period, the main priority was given to the preventive health services, especially to the control of highly prevalent communicable diseases. For this reason, vertical organizations, such as the malaria control dispensary and the syphilis and leprosy control dispensary, were established, and their health services were taken to the villages. Malaria control was spread throughout the country, whereas trachoma control was spread to the southern and southeastern regions and syphilis control was spread to the northern region. Tuberculosis control was first the responsibility of the nongovernmental organizations supported by the MoH. Later, it was administered by the ministry itself. In this period, it was believed that providing curative health services (hospitals) should be the responsibility of local governments, and thus, the MoH's responsibility was limited to coordinating and guiding these services. Because of this, model hospitals were mostly established in the big cities. As a result, preventive and curative health services were not integrated and were administered by central and local governments separately. At the provincial level, there were only district health officers. Because of expanding health services to rural areas, dispensaries (diagnostic and treatment centers) were established in the districts. Dispensaries, which had 5 to 10 beds, were responsible for providing free-of-charge health care with a physician and a health technician. The number of dispensaries increased from 90 in 1933 to 180 in 1936. Other than dispensaries, there were also mobile physicians, whose responsibility was to provide preventive and curative health care to the rural population. These mobile physicians regularly visited villages for 20 days of the month.[12]

As mentioned before, health manpower was insufficient at the beginning of this period. For this reason, priority was given to increasing the number of physicians and male nurses. Medical education was supported by scholarships and free dormitories. As a result, the number of physicians increased threefold between 1923 and 1935. At the same time, compulsory service was introduced for physicians because of the shortage and unequal distribution of them. By giving top priority to preventive health services, doctors working in preventive healthcare services were paid more than those in curative services. The important characteristic of this period was to enact the main health legislations consisting of 51 laws and 18 regulations, most of which are still in force.[8,12–13]

Unfortunately, accessible healthcare services to all people in the country could not be adequately implemented. After the Second World War, a new era commenced, and in 1946, the first national health plan was prepared. The objectives of this plan were not different from those accepted at the beginning of the Republic. The main difference was to establish a national health bank and health fund. According to this plan, the health services organization would be organized into seven different regions in the country. In each region, there would be a state hospital with 500 beds, special hospitals (such as maternity, child, and mental hospitals and a sanatorium), and nursing/midwifery graduate schools. Unfortunately, this plan was not carried out as intended, and instead, health centers were established with a new approach of integrated health services. A health center was established for every 40 villages (approximately 20,000 population), and it was responsible for the preventive and curative health care of this defined community. The health center, which had 10 to 25 beds, was staffed with 1 to 2 physicians and 11 other healthcare personnel (such as nurses, midwifes, and male nurses). In this way, population-based, integrated healthcare services were intended to be accessible to the entire population. Although the aim was to establish 1,000 health centers within 10 years, this was not implemented. The number of health centers increased from 16 in 1950 to 283 in 1960.[8,13–14]

In the postwar era, vertical organizations continued to serve as important centers for the control of communicable diseases because of postwar epidemics. In 1952, a new vertical organization for maternal and child health, serving a population of 30,000 to 50,000, was established under the MoH.[14] At the beginning of the 1950s, the MoH took over the hospitals run by local governments. Even though this change was important to integrate preventive and curative services, curative health services were given high priority, and preventive services were neglected. Despite this, curative health services were not sufficiently improved because of the lack of health personnel.

In 1945, the Social Insurance Institution (SSK) was established to provide retirement benefits to workers. In 1952, the Social Insurance Organization (SIO) developed its own healthcare facilities, including hospitals and dispensaries, and assigned its own health personnel.[8]

Since 1960

At the beginning of the 1960s, the population reached 27,755,000, 68% of whom were living in rural areas. There were 8,214 physicians; nearly half of them were specialists. Even though other health personnel increased in numbers over the years, there was still a shortage. The population per physician was 3,400, with 17,000 population per nurse and 8,600 population per midwife. The annual population increase rate was at the highest level of 2.9%; the infant mortality rate was also high, with 208 infant deaths per 1,000 live births. The MoH budget was 5.18% of the general budget in 1955, and reached its highest level of 5.27% in 1960.[12,14] At the provincial level, the healthcare system consisted of hospitals, health centers, district health officers, and vertically integrated organizations. Hospitals, not accessible to the entire population, were generally in the center of cities. The aim of establishing new health centers across the country could not be achieved completely. On the other hand, district health officers were busy with bureaucratic activities instead of health care. By the year 1960, it was apparent that the healthcare system and health status of the country would not improve with this model; therefore, different healthcare policies started to be discussed and a new law on socialization of health services, which was prepared by Dr. Nusret Fişek as an Undersecretary of the MoH, was enacted in 1961. After 1960, 5-year development plans began to be constructed, and programs regarding socialization policies were enacted in the First Five Years Development Plan. The implementation of the law was begun in 1963 and was gradually expanded to the entire country by 1984.[15]

The socialization law deals with the organization of all health services in the country, with the aim of providing of health services to the entire population on an equitable basis. The basic principles of this law are the following: (1) to deliver equitable and continuous health services, (2) to integrate health services horizontally, (3) to organize a referral healthcare system, (4) to ensure community participation in health services decision making, (5) to implement a population-based healthcare system, (6) to deliver health services with a teamwork approach, and (7) to give top priority to preventive health services. This socialization law with these principles remains in force at this time.[8,15]

According to the legislation, the MoH is responsible for health policy and health services. It is the main provider of primary and secondary health care and also partly of tertiary health care. The Provincial Health Directorates are responsible for health services at the provincial level. The main primary healthcare settings are "health centers" (Sağlık Ocağı) and "health houses." Health centers are responsible for the health of a defined community, up to 10,000 people. They give preventive, curative, and rehabilitative health care to the community, both in the health center as well as in people's homes as a holistic approach. Health services provided by health centers and health houses are free for the entire population. A team, which consists of a physician, a nurse, midwives, a health technician, a medical secretary, and sometimes a pharmacist and a dentist, work in each health center.[8,15]

Since 1963, the number of health centers has gradually increased, reaching 6,377 in 2006, with 10,317 population per health center.[16] The smallest primary healthcare unit is called a "health house," in which only one midwife works. Secondary and tertiary healthcare settings are hospitals. The MoH is mainly responsible for managing hospitals. The MoH runs state hospitals and also some specialist hospitals, such as maternity, psychiatric, children's, chest disease, and bone disease. University hospitals serve as referral centers, and there are also

private hospitals. Although there were some hospitals, which were administered by other ministries, SIO, or public institutions, in 2005, all of them were gathered under the MoH, with the exception of the military hospitals.[8,15]

There have been some problems in the implementation of this model, despite the fact that it is a more suitable model given the conditions of the country. The socialization law was put into practice successfully at the outset, but later, some changes were made to the implementation.[15] Some principles were neglected or not carried out, mainly because of lack of political stability. These neglected principles were as follows: having someone working full-time in the health centers, free healthcare services, organizational unity of health services at the provincial level, and the two-way referral system. At the same time, high priority was given to curative health services instead of preventive ones. Qualified health manpower for primary health care could not be trained. The shortage of buildings, supplies, and equipment for health care could not be adequately addressed. Vertical organizations were not closed, and community participation, which is one of the most important principles, could not be achieved.

In the 1980s, the economic system of Turkey began to change toward liberalization, and at the same time, "health reform" discussions commenced. A special unit for health reforms was formed in the MoH after 1990, and several projects were carried out with the support of the World Bank. Two National Health Congresses were held to discuss the proposed reforms, which aimed to make changes to the organization (office-based "family medicine services," instead of community-based health centers), funding (premiums instead of taxes), and manpower (contract-based work instead of civil servants). These proposals did not meet with general acceptance; there was also opposition from the Turkish Medical Association, health organizations, and some academics. Together with the political changes, the reform proposal could not be put into practice, but later on (in 2001), a rolling fund was implemented in health centers. In 2002, the reform discussions restarted with a different name, "health transformation program," but with the same context. Currently, the socialization law is still in practice, and there are 6,377 health centers providing community-based, holistic health care, whereas "family medicine services," as a pilot project, is limited to some cities. The changes related to the financing of health services have not yet been carried out; the Social Security and General Health Insurance law was passed in the Grand National Assembly, but its application was postponed.[11,14,17]

DESCRIPTION OF THE CURRENT HEALTHCARE SYSTEM

Although the main responsible governmental body in Turkey for the planning and implementation of health services is the MoH, it is not the sole provider. Besides the MoH, universities, armed forces, regional and district municipalities, and the private sector provide healthcare services. The central unit of the MoH controls and organizes urban and rural regional healthcare services. The central unit consists of planning, advisory, and evaluation bodies for national and regional health services. Health services in each regional district are administered by the regional health administrator. Regional health services are organized as a small model of national health services. Figure 15-2 shows the organizational structure of the MoH in Turkey.[11]

Regional health services are structured by socialized health services, as summarized earlier. According to the health services socialization law, which was passed

in 1961 and implemented in 1963, the main local health services units are health centers. These units provide primary healthcare services for 5,000 to 10,000 of the population. Distribution of health centers are established based on the distribution of the population. Usually 8 to 10 health centers are administered under one group. These group administration units function as an intermediate step between the regional health administration and the health center. Each health center has multiple "health houses," which are the most peripheral units of health services organization throughout the country. The fundamental role of health centers and health houses is to provide primary, secondary, and if necessary, tertiary health services with a holistic approach. These public health services are provided at homes and workplaces, as well as at the health center. A team consists of physicians, nurses, midwives, a health technician, and a driver. If the health center is serving a larger population, it may include a dentist, pharmacist, psychologist, social worker, laboratory technicians, or other health-related professionals. Health houses, on the other hand, station nurses and midwives, who mostly provide preventive health services for small communities, such as townships and villages. Other than these state-run health

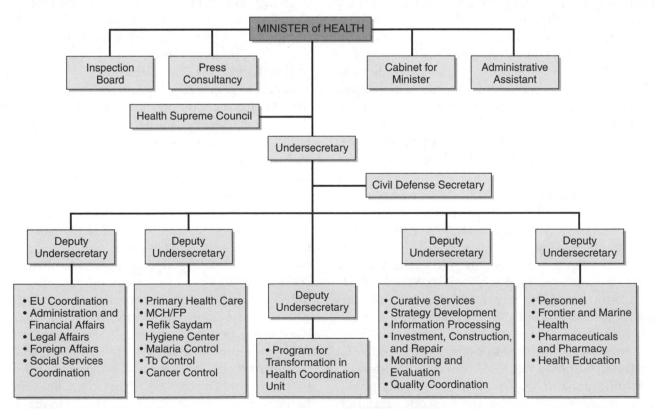

FIGURE 15-2 Organizational Structure of the Ministry of Health in Turkey
Ministry of Health, 2007.

units, private healthcare providers and occupational health services address additional the primary care needs of the community.[8,12]

General state hospitals, specialized hospitals, and university and training hospitals provide second- and third-level healthcare services nationwide. Although the socialization law requires a mutual referral chain between health centers and hospitals, today it is possible to bypass health centers to seek health care directly from hospitals. Besides the MoH, armed forces, universities, municipalities, and the private sector also provide hospital-based healthcare services.

After the 2002 general elections, the new cabinet initiated the "Health Transformation Program." Some of the main goals of this program were to limit MoH responsibilities as a planning and supporting government body, to start a national health insurance program, and to establish widely distributed and easily accessible healthcare services nationwide.[17] For this purpose, it was planned to initiate "family medicine practice" and transform state-owned hospitals into self-governing corporate entities. After the initial application, this program, and in particular general health insurance, received strong objections from the Turkish Medical Association, other professional associations, trade unions, and universities and was later canceled by the Supreme Constitutional Court. Nevertheless, the Family Medicine pilot program was initiated in 2005. Despite widespread opposition and without any systematic outcome evaluation, the program has continued to expand to the rest of the country.

Facilities

Primary Healthcare Facilities

Based on 2006 data,[16] there are 6,377 health centers in Turkey. Urban and rural distribution of these centers is 43.1% and 56.9%, respectively. The average population they serve is 10,317, which is quite close to the number (10,000) projected by socialization law. There are regional differences, however; population per health center in the northern districts (Black Sea) is 6,800, and in the northwestern districts (Marmara), it is 15,705. In Istanbul, the population per health center is 26,257, the highest in the country.

In addition to health centers, there are a few other vertically organized primary healthcare facilities in the urban areas of the country. Distribution of these MoH-run facilities is shown in Table 15-3.[16]

All of these centers work collaboratively with the health centers. Maternity, child health, and family

TABLE 15-3 Distribution of Primary Healthcare Facilities in Turkey

Primary healthcare facilities	Number
Health centers	6,377
Maternity, child health, and family planning centers	298
Tuberculosis (Tb) control centers	259
Malaria control dispensary	37

Source: Ministry of Health, 2007.

planning centers serve children and reproductive-age women. Tb control centers implement DOTS (Directly Observed Treatment Short-Course) nationwide. Malaria control dispensaries, however, are located only in those regions with endemic malaria.

Secondary and Tertiary Healthcare Facilities

In 2006, the total number of beds was 196,667 in 1,205 hospitals in Turkey. Although there are regional differences, the number of beds per 10,000 population is 27. In the most developed and the least developed sections of the country, the number of beds per 10,000 population is 27.6 and 12.5, respectively. Sixty-four percent of hospitals and 68% of beds are administered by the MoH. There are 52 training and education hospitals (7%) under the MoH. These and other university training and education hospitals provide 29% of the total number of beds in the country. The private sector also provides 25% of all hospitals and 7% of all beds in Turkey. The majority of private hospitals (41%) and beds (45%) are located in the most developed part of the country; only 3% of private hospitals and 2% of beds provided by the private sector are located in the least developed sections of the country.[18] Table 15-4 presents the distribution of hospitals and beds in the country.[18]

In addition to these general hospitals, there are specialty hospitals, such as those for obstetrics, children, chest diseases, cardiovascular diseases, mental health, eye diseases, physical therapy and rehabilitation, oncology, venereal diseases, leprosy, emergency and traumatology, occupational diseases, and dentistry.

Workforce

At the end of 2007, there were 98,634 physicians.[11] Overall, there is one physician per 716 persons in the country. Fifty-one percent of all physicians are specialized practitioners, and 58% of them are employed by the MoH.

TABLE 15-4 Distribution of Hospitals and Beds in Turkey

Administered by	Hospitals	Beds
MoH	769	133,168
Medical schools	56	29,700
Private sector	305	13,707
Other governmental	48	17,091
Associations, organizations, and so forth	27	3,001
Total	1,205	196,667

Source: Ministry of Health, 2007.

The rest of the specialized practitioners are mainly employed by universities. These physicians can work part-time in government hospitals and part-time in the private sector. In the last decade, the number of specialized practitioners has increased gradually. Almost three fourths of dentists practice in the private sector; therefore, there is a huge need for dentists in government health services. There is a significant regional disparity in the distribution of dentists; in some regions, there are 2,000 persons per dentist and in others 47,000 persons per dentist. The same problem arises regarding the distribution and need for nurses and midwives in Turkey. Today there is a huge need for midwives in primary care.[11,19–21]

The number of general practitioner physicians who work in the health centers is 15,020; there are 4,380 people per each general practitioner in the country. Table 15-5 shows the distribution of health personnel in health centers.[16] There are significant differences between the more and less developed regions of the country.

Technology and Equipment

Medical technology is one of the areas that clearly demonstrates Turkey's dependency on foreign technol-

TABLE 15-5 Distribution of Health Personnel in Health Centers

Health Personnel	Number	People per Personnel
General practitioner	15,020	4,380
Midwife	22,507	2,923
Nurse	12,921	5,092
Health technician	5,869	11,210

Source: Ministry of Heatlh, 2007.

ogy and finance. The main goal of investment in this area is to increase profit instead of technology development, research, or production. The numbers of computerized tomography (CT) and magnetic resonance imaging (MRI) are 566 and 254, respectively. There are seven CTs and three MRIs per 1 million people in the country; these numbers for CT and MRI, however, are 16 and 5 per 1 million people in the most developed region and 2 and 2 per 1 million people in the least developed region of the country. Almost half of all CTs (46%) and 58% of all MRIs are provided by the private sector (Table 15-6).[11,22]

In the total of 645 hemodialysis centers in the country, there are 9,844 dialysis units. Each serves an average of four patients, which is consistent with European Renal Association criteria.[18]

There has been a significant improvement in the pharmaceutical industry, especially since the 1950s. Today there are 42 production plants and 136 companies in this sector; 40 of these companies are under multinational corporations. The largest customers of these companies are the government facilities; the export–import ratio in the pharmaceutical industry is quite low (10%).[23]

From the beginning of and before the foundation of the Republic, Turkey has been quite successful in vaccine production and vaccination programs. Until the mid-1990s, Turkey produced its own vaccines against smallpox, rabies, Tb, pertussis, diphtheria, tetanus, typhoid fever, typhus, and cholera.[24] Unfortunately, privatization efforts in the late 1990s stopped national vaccination production and created an absolute dependence on imported vaccines.

EVALUATION OF HEALTHCARE SYSTEM

Cost

There are three main finance sources for healthcare services in Turkey: (1) the state budget, (2) social security organizations' budget, and (3) personal expenses.

The general state budget is financed from tax revenues, which is the major source for health services

TABLE 15-6 Distribution of CTs and MRIs in Turkey

	Total	Per 1 Million	MoH	University	Private
CT	566	7	222	86	258
MRI	254	3	65	41	148

Source: Ministry of Health, 2007.

finance in the country. Although they were merged under one umbrella in 2005, historically, there have been three different social security organizations in the country: the Civil Servants' Pension Fund (ES), the SSK, and the Social Security Organization for the Self-Employed (Bag-Kur). ES is funded from state employee salaries and with the state matching payments; this fund provides social and healthcare services for state employees, retirees, and their dependents. SSK provides the same services for workers who are employed in industry; this fund is supported by employers' payments as well as salary deductions. Bag-Kur, on the other hand, provides social and healthcare services for self-employed individuals, who pay funding premiums themselves. Social security coverage in Turkey is 87%. Sixty-one percent of those covered are under SSK. Twenty-eight percent are under Bag-Kur, and 11% are under the ES fund. Although official figures reflect that only 13% of the population is uncovered by any one of these social security funds, the national health accounts household health expenditure survey estimated that 33% of the population is not fully covered for healthcare expenses.[25] According to the National Household Survey,[26] the percentage of those not fully covered in urban and rural areas are 30% and 43%, respectively.

Since 1992, the healthcare expenditures of this uncovered population are compensated via another fund called "green card," which covers all healthcare expenditures of uncovered and/or poor people. Although all state funds have prescription coverage, there is a 20% co-payment for active employees and 10% co-payment for retirees. Besides these state funds, there are also private retirement and health insurance systems that provide private health coverage. Until 2001, all health centers provided free primary care services; since then, health centers have become fee-for-service and for-profit service providers.[11]

The MoH budget, which is funded from the general budget as well as hospital and primary healthcare services revenues, is 1.14% of the GDP, and 4.4% of the general budget in 2006.[16,19] Although these figures are increasing since the 2000s, it is still below the essential level and less than half of the WHO-recommended percentage. The budget portion for preventive healthcare services (the budget of the general directorate of primary health care) decreased from 31% in 2002 to 24% in 2006.[16] During the same budget period, the portion for curative services (the budget of the general directorate of curative services) increased from 40% to 67%[18]; however, with a health expenditure of 586 USD per person, Turkey is the lowest OECD country in health expenditure. The health expenditure for preventive health services is only 5 USD per person.[27]

In the year 2000, 63% of all healthcare expenditures were made through state institutions and 37% through the private sector. Three quarters of private sector expenditures and 28% of all healthcare service expenses are out of pocket.[25] According to the national household survey,[26] on average, 12% of household expenses were out-of-pocket medical expenses, approximately one third of the amount spent on groceries. More than one third (35%) of out-of-pocket household health expenses go to prescription costs. The remaining 65% covers other treatment services, laboratory fees, eyeglasses, hearing aids and other devices, and donations. Between 2002 and 2007, social security institutions' healthcare service purchases increased by 3% from state hospitals, 33% from university hospitals, and 64% from private hospitals. According to 2006 data, one third of all health expenses and 21% of state expenses go to prescription drug expenditures.[11] The estimated prescription drug expense per person is 134 USD annually.[28]

Quality

In primary health care, the number of annual outpatient services per person is 1.8 in health centers throughout the country. This figure differs between developed[5,19] and less developed[3,6] regions. One fifth of all outpatient services in health centers is supported by a laboratory diagnosis. As expected, only 6.4% of all outpatient applications are referred to secondary- or tertiary-level healthcare facilities.[16]

Home visits to high-risk populations, including children and pregnant women, are among the most important preventive services provided by the community health centers. In 2006, the average number of visits per baby was 5.2, per children 1.2, and per pregnant women 2.7.[16] Not only the quantity of home visits, but also the quality of service, education, and prenatal care is important in primary health care. Overall, 81% of all pregnant women received at least one health service, either education or care from a primary healthcare provider. This is much lower than optimal, as it means that nearly 20% of pregnant women did not receive any professional care during their pregnancy. Four of five deliveries occur in health institutions and 83% of all deliveries are supported by a health professional. As expected, these numbers are lower in rural communities than in urban settings. Deliveries via cesarean section consist of 21% of all labors, which is lower than many other countries. Other important indicators of the quality of primary healthcare services are family planning, maternity, and child health services. The 2003 Turkish Demography and Health Survey demonstrated that 71% of 15- to 49-year-old reproductive-age women use at least one family planning method. Although this number has increased over the years, only 43% of these women use a modern family planning technique.[10]

Nationwide vaccination services are provided by health centers and are free to all children and pregnant women. The routine vaccination schedule includes BCG, DTP, OPV, MMR, hepatitis B, and HiB vaccines. Despite the moderately high vaccination rates for BCG (88%), DTP (89%), OPV (95%), and measles (79%), full coverage among 12- to 23-month-old children is only 54%.[10] The vaccination rate is closely related to the mother's education and socioeconomic level.

The admission rate in state hospitals is 2.8 per 100. In university hospitals, it is 9.3%, and in private hospitals, it is 8%. The national average admission rate is 3.5%, whereas the overall admission rate is 3.5. According to 2006 data, the national bed occupation rate is 64%, and the patient turnout rate is 46 patients with an average 5 days of admittance. These rates are the highest in university hospitals and the lowest in private hospitals. The crude mortality rate among hospital admittances is 1.4%.[18]

Access

The national health accounts household health expenditures survey[25] demonstrated that the average annual healthcare usage per person is 4.6 office visits; only 0.3% of them are preventive services. The average hospital admittance per person is 0.1%. There is a significant disparity in access to health care between rural and urban populations, socioeconomic levels, and especially social security coverage. Examining the health technology and imaging use in hospital admittances shows that the average technology use, which is 69% among admitted patients, drops significantly among those without social security coverage. Medical technology was used for 100% of those with private health insurance. Technology and laboratory use among outpatient clinics is 12% and 15%, respectively. Overall, five of six persons with any health problem reported having access to health care. The most commonly reported problem in access is financial problems.[25,26]

In 2006, there were a total of 217,540,425 outpatient applications to all hospitals in the country. The average application per person was 3.0. Eighty-seven percent of all these admittances were made to government hospitals, 6% were made to university hospitals, and 7% were made to private hospitals.[18]

CURRENT AND EMERGING ISSUES AND CHALLENGES

Regarding health services and quality of life, the most important challenges Turkey faces today are poverty and economic and social disparities. As we discussed earlier, health expenditure takes up only a small percentage of the general budget; the budget slice for preventive health services and public health is continuously decreasing. On the other hand, the private sector is getting stronger in the healthcare industry. Social security funds do not fully cover every citizen, and out-of-pocket expenses are also increasing significantly. A major challenge in access to health care is unequal distribution of healthcare facilities and human power throughout the country.

The main problem today, however, is the current administration's "health transformation program." The first step of this program is to initiate family medicine as a primary healthcare provider. The second step is to transform hospitals into self-governing for-profit health enterprises. The third step is to start a nationwide health insurance system for the financing of new programs. All three steps of this new program represent a significant threat to population-based health services in the country. Instead of supporting and improving free, accessible, and widespread health centers as primary healthcare providers, the new program proposes a family medicine system as a model copied from the U.S. healthcare system. Current pilot implementations have not been evaluated according to the needs of the population.

There are major differences between the current holistic primary healthcare services and the proposed family medicine program. The primary healthcare services for community-based preventive, therapeutic, and rehabilitative healthcare services are provided by a team that includes physicians, nurses, a health technician, and so forth. The proposed family medicine program, on the other hand, provides individual-based healthcare services by a teamed-up physician and a nurse. Instead of a holistic approach to community health, regardless of community health needs, preventive and therapeutic health services are provided by different healthcare providers. Instead of community-based healthcare services, all of the services are provided in health institutions, and all healthcare services are proposed as private for-profit health services, instead of free, accessible, socialized healthcare services.

In the new transformation program, hospitals will become for-profit private enterprises. This will lead health care into an expensive market economy, which will increase the already excessive out-of-pocket expenses and exacerbate the problems with access to health care and the disparities in the community. The new private health insurance system will create a new burden of insurance premiums for limited services and will cover only those who pay their insurance premiums. The easiest way of evaluating the possible consequences of this transformation is to look at the current healthcare problems in the United States; it is not difficult to predict that this transformation will foster inequalities and will deepen the health and social disparities in the country.

ACKNOWLEDGMENTS

The authors thank Ms. Dana Kristine Weikart for language editing and review.

REFERENCES

1. AnaBritannica Turkish Edition, Cilt 21, İstanbul; 1990.
2. TC Anayasası, Resmi Gazete 9.07.1961-334. The Turkish Constitution. *State Official Journal.* July 09, 1961–334.
3. Anayasası TC. Resmi Gazete. The Turkish Constitution. *State Official Journal.* November 09, 1982-17863.
4. DİE. Türkiye İstatistik Yıllığı 2004, Ankara 2005 *SIS. Turkey's Statistical Yearbook 2004, Ankara 2005.*
5. Dokuzuncu kalkınma planı (2007–2013), Resmi Gazete, 1 Temmuz 2006. Ninth Development Plan (2007–2013). *State Official Journal.* July 01, 2006.
6. The World Bank Turkey at a glance. Retrieved April 6, 2008, from http://devdata.worldbank.org/AAG/tur_aag.pdf.
7. TÜİK, Nüfus İstatistikleri ve Projeksiyonlar. Retrieved April 6, 2008, from http://www.tuik.gov.tr/VeriBilgi.do?tb_id=39&ust_id=11.
8. Fişek NH. Halk Sağlığına Giriş, unpublished speech at Turkish Council, Ankara; 1985.
9. TÜİK. 2006 Yoksulluk Çalışması Sonuçları. Retrieved April 6, 2008, from http://www.tuik.gov.tr/PreHaberBultenleri.do?id=626.
10. Hacettepe Üniversitesi Nüfus Etüdleri Enstitüsü. *Türkiye Nüfus ve Sağlık Araştırması,* Ankara Turkey 2003, Ankara 2004. *Hacettepe University Institute of Population Studies. Turkey Demographic and Health Survey 2003, Ankara, 2004.*
11. T.C. Sağlık Bakanlığı, Türkiye'de Sağlığa Bakış, Ankara 2007 *The Ministry of Health of Turkey. Health at a Glance Turkey 2007, Ankara 2007.*
12. Aydın E. Türkiye'de sağlık teşkilatlanması tarihi, Ankara; 2002.
13. Sağlık Bakanlığı. Dr. Refik Saydam *Turkey 1881–1942,* USDIK Press, Ankara; 1982.
14. Soyer A. Sağlığın Öyküsü, unpublished speech at Turkish Council, İstanbul; 2004.
15. Öztek Z. Türkiye'de sağlık hizmetleri: sorunlar ve çözümler, *HASUDER raporu,* Ankara; 2007.
16. Sağlık Bakanlığı, *Temel Sağlık Hizmetleri Genel Müdürlüğü Çalışma Yıllığı.* 2006, Turkish Government Report, Ankara; 2007.
17. *The Ministry of Health of Turkey, Health Transition Program,* Ankara; 2008
18. Sağlık Bakanlığı, Yataklı Tedavi Kurumları Çalışma Yıllığı, Turkey Report 2006, Turkish Government Report, Ankara; 2007.
19. SB, Sağlık İstatistikleri 2004, Ankara 2005. *The Ministry of Health of Turkey. Health Statistics 2004, Ankara 2005.*
20. SB RSHMB Hıfzıssıhha Merkezi Müdürlüğü. Sağlıkta insan kaynakları mevcut durum analizi, Ankara 2007. *The Ministry of Health of Turkey. Analysis of Current Situation for Human Resources in Health Sector, Ankara 2007.*
21. *ÜAK,* Tıp-sağlık bilimleri eğitim konseyi başkanlığı, Türkiye'de tıp-sağlık bilimleri alanında eğitim ve insangücü planlaması. Bayındır Ü, Durak İ. Şubat; 2008.
22. Onur hamzaoğlu. Türkiye'nin sağlığını okumak. *Sürekli tıp eğitimi.* 2007;16(12):VI.
23. İlaç endüstrisi işverenleri sendikası. Türkiye'de ilaç endüstrisinin gelişimi. Retrieved April 6, 2008, from http://www.ieis.org.tr.
24. Toplum ve Hekim. *Panel: Türkiye Aşı Üretmeli mi? Üretebilir mi?* 2003;1885:398–400.
25. SB Ulusal Sağlık Hesapları Hane Halkı Sağlık Harcamaları 2002–2003, Ankara 2006. *The Ministry of Health of Turkey. Turkey National Health Accounts Household Health Expenditures 2002–2003, Ankara 2006.*
26. T.C.SB RSHMB Hıfzıssıhha Merkezi Müdürlüğü, Ulusal hane halkı araştırması, 2003, Ankara 2006, *The Ministry of Health of Turkey. National Household Survey 2003 Basic Findings, Ankara 2006.*
27. Sağlık H. *Türkiye ekonomi politikaları araştırma vakfı Sağlık politikaları ve ülkemizde sağlık harcamaları sorunu.* Ankara, Turkey; 2008.
28. Araştırmacı ilaç firmaları derneği, Türkiye 2006 yılı ilaç harcamaları değerlendirilmesi. Retrieved April 4, 2008, from http://www.aifd.org.tr/pdf/Haber/140.pdf.

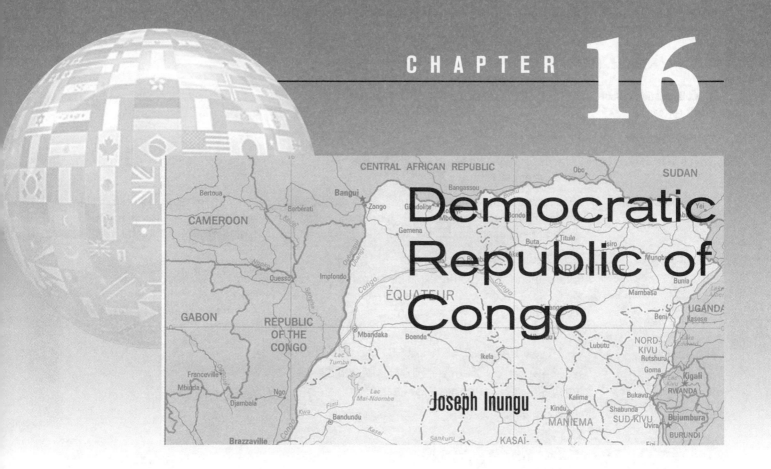

CHAPTER 16

Democratic Republic of Congo

Joseph Inungu

COUNTRY DESCRIPTION

TABLE 16-1 Congo

Nationality	Noun: Congolese (singular and plural)
	Adjective: Congolese or Congo
Ethnic groups	Over 200 African ethnic groups of which the majority are Bantu; the four largest tribes—Mongo, Luba, Kongo (all Bantu), and the Mangbetu-Azande (Hamitic)—make up about 45% of the population
Religions	Roman Catholic 50%, Protestant 20%, Kimbanguist 10%, Muslim 10%, other (includes syncretic sects and indigenous beliefs) 10%
Language	French (official), Lingala (a lingua franca trade language), Kingwana (a dialect of Kiswahili or Swahili), Kikongo, Tshiluba
Literacy	Definition: age 15 and over can read and write French, Lingala, Kingwana, or Tshiluba
	Total population: 65.5%
	Male: 76.2%
	Female: 55.1% (2003 est.)
Government type	Republic
Date of independence	June 30, 1960 (from Belgium)

(continues)

TABLE 16-1   Congo   (continued)

Gross Domestic Product (GDP) per capita	$300 (2007 est.)
Unemployment rate	Not applicable
Natural hazards	Periodic droughts in south; Congo River floods (seasonal); in the east, in the Great Rift Valley, there are active volcanoes
Environment: current issues	Poaching threatens wildlife populations; water pollution; deforestation; refugees responsible for significant deforestation, soil erosion, and wildlife poaching; mining of minerals (coltan—a mineral used in creating capacitors, diamonds, and gold), causing environmental damage
Population	66,514,506

Estimates for this country explicitly take into account the effects of excess mortality caused by AIDS; this can result in lower life expectancy, higher infant mortality, higher death rates, lower population growth rates, and changes in the distribution of population by age and gender than would otherwise be expected (July 2008 est.) |
| Age structure | 0–14 years: 47.1% (male 15,711,817/female 15,594,449)

15–64 years: 50.4% (male 16,672,399/female 16,875,468)

65 years and over: 2.5% (male 674,766/female 985,607) (2008 est.) |
| Median age | Total: 16.3 years
Male: 16.1 years
Female: 16.5 years (2008 est.) |
Population growth rate	3.236% (2008 est.)
Birth rate	43 births/1,000 population (2008 est.)
Death rate	11.88 deaths/1,000 population (2008 est.)
Net migration rate	1.24 migrant(s)/1,000 population (2008 est.)
Gender ratio	At birth: 1.03 male(s)/female
Under 15 years: 1.01 male(s)/female
15–64 years: 0.99 male(s)/female
65 years and over: 0.68 male(s)/female
Total population: 0.99 male(s)/female (2008 est.)
Infant mortality rate	Total: 83.11 deaths/1,000 live births
Male: 91.14 deaths/1,000 live births
Female: 74.83 deaths/1,000 live births (2008 est.)
Life expectancy at birth	Total population: 53.98 years
Male: 52.22 years
Female: 55.8 years (2008 est.)
Total fertility rate	6.28 children born/woman (2008 est.)
HIV/AIDS adult prevalence rate	4.2% (2003 est.)
Number of people living with HIV/AIDS	1.1 million (2003 est.)
HIV/AIDS deaths	100,000 (2003 est.)

Central Intelligence Agency. The World Fact Book, 2008. Retrieved November 18, 2008, from https://www.cia.gov/library/publications/the-world-factbook.

History

Although little is known about the early inhabitants of the Democratic Republic of Congo (DRC), it is commonly believed that pygmies lived in the Congo Basin before the Bantu groups moved into the area from the north and spread east and south about 2,000 years ago.[1] The early inhabitants of the Congo lived in small villages led by chiefs or dominant clan leaders. Over time, some of these chiefs conquered neighboring villages and established big kingdoms. A few of the well-known kingdoms are the kingdom of Kongo, Luba, Lunda, and Kuba.

The mouth of the Congo River and the lower course of the river were known to the Portuguese for 4 centuries. A succession of voyages down the West Coast of Africa resulted in the discovery of the Congo in 1484 by Diego Cao, leading to the establishment of commercial relationships between the kingdom of Kongo and Portugal. Missionaries were sent out later to convert people to Christianity.[2] It was not until Stanley's memorable journey and especially his discovery of the great Congo waterway in 1870 that Europe became interested in the black continent.[3]

In 1876, the African International Association was created in the aftermath of the meeting of about 40 world-known geographers convened in Brussels by King Leopold II of Belgium. The association was intended to be a joint effort of all the Western countries at the conference to carry out humanitarian projects in Equatorial Africa. Instead of working together, these countries organized independent expeditions to explore Africa. As each country claimed authority over portions of African land, a phenomenon known as the Scramble for Africa, the European powers were forced to organize the Berlin Conference of 1884–1885 to avoid potential conflict. To support Leopold II's professed aim of protecting Africans from Arab slavers and opening the country to missionaries and Western capitalists, the Berlin Conference legitimized his authority to develop the Congo. Later, he secretly bought off the foreign investors in the Congo and made it his private property. He named it the Congo Free State. Leopold II accumulated a vast personal fortune from ivory and rubber through Congolese slave labor. His brutal exploitation of the Congo eventually caused international outcry, prompting Belgium to take over its administration.[4]

The new colonial administration developed modern cities, built railroads and health care infrastructure, and encouraged immigration from neighboring countries to develop plantations and mining, which flourished in Katanga with the creation of the "Union Minière du Haut Kanga" in 1906.[5] At the same time, it gave privileges only to a small number of Congolese who adopted European culture. As in the rest of colonial Africa, the independence struggle that started in the late 1950s became a great national awakening in the Belgian Congo with people ready to shed fear in order to manifest their aspirations for freedom and their desire for a better and more secure future.[6] In 1956, a group of the Congolese elite published an important document called "le Manifeste de Conscience Africaine" (the African Conscience Manifest), requesting independence. In 1957, the Association des Bakongos, the first political party created in the Congo, won the first municipal elections in Leopoldville, the capital city. After a series of riots and civil unrest that started on January 4, 1959, Belgium realized how difficult it would be to maintain control over this vast country. Belgium organized a meeting of Congolese politicians in Brussels on January 20, 1960, where the independence date was decided. The country became independent on June 30, 1960, with Joseph Kasavubu as president and Patrice Emery Lumumba as prime minister.

Only a few weeks after independence, ethnic and personal rivalries, often encouraged by Belgian interests, began to pull the country apart. The Congolese army mutinied against their Belgian Officers in Kinshasa. Moise Tshombe, the provisional president of the richest province of the country, seceded on July 11, 1960, followed by Kasai, the second richest province of the country, crippling the government.

To reestablish order in the country, Prime Minister Lumumba sought assistance from the United Soviet Socialist Republic, an act viewed in the United States as an attempt for the United Soviet Socialist Republic to gain a foothold in sub-Saharan Africa. The United States started looking for ways to replace Lumumba as leader. On September 14, 1960, Colonel Joseph Mobutu, the army chief, overthrew the government. Patrice Lumumba was arrested, tortured, and sent to his political rival Moise Tshombe in Katanga, where he was assassinated with the help of Belgian paratroopers. Tshombe became prime minister. In 1963, Pierre Mulele, Lumumba's ally, launched a rebellion in the Kwilu while Antoine Gizenga, Lumumba's deputy prime minister, set up a rival government in Stanleyville. This rebellion was crushed with the help of Belgian, British, and U.S. troops.

At the end of the Cold War, Zaire ceased to be the anticommunist bastion. Mobutu was weakened. His regime's human rights abuses, his government corruption, and his massive embezzlement of government funds for personal use became the target of international criticism. Under pressure, Mobutu agreed to a multi-party system in April 1990. In 1992, he reluctantly organized a Sovereign National Conference in Kinshasa attended by more than 2,000 delegates of various political parties. The conference elected the Archbishop Laurent Monsengwo to chair the conference, along with Étienne Tshisekedi wa Mulumba, leader of the Union for Democracy and Social Progress, as prime minister. Mobutu created a parallel government with a new prime minister. The ensuing stalemate produced a compromise merger of the two governments into the High Council of Republic-Parliament of Transition in 1994, which maintained Mobutu as head of state and appointed Kengo Wa Dondo as prime minister.

After the war and genocide in neighboring Rwanda, thousands of Hutu, including the Rwandan Hutu military forces (Interahamwe), crossed the border to seek refuge in Eastern Congo. These Interahamwe started using the newly established Hutu refugee camps to attack Congolese Tutsi, as well as the new Tutsi-led government in Rwanda. Congolese Tutsi, with the assistance of the Tutsi-led government in Rwanda, formed a militia to defend themselves against the Interahamwe. Joined by various Congolese opposition groups, the Tutsi militia became the Alliance des Forces Démocratiques pour la Libération du Congo-Zaïre (AFDL) led by Laurent-Desire Kabila. The AFDL forces attacked the Hutu refugee camps looking for the Interahamwe. Emboldened by their success, the AFDL forces decided to oust Mobutu.

The elements of the AFDL started moving toward Kinshasa. Demoralized Mobutu's army did not oppose any significant resistance. To avoid a bloody confrontation in Kinshasa, President Mandela held peace talks between Mobutu and Kabila in May 1997. Facing the inevitable, Mobutu fled the country, and Kabila entered triumphal in Kinshasa on May 20, 1997. He proclaimed himself president and changed the name of the country to the DRC. With limited managerial skills, Laurent Kabila faced serious challenges holding his coalition together. A rift between him and his former allies, backed by Rwanda and Uganda, sparked a new rebellion. Troops from Angola, Chad, Namibia, Sudan, and Zimbabwe intervened to support Kabila's regime, turning the country into a vast battleground. In 1999, the Lusaka Accord was signed by all of the countries involved, as well as by most of the various rebel fractions. In January 2001, President Laurent Kabila was assassinated, and his son, Joseph Kabila, became president. He successfully negotiated the withdrawal of Rwandan forces occupying eastern Congo in October 2002. Two months later, the Pretoria Accord was signed by all rebel groups to end the fight in the Congo. This accord paved the way for the Congo's new power-sharing transitional government led by Joseph Kabila and four vice presidents (former rebel leaders). The transitional government held a successful constitutional referendum in December 2005 and organized elections for the presidency, National Assembly, and provincial legislatures in 2006. The newly elected National Assembly was installed in September 2006, and Joseph Kabila was inaugurated as president in December 2006.[7]

Despite the political progress, the instability continues in the Eastern part of the Congo. The rebel general, Laurent Nkunda, and his militia, made essentially of fellow Tutsi, have been fighting the Congolese Army since August 2007.

Size and Geography

With 2,345,408 square kilometers (905,567 square miles), the DRC is the third largest country in Africa after Algeria and Sudan. The DRC is located at the heart of Africa, astride the equator. It is limited clockwise from the Southwest by Angola, the Republic of Congo, the Central African Republic, the Sudan, Uganda, Rwanda, Burundi, Tanzania across Lake Tanganyika, and Zambia. A map of the DRC is shown in Figure 16-1.

Government and Political System

The DRC is a republic with a strong presidential system. Based on the new constitution passed on February 18, 2006, the government is divided into three branches. The executive branch is composed of (1) the President, Joseph Kabila; (2) the Prime Minister, Antoine Gizenga, appointed by the president; and (3) the cabinet, ministers appointed by the president. The legislative branch consists of a National Assembly with 500 seats. Sixty-one members are elected by majority vote in single-member constituencies, and 439 members are elected by open-list proportional representation in multimember constituencies. The members serve 5-year terms. The Senate has 108 seats, and members are elected by provincial assemblies to serve 5-year terms. The judicial branch consists of a Constitutional Court, an Appeals Court or Cour de Cassation, Council of State, High Military Court, and civil and military courts and tribunals.

There are several political parties. The most active are the Christian Democrat Party, Congolese Rally for Democracy, Convention of Christian Democrats, Forces of Renewal, Movement for the Liberation of the Congo, People's Party for Reconstruction and Democracy,

FIGURE 16-1   Map of Democratic Republic of Congo

Social Movement for Renewal, Unified Lumumbist Party, Union for Democracy and Social Progress, and Union of Mobutist Democrats.

When the country became independent from Belgium on June 30, 1960, Kinshasa was made the capital city. The country is divided into several administrative divisions, including 11 provinces: Bandundu, Bas-Zaire, Equateur, Haut-Zaire, Kasai-Occidental, Kasai-Oriental, Kinshasa, Maniema, North Kivu, Shaba, and South-Kivu.

Macroeconomics

Despite a vast potential of natural resources and mineral wealth, the DRC is one of the poorest countries in the world, with a per capita gross domestic product (GDP) of U.S.$300 in 2007 (Table 16-2). This is the result of years of mismanagement, corruption, and war. Agriculture is the mainstay of the Congolese economy, accounting for 55% of the GDP in 2007. Coffee, palm oil, rubber, cotton, sugar, tea, and cocoa are the most important cash crops, whereas cassava, plantains, maize, groundnuts, and rice make up the food crops.

Industry accounts for 11% of the GDP. Mining industries are concentrated in the Katanga region. Cop-per, cobalt, diamonds, and gold continue to dominate exports. Gecamines, the state-owned mining company, has been severely affected by corruption and mismanagement. Manufacturing and service sectors, concentrated in Kinshasa, accounted for 34% of the GDP in 2000. It consists of consumer goods, mainly food processing, textile manufacturing, beer, cigarettes, metalworking, woodworking, and vehicle assembly.[8]

The DRC is a low-income and severely indebted economy in Africa. It ranks 11th from the bottom of the United Nations Development Program Human Development Index. According to a CIA report, 23% (15 million of the adult population) are participating in the economy. No specific unemployment data are available; however, the OECD cites the unemployment rate as "very high." Wealthy Congolese, government officials, and businessmen live primarily in Kinshasa or Lubumbashi. The urban subbourgeoisie include teachers, clerks, and low-level bureaucrats who depend on the state for their salaries. The rest of the city inhabitants are involved in small trade to survive. Many of them are soft drink vendors, shoe repairmen, taxi drivers, salespeople, artisans, smugglers, or prostitutes. Rural peasants live on agriculture, fishing, and/or hunting.

TABLE 16-2　Principal Country Economic Indicators

GDP (purchasing power parity)	U.S.$19.07 billion
GDP (official exchange rate)	U.S.$8.738 billion
GDP (real growth rate)	7%
GDP (per capita)	U.S.$300

From the DRC Ministry of Labor, 2007.

The means of transportation are very limited in this vast country. The network of roads approximates 153,497 kilometers. Only 2,794 kilometers of the roads are paved, leaving the vast interior devoid of roads.

Railroads cover 5,138 kilometers in three discontinuous lines: one linking Kinshasa and Matadi, another in northeastern Congo, and another in southeastern Congo to export minerals. The inland waterways cover 15,000 km. The Congo River is the most significant waterway for passengers and freight between Kinshasa and Kisangani. The number of ports is limited because the country has a tiny Atlantic coastline of approximately 40 kilometers. Matadi on the mouth of the Congo River is the principal port but is not accessible by large vessels. Other important ports include the Atlantic port at Boma and inland ports at Kinshasa and at Ilebo on the Kasai River. In 2006, there were 234 reported airports in the country. The two principle airports are located in Kinshasa and Lubumbashi.

The educational system in the DRC consists of four levels. The kindergarten is a 3-year program for children 3 to 5 years of age. It is not mandatory. Primary school is a 6-year program divided into three levels of 2 years each, namely, an elementary level for children 6 to 7 years old, a middle level for children 8 to 9 years old, and a terminal level for children 10 to 11 years old.

Secondary school students can select the short or long cycle. The system offers a 2-year *cycle d'orientation* taken by all secondary school students. These students take intensive classes in mathematics, French, and sciences. Successful students can advance to a short cycle offering 2- and 3-year technical diploma programs or to a long cycle, which takes 4 years to complete. Long-cycle students can select the humanities scientifiques, litteraires, pedagogiques, or techniques. The Congo has three national universities located in Kinshasa, Lubumbashi, and Kisangani. Several private universities have grown recently to meet the needs of the young population. In addition, there are several higher-education institutions, as well as technical and teacher-training schools scattered around the country.

Demographics

The total population of the DRC was 65,751,512 in 2007, with a median age of 16.1 years (male, 15.8 years; female, 16.4 years) and a gender ratio of 0.985 male(s)/female. Approximately 48% of the general population is 15 years old or younger.[8] The age distribution of the population is shown in Table 16-3.

With a birth rate of 42.96 births per 1,000 population and a death rate of 10.34 deaths per 1,000 population, the DRC experienced a growth rate of 3.39% in 2007. The DRC has over 250 ethnic groups, with a majority Bantu. The four largest tribes are Mongo, Luba, Kongo, and Mangbetu-Azande, and they make up approximately 45% of the population.

French is the official language. Lingala, Swahili, Kikongo, and Tshiluba are the common national languages spoken in the Congo. The literacy rate is high compared with other African countries. Approximately 65.5% (male, 76.2%; female, 55.1%) of the population aged 15 years and older can read and write French, Lingala, Kikongo, Shwahili, or Tshiluba.

Despite the natural resources, the DRC is one of the poorest countries in the world. Nearly three of four Congolese live in absolute poverty, with no regular supply of food or drinking water. This precarious situation of the population means that nearly two thirds of the Congolese population is deprived of health care for lack of financial resources. According to the United Nations Development Program, nearly 90% of the population lives on less than 20 U.S. dollars per month.[9]

TABLE 16-3　Age and Gender Distribution in the DRC, 2007

Age Range	Percentage of Population	Gender Distribution Male	Gender Distribution Female
0–14 years	47.6	15,718,614 (23.90%)	15,557,058 (23.70%)
15–64 years	49.9	16,224,734 (24.7%)	16,571,549 (25.2%)
65 years and over	2.6	680,313 (1.06%)	999,244 (1.54%)

Central Intelligence Agency. The World Fact Book, 2008. Retrieved November 18, 2008, from https://www.cia.gov/library/publications/the-world-factbook.

Selected sociodemographic characteristics of the Democratic Republic of the Congo are summarized in Table 16-4.

Roman Catholic is the most popular religious affiliation in the DRC, accounting for 50% of the population, followed by Protestant 20%, Kimbanguist 10%, Islam 10%, and other indigenous religions 10%.

Infectious and parasitic diseases are major health threats, accounting for at least 50% of all deaths in the DRC. Malaria, tuberculosis, HIV/AIDS, river blindness, trypanosomiasis, and schistosomiasis are all endemic. Coexistence of malaria and HIV in the same geographic area poses serious public health problems. These problems are compounded by the growing resistance of malaria to antimalarial drugs. Vaccine-preventable diseases and other preventable diseases such as measles, diarrheal diseases, tetanus, diphtheria, pertussis, poliomyelitis, and tuberculosis continue to kill children and pregnant women. Life expectancy at birth is 57.2 years, but it is expected to have declined because the wars and the advent of HIV/AIDS.

BRIEF HISTORY OF THE HEALTHCARE SYSTEM

Pre-World War II

Improving the health condition of the indigenous population in the Congo was one of the most important social priorities of the colonial administration during the Congo Free State era. Unfortunately, the size of the country, the low population density, and the lack of existing means of communication (roads) hindered the effort to offer care and organize an effective health system. Moreover, the causal agents and the mode of transmission of diseases that were prevalent in the Congo, such as malaria and trypanosomiases, were not known to Belgian physicians. These factors affected the ability of the colonial authority to offer care to the indigenous population. The majority of them relied on traditional medicine for survival.

The organization of the health system in the Congo Free State occurred gradually. On August 1888, King Leopold signed a decree allowing the organization of medical services in important centers of the country. In 1899, health commissions were created in different administrative districts of the country to fight malaria and trypanosomiasis. In 1910, the School of Tropical Diseases was formed in Antwerp to study and lead the fight against endemic tropical diseases.

The organization of the medical service was accelerated between 1911 and 1928. The medical service became autonomous and was placed under the authority of the Colony General Governor in 1922. Although 34 hospitals existed in the Congo in 1920 with a total of 3,040 beds, this number increased to 190 hospitals in 1946 with 21,178 beds.[10]

During the war (1900–1945), the Research Medical Center of Brussels for Central Africa (CEMUBAC) was formed to control tuberculosis in the Congo. Several organizations such as missionaries, philanthropic

TABLE 16-4 Demographic Characteristics of the Democratic Republic of the Congo, 2007

Demographic and Socioeconomic Statistics	
Population	
Number	65,751,512
Annual growth rate	3.39%
Urban population (2008 date)	33.0%
Infant mortality rate (per 1,000 live births)	120.0
Total fertility rate	6.37
Crude death rate (per 1,000 population)	10.34
Net migration rate (per 1,000 population	1.28
Life expectancy at birth (years)	57.2

Central Intelligence Agency. The World Fact Book, 2008. Retrieved November 18, 2008, from https://www.cia.gov/library/publications/the-world-factbook.

organizations, and international agencies joined the colonial government effort to expand the healthcare system.

Post-World War II

The end of World War II saw the implementation of the Van Hoof Duren Plan aimed at building Medico-Surgical Centers at each of the 38 provincial capitals in the Congo. Each Medico-Surgical Center was expected to serve a network of 15 satellite dispensaries.[11]

Although the modern healthcare system in the DRC was inherited from colonization, it has been modified to meet the new political realities. The National Health System is divided into three levels.[12] The central level includes the Minister of Health Office, the General Secretariat office, and seven divisions and specialized programs. The eight divisions are (1) general services (Human Resources and Finance), (2) hospitals, (3) epidemiology, (4) primary care, (5) pharmacy and medicinal plants, (6) health promotion and training, (7) planning, and (8) 42 specialized programs including the National Institute for Biological Research and the Expanded Immunization Program.

The intermediary level includes the Provincial Health Division with seven divisions and the health districts. The Provincial Health Division is led by the Provincial Medical Inspector. He is the liaison between the province and the central administration. There are 11 provincial health divisions. Each of the 41 Health Districts is led by a Medical District Inspector. He is the liaison between the provincial medical inspector and the health zones.

The periphery level is essentially made of the "zones de santé" (health zones), considered to be the basic units of the primary healthcare system in the DRC. Each health zone is led by the medical director of the health zone. The country is currently divided into 515 health zones. Each health zone, covering a total population of 100,000 to 150,000, contains on average 1 referral hospital, 1 to 3 reference health centers, and 15 to 25 standard health centers. Each standard health center is staffed by at least one certified nurse providing basic preventive and primary care services to the 5 to 10 villages in the area. There are about 6,000 health centers in the DRC. Serious medical cases are referred upward to the reference health centers first and then to the hospital of reference. The primary health system of the DRC was considered one of the most efficient in Africa. Each health zone was expected to fit within the boundary of the political entity called a territory. External financial

assistance was instrumental in the development of the health zones in the DRC. Although the three levels were presented separately, it must be emphasized that they are interconnected in practice.

DESCRIPTION OF THE CURRENT HEALTHCARE SYSTEM

Facilities

Based on the 2001 Ministry of Health report,[13] there were 3 tertiary (national) hospitals, 11 provincial hospitals, 306 general hospitals, and more than 6,000 health centers in the DRC. Private hospitals or medical centers were not tallied. Because of the limited sources of information regarding the number of primary care clinics in the DRC, we relied on the 1985 Ministry of Planning report to describe the distribution of hospitals, as well as the health centers in the different regions. There is a high concentration of physicians in the capital city as compared with other regions.

Religious organizations, notably Roman Catholic, Protestant, and Kimbanguist churches, and international relief organizations provide the bulk of health care in the DRC, particularly in rural areas. About half of the hospitals and health units are run by religious and other private institutions. The state runs the remaining half.[14]

Workforce

Before 1960, the healthcare system in the DRC was staffed by white foreign physicians and nurses. During colonization, Belgium focused only on preparing the supporting staff. In 1926, three nursing schools opened in Kinshasa, Kisantu, and Katana followed by a new school to train assistant pharmacists in 1947. On October 12, 1954, Lovanium University Center opened in Kinshasa, with a medical school, followed by the opening of the University of Lubumbashi and Kisangani in 1956 and 1962, respectively. The precipitous exodus of Belgium from the DRC in 1960 created a vacuum in all of the vital sectors, including the healthcare system. On June 30, 1960, there were only two Congolese physicians and a handful of diploma nurses for the entire country. The new government turned to the United Nations and the World Health Organization to attract foreign expertise. About 131 foreign physicians arrived in the Congo in 1961.

The effort to train local medical personnel became a priority after independence. In 1960, a contingent of Congolese medical assistants was sent to Belgium and

France for an accelerated training in medicine to staff the hospitals in the Congo. In the 1970s, the High Institute of Medical Techniques opened in Kinshasa to train highly qualified technicians in various disciplines (nursing, radiology, administration, nutrition, midwifery, etc.). In 1987, a new School of Public Health opened in Kinshasa to train health educators, health managers, and epidemiologists.

Despite a very difficult start, the DRC made an appreciable effort in training healthcare personnel. The number of health personnel recorded in 2007 is shown in Table 16-5. There were 5,827 Congolese physicians in the country. As a result of repeated wars and the continued deterioration of the living conditions in the country, approximately 30% of Congolese physicians practice medicine in South Africa, in other African neighboring countries, or in the West. A similar exodus has been reported among nurses, pharmacists, laboratory technicians, and so forth. This exodus has deleteriously affected the healthcare system in the DRC.

Technology and Equipment

Because of repeated wars and mismanagement, state-run hospitals and health units are in a general state of despair. The physical infrastructure has not been renovated since independence. Many hospitals lack basic equipment and medical supplies to meet the needs of the population. Hospitalized patients are often asked to buy their own medicines and supplies in order to be treated. At the same time, Congolese dignitaries and their allies continue to seek care in South Africa or Europe to avoid the crumbling local hospitals.

EVALUATION OF THE HEALTHCARE SYSTEM

Cost

The health sector in the DRC is essentially funded from three sources: the state budget, external (bilateral and multilateral) contributions, and recovery of the cost and services from users (up to 70% of operating cost). In 2006, the national budget of the DRC was 1,089,365,970,124 Congolese franc (U.S.$2,551, 208,361). Of this budget, the Ministry of Health received 62,107,411,126 Congolese franc, representing 5.7% of the total budget. The evolution of the country health budget from 2000 to 2005 is shown in Figure 16-2.[15] The major socioeconomic indicators as well as the government expenditure on health are shown in Table 16-6.

After independence, the country maintained the health financing policy established in the Van Hoof Duren plan in 1945. This plan specifically prescribed a central government role in financing the state healthcare system.

The historical development of the health system in the DRC, like that of many other African countries, was marked by its institutional character and the critical role played by the central authority in providing all of the financial resources for the health system. For many, it is the responsibility of any government to finance the healthcare system to protect its citizens. With the gradual withdrawal of the state from its responsibility, the healthcare system relied on external (bilateral or multilateral) contributions and fee-for-service payments

TABLE 16-5   The Distribution of the Health Workforce in the DRC in 2007

Categories	Total Number in the DRC	Density per 1,000
Physicians	5,827	0.107
Nurses and midwives	28,789	0.529
Dentists and technicians	159	0.003
Environmental and public health workers	Not applicable	Not applicable
Laboratory technicians	512	0.009
Other health workers	1,042	0.019
Community health workers	Not applicable	Not applicable
Health management and support	15,013	0.270
Total	52,542	0.966

From the DRC Ministry of Labor, 2007.

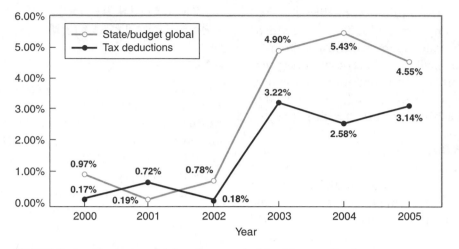

FIGURE 16-2   Evolution of the Country's Healthcare Budget, 2000–2005

from patients. As a result, the budget of the Ministry of Health continued to decline after independence. The 1985 Ministry of Health budget of $15,156,112 was six times less than the 1959 budget. Although foreign assistance represented only 33% of the health budget in 1959, it accounted for 80% of the Ministry of Health budget in 1985. The budget dropped from 4.1% in 1979 to 2.1% in 1984 and to 0.2% in 1990.[16] With the help of foreign partners such as religious organizations and private nongovernmental organizations, the current government is trying to rebuild the health system.

Quality

Once considered a model for sub-Saharan countries, the health system in the DRC has experienced serious challenges during the last 20 years because of poor management, a lack of resources and qualified manpower, and repeated civil wars. The current poor health indicators underscore the need for immediate actions to salvage the health system in the DRC. The infant mortality rate is 120 deaths per 1,000 live births. In 2004, 16% of children under 5 years had acute malnutrition. It is

TABLE 16-6   Socioeconomic Indicators for the DRC

Categories	
GDP (purchasing power parity) in billion	19.7
GDP per capita	$300
GDP real growth rate	7%
Total expenditure on health as a percentage of gross domestic product	4.0%
General government expenditure on health as a percentage of total expenditure on health	28.1%
Private expenditure on health as a percentage of total expenditure on health	71.9%
General government expenditure on health as a percentage of total government expenditure	5.7%
External resources for health as a percentage of total expenditure on health	19.1
Per capita total expenditure on health at international dollar rate	U.S.$15.3
Per capita government expenditure on health at international dollar rate	U.S.$4.3

From the DRC Ministry of Labor, 2007.

estimated that of the 1.2 million HIV-infected people only 5,000 have access to antiretroviral therapy. Malaria is endemic and claims many lives among children and pregnant women. Its resistance to existing medications compounds the problem. Other leading causes of death include upper respiratory infections, diarrheal diseases, and tuberculosis. Selected general health indicators in the DRC are shown in Table 16-7.

The quality of any health system depends not only on the number of qualified personnel and the adequacy of the existing infrastructures, but also on access to health services. The breakdown of the Congolese economy led to the gradual deterioration of the working conditions in the Congo forcing more than 20% of the physicians to look for work outside of the country. The exodus of Congolese physicians worsened an already precarious situation and exacerbated the imbalance in the distribution of physicians between rural and urban areas.

Access

In the last 10 years, many people have moved to urban areas in search of better jobs. These urban immigrants settle in the outskirts of big cities in temporary and substandard houses. The social norms that keep people's behavior in check in traditional communities disappear in big cities. Without a concomitant national job creation strategy, these immigrants live in abject poverty. Overcrowding, unhygienic living conditions, and poverty lead to malnutrition, diseases such as diarrhea, typhoid fever, HIV, tuberculosis, malaria, and death.

The health needs are overwhelming in the DRC. Unfortunately, the existing state-run hospitals and health units are ill equipped to address these needs. Pharmacies in these hospitals do not have the essential drugs to treat common diseases in the community. The June 2001 joint WHO-UNICEF mission estimated that over 70% of Congolese had no access to conventional medical care. Because of the lack of medical insurance, difficulty in accessing a healthcare center, especially in rural areas, and the horrible state of existing hospitals and health centers, the majority of Congolese turn to the informal sector. Many turn to traditional healers for care.

CURRENT AND EMERGING ISSUES AND CHALLENGES

Cultural Considerations

Many cultural issues, such as gender inequality, carnivorous diet, and widow inheritance, have an impact on health; however, there is one cultural belief that has far-reaching consequences in the lives of Congolese: the spiritual causes of disease. Congolese believe in the

TABLE 16-7　Morbidity and Mortality Indicators in the DRC, 2007

Categories	Total Number DRC
Infant deaths per 1,000 live births	120
Life expectancy at birth, total	45
Life expectancy at birth, male	44
Life expectancy at birth, female	46
Deaths per 1,000 population	19
HIV/AIDS prevalence (%)	5%
Moderate malnutrition, ages 1 to 4 years (%)	13.2%
Severe malnutrition, ages 1 to 4 years (%)	10.7%
< 5 fully immunized against tuberculosis (%)	55%
< 5 fully immunized against measles (%)	45%
Contraceptive use among married women, all methods, ages 15–49 years (%)	31%
Maternal deaths per 100,000 live births	990

From the DRC Ministry of Labor, 2007.

existence of a Supreme Being. They believe that the Supreme Being uses ancestors to reach them. For them, ancestors influence every aspect of their lives. That is why they offer sacrifices and gifts to appease them and attract their favors. Poor harvests, poor health and infertility, and death are often attributed to angry ancestors, enemies, or witches. When someone faces any of these situations, relatives have to determine whether it is of natural origin or whether it is caused by enemies or witches. They consult spiritual healers called *ngangas*, believed to have supernatural powers. If the *nganga* determines that a witch or enemy caused the sickness, his recommendations are put into practice. They often consist of wearing a talisman or drinking a mixture of herbs and clay called *nkisi*, specifically prepared to cure the patient. The effectiveness of the *nkisi* depends on how well the patient adheres to specific rules prescribed by the *nganga*. Unfortunately, the lack of knowledge about the active ingredients and its toxicity has led to cases of intoxication, liver damage, kidney failure, and death.

Influence of the International Monetary Fund, the World Bank, and the World Health Organization

As mentioned previously here, a significant portion of the healthcare budget comes from bilateral or multilateral contributions. The World Bank, the IMF, the Global Fund, USAID, and the European Union continue to play a critical role in financing specialized programs for HIV, malaria, and tuberculosis program, immunizations, and health zones, among others.

The World Bank and the International Monetary Fund were created in 1944 at Bretton Woods Conference intended to design international trade and finance. The World Bank is the world's largest multilateral development finance institution. In 1951, the World Bank extended its first loan of U.S.$41 million to support a 10-year development plan. The World Bank loans to the Congo increased significantly during Mobutu's regime. The country ranked fourth in terms of World Bank aid, after South Africa, Nigeria, and Sudan. Unfortunately, Mobutu skillfully deposited part of the money in his bank account in Europe. After several years of international isolation, the World Bank sponsored the "Friends of the Congo" conference on December 3, 2007, to normalize relationships.[17] The World Bank is currently in negotiation with Kabila's government.

The IMF/World Bank policies, like Structural Adjustment of the 1970s, had disastrous consequences in the country. The requirements to cut back on health, education, and public services, while promoting crops and other resources for export, were perceived as an institutionalization of colonialism. The resulting increased poverty in the country and the immense burden of debt further crippled Congo's ability to develop. On the other hand, the World Health Organization continues to be a valuable partner for the DRC. There are many nongovernmental organizations operating in the DRC. They play a critical role in channeling funds from international and Western countries directly to those in need.

Health Challenges Facing the Country

The history of the DRC is characterized by recurrent civil unrests and complex struggles for power. A combination of ethnic tensions, economic interests, and foreign involvement continues to drive political instability in the Congo. DRC has as many as 250 ethnic groups, speaking 700 local languages and dialects. When Belgium left the Congo precipitously, the struggle for power among these groups became open.

Years of civil war in the DRC resulted in massive population displacement that forced farmers to abandon their land and then led to food shortages. Massive displaced populations living in refugee camps led to the degradation of the environment, the development of severe malnutrition, and the development of diseases, such as HIV/AIDS, tuberculosis, and malaria. The new government in Kinshasa has failed to consolidate democratic institutions and promote accountable governance. The security forces are incapable of controlling the national territory. This fact has led to ongoing human rights abuses including widespread sexual violence.[18] Unless the political system is stabilized in the DRC, it is hard to see how a sustainable healthcare system can emerge in this country.

The health system in the DRC is facing several challenges. The number of hospitals in the Congo has not changed significantly since independence. The country is ill equipped to address the overwhelming and growing needs of the population. Malaria, tuberculosis, HIV/AIDS, and malnutrition are common health issues in the Congo. The breakdown of the health system in the DRC poses serious challenges to the new government. The government is unable to create a decent working environment or provide an appropriate wage to the physicians to prevent brain drain. As a result, the country continues to lose medical personnel to neighboring countries. The improvement of the health system must go hand and hand with the general improvement of the economy. The DRC is the third most populous country in Africa. With an economy in shambles, the majority of the people are unemployed and live in abject poverty. Poverty leads to diseases and deaths. Effort must be made to break the cycle of poverty. No country has been developed on external aid only. The time has come for Congolese to assume their destiny. With all of the natural resources, the DRC should be counted among the richest countries on the planet. With the right leadership, the country could be the jewel of Africa.

REFERENCES

1. African Wireless. Map of the Democratic Republic of the Congo. Retrieved February 19, 2008, from http://www.africanwireless.com/dr_congo_maps.htm.

2. Filippo P. *A report of the Kingdom of Congo and of the Surrounding Countries* [translated in English by Margarite Hutchinson, 1881]. London: John Murray; 1591.

3. Scott KJ. *The Partition of Africa*, 2nd ed. London: Edward Standford; 1894.

4. Johnstone R. Focus on the Democratic Republic of Congo. Let the Bible Speak Website, 2005. Retrieved February 14, 2008, from http://www.ltbs.org/magazine/LTBSVol021_16 17.pdf.

5. History World Website. History of the Democratic Republic of Congo. Retrieved February 14, 2008, from http://www.historyworld.net/wrldhis/PlainTextHistories.asp?history id=ad34.

6. Nzongola-Ntalaja G. The history of democracy in DR Congo. High Beam Website, 2006. Retrieved February 14, 2008, from http://www.encyclopedia.com/doc/1G1-1563 66428.html.

7. The Library of Congress. A Country Study: Zaire (Former). Country Studies, 2005. Retrieved February 15, 2008, from http://lcweb2.loc.gov/frd/cs/zrtoc.html.

8. Central Intelligence Agency. Democratic Republic of Congo. The World Factbook, 2008. Retrieved February 14, 2008, from https://www.cia.gov/library/publications/the-world-factbook/geos/cg.html.

9. Bell M. Child Alert: Democratic Republic of Congo Martin Bell reports on children caught in war. UNICEF Child Alert Website, 2006. Retrieved February 14, 2008, from http://www.unicef.org/childalert/drc/content/Child_Alert_DRC_en.pdf.

10. Ruppol JF. Apports de la Belgique en Afrique Centrale, dans le Domaine MEDICAL DE 1985 A CE Jour. Expose du Dr J.F Ruppol au Centre Royal Africain d'Outre-Mer. Site d'etude de la colonisation belge website. Retrieved February 11, 2008, from http://www.urome.be/fr2/reflexions/Ruppol.pdf.

11. Mwenyimali T. Problematiques de la Gestion des Ressources Humaines: Etat de la Question et Perspectives. Ministere de la Sante Publique Democratic Republic of Congo Website. Retrieved February 15, 2008, from www.minisanterdc.cd/revue_annuelle/ra2k5/gestion_ress_hum.ppt.

12. Ministry of Health. Organigramme du Ministere de la Sante. Ministere de la Sante Publique Democratic Republic of Congo Website. Retrieved February 16, 2008, from http://www.minisanterdc.cd/leministere/organigramme.htm.

13. Ministry of Health. Health-System Strengthening Strategy. Ministere de la Sante Publique Democratic Republic of Congo Website, 2005. Retrieved February 16, 2008, from http://www.minisanterdc.cd/Ressourcesofficielles/docs/srss/srss_rdc_web_en.pdf.

14. Library of Congress. Country Studies: Zaire. Library of Congress Website. Retrieved February 15, 2008, from http://lcweb2.loc.gov/frd/cs/zaire/zr_appen.html.

15. Kelotin D. Financement de l'Etat Pour la Strategie: Budget Ordinaire, Fonds PPTE et Appuis Budgetaires. Ministere de la Sante Publique Democratic Republic of Congo Website. Retrieved February 15, 2008, from http://www.minisanterdc.cd/revue_annuelle/ra2k5/financement_etat_pour_sante.ppt.

16. Ministry of Health. Health-system Strengthening Strategy Health. Ministere de la Sante Publique Democratic Republic of Congo Website. Retrieved February 14, 2008, from http://www.minisanterdc.cd/Ressourcesofficielles/docs/srss/srss_rdc_web_en.pdf.

17. Willame JC. The "Friends of the Congo" and the Kabila System. *A Journal of Opinion.* 1998:26(1); 3–6.

18. DRC Fast Updates. Fast Analytical Framework: DRC/Kivu. Swiss Peace Website, 2007. Retrieved February 17, 2008, from http://www.swisspeace.ch/typo3/fileadmin/user_upload/pdf/FAST/Analytical_Frameworks/2007/Kivu_Analytical_Framework_2007_09.pdf.

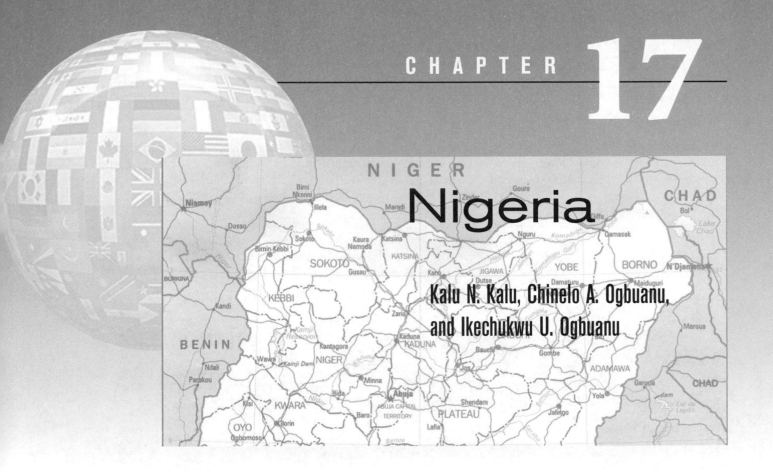

CHAPTER 17

Nigeria

Kalu N. Kalu, Chinelo A. Ogbuanu,
and Ikechukwu U. Ogbuanu

COUNTRY DESCRIPTION

TABLE 17-1 Nigeria

Nationality	Noun: Nigerian(s) Adjective: Nigerian
Ethnic groups	Nigeria, Africa's most populous country, is composed of more than 250 ethnic groups; the following are the most populous and politically influential: Hausa and Fulani 29%, Yoruba 21%, Igbo (Ibo) 18%, Ijaw 10%, Kanuri 4%, Ibibio 3.5%, Tiv 2.5%
Religions	Muslim 50%, Christian 40%, indigenous beliefs 10%
Language	English (official), Hausa, Yoruba, Igbo (Ibo), Fulani
Literacy	Definition: age 15 and over can read and write Total population: 68% Male: 75.7% Female: 60.6% (2003 est.)
Government type	Federal republic
Date of independence	October 1, 1960 (from the United Kingdom)
Gross Domestic Product (GDP) per capita	$2,200 (2007 est.)

(continues)

TABLE 17-1   Nigeria (continued)

Unemployment rate	5.8% (2006 est.)
Natural hazards	Periodic droughts; flooding
Environment: current issues	Soil degradation; rapid deforestation; urban air and water pollution; desertification; oil pollution—water, air, and soil; suffered serious damage from oil spills; loss of arable land; rapid urbanization
Population	138,283,240 Estimates for this country explicitly take into account the effects of excess mortality caused by AIDS; this can result in lower life expectancy, higher infant mortality, higher death rates, lower population growth rates, and changes in the distribution of population by age and gender than would otherwise be expected (July 2008 est.)
Age structure	0–14 years: 42.2% (male 29,378,127/female 28,953,864) 15–64 years: 54.7% (male 38,466,129/female 37,172,355) 65 years and over: 3.1% (male 2,046,309/female 2,266,456) (2008 est.)
Median age	Total: 18.7 years Male: 18.8 years Female: 18.6 years (2008 est.)
Population growth rate	2.382% (2008 est.)
Birth rate	39.98 births/1,000 population (2008 est.)
Death rate	16.41 deaths/1,000 population (2008 est.)
Net migration rate	.25 migrant(s)/1,000 population (2008 est.)
Gender ratio	At birth: 1.03 male(s)/female Under 15 years: 1.01 male(s)/female 15–64 years: 1.03 male(s)/female 65 years and over: 0.9 male(s)/female Total population: 1.02 male(s)/female (2008 est.)
Infant mortality rate	Total: 93.93 deaths/1,000 live births Male: 100.87 deaths/1,000 live births Female: 86.79 deaths/1,000 live births (2008 est.)
Life expectancy at birth	Total population: 47.81 years Male: 47.15 years Female: 48.5 years (2008 est.)
Total fertility rate	5.41 children born/woman (2008 est.)
HIV/AIDS adult prevalence rate	5.4% (2003 est.)
Number of people living with HIV/AIDS	3.6 million (2003 est.)
HIV/AIDS deaths	310,000 (2003 est.)

Central Intelligence Agency. The World Fact Book, 2008. Retrieved November 18, 2008, from https://www.cia.gov/library/publications/the-world-factbook.

History

Nigeria's independence from Britain was achieved on October 1, 1960, but from the outset, the new nation was challenged by regional and ethnic divisiveness that made it difficult to establish a common foundation for constitutional governance. The complications arose partly as a result of British colonial policy but more fundamentally because of the lack of a regional consensus on the viability of independence as well as a general unpreparedness by the indigenous elite to transform the anticolonial rhetoric into a wholesome nationalist culture. Although British colonial rule in Nigeria lasted for nearly a century, its duration and persistence depended largely on the ability of British colonialists to play one ethnic group against the other. The 1914 amalgamation by the British of the Northern, Southern, and Lagos Protectorates (which were up until then a collection of disjointed and virtually independent groups) into what is today's Nigeria set the stage for latter events that would exploit the deep-seated tensions that became the bane of the emergent postcolonial state.

In northern Nigeria, there existed a monolithic class system that distinguished the ruling oligarchy from the ordinary people. The dominant ethnic groups in the north were the Hausas and Fulanis, who could trace their origins to northern Africa. An opportune mix of itinerant and nomadic culture created the dynamic for a theocratic conquest of much of northern Nigeria by the Hausa-Fulani. The existent class system provided the British colonialists with a judicial and administrative infrastructure that facilitated a sort of "indirect rule" in the North. Because the emirs and other lower ranking officials in the emirate system were simply designated as colonial officers ruling their subjects on behalf of the British colonial state,[1] it created an additional privilege and authority that they were unwilling to give up easily, even at the price of independence. To secure the consent of northern leaders for independence, much of the feudal authority system in the region was left intact. This meant that, in the formative years of Nigeria's independence, two parallel authorities operated side by side, a paternalistic feudal authority in the north and a federal parliamentary authority for the rest of the country.

In the south, there was the relatively egalitarian society of the Igbos.[1] In order to replicate the system of indirect rule within that ethnic group, characteristically disposed to a decentralized, communal, and less paternalistic form of traditional governance, it became necessary for the British to impose their own stratification system by inventing a system of warrant chiefs who in addition to British military force were used to enforce colonial rule and authority.[1] Among the functions of the warrant chiefs or native officials were the collection of taxes for colonial administration, provision of cheap native labor for colonial public works, and the enforcement of colonial regulations and ordinances.

In western Nigeria's Yorubaland, especially within the Ile-Ife, Oyo, and Ibadan principalities, the semifeudal structure of Chiefs and Council of Elders also provided the British the opportunity to use the existing traditional authority to implement a *de facto* system of indirect rule but not to the extent possible in the north. More than anything, the system of indirect rule and the compromise to allow a quasiautonomous authority in the north retarded the process of national political integration as well as sectionalized consequent efforts at developing a truly Nigerian citizenship. From then on, the evolution of "national" political parties was regionalized. Political leadership became personalized, and objective government policy yielded to the allure of self-serving inclinations.

Size and Geography

The population of Nigeria is about 144 million people—the largest on the African continent and the eighth most populous in the world.[2] Nigeria (officially the Federal Republic of Nigeria) is located in West Africa on the Gulf of Guinea (part of the Atlantic Ocean). It is bounded by four other countries: Niger to the North, Chad and Cameroon in the East, and the Benin Republic to the West. Human habitation of the area now known as Nigeria dates back archaeologically to at least 9000 BC[3] (Figure 17-1).

Government and Political System

Nigeria is a federal republic with a president, a national assembly consisting of a Senate and House of Representatives, and a judicial system headed by a supreme court. With a modified system of federal government and 36 states spread across six geopolitical zones (southeast, south–south, southwest, northeast, northwest, north central), the central government in the capital city of Abuja has a great deal of authority over allocation of values, national policy, resource distribution, and infrastructural development. With nonexistent or ineffective state constitutions (if they exist), the central government holds sway in matters of program development, national security, and finance. Nigeria's brand of federalism has, in fact, come to reflect an awkward hybrid between

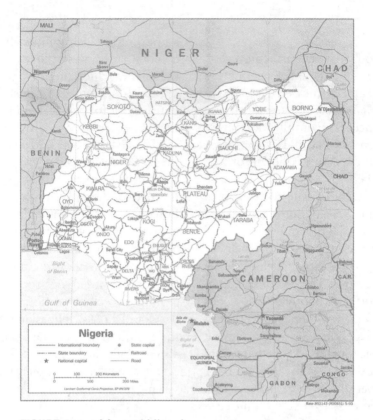

FIGURE 17-1 Map of Nigeria

popular consent and authoritarian regimentation. Much of this had not evolved as an accident of fate, but rather as a lingering consequence of the disagreements and compromises that befell the country for much of its 48 years of existence.

Macroeconomics

With an industrial production growth rate estimated at 3.1% (2007), 95% of Nigeria's export income comes from petroleum and petroleum-related products, whereas the rest comes from cocoa and rubber. As a result of the country's indigenization decree of the late 1970s and the consequent privatization schemes, the private sector has become more prominent in the ownership and management of key industrial facilities. This, however, has continued to create a situation in which a sizable proportion of the nation's wealth is concentrated in the hands of a narrow and select economic oligarchy.

The petroleum economy has remained the principal source of the country's wealth and foreign exchange earnings, especially since the end of the civil war, which lasted from 1967 to 1970. Although the first oil well was drilled in Oloibiri (Niger Delta) in 1956, it took major

shifts in the international demand and supply of oil in the early 1980s to generate an overwhelming reliance on the oil sector for the revenue needed to support the nation's developmental programs.

As pointed out by the CIA World Factbook,[4] Nigeria's former military rulers failed to diversify the economy away from its overdependence on the capital-intensive oil sector, which provides 20% of GDP, 95% of foreign exchange earnings, and approximately 80% of budgetary revenues. The largely subsistence agricultural sector has failed to keep up with rapid population growth, and the country, once a large net exporter of food, now must import food to feed its growing population.

After the signing of an International Monetary Fund (IMF) standby agreement in August 2000,[5] Nigeria received a debt-restructuring deal from the Paris Club and a $1 billion credit from the IMF, both contingent on economic reforms. Nigeria pulled out of its IMF program in April 2002, after failing to meet spending and exchange rate targets, making it ineligible for additional debt forgiveness from the Paris Club. In later years, the government has begun showing the political will to implement the market-oriented reforms urged by the IMF, such as to modernize the banking system, to curb inflation by blocking excessive wage demands, and to resolve regional disputes over the distribution of earnings from the oil industry. In 2003, the government began deregulating fuel prices, announced the privatization of the country's four oil refineries, and instituted the National Economic Empowerment Development Strategy, a domestically designed and run program modeled on the IMF's Poverty Reduction and Growth Facility for fiscal and monetary management. In November 2005, Nigeria won Paris Club approval for a debt relief deal that eliminated $18 billion of debt in exchange for $12 billion in payments—a total package worth $30 billion of Nigeria's total $37 billion external debt. The deal requires Nigeria to be subject to stringent IMF reviews.

The gross domestic product (GDP) rose strongly in 2007, based largely on increased oil exports and high global crude prices. The GDP real growth rate was 6.1% (2007) with a GDP per capita of $2,200. The agricultural sector accounted for 17.6%, whereas industry and services accounted for 53.1% and 29.3%, respectively. Despite oil revenues, Nigeria remains essentially an agro-based economy, with the agricultural sector accounting for 70% of the labor force, industry 10%, and services at 20%. With approximately 60% of the population living below the poverty line, the per capita annual income remains at approximately $300. With an external debt account of about $5.815 billion, increasing oil revenues helped to boost the country's foreign exchange reserves to $50.33 billion (as of December 2007) and its stock of domestic foreign direct investment to an estimated volume of $31.66 billion.

Because of the centrality of oil in the macroeconomy, serious market failures have become more salient. The role of the state in mediating between public ownership (property rights) and private capital in the free market creates a situation where politics, not markets, determines the incentives of ownership. Hazem and Luciano wrote that because "the state receives revenues which are channeled to the economy through public expenditure, the allocation of these public funds between alternative uses has great significance for the future development pattern of the economy."[6] Because most public infrastructures are not profit making, they must be supported by continuous appropriation of public funding generated through external rents, despite the performance of other sectors of the domestic macroeconomy.

Even though state expenditures on public sector infrastructures can help to create jobs, thereby reducing unemployment, it can also provide additional sources for extracting legal and illegal rents (corruption) from the public treasury. Although Nigeria is heavily dependent on oil-related rents (income received by a country for use of its natural resources by outside parties), the vast majority of this wealth benefits a tiny fraction of the population.[7] Nigeria's ruling classes, exploiting their influence on and dominance of the government, are able to appropriate oil rents for their own benefit. This points to an important factor in the development process—that is, renter economies rarely spread the wealth, but rather concentrate it in the hands of those who control political power.

With a total land mass of about 923,768 km², the country operates a total of 194,394 km of road network. There are three major seaports with terminals in Port Harcourt, Calabar, and Lagos. The railways system with a total line of about 3,505 km has suffered maintenance problems over the years. This is due partly to the fact that land and air traffic have become the predominant means of transportation since the end of the civil war in 1970, as well as the rising affluence and occupational mobility attributable to the oil economy. The country maintains about 70 airports, with 36 having fully paved runways.

Demographics

The annual population growth rate is about 2.4%.[8] The median age of the population is about 18.63 years, with an adult literacy rate of 75.7% for males, 60.6% for females, and 68% for both genders (Table 17-2). From 1999 to 2005, the net primary school enrollment for males and females was 64% and 57%, respectively.[8] In 2003, the majority of the population (70.8%) was living below the poverty line (less than US$1 per day). The gross national income per capita in 2005 was 1,040 (international dollars).[8] The two major religions in Nigeria are Christianity (mainly in the southern region) and Islam (northern region). Rural–urban migration is estimated at about 5.3%.[9] The United Nations estimated that in 2005 the population density was 153 people per square kilometer, with 48.3% living in the urban centers and 51.7% residing in rural areas.[10]

Although three major ethnic groups (Ibo, Hausa, and Yoruba) constitute over 40% of the population, there are also numerous subethnic tertiary groups that complement the more than 250 ethnolingual distinctions in the country. The official language in Nigeria is English, but it has been estimated that 521 different languages are spoken across the country. The three major indigenous languages spoken in Nigeria are Hausa, Yoruba, and Ibo.

TABLE 17-2   Comparisons of Demographics of Nigeria with the United States

Indicator	Nigeria (Year)	United States (Year)
Total population (in thousands)	144,700 (2006)[2]	298,213 (2005)[8]
Per capita GDP in international dollars[8]	1,040 (2005)	41,950 (2005)
Annual population growth rate[8] (%)	2.4	1.0
Adult literacy rate—total[11] (%)	68	97
Adult literacy rate—male[11] (%)	75.7	97
Adult literacy rate—female[11] (%)	60.6	97
Dependency ratio[11] (per 100)	90	51
Median age—total[11] (years)	18.63	36.27
Total fertility rate[12]	5.7 (2004)	2.0 (2004)

Data are from the World Health Organization (WHO), *World Health Report 2006.*

BRIEF HISTORY OF THE HEALTHCARE SYSTEM

Pre-World War II

The beginning of modern medical and health services in Nigeria has a historical precedent that predates the Amalgamation Decree of 1914 that united the Northern and Southern Protectorates to form what is today's Nigeria. As pointed out in the United States' Library of Congress Country Studies,[13] Western medicine was not formally introduced into Nigeria until 1860, when the Sacred Heart Hospital was established by Roman Catholic missionaries in Abeokuta. For much of the colonial period, modern healthcare facilities in Nigeria were provided through religious missions.

Although Roman Catholic missions predominated (accounting for about 40% of the total number of mission-based hospital beds by 1960), there were a total of 118 mission hospitals compared with 101 government hospitals.[14] Roman Catholic missions were concentrated in the southeastern and midwestern parts of the country, whereas the Sudan United and the Sudan Interior Missions focused on the middle belt region and the Islamic North, respectively. Together, they operated 25 hospitals or other facilities in the northern half of the country, and many of the mission hospitals remained an important component of the healthcare network into the 1990s.

The missions also played an important role in medical training and education, providing training for nurses and paramedical personnel and sponsoring basic education as well as advanced medical training (often in

Europe) for many of the first generation of Western-educated Nigerian doctors. This helped to lay the foundation for a wider distribution and acceptance of the efficacy of modern medical care to a majority of the indigenous population. The British colonial government began providing formal medical services with the construction of several clinics and hospitals in Lagos, Calabar, and other coastal trading centers in the 1870s. The hospital in Jos (Plateau state) was built in 1912 after the beginning of tin mining in that part of the country and partly because the temperate climate in that region made habitation for Europeans much more appealing than in the more arid savannah region in the north. Unlike the missionary facilities, the colonial hospitals were initially for the sole use of Europeans, and this privilege was later extended to African employees of European establishments.

World War I had a greatly detrimental effect on medical services in Nigeria because of the large number of medical personnel (both European and African) who were pulled out to serve in Europe. After the war, medical facilities were expanded substantially, and a number of government-sponsored schools for the training of Nigerian medical assistants were established. Although a number of Nigerian physicians were trained in Europe, they were not permitted to practice in colonial government hospitals unless they were there specifically to treat an African patient. This practice led to protests and to the frequent involvement of doctors and other medical personnel in the nationalist movements of the period.

Since World War II

The end of World War II brought about a dramatic shift in the attitude of the colonial government toward indigenous health care. In 1946, a 10-year health development plan was announced. The health plan established the Ministry of Health to coordinate health services throughout the country, including those provided by the government, private companies, and missions. The plan also allocated funds for hospitals and clinics, most of which were concentrated in the main cities; however, little funding was appropriated for rural health centers, and there was also a strong imbalance between the allocation of facilities to southern areas compared with those in the north.[15] In 1948, the University of Ibadan was established, which included the country's first full faculty of medicine and university hospital. In addition, a number of nursing schools were established, as were two schools of pharmacy. By 1960, the country had 65 government nursing or midwifery training schools.

The problems of geographic maldistribution of medical facilities among the regions and of the inadequacy of rural facilities persisted into the 1980s. There were also significant disparities within each of the regions. For example, in 1980, there was an enormous discrepancy between Lagos with 2,600 people per physician versus the extremely rural region of Ondo with 38,000 people per physician.[16] Across the urban–rural divide, many of the specialized physicians preferred to establish their practices in the urban areas, and few moved to the rural areas. The few doctors who did work in the rural areas did so as part of their requirement to serve in the National Youth Service Corps[16]—a national Peace Corps–type program established in 1973.

DESCRIPTION OF THE CURRENT HEALTHCARE SYSTEM

The three tiers of care stipulated under the National Health Policy are primary, secondary, and tertiary levels. These levels are supervised respectively by the three tiers of government (local, state, and federal), with some overlap in responsibilities.[17,18]

The federal government launched its Primary Health Care (PHC) plan in August 1987, which then President Ibrahim Babangida announced as the cornerstone of the country's health policy.[19] The policy also spells out the functions of each tier of government and provides for the establishment of the advisory National Council on Health chaired by the Federal Minister of Health.[20] Other bodies set up by the policy include the State Health Advisory Committees and Local Government Health Committees.[20] Its main objectives were to accelerate healthcare personnel development, to improve collection and monitoring of health data, to ensure availability of essential drugs in all areas of the country, to implement an Expanded Programme on Immunization, to improve nutrition and promote health awareness, to develop a national family health program, and to develop oral dehydration therapy for treatment of diarrheal disease in infants and children. The Federal Ministry of Health in collaboration with participating local government councils was charged with the implementation of these programs.

The National Health Policy was revised in 1996[18] and later in 2004. This policy is based on the fundamental principles of the second National Development Plan (1970–1974), which describes five national goals: a free and democratic society; a just and egalitarian society; a united, strong, and self-reliant nation; a great and dynamic economy; and a land of full opportunities for all citizens.[18–21] This policy states that health development shall be seen not solely in humanitarian terms but as an essential component of the package of social and economic development as well as an instrument of social justice.

Facilities

According to the National Health Policy, the federal government is responsible for formulation, strategic guidance, coordination, supervision, monitoring, and evaluation at all levels. It also has operational responsibility for disease surveillance, essential drug supply, and vaccine management and for the provision of specialized care through tertiary institutions such as university teaching hospitals and federal medical centers.[17,20] Some state governments also provide tertiary care through state-owned teaching hospitals.[17] These tertiary centers serve as referral institutions for secondary health facilities but may also provide some PHC services through their general outpatient departments (Figure 17-2).

Service delivery is through PHC centers, health clinics, and health posts. The Library of Congress Country Studies[15] pointed out that in 1979 there were 562 general hospitals, supplemented by 16 maternity and pediatric hospitals, 11 armed forces hospitals, 6 teaching hospitals, and 3 prison hospitals. In addition, general health centers were estimated to number slightly less than 600, general clinics 2,740, maternity homes 930, and maternal health centers 1,240. In addition to the public health

Overview of the Healthcare System

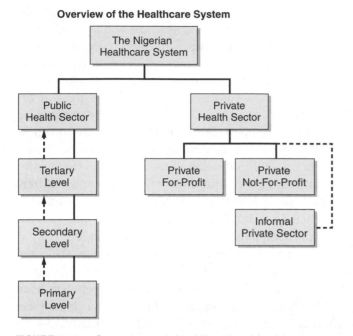

FIGURE 17-2 Overview of the Nigerian Healthcare System

sector, the private health sector plays a major role in healthcare delivery in Nigeria. Private providers are broadly divided into private for-profit providers and private not-for-profit providers (including voluntary or missionary agencies).[22,23] These private providers offer a mixture of services ranging from primary to tertiary care, depending on their infrastructure and staffing levels. There is also the informal healthcare system, consisting of unregistered healthcare providers, operating outside of the organized and monitored formal healthcare system.[24,25] Most Nigerians resort to the informal system for common ailments, usually because of financial constraints.

According to available data from the Federal Ministry of Health, in 1999, there were 18,258 registered PHC facilities, 3,275 secondary facilities, and 29 tertiary facilities across the country.[20] The public sector accounted for 67% of PHC facilities, 25% of secondary facilities, and 97% of the tertiary facilities.[20] A nationwide survey of health facilities showed that less than 4% of existing facilities in 1991 were owned by missions and other voluntary agencies.[23] The most recent data from the Ministry of Health[26] showed that in 2005 there were 20,278 PHC, 3,303 secondary, and 59 tertiary facilities. The public sector accounted for 67.6% of the PHC, 25% of the secondary, and 100% of the tertiary facilities. Al-

though there is overall increase in the number of facilities, there has not been much change with regard to the proportion of ownership when compared with equivalent 1999 figures.

Primary health centers are present in every district of each of the 774 local government council areas,[24] and the local government authorities are directly responsible for them; however, the Federal Ministry of Health through the National Public Health Care Development Agency develops policies and the PHC physical structures and supervises the operation of these centers.[17] Characteristically, hospitals are divided into general wards, which provide both outpatient and inpatient care on a fee-for-service basis, and amenity wards, which charge higher fees but offer better aesthetic and therapeutic conditions. The general wards are usually crowded and require long waits for registration as well as for treatment. Inpatient hospitalization in the general wards can be sometimes quite challenging. Patients frequently do not see a doctor but only a nurse or other practitioner.

In some cases, patients need to pay bribes in order to receive medical care. Because of limited space, beds are put in corridors, and some patients even sleep on the floors, regardless of whether they themselves or others around them are contagious. Although some family members offer to bring food to their relatives in the hospital, the hospital-provided food is often prepared and served under very unhygienic conditions. Most of the Nigerian elite do not have to see or witness these conditions; they usually travel abroad to the West for medical care, either for periodic medical checkups or when a serious or recurrent medical ailment exists.

Workforce

The objective of primary health care is the provision of inexpensive and simple treatment of everyday ailments that do not require specialist care as well as preventive medicine for the promotion of health.[24] Referrals are made, when needed, to secondary and tertiary health centers. General practitioners, community health doctors, registered nurses, and community health officers staff these health centers. Community health extension workers head the smaller health clinics and health posts. They are assisted by voluntary village health workers and traditional birth attendants.[24] These healthcare workers receive training for varying lengths of time on basic preventive health and maternity services. The 36 state governments and the federal capital territory are also responsible for the provision of the secondary level of care through general hospitals.[17] The general hospitals are managed by the state health management boards.[24]

Nigeria, like many African countries, is facing a serious shortage of health workers. According to the WHO,[8] in 2003, there were 34,923 physicians in the country (0.28 per 1,000 population), 127,580 nurses (1.03 per 1,000 population), and 12 hospital beds per 10,000 population in 2000.[8] Comparable figures for the United States for 2000 are 730,801 physicians (2.56 per 1,000 population) and 2,669,603 nurses (9.37/1,000 population; Table 17-3).

One of the factors contributing to this shortage is the emigration of healthcare professionals from the country. Thousands of Nigerian-trained doctors continue to migrate annually for various reasons, including poor remuneration, limited spaces for postgraduate medical residency training, dilapidated medical infrastructure, and poor job satisfaction.[27,28] The state of the healthcare system has been worsened by this progressive shortage of doctors and nurses. In 2005, there were 2,392 Nigerian doctors practicing in the United States and 1,529 in the United Kingdom.[29] Even Nigerian doctors who have completed their postgraduate medical

residency training overseas are unwilling to return to the country because of limited incentives.[30]

Medical training in Nigeria is also in dire need of reform. The undergraduate medical education terminates with a Bachelor of Medicine and Bachelor of Surgery Degree after 6 years of study (1 year spent in premedical/basic sciences training and 5 years for medical/clinical training). Immediately after completion of the medical training is a 1-year of internship, or *housemanship*, in an accredited teaching hospital or general hospital. After the internship is completed, doctors begin a 1-year service to the nation usually in rural areas in dire need of medical personnel (the National Youth Service Corps). Postgraduate training can then commence after the completion of the National Youth Service Corps.

Since 1948, when the University College Hospital, Ibadan was established as a college branch of University of London, there has not been substantial modification to the curriculum. Efforts made to reform the curriculum regionally and nationally have failed. There are also varying levels of compliance by the different medical schools to the minimum standards set by the regulatory bodies (National Universities Commission and the Medical and

TABLE 17-3 Comparative Healthcare Professionals/Workforce

Indicators	Nigeria (Year)	United States (Year)
Physicians	34,923 (2003)	730,801 (2000)
Physicians (density per 1,000 population)	0.28 (2003)	2.56 (2000)
Nurses	127,580 (2003)	2,699,603 (2000)
Nurses (density per 1,000 population)	1.03 (2003)	9.37 (2000)
Dentists	2,482 (2003)	463,663 (2000)
Dentists (density per 1,000 population)	0.02 (2003)	1.63 (2000)
Pharmacists	6,344 (2004)	249,642 (2000)
Pharmacists (density per 1,000 population)	0.05 (2004)	0.88 (2000)
Community health workers	115,761 (2004)	Not available
Community health workers (density per 1,000 population)	0.91 (2004)	Not available
Lab technicians	690 (2004)	651,035 (2000)
Lab technicians (density per 1,000 population)	0.01 (2004)	2.28 (2000)
Other health workers	1,220 (2004)	4,138,567 (2000)
Other health workers (density per 1,000 population)	0.01 (2004)	14.52 (2000)

Data are from *World Health Statistics, 2007.*

Dental Council of Nigeria).[31] There are currently about 20 accredited medical schools in Nigeria, most of which are established by the federal government.[11]

Technology and Equipment

Most medical equipment in use in Nigeria today is outdated and needs replacement, requiring both financial resources and a trained workforce. Because of shortages in electricity and equipment spare parts in the early 1980s, expensive medical equipment could not be operated. As the cost of imported goods skyrocketed, public healthcare facilities became unable to handle the healthcare needs of the population. At this time, private facilities, although largely unregulated, began to fill the void left by the public healthcare sector.[16] As the demand for modern medical care far outstripped its availability and government hospitals deteriorated, medical personnel, drugs, and equipment were increasingly provided by the private sector.[32]

Today, the country still suffers from endemic shortage of modern medical equipment such as computed tomography scanners, X-rays, computerized testing, and diagnostic equipment. Items such as surgical and cardiovascular equipment needed for more sophisticated medical procedures are limited. Where such equipment is available, very little of it remains in serviceable condition. Upkeep, maintenance, and inspection of available equipment remain persistent problems.

EVALUATION OF THE HEALTHCARE SYSTEM

A National Health Insurance Scheme (NHIS) was first introduced in Nigeria in 1962 as a compulsory scheme for public service workers. In 1999, the scheme was modified to cover more people and introduced by the NHIS Act 35 of 1999.[18] This scheme of mandatory payroll deductions allows each insured person to decide at which health center to register. A healthcare provider registered under the scheme would provide a defined range of services as needed for a capitation for each patient.[33] Health maintenance organizations are also expected to play a major role in coordination of the health centers while the overall regulation of the scheme rests with the NHIS Council. The major objectives of the scheme are to ensure that every Nigerian has access to adequate healthcare services, to protect families from financial hardship caused by huge medical bills, and to limit the rise in the cost of and to ensure efficiency in healthcare services.[18,33]

Cost

Health care is financed in Nigeria through a variety of sources including budgetary allocations from government at all levels (federal, state, and local), loans and grants, private sector contributions, and out-of-pocket expenses.[20] The public health sector is financed with an allocation from the Federation Account's general revenue. This allocation is made to the various levels of government based on a preagreed revenue allocation formula. The general mechanism for mobilization of revenue includes royalties and fees from the oil sector; general tax revenue, including a value-added tax; social health insurance; cost recovery, including user fees in public health facilities; and external aid in terms of loans, donations, and grants.[18] The percentage of allocation by the government to the health sector has always been about 2% to 3% of the national budget, although this has increased marginally in recent times.[18] Health expenditure as a percentage of total federal recurrent expenditure was 2.55% in 1996, 2.96% in 1997, 2.99% in 1998, 1.95% in 1999, and 2.5% in 2000.[20] In 2004,[8] general government expenditure on health as a percentage of total government expenditure was 3.5% (Table 17-4).

According to the World Bank, per capita public spending for health care in Nigeria is less than US$5.[18,20] This is far below the US$34 recommended by the WHO for low-income countries.[20] The reduction in health spending in the late 1980s was due to the Structural Adjustment Programs (SAPs), which de-emphasized spending on health and social services.[20] The United Nations Development Programme's *Human Development Report* 2003 shows that Nigeria's public expenditure on health as a percentage of GDP was 1% and 0.05% in 1990 and 2000, respectively. The private health sector is mainly financed through out-of-pocket expenses and also through donations from voluntary or missionary agencies (local and international).

Some employers such as oil companies and other large organizations also finance health care by establishing company-owned clinics where employees receive primary- and secondary-level health care. Other employers engage in retainership with private providers.[18] Retainership is a financing mechanism whereby employees can benefit from health services up to a prescribed monthly limit through a contracted private provider. The provider is reimbursed retrospectively at agreed intervals. In some scenarios, the employees pay the bills

TABLE 17-4 Core Health Expenditure Indicators (2004)

Indicators	Nigeria	United States
Total expenditure on health as percentage of GDP	4.6	15.4
General government expenditure on health as percentage of total expenditure on health	30.4	44.7
Private expenditure on health as percentage of total expenditure on health	69.6	55.3
General government expenditure on health as percentage of total government expenditure	3.5	18.9
External resources for health as percentage of total expenditure on health	5.6	0.0
Social security expenditure on health as percentage of general government expenditure on health	0.0	28.0
Out-of-pocket expenditure as percentage of private expenditure on health	90.4	23.8
Private prepaid plans as percentage of private expenditure on health	6.7	66.4
Per capita total expenditure on health at average exchange rate (US$)	23	6,096
Per capita total expenditure on health at international dollar rate	53	6,096
Per capita government expenditure on health at average exchange rate (US$)	7	2,725
Per capita government expenditure on health at international dollar rate	16	2,725

Data are from *World Health Statistics, 2007.*

up front and are later reimbursed by their employers. In other cases, employees are paid "medical allowances" as part of their fringe benefits. They are at liberty to spend these allowances in whichever facility they choose. These various forms of employee medical benefit schemes are an important part of "private health insurance" in Nigeria.

Private expenditure on health care accounts for 69.6% of the total health expenditure, whereas government expenditure on health accounts for the remaining 30.4%.[8] Out-of-pocket payments account for 90.4% of private healthcare expenditure, whereas prepaid plans account for 6.7%.[8] The total expenditure on health as a percentage of the GDP was 5% in 2003 and 4.6% in 2004.[8] In comparison, the corresponding figure for the United States was 15.2% of GDP in 2003 and 15.4% in 2004.[8,12,34]

Quality

Among the various health-related ailments that affect most Nigerians, communicable diseases exert a great toll. Notable among them are malaria, tuberculosis, diarrhea, poliomyelitis, and most recently HIV/AIDS (Table 17-5). According to the Federal Ministry of Health, the prevalence of HIV among pregnant women was 5% in 2003.[35] Nigeria has the third highest burden of infection in the world with an estimated 4 million people living with HIV.[36]

The average life expectancy at birth is 47 years for males and 48 years for females[8] (Table 17-6). The adult mortality rate (probability of dying between 15 and 60 years) is 461 per 1,000 population for males and 421 per 1,000 population for females.[8] Although the infant mortality rate is 101 per 1,000 live births, the under-5 mortality for both genders is 194 per 1,000 live births.[8] Needless to say, the maternal and child health statistics in Nigeria remain abysmal. The maternal mortality rate ranges from 800 to 1,500 per 100,000 and is one of the worst in the world.[9,20] Some of the common causes of maternal mortality are obstetric hemorrhage, sepsis, and pre-eclampsia/eclampsia.[38,39] The high maternal mortality rate may be because only approximately 35% of births are attended by skilled health personnel. In addition, prenatal coverage is low, with about 47% of women attending at least four prenatal visits per year.

Access

In Nigeria, access to quality health care is dictated by the ability to pay. Because of this, many individuals and families are unable to engage in the kinds of preventive

TABLE 17-5 Infectious Disease Morbidity Statistics for Nigeria and the United States

Indicator	Nigeria (Year)	United States (Year)
HIV prevalence among adults aged ≥ 15 years/100,000 population[8]	3,547 (2005)	508 (2005)
Tuberculosis prevalence per 100,000 population[8]	536 (2005)	3 (2005)
Tuberculosis incidence per 100,000[8]	283 (2005)	5 (2005)
Number of confirmed polio cases[8]	1,099 (2006)	0 (2006)
Malaria cases (per 100,000)[11]	2,103	0.52
HIV: estimated mother–child transmissions (thousands)[37]	4,200 (2005)	
HIV: estimated pediatric infections, 0–14 years (thousands)[37]	240 (2005)	
HIV: estimated number of children orphaned by AIDS, 0–17 years (thousands)[37]	930 (2005)	

Data are from WHO, *World Health Statistics, 2007.*

medicine or practices (such as early immunization or vaccination) necessary to avoid future, more expensive hospitalization. Nigeria has a low birth weight rate of 17%, and only 13% of infants complete their immunization schedule before their first birthday.[9] In 2005, for example, 35% of infants received the measles vaccine compared with 93% in the United States (Table 17-7). Payment to the various provider groups and for different services (private and government hospitals, general practitioners, specialists, maternity services, immuniza-

tions) is mainly by fee-for-service, and very few can afford to pay.

Before 1986, free medical services, including food for hospitalized patients, were provided in public hospitals; however, because of the economic recession in the 1980s, the ill-fated SAP was introduced with the support of the IMF and the World Bank.[22] Some of the requirements of SAP included the rationalization and introduction of "user fees" in public health facilities. Whether these user fees were paid by individuals with or without

TABLE 17-6 Primary Health Indicators

Indicator	Nigeria (Year)	United States (Year)
Life expectancy at birth (years)—males	47 (2005)	75.0 (2005)
Life expectancy at birth (years)—females	48 (2005)	80.0 (2005)
Healthy life expectancy (HALE) at birth (years)—males	41 (2002)	67 (2002)
Healthy life expectancy (HALE) at birth (years)—females	42 (2002)	71 (2002)
Adult mortality rate (per 1,000 population)—males	461 (2005)	137 (2005)
Adult mortality rate (per 1,000 population)—females	421 (2005)	81 (2005)
Under-5 mortality rate (per 1,000 population)—both genders	194 (2005)	8 (2005)
Infant mortality rate (per 1,000 live births)—both genders	101 (2005)	7 (2005)
Neonatal mortality rate (per 1,000 live births)—both genders	47 (2004)	4 (2004)
Maternal mortality ratio (per 100,000 live births)—both genders	800 (2000)	14 (2000)
Average annual cigarette consumption per adult[40]	188 (1992–2000)	2,193 (1992–2000)

Data are from *World Health Statistics, 2007.*

TABLE 17-7 Health Service Coverage (Percentages)

Indicator	Nigeria (Year)	United States (Year)
Immunization coverage among 1-year-olds—measles	35 (2005)	93 (2005)
Immunization coverage among 1-year-olds—DTP3[a]	25 (2005)	96 (2005)
Immunization coverage among 1-year-olds—hepatitis B[b]	Not available (2005)	92 (2005)
Prenatal coverage (at least one visit)	61 (2003)	Not available
Prenatal coverage (at least four visits)	47 (2003)	Not available
Births attended by skilled health personnel	35 (2003)	99 (2003)
Contraceptive prevalence rate	12.6 (2003)	72.9 (2002)

[a] Three doses of diphtheria-tetanus toxoid-pertussis vaccine.

[b] Three doses of hepatitis B vaccine.

Data are from *World Health Statistics, 2007.*

reimbursement by their employers or by the employers directly, payments were made on a fee-for-service basis.

Such fees were usually set arbitrarily by providers, and in general, fees accessed by public health facilities were much cheaper than those accessed by private providers. In 1992, however, the Guild of Medical Directors introduced new billing guidelines and fee schedules for provider reimbursement in the private health sector in order to harmonize fees across the country and reduce price competition to levels that posed a minimal threat to ethical medical practice.[23] Nevertheless, the policy remains highly unregulated.

The Bamako Initiative was introduced by the African Ministers of Health meeting in 1987, with financial support from several organizations, including the WHO, the United Nations International Children's Emergency Fund, and the United Kingdom's Department of International Development.[25,41] It was adopted by the Nigerian government in 1988. The main aim of the initiative was to strengthen the primary healthcare infrastructure through the introduction of user fees. The revenue generated was to be used to improve the availability and affordability of essential drugs and to improve health center infrastructures; however, this initiative has been criticized as placing too much emphasis on drugs to the detriment of other aspects of the health system.[41] The introduction of the user fees in public healthcare facilities and the subsequent rise in healthcare costs limited access and made it prohibitive for many citizens to seek needed healthcare services in a timely manner. Many sought relief through unregulated private health facilities, drug vendors, and traditional healers,[25] thereby worsening their health status.

CURRENT AND EMERGING ISSUES AND CHALLENGES

Despite the receding influence of such endemic diseases as yellow fever, health problems in Nigeria remain acute. Malaria and tuberculosis have become the most prevalent, with children accounting for 75% of registered deaths associated with malaria. In 2000, 30% of childhood mortality was attributable to malaria, whereas 20% was attributable to diarrheal diseases. There have also been major outbreaks of cerebrospinal meningitis—a potentially fatal inflammation of the membranes of the brain and spinal cord—in parts of northern Nigeria.[42] In 1999, the prevalence of malnutrition for children under the age of 5 years was 46%. In 1995, Nigeria suffered the highest number of measles cases reported among all countries in Africa. Nigerians also experience high incidence rates of schistosomiasis, guinea worm, trachoma, river blindness (onchocerciasis), and yaws.[43] In March 1987, the presence of AIDS was officially confirmed in the country, but since then, the infection rate has reached epidemic proportions, with an estimated 3.5 million (including 5.8% of the adult population) living with HIV/AIDS in 2001 and deaths the same year numbering 170,000.[43]

Over the last couple of years, a program for the eradication of river blindness and malaria has been undertaken in cooperation with the WHO. In December 2006, the World Bank approved a US$180 million Malaria Control Booster Project. This project is billed as Africa's largest and is expected to support national coverage of malaria control interventions in 7 of the 36 states of the federation.

The government is also working to control the spread of sexually transmitted diseases, including HIV/AIDS, through public education and behavior change. A report by the National AIDS and Sexually Transmitted Diseases Control Program indicated that 20% of the current AIDS cases in the country were civil servants, 18% were housewives and businessmen, 11% were farmers, and 8% were students. An earlier United States National Intelligence Council study highlighted the rising HIV/AIDS problem through 2010 in five countries that had large populations at risk for HIV infection: Nigeria, Ethiopia, Russia, India, and China. In response, Nigeria was designated as 1 of 15 countries worldwide to be assisted under the U.S. President's Emergency Plan for AIDS Relief. The United States Agency for International Development has been working with the Nigerian government to make antiretroviral treatment available to approximately 350,000 people living with HIV/AIDS, as well as provide health and social services to close to 2 million HIV-positive people. This partnership is also making efforts toward prevention and care of people with a co-morbidity of HIV and tuberculosis.[44]

In addition to the "brain drain" of professional health workers in Nigeria, counterfeit drugs have posed a major challenge to the health of Nigerians. Factors that have facilitated drug counterfeiting in Nigeria include corruption, poor drug control systems, and poor interagency cooperation. The extent of the corruption overwhelmed the ability of the National Drug Regulatory Agency to police. As a result, in 1993, a new agency was formed with autonomy and extra powers.[45] This new agency, the National Agency for Food and Drug Administration and Control, has taken major strides to reduce the counterfeit drug problem and has made tremendous progress initially unthinkable in the Nigerian system. In collusion with corrupt government and customs officials, the subterranean economy that traffics in the importation of illegal pharmaceuticals and drugs has continued to undermine National Agency for Food and Drug Administration and Control efforts to achieve an overwhelming sense of regulatory efficacy.

Nigeria has a great need to address the issue of lack of clean drinking water. Millions of Nigerians are afflicted annually by various water-borne diseases, worms, and parasites. As a serious public health issue, water provides a common link—either through drinking or bathing—for the transmission of infectious diseases, as well as providing a breeding ground for harmful pathogens.

Nigeria also suffers from a rising level of *e-waste* (a litany of used electronic gadgets such as computers, ra-dios, cell phones, and televisions) that are indiscriminately discarded around cities, with some ending up in dumpsites where they are burned. Among them are millions of used cell phone "sim cards." To date, very little or no testing has been done regarding the chemical decomposition of these types of materials and their implication for the integrity of the groundwater as well as public health.

Nigeria today could also be termed a "plastic society." The streets of the major cities and urban centers are littered with little plastic sachets used for packaging and selling drinking water. After use, people dispose of them in the streets. When it rains, the plastic sachets block the drains and clog the gutters causing the drains to overflow, flooding streets and homes. Because these polyethylene plastic products are essentially nonbiodegradable, they litter the ground for years. In most cases, they are scooped up and burned in open incinerators, further emitting harmful toxic fumes into the air.

Cherry-Picking: A Two-Tiered System

One of the most critical problems confronting the delivery of health care in Nigeria is the perennial low level of government commitment to the healthcare sector. Although the budgetary allocations for health care average 2% to 3%, in some specific instances, because of corruption and other factors, statistics indicate that the actual amount released from the national budget is as low as 30% to 40% of the budgeted amount.[18] According to the WHO, the federal government "recurrent health expenditure as a share of total federal government recurrent expenditure stood at 2.55% in 1996, 2.96% in 1997, 2.99% in 1998, declined to 1.95% in 1999, and rose to 2.5% in 2000."[20,46] Hence, beyond budgetary allocations, a concern in funding the healthcare sector in Nigeria is the growing gap between budgeted figures and the actual funds released from the treasury for health activities. Although much of the expenditures go into administering the health personnel system, a sizable proportion of the funds are lost as a result of waste, mismanagement, and official malfeasance. The government also needs to take a more proactive role in ensuring a competitive patient cost-sharing system while regulating arbitrary cost increases as well as insurance risk exposure. According to Laurence A. Graig, "Such competition should be regulated in the sense that a risk equalization fund ensures that insurance funds compete for members on factors other than risk status."[47]

The WHO ranked Nigeria 187th of 191 countries in overall health systems performance.[48] In the area of responsiveness to people's nonmedical expectations (i.e., respect for persons [respect for dignity, confidentiality, autonomy] and client orientation [prompt attention, quality of amenities, access to social support networks, choice of provider/facility]), Nigeria ranked 149th. For comparison, the United States ranked 37th in overall systems performance and 1st in terms of responsiveness. In a recent satisfaction study involving 250 inpatients at a teaching hospital in Edo State, Nigeria, the authors found that only 93 of the 250 patients (37.2%) claimed to have received adequate information concerning their disease condition.[49] As regards friendliness, 136 of the patients (54%) evaluated the doctors as very friendly, whereas 6 (2.4%) perceived the doctors to be unfriendly. In contrast, 32 patients (12.8%) judged the nurses very friendly, whereas 76 (30.6%) felt that the nurses were unfriendly.

Another problem worthy of mention is the fact that there is little or no long-term care both in terms of facilities and the needed professionals to provide that service. Also, mental care is very rudimentary in Nigeria. The majority of mental health services are concentrated in only eight regional psychiatric centers and psychiatric departments of medical schools and in a few general hospitals. Because of the local belief systems, these formal systems face competition from native herbalists and faith healing centers. The ratio of psychologists and social workers is 0.02 to 100,000 population.[50]

In Nigeria, there is a clear demarcation between the health-seeking behavior of the "haves" and "have-nots." Wealthier individuals usually seek health care in well-equipped hospitals and private clinics. On the other hand, those who are financially challenged are more likely to use the "informal" private health sector or, at best, the primary health centers, which are usually chronically understaffed. Traditional medicine healers, drug peddlers, and others who practice in the informal sector usually prescribe "mixtures" of drugs without regard to appropriate dosage regimen and manufacturers' safety standards. Treatments prescribed are usually based on conjectured diagnoses without any form of laboratory workup.[25]

Equally troublesome is the lack of a safety-net system for the poor. In a system in which health care is mainly paid for out of pocket, there is no safety net for individuals who are below the poverty line (which is arbitrarily defined as earning less than $275 annually).[24] Few public health facilities and even fewer private health facilities accommodate patients who cannot afford to pay for treatment. Some missionary-run health facilities occasionally hold medical outreaches to provide a wide range of services (outpatient services, general surgery, eye clinics, etc.) free of charge or for very minimal fees. Many poor patients bear their illnesses without seeking medical attention while waiting for the next free medical outreach; however, if the government succeeds in its effort to initiate a social health insurance scheme, this would allow cross-subsidization in the health sector—in the sense that the scheme gives access to health care to people who cannot afford it—provided by the contribution of members who are financially able.[51]

Apart from the healthcare system, several other supporting systems such as road, transportation, electricity, water, and sewage also suffer from inadequate infrastructure. According to the WHO, in 2004, 67% of the urban population and 31% of rural population had access to improved drinking water sources.[8] The proportion of the population with access to improved sanitation was 53% and 36% for the urban and rural areas, respectively.[8] There have also been several ethnic and religious uprisings in the country, which have led to the loss of lives and property and to an overburdening of the fragile healthcare system. This instability and security issues have discouraged potential investors, thereby negatively impacting growth in the economic and health sector.[11] Hence, for meaningful progress to be made in the healthcare system, there have to be equivalent improvements in other related sectors of the Nigerian society and economy.

At the Nigerian National Health Conference held in November 2006,[52] participants representing stakeholders from within and outside the country identified priorities to sustain the current health reforms. The goal of this conference was to develop a health agenda for Nigeria in the 21st century with subsequent dissemination to stakeholders. Some of the observations endorsed at the conference were that Nigeria still has one of the worst health indices in the world and accounts for 10% of the world maternal deaths but 2% of the world population (2000 figures); the health system is still underfunded with per capita expenditure of US$9.44 on health; and key correlates of ill health such as hunger, poverty, illiteracy, poor sanitation, gender inequalities, and unemployment are still prevalent in the society.

Following these observations, several resolutions and recommendations were made and endorsed by the conference—the establishment of a special system of social welfare for the disadvantaged and vulnerable groups, promotion and legitimization of public–private partnership in all aspects of the health system to ensure sustainability of the healthcare system, and an increase in Nigeria's per capita expenditure on health from US$ 9.44 to the WHO-recommended US$34. In addition, the conference endorsed a new, competitive welfare and compensation package for healthcare practitioners in the private and public health sectors.[52]

Successfully managing health promotion and education must be seen as a collective responsibility between citizens, the government, and the medical or health research centers. To the extent that a healthy population is an active population, the negative effects of disease and illness can be offset by an active and energetic workforce fully engaged in the nation's productive process. Rather than speaking in broad generalities, the nation's health policy must speak to the specifics—the need to isolate chronic epidemiological issues (such as malaria, HIV/AIDS, sexually transmitted diseases, yellow fever, and water-borne parasites) and to exercise the political will necessary to address the specific needs of marginalized groups or at-risk populations. There should be an increased commitment of resources to understanding the environmental conditions, cultural, and biological circumstances that make certain types of pathologies more prevalent or chronic in the Nigerian context so that intervention or preventive measures can be taken to mitigate their more costly and public health effects.

The ongoing shift toward social health insurance is welcome in principle, but the means to achieving optimal public–private sector mix in the design of health plans remains a major challenge, as long as the triple issues of cost, access, and quality are not taken seriously. Affordable health care on demand is a key objective that should inform government healthcare policy making.

REFERENCES

1. Badru Padre. *Imperialism and Ethnic Politics in Nigeria, 1960–1966.* Trenton, NJ: Africa World Press; 1998, pp. 69–71.

2. The World Bank. *World Development Indicators Database.* New York: The World Bank; April 2007.

3. McIntosh SK, McIntosh RJ. Current directions in West African prehistory. *Annual Review of Anthropology.* 1983;12: 215–258.

4. The CIA World Factbook. Retrieved February 28, 2008, from https//www.cia.gov/library/publications/the-world-factbook/print/ni.html.

5. US General Printing Office. *Nigeria: CIA World Factbook.* Washington, DC: US General Printing Office; 2008.

6. Hazem B, Luciano G, eds. *The Rentier State,* vol. II. New York: Croom Helm; 1987, p. 12.

7. Omeje K. Oil conflict and accumulation politics in Nigeria. Report from Africa: population, health, environment, and conflict. *ECSP Report.* 2007;12:45:44–49. Retrieved January 10, 2008, from http://www.eia.doe.gov/emeu/cabs/orevcoun .html.

8. World Health Organization. *World Health Statistics 2007.* Geneva, Switzerland: WHO; 2007.

9. Labiran A. *Social Determinants of Health: Nigerian Perspective. The Regional Consultation of the Commission on Social Determinants of Health.* Brazzaville, Congo: DRC Government Publications; 2005.

10. The United Nations. *World Population Prospects: The 2005/2006 Revision and World Urbanization Prospects.* New York: U.N. Press; 2006.

11. Okafor C, Follen M, Adewole I. Opportunities to improve health systems in Africa: a comparative overview of healthcare challenges for stakeholders and strategic planners. *Gynecol Oncol.* 2007;107(1 Suppl 1):S86–S93.

12. World Health Organization. *The World Health Report 2006: Working together for health: World Health Organization.* Geneva, Switzerland: WHO; 2006.

13. The United States Library of Congress Country Studies and the CIA World Factbook: Nigeria: History of Modern Medical Services; 1991. Retrieved March 30, 2008, from http://www.photius.com/countries/nigeria/society/nigeria_society_history_of_modern_me~10005.html.

14. Library of Congress Country Studies and the CIA World Factbook, p. 2. Retrieved March 30, 2008, from http://www .photius.com/countries/nigeria/society/nigeria_society_history_of_modern_me~10005.html.

15. Library of Congress Country Studies and CIA World Factbook, p. 3. Retrieved March 30, 2008, from http://www .photius.com/countries/nigeria/society/nigeria_society_history_of_modern_me~10005.html.

16. Library of Congress Country Studies and CIA World Factbook, p. 4. Retrieved March 30, 2008, from http://www .photius.com/countries/nigeria/society/nigeria_society_history_of_modern_me~10005.html.

17. Onwujekwe O, Uzochukwu B. Socio-economic and geographic differentials in costs and payment strategies for primary healthcare services in Southeast Nigeria. *Health Policy.* 2005;71(3):383–397.

18. Petu A. Health financing reforms: the Nigerian experience. *African Health Monitor.* 2005;6(1):33–34.

19. The Library of Congress Country Studies and the CIA World Factbook, 1991. Retrieved February 18, 2008, from http://www.photius.com/countries/nigeria/society/nigeria_society_primary_health_care_~10006.html.

20. World Health Organization. *WHO Country Cooperation Strategy: Federal Republic of Nigeria, 2002–2007.* Geneva, Switzerland: WHO; 2007.

21. World Health Organization. *Health Systems Policies and Service Delivery.* Nigeria: Ministry of Health; 2006.

22. Alubo O. The promise and limits of private medicine: health policy dilemmas in Nigeria. *Health Policy Plan.* 2001;16(3):313–321.

23. Ogunbekun I, Ogunbekun A, Orobaton N. Private health care in Nigeria: walking the tightrope. *Health Policy Plan.* 1999;14(2):174–181.

24. Akanji BO, Ogunniyi A, Baiyewu O. Healthcare for older persons, a country profile: Nigeria. *J Am Geriatr Soc.* 2002;50(7):1289–1292.

25. Uzochukwu BS, Onwujekwe OE. Socio-economic differences and health seeking behavior for the diagnosis and treatment of malaria: a case study of four local government areas operating the Bamako initiative programme in southeast Nigeria. *Int J Equity Health.* 2004;3(1):6.

26. Federal Ministry of Health, Nigeria. *National Health Indicators 2008.* Nigeria: Ministry of Health; 2008.

27. Arah OA, Ogbu UC, Okeke CE. Too poor to leave, too rich to stay: developmental and global health correlates of physician migration to the United States, Canada, Australia, and the United Kingdom. *Am J Public Health.* 2008;98(1): 148–154.

28. Clark DA, Clark PF, Stewart JB. The globalization of the labour market for health-care professionals. *International Labour Review.* 2006;145.

29. Mullan F. The metrics of the physician brain drain. *N Engl J Med.* 2005;353(17):1810–1818.

30. World Health Organization. *Managing Brain Drain and Brain Waste of Health Workers in Nigeria, 2006.* Geneva, Switzerland: WHO; 2006.

31. Ibrahim M. Medical education in Nigeria. *Med Teach.* 2007;29(9):901–905.

32. Library of Congress Country and CIA World Factbook, p. 4–5. Retrieved October 23, 2008, from www.ciafactbook.gov

33. Federal Republic of Nigeria. *National Health Insurance Scheme Decree 1999.* Nigeria: Ministry of Health; 1999.

34. Organisation for Economic Co-operation and Development. *OECD Health Data 2006: How Does the United States Compare?* New York: OECD Publications; 2006.

35. Federal Ministry of Health Nigeria. *National HIV Seroprevalence Sentinel Survey.* Nigeria: Ministry of Health; 2004.

36. Idigbe EO, Odutolu O, Okonkwo P, et al. Evaluation of the Nigerian national antiretroviral (ARV) treatment training programme. *SAHARA J.* 2006;3(3):488–502.

37. UNICEF: At a Glance: Nigeria Statistics. Retrieved February 28, 2008, from http://www.unicef.org/infobycountry/nigeria_statistics.html.

38. Onah HE, Okaro JM, Umeh U, Chigbu CO. Maternal mortality in health institutions with emergency obstetric care facilities in Enugu State, Nigeria. *J Obstet Gynecol.* 2005; 25(6):569–574.

39. Aboyeji AP, Ijaiya MA, Fawole AA. Maternal mortality in a Nigerian teaching hospital: a continuing tragedy. *Nigeria Health.* 2007;37(2):83–85.

40. United Nations Human Development Report 2002, Deepening Democracy, 172. New York: UN Press; 2002.

41. Uzochukwu BS, Onwujekwe OE, Akpala CO. Effect of the Bamako-Initiative drug revolving fund on availability and rational use of essential drugs in primary health care facilities in south-east Nigeria. *Health Policy Plan Trop Doct.* 2002; 17(4):378–383.

42. The Library of Congress Country Studies and the CIA World Factbook, 1991, p. 3. Retrieved November 23, 2008, from www.ciafactbook.org

43. Encyclopedia of Nations. Nigeria: Health. Retrieved February 18, 2008, from http://www.nationsencyclopedia.com/Africa/Nigeria-Health.html.

44. United States Agency for International Development. Nigeria: USAID Strategy in Nigeria. Retrieved February 18, 2008, from http://www.usaid.gov/locations/sub_saharan_africa/countries/nigeria.

45. World Health Organization. *Report of Pre Eleventh ICDRA Satellite Workshop on Counterfeit drugs.* Madrid, Spain, February 13–14, 2004. Geneva, Switzerland: WHO; 2004.

46. World Health Organization. Health financing and social protection. Retrieved February 18, 2008, from http://www.who.int/countries/nga/areas/health_financing/en/index.html

47. Graig LA. *Health of Nations.* Washington, DC: CQ Press; 1999, p. 178.

48. World Health Organization. Health Systems: Improving Performance. *The World Health Report 2000.* Geneva, Switzerland: WHO; 2000.

49. Ofovwe CE, Ofili AN. Indices of patient satisfaction in an African population. *Public Health.* 2005;119(7):582–586.

50. Ayonrinde O, Gureje O, Lawal R. Psychiatric research in Nigeria: bridging tradition and modernization. *Br J Psychiatry.* 2004;184:536–538.

51. Okonkwo A. Nigeria set to launch health insurance scheme. *The Lancet.* 2001;358(9276):131.

52. Federal Republic of Nigeria. Federal Ministry of Health. Conference Communiqué: Nigerian National Health Conference (NHC2006), November 28–29, 2006. Abuja, Nigeria: Ministry of Health; 2006.

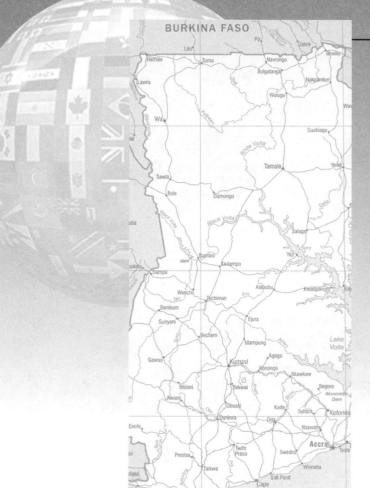

CHAPTER 18

Ghana

Ahmed Adu-Oppong,
Lois Kisiwaa-Ameyaw, and
Beatrice Wiafe Addai

COUNTRY DESCRIPTION

TABLE 18-1 Ghana

Nationality	Noun: Ghanaian(s)
	Adjective: Ghanaian
Ethnic groups	Akan 45.3%, Mole-Dagbon 15.2%, Ewe 11.7%, Ga-Dangme 7.3%, Guan 4%, Gurma 3.6%, Grusi 2.6%, Mande-Busanga 1%, other tribes 1.4%, other 7.8% (2000 census)
Religions	Christian 68.8% (Pentecostal/Charismatic 24.1%, Protestant 18.6%, Catholic 15.1%, other 11%), Muslim 15.9%, traditional 8.5%, other 0.7%, none 6.1% (2000 census)
Language	Asante 14.8%, Ewe 12.7%, Fante 9.9%, Boron (Brong) 4.6%, Dagomba 4.3%, Dangme 4.3%, Dagarte (Dagaba) 3.7%, Akyem 3.4%, Ga 3.4%, Akuapem 2.9%, other 36.1% (includes English [official]) (2000 census)
Literacy	Definition: age 15 and over can read and write
	Total population: 57.9%
	Male: 66.4%
	Female: 49.8% (2000 census)

(continues)

TABLE 18-1 Ghana (continued)

Government type	Constitutional democracy
Date of independence	March 6, 1957 (from the United Kingdom)
Gross Domestic Product (GDP) per capita	$1,400 (2007 est.)
Unemployment rate	11% (2000 est.)
Natural hazards	Dry, dusty, northeastern harmattan winds occur from January to March; droughts
Environment: current issues	Recurrent drought in north severely affects agricultural activities; deforestation; overgrazing; soil erosion; poaching and habitat destruction threatens wildlife populations; water pollution; inadequate supplies of potable water
Population	23,382,848 Estimates for this country explicitly take into account the effects of excess mortality caused by AIDS; this can result in lower life expectancy, higher infant mortality, higher death rates, lower population growth rates, and changes in the distribution of population by age and gender than would otherwise be expected (July 2008 est.)
Age structure	0–14 years: 37.8% (male 4,470,382/female 4,360,359) 15–64 years: 58.7% (male 6,852,363/female 6,866,470) 65 years and over: 3.6% (male 386,150/female 447,124) (2008 est.)
Median age	Total: 20.4 years Male: 20.2 years Female: 20.7 years (2008 est.)
Population growth rate	1.928% (2008 est.)
Birth rate	29.22 births/1,000 population (2008 est.)
Death rate	9.39 deaths/1,000 population (2008 est.)
Net migration rate	−0.55 migrant(s)/1,000 population (2008 est.)
Gender ratio	At birth: 1.03 male(s)/female Under 15 years: 1.03 male(s)/female 15–64 years: 1 male(s)/female 65 years and over: 0.86 male(s)/female Total population: 1 male(s)/female (2008 est.)
Infant mortality rate	Total: 52.31 deaths/1,000 live births Male: 56.64 deaths/1,000 live births Female: 47.85 deaths/1,000 live births (2008 est.)
Life expectancy at birth	Total population: 59.49 years Male: 58.65 years Female: 60.35 years (2008 est.)
Total fertility rate	3.78 children born/woman (2008 est.)
HIV/AIDS adult prevalence rate	3.1% (2003 est.)

(continues)

TABLE 18-1 Ghana (continued)

Number of people living with HIV/AIDS	350,000 (2003 est.)
HIV/AIDS deaths	30,000 (2003 est.)

Central Intelligence Agency. The World Fact Book, 2008. Retrieved November 18, 2008, from https://www.cia.gov/library/publications/the-world-factbook.

History

The Republic of Ghana was named after the medieval Ghana Empire of West Africa Ancient Ghana. Geographically, Ancient Ghana was approximately 500 miles (800 km) north of the present Ghana and occupied the area between Rivers Senegal and Nigeria. The actual name of the Empire was Ouagadougou. Ghana was the title of the kings who ruled the kingdom. The word "Ghana" means "Warrior King."[1] Ancient Ghana was controlled by Sundiata in 1240 AD and absorbed into the larger Mali Empire, which reached its peak of success under Mansa Musa in approximately 1307. Around 1235, a Muslim leader named Sundiata united warring tribes. He then brought neighboring states under his rule to create the Mali Empire. Its capital city was called Kumbi-Saleh. Ancient Ghana derived power and wealth from gold and the introduction of the camel during the Trans-Saharan trade. The Islamic community at Kumbi-Saleh remained a separate community quite a distance away from the King's palace. It had its own mosques and schools, but the King retained traditional beliefs. He drew on the bookkeeping and literary skills of Muslim scholars to help run the administration of the territory.[2]

There were numerous reasons for the decline of Ghana. The King lost his trading monopoly, at the same time the drought began and had a long-term effect on the land and its ability to sustain cattle and cultivation. On March 6, 1957, when the leaders of the former British colony of the Gold Coast sought an appropriate name for their newly independent state, the first African nation to gain its independence from colonial rule, they named their new country after ancient Ghana. The choice was more than merely symbolic because modern Ghana, like its namesake, was equally famed for its wealth and trade in gold. The growth of trade stimulated the development of early Akan states located on the trade route to the gold fields in the forest zone of the south.[3]

Of the components that would later make up Ghana, the state of Asante was to have the most cohesive history and would exercise the greatest influence. The Asante are members of the Twi-speaking branch of the Akan people. The groups that came to constitute the core of the Asante confederacy moved north to settle in the vicinity of Lake Bosumtwe. Before the mid-17th century, the Asante began an expansion under a series of militant leaders that led to the domination of surrounding peoples and to the formation of the most powerful of the states of the central forest zone.

The Europeans arrived in Gold Coast in the late 15th century. The Portuguese were the first to arrive. By 1471, under the patronage of Prince Henry the Navigator, they had reached the area that is now known as the Gold Coast because Europeans knew the area as the source of gold that reached Muslim North Africa by way of trade routes across the Sahara.[4] The initial Portuguese interest in trading for gold, ivory, and pepper increased so much that in 1482 the Portuguese built their first permanent trading post on the western coast of present-day Ghana. This fortress, Elmina Castle, constructed to protect Portuguese trade from European competitors and hostile Africans, still stands. With the opening of European plantations in the New World during the 1500s, which suddenly expanded the demand for slaves in the Americas, trade in slaves soon overshadowed gold as the principal export of the area. During the 17th and 18th centuries, other European adventurers emerged on Gold Coast. First Dutch and later English, Danish, and Swedish were granted licenses by their governments to trade overseas. On the Gold Coast, these European competitors built fortified trading stations and challenged the Portuguese. Sometimes they were also drawn into conflicts with local inhabitants, as Europeans developed commercial alliances with local chiefs.[5]

The principal early struggle was between the Dutch and the Portuguese. With the loss of Elmina in 1642 to the Dutch, the Portuguese left the Gold Coast permanently. The next 150 years saw drastic changes and uncertainty, marked by local conflicts and diplomatic maneuvers, during which various European powers struggled to establish or to maintain a position of dominance in the profitable slave trade. There were short-lived ventures by the Swedes and the Prussians.[6] The Danes remained until 1850, when they withdrew from the Gold Coast. The British gained possession of all Dutch coastal forts at the end of the 19th century, thus making them the dominant European power on the Gold Coast until March 6, 1957, when the new republic of Ghana was born with Osagyefo "liberator" Dr. Kwame Nkrumah as its first president. It was during the first republic that healthcare facilities were built to take care of the indigenous Ghanaian population.

Size and Geography

Until March 1957, Ghana was known to the world as the Gold Coast. The Portuguese who came to Ghana in the 15th century found so much gold between the rivers Ankobra and Volta that they named the place Mina, meaning *mine*. English colonists later adopted the Gold Coast. The Republic of Ghana occupies an area of 239,460 km^2 (92,440 square miles), and it borders Côte d'Ivoire (also known as Ivory Coast) to the west, Burkina Faso to the north, Togo to the east, and the Gulf of Guinea to the south. Ghana is made of 10 administrative regions and 110 administrative districts with a decentralized system of administration. Within this arrangement, the national level is responsible for policy and strategy development. The regional level is the intermediate level responsible for translating national policy into regional strategies and coordination of district actions. The district is the level at which all government policies are implemented. The district assemblies are the highest political and administrative authority at the local level. The district assemblies, through their subcommittees, harmonize and coordinate plans and activities of all decentralized ministries. They also facilitate grassroots participation and community involvement in socioeconomic development programs and activities. The district assemblies are generally supportive of decentralized departments. Undoubtedly, the district assemblies are very important in the implementation and sustainability of a multisectoral response to healthcare systems.

Government and Political System

Ghana was formerly known as Gold Coast when it was a colony of Great Britain. On March 6, 1957, the former British colony of Gold Coast became the first country in sub-Saharan Africa to shake off colonial rule, inspiring liberation struggles around the continent. It obtained its independence under its first president Osagyefo "Redeemer" Dr. Kwame Nkrumah, the founding father of Pan-Africanism and a figurehead among Africa's independence leaders with his concept of African Liberation through the concept of socialism.[7] Ghana was created as a parliamentary democracy at independence in 1957, followed by alternating military and civilian governments. In January 1993, military government gave way to the Fourth Republic after presidential and parliamentary elections in late 1992. The 1992 constitution divides powers among a president, parliament, cabinet, Council of State, and an independent judiciary. The government is elected by universal suffrage. Ghana is a multiparty constitutional democracy with a democratically elected government. Since January 1993 when Ghana ushered in the Fourth Republic, four presidential and parliamentary elections have been held successfully. John Agyekum Kufuor was re-elected in December 2004 and sworn into office for a second and final 4-year term in January 2005. John Atta-Mills was sworn into office in January 2009. The three traditional "three arms of government" are as follows: the President (executive), the Parliament (the legislature), and the judiciary. The legislature is perhaps the most important in the practice of democracy. This is because it is the institution through which the people are represented in government; however, parliamentary practice in Ghana is arguably the most underdeveloped of the three. This is as a result of frequent military interventions in the governance of the country. Historically, whenever there has been an interruption in government, Parliament is the first casualty. While the dismissed Head of State is immediately replaced and the judiciary constituted, Parliament is dissolved. The function of Parliament is then taken over by the executive, which monopolizes legislation.[8] This unfortunate trend has affected the smooth evolution of the institution and stunted its growth. This explains why despite its long history of existence the legislature is still seen as an infant institution.

The Republic is based on a parliamentary system of government with an elected president and a national parliament. The country is divided into 10 regions and 110 administrative districts. Each district is presided over by an elected district assembly with responsibility for policy development and planning to harness local resources for social and economic development. The district assembly is the basic unit of government administration and is constituted as the planning authority for the district. There are various subdistrict administrative structures and subordinate bodies of the district assemblies—the submetropolitan district councils, urban/town/zonal area councils, and unit committees. The latter form the base structures of the new local government system, with units comprising settlements or groups of settlements with a population of 500–1,000 in rural areas and at least 1,500 in urban areas. There are 10 regional cocoordinating councils that are administrative rather than political policy-making bodies. Their functions include the coordination of the plans and programs of district assemblies in the region and monitoring and evaluation of programs and projects.[9]

Judicial System

The legal system is based on Ghanaian common law, customary (traditional) law, and the 1992 constitution. Court hierarchy consists of Supreme Court of Ghana (highest court), Court of Appeal, and High Court of Justice. Beneath these bodies are district, traditional, and local courts. Since independence, courts are relatively independent; this independence continues under the Fourth Republic. Lower courts are being redefined and reorganized under the Fourth Republic.

Council of State

The Council of State, a small body of prominent citizens of proven character, advises the President on national issues. It is analogous to the Council of Elders in the traditional political system.

District Assemblies

The local government system consists of Regional Cocoordinating Council, a four-tiered Metropolitan, and a three-tiered Municipal/District Assemblies Structure. The assemblies are either metropolitan (population over 250,000), municipal (population over 95,000), or district (population 75,000 and over). There are 3 Metropolitan Assemblies, 4 Municipal Assemblies, and 103 District Assemblies.

Politics

Political parties became legal in mid-1992 after a 10-year hiatus. Under the Fourth Republic, major parties are the National Democratic Congress, led by Jerry John Rawlings, which won presidential and parliamentary elections in 1992; the New Patriotic Party, which won the presidential and parliamentary elections in 2000 and 2004, led by His excellency John Agyekum Kuffour; the People's National Convention, led by former president Hilla Limann; and (new) the People's Convention Party, successor to Kwame Nkrumah's original party of the same name. The 11 registered parties in the 2008 elections are as follows: the Convention Peoples Party, the Democratic Peoples Party, Every Ghanaian Living Everywhere, the Great Consolidated Popular Party, the Ghana National Party, the National Democratic Congress, the New Patriotic Party, the National Reform Party, the Peoples National Convention Party, the United Ghana Movement, and the Ghana Democratic Republican Party.[6]

Macroeconomics

Since its independence in 1957, Ghana has experienced different political regimes with different economic results and social outcomes. During the 1980s, the government's tax base diminished by falling income and production. The resulting large deficit led to rising inflation and a large external debt burden. It also resulted in lower expenditure and a general neglect of the country's infrastructure and its educational and health services. It is estimated that about 2 million Ghanaians left the country, including 14,000 teachers. Health personnel were very demotivated, and many chose to emigrate. It is also estimated that 60% of medical doctors who graduated in the 1980s were employed outside of Ghana.[10]

In January 2001, the economy of Ghana was again facing crisis. Inflation was running at 41%, whereas the budget deficit as well as external and domestic debts stood at unsustainable levels. This macroeconomic context had a negative impact on expenditure in social sectors and poverty reduction activities as the government found it increasingly difficult to meet its counterpart funding obligations to donor-supported projects, including the social sectors. With strong donor support, the government of President Kufuor adopted and implemented prudential fiscal and monetary measures that resulted in macroeconomic stability and economic growth and investor confidence. The inflation rate decreased from 40.5% by the end of 2000 to 10.5% at the end of first quarter 2004. In terms of economic progress, the increase in fuel prices put Ghanaian economy under pressure. The level of fuel prices and government subsidy is discussed in Ghana as the country strives to adjust to increased prices.[11] Ghana remains somewhat dependent on international financial and technical assistance as well as the activities of the extensive Ghanaian in the diaspora. Gold, timber, cocoa, diamond, bauxite, and manganese exports are major sources of foreign exchange. An oil field that is reported to contain up to 3 billion barrels (480,000,000 m^3) of light oil was discovered in 2007. Oil exploration is ongoing, and the amount of oil continues to increase. The domestic economy continues to revolve around subsistence agriculture, which accounts for 50% of GDP and employs 85% of the work force. The average annual real economic growth rate per

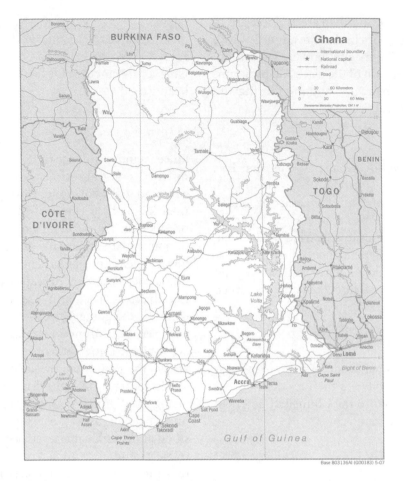

FIGURE 18-1 Map of Ghana

capita was −1.1% and 1.9%, respectively, for the periods 1980–1990 and 1991–2003. Household final consumption expenditure per capita decreased annually by −0.8 and increased by 1.6 during the periods 1980–1990 to 1990–2001. The Human Development Index was 0.439, 0.511, and 0.568, respectively, in 1975, 1990, and 2002. The undernourished proportion has decreased from 35% to 25% between 1990–1992 and 1999–2001. The prevalence of HIV/AIDS in Ghana is low compared with the African epidemiological situation. In 2003, the prevalence rate was 3.1%.[12] Life expectancy increased from 49.9 years to 57.9 between 1970–1975 and 2000–2005. The country has, since July 2007, embarked on a currency redenomination exercise, from cedi (¢) to the new currency, the Ghana cedi (GH¢). The transfer rate is 1 Ghana cedi for every 10,000 cedis. The new Ghana cedi is now exchanging at a rate of $1 USD = Gh¢ 0.93.[13] Ghana is the world's second largest cocoa producer, and its track record of economic reform over the past few years has boosted growth. It is also Africa's second biggest gold producer after South Africa.

The Ghanaian economy is benefiting from one of the most successful reform programs in Africa, with increased growth reflecting strong economic fundamentals underpinned by anti-inflationary monetary policy and fiscal consolidation. It is now apparent that the private sector is responding positively. The economy seems to be on the cusp of becoming an emerging market. The improving policy environment has contributed to a recent upsurge in economic growth, with real gross domestic product (GDP) growth reaching an estimated 6.2% in 2006 from the average annual rate of 5.5% during 2000–2005.[14] Recent strong performance has enabled Ghana to accelerate implementation of its poverty reduction strategy. Economic growth is becoming broader based, although the agricultural sector still dominates economic activity. The track record in strengthening democracy and a stable political environment bodes well for continuing economic expansion; however, the political situation could be improved further by tackling growing perceptions of corruption in public life. Ghana also benefitted from $4.2 billion of multilateral debt relief after the 2005 G8 summit in Gleneagles, Scotland.[15]

Demographics

Ghana has a population of 23 million (2007 estimates),[16] of which 52% are female 48% are male, with 9.2 million persons 15–49 years old. Life expectancy of the total population is 59.12 years, the male is 58.31 years, and the female is 59.95 years. The illiteracy rate is 42.1%.[17] More than half live in rural settings. English is the official language of business and instruction; other local dialects include Akan (majority), Ga, and Ewe: Akan 45.3%, Mole-Dagbon 15.2%, Ewe 11.7%, Ga-Dangme 7.3%, Guan 4%, Gurma 3.6%, Grusi 2.6%, Mande-Busanga 1%, other tribes 1.4%, other 7.8% (2000 census). The Christian population is 68.8%, with the following distributions by denominations (Pentecostal/Charismatic 24.1%, Protestant 18.6%, Catholic 15.1%, other 11%). Muslim is 15.9%, traditional African religion Animism 8.5%, other 0.7%, and none 6.1% (2000 census).[15] Ghana's consistent growth of approximately 5% per annum over the last 15 years has resulted in one of the fastest rates of poverty reduction in Africa. Acute poverty—income of less than $1 a day—fell from 51% in the early 1990s to 35% in 2006. Most poverty is still rural, although the figures available indicate a slight increase in urban areas, from 7% to 9% in 2006.[18] Relentless urbanization is shifting the pattern of poverty, with youth facing the most difficulty, as Ghana struggles to create formal sector jobs and provide services for the growing urban population.[19]

BRIEF HISTORY OF THE HEALTHCARE SYSTEM

Pre–World War II

Until October 19, 1923, when the Korle Bu Teaching Hospital, formerly known as the Gold Coast Hospital, was opened by the then Governor of the Gold Coast, Sir Gordon Guggisberg, health services were solely for Europeans. There were only European physicians who treated only the settlers. The majority of the indigenous Ghanaian population practiced traditional African medicine. After the opening of the Gold Coast Hospital, the indigenous population of Accra was able to receive the European health care at a minimal cost. Korle Bu Hospital had less than 200 beds and treated up to 200 patients daily.[20] At that time, Korle Bu was described as the finest hospital in Africa, on account of its impressive array of fine buildings and a cadre of competent staff, who provided excellent medical services to the population of Ghana in general, and the city of Accra in particular. Korle Bu Hospital, from its inception, has been used for the training of practical nurses, nurse anesthetists, dispensers, midwives, and other para medical staff.

Since World War II

In 1946, a Nurses Training College was opened at Korle Bu to train a higher level of staff registered nurses for the hospital and for the entire country. In April 1963, the government made Korle Bu Hospital the teaching hospital for the University of Ghana Medical School.[21] After independence, medical services became free to all citizens of Ghana and were financed by the government. Under the leadership of Dr. Kwame Nkrumah, Ghana set up a National Health Service, which was fully financed from state revenue. Again during this time because of the lack of facilities in the rural areas, the quality of care received there was very poor; however, the concept during that time was concentrated on vaccine-preventable diseases, and everybody (including the rural areas) had access to available vaccinations. It was the belief of the Nkrumah administration that health before wealth was more than just an old adage; it developed programs that aim to protect and improve the health of people to help in the battle against poverty.[22] The government was committed to the objective of health for all. Good health boosts labor productivity, educational attainment, and income and thus reduces poverty. A country's economic development is closely interrelated with the health status of its population, and efficient and equitable healthcare system is therefore an important instrument in breaking the vicious circle of poverty and ill health. Until 1983, Ghana's health system was financed mainly out of the national budget.[23]

By the early 1980s, Ghana was experiencing balance of payments crisis, which was soon generalized into an economic crisis that affected all sectors of the economy. Thus, not only did Ghana experience a general decline in agricultural productivity and exports that included declining world prices for cocoa and gold, but there was also a shortfall in foreign exchange earnings, which impacted negatively on import-dependent manufacturing firms. Furthermore, consumer goods shortages, inflationary pressures, and unemployment gradually built up and resulted in deficit financing via external borrowing, making the situation worse. By this time, Ghana's balance of payments was in disarray; budget deficits were ballooning, and foreign investment flows had nearly dried up.[24]

In Ghana and across Africa, structural adjustment was foisted on one country after the other, and efforts were made to dismantle agricultural marketing boards, privatize, commercialize, liquidate state-owned enterprises, deregulate various aspects of the economy, reduce the size of the state bureaucracy through civil service retrenchments, encourage the private sector, and promote the embrace of the market. Structural adjustment was very much concerned about balancing budgets and servicing public debt both domestic and external. To do this, there were budget cuts on social spending, with education and health bearing the heaviest brunt. Slowly but surely, in 1978, the government was forced to introduce cost recovery into the health system in Ghana.[25] This was popularly known as "cash and carry." This system was a product of the structural adjustment program that the International Monetary Fund and the World Bank had prescribed and that Ghana readily adopted. It involved the wholesale withdrawal of government subsidies on health delivery. Under the cash-and-carry system, patients were asked to pay for full cost of medication and care. Because of economic crises and mismanagement, the government had to reduce spending on health and social affairs. Less money was available for health. The government was not able to finance the health system via general taxation. The Bamako Initiative reform (1988) also instituted the introduction of user fees in government health facilities, the joint management of the resources generated by health staff and the community, and the decentralization of the health sector. The rationale behind full cost recovery was that there would be an increase in resources to the healthcare facilities that would allow them to expand and upgrade their services, improve access to health care, improve patients' care, and have better efficiency because of the increased revenue from charges. Furthermore, there was the presumption that cost recovery would help reduce unnecessary visits by patients who would abuse the system because it was free. The evidence gathered thus far suggests that none of these assumptions materialized. Since its introduction, cash and carry appeared to have carried away health services from the people. The cash-and-carry system could best be described as "stinking and dehumanizing" because patients who did not have the ability to pay for medical services were turned away from hospitals only to die at home. The disabled, poor, and accident victims were being asked to pay on the spot before getting medical attention.[26] To make matters worse, cost recovery was introduced at a time when many

people had been laid off from the public sector and income levels were extremely low. Many poor people were turned away from health centers for lack of funds.[27]

Unfortunately, the poor were simply priced out of hospital care, and a two-tiered healthcare system came into operation with better facilities for those who could afford to pay. Once again, women and children bore the brunt of such harsh policies. The introduction of user fees further impoverished the majority of Ghanaians, and it devastated their ability to sustain a livelihood for a long time. Some people, especially the poor living below the poverty line, had to borrow money, took out loans, sold their animals or furniture, dissolved their little savings, cut down on buying food, and even stopped sending their children to school in order to pay for health care. The process of borrowing money from extended family delayed treatment and, in many cases, caused deterioration of the illness or even death. In other cases, people did not seek medical treatment because they could not afford it, which often increased their morbidity and mortality.[28]

It was welcomed news when in 2004 the government rekindled the need for social equity to be a key part of healthcare policy through the establishment of the National Health Insurance Scheme (NHIS) to replace the cash-and-carry system. If Ghana is to attain the Millennium Development Goals and Middle-Income Status by 2015, the main goals of the health ministry should be threefold, namely increasing public access to health care, improving the quality and efficiency of healthcare delivery, and finally, improving and increasing programs of education on curative and preventive health care.

DESCRIPTION OF THE CURRENT HEALTHCARE SYSTEM

There are four main categories of healthcare delivery systems in Ghana: the public, private for profit, private not for profit, and traditional systems.[29] The public health system, centered on the Ministry of Health (MOH), has a hierarchical organizational structure from the central headquarters in Accra to the regions, districts, and subdistricts. Services are delivered through a network of facilities, with health centers and district hospitals providing primary healthcare services, regional hospitals providing secondary health care, and two teaching hospitals—the Korle Bu Hospital and the Komfo Anokye Teaching Hospital (KATH)—at the apex providing tertiary services. The two teaching hospitals also play a key role in teaching and research—offering facilities for the training of doctors and other health professionals and for medical and public health research. KATH serves about half of the 23 million people of Ghana as well as the neighboring Burkina Faso and the Cote d'Ivoire as the main tertiary referral centre.

Facilities

There are a total of 163 hospitals and 692 community health centers in Ghana.[30] The breakdown of the hospitals is as follows: 2 teaching hospitals, 8 regional hospitals, 48 district hospitals, 23 government funded hospitals (including military hospitals), 43 charity hospitals, and 39 private hospitals. Services are delivered through a network of facilities: health centers and district hospitals provide primary healthcare services. Regional hospitals provide secondary health care, whereas two teaching hospitals are at the apex to provide tertiary services. Health care is structured in a four-tiered system. Level A comprises health systems at community level, including trained birth attendants and community health workers. Level B comprises health posts and health centers at subdistrict level. Level C comprises hospitals that function as district referral units. Regional and teaching hospitals make up level D, as they provide tertiary services.

- National
- Regional
- District
- Subdistrict

National

The national level is made up of the MOH, where health policy is formulated, the health system is monitored, and evaluation of progress in achieving targets is conducted. The second entity within the national level is the Ghana Health Services, which is responsible for the resources allocation and the creation of partnership with the private sector.

Regional

There are 10 regional health administrations that serve as link between the national and district levels and allocate resources within the region. The regional and district hospitals are set up as part of a national policy, which ensures that every region and district should have a befitting health facility; however, that is not the case for all regions and districts in the country, more especially now that new districts are springing up in conformity to the decentralization policy. The regional hospitals

depend on district hospitals for their patient load. The majority (68%) of the dentists in Ghana work in public regional hospitals. There is usually a dentist, two or three dental surgery assistants, and one or more dental laboratory technicians, depending on the size of the catchment area. The dentist is responsible to the chief medical officer of the hospital. Unlike the medical profession, dentistry has no representation at the regional, district, or community levels.

District

The focal point of the healthcare system is at the district level, where the implementation of the national healthcare strategy takes place. The district level is concerned with operational planning and implementation of service within the district. It is responsible for the construction of health facilities: hospital, health centers, and community health clinics. This is the key level of management of the primary healthcare system and provides leadership in district health care. The attempt to provide middle, paradental personnel to provide oral health services in the district and rural areas, especially to school children, was defeated when the 15 dental therapists trained overseas in the late 1970s ended up in schools within Accra, the capital. There are presently only 14 dental clinics in the 110 districts in the country.

Subdistrict Levels

Community-Level Health Centers   These provide outpatient services to relieve the district and regional hospitals of all but their most specialized functions. Health centers usually serve a catchment area of about 8 km^2 and provide the first point of contact with health personnel from the MOH. There is no dental equivalent to the delivery system at this level, except for the odd outreach program by the already understaffed dental team from the regional hospitals.[31]

Health Centers, Health Posts, and Rural Clinics This is the smallest unit at the broad base of the three-tiered system where minor cases like cuts and wounds are treated with serious cases referred to the health centers or the district hospitals. These stations are run by Community Clinic Attendants and function as first-aid stations and health observational posts. There is no equivalent oral health delivery system at this level.

Community-Based Health Planning and Services Community Level   This is a new system of healthcare delivery introduced in the country some few years ago based on a research carried out by the Navrongo Health Research Centre. It is similar to the primary healthcare concept, but a qualified health worker, called community health officer, normally minds this program. Community health nurses are mostly reoriented to assume this position. Now it has been integrated into their training program. This system is operated on zonal basis in a giving subdistrict. The requirement for setting up the community-based health planning and services zone is similar to that of the health center. One distinct feature is that community-based health planning and services zones are normally established at the remote areas comprising a number of communities with a population of between 3,000 and 4,000. Its emphasis is more on health promotion (preventive health) than curative health.

Workforce

The nation has three medical schools that are responsible for training physicians. They are the University of Ghana Medical School in Accra, Kwame Nkrumah University of Science and Technology Medical School in Kumasi, and the University of Cape Coast School of Medical Sciences in Cape Coast. There are two teaching hospitals in the nation that are responsible for training the healthcare workforce. These teaching hospitals are Korle Bu Teaching Hospital in Accra and KATH in Kumasi.

Besides these two teaching institutions, there are a number of other institutions, with links to the MOH, located at Korle Bu, that are also involved in training the healthcare workforce in Ghana. These are as follows: the Nurses Training School, the Public Health Nurses Training School, the Midwifery Training School, the School of Hygiene, the Disease Control Division of the MOH, the Health Education Unit of the MOH, and the Center for Health Statistics of the MOH. In addition, several other institutions, with their own administration and budgets, have links with Korle Bu hospital. These include the University of Ghana Medical School, the Blood Bank, the Health Laboratory Services, and the Public Health Reference Laboratory. Komfo Anokye Hospital in Kumasi is host to other institutions attached to the MOH and also has links with several autonomous institutions responsible for training the healthcare workforce. These include the Nurses Training School, the Midwifery Training School, the Medical School of the University of Science and Technology, the Blood Bank, and the Health Laboratory Services. These institutions have been able to train adequate workforce for the system; hence, workforce training has not been the

issue in Ghana—the issue has been retention. The lack of ability of the system to craft adequate compensation and pay structures to retain the trained workforce has led to the migration of the healthcare workforce to developed countries for greener pastures.[32] A World Health Organization (WHO) report on international migration stated that by the end of 2005 Ghana lost over 50% of her highly skilled labor. Of this, 90% were healthcare professionals.[33] Ghana was the only country to lose most of its professionals during the 1980s. Currently, there is only one doctor per 160,000 population in the country. The test is to train and retain those coming through medical schools. The onus is on the government to pay the medical professionals decent wages plus generous incentives to encourage them to stay in Ghana.[34]

Technology and Equipment

The provision of equitable, quality, and efficient health care requires an extraordinary array of properly balanced and managed resource inputs. Physical resources such as fixed assets and consumables, often described as healthcare technology, are among the principal types of those inputs. Technology is the platform on which the delivery of health care rests and the basis for provision of the majority of health interventions. Technology generation, acquisition, and utilization require massive investment, and related decisions must be made carefully to ensure that the best match between the supply of technology and health system needs, the appropriate balance between capital and recurrent costs, and the capacity to manage technology throughout its life. There is a large need for new medical equipment to equip the new facilities that are being built and the existing facilities that are being expanded and/or refurbished. Much of the existing equipment is also obsolete or broken and cannot be repaired locally because of a lack of spare parts or maintenance expertise. This need is expected to increase as more of the planned projects are started. Future demand will increase as there has been a recognized need to improve the health service in Ghana, and this is being addressed as funds become available.[35] Doctors try to improve information in various ways, frequently by prescribing tests. An ideal test is cheap, produces no adverse side effects, and is accurate in two senses: It always identifies pathology when it is present and confirms its absence when it is not present. Even accurate and safe tests can be worthless—for instance, when no effective treatment is available. If resources dedicated to health care are limited, something has to be sacrificed (rationing), and this is the case in Ghana when it comes to diagnostic or treatment procedures that require pieces of high-tech equipment that are either not available or scarce in the nation. Other nations have rationed health care for years by setting healthcare budgets or regulated fees, effectively controlling the numbers of hospitals or the amount of medical equipment or other devices. First, how can rationing be done "rationally"? As British economist Alan Williams put it, "Only when we can be satisfied that the most valuable thing that we are not doing is less valuable than the least valuable thing that we are doing, can we be sure that we are being efficient in the pursuit of welfare."[36] The country depends on Ghanaians in the diaspora, nongovernmental organization, and bilateral and multilateral donors for donations of pieces of technological equipment in the medicine field. The technological donations have been in the form of new, used, refurbished, and/or rehabilitated medical equipment, mobile medical services, and equipment, as was the case on October 3, 2007, when GE Vice President of Corporate Citizenship visited the KATH in Kumasi to commission the product donations, which provide the much-needed infrastructure and technology to enable lifesaving health care. These include a fluoroscopy unit for radiology, ultrasounds, incubators, monitors, lighting, electrical distribution equipment, water purification, and Internet connectivity.[37]

EVALUATION OF THE HEALTHCARE SYSTEM

Cost

The cost of health service delivery can simply be grouped into two: the capital cost and the recurrent cost. The capital cost is the hardware cost that includes the provision of healthcare facilities—such as building hospitals, maintaining the healthcare facilities, and training health service providers. These costs have always been borne by government under all of the previous health financing schemes. The health insurance system being implemented falls short of taking care of these costs.

The other cost is the recurrent cost—the cost associated to the consumables and other supplies such as medical supplies (disinfectants, surgical masks, syringes, etc.), drug cost, laboratory inputs, fuel for ambulance, and servicing of equipment. This is the cost, or probably part of this, that users of health service are usually asked to pay. It must be mentioned here that the cost as passed on the "ordinary Ghanaian" is usually not the full recurrent cost. The average cost of hospital admission varies tremendously from region to region and among districts. The average cost of hospital admissions at St. Theresa's Hospital at Nkoranza is about 81,131 cedis ($9.00) for general admissions and 26,234 cedis ($3.00) for normal deliveries. Although this may look inexpensive by the Western standards, the annual income for most people in this region is approximately $10. This is a district hospital, and the cost goes up as one is referred to the regional hospital for other care that is not available at the district.

Finance

Identifying and quantifying the variety of health finance flows are challenging exercises. Where data are available, they are not collected or managed systematically as Ghana lacks a central entity responsible for carrying out these tasks. Accordingly, even the MOH acknowledges that its figures must be treated with care.[38] Often, particularly in the case of flows that bypass the Ministry's budget, data are not even available. Rising allocations from the central government have allowed Ghana to reach the 2001 Abuja Declaration target of allocating 15% of the annual budget to improvements in the health sector. Derived mostly from national sources, these allocations are augmented by three foreign sources. To begin, a number of donors (including the World Bank, the United Kingdom, the European Union, and the African Development Bank) have begun using general budget support as an aid modality through the Multi-Donor Budget Support initiative. As budget support has generally not been tied to specific sectors, measuring the extent of its use for health is practically impossible. The share of health finance channeled through central government is likely to increase in the future as several donors are currently considering a move to budget support. Other sources of central government allocations to the health sector include commercial lending (15%) and debt relief (0.2%, from the Heavily-Indebted Poor Country initiative). The budget of the MOH distinguishes between three sources of funding: allocations from central government (which accounted for 59.2% of the Ministry's total budget of $435 million in 2005), support from bilateral and multilateral donors (27.2%), and internally generated funds from private households (13.6%). The distinction between three sources of health finance, used in most government documents, paints a simplified picture, which does not capture adequately the various financing channels and actors in Ghana's health sector (Figure 18-2). First, it is important to understand that funds from central government are derived from different sources, including foreign ones. Second,

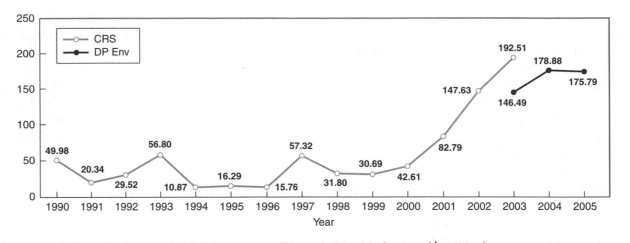

FIGURE 18-2   Official Development Assistance to Ghana's Health Sector ($ million)

Author calculations based on data from DAC Creditor Reporting System (CRS) 2006 and Ghana Development Partner Envelope Overview (DP Env) 2006 on health in Ghana compared to the public sector's contribution of 35 percent.

donors use diverse channels to achieve health outcomes. Third, a large degree of private finance bypasses the MOH's budget. Finally, new actors such as foundations, global funds, and nongovernmental organizations (NGOs) have important roles to play in financing health.

Donors have an important stake in the healthcare sector in Ghana, providing 27.2% of the Ministry's budget. Their support for health increased sixfold between 1999 and 2003, from $30.7 million to $192.5 million (Figure 18-3). This can be seen as part of a larger global shift of Official Development Assistance toward

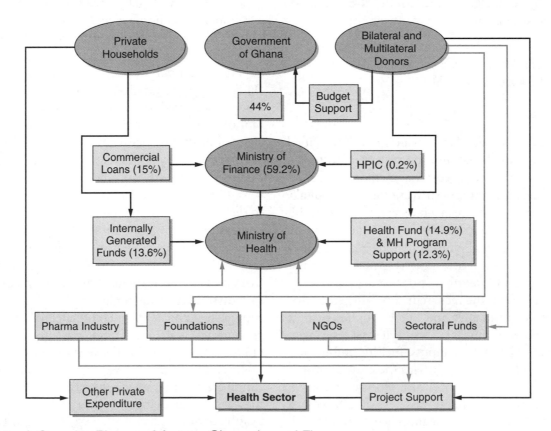

FIGURE 18-3   A Complex Picture of Actors, Channels, and Flows

Author created from percentages data derived from the Ministry of Health 2007.

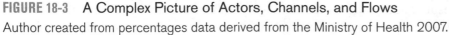

the social sectors, encouraged by the adoption of the Millennium Development Goals and the Poverty Reduction Strategy Initiative of the World Bank; however, the volumes actually disbursed in Ghana may differ from those pledged and reported to the Development Assistance Committee. In 2003, for example, Official Development Assistance disbursements confirmed by local development agencies fell significantly below Development Assistance Committee figures. The primary reason behind such discrepancies is that local agencies will not necessarily have figures for aid that is not channeled through or managed by them. This may include the remuneration of experts providing technical assistance in Ghana's health sector or scholarships to Ghanaian medical students at universities in donor countries. Health financing in Ghana is partly based on a cash-and-carry system, requiring users to pay for a proportion of health services out of their own pockets. Funds from private households, in the form of user fees for drugs and other consumables, constitute 13.6% of the budget of the MOH[39]; however, WHO figures suggest that those that bypass the budget dwarf households' contributions through the Ministry's budget. According to the WHO National Health Account initiative, between 1998 and 2004, private spending constituted around 65% of the total expenditure on health in Ghana compared with the public sector's contribution of 35%.[40] Remittances, the single most important private capital inflow to Ghana, have become a major contributor to household income and, indirectly, to household expenditure on health; however, figures from various sources differ greatly. For 2005, the IMF's Balance of Payments Statistics report private transfers at below $100 million, whereas the Bank of Ghana reports a vastly higher figure: $1.52 billion. The latter figure is based on household surveys, which may provide a more accurate picture, as it includes informal transfer channels not captured by the IMF. Although the use of private capital inflows cannot be determined with certainty, evidence from Ghana suggests that remittances help households cover emergency expenses, for example, in the case of major illnesses.[41] Figure 18-2 shows new actors that have begun financing health in Ghana. They are NGOs, global funds, private donors, the pharmaceutical industry, and private foundations, as well as private commercial capital flows.

NGOs

As estimated by the National Coalition of Health NGOs, 400 NGOs are active in the Ghanaian health sector, with a large majority acting as implementing agencies for donor-funded projects. This means that their self-generated financial contribution to the sector is minimal. Nevertheless, their proximity to local institutions and marginalized individuals, especially in remote areas, renders them a crucial part of the healthcare system. Faith-based NGOs such as the Christian Health Association of Ghana or the Catholic Secretariat, which represents the Catholic Church, are particularly important in Ghana.

Global Funds

Global funds have had a tremendous impact on health sector finance in recent years. The two largest global funds in the Ghanaian health sector are the Global Fund and the GAVI Alliance. Since 2000, the former has disbursed $42 million of the $93.4 million pledged in its grant agreement with Ghana, directing funds to fighting malaria (44%), HIV/AIDS (36%), and tuberculosis (20%). The GAVI Alliance has disbursed around $20 million to Ghana since 2000, targeting hepatitis B (a total of $45 million pledged) and yellow fever ($4.5 million) in a multiyear immunization plan (2002–2006) and providing cash support for immunization services ($3.6 million) and injection safety ($855,000).[42]

Private Donors

It is particularly difficult to determine an exact figure for private donations. They are neither recorded systematically nor captured by national statistics. According to the MOH, it administered a total of $176 million in financial and in-kind donations between 2004 and 2005. Although these numbers must be treated with caution, they show that private donations constitute a considerable inflow to the sector, especially bearing in mind that the Ministry's total annual budget (excluding donations) amounted to only $435 million in 2005. Some private donors use informal financing channels, meaning that the magnitude of Ghana's total receipts is almost certainly even larger. The Catholic Secretariat, for example, reported donations of $160,000 in 2004.

The Pharmaceutical Industry

Of the 14 pharmaceutical companies contacted, only one (Pfizer) provided details of program support through in-kind contributions. In 2005, the company delivered $1.6 million worth of Zithromax to fight trachoma (International Trachoma Initiative) and $320,000 worth of Diflucan to fight opportunistic infections, that is, infections that predominantly affect people with a poorly functioning or suppressed immune system (Diflucan Partnership

Program).[43] Pfizer also engages in Ghana through the Pfizer Foundation, which provides grants for training and capacity-building activities in the health sector. Other pharmaceutical industry activities have been captured by the International Federation of Pharmaceutical Manufacturers and Associations (2004 and 2005).[44] Thus, GlaxoSmithKline supports malaria prevention in Ghana through the African Malaria Partnership, and Merck & Co. has supported the dissemination of healthcare materials, together with the International Council of Nurses and Elsevier Science. Finally, Abbott Laboratories and Boehringer Ingelheim have donated Viramune and Determine within the framework of their joint initiative for the prevention of mother-to-child transmission of HIV.

Private Foundations

Information on the activities of foundations in Ghana remains incomplete. Among the 11 foundations contacted, the Gates Foundation appears to be the largest sponsor of health-related projects. It granted $16.4 million between 2000 and 2005. The Rockefeller Foundation reports $3.4 million in grants to Ghana between 1999 and 2005, including projects by the MOH, the Forum of African Women, and the University of Ghana. European foundations are also gaining in importance. The U.K.-based Wellcome Trust, for example, granted $903,000 to Ghanaian health projects between 2000 and 2006.[45]

Private Commercial Capital Flows

Like many other low-income countries, Ghana has not yet attracted large amounts of private commercial capital. Although the importance of Foreign Direct Investment is gradually growing, these investments have predominantly concentrated on the mining and manufacturing industries, with no investment projects identified in the health sector. Commercial bank loans, on the other hand, are important when used to finance health infrastructure projects. In 2005, they constituted 15% of the total budget of the MOH.

NHIS

Households in many developing countries face the constant risk of having to finance the treatment of serious illnesses directly out of pocket. Health insurance systems, both public and private, based on prepayment or risk pooling, could help alleviate the exposure to these risks significantly.[46] The Ghanaian government in 2005 introduced the NHIS, to replace the cash-and-carry system in the hope of easing the overall burden borne by private households. The law underpinning the NHIS makes membership of an insurance scheme compulsory, with households expected to make premium payments in line with their "ability to pay."[47] The scheme is run by local mutual health organizations. There is the consideration of a unique identification system that would allow patients to cross district lines for specialist care. Medical informatics would help create standards for electronic exchange of financial and administrative data and also standards for unique identifiers, code sets, security, and privacy; however, this will require a tremendous investment in technology that is currently not available at the local level. With insurance schemes so far only having existed at the community level, the ultimate aim is to make the NHIS the main purchasing mechanism for health services throughout the country. This well-intended initiative is not founded on solid grounds, with doubts having been voiced regarding its financial sustainability.[48] Determining acceptable contribution levels will be a key challenge and will rely on better information on household income. Further information would allow the government to make a better distinction between those who could pay higher contributions for quality packages and those who must remain exempt from payments, which currently include the core poor, indigenous people, and children with insured parents. The National Health Insurance Levy was introduced on August 1, 2004, to provide "seed money" for the NHIS. The levy is a disguised value-added tax (VAT) charge (2.5%) on some goods and services, and thus, consumers in Ghana are paying the levy. VAT is a consumption tax administered in Ghana. The tax regime that started in 1998 had a single rate but in September 2007 entered into a multiple-rate regime. In 1998, the rate of tax was 10% and amended in 2000 to 12.5%; however, with the passage of Act 734 of 2007, a 3% VAT Flat Rate Scheme began to operate for the retail distribution sector. This allows retailers of taxable goods under Act 546 to charge a marginal 3% on their sales and account on same to the VAT service. It is aimed at simplifying the tax system and increasing compliance. It is the hope of the government that if properly monitored it would ultimately increase tax revenue in the country. The premium is set at $8.00 per year. People under 18 years old, those over 70 years old, and the indigent are exempt from premium payment. An entire family unit must enroll in the plan. The benefits package covers 95%

of disease burden in Ghana, and there are no co-payments or deductibles. The NHIS is funded by premiums, sales tax, and social security contributions.

Quality

An effective health service delivery does not only depend on being able to pay for drugs or other consumables but also has the state-of-art facilities that effectively promote diagnosis, treatment, and the necessary environment for recovery when one falls ill and well-qualified and motivated health personnel to use and manage those facilities. The ideal alternative is to have an environment that shields people from falling ill—having the appropriate environment to reduce infections and other noncommunicable diseases. Ghana needs massive capital investments in the health and social service sectors to ensure such an ideal health environment. Ghanaians deserve good health facilities; indeed, all of the regional hospitals and district hospitals should be like those of Sunyani, Ho, or the Cape Coast hospitals. (For those who have not been to any of these mentioned hospitals, the facilities can be compared with any standard hospital in the United States or Western Europe). Because of the lack of diffusion of the state-of-the-art technology in the country diagnosis and because treatment of tertiary diseases is not up to par with the expected quality by the developing standard, the country preventive care methods are top-notch quality. There exists an unequal distribution of healthcare delivery across the country. There are severe disparities among regions and districts and between rural and urban areas in terms of healthcare quality and access to services.

Access

The country lacks adequate infrastructure to care for its citizens. There is also a disparity in the availability of healthcare facilities in the nation between the rural and urban areas. As a result, access to health care in the rural areas is not only difficult but also lacks the standard of quality deserved. With the introduction of the NHIS advertising, more people are signing on to the concept of insurance that has open access to most people who could not afford to visit the hospital without the insurance. Figure 18-4 demonstrates the increased access to health facilities in the Nkoranza district after the introduction of the NHIS pilot project. Similar increases have been reported in all the districts. The pilot project began in 2003, and from that point on, there was an increased in use in all of the health centers and hospitals in the Nkoranza district.

The effects of insurance enrollment on access to and costs of health care have potential implications for the NHIS in Ghana. One concern often raised in connection with prepayment schemes is whether the premiums are affordable to the target population. The data from this study offer arguments for and against the premiums set

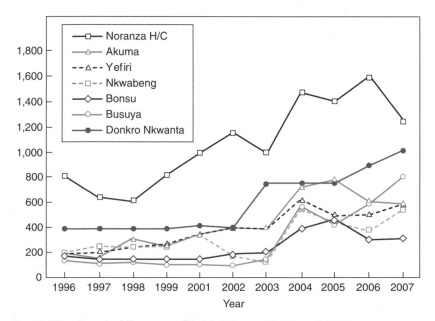

FIGURE 18-4   Outpatient Utilization in Nkoranza District from 1996 to 2007
Data from the evaluation of the Nkoranza Insurance Pilot project.

by the government of Ghana for the NHIS. A few findings signal potential problems with the government-established premium of 72,000 cedis per adult. The NHIS premium structure requires that household adults pay this amount, and all dependents within the household will be covered. Thus, for a family of five with two parents, the annual premium would be 144,000 cedis,[49] falling between the annual total of 125,000 for the Nkoranza scheme and 200,000 cedis for the Okwahuman scheme. Referring specifically to Nkoranza, the household data revealed that half of currently uninsured households were previously enrolled in the scheme. Nearly 80% of formerly insured households cited expensive premiums as the reason for ending their membership. Among households that have never enrolled, 60% cited the same reason for not enrolling, indicating an inability to afford premiums that were lower than those proposed under the NHIS. Also, regression analysis of individual predictors of enrollment found wealth to be a significant factor, suggesting that families with fewer resources would be less likely to join a prepayment scheme; however, the results also lend support to the established premium structure and rates, perhaps more convincingly than arguments against them. First, although some families in Nkoranza indicated that they could not afford the somewhat lower premiums for that CBHI scheme, larger families would benefit from the NHIS structure, as regardless of the number of dependents, the total family cost would be the same (i.e., 144,000 cedis). Second, the NHIS offers more comprehensive benefits, including outpatient curative care and normal delivery care, making it a better value for families. Third, reviewing average payments made by uninsured patients for inpatient and delivery care, which ranged from 125,000 to 490,000 cedis per episode/event, the cost of 144,000 cedis for an entire family seems quite reasonable. Although exemption policies and practices may need to be flexible to respond to the needs of a given community, the NHIS premium structure and rates seem to be within reach of the majority of Ghanaians.

CURRENT AND EMERGING ISSUES AND CHALLENGES

In the health sector, some of the persisting challenges are as follows: Malaria continues to be the major cause of high morbidity as well as mortality; the HIV/AIDS epidemic has the potential to drain resources in the health sector, as well as important human resources needed to develop the country further. High migration to devel-oped countries of trained health workers, particularly doctors and nurses, continues to hamper the effective provision of health services, especially at regional and district levels, and the lack of proper sanitation in the urban areas poses a greater threat for outbreaks.

Apart from human resource management, a major challenge for Ghana's health sector is the unequal distribution of healthcare delivery across the country. There are severe disparities among regions and districts and between rural and urban areas in terms of healthcare quality and access to services. As a result, diseases such as malaria are significantly more prevalent in rural than in urban areas. Malaria remains the main cause of mortality and morbidity in Ghana, accounting for about 21% of the under-5 mortality rate and 40% of outpatient morbidity. The government appears to be tackling this problem by making efforts to reduce the burden of malaria. It launched a new Malaria Drug Policy in 2005 and, under its Intermittent Prevention Treatment strategy for malaria, adopted the new amodiaquine–artesunate drugs combination for prevention and treatment. In 2006, the Ghana Health Service changed the recommended dose of this drug for malaria, after controversy over side-effects also scaled-up Insecticide Treated Nets (ITNs) distribution across the country. Over 5 million ITNs were procured for distribution, and ITN utilization increased by 32.7% for pregnant women and 31.0% for children less than 5 years old.

In 2006, the government achieved its target of reducing the prevalence rate of HIV/AIDS to 2.3%; the recorded prevalence rate was 3.7%,[50] as more antiretroviral therapy sites became operational. By the end of 2006, the government had a 2-year stock of antiretroviral drugs. Nonetheless, the exodus of doctors and other health service personnel continues to be a problem for health service delivery.

Available data indicate that between 1999 and 2005 around 50% of doctors trained in Ghana left the service.[51] The government has used incentives to try to stem this tide without much success. Incentives include the distribution of saloon cars to doctors working in deprived areas and enhanced salaries and pensions.

In Ghana, a lack of access to clean water and sanitation systems is a central public health concern, contributing to 70% of diseases in Ghana. There is substantial variation in access to clean, affordable water and sanitation, depending on income, between rural and urban areas and across regions in Ghana. According to the Ghana Water Sector Restructuring Secretariat, in 2005, only 46% of the total population had access to piped water.[38] The figure falls to 22% for those classified as poor. Uninterrupted access to treated and piped water is only significant in some urban areas. Average urban access is 46%, whereas in rural areas, only 35% of the population has access. Access to proper sanitation is equally dismal. Again, according to the Water Sector Restructuring Secretariat, the percentage of the population with access to improved sanitation facilities is approximately 40% in urban areas and 35% in rural areas. To meet the Millennium Development Goals, water supply coverage for the urban areas will have to be increased to 88%, and sanitation coverage must be increased to 80%.

Ghana is known as one of the African countries with the highest rate of brain drain in the medical sector. It is estimated that about a third of Ghana's trained health personnel left the country in the period from 1993 to 2002.[52] The health sector is facing another challenge, namely the difficulty in attracting and retaining qualified health personnel in rural and deprived areas. The government is continuing its efforts to reverse the brain drain in the health sector and has among others set up a vehicle revolving fund for health workers in 2002.[53] To further retain and attract qualified people in the country, Ghana will have to review its civil service conditions in order to increase economic efficiency and the social sector service delivery.

REFERENCES

1. Jackson JG. *Introduction to African Civilizations*, 2nd ed. Chaleston, SC: Kensington Publishing Corp, Citadel Press; 2001.

2. Stearns PN, Langer WL. *The Encyclopedia of World History: Ancient, Medieval, and Modern*, 6th ed. New York: Houghton Mifflin Books; 2001.

3. Buah FK. *History of Ghana*. London: Macmillan Education Ltd.; 1980.

4. Nkrumah, K. *Revolutionary Path*. New York: International Publishers; 1973.

5. MacLean I. *Rational Choice and British Politics: An Analysis of Rhetoric and Manipulation from Peel to Blair*. Oxford: Oxford University Press; 2001.

6. Ghana Information Services Department. *Ghana: A Brief Guide*. Accra: GIS Publication; 1994.

7. Nkrumah I. *Neo-Colonialism: The Last Stage of Imperialism*. New York: International Publishers; 1965.

8. Nyinah JB. Ghana's parliament: a brief history. Ghana Home Website, 2003. Retrieved February 20, 2008, from www.ghanaweb.com/GhanaHomePage/features/artikel.php?ID=3901.

9. Ghana Ministry of Health. *Health Sector Program of Work: Bridging the Inequality Gap: Addressing Emerging Challenges With Child Survival*. Accra: MOH Report; 2005.

10. Vujicic M, Zurn P, Daillo K, Adams O, Dal Poz M. The role of wages in the migration of health care professionals from developing countries. *Human Resources for Health*. 2004;2:3–8.

11. Ocquaye M. Govt. can't reduce fuel prices. *Daily Graphic*. March 2, 2005, p. A1.

12. Adu-Oppong A, Grimes RM, Ross MW, Risser J, Gladstone K. Social and behavioral determinants of consistent condom use among female commercial sex workers in Ghana. *AIDS Education and Prevention*. 2007;19:160–172.

13. Adams O, Stilwell B. Health professionals and migration. *Bulletin of the World Health Organization*. 2004;82:8–16.

14. World Bank. *Global Economic Prospects 2006: Economic Implications of Remittances and Migration*. Washington, DC: World Bank Report; 2006.

15. OECD. News and Ideas from the OECD Development Assistance Committee. Paris: DAC Secretariat. *DAC News*. 2006;4:23–27.

16. African Economic Outlook 2003/2004—Country Studies. OECD website, 2005. Retrieved January 15, 2008, from http://www.oecd.org/dataoecd/24/28/32429910.pdf.

17. Program of work of the OECD development centre 2007–2008. OECD website, 2008. Retrieved February 12, 2008, from http://www.oecd.org/dataoecd/54/57/39782186.pdf.

18. Ghana Health Services. Poverty Reduction Strategy 2005–2008. *An Agenda for Growth and Prosperity*. 2006;1:22–20.

19. Berry L. *Ghana: A Country Study*. Washington, DC: Federal Research Division, Library of Congress; 1995, pp. 81–82.

20. Twumasi PA. *Medical Systems in Ghana: A Study in Medical Sociology*. Accra: Ghana Publishing Corporation; 1975.

21. Bossert TJ, Beauvais JC. Decentralization of health systems in Ghana, Zambia, Uganda and the Philippines: a comparative analysis of decision space. *Health Policy and Planning*. 2002;17:14–31.

22. Agyapong IA. Reforming health service delivery at the district level in Ghana: the perspective of a district medical officer. *Health Policy and Planning*. 1999;14:59–69.

23. Gaines K. *On Nkrumah Assassination by CIA: American Africans in Ghana, Black Expatriates and the Civil Rights Era*. Chapel Hill, NC: The University of North Carolina Press; 2006.

24. Bonsi SK. *Studies on an Appropriate Mechanism for Exemptions from Charges for Drugs and Curative Care in Government Health Facilities in Ghana*. Accra: MOH Report; 2001.

25. World Health Organization. *Macroeconomics and Health: Investing in Health for Economic Development*. Geneva: World Health Organization Report; 2001.

26. Sikosana PL, Dlamini N, Issakov A. *Health Sector Reform in Sub-Saharan Africa: A Review of Experiences, Information Gaps and Research Needs*. Geneva: World Health Organization Report; 1997.

27. Asante AD, Zwi AB, Ho MT. Equity in resource allocation for health: a comparative study of the Ashanti and Northern Regions of Ghana. *Health Policy*. 2006;78:135–148.

28. Reporters without Borders. Worldwide Press Freedom Index 2006. Available at Worldwide Press Freedom website.

Retrieved February 24, 2008, from www.reporterssan frontiers.org.

29. Adjei S. Assessing the effect of primary health on mortality in Ghana. *Journal of Bio-social Science.* 1989;10(Suppl): 115–125.

30. Ministry of Health. *Health Sector Program of Work 2002: Ghana-Accra: Report of the External Review Team.* Ghana: Ministry of Health; 2003.

31. Ministry of Health. *Health Sector Five-Year Program of Work: 2002–2006.* Accra: MOH Report; 2006.

32. Adusei K, Akor SA, Oppong-Mensah D. *Ministry of Health Oral Health Policies and Medium Term Strategic Plan.* Accra: Oral Health Unit of the Ministry of Health Report; 2000.

33. Ministry of Health. *Human Resource Policies and Strategies for the Health Sector 2002–2006.* Accra: Ministry of Health Report; 2006.

34. World Health Organization. Migration and health workers special issue. *Bulletin of the World Health Organization.* 2004;82:559–636.

35. Adams O, Stilwell B. Health professionals and migration. *Bulletin of the World Health Organization.* 2004;82:550–558.

36. International Market Research. Healthcare Products and Services in Ghana. Retrieved March 2, 2008, from http://strategis .ic.gc.ca/epic/site/imr-ri.nsf/en/gr123482e.html.

37. Business Wire: GE Expands Healthcare Initiative to Hospitals in Ghana: Partner initiative to provide medical and infrastructure equipment across Africa, October 3, 2005. Retrieved March 1, 2008, from http://findarticles.com/p/ articles/mi_m0EIN/is.

38. Organisation for Economic Co-operation and Development. *Creditor Reporting System.* Paris: Development Assistance Center Report; 2006.

39. Ministry of Health. *Pause...Get it Right...Move on—Review of Ghana Health Sector, 2005 Program of Work.* Accra: Main Sector Review Report; 2006.

40. Organisation for Economic Co-operation and Development. *Creditor Reporting System.* Paris: Development Assistance Center Report; 2006.

41. African Development Bank. African Development Report. Natural resources for sustainable development in Africa. Available at African Development Bank website, 2007. Retrieved March 12, 2008, from http://www.afdb.org/pls/ portal/docs/page/adb_admin_pg/documents/economics andresearch/ad%20summary-2007.pdf.

42. United States AID for International Development. *Private Remittances Flows to Ghana.* Washington, DC: Country Report; 2005.

43. Hudson Institute. *A Review of Pharmaceutical Company Contributions—HIV/AIDS, Tuberculosis, Malaria, and Other Infectious Diseases.* Washington, DC: Center for Science in Public Policy Report. Hudson Institute; 2004.

44. International Federation of Pharmaceutical Manufacturers Associations. *Building Healthier Societies through Partnerships.* Geneva: International Federation of Pharmaceutical Manufacturers Associations Report; 2005.

45. World Health Organization. *Macroeconomics and Health: Investing in Health for Economic Development.* Geneva: World Health Organization Report; 2001.

46. United Nations Development Program. *International cooperation at a crossroads: aid, trade and security in an unequal world.* New York: United Nations Development Program Human Development Report; 2005.

47. Drechsler D, Jütting J. Is there a role for private health insurance in developing countries? *German Institute for Economic Research.* 2005;15:123–138.

48. Ghana Ministry of Health. *Health Sector Five-Year Program of Work—2002–2006.* Accra: Ministry of Health Report; 2006.

49. Léger F. *Financial Assessment of the National Health Insurance Fund.* Geneva: International Labor Organization Report; 2006.

50. Wilbulpoprasert S. Inequitable distribution of doctors: can it be solved? *Human Resources Development Journal.* 1999;3: 2–22.

51. Sulzbach S, Garshong B, Owusu-Banahene G. *Evaluating the Effects of the National Insurance Act in Ghana.* Accra: USAID & Partners for Health Reform Report Order No. TE 090; 2005.

52. Ghana Ministry of Health. *Health Sector Program of Work: Bridging the inequality gap: Addressing Emerging Challenges with Child Survival.* Accra: Ministry of Health Report; 2005.

53. African Development Bank. *2003–2004 African Economic Outlook.* Paris: OECD Report; 2004.

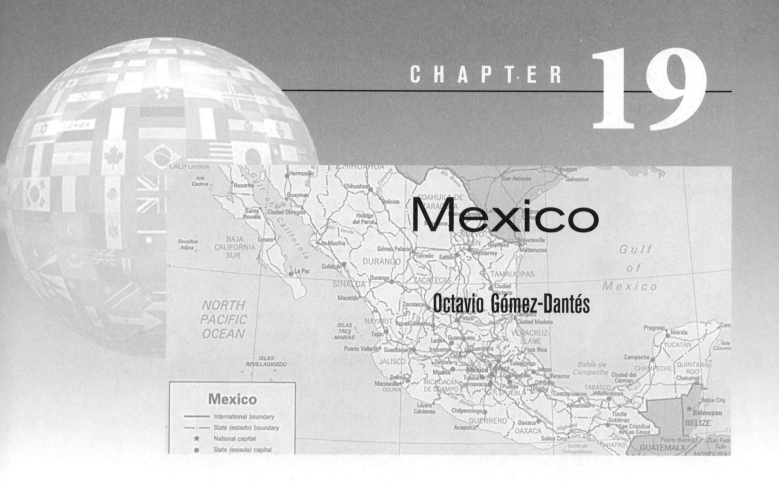

CHAPTER 19

Mexico

Octavio Gómez-Dantés

COUNTRY DESCRIPTION

TABLE 19-1   Mexico

Nationality	Noun: Mexican(s) Adjective: Mexican
Ethnic groups	Mestizo (Amerindian-Spanish) 60%, Amerindian or predominantly Amerindian 30%, white 9%, other 1%
Religions	Roman Catholic 76.5%, Protestant 6.3% (Pentecostal 1.4%, Jehovah's Witnesses 1.1%, other 3.8%), other 0.3%, unspecified 13.8%, none 3.1% (2000 census)
Language	Spanish, various Mayan, Nahuatl, and other regional indigenous languages
Literacy	Definition: age 15 and over can read and write Total population: 91% Male: 92.4% Female: 89.6% (2004 est.)
Government type	Federal republic
Date of independence	Independence Day, September 16, 1810
Gross Domestic Product (GDP) per capita	$12,500 (2007 est.)

(continues)

TABLE 19-1 Mexico (continued)

Unemployment rate	3.7% plus underemployment of perhaps 25% (2007 est.)
Natural hazards	Tsunamis along the Pacific coast; volcanoes and destructive earthquakes in the center and south; and hurricanes on the Pacific, Gulf of Mexico, and Caribbean coasts
Environment: current issues	Scarcity of hazardous waste disposal facilities; rural to urban migration; natural freshwater resources scarce and polluted in north, inaccessible and poor quality in center and extreme southeast; raw sewage and industrial effluents polluting rivers in urban areas; deforestation; widespread erosion; desertification; deteriorating agricultural lands; serious air and water pollution in the national capital and urban centers along the U.S.–Mexico border; land subsidence in Valley of Mexico caused by groundwater depletion; the government considers the lack of clean water and deforestation national security issues
Population	109,955,400 (July 2008 est.)
Age structure	0–14 years: 29.6% (male 16,619,995/female 15,936,154) 15–64 years: 64.3% (male 34,179,440/female 36,530,154) 65 years and over: 6.1% (male 3,023,185/female 3,666,472) (2008 est.)
Median age	Total: 26 years Male: 24.9 years Female: 27 years (2008 est.)
Population growth rate	1.142% (2008 est.)
Birth rate	20.04 births/1,000 population (2008 est.)
Death rate	4.78 deaths/1,000 population (2008 est.)
Net migration rate	−3.84 migrant(s)/1,000 population (2008 est.)
Gender ratio	At birth: 1.05 male(s)/female Under 15 years: 1.04 male(s)/female 15–64 years: 0.94 male(s)/female 65 years and over: 0.82 male(s)/female Total population: 0.96 male(s)/female (2008 est.)
Infant mortality rate	Total: 19.01 deaths/1,000 live births Male: 20.91 deaths/1,000 live births Female: 17.02 deaths/1,000 live births (2008 est.)
Life expectancy at birth	Total population: 75.84 years Male: 73.05 years Female: 78.78 years (2008 est.)
Total fertility rate	2.37 children born/woman (2008 est.)
HIV/AIDS adult prevalence rate	0.3% (2003 est.)
Number of people living with HIV/AIDS	160,000 (2003 est.)
HIV/AIDS deaths	5,000 (2003 est.)

Central Intelligence Agency. The World Fact Book, 2008. Retrieved November 18, 2008, from https://www.cia.gov/library/publications/the-world-factbook.

History

Mexico is the largest Spanish-speaking country in the world and the nation with the largest indigenous population in the Americas (10.2 million). Around 5,000 years ago, ancient Meso-American Indians domesticated corn.[1] This agricultural revolution, among other things, allowed for the construction of advanced civilizations, which were conquered by the Spaniards in 1519. Independence from Spain was achieved in 1821. A war with the United States in 1846 to 1848 ended with Mexico losing half of its territory.[2] In 1864, the French invaded Mexico and ruled until 1867. A major revolt against a long-standing dictatorship produced the Mexican Revolution in 1910, which resulted in the death of 10% of the nation's population.[3] Since then, Mexico has struggled to build a stable democratic regime able to respond to the demands of an increasingly urban and educated population.

Size and Geography

Mexico covers 1.9 million square miles of land, 13% of which is arable.[4] To the north, it borders with the United States of America and to the south with Guatemala and Belize (Figure 19-1).

Government and Political System

Mexico is a federal presidential representative democratic republic whose government is based on a congressional, multiparty electoral system. The president of the country is both head of state and head of government. The federal government is divided into three branches: executive, legislative, and judicial, as established by the political Constitution published in 1917. The 32 constituent states of the federation also have a republican form of government based on a local congressional system.

Macroeconomics

Mexico's gross domestic product (GDP) was $839.8 billion in 2006, with a per capita GDP of $8,006.[5] Its human development index is 0.821, above the world average of 0.742 and ranking 53 out of 177 countries.[6] Inequality, as measured by the Gini index (a Gini coefficient of 0 represents perfect equality, and a value of 1.0 perfect inequality), is 0.54, which is higher than all other high human development countries except for Brazil.[7]

The principal source of its GDP is services (64.0%), with industry (mainly manufacturing and mining) running second (24.8%) and agriculture representing a

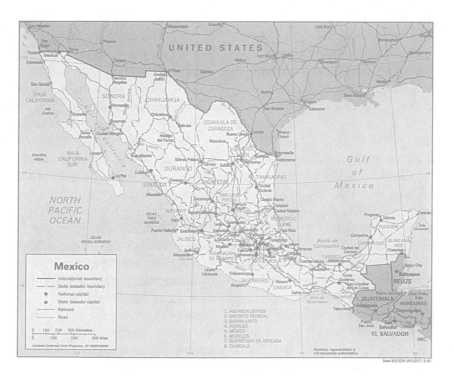

FIGURE 19-1 Map of Mexico

relatively small and declining portion (5.0%).[5] Mexico's annual economic growth rate for the period from 2001 to 2006 was 2.3%, with unemployment at 3.2% of the labor force.[5]

Infrastructure

Mexico has 222,360 miles of highways, 77% of which are paved, as well as 556,700 buses and 14.3 million registered vehicles.[8] The railway system includes 16,663 miles of railways, 1,119 locomotors, and 36,507 railcars. There are 108 ports on the Mexican coasts and 2,348 merchant ships. Finally, there are 85 airports and 1,440 aerodromes in the country, providing services to 1.5 million flights that carry 69.4 millions passengers annually.

Demographics

Mexico has a population of 107.5 million (2006).[9] The proportion of women (50.3) and men (49.7) has remained stable in the past years. Recent projections estimate a population of 111.6 million for 2010, with an annual growth rate of 0.85%. Around 10% of its population (10.2 million) is indigenous and concentrated in 2,443 municipalities, mostly located in the southern states of the country.[10]

Three phenomena mark the recent demographic development of Mexico[9,11]: (1) a reduction in the general mortality rate from 16 deaths per 1,000 population in 1950 to 4.8 per 1,000 in 2006, mostly explained by a decline in infant mortality from 79 per 1,000 live births in 1970 to 18.1 in 2006; (2) an increase in life expectancy at birth from 49.6 years in 1950 to 78.1 years in women and 73.2 in men in 2006; and (3) a reduction in total fertility rate from 6.8 children per woman of reproductive age in 1970 to 2.2 children in 2006.

These phenomena are generating an aging process, which implies an increasing participation of older adults (65 years of age and older) in the population structure, whose base is shrinking. Children under 5 will account for only 6.6% of the total population in 2050. In contrast, older adults will account for 11.8% of the population in 2030 and 21.2% of the total population in 2050.[9]

Mexico has also being experiencing an accelerated urbanization process. Today, 7 of every 10 Mexicans live in one of the 360 cities that exist in the country, and approximately 35% of the population lives in one of the nine cities with 1 million inhabitants or more.[12] This process is associated with a parallel process of population dispersion in small communities.[13] In 1970, there were 54,000 communities in Mexico with less than 100 inhabitants, where 3% of the population dwelled. By 2000, this figure had increased to 130,000 communities, where 2.5% of the population resided. This phenomenon increases the problems of access to health services of a rural, dispersed population with major health needs.

Education

The average years of schooling in Mexico is 8.1 compared with 6.0 in Latin America and 9.5 in OECD countries.[14] Elementary education is completed by 93.4%, whereas 22.3% of the population completes college. As in other areas, there are important regional differences. Poorer states tend to perform badly in education completion compared with the richer northern states of the country. The illiteracy rate among teenagers and adults is 7.9%; however, recent estimates suggest that around 50% of teenagers may be functionally illiterate.[15]

Mortality and Morbidity

The increase in life expectancy and the growing exposure to risks related to unhealthy lifestyles are modifying the main causes of disease, disability, and death. Mexico is going through an epidemiological transition characterized by an increasing predominance of noncommunicable diseases and injuries. In 1950, around 50% of all deaths in the country were due to common infections, reproductive events, and ailments related to malnutrition. Today, these diseases represent less than 15% of total deaths.[16] Noncommunicable diseases and injuries are now responsible for more than 85% of total deaths.

In contrast with what happened in developed countries, however, in Mexico, posttransitional ailments coexist with pretransitional diseases. Noncommunicable diseases are increasingly dominating the epidemiological profile, but common infections, reproductive ailments, and diseases related to malnutrition are still affecting an important number of Mexicans, especially those living in poverty conditions. In the central state of Mexico, for example, mortality rates for acute respiratory infections are 11 times higher than those in the northern state of Durango.[17] Maternal mortality figures in the southern state of Guerrero are two times higher than those for the country as a whole and four times higher than those the northern state of Coahuila.[17] Finally, malnutrition, although decreasing in the general population, is still common among poor children. Mortality rates caused by malnutrition in children under 5 years old are 12 times higher in the southern state of Puebla than in the northern state of Nuevo Leon,[17] and stunting, which affects 1.2 million Mexican children under 5, is five times more frequent in the rural areas of the southern part of Mexico than in the urban communities of the north of the country.[18]

Poor populations are also being affected by emerging risks and noncommunicable diseases. The southern state of Yucatan, for example, shows higher mortality rates because of cardiovascular diseases than Mexico City, both in women and men.

BRIEF HISTORY OF THE HEALTHCARE SYSTEM

The origins of the modern Mexican health system date back to 1943, when three important institutions were created: the Ministry of Health (MoH), the Mexican Institute for Social Security (IMSS), and Mexico's Children Hospital (the first of what are now 12 National Institutes of Health, charged with tertiary care, training of specialists, and performing scientific research). The IMSS was created to tend to the needs of the industrial workforce (in 1960, a similar institution for federal civil servants was created, the Institute for Security and Social Services for Government Employees [ISSSTE]), whereas the MoH was assigned the responsibility of caring for the urban and rural poor.[19]

The prevailing model of healthcare delivery, which was mostly hospital based and specialty oriented, produced a dramatic increase in the costs of health care. In addition, health services were not reaching an important proportion of the rural poor. Furthermore, many households had to mobilize their own resources to access care in an unregulated private market.

Health conditions were also changing. Between 1940 and 1970, Mexico witnessed an important transformation of its epidemiologic profile. Common infections, though persistent, showed a significant decline, whereas

TABLE 19-2   Basic Demographic and Health Indicators, Mexico 2006

Total population	107,525,207
Population 60 years of age and older (%)	7.1
Life expectancy at birth male/female	72.7/77.6
Death rate per 1,000 population	4.8
Infant mortality rate per 1,000 live births	18.1
Maternal mortality ratio per 100,000 live births	60.1
Prevalence of diabetes as percentage of population aged 20–69	10.7
Prevalence of hypertension as percentage of population aged 20–69	29.2
Births attended by trained personnel (%)	94.1
Vaccination coverage (%)	
• Children < 1	95.8
• Children 1–4 years of age	98.3
Population with public health insurance (%)	60.1
Uninsured population (%)	39.9
Total expenditure in health as a percentage of GDP	6.5
Per capita expenditure in health (US$)	866.4
Public expenditure in health as a percentage of total health expenditure	47.1

From Gómez-Dantés O, Becerril V. El siste'de México. Retrieved August 20, 2008, from http://www.observatoride lasalud.com.

noncommunicable diseases and injuries experienced a sharp increase. There was a perceived need for changes that could adapt the health system to the new health conditions and meet the demands for equitable and cost-effective services.

The response to this situation was an effort to extend basic health care to underserved populations through two programs, one for the rural poor and the other for poor urban communities. The economic crisis of the early 1980s, however, limited their prospects.

In the search for new approaches to extend access and improve the efficiency and quality of care, a healthcare reform was launched in 1983.[20] A constitutional amendment establishing the right to the protection of health was introduced. A new health law was published, replacing an old-fashioned sanitary code. Health services for the uninsured population were decentralized to state governments. Finally, limited coverage of health services resulted in a program that included the construction of health centers and district hospitals. The force guiding this program was the primary healthcare model, which implied a greater emphasis on first-level care, a proper mix of technologies, and the promotion of community participation; however, the possibility of extending comprehensive health services to all was not reached until the initial years of the new millennium.

In the 1990s, several national health accounts studies revealed that more than half of total health expenditures in Mexico were out of pocket. This was due to the fact that half of the population lacked health insurance. The high levels of out-of-pocket expenditure exposed Mexican families to catastrophic financial episodes. In fact, in 2000, nearly 3 million Mexican households suffered catastrophic health expenditures.[21] Not surprisingly, Mexico performed poorly on the international comparative analysis of fair financing developed by the World Health Organization as part of the *World Health Report 2000*.[22] The poor results motivated the development of additional analysis that showed that impoverishing health expenditures were concentrated among the poor and uninsured households.

The products of this analysis generated the advocacy tools to promote a legislative reform that established the System for Social Protection in Health, approved by a large majority of the Mexican Congress in 2003.[23] This system is mobilizing public resources by a full percentage point of GDP over a period of 7 years to provide health insurance through the *Seguro Popular* to all of those ineligible for social security: the self-employed, those out of the labor market, and those working in the informal sector of the economy.

DESCRIPTION OF THE CURRENT HEALTHCARE SYSTEM

The Mexican health system includes two sectors, public and private.[24] The public sector comprises the social security institutions (IMSS, ISSSTE, the social security institutions for oil workers [PEMEX], the armed forces [SEDENA and SEMAR]), *Seguro Popular*, and the institutions offering services to the uninsured population, including the MoH, the State Health Services (SESA), and the IMSS-Oportunidades Program. These institutions own and run their health facilities and employ their own staff, except for *Seguro Popular*, which buys services for its affiliates from the MoH and the SESA. The private sector includes facilities and providers offering services mostly on a for-profit basis.

Social security institutions are financed with contributions from the government, the employer (which in the case of ISSSTE and the social security institutions for oil workers and the armed forces is also the government in its role as employer), and the employee. The MoH and the SESA are financed with federal and state government resources, coming from general taxation and small contributions that users pay when receiving care. The IMSS-Oportunidades program, which is directed to the rural poor of 17 states, is financed with federal resources, although the program is operated by IMSS. Finally, *Seguro Popular* is financed with federal and state government contributions and family contributions, with total exemption for those families in the bottom 20% of income distribution.

The services of the private sector are financed mostly with out-of-pocket payments. A small portion of private health expenditure in Mexico comes from private insurance premiums.

Facilities

The Mexican health system has 23,269 health units, not counting the medical offices of the private sector; 4,103 are hospitals, and the rest are ambulatory clinics.[16]

Of the total number of hospitals, 1,121 are public and 3,082 private, for a rate of 1.1 hospitals per 100,000 population; however, there are regional differences. The state of South Baja California has 3.2 hospitals per 100,000 population, whereas the state of Mexico has only 0.5 per 100,000 population. Of the total number of public hospitals, 628 belong to social security institutions and the rest to those institutions that care for the population without social security; 86% are general hospitals, and the rest are specialty hospitals.

In terms of size, public hospitals are classified as hospitals with 30 beds or less and hospitals with more than 30 beds. Sixty-four percent of social security hospitals and 54% of hospitals for the population without social insurance have more than 30 beds. In the private sector, most hospitals are small maternity clinics. Around 69% of private health hospitals have less than 10 beds and only 6.2% have more than 25 beds.

Regarding hospital beds, in 2005, there were 78,643 beds in the public sector; 53.7% belonged to social security hospitals, and the remainder to the MoH, the SESA, and the IMSS-Oportunidades Program.[16] This means that there are 0.74 beds per 1,000 population in the public sector.

Public institutions also count with around 19,000 public ambulatory units and 2,990 operating rooms.[16] The number of operating rooms per 1,000 population in the public sector is 2.7, with important differences among states and institutions. No reliable figures for the private sector are available.

Workforce

According to the OECD, there were 1.8 doctors per 1,000 population in 2005, an increase of 50% in 10 years, although the doctor-to-population ratio in Mexico remains well below the OECD average (3.0) and that of other Latin American countries, such as Argentina (3.0) and Uruguay (3.6).[25] There are important regional differences. Mexico City has four doctors per 1,000 population, whereas Puebla and Chiapas have less than one per 1,000 population.

The availability of nurses in 2005 (2.2 nurses per 1,000 population) was also below the OECD average of 8.6.[25] In this matter, there are also regional differences. Mexico City has 5 nurses per 1,000 population, whereas the state of Mexico has only 1 per 1,000 population.

Mexico has 82 medical schools and 593 nursing schools. Sixty-nine of those medical schools are affiliated with the Mexican Association of Medical Schools, and 44 are certified.

Technology and Equipment

Regarding high-tech specialty medical equipment and procedures, Mexico has 360 computed tomography scanners (CTs) for a rate of 3.6 CTs per mission population (175 in the public sector and 185 in the private sector). This is the lowest figure for OECD countries, which on average have 20.6 CTs per million population.[25] Mex-

ico has 139 radiation therapy units, for a rate of 1.3 per million population, the lowest of all OECD countries, which on average have 6.2 units per million population. Finally, Mexico presents the lowest number of mammographs per capita of all OECD countries, with 4.5 per million population.

EVALUATION OF THE HEALTH SYSTEM

Cost

Total health expenditure in Mexico was 6.5% of GDP in 2006, well below the OECD average (9%) and below the Latin American average (6.8%), but up from 5.5% in 2000.[26,27] Health expenditure per capita in that same year was US$866.4, once adjusted for purchasing power parity. This compares with an OECD average of US$2,759 and a Latin American average of US$222.

Mexico's public expenditure on health as a percentage of total health expenditure in 2006 was 47.1%, up from 40.4% in 1990 but still the third lowest of OECD countries, which average 72.5%. Public health expenditure includes all resources of the social security institutions (IMSS, ISSSTE, and the social security institutions for oil workers and the armed forces), the MoH, the SESA, and the IMSS-Oportunidades Program. In 2006, total public health expenditure amounted to US$43,595 million. IMSS accounted for 48.4% of this expenditure, followed by the MoH/SESA/*Seguro Popular* (33.5%) and ISSSTE (8.6%). Public per capita expenditure was US$406, with important differences among populations. For those covered by social security institutions, US$536 were spent per capita versus US$296 for the population without social security coverage. In 2000, public per capita expenditure for social security beneficiaries was 2.5 times higher than public per capita expenditure for the population without social security coverage. This difference declined in 2006 to only two times thanks to the mobilization of resources for the *Seguro Popular*.

Private expenditure, which includes all direct or indirect payments made by households in exchange for health services and products, accounts for 52.5% of total health expenditure in Mexico. This is a much larger portion than the average OECD country (17.5%) and a larger portion than Argentina (43.5%) and Colombia (23.7%) but lower than Brazil (57.2%) and Uruguay (65.2%).[25,28]

Ninety-five percent of private health expenditure is out of pocket. The remaining 5% is paid as private insurance premiums. In Argentina, Brazil, Colombia, and Uruguay, out-of-pocket expenditures account for 64%, 67.1%, 72.4%, and 26.6% of total private health expenditure, respectively.[28] This means that Mexico has the highest level of out-of-pocket expenditures of middle-income countries in Latin America. This type of expenditure exposes households to catastrophic financial events. In 2000, an estimated 3 to 4 million Mexican families suffered catastrophic or impoverishing health expenditures[21]; however, several studies showed that by 2006 this figure had declined because of the implementation of several programs to combat poverty and the *Seguro Popular*.[29]

Quality

Quality of health care has been a permanent challenge of the Mexican health system. A quality assessment conducted between 1997 and 1999 in more than 1,900 public health centers, and 214 general public hospitals documented serious problems with waiting lists and waiting times, drug supply in both ambulatory settings and hospitals, medical equipment, and medical records. Historically, public health agencies have operated as monopolies with little consumer choice, poor responsiveness to consumer needs, and lack of concern for quality. Furthermore, few health facilities, public or private, were subjected to a formal accreditation process.

Several initiatives have been recently implemented to improve technical and interpersonal quality of care. These initiatives have been designed to improve standards of quality in service delivery while enhancing the capacity of citizens to demand accountability. A central component of these initiatives was the strengthening of the certification process for public and private health units, which is now coordinated by the National Health Council, an institution created in 1917 as the highest policy-making body in the sector. As of 2006, 223 public hospitals (19.9%) had been certified.[17] The institution with the highest percentage of certified hospitals was IMSS, with 42%. The National Health Council also certified 304 private hospitals in 2006. This process was reinforced by a disposition incorporated to the General Health Law in 2003 requiring the accreditation of all units providing services to the *Seguro Popular*. In 2006, 38 hospitals and 1,408 ambulatory clinics, all from the SESA, had completed the accreditation process.

Initiatives to improve the availability of basic inputs have also been designed. A regular external measurement of the availability of drugs in public institutions was implemented as a monitoring tool of a program designed to improve access to essential drugs in the public sector. In 2002, these measurements showed that only 55% of prescriptions in ambulatory clinics of the MoH were fully filled. By 2006, this figure had increased to 79% in ambulatory clinics of the MoH and to 89% in ambulatory clinics of the MoH that serve *Seguro Popular* beneficiaries.[30] Percentages in ambulatory clinics of social security institutions in 2006 were consistently above 90%.

A national system of indicators was also implemented to monitor quality of care by state and institution. This monitoring system includes indicators for waiting times for ambulatory and emergency care, waiting times for elective interventions, and distribution and dispensing of pharmaceuticals.

Regarding overall satisfaction, the National Health and Nutrition Survey 2006 indicates that 81.2% of health service users consider healthcare services either "good" or "very good."[18] Social security institutions providing services to oil workers and the armed forces show the highest satisfaction levels (96.6%), followed by private services (91.1%).

According to this same survey, waiting times tend to be too long. IMSS is the institution with the highest average waiting time in ambulatory settings (91.7 minutes), followed by ISSSTE (78.7 minutes). In contrast, average waiting time in the private sector is only 29.2 minutes.

One of the most frequent complaints in public services is related to waiting times for elective surgeries and their cancellation. A national responsiveness survey implemented in 2004 indicates that the percentage of canceled surgeries in public hospitals is 18.2%, with similar figures for all public institutions.[31] Almost half of these canceled surgeries are canceled after the patient has been hospitalized. The main causes of cancellation are related to problems in health services, including lack of inputs, surgery rooms, and medical personnel.

Access

The mobilization of additional public resources for *Seguro Popular* created the financial conditions to expand the coverage of health insurance in Mexico. As a result, the proportion of the population with social protection for health increased by 20% between 2003 and 2007. According to Article 4 of the Mexican Constitution, the protection of health is a social right; however, not all Mexicans have been equally able to exercise it. In 2003, half of the population, by virtue of its occupational status, enjoyed the legislated protection of social security, whereas the other half was left without access to any form of health insurance. A very large fraction of this population received health care at units of the MoH, which implies the transfer of health benefits to vulnerable populations under a public charity scheme.

The Mexican health system is a segmented system with three broad categories of beneficiaries:[24] (1) workers of the formal sector of the economy, retired population, and their families; (2) self-employed, workers of the informal sector of the economy, unemployed, and their families; and (3) the population with the ability to pay.

The workers of the formal sector of the economy and their families are the beneficiaries of social security institutions, which in 2000 covered 45.6 million people (Table 19-3). IMSS covered 80% of this population and ISSSTE another 18%, and the remainder was covered by the social security institutions for oil workers and the armed forces. The second category (self-employed, workers of the informal sector of the economy, unemployed, and their families) was covered until 2003 by services of the MoH, the SESA, and the IMSS-Oportunidades Program. In 2000, this population amounted to 48.9 million people. The third category is the users of private health services, mostly upper- and middle-class individuals; however, the poor and those affiliated with social security institutions also use them on a regular basis. According to the National Health and Nutrition Survey 2006, 25% of beneficiaries of social security institutions regularly use private health services, mostly ambulatory care.[18]

The recently created System of Social Protection in Health has extended public health insurance. As mentioned previously, in 2000, only 45.6 million Mexicans (45.4% of the total population) had access to social insurance. In 2006, this figure reached 48.9 million. Added to this are the 15.6 million affiliated with the *Seguro Popular* between 2004 and 2006. In total, 60.1% of the Mexican population has social protection in health. (There are also 5.3 million people with private health insurance, many of which are also affiliated to a social security agency.) This leaves 43 million Mexicans without public health insurance, most of whom will become affiliated with the *Seguro Popular* in the course of the following 4 years.

In general terms, those affiliated with social security institutions have access to a broad, but not explicitly defined, package of health services. This includes ambulatory and hospital care. Coverage includes drugs as well. Those affiliated with the *Seguro Popular* have access to 255 essential interventions and the respective drugs. In addition, they have access to a package of 18 high-cost interventions for the treatment of acute neonatal conditions, cancer in children, cervical and breast cancer, and HIV/AIDS, among others. The uninsured population has access to a limited package of benefits that vary considerably depending on the population. Uninsured individuals living in large urban areas have access to a relatively large package of services, in contrast with the uninsured rural poor that tend to have access only to limited ambulatory care on an irregular basis.

Public Health Services

Public health services are provided by the MoH to the entire population, regardless of its affiliation status to any particular health institution. These services include health promotion, risk control, and disease prevention activities, including vaccination and epidemiological surveillance.

The MoH is also responsible for the generation of information on health conditions and health services and for the evaluation of the national and state health systems, health institutions, health policies, programs, and services. Salient among the monitoring and evaluation activities is the annual publication of *Salud: México*, a comparative report of the performance of state health systems and health institutions, and the *Observatory on Hospital Performance*, which monitors the performance of public hospitals. The Federal Commission for Protection against Health Risks was created in 2001 with the mission of regulating products and services

TABLE 19-3 Health Coverage, Mexico, 2000 and 2006

	2000		2006	
Population with social security	45,604,713	45.3%	48,913,644	45.5%
Population with *Seguro Popular*	–	–	15,672,374	14.5%
Uninsured population	48,913,644	54.7%	42,939,189	39.9%
Total population	100,569,263	100%	107,525,207	100%

related to health, including drugs and medical equipment, occupational and environmental exposures, basic sanitation, food safety, and health-related advertisement.

CURRENT AND EMERGING ISSUES AND CHALLENGES

Improvements have been made toward increasing the coverage of health care in Mexico while also improving the quality of the available services. Evidence shows that the recent reforms are expanding access to comprehensive health care, with the promise of extending it to all by 2010. Mexico, however, continues to face difficulties, mostly related to the challenges posed by emerging diseases. Efforts in controlling common infections, reproductive problems, and malnutrition yielded significant progress; however, after certain benchmarks, such as increased immunization coverage and reductions in deaths caused by diarrhea and acute respiratory infections, were reached, the prevalence of noncommunicable diseases began to increase, creating enormous pressures on the health system. Salient among the challenges related to the new epidemiological profile is a critical need for additional public funding to extend access to costly interventions for noncommunicable ailments, such as cardiovascular and cerebrovascular diseases, cancer, mental health problems, and the complications of diabetes. Another challenge facing the reformed system is to achieve the right balance between additional investments in public health activities on the one hand and personal curative health services on the other. Finally, additional improvements in the quality of care are still expected. To accomplish this goal, several areas must be strengthened: (1) technical quality of care; (2) availability of drugs in hospital settings; (3) availability of care during evenings and weekends; and (4) waiting times for ambulatory, emergency care, and elective interventions.

Narrowing health gaps also remains a challenge. These gaps are concentrated in rural, dispersed, and indigenous communities, especially in the southern states of the country. The main cause of these problems is poverty, and its final solution depends on the possibility of improving the general level of well-being in these populations. Nevertheless, the experience of 20 years of consistent investments in public health in Mexico shows that, despite the existence of extended poverty, it is possible to considerably reduce the burden of communicable diseases through highly effective and accessible interventions.[31,32]

REFERENCES

1. Covarrubias M. *The Eagle, the Jaguar, and the Serpent. Indian Art of the Americas*. New York: Alfred A. Knopf; 1954.
2. González L. El periodo formativo. In: Cosío-Villegas D, coordinator. *Historia Mínima de México*. Mexico City: El Colegio de México; 1994, pp. 75–118.
3. Blanquel E. La revolución mexicana. In: Cosío-Villegas D, coordinator. *Historia Mínima de México*. Mexico City: El Colegio de México; 1994, pp. 119–156.
4. Aguayo-Quezada S. *El Almanaque Mexicano 2008*. Mexico City: Aguilar; 2008.
5. Banco de México. Estadísticas. Retrieved April 23, 2008, from http://www.banxico.org.mx.
6. UNDP. *Human Development Report 2006*. New York: Oxford University Press; 2007.
7. NationMaster. Economy statistics. Distribution of family income. Gini index by country. Retrieved March 10, 2008, from http://www.nationmaster.com.
8. Secretaría de Comunicaciones y Transportes. Infraestructura, transporte y comunicaciones. Retrieved March 10, 2008, from http://www.sct.gob.mx.
9. Consejo Nacional de Población. Proyecciones de población de México 2000–2050. Retrieved March 10, 2008, from http://www.conapo.gob.mx/00cifras/5.htm.
10. Comisión Nacional para el Desarrollo de los Pueblos Indígenas, Programa de las Naciones Unidas para el Desarrollo. *Informe sobre Desarrollo Humano de los Pueblos Indígenas de México 2006*. México City: CNDPI, PNUD; 2006.
11. Partida V. *Veinticinco años de transición epidemiológica en México. En: CONAPO. La situación demográfica de México 1999*. Mexico City: CONAPO; 1999.
12. Garza G. Evolución de las ciudades mexicanas en el siglo XX. *Revista de Información y Análisis*. 2002;(19):7–16.
13. Reyna-Bernal A, Hernández-Esquivel JC. *Poblamiento, desarrollo rural y medio ambiente. Retos y prioridades de la política de población. En: CONAPO. La situación demográfica de México 2006*. Mexico City: CONAPO; 2006.
14. Secretaría de Educación Pública. *Sistema educativo de los Estados Unidos Mexicanos. Principales Cifras: Ciclo Escolar 2005–2006*. Mexico City: SEP; 2007.
15. Worldfund. Education gap. Retrieved March 5, 2008, from http://www.worldfund.org/index.php?q=Education-Gap.html.
16. Secretaría de Salud. *Programa Nacional de Salud 2007–2012*. Mexico City: Secretaría de Salud; 2007.
17. Secretaría de Salud. *Salud: México 2006*. Mexico City: Secretaría de Salud; 2007.
18. Oláiz-Fernández G, Rivera-Dommarco J, Shamah-Levy T, et al. *Encuesta Nacional de Salud y Nutrición 2006*. Mexico City: Secretaría de Salud, Instituto Nacional de Salud Pública; 2006.
19. Frenk J, Sepúlveda J, Gómez-Dantés O. Evidence based health policy: three generations of reform in Mexico. *Lancet*. 2003; 362(9396):1667–1671.
20. Soberón G. El cambio estructural en la salud. *Salud Pública de México*. 1987;29:127–140.

21. Secretaría de Salud. *Programa Nacional de Salud 2001–2006. La democratización de la salud en México. Hacia un sistema universal de salud.* Mexico City: Secretaría de Salud; 2001, p. 57.

22. World Health Organization. *World Health Report 2000. Health Systems: Improving Performance.* Geneva: World Health Organization; 2000.

23. Frenk J, Knaul F, Gómez-Dantés O, et al. *Fair Financing and Universal Social Protection. The Structural Reform of the Mexican Health System.* Mexico City: Secretaría de Salud; 2004.

24. Gómez-Dantés O, Becerril V. El sistema de salud de México. Retrieved August 20, 2008, from http://www.observatori delasalud.

25. OECD. *Health At A Glance 2007. OECD Indicators.* Paris: OECD; 2007.

26. Secretaría de Salud. *Sistema de Cuentas en Salud a Nivel Federal y Estatal (SICUENTAS).* Mexico City: Dirección General de Información en Salud, Secretaría de Salud; 2006.

27. Organisation for Economic Co-operation and Development, OECD Health Data 2007. Retrieved March 10, 2008, from http://www.oecd.org/health/healthdata.

28. World Health Organization. *World Health Report 2006. Working Together for Health.* Geneva: World Health Organization; 2006.

29. Knaul FM, Arreola-Ornelas H, Méndez-Carniado O, et al. Evidence is good for your health system: policy reform to remedy catastrophic and impoverishing health spending in Mexico. *Lancet.* 2006;368:1828–1841.

30. Secretaría de Salud. Evaluación del surtimiento de medicamentos a la población afiliada al Seguro Popular de Salud. In: Secretaría de Salud. *Sistema de Protección Social en Salud. Evaluación de procesos.* Mexico City: Secretaría de Salud; 2006, pp. 59–78.

31. Secretaría de Salud. *Observatorio del Desempeño Hospitalario 2005.* Mexico City: Secretaría de Salud; 2006.

32. Sepúlveda J, Bustreo F, Tapia R., Improvement of child survival in Mexico: the diagonal approach. *Lancet.* 2006;368: 2017–2027.

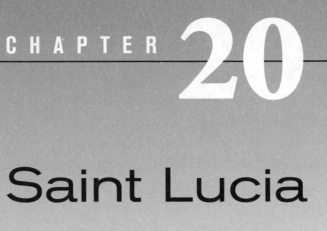

CHAPTER 20

Saint Lucia

Damian E. Greaves
and Omowale Amuleru-Marshall

COUNTRY DESCRIPTION

TABLE 20-1 Saint Lucia

Nationality	Noun: Saint Lucian(s)
	Adjective: Saint Lucian
Ethnic groups	Black 82.5%, mixed 11.9%, East Indian 2.4%, other or unspecified 3.1% (2001 census)
Religions	Roman Catholic 67.5%, Seventh Day Adventist 8.5%, Pentecostal 5.7%, Rastafarian 2.1%, Anglican 2%, Evangelical 2%, other Christian 5.1%, other 1.1%, unspecified 1.5%, none 4.5% (2001 census)
Language	English (official), French patois
Literacy	Definition: age 15 and over has ever attended school
	Total population: 90.1%
	Male: 89.5%
	Female: 90.6% (2001 est.)
Government type	Parliamentary democracy

(continues)

TABLE 20-1   Saint Lucia (continued)

Date of independence	February 22, 1979 (from the United Kingdom)
Gross Domestic Product (GDP) per capita	$4,800 (2005 est.)
Unemployment rate	20% (2003 est.)
Natural hazards	Hurricanes and volcanic activity
Environment: current issues	Deforestation; soil erosion, particularly in the northern region
Population	172,884 (July 2008 est.)
Age structure	0–14 years: 28.9% (male 25,786/female 24,169) 15–64 years: 66% (male 56,346/female 57,725) 65 years and over: 5.1% (male 3,212/female 5,646) (2008 est.)
Median age	Total: 26 years Male: 25.2 years Female: 26.9 years (2008 est.)
Population growth rate	1.305% (2008 est.)
Birth rate	18.89 births/1,000 population (2008 est.)
Death rate	4.99 deaths/1,000 population (2008 est.)
Net migration rate	−0.84 migrant(s)/1,000 population (2008 est.)
Gender ratio	At birth: 1.07 male(s)/female Under 15 years: 1.07 male(s)/female 15–64 years: 0.98 male(s)/female 65 years and over: 0.57 male(s)/female Total population: 0.97 male(s)/female (2008 est.)
Infant mortality rate	Total: 12.46 deaths/1,000 live births Male: 13.56 deaths/1,000 live births Female: 11.27 deaths/1,000 live births (2008 est.)
Life expectancy at birth	Total population: 74.32 years Male: 70.77 years Female: 78.12 years (2008 est.)
Total fertility rate	2.11 children born/woman (2008 est.)
HIV/AIDS adult prevalence rate	Not available
Number of people living with HIV/AIDS	Not available
HIV/AIDS deaths	Not available

Central Intelligence Agency. The World Fact Book, 2008. Retrieved November 18, 2008, from https://www.cia.gov/library/publications/the-world-factbook.

History

Saint Lucia is a small island developing state in the Caribbean located approximately 62 degrees west and 14 degrees north. Although the circumstances of its discovery still provide controversy, there is agreement that it occurred on or around December 13, 1502. That is the date that is now celebrated as Discovery Day. The indigenous people were Arawaks in the earliest periods, and later the Caribs dominated as Europeans made several attempts to colonize the island in the early 17th century. The French ultimately settled in the island, signing a treaty with the local Caribs in 1660, but this did not settle the matter. The French and the British battled for a number of years for ownership of Saint Lucia until the British finally secured it in 1814. Saint Lucia formed part of the British Windward Islands Colony until this was dissolved. It became a member of the West Indies Federation of 1958–1962 and an independent nation in 1979.[1]

Size and Geography

Saint Lucia is located in the eastern Caribbean Sea on the boundary with the Atlantic Ocean. It is situated north of the islands of St. Vincent and the Grenadines, northwest of Barbados and south of Martinique. It is 27 miles long (north to south) by 14 miles wide (east to west), with a total area of 616 km^2 (Figure 20-1). The island state is subdivided into one capital city, Castries, and three major towns: Vieux-Fort, Soufriere, and Gros Islet. There are also six villages: Anse la Raye, Canaries, Choiseul, Dennery, Laborie, and Micoud.

The island of Saint Lucia is considered one of the most mountainous islands in the Caribbean. Its highest peak is Mount Gimie, which is 3,146 ft above sea level. The world famous Pitons, located in Soufriere on the western side of the island, are considered to be the island's most famous landmark and achieved World Heritage status in June 2004. With its drive-in volcano and the Sulfur Springs as a distinctive feature, Saint Lucia stands among very few islands in the world that possess this natural wonder.[2]

Saint Lucia forms part of the regional grouping called the Caribbean Community (CARICOM) and a subregional grouping called the Organization of Eastern Caribbean States (OECS). Saint Lucia is, in fact, home to the OECS headquarters. It also forms part of the Windward Islands subgrouping, which comprises Saint Lucia, Dominica, St. Vincent and the Grenadines, and the tri-island state of Grenada.

The population is largely of African origin, representing between 80% and 90% of the total population,

depending on the construction of the mixed-race minority. The dominant religion is Roman Catholicism, although in more recent times, a large Protestant minority has emerged. The official language of the country is English, but an Afro-French Creole is widely spoken.

The majority of the population lives in the coastal areas and in the less mountainous areas in the interior. A good network of roads links the various communities and villages to the main towns in the north and the south of the island. In addition, the island's telecommunications system effectively covers the remote villages as well as the main population centers.

Government and Political System

Saint Lucia's political system and government are patterned after the Westminster model, identified with British colonial traditions. After almost 165 years of British rule, the country gained its independence in 1979. The executive branch of government comprises the Prime Minister and the Cabinet of Ministers, whereas the Parliament and the Senate constitute the legislative branch. Parliamentary elections are held every 5 years for 17 parliamentary seats. Political, fiscal, and administrative decentralization is the responsibility of government. Currently, there is no real representative local

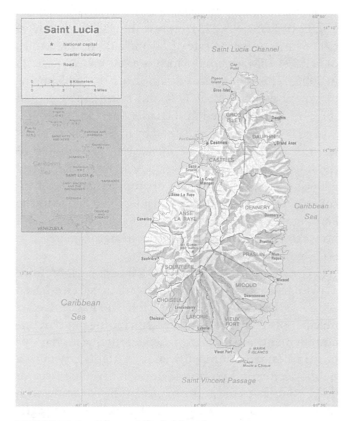

FIGURE 20-1 Map of Saint Lucia

government; however, a system of local administration is in place in the various towns and villages, comprising district councils made up of nominated representatives. In 1997, the St. Lucia Labour Party took office, pronouncing local government reform. Nevertheless, little has progressed on this issue beyond formal study with the support of the Caribbean Development Bank, where one can find recommendations on the modalities of implementing local government reform.

Like other countries that have acquired the Westminster model, each government Ministry in Saint Lucia is responsible for the implementation of policies and plans for its sector. National development plans are, therefore, based on the plans submitted by each ministry and through consultations with each ministry. These plans normally cover a three-year period and are submitted to the Cabinet of Ministers for approval.

Macroeconomics

Saint Lucia is classified as a lower- to middle-income country by the World Bank, and the economy is characterized by a high degree of openness. Like the rest of the countries in the Eastern Caribbean Currency Union, the island faces serious economic challenges caused primarily by a combination of domestic and external factors.[3] In 2006, the island recorded a gross domestic product (GDP) of EC$1,407.17M, representing a growth rate of 5.02 with an inflation rate of 2.3 and a domestic savings of EC$394.18M. Unemployment was estimated at 15.7% in 2006.[4] This represents a decline from the 2005 unemployment estimation of 17% and is much lower than the over 20% recorded in the latter years of the 1990s. Such a decline can be explained by investment in physical infrastructure and the increase in the number of the hotel rooms. As the Poverty Assessment Report of 2006 suggests, the expansion of employment largely in construction did not bring considerable change to the employment status of women. Single, female-headed households derived fewer benefits from this increase in employment.

The country has experienced a transformation from a primary commodity economy to a service-based economy, led by the tourism sector. The nation faces a number of economic challenges, including poverty, unemployment, a need for higher-level educational opportunities, poor competitiveness, a highly centralized public sector, and economic uncertainty. One issue of grave concern to the performance of the economy, with regard to its structure, has been the decline in the agri-cultural sector in general and the banana industry in particular. There have been attempts at diversification of agriculture, but the size of exports of nonbanana agricultural commodities and the modest level of growth overall are daunting; indeed, nonbanana agriculture has also suffered a decline. This means, therefore, that production and exports of nonbanana agriculture were unable to replace bananas in terms of employment and production.

A major economic challenge in recent times has been the astronomical increase in international oil prices in 2007–2008 compared with previous periods. This has had implications for domestic transportation–related taxi fares and public transportation costs. Indeed, government has a vested interest in ensuring that transportation costs are not subject to rapid escalation in prices. A more challenging corollary to escalating oil prices for many people is the rapid rise in food prices and ultimately in the cost of living.

These economic woes are compounded by the absence of timely and reliable information to measure scientifically and objectively the extent of the consequent problems in order to inform the requisite corrective measures and decision making. In this context, a culture of information gathering and information analysis and orientation to informed decision making requires public sector reform to correct a tradition of blind decision making and enable the country to manage prevailing challenges more efficiently and effectively.

Demographics

Saint Lucia's population is approximately 166,838 according to preliminary estimates in 2006. This represents a slight increase of approximately 1.4%, or 2,251 persons. The birth rate increased to 14.4 per 1,000, after a downward trend over the previous 6 years. The death rate also increased from 7.4 in 2005 to 7.9 per 1,000 in 2006. Male births and deaths continue to outnumber those of females, with males contributing 52% of total births and 54% of total deaths. An analysis of the population by gender indicates that 51% (85,159) were females and 49% (81,679) were males. The 2006 estimates also indicate a youthful population with persons aged 10 to 14 years (17,231) and 15 to 19 years (17,645), accounting for 20.9% of the population.[5]

According to the last population estimate, 65.2% of Saint Lucians comprised the economically active proportion of the adult population (individuals aged 15 to 64). There has been an increase in the labor force, exerting an upward pressure on the unemployment rate. The dependency ratio (i.e., the ratio of dependent adults and children to economically active adults) reached 1:1.9.[6]

Saint Lucia has made great strides in improving the health of residents since independence, but major health challenges still face the country. Some of these are new challenges from emerging diseases that require sound planning and a well-coordinated response. The five leading causes of mortality for 1996–1999, when examining percentage of total deaths, were heart diseases (19%), malignant neoplasm (14%), cerebrovascular diseases (12%), diabetes mellitus (9%), and accidents and adverse effects (5%). This pattern mirrored that of the period from 1992 to 1995.[6] In the case of infants, the records for 1996–1999 indicated that the five leading causes of death were perinatal conditions (52%), congenital anomalies (13%), heart diseases (3%), intestinal infectious diseases (3%), and accidents (3%). For the period from 1992 to 1995, the first two leading causes were the same, whereas accidents were not among the leading causes of infant deaths. Among children under 5 years, the percentage of deaths from diarrheal diseases for 1996–1999 was 5% compared with 3% for 1992–1995.

Individuals in the age 15 to 44 category accounted for 55% and 53% of all deaths from accidents and violence for the 1992–1995 and the 1996–1999 periods, respectively. The 60 years or older age category represented 82% and 80% of all deaths from heart diseases, 81% and 87% from diabetes mellitus, and 73% and 63% from malignant neoplasms, respectively, for the two periods. The proportion of all deaths from malignant neoplasm attributed to the age 45 to 49 group increased from 13% to 25%. A total of 149 cases of tuberculosis were reported for 1993–1999 ranging between 11 and 35 cases, giving an average of 19 cases per year.[7]

Social Context

In 1995, a poverty assessment found that 25.1% of the population was poor, and indeed, 7.1% was indigent. The assessment conducted 10 years later revealed that poverty had worsened in that it then stood at 28.8%. Ironically, the measured rate of indigence fell substantially to 1.6% of the population. Moreover, the more recent study also showed that, although measured poverty increased, economic inequality fell across Saint Lucia. The consultants on this project submitted that the finding of increased poverty did not mean that the poor were worse off, suggesting that comparisons of indigence are

"purer" insofar as they ignore relative factors that intervene in poverty comparisons.[5]

Another important piece of information revealed by the 2005 assessment is that poverty is primarily a rural phenomenon with rural districts exhibiting prevalence rates in excess of 35%. This level of poverty has been attributed to a lack of jobs and of opportunities to earn an income. Other causes included a lack of education, few skills, and a lack of self-esteem. In the rural areas, the impact of the decline in competitiveness of the banana industry cannot be discounted. A number of social problems have followed the associated structural difficulty experienced in the Saint Lucian economy. In addition to the rapid growth of slums in the urban areas, there is the developing informal sector, and underground economy, integrating the country into the international narco-trafficking industry as a transshipment point for drugs.

In Saint Lucia, there is evidence that a drug culture seems to be inserting itself as an important new source of resources for common economic activities. The predictable upsurge in drug trafficking and other drug-related crime has also been noted. Increasing numbers of young people are becoming involved in trafficking and the use of illegal drugs. Some of the marginalized urban communities are demonstrating conditions characteristic of social anomie. This tends to exacerbate other sociocultural challenges, including the decline of the extended family that has resulted in many older persons living alone.[5]

BRIEF HISTORY OF THE HEALTHCARE SYSTEM

Pre–World War II

Before the late 1880s, most health institutions on the island were military institutions, and there were two military hospitals. The island's main hospital came to be established in the late 1880s. In the early to mid-1900s, between the two World Wars, public health developments were along environmental lines, with sanitation and mosquito control being the major focus. The Mosquito Act of 1935 provides a case in point. The 1938 Moyne Commission Report was quite damning of the British for the underdevelopment of health and welfare of persons in Caribbean territories, including Saint Lucia. This gave rise to the decision by the British to build health centers in parts of the island in the 1940s.

By 1946, the Soufriere Hospital was built in the southwest in the town of Soufriere, with St. Jude Hospital being built by the American armed forces during World War II, in Vieux-Fort in the south of the island.

Since World War II

Health center expansion continued during the 1950s to the 1970s so that by the end of the 1970s there were 34 health centers across Saint Lucia. The modern era, from 1980, saw the introduction of the Gros Islet Polyclinic, the Tapion Private Hospital in 1996, and the development of several private medical facilities.

Before the 1980s, the health system of Saint Lucia could be described as highly centralized, with a measure of partial decentralization mainly at the hospital level. There were four hospitals located in various towns and villages: in Vieux-Fort in the south, in Soufriere in the southwest, in Dennery in the east, and in Castries, the capital city, in the north. In more recent times, Gros Islet, in the extreme north of the island, became the location of a polyclinic offering multiple services.

In 1979, the country ratified the Alma Ata Declaration, during which time its health system experienced radical reform. At the community level, access to health care increased through the introduction of the Primary Health Care approach, which resulted in further decentralization of health services with the construction of 34 health centers. This decentralized health structure helped to bring the services closer to the communities in which the clients lived and worked, and thus, access to the health services was increased. Ironically, this period was also characterized by the subsequent implementation of the Selective Primary Health Care alternative, with a focus on growth monitoring, oral rehydration, breastfeeding, immunization, female education, family planning, and food supplementation, popularly known as the *GOBI-FFF* formula. As these vertical programs took hold, less emphasis began to be placed on the role of the community and the involvement of the people in decision making. It can, therefore, be suggested that the failure to collaborate with communities at that time was a feature that militated against the cause of sustainable health promotion. As a result of this shortcoming, the responsibility for one's own health had not been nurtured, and the assumption of this responsibility by affected persons remains a challenge even today. This might explain why health is not a priority in many households and communities.[8]

It was during the earlier phase of this era that Regional Health Teams comprising multidisciplinary groups of health and social service providers were activated. By the mid-1980s, this forward-looking, biopsychosocial approach was largely deemed to be successful. Despite its success in facilitating increased access to comprehensive services in communities, these interdisciplinary structures were permitted to fall apart over the intervening years. This can be attributed to a number of factors, including attrition, lack of career mobility, limited financial resources, and managerial authority. Essentially, the Regional Health Team structure had not been permitted to become institutionalized.

By the 1990s, these failures of the system motivated calls for health reform and, ultimately, a national strategic plan for health. Citizens began registering their complaints and dissatisfaction with the system, chronicling complaints of insufficient staff and medical supplies, as well as long waiting times, particularly with secondary health services. The declining morale of the staff also complicated this situation. The Ministry of Health responded by beginning to examine plans and strategies for health sector reform. A health sector reform secretariat commenced work in 1998, producing a discussion document outlining the way forward to health reform in Saint Lucia.

By the year 2000, a document referred to as the Health Sector Reform Proposals (2000) was developed and formed the foundation for the National Health Strategic Plan 2006–2011. This plan outlines a strategic road map for the reforms as the way forward for action and change in the health system of Saint Lucia.[9] Major problems that continue to affect the country's health situation, or the performance of the health services sector, include a high level of poverty, financial and human resources limitations, low levels of education, unhealthy lifestyles, and reluctance to pay for health services within the public sector.[10]

DESCRIPTION OF THE CURRENT HEALTHCARE SYSTEM

In Saint Lucia, healthcare services are largely administered and delivered by the public sector. The provision of health services by the private sector, however, is a growing phenomenon. It is regulated by the Public Health Law of 1975, a piece of legislation that seems to be in need of modernization. There are eight objectives of the Saint Lucia health system:

1. The provision of efficient quality health care
2. The maintenance of an adequate program of primary and preventative health care
3. Greater equity in the allocation and use of health resources
4. The design and implementation of comprehensive and integrated programs for the prevention and treatment of chronic disease, the rehabilitation of the disabled, and the treatment and care of the older population
5. The improvement and sustainability of mental health services to the level of contemporary international standards
6. The reduction of the incidence of environmental problems
7. The promotion of a high standard of industrial and occupational health and safety
8. Improvement in the system of health financing, making it more affordable and sustainable[11]

In general, the Ministry of Health is responsible for the organization of resources and services for the health of the nation. For this purpose, it is organized into subdivisions, which are responsible for the various health programs, including preventive services, health education and promotion, environmental health, hospital, and curative services. There are heads of departments who are responsible for the overall management and development of programs and the available staff, including program managers, who operate specific health programs.

Facilities

There are currently 32 health centers, one polyclinic located in the town of Gros Islet in the north, and two district hospitals, one located in Dennery in the east and the other located in Soufriere in the southwest. Two of the original 34 health centers, one in Boguis, Babonneau, and the other in Marchand, Castries, had to be decommissioned. In the case of the Boguis health center, earth movements in the latter part of the 1990s prompted the decision to condemn this facility. The Marchand Health Center closed its doors to the public because of its unsuitable location. This facility was considered to be located on a very busy road. Moreover, the noise and dust that both patients and staff were subjected to compromised quality patient care. In addition, blood pressures could not be taken properly and staff members reported that talking to patients above the noise level was impossible.[12]

The government health centers represent a well-distributed network that serves the various communities in the country. This network was established on the basis of population distribution, transportation routes, and the unwritten policy guidelines that each health center should serve a catchment population within a minimum of three miles. This network is adequate to meet the needs of the population.[9] Currently, health centers function, for the most part, as clinical service points delivering mainly curative medical care and some preventive services. Some of these other services include various health programs and health development activities in the areas of chronic, noncommunicable and sexually transmitted diseases, and mental health care. The vision is that through the reform process, these community-based institutions will assume a larger role as the health provision units of the community and serve as the interface between the people and the health system.[9]

The health and education, nutrition, environmental health, and community nursing departments are primarily responsible for the delivery of preventive care, whereas secondary care is provided by the two general hospitals, Victoria and St. Jude, located in the northern and southern parts of the island, respectively. Some basic secondary care is also provided by the two district hospitals located in the town of Soufriere and the village of Dennery. Indeed, the mandate of the district hospitals lies in the area of primary care, in addition to some scaled-down secondary services. The psychiatric hospital (Golden Hope Hospital) and the drug detoxification and rehabilitation center (Turning Point), located in the north of the island, and are the only institutions involved in what might be considered rehabilitative care.[12]

Workforce

It is a truism that the health workforce is the single most important element of healthcare delivery. Moreover, the availability of appropriately trained and motivated medical, nursing, and support staff is critical. A serious challenge to the health system is the ability of the system to retain its health workforce, particularly in certain critical areas or specialties.

In the Saint Lucian context, there are many varied professions and skills involved in the health services. Doctors and nurses comprise the bulk of the health professionals employed in the public sector. Over the years, the numbers of various professionals have increased, and this is a reflection of an expansion in the types of services provided. According to the Pan American Health

Organization's (PAHO) published profile on Saint Lucia's Health System and Services in 2001, there was an increase in all types of selected health personnel per 10,000 population in the 1996 and 1997 period, compared with the earlier period of 1988 and 1989.[7] Even then, however, the ratio of physicians per 10,000 population was still less than 1 in the 1996 and 1997 period, compared with Grenada, for example, in which the ratio was considerably higher at 8 per 10,000 population for the same period.[13] As another OECS comparison, Dominica posted a similar ratio of 8.3 physicians per 10,000 population a few years later.[14] The ratio of general practitioners to specialists in 1997–1998 ranged between 1:3.1 and 1:4.1 in Saint Lucia, comparing favorably with St. Kitts and Nevis, where the ratio was 1:2,[15] and Dominica, where the ratio was 1:1.7 in 2002.[14]

In 1997, the majority of physicians (64%), nurses (72%), and nursing auxiliaries (64%) worked in the acute general hospitals, whereas the majority of other health professionals worked in primary care services. In these services, the ratio of general practitioners to specialists was 7.5:1 compared with the acute general hospitals and private sector where the ratios were 1:1 and 0.8:1, respectively. This same report further lamented the absence of a systematic measurement of the productivity of health personnel in the public main institutions.[7]

Special mention needs to be made of the workforce in the primary healthcare services. In Saint Lucia, the community health nurse, community health aide, and the health center attendant comprise the core staff for the delivery of nursing services at the health center. These personnel form the core team for the delivery of primary healthcare services at the community health centers. Other professionals, such as the nutritionist, family nurse practitioner, pharmacist, public health nurse, and the district medical doctor, visit the health center on a periodic basis. In addition to these, other members of the primary health team include the dentist and ancillary dental staff, the mental health officer, the dermatologist, and the pediatrician. The dermatology and pediatrics clinics are conducted periodically at select health centers. The teams also include an environmental health officer, a health educator, and a family life educator, who function mainly in the schools.

Carr and Wint, in their assessment of the structure and operations of the primary healthcare system in Saint Lucia, suggested that the staff mix appeared to be appropriate for the delivery of the services but lamented their less than adequate numbers. Particular concern about the sharing of nurses among health centers was expressed, raising the possible result of compromised services leading ultimately to the underutilization of those facilities.[9]

Technology and Equipment

There is evidence that the need for improvement in basic technology and equipment exists in Saint Lucia. The 2001 PAHO country report on the health systems and services profile identified a total of 501 beds in the public sector in 1999, with 244 of these in the acute general hospitals and 162 in the psychiatric hospital.[7] The private hospital began operations in 1998. To date, it has a total of 23 beds.[9] In relation to various types of equipment, the report further points out that basic diagnostic imaging equipment is available at the acute general hospitals in the public sector and the private hospital and the offices of private practitioners in the private sector. Indeed, a total of 29 such pieces of equipment was available in the private sector and 17 in the public sector in 1999. In addition, there are two clinical laboratories in the public sector, one in each acute general hospital and three in the private sector. The country has one blood bank; nevertheless, the two acute general hospitals maintain their own supply of blood for the purpose of transfusions.[7]

Global communications via the Internet and telemedicine, for example, have sensitized providers and consumers of health care to new technologies such as organ replacement and magnetic resonance imaging. The demand for their introduction into Saint Lucia is great. It is therefore critical that there be continuous technology assessment to determine carefully each technology's suitability and cost in the local context.

EVALUATION OF THE HEALTHCARE SYSTEM

In this section, attention is given to financing healthcare services in Saint Lucia, on their consequent quality, and on issues of access to these services.

Cost

There is a common perception that the existing system of healthcare financing across the CARICOM region is inimical to sustainability in its present form.[7] Essentially, the existing system fails to encourage the quality improvements that are necessary. This is further exacerbated by growing uncertainty and related economic challenges that constrain available resources. There is no doubt that health financing in countries such as Saint

Lucia, facing demographic and epidemiological challenges, is being proposed against a backdrop of competing financial demands. Sources of financing and the mechanisms through which resources are allocated within the health system have a direct impact on the health status of the population.

A financing mechanism must be informed by policy goals and principles that guide the delivery of health care within the system. Furthermore, the financing mechanism must demonstrate its ability to achieve desired targets and outcomes while having the capability of meeting the financial requirements of a comprehensive health system. A good health financing system is one that can be responsive to all levels of healthcare delivery, achieve financial sustainability, and ensure equitable access to health services. In 2001, PAHO suggested that the information on the financing of Saint Lucia's public health system was both timely and reliable; however, the same was not noted about the private sector.

Traditionally, the health sector in Saint Lucia derived its financing from a variety of mechanisms: public financing, user fees, loans, grants and donations (external sources), and private insurance. Currently, health services in Saint Lucia are funded from four principal sources: the consolidated fund, donor contributions, out-of-pocket payments, and private insurance schemes. The health sector is generally operated by publicly financed and publicly provided services. It is estimated that these various sources enable a per capita health expenditure of approximately US$188. Approximately half of this expenditure is covered directly from the government or from donors. To date, Saint Lucia's level of per capita health expenditure is indirect, through insurance. The remainder comes from public sources. It would be apparent that Saint Lucia's pattern of relative underfinancing holds true for the proportion of GDP devoted to health. Nevertheless, one can contend that if the performance of the economy is taken into account, the health expenditure of the country is comparable to states with similar levels of national income (Tables 20-2 and 20-3).[16]

The Ministry of Health uses the traditional method of budgetary transfers through line-item allocations to specific programs and facilities. Health workers who function within the public facilities are paid for the services that they provide by a salary and sometimes on a combined basis of salary and fee for service. It can be argued that the health system of Saint Lucia is financed more on traditional patterns of expenditure rather than on research and evidence-based decision making. This difficulty arises from the lack of decentralization in the area of institutional management where the central Ministry of Health remains both the provider and purchaser of health services. Internal mechanisms to ensure accountability are weak, which results in equally weak attempts at provider regulation.[16]

Most of the funds provided to the sector are derived from internal sources, in particular, from the consolidated fund of the government treasury. Financing from external agencies is received through grants and loans. Between 1993 and 1999, grants accounted for all of the funds received from external sources, except for 1993 and 1998, when loans represented 30% and 19% of all external funding, respectively. External funds accounted for only 2% of the total budget of the Ministry of Health in 1999 and ranged between 8% and 2% between 1993 and 1999.[17] External funds are used mainly for capital projects.

The government finances private insurance through income tax breaks. Provision is also made for individuals to claim returns on income tax for medical bills and medical insurance. Medical insurance is tax deductible up to the total premium amount, as are medical bills beyond US$150.[7]

A decreasing trend in public spending on health was recorded between 1997 and 2000. It was observed that the per capita health expenditure and the health sector's share of the total expenditure for 1999 were lowest for the period of 1993 to 1999, despite the fact that total public spending on social services as a percentage of GDP increased steadily to its highest level for the same period. For this period, data regarding the distribution of the health budget by the selected functions are only available for the public sector for 1998 and 1999. It revealed that about 50% of the total health budget in the public sector was spent on curative care. Health promotion and preventive care, on the other hand, consumed about 21%, whereas production/purchase of supplies accounted for approximately 10% of the budget. Less than 0.5% was budgeted for the training of health workers.[17]

In the recent past, health expenditure has grown considerably. According to the National Strategic Plan for Health (2006–2011), health expenditure grew by 40% between 2001 and 2006, from EC$61.7M to EC$86M.[7] The document further noted that the upward trend could be attributed to the growing demands placed on the public health system by the country's changing demographic and epidemiological profile. Indeed, the public health budget of 2006–2007 accounted for 9.18% of the total health budget. The resources allocated to the

TABLE 20-2   Health Expenditure in Caribbean Countries, 1997–2001

Indicators	Antigua	Bahamas	Barbados	Belize	Dominica	Grenada	Guyana	Jamaica	St. Kitts/Nevis	Saint Lucia	St. Vincent	Surinam	Trinidad & Tobago
THE%GDP	5.4	5.6	6.1	5	5.9	4.9	5	6.4	4.8	4.3	6.1	9.8	4.3
PHE%THE	39	43	34	51	27	31	17	49	34	36	37	41	55
GHE%THE	61	57	66	49	73	69	83	51	66	64	63	59	45
GHE&TGE	14	15	12	5.5	12	12	9.3	6.2	11	8.5	9.1	17.7	6.6
ERH%THE	3	43	4	4	2		4	3	7	0.6	1.5	12	4
SSHE%GHE										24		30	
OOP%THE	39	43	6	51	27	31	17	34	34	36	37	16	48
THE% (US$)	487	798	562	147	200	223	48	178	344	188	167	169	239
THE% (PPP$)	540	1,029	844	251	292	372	191	229	515	257	324	396	367

Data from WHO Report, 2004.

* THE–Total Health Expenditure
* GHE–Government (Public) Health Expenditure
* OOP–Out-of-Pocket Expenditure
* PHE–Private Health Expenditure
* ERH–External Resources for Health
* SSHE–Social Security Health

TABLE 20-3 Health Expenditure in Relation to Population and GDP, 2001

Country	Population	GDP per Capita (US$)	GDP per Capita (PPP$)	THE per Capita (US$)	THE Cap per (PPP$)	THE % GDP	GHE % GDP	PHE % GDP
OECS								
Antigua	76	9,055	10,931	497	600	5.5	3.2	2.3
Dominica	71	3,697	5,802	252	395	6.8	4.4	2.4
Grenada	103	3,881	7,099	198	362	5.1	2.7	2.4
Monsterrat	4.3	8,070	Not applicable	436	Not applicable	5.4	3.3	2.1
St. Kitts-Nevis	46	7,451	10,693	425	610	5.7	3.6	2.1
Saint Lucia	158	4,184	4,844	204	236	4.9	2.8	2.1
St. Vincent	112	3,112	5,714	190	349	6.1	4.2	1.9
Other Caribbean								
Belize	256	3,145	5,768	198	363	6.3	1.9	4.4
Bahamas	307	16,249	17,082	1,069	1,124	6.6	2	3.7
Barbados	270	9,444	14,811	734	1,151	7.8	3.9	3.9
Guyana	764	943	4,268	50	362	5.3	4.2	1.1
Jamaica	2,627	2,982	3,745	191	240	6.8	2.9	3.9
Trinidad and Tobago	1,267	7,068	9,785	432	598	6.1	2.1	4
Surinam	432	1,914	5,086	153	406	9.4	5.6	3.8

Data are for Saint Lucia from Saint Lucia at Independence: National Archives Authority of Saint Lucia, 1997. Data for Guyana, Jamaica, and Surinam are derived from World Health Organization Estimates for 2001(WHO Annual Report, 2004).

public health sector remain insufficient to respond adequately to the increasing healthcare needs of the population. At present, the health sector, comprising public, private, and nongovernmental institutions, provides health care to a large number of people; however, only a small fraction of the realistic cost of this service is recovered. In recent times, there has been increasing demand for overseas care, such that the Ministry of Health is finding it increasingly difficult to meet the demands of health care with the existing budget and structures.

Patients seeking care in health facilities pay out-of-pocket user fees for medical and hospital care, confinements, dental or ophthalmologic care, or laboratory exams. They are also required to make a co-payment for drugs in health centers and hospitals.

Information is available on out-of-pocket expenditures through the government health system. User fees are levied at all government health facilities according to a fee scale determined by the government.[7] These same regulations determine the exemptions and subsidized rates that are extended to various categories of people on the basis of age, occupation, income, or condition. A further large group of nonpayers are members of the National Insurance Corporation who are not really exempted in that their costs are presumed to be covered by the annual contribution that the National Insurance Corporation makes to the Ministry of Health's revenue. Data are not available on the number of people exempted or the total number of exemptions, except for those that deal with exemptions for drugs.

Quality and Access

Quality concepts in health have evolved over the years from the early concepts of quality control, through concepts of quality assessment, quality assurance, total quality management, continuous quality improvement, and quality of care development to clinical governance. Currently, the concept has expanded to quality systems where the requirement is to have a national quality strategy that addresses all aspects of quality at all levels. This is at the heart of the argument for the integrated nature of health care. This national quality system includes the public and private and nongovernmental sectors, and it applies to administrators as much as it applies to service providers.[10]

In Saint Lucia over the years, there has been an increasing demonstration of dissatisfaction with existing health services and the delivery of the health system. This is clearly conveyed by the Health Sector Reform document of Saint Lucia. This document underscores the point that the country needs a system of care that promotes wellness through the implementation of the Primary Health Care model. According to the document, Saint Lucia still continues to direct its resources and persists with arrangements that support the curative medical care approach to the delivery of health services. The authors of the health reform document further lamented the share of government expenditure allocated to the secondary care system, that is, the hospitals, which over the years averaged around 45% of the annual recurrent expenditure of the Ministry of Health. The system is also bedeviled by poor communication and inadequate health information, with a miniscule amount spent on preventive services, training of staff, and health promotion.[10]

In addition, consultations conducted with the citizens of the country revealed a general perception of a lackluster performance from health institutions. Respondents believed that health centers should expand the current services offered to include laboratory tests, X-rays, and specialist services. There was also a general view that the centers' working hours should be extended to provide care after normal working hours and that more basic equipment and medical personnel should be available at these community health centers. People also generally lamented the length of time that patrons had to spend waiting before seeing a doctor.[12]

Carr and Wint, in their analysis of the primary health care services in Saint Lucia, suggested that there was a host of areas in which these services could be strengthened, confirming the areas of shortcomings highlighted by the public consultations of the year 2000. Additionally, although they paid tribute to the professionals at the health centers, whom they described as well trained to carry out their specific functions, they lamented the absence of written guidelines for the delivery of services. The consultants further advanced a concern about the inadequacy of the medical records system to support efficient services and ensure continuity of care.[9] The laboratory services provided at the majority of health centers are restricted to the collection of samples that is sent to the hospital for testing. The result of this inefficiency is considerable delay in obtaining test results, thus compromising the quality of the services delivered. The access to Pap smear results is an example in which delays in the receipt of timely results from the Victoria Hospital have seriously affected the perceived quality of services delivered to the clients[12]; however, efforts supported by the Senior Management Team in the Ministry of Health have recently been made to reduce the time taken to provide laboratory results.

In the assessment of the quality of services delivered at the health centers as part of the preventive care thrust of the health system of Saint Lucia, staff at most health centers perceived that the supplies they received were adequate for the provision of quality care, despite periodic shortages of items such as dressings, plaster, and pharmaceutical items.[9] These pharmaceutical shortages affect patients who are distressed by chronic diseases and may be a contributing factor to the pressure faced by the Accident and Emergency Hospital Unit and staff. This periodic absence of basic services at the health centers has given rise to a situation in which health centers and even the district hospitals at Dennery and Soufriere are bypassed even for minor ailments.[9]

Another barrier to the utilization of community health centers is the major issue of overcrowding at the District Medical Officer's clinics. At most of the health centers, more than 50 clients present at each of these 4-hour clinics, causing a decline in the quality of care provided. Of even greater concern is the fact that hardly any screening of clients takes place by the family nurse practitioner or other health professional.[9]

Current supervisory practices at the health centers are perceived to contribute to the inadequate quality of care. Supervisory practices involve very little assessment of the quality of care delivered to patients in keeping with protocols. There is, instead, an inordinate amount of attention paid to quantitative data and in-service training. Although these are important aspects of the supervisory function, greater attention needs to be paid to the evaluation of the quality of services delivered and the impact of these services on the health of clients.[12]

Another barrier that has been identified relates to the system of referral of patients between hospitals and health centers. Information on patients is not being effectively transferred from the hospital to the health center to ensure proper follow-up care. Similarly, the transfer of information from the health centers to the hospital is no more effective. This can be attributed to the absence of a single form for use by both levels of care.[9] In addition, many patients bypass the health centers and self-refer to the hospitals. Indeed, the referral system would be enhanced by a closer working relationship and better communication between the hospital staff and the health center staff.

There is general agreement among researchers on health quality and access issues in Saint Lucia that while the basic package of primary healthcare services cover the important areas of maternal and child health, chronic diseases including cancer screening, and dental health, there is inadequate reach at the level of health center staff into areas such as mental health and the control of STI/HIV/AIDS. There is also almost a total lack of health programs targeting adolescent health. Even when services are somewhat available, they are sporadic and uneven. There is no structured policy or plan for the delivery of certain services such as dental services. Moreover, some specialist services such as dermatology, psychiatry, and pediatrics are only provided at select health centers. This means that services are distributed inequitably, with the majority concentrated in the northern zone of the island.

An examination of the impact of fees on the access to health center–based services is inconclusive. Anecdotal information suggests that the introduction in 1996 of the fee to see the District Medical Officer caused a reduction in the number of patients; however, there is also the converse point of view that the lack of a fee for service has contributed to the overutilization and abuse of the services.[9] The March 2000 Health Sector Reform document examined this issue of fees and payment, suggesting that community consultations revealed much concern regarding the escalating cost of health care. The question of paying for health and financing the healthcare system generated much discussion. Although users indicated a willingness to pay for health care, they would do so only if services were improved. The idea of "cash on delivery" was, however, rejected with a preference for prepayment, insurance, or taxation or a billing system

expressed instead.[9] Another factor to be taken into consideration is the cultural belief that public services are provided by government and that people ought not to pay for essential public services. It was clear from the views expressed by community residents that they were not happy with the delivery of the services in the public system and also objected to paying "cash on delivery."

Indeed, factors such as the cost of health care and the system of payments, as well as the perceived poor quality of services, severely compromised access. It is clear that there is a need to pay attention to these impediments to health care. With regard to the system of payments, the Health Sector Reform Committee saw the need to change the system of payments so that clients who need care would not have to pay before the service is delivered. The committee also recommended the need to develop a system that allows persons who cannot afford to pay to get health care when they need it.

Quality and access issues in health care must also be approached from the aspects of effective management in addition to the way in which the health services are organized. The health reform document of 2002 highlighted these issues by demonstrating that a large portion of the health challenges derived from ineffective management and the malorganization of scarce human, financial, and physical resources. This underscores the need for an evaluation of the management of the health system as well as the need for greater emphasis on greater community involvement in managing local health services.

In all of this, the Ministry of Health cannot escape the required scrutiny. There is the prevailing consensus that the ministry needs to examine critically its various functions, including the way it organizes and manages health, provides health care, and finances healthcare delivery. The health sector reform document was developed from the analysis of community consultation reports, which revealed a need for stricter regulations in all of these areas of the health system.[9] Undoubtedly, clear rules and guidelines ought to be a precursor to all issues relating to quality, equity, and efficiency. Monitoring and evaluation of the activities of the health system, if it occurs, would confirm that in the absence of rules and guidelines, quality, equity, and efficiency would remain largely illusive.

Other concerns were highlighted in the consultations held across the country. One such concern was the price and dispensation of drugs. General dissatisfaction was expressed about the affordability of the drugs and the availability at the times needed. There was also a concern that the health and safety of the client should never be jeopardized. Another area of concern was the quality of care provided by doctors and medical staff who straddled the private and public sectors. This particular aspect of the health system was seen as a situation that compromised the quality of care in the public sector and potentially placed barriers to access to various services. Added to this distressing phenomenon was the perception that the roles and functions of doctors in the delivery of health services warranted elucidation. The access to health services at health institutions was a further source of disquiet among patrons. A myriad of questions was raised with respect to this area of concern. These included the opening hours, the waiting times, and access to doctors.

One of the interesting elements of an environmental health nature raised was the handling and sale of food in public places. It was felt that greater attention needed to be placed on regulations and frequent monitoring in this area, particularly the aspect of outdated food items. The existing situation with regard to the Environmental Health Division of the Ministry of Health is one characterized by the absence of strong and effective leadership, exacerbated by a lack of clarity of its mission. It can be logically concluded that the role the division is expected to fulfill should determine the measure of its authority and resources to undertake its mandate.[12]

CURRENT AND EMERGING ISSUES AND CHALLENGES

Current National Agenda Health Priorities

Saint Lucia's National Strategic Plan for Health (2001–2006), which resulted from the health sector reform effort, established 12 priority health area programs. These areas are comprehensive in nature and designed to mobilize resources in a coordinated and synergistic manner, targeted at the priority health challenges.[12] These priority health areas include communicable diseases, noncommunicable diseases, sexual and reproductive health, child and adolescent health, environmental health, oral health, emergency medical services, mental health and substance abuse, food and nutrition, violence and injuries including gender-based violence, eye health, and disabilities and social protection.[12] It is hoped that through a focus on these priority areas, the health and well-being of all would be taken care of in a manner that reduces inequalities in access to high-quality health services.

Health Plans and Projects in Response to Health Agenda Priorities

The aforementioned health priorities emerged as responses to the various challenges being faced by the healthcare system in Saint Lucia. These challenges are all outlined in the recently completed National Strategic Plan for Health, 2006–2011. The document highlights the fact that the health system requires strengthening to respond effectively and efficiently to the new challenges. It prescribes an intersectoral approach and the requisite political commitment at all major decision-making levels.

There is recognition that communicable and noncommunicable diseases threaten the health and well-being of all Saint Lucians. High rates of morbidity and mortality have been attributed to chronic diseases and sexually transmitted infections, a distinction that, in some cases of cancer, is becoming increasingly blurred. Moreover, there appears to be an increase in the incidence and prevalence of certain psychological conditions as the society develops. In the face of this situation, attention needs to be paid to the care and support of the mentally challenged.

The health infrastructure in Saint Lucia is also recognized to be in urgent need of major improvements. An effort has been made to rationalize and upgrade all health centers to enhance their efficiency and utilization in the health delivery system. This will require a continuous quality improvement system as part of a general thrust toward creating a quality health promotion environment. The human resources issue is of paramount importance in Saint Lucia as it is for the entire region. Currently, there is the perennial challenge of ensuring adequate numbers of healthcare professionals and allied healthcare workers with the requisite skills mix for the delivery of healthcare services. Of equal importance is the need to ensure greater accountability from all levels of staff in the execution of their duties.

The capacity of the national emergency medical system requires improvement to ensure effective, appropriate, and timely dispatch, stabilization, and transfer of patients. The system also needs to be fully integrated with available hospital emergency rooms. All of this takes place against the backdrop of the increase in the incidence and prevalence of intentional and unintentional injuries and other life-threatening emergencies. Indeed, the widening gap between health resources and expressed needs poses its own challenges. This places serious demands on the health sector to satisfy the expectations of clients and to ensure that all persons in need of care are able to access the services that they require, with life-preserving quality.

Another key challenge is associated with the management and analysis of data and dissemination of information. The architects of the National Strategic Plan for Health have specifically highlighted the need to improve the surveillance and access and impact of pharmaceutical services and products. There is a dire need to monitor the activities of all stakeholders from private, public, and nongovernmental organizations, as well as all categories of medicine. Similarly, the recognition that men and women have different health needs requires that gender mainstreaming is instituted in order to address these differences equitably in all health sector policies and programs.[10]

The response to the challenges falls under the broad rubric of a national health development strategy outlined in a document called the National Strategic Plan for Health. This document confirms the Ministry of Health's plan and commitment to the Primary Health Care approach, which it sees as the platform and core component of the national health development strategy. The key principles to guide this process are (1) equity, when access to health care is regarded as a fundamental human right; (2) efficiency, with the objective of providing client-centered and responsive health care; and (3) effectiveness, with the aim to ensure value for money. The ultimate of these three principles is to ensure that all health interventions are responsive to client needs and that the health services are managed in an environment that guarantees accountability and promotes quality.

A Broad Caribbean Perspective

The current and emerging issues and challenges facing Saint Lucia cannot be divorced from what generally obtains in the rest of the CARICOM region or the subregional grouping of the Organization of Eastern Caribbean States. In several aspects, what obtains in one country is generally mirrored in others, notwithstanding some peculiarities. Thus, in the executive summary of the Caribbean Commission on Health and Development Report (2005), the distinguished authors alluded to the fact that (p. XIII)[15]

> Some of the most dramatic advances over the past half-century have been seen in health. . . . Political leaders and populations perceive a moral as well as a political imperative to ensure that health gains continue and are not eroded.

Despite these gains, these authors did not lose sight of the challenges that the region continued to face. Es-

sentially, the various countries of the region have to contend with their vulnerable open economies and their small size, which place limitations on resources that are available to be devoted to health. There is also the high cost of maintaining a health sector that seeks to improve the condition of public health and at the same time respond to the increasing demands for improvement in the quality of curative services. The latter takes place against the backdrop of the influence of information from other cultures and societies. Moreover, the ever-present threat of natural hazards that become full-fledged disasters in the face of inadequate preparations cannot be overlooked.

Within the Caribbean, at a regional level, there are important political and economic developments that are relevant to health. These political and economic changes are characterized by arrangements for functional cooperation, especially related to the free movement of people and the development of the Caribbean Single Market and Economy. The Caribbean is at present in the midst of a demographic and related epidemiological transition producing health risks associated with underdevelopment and development simultaneously. By and large, chronic noncommunicable diseases are firmly fixed as major causes of mortality, with HIV/AIDS growing in significance and other communicable diseases continuing to form part of the epidemiological reality of the region. As noted, the threat of natural disasters, especially hurricanes, is always present in the face of a growing burden of violence and unintentional injuries. The rising epidemic of obesity, a common risk factor in many chronic, noncommunicable diseases, also has to be seriously addressed. Finally, there are communicable diseases, such as dengue and food-borne threats, that still occur in epidemic form in some countries of the region. A fundamental approach across countries in the region would have to take into account a transformation of the socioeconomic environment through policies targeting primary determinants of health.

The Caribbean Commission on Health and Development Report outlines the many health challenges of the regional health systems, which are inextricably linked to economic realities. Caribbean countries are among the most heavily indebted, and domestic debt seems to be on the rise.[10] The challenge of facing the increasing liberalization of trade at the same time that there is erosion of the traditional preferences for many of the region's primary products poses economic challenges that present a reality pregnant with prospects of instability.

A major test for the countries of the Caribbean is the execution of their individual health plans. This is due to the lack of good health information systems, an organized form of collecting surveillance data, and presenting evidence for decision making. Furthermore, the entire region is plagued with the challenges of effective decentralization and workforce development and management, as evidenced by the shortages of many categories of health workers, particularly nurses. Furthermore, across the region, there is the ubiquitous challenge of the financing of the health services where the growing use of user fees in the acquisition of public services to compensate for shortfalls in public spending lingers as a fundamental issue that warrants attention. The issue of user fees continues to generate debate, particularly as it affects the most vulnerable segments of the population. Indeed, deficiencies in public health leadership are not to be discounted, as there are major vacua across the region in what have been described as essential public health functions.

REFERENCES

1. *Saint Lucia at Independence.* St. Lucia: National Archives Authority of Saint Lucia; 1997.
2. *Pitons Management Area & Soufriere Region Integrated Development, 2007.* St. Lucia: Ministry of Physical Planning, the Environment, Housing, Urban Renewal & Local Government; 2007.
3. *Organization of Eastern Caribbean States Human Development Report.* Grenada: OECS Secretariat; 2002.
4. Statistical Department: Ministry of Finance. *Statistical Report.* St. Lucia: International Financial Services and Economic Affairs; 2006.
5. *Poverty Assessment, Saint Lucia: 2006.* Saint Lucia: Ministry of Finance, International Financial Services and Economic Affairs; 2006.
6. *Saint Lucia Social and Economic Review, 2007.* Saint Lucia: Ministry of Finance, International Financial Services and Economic Affairs; 2007.
7. *Health Systems and Services Profile of Saint Lucia, 2001.* Retrieved March 7, 2008, from Health _ System_ profile-St_ Lucia_2001.
8. *Report of Chief Medical Officer.* St. Lucia: Ministry of Health, Human Services, Affairs and Gender Relations; 2002.
9. Carr P, Wint B. *Assessment of the Current Structure and Operations of the Primary Health Care System in Saint Lucia.* St. Lucia: Ministry Report; 2002.
10. *National Strategic Plan for Health (2006–2011).* Saint Lucia: Ministry of Health, Human Services, Family Affairs and Gender Relations; 2005.
11. *Health Sector Reform Proposals.* Saint Lucia: Ministry of Health, Human Services, Family Affairs and Gender Relations; March 6, 2000.
12. *Health Systems and Services Profile of Grenada Carriacou and Petite Martinique, 2001.* Grenada: Ministry of Health Publications; 2001.
13. *Health Systems and Services Profile of Dominica 2002.* Dominica: Ministry of Health Publications; 2002.
14. *Health Systems and Services Profile of St. Kitts/Nevis, 2002.* Ministry of Health Publications–St. Kitts/Nevis_2002.
15. Pan American Health Organization/World Health Organization. *Report of the Caribbean Commission on Health and Development, 2005.*
16. *Universal Health Care National Health Insurance Task Force Report.* November 2, 2003.
17. Ministry of Health, Human Services, Family Affairs and Gender Relations. *Hospital Regulations.* 1992:68.

Challenges and Opportunities

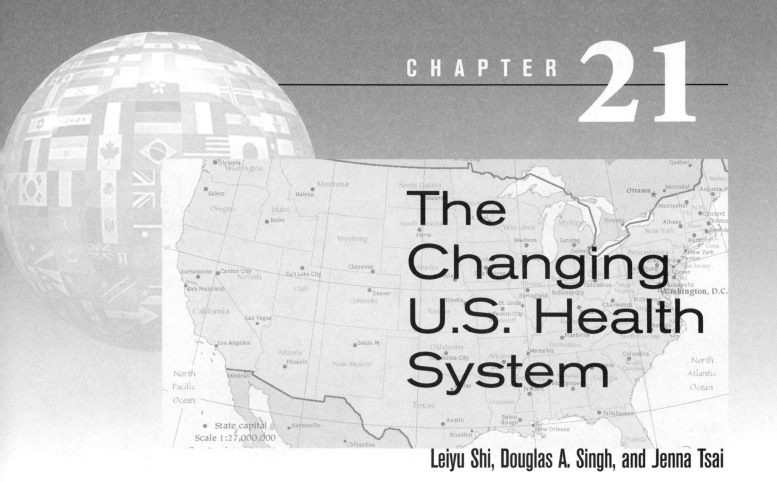

CHAPTER 21

The Changing U.S. Health System

Leiyu Shi, Douglas A. Singh, and Jenna Tsai

INTRODUCTION

The United States has a unique system of healthcare delivery. Unlike other developed countries where health care is perceived as a "right" and almost all citizens are entitled to receive at least basic healthcare services, the United States has a significant number of people who are without health insurance. The United States also witnesses significant disparities in health status across racial/ethnic and socioeconomic groups and between those insured and uninsured. The U.S. healthcare delivery "system" is not a system in the true sense, even though it is called a system when reference is made to its various features, components, and services. The system is fragmented because there are numerous private insurance plans and tax-supported public programs. The system has periodically undergone incremental changes, mainly in response to concerns with cost, access, and quality. In spite of these changes, providing at least a basic package of health care at an affordable price to every American remains an unrealized goal. People outside the United States sometimes wonder why Americans do not have a national healthcare system. The answers lie in the way the American culture was shaped by history that resulted in self-reliance, an aversion to unreasonable taxes, and a preference for limited government. Also, within the country today, sentiments about healthcare are paradoxical. Influenced by the American media, Americans have come to believe that the healthcare system may be in need of major reform, but at an individual level, they are overwhelmingly satisfied with their own care.

The main objective of this chapter is to give a general overview of the United States as a nation and to furnish a broad understanding of the healthcare delivery system. For a more in-depth understanding and systematic analysis of U.S. healthcare, readers may wish to consult additional textbooks, including those by the authors.[1,2]

COUNTRY DESCRIPTION

TABLE 21-1   United States

Nationality	Noun: American(s)
	Adjective: American
Ethnic groups	White 81.7%, black 12.9%, Asian 4.2%, Amerindian and Alaska native 1%, native Hawaiian and other Pacific islander 0.2% (2003 est.)
	A separate listing for Hispanic is not included because the U.S. Census Bureau considers Hispanic to mean a person of Latin American descent (including persons of Cuban, Mexican, or Puerto Rican origin) living in the United States who may be of any race or ethnic group (white, black, Asian, etc.)
Religions	Protestant 51.3%, Roman Catholic 23.9%, Mormon 1.7%, other Christian 1.6%, Jewish 1.7%, Buddhist 0.7%, Muslim 0.6%, other or unspecified 2.5%, unaffiliated 12.1%, none 4% (2007 est.)
Language	English 82.1%, Spanish 10.7%, other Indo-European 3.8%, Asian and Pacific island 2.7%, other 0.7% (2000 census)
	Hawaiian is an official language in the state of Hawaii
Literacy	Definition: age 15 and over can read and write
	Total population: 99%
	Male: 99%
	Female: 99% (2003 est.)
Government type	Constitution-based federal republic; strong democratic tradition
Date of independence	July 4, 1776 (from Great Britain)
Gross Domestic Product (GDP) per capita	$46,000 (2007 est.)
Unemployment rate	4.6% (2007 est.)
Natural hazards	Tsunamis, volcanoes, and earthquake activity around Pacific Basin; hurricanes along the Atlantic and Gulf of Mexico coasts; tornadoes in the midwest and southeast; mud slides in California; forest fires in the west; flooding; permafrost in northern Alaska, a major impediment to development
Environment: current issues	Air pollution resulting in acid rain in both the United States and Canada; the United States is the largest single emitter of carbon dioxide from the burning of fossil fuels; water pollution from runoff of pesticides and fertilizers; limited natural freshwater resources in much of the western part of the country require careful management; desertification
Population	303,824,646 (July 2008 est.)
Age structure	0–14 years: 20.1% (male 31,257,108/female 29,889,645)
	15–64 years: 67.1% (male 101,825,901/female 102,161,823)
	65 years and over: 12.7% (male 16,263,255/female 22,426,914) (2008 est.)
Median age	Total: 36.7 years
	Male: 35.4 years
	Female: 38.1 years (2008 est.)
Population growth rate	0.883% (2008 est.)
Birth rate	14.18 births/1,000 population (2008 est.)

(continues)

TABLE 21-1   United States (continued)

Death rate	8.27 deaths/1,000 population (2008 est.)
Net migration rate	2.92 migrant(s)/1,000 population (2008 est.)
Gender ratio	At birth: 1.05 male(s)/female
	Under 15 years: 1.05 male(s)/female
	15–64 years: 1 male(s)/female
	65 years and over: 0.73 male(s)/female
	Total population: 0.97 male(s)/female (2008 est.)
Infant mortality rate	Total: 6.3 deaths/1,000 live births
	Male: 6.95 deaths/1,000 live births
	Female: 5.62 deaths/1,000 live births (2008 est.)
Life expectancy at birth	Total population: 78.14 years
	Male: 75.29 years
	Female: 81.13 years (2008 est.)
Total fertility rate	2.1 children born/woman (2008 est.)
HIV/AIDS adult prevalence rate	0.6% (2003 est.)
Number of people living with HIV/AIDS	950,000 (2001 est.)
HIV/AIDS deaths	17,011 (2005 est.)

Central Intelligence Agency. The World Fact Book, 2008. November 18, 2008, from https://www.cia.gov/library/publications/the-world-factbook.

History

The first Americans are believed to be people who crossed from Asia to North America over a narrow land strip that is now submerged below the Bering Strait that connects Siberia to Alaska.[3] This migration likely occurred millennia before the white man arrived from Europe. Gradually, many of these Native Americans, as we call them today, migrated southward. By the time the Europeans arrived, the indigenous population had spread throughout the North American continent.

In the 15th century, European sailors began exploring new routes to India by sailing west from Spain and Italy. The modern history of the Americas begins with the voyage of Christopher Columbus, who crossed the Atlantic and reached the Bahamas in 1492.[3] In subsequent expeditions, he discovered other islands in the Caribbean Sea. Although Columbus is credited with discovering the New World, he never reached the continent of North America[4]; however, after the New World had been discovered, other explorers such as Juan Ponce de León and John Cabot reached North America's eastern shores. The voyage of John Cabot, an Italian, was commissioned by the British king. Cabot's voyage to North America later provided the basis for England's claim over the continent. Later, King Francis I of France sent Giovanni da Verrazano, an Italian adventurer, and subsequently Jacques Cartier, a French explorer, to lay claims on parts of North America on behalf of France. The Dutch hired Henry Hudson, an English navigator, who also reached North America. However, America was named after another Italian explorer, Amerigo (Latin: Americus) Vespucci, who likely explored the American coast further than any navigator of his time in at least two voyages; the accounts of his voyages were published in Europe.[5]

The first European colony in what would become the United States was established by neither England nor France but by the Spanish forces of Pedro Menéndez in what is now Florida. Menéndez destroyed a group of French settlers in northern Florida in 1565. The British sent Walter Raleigh, who in 1585 established the first British colony in Roanoke Island off the coast of North

Carolina. Although this colony did not last long, the British finally succeeded in establishing a colony in Jamestown, Virginia, in 1607. This was the first permanent English settlement in what later became the United States. Virginia soon became prosperous by growing tobacco plantations. These plantations required a labor force in excess of the available supply. In 1619, a Dutch ship brought the first African slaves to Virginia. By the 18th century, slavery became an integral part of the economic and social composition of Virginia.[6] Around 1795, the rapid increase in cotton cultivation brought slaves to other parts of the South.[7]

The early 1600s saw the beginning of a great tide of emigration from Europe to North America. Between 1620 and 1635, economic difficulties swept England. Many people could not find work. Even skilled artisans could earn little more than a bare living. Poor crop yields added to the distress. Other European emigrants left their homelands to escape political oppression, to seek freedom to practice their religion, or to find opportunities denied them at home. Britain continued to establish colonies in Plymouth (now Massachusetts), Maryland, Rhode Island, Connecticut, the Carolinas, New Jersey, and Pennsylvania. The New England colonies flourished from profits gained through commerce in fishing. The French established their settlements in what is now Quebec, Canada, and in Alabama and Louisiana. The Dutch established some scattered footholds, but theirs was never a strong colony in terms of political power or stability.[6] The Spaniards also established settlements mainly in the southern parts of North America. Around 1732, Britain founded a colony in Georgia to avert any threats of Spain's expansion into South Carolina.[6] In 1664, under the threat of an armed conflict, the Dutch surrendered New Amsterdam to the British, and the colony was renamed New York.[3] The French lost control of their colonies after they were defeated by the British. The British now had 13 colonies, all located east of the Mississippi River, that were secure for the first time in almost a century from attack by another power.[6]

A chain of events led to the War for American Independence. The Anglo-French wars were fought in both America and Europe and had dragged on from 1689 to 1763. The British wanted the colonies to bear part of the burden of new taxes. The American Revenue Act (Sugar Act) of 1764 and the Stamp Act of 1765 were passed by the British Parliament as means of raising revenues from Americans. The Currency Act of 1764 prohibited the American colonies from issuing paper currency. The Townshend Revenue Act of 1767 imposed taxes on tea, lead, paper, glass, and paint imported into the colonies.[6]

The Americans bitterly resented these taxes. Boycotts, protests, and skirmishes between the citizens and British troops posted in Boston brought on the Boston Massacre of 1770 in which three Bostonians were killed and two were mortally wounded. The incident inflamed public opinion.[6] The Tea Act of 1773 gave the British East India Company monopoly status to sell tea to the colonies. This action resulted in what is referred to as the Boston Tea Party in which American radicals boarded the ships carrying prime tea and dumped about 350 chests of tea into Boston harbor as a gesture of protest. Retaliation from Britain brought on the Coercive Acts of 1774. Although these acts were designed to coerce the Massachusetts colony into submissiveness, they had the opposite effect.[6] The American Revolution was born as a result of what Americans generally believed to be tyranny under Great Britain. Later, the framers of the Constitution were careful to place limits on the government's power over individual freedoms.

Not surprisingly, the revolutionary war began in the Boston area with fighting between armed citizens and British forces in 1775. On June 10, 1776, the Continental Congress appointed a committee under the leadership of Thomas Jefferson to draft the Declaration of Independence. On July 4 of that year, Congress approved the Declaration of Independence, according to which the 13 colonies in North America were "free and independent states" and became the United States of America. The Revolutionary War came to an end on October 19, 1781, when the American army under the command of George Washington and with the help of the French defeated the British forces at Yorktown, Virginia. In 1783, the Treaty of Paris endorsed the independence of the colonies from Great Britain. In 1789, George Washington became the first president of the United States.

When the population of a state reached 60,000 free inhabitants, it was eligible to join the union (United States). During Washington's tenure as president, Vermont, Kentucky, and Tennessee were added to the union. In later years, the country acquired land from France, Spain, Great Britain, Mexico, and Russia and annexed the Republic of Texas and the Republic of Hawaii. Alaska and Hawaii were the 49th and 50th states, respectively, to join the union in 1959. The United States also has a number of territories, all islands or groups of islands, that are under the jurisdiction of the federal government. The main territories are Puerto Rico, U.S. Virgin Islands, American Samoa, Guam, and Northern Mariana Islands. The nation's capital is Washington, DC (District of Columbia), which is a federal district.

Size and Geography

The total area of the United States is 3.79 million square miles (9.83 million km²). Ninety-three percent of this area is land (Figure 21-1). The estimated population in July 2007 was 301.6 million.[8] The United States occupies roughly 6.5% of the world's surface (about the same as China, and a little over half as much as Russia) and has about 4.5% of the world's population.

Forty-eight states and the District of Columbia are situated between Canada and Mexico and between the Atlantic and Pacific Oceans. Alaska and Hawaii are physically separate from the rest of the country (see the U.S.

map). Alaska occupies the northwestern corner of the North American continent, with Canada to its east and Russia to the west across the Bering Strait. Hawaii consists of eight major islands and over a hundred small ones. The main Hawaiian islands are located approximately 2,400 miles (3,900 kilometers) southwest of the U.S. mainland in the mid-Pacific. The 50 states have significantly different sizes. Alaska is the largest state and is about 425 times bigger than the smallest, Rhode Island. The three largest states, Alaska, Texas, and California, make up about 30% of the entire country. The most populous states are California (36.5 million), Texas (23.5 million), and New York (19.3 million). Wyoming (515,000),

FIGURE 21-1 Map of the United States

Vermont (624,000), and North Dakota (636,000) have the least number of people.[9]

Government and Political System

The United States is a representative republic in which those who govern are popularly elected by those who are governed. All U.S. citizens who have attained the age of 18 have the right to vote. As the supreme law of the land, the Constitution of the United States (adopted on September 17, 1787) incorporates several key principles of government: (1) government by the people, which means that it is the people who form the government; (2) limited government, which means that government can only do what the people allow it to do through exercise of a duly developed system of laws[10]; (3) federalism, according to which the central government shares sovereign powers with the state governments[10]; (4) separation of powers, which divides political power between the three branches of government: the legislative, the executive, and the judicial; (5) checks and balances that emanate from separation of powers and enable inspection and restraint of one part of the political system by another[7]; (6) respect for individual worth, a principle that was first embraced in the Declaration of Independence and that has been used as a measure of the value of social institutions to individuals[7]; and (7) equal opportunity, which stresses individual worth by making available to each individual the opportunity to develop his or her abilities and interests[7]; and (8) a Bill of Rights that protects individual liberties against violations by the government. These rights were added to the Constitution in the form of 10 amendments that were ratified by all states in 1791. The First Amendment protects the right to freedom of religion and freedom of expression from government interference.

The federal government has three branches: legislative (the Senate and House of Representatives), executive (the president and cabinet departments), and judicial (federal courts and the U.S. Supreme Court). Each of the states also has its own constitution and its own legislative, executive, and judicial branches. In general, the states can do anything that is not prohibited by the U.S. Constitution or is contrary to federal policy. The major reserved powers of the state include the authority to regulate commerce within the state and to exercise police powers. The latter refer to the state's right to pass and enforce laws that promote health, safety, welfare, and morality.[10]

Two political parties have traditionally dominated the political process. Other minor party groups have appeared on the political scene, but none has succeeded in replacing the two major parties,[7] currently the Republican and Democratic parties.

In response to issues that politicians believe their constituents face, the government makes decisions and takes actions that are broadly referred to as *public policy*. Policies can take the form of new laws, repeal of existing laws, interpretation and implementation of laws, executive orders, or court rulings. Throughout the policy-making process, the system of constitutional checks and balances prevails. The president often plays an important leadership role in key policy issues.

The Constitution grants Congress the power to make laws. The legislative process is often cumbersome as a bill (before it becomes law) goes through both houses of Congress and various committees and subcommittees. Various organizations, called interest groups, which represent common objectives of their members, try to influence policy makers to protect their members' interests. In the end, if the president signs the approved bill, it becomes law. The president also has the power to veto (overturn) a bill passed by Congress. Unless a presidential veto is overruled by a two-thirds majority of the Congress, it fails to become law. Even after a law has been passed, policy making continues in the form of interpretation and implementation by the federal agency responsible for implementing the law. For example, the Department of Health and Human Services oversees more than 300 programs related to health and welfare services. It is responsible for 12 different agencies that deal with such diverse areas as issues related to public health, approval of new drugs, healthcare research, services for older persons, and substance abuse.

Macroeconomics

America is called a "land of plenty." The nation is richly blessed with natural resources. In large part, the nation's spectacular economic growth has been credited to the enterprising way in which Americans have used the nation's resources.[7] The seeds of American capitalism are found in the Constitution. At the foundation of American capitalism is the belief that individuals know best what is in their self-interest. Americans believe that their market economy and its political system provide avenues for individuals to act in their own interest and realize achievement limited only by one's own potential and motivation. The economic system in the United States is based largely on the principles of free market, open competition, profit motive, and private ownership of the means of production. These forces unleash human potential to maximize productivity and innovation and to produce and distribute goods and services that people value. A significant majority of Americans believe that the marketplace provides people with the opportunity to succeed and that hard work is the ticket to success.[11]

The United States has the largest and most technologically advanced economy in the world. Components of the gross domestic product (GDP) in 2006 are shown in Table 21-2. Even though the service sector of the economy has grown, the United States has a thriving manufacturing sector in industries such as petroleum, steel, aerospace, defense, telecommunications, computers, chemicals, electronics, mining, pharmaceuticals, and consumer goods.

U.S. residents enjoy one of the highest standards of living in the world. The labor force is among the most productive, and unemployment is relatively low (4% to 9%). Roughly one third of the civilian labor force has college degrees. Both full- and part-time workers on an average work about 39.2 hours per week. The median

weekly earning for full-time workers is $671. Among employed civilians, approximately 15% work for various levels of government; the remaining 85% are employed in the private sector.[8] In 2006, the size of the average American family was 3.2, and the median annual family income (inflation adjusted) was $58,526.[12]

Demographics

America is a nation of immigrants and minority groups. In 2006, 12.4% of the total population was foreign born. Between 2000 and March 2006, almost 9 million foreign-born individuals entered the country. Hispanics/Latinos represent the largest number of foreign-born residents (Table 21-3).

The fertility rate per 1,000 women in the U.S. population has declined from 70.9 in 1990 to 66.7 (estimated) in 2005. Age-adjusted death rates have also declined from 939 per 100,000 population in 1990 to 801 in 2004.[8]

TABLE 21-2 Components of the U.S. GDP, 2006

	Billions of Dollars	Percentage
Total GDP	13,247	100.0
Consumption	9,269	70.0
Goods	3,785	28.6
Services	5,484	41.4
Private investment	2,213	16.7
Government spending	2,528	19.1
Federal	927	7.0
State and local	1,601	12.1
Exports minus imports	−763	−5.8

Source: U.S. Census Bureau. *Statistical Abstract of the United States, 2008.* p. 429.

TABLE 21-3 Foreign-Born Population, 2005

Region	Population (Thousands)	Percentage
Total	35,689	100.0
Latin America (Caribbean, Central America, South America)	19,019	53.3
Asia	9,534	26.7
Europe	4,870	13.6
Africa	1,252	3.5
Other	1,014	2.8

Source: U.S. Census Bureau. *Statistical Abstract of the United States, 2008.* p. 44.

Hence, immigration is a critical factor in determining the nation's labor force. The "intermediate" projection (the most likely outcome) suggests that net migration to the United States will decline from 1.075 million in 2007 to 1 million in 2010 and to 950,000 per year starting 2020.[13]

Table 21-4 provides the racial/ethnic mix, age categories, and gender mix of the U.S. resident population. In 2005, life expectancy at birth was 77.8 years (80.4 years for females; 75.2 years for males; 78.3 years for whites; 73.2 years for blacks). A person aged 65 years could expect to live to an age of 83.7 years, and a person aged 85 years could expect to live to an age of 91.8 years.[14]

In 2006, 12.3% of the U.S. population lived in poverty (annual income of less than $20,000 for a family of four). The poverty rate was higher among blacks (24.3%) and Hispanics (20.6%).[15] In 2000, when the last U.S. census was taken, 79% of the population lived in urban areas. Poverty rates vary by rural versus urban residence. In 2002, 14.2% of the rural population compared with 11.6% of the urban population was poor.[16]

The religious makeup of the U.S. population in 2007 was 51.3% Protestant, 23.9% Roman Catholic, 1.7% Mormon, 1.6% other Christian, 1.7% Jewish, 0.7% Buddhist, 0.6% Muslim, 2.5% other or unspecified, 12.1% unaffiliated, and 4% none.[17]

BRIEF HISTORY OF THE HEALTHCARE SYSTEM

Pre-World War II

Medical Services in Preindustrial America

From Colonial times to the beginning of the 1900s, medical education and practice were far more advanced

TABLE 21-4 Racial/Ethnic Mix, Age Categories, and Gender Mix of the U.S. Resident Population, 2006

Race/Ethnicity	Population (Thousands)	Percentage
Total resident population	299,399	100.0
White	239,746	80.0
Black/African American	38,343	12.8
Asian	13,159	4.4
American Indian/Alaskan Native	2,903	1.0
Native Hawaiian/Pacific Islander	529	0.2
Two or more races	4,719	1.6
Hispanic or Latino origin (may be of any race included above)	44,321	14.8
Age categories		
5–14	60,755	20.3
15–29	63,144	21.1
30–49	86,171	28.8
50–64	52,067	17.4
65–74	18,917	6.3
75–84	13,047	4.4
85 and over	5,297	1.8
Gender mix		
Male	147,512	49.3
Female	151,886	50.7

Source: U.S. Census Bureau. *Statistical Abstract of the United States, 2008*. pp. 9, 11.

in Great Britain, France, and Germany than they were in the United States. The practice of medicine in the United States had a strong domestic rather than a professional character because medical procedures were primitive. Medical education was not grounded in science. Consequently, medical practice was more a trade than a profession. The nation had only a handful of hospitals that existed in very large cities such as New York, Boston, and Philadelphia. There was no health insurance—private or public.

Since World War II

Medical Services in Postindustrial America

The postindustrial era is marked by the growth and development of a medical profession that benefited from urbanization, new scientific discoveries, and reforms in medical education. American physicians became professionally organized and to this day have been a powerful force in resisting proposals for a national health care program.

The system for delivering health care in America took its current shape during this period. Private practice of medicine became firmly entrenched as physicians became a cohesive profession, opted for specialization, and gained power and prestige. The hospital emerged as a repository for high-tech facilities and equipment.

History of Health Insurance

The first broad-coverage health insurance in the United States emerged in the form of workers' compensation. It was originally designed to make cash payments to workers for wages lost because of job-related injuries and diseases. Later, compensation for medical expenses and death benefits to the survivors were added.

Health insurance began in the form of disability coverage that provided income during temporary disability caused by bodily injury or sickness. During the early 1900s, medical treatments and hospital care became socially acceptable; however, they were also becoming increasingly more expensive, and people could not predict their future needs for medical care or the costs. These developments pointed to the need for some kind of insurance to spread an individual's financial risk over a large number of people. Between 1916 and 1918, 16 state legislatures, including New York and California, attempted to enact legislation compelling employers to provide health insurance, but the efforts were unsuccessful.

Health insurance became a permanent feature of employment benefits during World War II. During this period, wages were frozen, and employees accepted employer-paid health insurance to compensate for the loss of increments to their salaries. Thus, health insurance became an important component of collective bargaining between unions and employers. Subsequently, employment-based health insurance expanded rapidly, and private health insurance became the primary vehicle for the delivery of healthcare services in the United States. It is estimated that private health insurance grew from a $1 billion industry in 1950 to an $8.7 billion industry by 1965.

Before 1965, private health insurance was the only widely available source of payment for health care, and it was available primarily to middle-class working people and their families. The older population, the unemployed, and the poor had to rely on their own resources, on limited public programs, or on charity from hospitals and individual physicians. In 1965, Congress passed the amendments to the Social Security Act that created the Medicare and Medicaid programs. The government thus assumed direct responsibility to insure two vulnerable population groups—the older and the poor persons.

Although adopted together, Medicare and Medicaid reflected sharply different traditions. Medicare was upheld by broad grassroots support and, being attached to Social Security, had no class distinction. Medicaid, on the other hand, carried the stigma of public welfare. Medicare had uniform national standards for eligibility and benefits; Medicaid varied from state to state in terms of eligibility and benefits. Medicare covered anyone at or over the age of 65 years. Medicaid became a *means-tested* program, which confined eligibility to people below a predetermined income level. Consequently, many of the poor did not qualify because their incomes exceeded the means-test limits.

The creation of Medicare and Medicaid had a drastic impact on both federal and state budgets, but the federal government bore the greatest brunt. Federal healthcare expenditures increased at an average annual rate of 30%, whereas total federal expenditures increased at a rate of only 11.3%. To curb inflation, President Richard Nixon implemented the Economic Stabilization Program in 1971. Under this program, wages and prices were frozen, including those in the healthcare industry. The Health Maintenance Organization (HMO) Act of 1973 was passed during the Nixon administration after price controls had failed to be effective. The main rationale behind the new law was to create competition in the healthcare marketplace. The law required employers with more than 25 workers to offer an HMO plan as an alternative to the standard health insurance plans which were already in wide use.

During the 1990s, managed care was largely credited with containing double-digit inflation in healthcare costs. The beginning of the 21st century, however, has once again been marked with a pickup in healthcare spending. At the same time, somewhere between 15% and 17% of the U.S. population is not covered under either a private or public health insurance program.

DESCRIPTION OF THE CURRENT HEALTHCARE SYSTEM

Facilities

Health care is the largest industry in the United States. From a technological standpoint, the nation has a highly developed infrastructure for the delivery of medical services. The nation has ultramodern healthcare facilities, high-caliber medical schools, university-based curricula to prepare healthcare managers and public health professionals, research organizations, a large pharmaceutical industry, manufacturers of medical devices, and providers of long-term care and rehabilitation services. The private sector owns most of the infrastructure. The government, however, plays a critical supportive role. The public health infrastructure, for example, is in the public domain. The government is also a major financier of health services research and medical education. It operates the military and veterans health systems (discussed later). It supports the delivery of care for certain vulnerable populations (discussed later) and funds the Indian Health Service for Native Americans. By having state-of-the-art technology, the United States offers medical services by highly trained physicians in its world-renowned facilities that are the envy of the world. On the other hand, this focus on high technology and specialization has certain negative effects. It raises the cost of medical care, which produces imbalances in access to health insurance. It also influences medical education, practice of medicine, and technology-driven competition among hospitals.

Workforce

In 2005, there were 762,000 professionally active doctors of medicine in the United States, which amounted to 23.8 physicians per 10,000 civilian population. Roughly 78% of the physicians work in private office-based practice; the rest work in hospitals or other professional settings related to teaching, research, or administration.[18] Approximately 24% of all practicing physicians are graduates of foreign medical schools; however, they must take rigorous examinations and undergo further training before they can practice in the United States. Although compared with most European nations the United States has an aggregate oversupply of physicians, their distribution shows certain imbalances. A lopsided focus on technology has over time caused the supply of medical specialists to far outpace the supply of primary care physicians. For example, in 2005, 40.4% of the physicians worked in primary care, 12.3% in family medicine and general practice, 15% in internal medicine, 5.5% in obstetrics and gynecology, and the remaining in various medical specialties.[19] Besides a specialty-oriented medical education, disparities in income offer another reason why the majority of medical students in the United States opt for specialty training. For example, according to data from the American Medical Association, general surgeons can make 40% to 80% more than physicians in family practice. A high proportion of specialists in medicine drive the use of technology and the cost of health care. Besides imbalances in primary and specialty care, locations outside metropolitan areas experience shortages of physicians. About 17% of the U.S. population lives in nonmetropolitan areas, but only 9% of the physicians practice in these areas.[18] People needing medical care in these areas may experience increased travel time to see a physician, which can deter timely and appropriate health care. Scarcity of physicians may result in higher caseloads for physicians so that patients face increased time to get an appointment and wait longer in the physician's office before they receive care.

Nurses constitute the largest group of healthcare professionals. Like physicians and other healthcare professionals, nurses must be licensed to practice in their respective state of employment. Depending on their level of education and competency assessment, nurses can be licensed as registered nurses (RNs) or as licensed practical/vocational nurses (LPNs/LVNs); 77% of all nurses are RNs. RNs must complete a 4-year bachelor's degree, a 4-year diploma, or a 2-year or 3-year associate's degree. Nurses can also specialize beyond their RN training to become advanced practice nurses.

Dentists, optometrists, psychologists, podiatrists, pharmacists, and chiropractors must complete doctoral-level education to qualify for a license in their respective fields. Audiologists and speech/language pathologists must have master's level preparation. Healthcare professionals who generally are required to complete a 4-year bachelor's degree include physical therapists, occupational therapists, clinical laboratory technologists, and dietitians. Educational requirements for numerous other types of allied health professionals vary from one state to another, but require between one and four years of training.

Inpatient Institutions

Depending on patient needs, institutional care that requires an overnight stay is delivered in general acute-care hospitals, specialty hospitals that include rehabilitation hospitals and psychiatric facilities, and long-term care facilities. The construction and operation of these institutions is governed by federal laws; state regulations; city ordinances; standards of the Joint Commission on Accreditation of Healthcare Organizations; and codes for building, fire protection, and sanitation. The Joint Commission on Accreditation of Healthcare Organizations is a private nonprofit organization that sets standards and accredits various types of healthcare facilities on ongoing verification of compliance with the standards.

The military medical care system and the Veterans Administration (VA; described later) operate federal hospitals that are inaccessible by the general public. Most of the remaining hospitals, numbering almost 5,000 and operating over 800,000 beds, are accessible by the general public and are called community hospitals. In 2005, the United States had 2.7 community hospital beds per 1,000 resident population,[18] far fewer than what most developed countries have. Hospitals in the United States come under three main types of ownership: private nonprofit, private for profit, and government owned. Private nonprofit organizations, such as community associations and churches, operate nonprofit hospitals. By law, these hospitals must reinvest the profits in the hospitals' operations and cannot distribute them to any individuals. For-profit hospitals are proprietary or investor owned. They are operated for the financial benefit of the stockholders; however, hospitals operate in a competitive environment, and they must often compete on the basis of high-quality, cost-efficient services. In 2005, 70% of the nation's community hospital beds were operated as nonprofit. Fourteen percent were operated as for profit, and 16% were operated by state or local governments.[18] Approximately 400 teaching hospitals (including 64 VA medical centers) belong to the Council of Teaching Hospitals and Health Systems. These hospitals generally have substantial teaching and research programs, are affiliated with medical schools of large universities, and train the majority of physician residents in the United States.

Specialty hospitals in the United States are establishments that primarily treat specific types of medical conditions (such as cardiac conditions or orthopedics), provide specialized rehabilitation care, or specialize in treating certain types of patients (such as women or children). The exact number of such hospitals is unknown, but their numbers are increasing. In addition, there are nearly 3,000 mental health institutions (over 212,000 beds) that provide 24-hour hospital and residential treatment. Approximately 16,000 nursing homes with 1,716,000 beds deliver 24-hour long-term care to mostly older patients.[18] Nursing homes mainly provide skilled nursing care, which is medically oriented care approved by a physician and provided by and under the direction of licensed nurses for complex chronic conditions and often includes rehabilitation therapies. In addition to these nursing homes, there are a large number of assisted living and personal care facilities that mainly provide assistance with activities of daily living.

Outpatient Settings

Outpatient (ambulatory care) services are delivered in a variety of settings, depending on factors such as the type of care needed, location, and whether the person has health insurance. Development of new technology and innovations in payment methods to providers have led to a decline in the utilization of inpatient hospitals and an expansion of outpatient services in both volume and scope. Many procedures that previously required a hospital stay are now performed on an outpatient basis. In the United States, an average of 2.7 community hospital beds per 1,000 population and an average length of stay of 5.6 days are among the lowest in the world. Consequently, many hospitals provide both inpatient and outpatient services to remain profitable. In 2005, 7.7% of all ambulatory visits occurred in hospitals' outpatient units (an increase from 6.2% in 1992). Of course, most outpatient visits take place in physicians' offices (82.4% in 2005). Hospital emergency rooms, however, are commonly used by the insured and the uninsured alike for both urgent and nonurgent conditions. Heavy use for nonemergencies results in overcrowding and waste of resources. For nonurgent care, emergency rooms are often used by those who do not have routine access to primary care. In 2004–2005, 5.4% of children under the age of 18 and 18% of adults did not have a usual source of health care.[18] Since the creation of the

State Children's Health Insurance Program (SCHIP; discussed later), the proportion of children who do not have a usual source of health care has declined from 7.7% in 1993–1994.

Home health care has been among the fastest growing sectors in U.S. health care. Over 70% of home health patients are older. Home care commonly includes part-time or intermittent nursing care, rehabilitation services, nutritional consultations, and assistance with activities of daily living. Since the early 1980s, specialized high-technology home therapies have proliferated. They include intravenous antibiotics, oncology therapy, hemodialysis, nutrition, ventilator care, and tele-home health technologies for remote in-home patient monitoring. Overall, home health care has proven to be cost-effective because it decreases the use of hospitals, emergency departments, and nursing homes.

Other main outpatient settings in the United States include walk-in clinics that provide the convenience of evening and weekend hours with no prior appointments, urgent care centers that operate 24 hours a day 7 days a week, free-standing surgicenters that perform outpatient surgeries, laboratories, imaging centers, dialysis centers, pharmacies, and rehabilitation centers. Retail medical clinics have started to open in major stores where people commonly shop for everyday things.

The federal government provides funding for more than 1,100 community health centers. These centers are located in defined medically underserved areas where they provide primary care, mental health care, and dental care to mostly low-income and uninsured populations.

Public Health

Public health services in the United States are typically provided by local health departments, and the range of services offered varies greatly by locality. The programs are generally limited in scope. They include well-baby care, venereal disease clinics, family planning services, screening and treatment for tuberculosis, and outpatient mental health care.

The Subsystems of U.S. Healthcare Delivery

The United States does not have a well-integrated and coordinated healthcare delivery system enjoyed by everyone. Instead, there are multiple subsystems developed either through market forces or as a result of policy initiatives to address the needs of certain population segments. The major subsystems are described later here.

The Managed Care System

Managed care is a system of healthcare delivery that (1) seeks to achieve efficiencies by integrating the basic functions of healthcare delivery, (2) employs mechanisms to control (manage) utilization of medical services, and (3) determines the price at which the services are purchased and consequently how much the providers get paid. It is the most dominant healthcare delivery system in the United States today and is available to most Americans.

The primary financiers of the managed care system are employers and the government; however, it is not a private–public partnership. Employers purchase insurance for their own employees, but they do so voluntarily. As a result, many small employers do not provide health insurance to their employees. On the other hand, because employer-based health insurance requires cost sharing, many workers choose not to participate even when the employer pays the bulk of the premium costs. Because of variations in the government programs, beneficiaries are either required to obtain healthcare services through a managed care organization (MCO) or through alternative mechanisms. There are two main types of MCOs: HMOs and preferred provider organizations (PPOs). An MCO functions like an insurance company and promises to provide healthcare services contracted under the health plan to the enrollees of the plan.

The term *enrollee* or member refers to the individual covered under the plan. The contractual arrangement between the MCO and the enrollee—including the array of covered health services that the enrollee is entitled to—is referred to as the health plan (or "plan," for short). The health plan generally uses selected providers from whom the enrollees can choose to receive routine services. HMOs typically require in-network access—that is, the enrollees must receive services from the providers selected by the HMO. PPOs, on the other hand, allow out-of-network access—that is, the enrollees can choose to receive services either from providers that participate in the PPO's selected network or from providers that are not part of the network. The enrollee incurs higher out-of-pocket costs when out-of-network providers are used. Nevertheless, because of the option to choose one's providers, PPO plans have been more popular than HMO plans. In HMOs particularly, primary care providers or generalists manage routine services and determine the appropriateness of referrals to higher-level or specialty services. In these plans, generalists are often referred to as gatekeepers. Some HMOs may deliver services partially through the plan's own hired physicians, but most services are delivered through contracts with providers such as physicians, hospitals, and diagnostic clinics.

Although the employer finances the care by purchasing a plan from an MCO, the MCO is the one responsible for negotiating with providers. HMOs typically use capitation arrangements to pay providers. Under *capitation*, a negotiated fixed amount per enrollee is paid each month to the provider. This fixed amount is commonly referred to as the per-member-per-month rate. Risk is shared between the HMO and the provider who receives the per-member-per-month rate because in exchange for this payment the provider is obligated to deliver whatever contracted services the enrollees might need. PPOs commonly pay the providers a discounted fee that has been negotiated between the PPO and the provider. Providers are willing to discount their services in exchange for being included in the PPO's network and being guaranteed a patient population. As insurers, health plans must make actuarial projections of the expected cost of healthcare utilization. They bear the risk that the cost of services delivered could exceed the premiums collected. By underwriting this risk, a plan assumes the role of insurer.

The Military and Veterans Systems

The military medical care system is available free of charge to active-duty military personnel. It is a well-organized and highly integrated system operated by the U.S. Department of Defense. Comprehensive services cover prevention as well as treatments provided by salaried healthcare personnel. Routine ambulatory care is often available at a dispensary, sick bay, first-aid station, or medical station located close to the military personnel's workplace. Routine hospital services are provided in dispensaries located in military bases, in sick bays aboard ships, or in small base hospitals. Complicated hospital services are provided in regional military hospitals. Dependents of service members, retirees and their dependents, and survivors of deceased members can receive medical care through an insurance program called TriCare. This program permits the beneficiaries to receive care from military as well as private medical care facilities. Although patients have little choice regarding how services are provided, in general, the military medical care system provides high-quality health care.

War veterans are entitled to receive a wide array of medical and long-term care services through facilities operated by the VA. The VA system provides a broad spectrum of medical, surgical, and rehabilitative care. It is one of the largest and one of the oldest formally organized healthcare systems in the world. The VA, predecessor to the current Department of Veterans Affairs, was established in 1930. In addition to medical care, its mission includes education, training, research, and contingency support and emergency management for the Department of Defense medical care system. The VA system operates 155 medical centers, with at least one located in each state, Puerto Rico, and the District of Columbia. VA facilities also include 1,400 sites of care (outpatient clinics, nursing homes, rehabilitation centers, etc.). In 2006, almost 5.5 million people received care in VA facilities. The VA delivery system is organized under 21 geographically distributed Veterans Integrated Service Networks. Healthcare spending for 2007 is projected to be approximately $35 billion.[20]

The System for Vulnerable Populations

In 1965, the U.S. Congress passed two major amendments to the Social Security Act that created the Medicare and Medicaid programs, and the government assumed direct responsibility to pay for some of the health care on behalf of two vulnerable population groups—the older and the poor.[21] Medicaid and Medicare are prime representations of the public sector in the amalgam of private and public approaches for providing access to health care in the United States. Originally created for older persons, the Medicare program now covers nearly 43 million Americans that also include low-income disabled individuals below the age of 65 and people who have end-stage renal disease. The Medicaid program finances healthcare services for the indigent who have to qualify based on assets and income, which must be below the threshold levels established by each state. The program serves nearly 45 million poor Americans. In 1997, the SCHIP was enacted to provide health insurance to children living in low-income families that did not qualify for Medicaid. Of the 77 million children in the United States, about 45% are enrolled in either Medicaid or SCHIP. In the three main public programs, the government finances the insurance, but healthcare services are received mainly through private providers. Medicaid and SCHIP enrollees incur little out-of-pocket costs, but Medicare is estimated to pay for approximately half of an average enrollee's healthcare costs. This is mainly due to high deductibles, co-payments, and certain noncovered services such as dental services, vision care, hearing aids, and gaps in prescription drug coverage that was added to the program in 2005. Poor enrollees can qualify for both Medicaid and Medicare, in which case Medicaid pays for the gaps in Medicare coverage. Most others purchase private health insurance called Medigap to pay for noncovered Medicare expenses.

Other vulnerable populations, particularly the uninsured, those of minority and immigrant status, and those living in geographically or economically disadvantaged communities, receive care from safety-net providers that include community health centers, physicians' offices, hospital outpatient departments, and emergency rooms, of which community health centers are expressly designed for the underserved. Consistent with their unique role and mission, safety-net providers offer comprehensive medical and enabling services (e.g., language interpretation, transportation, outreach, and nutrition and social support services) targeted to the needs of vulnerable populations.

For over 40 years, federally funded health centers have provided primary and preventive health services to rural and urban underserved populations. The Bureau of Primary Health Care within the Department of Health and Human Services, Health Resources and Services Administration provides federal support for community-based health centers that include programs for migrant and seasonal farm workers and their families, homeless persons, public housing residents, and school-age children. In addition to essential primary care and preventives services, health centers provide enabling services such as case management, transportation, health education, language translation, and childcare. These services facilitate regular access to care for predominantly minority, low-income, uninsured, and Medicaid patients. By the end of calendar year 2006, the nationwide network of 1,000 reporting health centers delivered essential primary and preventive care at more than 4,000 sites serving 15 million users or more than 30% of the nation's 50 million underserved persons.[22] Health centers have contributed to significantly improved health outcomes for the uninsured and Medicaid populations and reduced disparities in health care and health status across socioeconomic and racial/ethnic groups.[23,24]

America's safety net, however, is by no means secure, and the availability of safety-net providers varies from community to community. Vulnerable populations residing in communities without safety-net providers have to forgo care or seek care from hospital emergency rooms if such services are available in the areas where they live. Safety-net providers face enormous demand pressures particularly in communities that may have an increasing number of uninsured and poor. The inability to shift costs for uncompensated care onto private insurance has become a significant problem because revenues from Medicaid, the primary source of third-party financing for core safety-net providers, are inadequate because of funding constraints.

The Indian Health System

American Indians and Alaska Natives (Native Americans) are the only ethnic group for which the federal government has taken direct responsibility for health care. Also, as citizens of the United States, Native Americans are eligible to participate in all public, private, and state health programs available to the general population. The Indian Health Service (IHS), an agency of the federal government, is the principal healthcare provider and health advocate for Native Americans. The agency provides health services to approximately 1.9 million Native Americans who belong to more than 562 federally recognized tribes in 35 states. The policy of self-determination underlies healthcare services for Native Americans. Accordingly, the tribes have three options for receiving health care: (1) directly from the IHS, (2) through contracting with the IHS to have the administrative control, operation, and funding for health programs transferred to American Indian and Alaska Native tribal governments, or (3) through compacting with the IHS and assuming even greater control and autonomy for the provision of their own healthcare services. The IHS operates 46 hospitals and over 600 health centers, clinics, and health stations.[25]

Integrated Delivery Systems

An integrated delivery system (IDS) may be defined as a network of organizations that provides or arranges to provide a coordinated continuum of services to a defined population and is willing to be held clinically and fiscally accountable for the outcomes and health status of the population. For over a decade now, organizational integration to form IDSs has been the hallmark of the U.S. healthcare industry. Integration in the U.S. healthcare delivery system has occurred in response to cost pressures, development of new alternatives for the delivery of health care, the growing power of MCOs, and the need to provide services more efficiently to populations spread over large geographic areas. An IDS represents various forms of ownership and other strategic linkages among major participants such as hospitals, physicians, and insurers. The objective is to achieve greater integration of healthcare services along the continuum of care.

EVALUATION OF THE HEALTHCARE SYSTEM

The healthcare system of a nation is influenced by external factors including the political climate, economic development, technological progress, social and cultural values, the physical environment, and population characteristics such as demographic and health trends. The combined interaction of these forces influences the course of healthcare delivery in the United States. In the following sections, we summarize the basic characteristics that differentiate the U.S. healthcare delivery system from that of other countries.

No Central Governing Agency and Little Integration and Coordination

The U.S. healthcare system provides a conspicuous contrast to the healthcare systems of other developed countries. The centrally controlled, universal healthcare systems of most developed countries authorize financing and delivery of health care for all residents. The U.S. system is not centrally controlled and has a very complex structure of financing, insurance, delivery, and payment mechanisms. Private financing, which is predominantly through employers, accounts for approximately 54% of total healthcare expenditures; the government finances the remaining 46%.

The main characteristics of U.S. healthcare system are as follows:

- No central governing agency and little integration and coordination
- A technology-driven delivery system focusing on acute care
- High on cost, unequal in access, and average on outcome
- Delivery of health care is under imperfect market conditions
- Government as subsidiary to the private sector
- Market justice versus social justice pervasive throughout health care
- Multiple players and balance of power
- Quest for integration and accountability

The less complex structure of a centrally controlled healthcare system improves efficiency by managing total expenditures through global budgets and by governing the availability and utilization of services through central planning. Because the United States has such a large private system of financing, insurance, and delivery, the majority of insurers as well as providers are private businesses, independent of the government. Nevertheless, the federal and state governments play an important role in healthcare delivery. They finance healthcare services for publicly insured patients, such as those covered under Medicare and Medicaid. They also determine public sector expenditures and establish reimbursement rates for services delivered to Medicare and Medicaid patients. The government uses various payment mechanisms for providers. Currently, almost all inpatient and home healthcare services delivered to Medicare and Medicaid patients are reimbursed according to a variety of prospective payment methods. Physician reimbursement rates are derived using complex formulas that take into account factors such as time, skill, and intensity of physician work. Beginning in 1983, a gradual departure occurred from the previous cost-based reimbursement methods. The government also formulates standards of participation through health policy and regulation and requires providers to comply with the standards and receive federal certification in order to deliver care to Medicare and Medicaid patients. Certification standards are also regarded as minimum standards of quality in most sectors of the healthcare industry.

The insurance and delivery functions are separated in the main government programs (Medicare, Medicaid, and SCHIP) because the government insures, but services are delivered through the private sector. Even in the military and VA systems, some services are contracted through the private sector.

A Technology-Driven Delivery System Focusing on Acute Care

The United States has been the hotbed of research and innovation in new medical technology. Because of its cost implications, almost all nations try to limit the diffusion and utilization of technology through central planning and control. Lack of such controls in the United States promotes innovation, rapid diffusion, and utilization of new technology. Growth in science and technology often creates demand for new services despite shrinking resources to finance sophisticated care. Other factors contribute to increased demand in expensive technological care: Patients assume that the latest innovations offer the highest quality, physicians want to try the latest gadgets, and competition among hospitals is often driven by the acquisition of technology. After organizations acquire new equipment and facilities, they are often under pressure to recoup the capital investments. Legal risks for providers and health plans alike may also play a role in discouraging denial of new technology.

Although technology has ushered in a new generation of successful interventions, the negative outcomes resulting from its overuse are many. For example, the expense of highly technical interventions increases insurance payments to providers. Insurance premiums rise, and it becomes more difficult for employers to expand coverage. Broad exposure to technology early in medical training affects not only clinical preferences but also future professional behavior and practice patterns. Because medical specialization revolves around technology, an oversupply of specialists in the United States has compounded the rate of technology diffusion. In this technology-driven environment, the healthcare system suffers from inadequate resources and mechanisms to address the growing needs of people with chronic conditions and co-morbidities. Given the rising number of older persons in the U.S. population, the system that is primarily driven by the acute-care model will be overburdened unless appropriate steps are taken to shift resources from acute to chronic care.

High Cost, Unequal Access, and Mixed Outcomes

Although data on healthcare spending in various countries are not always comparable because of differences in accounting for the expenditures, experts generally agree that compared with any other developed country in the world, United States spends the most. For example, in 2006, U.S. healthcare spending was $7,026 per capita, or 16% of the GDP.[26] The average annual healthcare cost inflation between 2000 and 2006 was 7.6% compared with an average annual increase of 5.0% in the nation's GDP. High cost of health care has ramifications for the expansion of health insurance to the uninsured, the long-term solvency of publicly financed programs, and other issues of equity and health disparities that remain unaddressed.

Access means the ability of an individual to obtain healthcare services when needed. In the United States, access is restricted to (1) those who have health insurance through their employers, (2) those covered under a government healthcare program, (3) those who can afford to buy insurance out of their own private funds, and (4) those who are able to pay for services privately. Health insurance is the primary means for ensuring access, although some uninsured Americans receive care through the safety net. In early 2005, 41.7 million Americans of all ages (14.4% of the population) were uninsured—that is, they were not covered under a private or public health insurance program.[27]

For consistent, basic, and routine primary care, the uninsured are unable to see a physician unless they can pay the physician's fees. Those who cannot afford to pay generally wait until health problems develop, at which point they may be able to receive services free of charge in a hospital emergency department. The Emergency Medical Treatment and Labor Act of 1986 requires screening and evaluation of every patient, necessary stabilizing treatment, and admitting when necessary, regardless of ability to pay. Uninsured Americans therefore are able to obtain medical care for acute illness. Hence, one can say that the United States does have a form of universal catastrophic health insurance even for the uninsured.[28]

It is well acknowledged that absence of insurance inhibits the patients' ability to receive well-directed, coordinated, and continuous health care through access to primary care services and, when needed, referral to specialty services. Experts generally believe that inadequate access to basic and routine primary care services is the main reason that the United States, in spite of being the most economically advanced country, lags behind other developed nations in measures of population health such as infant mortality and overall life expectancy. This belief, however, remains largely unsubstantiated, mainly in view of the fact that health status of a population is based on many factors that include individual lifestyles and behaviors.

Delivery of Health Care Under Imperfect Market Conditions

Under national healthcare programs, patients have varying degrees of choice in selecting their providers; however, true economic market forces are virtually nonexistent. In the United States, even though the delivery of services is largely in private hands, health care is only partially governed by free market forces. The delivery and consumption of health care in the United States do not quite meet the basic tests of a free market, as described later here. Hence, the system is best described as a quasimarket or an imperfect market. These are some key features characterizing free markets:

In a free market, multiple patients (buyers) and providers (sellers) act independently. In a free market, patients should be able to choose their provider based on price and quality of services. If it were this simple, patient choice would determine prices by the unencumbered interaction of supply and demand. Theoretically at least, prices are negotiated between payers and providers; however, in many instances, the payer is not the patient but a managed care organization, Medicare, or Medicaid. Because prices are set by agencies external to the market, they are not freely governed by the forces of supply and demand.

For the healthcare market to be free, unrestrained competition must occur among providers on the basis of price and quality. Generally speaking, free competition exists among healthcare providers in the United States. The consolidation of buying power into the hands of private health plans, however, has forced providers to form alliances and integrated delivery systems on the supply side. In certain geographic sectors of the country, a single giant medical system has taken over as the sole provider of major healthcare services, restricting competition. As the healthcare system continues to move in this direction, it appears that only in large metropolitan areas will there be more than one large integrated system competing to get the business of the health plans.

A free market requires that patients have information about service options. Free markets operate best when consumers are educated about the products they are using. Patients, however, are not always well informed about the decisions that need to be made regarding their care. Choices involving sophisticated technology, diagnostic methods, interventions, and pharmaceuticals can be difficult and often require physician input. Acting as advocates, primary care providers can reduce this information gap for patients. Recently, healthcare consumers have taken more initiative to educate themselves using Internet resources for gathering medical information. Pharmaceutical product advertising is also having an impact on consumer expectations and increasing awareness of available medications.

In a free market, patients have information on price and quality for each provider. Current pricing methods for healthcare services further confound free market mechanisms. Hidden costs make it difficult for patients to gauge the full expense of services ahead of time. Item-based pricing, for example, refers to the costs of adjunct services that often accompany major procedures such as surgery. Patients are usually informed of the surgery's cost ahead of time but cannot anticipate the cost of anesthesiologists and pathologists or hospital supplies and

facilities, thus making it extremely difficult to ascertain the total price before services have actually been received. Package pricing and capitated fees can help overcome these drawbacks by providing a bundled fee for a package of related services. Package pricing covers services bundled together for one episode, which is less encompassing than capitation. Capitation covers all services an enrollee may need during an entire year.

In recent years, care quality has received much attention. Performance rating of health plans has met with some success; however, apart from sporadic news stories, the public generally has scant information on the quality of healthcare providers.

In a free market, patients must directly bear the cost of services received. The purpose of insurance is to protect against the risk of unforeseen catastrophic events. Because the fundamental purpose of insurance is to meet major expenses when unlikely events occur, having insurance for basic and routine health care undermines the principle of insurance. Health insurance coverage for minor services, such as colds, coughs, and earaches, amounts to prepayment for such services. There is a moral hazard that after enrollees have purchased health insurance they will use healthcare services to a greater extent than if they had to pay for such services themselves. Even certain referrals to higher-level services may be forgone if the patient has to bear the full cost of these services.

Moral hazard can be contained by a new type of health insurance arrangement that seems to be gaining some initial momentum. Under certain qualifying conditions, individuals can have a Health Savings Account (HSA), which is a tax-sheltered trust account that the individual owns for the purpose of paying qualified medical expenses. The HSA account works in conjunction with a high-deductible health plan. In order to have an HSA, the individual must enroll in an high-deductible health plan. Healthcare expenses are paid out of the HSA. Insurance kicks in once the annual deductible is met. The minimum annual deductibles for 2007 were $1,100 for an individual plan and $2,200 for a family plan.

In a free market for health care, patients as consumers make decisions about the purchase of healthcare services. In addition to the factors discussed earlier, at least two more factors limit the ability of patients to make decisions. First, decisions about the utilization of health care are often determined by need rather than price-based demand. Need has generally been defined as the amount of medical care that medical experts believe a person should have to remain or become healthy.[29] Second, the delivery of health care can result in demand creation. This follows from self-assessed need, which when coupled with moral hazard leads to greater utilization. This creates an artificial demand because prices are not taken into consideration. Practitioners who have a financial interest in additional treatments also create artificial demand,[30] commonly referred to as provider-induced demand.

Government as Subsidiary to the Private Sector

In most other developed countries, the government plays a central role in the provision of health care. In the United States, the private sector plays the dominant role. This can be explained to some degree by the American tradition of reliance on individual responsibility and a commitment to limiting the power of the national government. As a result, government spending for health care has been largely confined to filling in the gaps left open by the private sector. These gaps include environmental protection, support for research and training, and care of vulnerable populations.

Market Justice Versus Social Justice Pervasive Throughout Health Care

Market justice and social justice are two contrasting theories that govern the production and distribution of healthcare services in the United States. The principle of market justice ascribes the fair distribution of health care to the market forces in a free economy. Medical care and its benefits are distributed on the basis of people's willingness and ability to pay.[31] In contrast, social justice emphasizes the well-being of the community over that of the individual; thus, the inability to obtain medical services because of a lack of financial resources would be considered unjust. A just distribution of benefits must be based on need, not simply one's ability to purchase it in the marketplace. In a partial public and private healthcare system, the two theories often operate side by side; however, market justice principles tend to prevail. Unfortunately, market justice results in the unequal allocation of healthcare services, neglecting critical human concerns that are not confined to the individual but have broader negative impacts on society.

Multiple Players and Balance of Power

The U.S. healthcare system involves multiple players. The key players in the system have been physicians, administrators of health service institutions, insurance companies, large employers, and the government. Big business, labor, MCOs, insurance companies, physicians, and hospitals make up the powerful and politically active special interest groups represented before lawmakers by high-priced lobbyists. Each player has a different economic interest to protect. The problem is that the self-interests of each player are often at odds. For example, providers seek to maximize government reimbursement for services delivered to Medicare and Medicaid patients, but the government wants to contain cost increases. The fragmented self-interests of the various players produce countervailing forces within the system. One positive effect of these opposing forces is that they prevent any single entity from dominating the system. In an environment that is rife with motivations to protect conflicting self-interests, achieving comprehensive system-wide reforms is next to impossible, and cost-containment remains a major challenge. Consequently, the approach to healthcare reform in the United States is characterized as incremental or piecemeal.

Quest for Integration and Accountability

The use of primary care as the organizing hub for continuous and coordinated health services was recognized in the United States. It was envisioned that through primary care other healthcare services would be integrated in a seamless fashion. Although this model gained popularity with the expansion of managed care, its development stalled before it could reach its full potential. The large-scale transition of healthcare delivery to the managed care system in the 1990s was met with widespread criticism, which turned into a backlash from consumers, physicians, and legislators. As a result, various compromises were reached. The HMO model that was based on primary care and gatekeeping became less popular than was initially foreseen by its proponents. A compromised PPO model has become dominant in U.S. healthcare delivery; however, current political debates seem to recognize the need for a primary care–based model of healthcare delivery. The model also emphasizes the importance of the patient–provider relationship and how it can best function to improve the health of each individual; however, such a system would fall short of meeting any population-wide objectives without universal access to basic health care. In 2007, the state of Massachusetts implemented a program that promises to achieve nearly universal health coverage in the state. Under legal penalties, the program calls for all residents to obtain health insurance and for all employers to offer a basic insurance plan that workers can buy with pretax dollars. Government subsidies will be made available to low-income individuals to buy insurance; the indigent will have their premiums paid by the state. A central clearinghouse will broker the purchase of insurance and will establish rules and procedures. Naturally, other states will be closely observing whether the Massachusetts plan can deliver universal access within reasonable cost parameters.

Integral to the relationship between patients and providers is the concept of accountability. For providers, accountability means delivery of care that is efficient, ethical, and of a high quality. From the patient's standpoint, it means taking individual responsibility to safeguard one's own health and to use available resources sensibly.

CONCLUSION

The United States does not have a well-integrated healthcare delivery system for all citizens. Instead, there are multiple subsystems developed either through market forces or through public initiatives to address the needs of certain population segments. The subsystems include managed care, the military and VA systems, the system for vulnerable populations, and the emerging integrated delivery system. The basic features that characterize the unique healthcare delivery system in the United States include the absence of a central agency to govern the system, little integration and coordination, a technology-driven delivery system focusing on acute care, a costly system that produces unequal access and average outcomes, delivery of health care under imperfect market conditions, government as subsidiary to the private sector, the conflict between market justice and social justice, multiple players and balance of power, and quest for integration and accountability.

REFERENCES

1. Shi L, Singh DA. *Delivering Health Care in America: A Systems Approach*, 4th ed. Sudbury, MA: Jones and Bartlett Publishers, Inc.; 2008, p. 649.
2. Shi L, Singh DA. *Essentials of the US Health Care System.* Sudbury, MA: Jones and Bartlett Publishers, Inc.; 2005.
3. Bedford HF, Colbourn T. *The Americans: A Brief History to 1877*, part 1. New York: Harcourt Brace Jovanovich, Inc.; 1972.
4. Konstam A. *Historical Atlas of Exploration: 1492–1600.* New York: Checkmark Books; 2000.
5. Bryant WC, Gay SH, Brooks N. *Scribner's Popular History of the United States.* New York: Charles Scribner's Sons; 1897.
6. Bradley HW. *The United States 1492–1877.* New York: Charles Scribner's Sons; 1972.
7. Karlen HM. *The Pattern of American Government*, 2nd ed. Beverly Hills, CA: Glencoe Press; 1975.
8. U.S. Census Bureau. *Statistical Abstract of the United States: 2008.* Washington, DC: General Printing Office; 2008.
9. U.S. Census Bureau. State and County QuickFacts, January 2008. Retrieved May 6, 2008, from http://quickfacts.census.gov/qfd/states/38000.html.
10. Sidlow E, Henschen B. *America at Odds: An Introduction to American Government*, 2nd ed. Belmont, CA: Wadsworth, a Division of Thomson Learning, Inc.; 2000.
11. Gosling JJ. *Economics, Politics, and American Public Policy.* Armonk, NY: ME Sharpe; 2008.
12. U.S. Census Bureau. Income, Earnings, and Poverty Data from the 2006 American Community Survey. Washington, DC: U.S. Census Bureau; 2007. Retrieved March 19, 2008, from http://www.census.gov/prod/2007pubs/acs-08.pdf.
13. Social Security Administration. *The 2007 Annual Report of the Board of Trustees of the Federal Old-Age and Survivors Insurance and Federal Disability Insurance Trust Funds.* Washington, DC: U.S. Government Printing Office; 2007.
14. Kung HC, Hoyert DL, Xu J, Murphy SL. *Deaths: Final Data for 2005. National Vital Statistics Reports*; vol. 56, no. 10. Hyattsville, MD: National Center for Health Statistics; 2008.
15. DeNavas-Walt C, Proctor BD, Smith J. *Income, Poverty, and Health Insurance Coverage in the United States: 2006.* Washington, DC: U.S. Government Printing Office; 2007.
16. Jolliffe D. Rural Poverty at a Glance. Rural Development Research Report No. (RDRR-100), July 2004. Retrieved May 7, 2008, from http://www.ers.usda.gov/publications/rdrr100.
17. Central Intelligence Agency. 2008. The 2008 World Factbook. Retrieved August 20, 2008, from https://www.cia.gov/library/publications/the-world-factbook/index.html.
18. National Center for Health Statistics. *Health, United States, 2007.* Hyattsville, MD: U.S. Department of Health and Human Services; 2007.
19. American Medical Association. 2007. 2005 data published by the US Department of Labor, Bureau of Labor Statistics. Retrieved May 4, 2008, from http://www.bls.gov/oco/ocos074.htm.
20. Department of Veterans Affairs. *Fact sheet: Facts about the Department of Veterans Affairs.* Washington, DC: VA Office of Public Affairs; 2007.
21. Potter MA, Longest BB. The divergence of federal and state policies on the charitable tax exemption of nonprofit hospitals. *Journal of Health Politics, Policy and Law.* 1994;19(2): 393–419.
22. Bureau of Primary Health Care. *BPHC-UDS Annual Report.* Washington, DC: BPHC; 2007.
23. Politzer RM, Schempf AH, Shi L, Starfield B. The future role of health centers in improving national health. *Journal of Public Health Policy.* 2003;24(3):296–306.
24. Shi L, Politzer R, Regan J, Lewis-Idema D, Falik M. The impact of managed care on vulnerable populations served by

community health centers. *Journal of Ambulatory Care Management.* 2001;24(1):51–66.

25. Indian Health Service. IHS Fact Sheets, January 2008. Retrieved May 4, 2008, from http://info.ihs.gov/Profile08.asp.

26. Catlin A, Cowan C, Hartman M, et al. National health spending in 2006: a year of change for prescription drugs. *Health Affairs.* 2008;27:14–29.

27. Cohen RA, Martinez ME. Health insurance coverage: Estimates from the National Health Interview Survey, January–March 2005. Retrieved from http://www.cdc.gov/nchs/nhis.htm.

28. Altman SH, Reinhardt UE. Introduction: where does health care reform go from here? An uncharted odyssey. In Altman SH, Reinhardt UE, eds. *Strategic Choices for a Changing Health Care System* (xxi–xxxii). Chicago: Health Administration Press.

29. Feldstein PJ. *Health Care Economics*, 4th ed. New York: Delmar Publishing; 1993.

30. Hemenway D, Fallon D. Testing for physician-induced demand with hypothetical cases. *Medical Care.* 1985;23(4): 344–349.

31. Santerre RE, Neun SP. *Health Economics: Theories, Insights, and Industry Studies.* Chicago: Irwin; 1996.

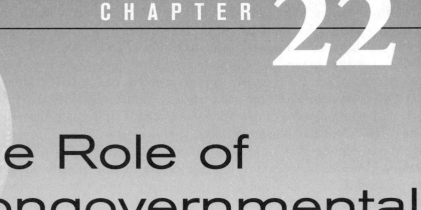

CHAPTER 22

The Role of Nongovernmental Organizations in Global Health

Matthew W. Walker, James Allen Johnson III, and Gerald R. Ledlow

INTRODUCTION

Nongovernmental organizations (NGOs) serve in a wide and varied spectrum of advocacy and operations around the globe. From locally based groups meeting in private homes to global giants with budgets in the hundreds of millions of dollars, NGOs throughout the world make significant contributions nationally and internationally based on their unique missions. By definition, NGOs are independent from government influence, and therefore, they are often in a unique position to address issues that governments are unable or unwilling to address effectively. NGOs provide leadership and resources for producing and advocating public policy and operate in spheres where government officials are constrained by bureaucratic or political considerations. According to a 1997 United Nations (UN) working paper, the strength of NGOs lies in their "proximity to their members or clients, the flexibility and the high degree of people's involvement and participation in their activities, which leads to strong commitments, appropriateness of solutions and high acceptance of decisions implemented."[1]

The Duke University Directory of Development Organizations lists 51,500 very diverse organizations.[2] Al-though this number may seem high, it is small in comparison to the amount of resources controlled and distributed by these organizations. The biggest of them, World Vision, had annual expenses for 2007 of over $977 million USD,[3] greater than the gross domestic product (GDP) of the nation of St. Lucia in the same year ($958 million) and as much as 20 times the GDP of some of the smallest countries in the world.[4] Based on firm financial growth, several NGOs are large and continue to expand in both funding and mission. Today, NGOs in Africa manage nearly $3.5 billion in external aid compared with slightly less than $1 billion in 1990.[5]

NGOs AND THE UN

NGOs are part of a spectrum of international organizations that include foundations, development banks, UN agencies, bilateral agencies, and International Government Organizations like the World Health Organization (WHO). Having participated in the work of the UN from its inception, NGOs first took a role in formal UN deliberations through the Economic and Social Council in 1946. Initially, 41 NGOs were granted consultative status by the council, and by 1992, more than 700 NGOs had attained that level of credibility. The number has been steadily increasing ever since, and today, 3,052 NGOs have been granted consultative status by the UN.[6]

Many UN agencies routinely consider reports from NGOs, alongside official reports from governments, when considering policy or operational revisions.[7] During a 2007 workshop organized by the UN, Renee van de Weert, United Nations Children Fund (UNICEF) senior adviser on child survival, highlighted the important role of NGOs as local whistle-blowers in emergency situations. Giving examples of how NGOs successfully drew media attention to the issue of child soldiers in the Democratic Republic of Congo, van de Weert also recognized the role of the French NGO, Action contre la Faim, in raising awareness about malnutrition in Darfur and mobilizing UNICEF in the region.[8]

The UN itself provides aid through its many humanitarian branches. The largest of which include the World Food Program, whose projects benefited 24.3 million people in 2006,[9] and the United Nations Development Program, which is currently on the ground in over 166 countries.[10] Other UN humanitarian branches include the High Commission for Refugees, with projects in over 110 countries,[11] and UNICEF, which aids children in 190 countries.[12] Also, agencies of the UN, such as the WHO and UNAIDS, are world leaders in the monitoring and prevention of disease. The UN sponsors a variety of other human development programs and agencies, including

- FAO—Food and Agriculture Organization
- ILO—International Labor Organization
- IPCC—International Panel on Climate Change
- IAEA—International Atomic Energy Agency
- UNEP—United Nations Environmental Program
- UNFPA—United Nations Population Fund
- OHCHR—Office of the United Nations High Commissioner for Human Rights
- UNHRC—United Nations Human Rights Council
- UN-HABITAT—United Nations Human Settlements Program

WHAT IS AN NGO?

Although the importance of NGOs in terms of health and development is clear, the term *NGO* remains vaguely defined. The Duke University Library, which has accumulated the most encompassing directory of NGOs available today, defines NGOs as "legal entities created by private individuals, private organizations, publicly traded organizations, or in some combination where governmental influence, supervision and management are removed, or at least greatly minimized, from the NGO's strategic and operational mission."[13] According to Peter Willetts, a professor at City University in London, the term "nongovernmental organization" or NGO, came into currency in 1945 because of the need for the UN to differentiate in its charter between participation rights for intergovernmental specialized agencies and those for international private organizations. At the UN, virtually all types of private bodies can be recognized as NGOs. They only have to be independent from government control, not seeking to challenge governments either as a political party or by a narrow focus on human rights, nonprofit making and noncriminal."[14] The definition generally used by the Peace Corps to define an NGO is "a specific type of organization that is not part of government and that possesses the following four characteristics:

- Works with people to help them improve their social and economic situations and prospects
- Was formed voluntarily
- Is independent, controlled by those who have formed it or by management boards representing the organization's stakeholders
- Is not for profit; although NGOs engage in revenue-generating activities, the proceeds are used in pursuit of the organization's aims"[15]

CLASSIFYING NGOs

Nationally and internationally, the broad range of NGOs has become so expansive that the establishment of a single classification system is exceedingly difficult. The World Bank classifies NGOs into two categories *operational* and *advocacy*.[16] According to the WHO definition, the primary purpose of an operational NGO is the design and implementation of development-related projects, as opposed to advocacy NGOs, which assert a primary purpose to defend or promote a specific cause. NGOs can be further classified as being either relief oriented or development oriented by the development status of the countries in which they work, by the nature of their work, whether they are faith based or secular or any combination of the above. Because of this seemingly unending variation, a long list of acronyms has been developed in order to aid in the classification of NGOs. Some examples of these include the following:

- FONGOS—Funder-Organized NGOs
- RINGO—Religious International NGO
- PVO—Private Voluntary Organization
- CBO—Community-Based Organization
- CSO—Civil Society Organization
- BONGO—Business-Organized NGOs
- TANGO—Technical Assistance NGO

A Look at Some of the Largest International NGOs

The following section summarized the NGO "Global Giants," who have hundreds, even thousands, of employees, and budgets in the hundreds of millions of dollars. The short list later here represents some of the biggest and most established NGOs working in the world today.

CARE

Founded in 1945 to provide relief to World War II survivors, CARE is committed to promoting social change and ending global poverty in over 60 countries. A leading humanitarian organization fighting global poverty, CARE believes that women are essential in regard to helping families and entire communities escape poverty. Women are at the heart of CARE's community-based efforts to improve basic education, prevent the spread of HIV, increase access to clean water and sanitation, expand economic opportunity, and protect natural resources. CARE also delivers emergency aid to survivors of war and natural disasters.[17]

Carter Center

The Carter Center was founded in 1982 by former U.S. president Jimmy Carter and former first lady Rosalynn Carter. The Carter Center has helped to improve the quality of life for people in over 70 countries worldwide. Led by the Carters and an independent board of trustees, the center seeks to prevent and resolve conflicts, enhance freedom and democracy, and improve health. The Carter Center is guided by a fundamental commitment to human rights and the alleviation of human suffering by both engaging with those at the highest levels of government and working side by side with poor and often forgotten people.[18]

Catholic Relief Services

Founded in 1943 under the name War Relief Services, Catholic Relief Services (CRS) changed its name officially in 1955. Providing assistance to 80 million people in more than 100 countries and territories throughout the world, CRS approaches emergency relief and long-term development holistically, ensuring that all people, especially the poorest and most vulnerable, are able to participate in the very fullness of life—to have access to basic necessities, health care, and education—all within peaceful, just communities. To achieve this, CRS focuses on six key areas of service: emergencies, hunger, education, health, peace, and helping at home.[19]

Center for Gender and Health Equity

The Center for Gender and Health Equity (CHANGE) was founded in 1994 as an advocacy NGO, focused on the effects of U.S. international policies on the health and rights of women, girls, and other vulnerable populations throughout the world. CHANGE's overarching goal is to ensure that U.S. international policies and programs promote sexual and reproductive rights and health through effective, evidence-based approaches to prevention and treatment of critical reproductive and sexual health concerns, and through increased funding for critical programs.[20]

Christian Children's Fund

Established by a Presbyterian minister in 1938 to aid Chinese orphans during the Sino-Japanese War, the Christian Children's Fund (CCF) assists more than 13.2 million children and family members in 31 countries, regardless of race, creed, or gender. Within the context of alleviating child poverty, vulnerability, and deprivation, the CCF creates programs in a variety of different areas that provide practical assistance to impoverished communities and plant the seeds of self-sufficiency. CCF's integrated development model is made up of interventions in six primary sectors: early child development, health and sanitation, education, nutrition, sustainable livelihoods, and emergency and disaster relief.[21]

Episcopal Relief and Development

Originally the Presiding Bishop's Fund for World Relief, the Episcopal Relief and Development (ERD) was founded in 1940 to assist refugees fleeing Europe during World War II. In 2000, the organization's name was officially changed to ERD. ERD has served the needs of the poor and oppressed in over 100 countries worldwide by working with Anglican and Episcopal partners to provide emergency assistance, such as food, water, and shelter, in times of disaster. The ERD addresses the United Nation's Millennium Development Goals through their food security and primary health programs and offers long-term solutions to help people sustain safer, healthier, and more productive lives.[22]

Human Rights Watch

The largest human rights organization based in the United States, Human Rights Watch, conducts fact-finding investigations into human rights abuses in all regions of the world. Founded in 1978 as Helsinki Watch to monitor human rights in the Soviet bloc countries, Human Rights Watch publishes dozens of books and reports every year, generating extensive coverage in local and international media. Human Rights Watch also meets with government officials to urge changes in policy and practice. In extreme circumstances, Human Rights Watch presses for the withdrawal of military and economic support from governments that egregiously violate the rights of their people.[23]

International Committee of the Red Cross

With its headquarters in Geneva, Switzerland, the International Committee of the Red Cross (ICRC) was founded in 1863 to protect the lives and dignity of victims of war and internal violence and to provide them with assistance. Today, the ICRC is based in around 80 countries and has a total of more than 12,000 staff. An impartial, neutral, and independent organization, the ICRC directs and coordinates international relief activities and endeavors to prevent suffering by promoting and strengthening humanitarian law and universal humanitarian principles.[24]

Médecins Sans Frontières/Doctors Without Boarders

Médecins Sans Frontières (MSF) is an independent humanitarian medical aid agency that is committed to two objectives: providing medical aid wherever needed, regardless of race, religion, politics, or gender, and raising awareness of the plight of the people they help. Founded in 1971, MSF has 19 country offices and provides emergency medical aid in nearly 60 countries. MSF teams are comprised of doctors, nurses, and other professionals, medical and nonmedical, working alongside locally hired staff.[25]

Oxfam International

The name "Oxfam" comes from the British group Oxford Committee for Famine Relief founded in 1942 during World War II. Oxfam International is a confederation of 13 independent NGOs working with over 3,000 partners in over 100 countries with the common goal of ending global poverty and related injustice. Oxfam works with communities, allies, and partner organizations, undertaking long-term development, emergency work, and research and campaigning for a fairer world. Oxfam works on a broad range of issues, including trade, conflict, debt and aid, and education.[26]

Partners in Health

Founded by Dr. Paul Farmer in 1987 to deliver health care to the poorest areas of Haiti, Partners in Health's (PIH) headquarters is located in Boston, Massachusetts. Today, PIH has programs in nine countries on four continents. With a mission to provide a preferential option for the poor in health care, PIH works globally to bring the benefits of modern science to those most in need through service delivery, training, research, and advocacy.[27]

Pathfinder International

Officially established in 1957 as the Pathfinder Fund, Pathfinder International provides women, men, and adolescents throughout the developing world with access to quality family planning and reproductive health information and services. Pathfinder works to halt the spread of HIV/AIDS, to provide care to women suffering from the complications of unsafe abortions, and to advocate for sound reproductive health policies in the United States and abroad.[28]

Relief International

Relief International (RI) currently works in 15 countries, predominantly in the Middle East and Africa, as a humanitarian nonprofit agency that provides emergency relief, rehabilitation, development assistance, and program services to vulnerable communities. RI is solely dedicated to reducing human suffering and is nonpolitical and nonsectarian in its mission.[29]

Rotary Club International

Formed in 1905 as a service club in Chicago, the Rotary name derived from the early practice of rotating meetings among members' offices. Dedicated to its motto, "Service Above Self," the Rotary's popularity spread rapidly; by 1921, Rotary clubs had been formed on six continents, and the organization adopted the name Rotary

International a year later. In 1985, Rotary members made a commitment to immunize the world's children against polio and teamed up with the WHO, UNICEF, and the Centers for Disease Control (CDC) to become a spearheading partner in the Global Polio Eradication Initiative. Thanks to Rotary and its partners, more than 5 million instances of childhood paralysis and 250,000 deaths have been prevented worldwide.[30]

Salvation Army International

Although the Christian-based movement that led to the Salvation Army started in 1865, the Salvation Army as an organization was founded in 1878. With its international headquarters located in London, England, the Salvation Army is committed to the advancement of education, the relief of poverty, and other charitable objectives beneficial to society or the community of mankind as a whole. The Salvation Army works in over 110 countries worldwide.[31]

World Vision

World Vision is a Christian humanitarian organization that is dedicated to working with children, families, and their communities worldwide to reach their full potential by tackling the causes of poverty and injustice. World Vision began caring for orphans and other children in need first in South Korea in 1950 and then expanding throughout Asia. Eventually, World Vision expanded to more than 90 countries and embraced larger issues such as community development and advocacy for the poor. World Vision's child sponsorship program has been very popular in attracting donors who send funds each month to provide support for sponsored children and projects.[32]

COUNTRIES AND NGO DIVERSITY

The following section lists examples of NGOs actively working in countries discussed in this book. A diverse sample of NGOs was chosen in order to present an overview as to the broad range of work they perform on a global scale and in certain instances to highlight some of the important health issues affecting respective countries. Readers should notice distinct differences in the type of projects that NGOs conduct in relation to the development status of the country in which they work. NGOs with projects in developing countries tend to function operationally, focusing on meeting the exis-

tential needs of their target populations, whereas NGOs in developed countries are often designed to serve social needs or administer foreign aid. Immense variation can be found in terms of sectors of development. From vocational training for indigenous Australians to microcredit in Vietnam, NGOs use incredibly diverse methods to address health, economic, and social inequalities throughout the world.

Australia

OzGREEN

An environmental advocacy organization established in 1992, OzGREEN is a leading Australian provider of environmental awareness and education programs. OzGREEN projects and staff have received a number of awards including the Environmental Educators of the Year Award (1998) and UN Media Peace Awards (1991, 1994). Focused around water conservation, OzGREEN projects encompass a broad range of issues, including the hosting of Youth Congresses aimed at developing vision and action plans for the future of the Murray Darling River Basin.[33]

Indigenous Community Volunteers

Indigenous Community Volunteers (ICV) is a social advocacy and operational organization dedicated to providing indigenous Australians with new skills. Using a needs-based model, ICV approaches organizations or individuals to identify needs and then matches projects with volunteers in order to address those needs. ICV relies on a dedicated base of Australian volunteers willing to share their skills in business planning, corporate governance, office administration, information technology, and many other areas. Skills-transfer projects such as these lead to employment, self-employment, and community development.[34]

Cambodia

Samaritan's Purse

Samaritan's Purse is a nondenominational evangelical Christian organization with a mission of providing spiritual and physical aid to hurting people around the world. One of the largest faith-based international NGOs, Samaritan's Purse reported assets of over 192 million USD in 2006.[35] Samaritan's Purse is highly active in Cambodia where, among other projects, they have sponsored a community of land mine victims, through the construction of wells, latrines, a paved road, a schoolhouse, and livestock and agriculture programs.[36]

Khmer HIV/AIDS NGO Alliance

A Cambodian NGO at the forefront of the fight against HIV/AIDS, Khmer HIV/AIDS NGO Alliance (KHANA) envisions a Cambodia where all people, particularly those who are vulnerable, have equal access to effective, nondiscriminatory HIV prevention, care, and support services. KHANA collaborates with the Cambodian government and a host of grassroots organizations all over the country to carry out projects that address prevention, advocacy, awareness raising, and a variety of other initiatives and activities.[37]

Canada

Canadian Diabetes Association

Established over 50 years ago, the Canadian Diabetes Association is a charitable organization with a presence in more than 150 communities across the country. The association's mission is to promote the health of Canadians through diabetes research, education, service, and advocacy. Offering a wide range of programs and services, their projects include summer camps for young people with type 1 diabetes, insurance resources, and diabetes information developed especially for use by Aboriginal communities.[38]

Coaching Association of Canada

The Coaching Association of Canada is a not-for-profit amateur sport organization with the mandate to improve the effectiveness of coaching across all levels of the sport system. Established in 1970, the Coaching Association of Canada launched the National Coaching Certification Program in 1974 and, since its inception, has developed into a world leader in coach training and certification. Each year, more than 50,000 coaches take a National Coaching Certification Program workshop, and since it began, more than 900,000 coaches have participated in the program.[39]

D.R. Congo

HIRC International Rescue Committee

Requested by Albert Einstein in 1933, the International Rescue Committee (IRC) is a leading secular, international, operational NGO focused on relief and humanitarian aid. The IRC is consistently given high marks by charity watchdog groups, earning an A from the American Institute of Philanthropy, and named as one of 10 gold star charities by the Forbes Investment Guide.[40, 41] The IRC is one of the largest providers of humanitarian aid in the Democratic Republic of the Congo, providing critical health and emergency response services to those displaced by violence and addressing sexual violence by providing emergency care, counseling, prevention measures, advocacy, and other support services.[17]

Africare

As the oldest and largest African American–led organization in its field, Africa is Africare's specialty. Africare reaches families and communities in 25 countries in every major region of sub-Saharan Africa. Founded in 1970, Africare has delivered more than 710 million USD in assistance through projects focused on HIV/AIDS, food security and agriculture, water resource development, vocational training, and others. In March 2005, Africare opened its first office in the D.R. Congo. There, Africare is providing community-based support to AIDS orphans and other vulnerable children in the capital of Kinshasa.[42]

Germany

The German Music Council or Deutscher Musikrat

Representing over 8 million music-loving citizens, the German Music Council is the largest cultural association in Germany.[43] Through the promotion of the status of music in society and the continued development of musical culture, the German Music Council supports improvements in the artistic and social situation of musicians and music teachers. Deutscher Musikrat also sponsors young talent competitions and events such as "Jugend musiziert" (Young People Play Music) and "Jugend jazzt" (Young People Play Jazz).[44]

Komen Deutschland (Komen)

An affiliate of the Susan G. Komen foundation, the world's largest grassroots network of breast cancer survivors and activists,[45] Komen Deutschland supports projects throughout the country that improve care and promote education and research. Throughout the calendar year, Komen Deutschland solicits funds from businesses and individuals countrywide; however, the majority of funds are raised through annual events such as the Pink Tie Ball and Race for the Cure. Overall, since the founding of the Komen Foundation in Germany, approximately 840,000 euros have been raised in the name of breast cancer prevention.[46]

Ghana

International Trachoma Initiative

Founded in 1998, the International Trachoma Initiative is dedicated to the elimination of blinding trachoma, the world's leading cause of preventable blindness. Working in countries where the WHO has documented widespread disease, International Trachoma Initiative collaborates with national ministries of health and other partners to identify regions where trachoma control will be targeted, develop a plan for implementing a prevention and treatment strategy, and mobilize people and resources.[47]

Oxfam

As part of their Water for Survival Program in Ghana, Oxfam is working with Water Aid UK, and local partner Rural Aid, to provide hand-dug wells with pumps and ventilated pit latrines. Water and sanitation initiatives are complemented by hygiene education activities to ensure that the health benefits for the community can be maximized.[48]

Grenada and West Indies

Grenada Planned Parenthood Association

A Member Association of the International Planned Parenthood Federation, the Grenada Planned Parenthood Association (GPPA) is a member of a global network spanning 149 countries.[49] The aim of GPPA is to provide the population of Grenada and the West Indies with the knowledge and the means to choose whether, when, and how many children to have by providing family planning information and education on a national scale. Disseminating its message through the media and community meetings, the GPPA endeavors to work toward a balance between human numbers, human needs, and Grenada's natural resources.[50]

International Coral Reef Action Network

Established in 2000 with a historic grant from the United Nations Foundation, the International Coral Reef Action Network is an innovative and dynamic network of many of the world's leading coral reef science and conservation organizations. The network consolidates technical and scientific expertise in reef monitoring and management to create strategically linked actions across local, national, and global scales. The International Coral Reef Action Network seeks to put mechanisms in place that support the translation of findings into direct on-the-ground action throughout the world's major coral reef regions.[51]

India

Heifer

Heifer International was founded on the belief that ending hunger begins with giving people the means to feed themselves. Heifer helps families move toward self-reliance through gifts of livestock and training in environmentally sound agriculture. Recipient families pass on the gift by sharing one or more of their animals' offspring with other struggling families. Heifer International is funded by the Heifer Foundation, which was established in 1990 to generate ongoing support for the work of Heifer International. As of December 31, 2006, the foundation's assets and commitments totaled over 82.5 million USD.[52] In India, Heifer International has worked on Angora rabbit wool production, camels for economic development, goat and pig projects in both rural and urban areas, and integrated livestock projects for rural women.[53]

Operation Smile

Founded in 1982, Operation Smile coordinates more than 30 medical mission sites in 26 countries annually repairing children's cleft lips and cleft palates.[54] Since Operation Smile's first mission to India in 2002, volunteers have provided free medical evaluations to more than 3,400 patients and life-changing surgery to more than 1,300 children and young adults. In 2007, Operation Smile India opened a cleft care clinic in Kolkata to provide year-round treatment and follow-up care for children throughout the country.[55]

Ireland

Crisis Housing Caring Support

Located in Galway, Western Ireland, Crisis Housing Caring Support was originally established by the Galway Diocese of the Catholic Church. Crisis Housing Caring Support supports people who are homeless or at risk of homelessness, women and children who experience domestic violence, and older people who are isolated by providing emergency accommodation and support services, refuge and outreach services, and senior support services, including community catering and a day center for older people.[56]

Irish Kidney Association

Founded in 1978, the Irish Kidney Association is a charitable voluntary organization that is dedicated to helping patients and families to live as normal a life as possible, given the presence of the kidney-related illness. By providing information on kidney diseases, associated medical scenarios, and social benefits and entitlements, the IKA takes a holistic approach to the needs of the individual by offering assistance across all aspects of life—medical, social, and psychological.[57]

Japan

Children Without Borders or Kokkyo naki Kodomotachi

Kokkyo naki Kodomotachi is a humanitarian educational association established in 1997 with the purpose of supporting children throughout Asia. By fostering exchange among the youth of the world, the organization hopes to inform children in developed countries of the circumstances of underprivileged children. Kokkyo naki Kodomotachi offers a video workshop in which youths are taught the basic usage of digital video cameras so that they may express themselves (problems, anxiety, feelings, etc.) in a different manner. These types of workshops have been organized in Cambodia, Indonesia, and India since 2004.[58]

Engineering and Consulting Firms Association

The Engineering and Consulting Firms Association is a nonprofit, independent organization that was established in 1964 for the purpose of contributing to international development through the application and transfer of technology. By means of consulting services, participants pass on Japanese technology and experience in order to aid in the development of new fields and to achieve improved working environments. The Engineering and Consulting Firms Association encourages and facilitates the application of state-of-the art technology in developing countries by coordinating with governments and international organizations.[59]

Jordan

Refugees International

As a global advocacy NGO, Refugees International (RI) generates lifesaving humanitarian assistance and protection for displaced people around the world and works to end the conditions that create displacement. Based on up-to-date information gathered in the field, RI provides governments, international agencies, and NGOs with effective solutions to improve the lives of displaced people by recording the need for basic services such as food, water, shelter, protection from harm, health services, and access to education. In Jordan, RI works primarily with Palestinian and Iraqi refugees. Other refugee groups in Jordan include Sudanese, Syrians, and Sri Lankans.[60]

Islamic Relief

Islamic Relief is an international relief and development NGO that is dedicated to alleviating the poverty and suffering of the world's poorest people. As well as responding to disasters and emergencies, Islamic Relief promotes sustainable economic and social development by working with local communities. In 1997, Islamic Relief extended its Orphans Sponsorship Program to Jordan. Hundreds of orphans have benefited from the program over the years, and more than 300 Palestinian orphans are currently being sponsored by donors from all over the world. Islamic Relief also carries out seasonal Ramadhan and Qurbani projects in Jordan distributing food to around 25,000 people so far.[61]

Korea

Disabled Persons International Korea

Disabled Persons International Korea (DPI) is an international organization that promotes awareness of disability issues and raises the voices of disabled people. The goal of DPI is to assist in the creation of a society where disabled people can participate on an equal basis by promoting the understanding of disabled people's rights. Initiated as a member country in 1986, DPI Korea has been working hard toward introducing various disabled rights issues in Korea. Active in five locations—Seoul, Jeju, Choong-nam, Daegu, Incheon—DPI Korea's main activities include the sponsoring of computer training for disabled people, a women's academy of disability, and the Sae-nal library.[62]

Korean Association for Suicide Prevention

The Korean Association for Suicide Prevention is dedicated to preventing suicidal behavior, alleviating the effects of suicide, and providing a forum for academics, mental health professionals, crisis workers, volunteers, and suicide survivors. The organization aims to raise awareness through public meetings, mass media presentations and interviews and by the hosting of a National Suicide Prevention Day. The Korean Association for Suicide Prevention is a member of the International Association for Suicide Prevention.[63]

Mexico

Comisión de Apoyo a la Unidad y Reconciliación Comunitaria

Translated as the Commission of Assistance Toward Community Unity and Reconciliation, Comisión de Apoyo a la Unidad y Reconciliación Comunitaria (CORECO) is an advocacy NGO founded in 1996 in San Cristóbal de Las Casas, Chiapas, Mexico. CORECO collaborates with communities and civil organizations in an effort to foster unity and peace with justice and dignity. CORECO offers assistance in the form of conflict resolution workshops so that persons, communities, and organizations in conflict can find their own ways to resolve problems.[64]

Project HOPE (Health Opportunities for People Everywhere)

Since 1958, project HOPE has worked to make health care available for people around the globe, especially children. Perhaps most well known for its refitted Navy ship, donated by President Eisenhower, Project HOPE traveled the world with American doctors, nurses, and technologists to share skills and knowledge with people of developing nations. In Mexico, project HOPE's work includes diabetes education and the administration of a regional HIV/AIDS Education and Training Center.[65]

New Zealand

Fred Hollows Foundation

An independent, politically unaligned, and secular nonprofit organization, the Fred Hollows Foundation is dedicated to facilitating comprehensive and quality eye care in developing countries. The foundation carries on the work of the late Professor Fred Hollows (1929–1993), an eye surgeon of international renown and strong advocate for social justice. The foundation works for a world where no person is needlessly blind by focusing on the prevention of blindness and restoring sight for people who are blind from cataracts or other disorders. In late 2006, the foundations in New Zealand, Australia, and the United Kingdom joined together to establish the Fred Hollows Foundation International, a new global network to enhance foundation operations around the world.[66]

Rotorua Adventure Therapy Aotearoa Incorporated

Rotorua Adventure Therapy Aotearoa Incorporated (RATA) became an incorporated society in 2004. RATA Inc. is one of the first organizations to be established for the sole purpose of forwarding the professional practice of adventure therapy. Adventure therapy is an internationally recognized form of therapy that combines various physical and psychological activities, often in an outdoor natural setting, with therapeutic change processes. Based in Rotorua, Aotearoa, New Zealand, RATA's programs include hiking, camping, kayaking, rock climbing, abseiling, high ropes courses, mountain biking, and the use of team initiative activities in both outdoor and indoor settings. Client groups include young people, older persons, people with disabilities, youth groups, and those with mental health disabilities.[67]

Nigeria

Direct Relief International

Direct Relief focuses on strengthening existing, fragile health systems in poor areas by providing resources that enable local health workers to address community needs. Direct Relief's medical assistance programs equip health professionals working in resource-poor communities to better meet the challenges of diagnosing, treating, and caring for people. Direct Relief has provided nearly $1.2 million in medical material assistance to Nigeria since 2000, focusing on preventive health care and medical supplies. They provide free health screenings, diagnosis and treatment, nutritional counseling, and referrals in four rural communities within the Niger Delta region.[68]

Girls Power Initiative

Girls Power Initiative (GPI) is a Nigerian youth development organization founded in 1993 to address the challenges facing girls in the Nigerian society and equip them with information, skills, and opportunities to grow into self-actualized young women. GPI seeks to empower girls by promoting sexual and reproductive health rights through educational programs, counseling, referral services, and social action. GPI's many activities include the sponsoring of local, national, and international seminars and workshops committed to managing and educating girls into healthy self-reliant, productive, and confident women.[69]

Peru

ProWorld (ProPeru)

ProWorld's mission is to promote social and economic development, empower communities, and cultivate educated, compassionate global citizens. Funded by the tuition of its volunteers, ProWorld seeks to develop lasting relationship with community partners through needs-based projects in Peru, Belize, Mexico, Thailand, and India. Among its many projects in Peru, ProPeru has installed cleaner burning stoves in indigenous communities throughout the Sacred Valley, helping to reduce the host of respiratory illnesses and eye maladies resulting from inadequate ventilation when preparing food indoors.[70]

Socios en Salud (PIH)

Since 1994, Partners in Health's sister organization in Peru, Socios en Salud (SES), has been treating disease and training community members to provide prevention and care for their neighbors in the shantytowns around Lima. Based in the northern Lima town of Carabayllo, SES is now Peru's largest nongovernmental healthcare organization, serving an estimated population of 700,000 inhabitants, many of whom have fled from poverty and political violence in Peru's countryside. As a valued partner to Peru's Ministry of Health, SES has also had an impact on national policies for prevention and treatment of drug-resistant tuberculosis and HIV and provides important training and support to help implement those policies nationwide.[71]

Portugal

Sociedade Portuguesa de Alergologia e Imunologia Clínica

The Portuguese Society of Allergology and Clinical Immunology was established in 1950. A nonprofit advocacy society, the Sociedade Portuguesa de Alergologia e Imunologia Clínica is dedicated to the promotion of the study of allergy and clinical immunology. The society publishes the bimonthly *Journal of Immunoallergology* in Portuguese and English, organizes annual meetings of the Portuguese Society of Allergology and Clinical Immunology, and promotes the annual attribution of three scientific awards and two scholarships.[72] The Sociedade Portuguesa de Alergologia e Imunologia Clínica has been a key motivator in the establishment of Portugal's National Program of Asthma Control.[73]

Stop Tuberculosis Partnership (Stop TB)

The Stop TB Partnership was established in 2000 to realize the goal of eliminating tuberculosis as a public health problem and, ultimately, to obtain a world free of tuberculosis. It comprises a network of international organizations, countries, and donors from the public and private sectors to achieve this goal. As Stop TB's recently appointed special envoy to the UN, the former president of Portugal Jorge Sampaio has rallied celebrity support in his home country to promote the I Am Stopping TB Campaign, which was the slogan for the 2008 World Tuberculosis Day.[74]

Russia

Moscow Helsinki Watch Group

Re-established in 1989, the Helsinki Watch Group is an influential human rights monitoring NGO whose mission is to assist human rights observation and democracy development in Russia.[75]

No to Alcohol and Drug Abuse

Among the first NGOs in Russia established in the area of substance abuse and prevention, the No to Alcohol and Drug Abuse (NAN) Foundation's primary goal is to counteract the consequences of chemical dependency in Russian society. With 15 years of experience in this field, NAN has developed a range of well-established preventive and rehabilitation programs. By providing education, vocational and life skills training, and material, psychological, and legal assistance NAN hopes to promote healthy lifestyles, community awareness, and mobilization.[76]

Taiwan

Buddhist Lotus Hospice Care Foundation

Set up by members of the Buddhist Medical Union in 1994, the Buddhist Lotus Hospice Care Foundation assists patients and family members to practice Buddhist ceremonial procedures for passing of loved ones. Volunteers, friends, and relatives pray for 8 hours at the death of the patient then for 49 days after death. It is believed that this continuous praying helps to raise the soul to the next world and comforts bereaved family members. The foundation's major goals are to provide Buddhist spiritual care, to promote filial doctrine, and to establish a model of Buddhist terminal care in Taiwan. The first hospice in a Buddhist hospital was opened 1996 in the Tzu-Chi Hospital in Hualien, eastern Taiwan. Now, there are 15 hospital-based hospices in Taiwan, with about 200 beds in total.[77]

Garden of Hope Foundation

The Garden of Hope Foundation was established in 1988 to help disadvantaged girls and young women. In particular, the foundation targets victims of sexual abuse and family violence. From one halfway house, their services have grown to include shelters and service centers island-wide, providing everything from counseling and temporary housing to employment training, social work, and legal aid. The Garden of Hope Foundation also contributes to research and government discussions on policy and has been essential to the creation of several key laws involving child welfare and women's rights.[78]

Turkey

Mother Child Education Foundation (AÇEV)

Founded in 1993, as the result of a highly successful pilot project entitled the Mother Child Education Program, AÇEV's mission is to make a lasting contribution to society and to improve the quality of individuals' lives through education. In its two main areas of expertise, early childhood and adult education, AÇEV develops and implements various training programs and projects both within Turkey and abroad. AÇEV's Mother Child Education Program targets 5- to 6-year-old children who do not have the opportunity to receive preschool education by offering a home-based education program.[79]

Türkiye Erozyonla Mücadele Ağaçlandırma

The Türkiye Erozyonla Mücadele Ağaçlandırma (TEMA) Foundation (the Turkish Foundation for Combating Soil Erosion, for Reforestation and the Protection of Natural Habitats) was founded in 1992. TEMA considers soil to be one of Turkey's most precious resources and therefore pursues its primary goal: to raise public awareness about the dangers of desertification resulting from widespread soil erosion within Turkey. The foundation, with the support of the Ministry of Environment and Forestry, has planted 2.2 million saplings over an area of 2.350 hectares under 25 different reforestation projects.[80]

United Kingdom

Minds Against Malaria

Funded by a $40 million grant from the Bill & Melinda Gates Foundation to the London School of Hygiene and Tropical Medicine, this operational NGO is bringing interdisciplinary coordination to a new level. Minds Against Malaria will join with European and African partners to identify and establish several centers for malaria research and training with the hopes of stimulating more rapid development of vaccines, drugs, and other control methods.[81]

Parkinson's Disease Society

The Parkinson's Disease Society is the leading charity in the United Kingdom that is dedicated to supporting all people affected by Parkinson's disease. Established in 1969, the society has funded research that has led to advances in the search for the cause of Parkinson's, better medical and surgical treatments, and better therapies and equipment and toward finding a cure. Entirely funded by charitable donations, the organization has a network of over 330 branches and support groups located throughout the United Kingdom.[82]

United States

American Red Cross

Comprised of almost 97 million volunteers and staff in 186 countries, the International Federation of Red Cross and Red Crescent societies make up the largest humanitarian network in the world. The federation's vision is to strive, through voluntary action, for a world of empowered communities, better able to address human suffering and crises with hope, respect for dignity, and a concern for equity. The American Chapter of the Red Cross was established by Clara Barton in 1881 and acts primarily as an operational NGO by working with the U.S. government and other humanitarian organizations to provide for the basic needs of people affected by emergencies and disasters at home and abroad.[83]

March of Dimes

In 1939, the National Foundation for Infantile Paralysis was established by Franklin D. Roosevelt, himself a victim of poliomyelitis, to combat the growing polio epidemic in the United States. As a grassroots fund-raising effort, the national foundation asked the American public to send dimes to President Roosevelt at the White House. The effort was called the March of Dimes, and after the arrival of thousands of pounds of dimes, the March of Dimes became the official name of the foundation. Having played an essential part in conquering the polio epidemic in the United States, the March of Dimes now focuses on improving the health of babies by preventing birth defects, premature birth, and infant mortality through research, community service, education, and advocacy.[84]

Vietnam

Grameen Foundation

In 1976, with only $27 from his own pocket, Dr. Muhammad Yunus established the Grameen Bank in the Bangladeshi village of Jobra and effectively pioneered the now popular sector of development called microcredit. The Grameen Foundation's mission is to enable the poor to create a world without poverty. With tiny loans, financial services, and technology, the foundation helps the poor, mostly women, to start self-sustaining businesses. The Grameen method requires no collateral for a loan, no legal instrument, and no group guarantee or joint liability and has loan recovery rates over 98%. In Vietnam, three organizations using the Grameen Bank model cover 16 provinces and have given loans to 130,000 poor families. Dr. Muhammad Yunus and Grameen Bank of Bangladesh were awarded the Nobel Peace Prize in 2006.[85]

Vietnam Assistance for the Handicapped

Founded in 1991 to assist war amputees, the overall purpose of Vietnam Assistance for the Handicapped (VNAH) is to assist the disabled in Vietnam to overcome disabilities and to lead a richer and fuller life. VNAH offers technical assistance to regional prosthetics clinics and wheelchair factories to aid in the production of high-quality, low-cost products. Also offering vocational training, the VNAH aims to promote programs and policies at the national level that integrate the dis-

abled into all aspects of their community's social and economic affairs.[86]

NGO GLOBAL ROLE

NGOs have become increasingly influential in world affairs. They often impact the social, economic, and political activities of communities and the country as a whole. NGOs address a host of issues, including, but not limited to, women's rights, environmental protection, human rights, economic development, political rights, or health care. In numerous countries, NGOs have led the way in democratization, in battling diseases and illnesses, in promoting and enforcing human rights, and in increasing standards of living.[87]

NGOs have played a significant role in global socioeconomic, ethical, health, and human rights culture. It is difficult to estimate the comprehensive value of NGOs over the past 60 years (since the establishment of the UN charter); however, it is clear that NGOs will continue to play an important role into the future considering the varied nature of their work (refer to Table 22-1 to get a sense of this fact). NGOs, depending on their operational or advocacy mission, will continue to improve the human condition one child, one family, one community, and one nation at a time; their overall efforts are focused on making our world a better place in which to exist and ultimately thrive.

Table 22-1 provides a quick summary of the NGOs described in this chapter and the sectors of development in which they work in relation to each country described in this book. The acronyms and abbreviations relate to the previous summary descriptions.

TABLE 22-1 Select Operational and Advocacy NGOs with Country-Specific Missions

Country	Operational NGO Example	Advocacy NGO Example	Country	Operational NGO Example	Advocacy NGO Example
Australia	OzGREEN	ICV	**Mexico**	HOPE	CORECO
Cambodia	Samaritan Purse KHANA		**New Zealand**	Fred Hollows RATA	
Canada	Canadian Diabetes Association	Coaching Association of Canada Canadian Diabetes Association	**Nigeria**	Direct Relief International GPI	GPI
D.R. Congo	Africare IRC		**Peru**	ProWorld PIH	ProWorld
Germany		Deutscher Musikrat Kolmen	**Portugal**		Sociedade Portuguesa de Alergologia e Imunologia Clínica Stop TB
Ghana	Oxfam International Trachoma Initiative		**Russia**	NAN	Moscow Helsinki Watch Group
West Indies		GPPA International Coral Reef Action Network	**Taiwan**	Buddhist Lotus Hospice Care Foundation Garden of Hope Foundation	Buddhist Lotus Hospice Care Foundation Garden of Hope Foundation
India	Heifer Operation Smile		**Turkey**	AÇEV	TEMA
Ireland	Crisis Housing Caring Support	Irish Kidney Association	**U.K.**		Minds Against Malaria Parkinson's Disease Society
Japan		Kokkyo naki Kodomotachi Engineering and Consulting Firms Association	**U.S.A.**	American Red Cross	March of Dimes
Jordan	RI Islamic Relief		**Vietnam**	Grameen VNAH	VNAH
Korea		DPI Korean Association for Suicide Prevention			

REFERENCES

1. United Nations Department of Economic and Social Affairs. Retrieved from http://esa.un.org/coordination/ngo/new/index.asp?page=intro.

2. Duke University website. Retrieved March 28, 2007, from http://library.duke.edu/research/subject/guides/ngo_guide/ngo_issues.html.

3. Annual Review, Financials. World Vision website. Retrieved March 28, 2007, from http://www.worldvision.org/resources.nsf/main/2007_financials.pdf/$file/2007_financials.pdf?Open&lid=3057&lpos=lft_txt_ar2007pdf.

4. International Monetary Fund, World Economic Outlook Database, April 2008. Data for 2007. New York: IMF; 2008.

5. Ofosu-Appiah B. Making NGOs More Effective and Responsive in a Globalized World. African Path; March 2008. Global Policy Forum website. Retrieved March 28, 2007, from http://www.globalpolicy.org/ngos/intro/growing/index.htm.

6. NGLS U.N. Non-Governmental Liaison Service 2007. The Roll NGOs Play in Making the UN Accountable. Report from the engagement workshop at the CIVICUS World Assembly Glasgow, May 2007. Glasgow: Civicus; 2007.

7. Kavan J. Aim of Millennium Development Goals is to Enable People to Live in Dignity, Safety. The President of the United Nations General Assembly address, to the fifty-sixth Annual DPI/NGO Conference, 2003. New York: UN Press; 2003.

8. U.N. Non-Governmental Liaison Service 2007. The Roll NGOs Play in Making the UN Accountable. Report from the engagement workshop at the CIVICUS World Assembly Glasgow, May 2007. Glasgow: Civicus; 2007.

9. World Food Program website. Retrieved August 20, 2008, from http://www.wfp.org/food_aid/introduction/index.asp?section=12&sub_section=1.

10. United Nations Development Program website. Retrieved March 29, 2008, from http://www.undp.org/about/.

11. United Nations High Commission for Refugees website. Retrieved August 20, 2008, from http://www.unhcr.org/basics.html.

12. UNICEF website. Retrieved August 20, 2008, from http://www.unicef.org/about/who/index_introduction.html.

13. Duke University website. Retrieved March 28, 2008, from http://library.duke.edu/research/subject/guides/ngo_guide/ngo_issues.html.

14. Willetts P. What Is a Non-Governmental Organization? Retrieved March 28, 2008, from http://www.staff.city.ac.uk/p.willetts/CS-NTWKS/NGO-ART.HTM.

15. Peace Corps. 2003 An NGO training guide for Peace Corps Volunteers. Peace Corps Information Collection and Exchange. Publication number MOO7O. Retrieved April 2, 2008, from http://www.peacecorps.gov/multimedia/pdf/library/M0070_all.pdf.

16. Duke Universities Library website: World Bank and NGOs. Retrieved August 20, 2008, from http://library.duke.edu/research/subject/guides/ngo_guide/igo_ngo_coop/ngo_wb.html.

17. CARE website. Retrieved April 8, 2008, from http://www.care.org/about/index.asp.

18. Carter Center website. Retrieved April 11, 2008, from http://www.cartercenter.org/about/index.html.

19. Catholic Relief Services website. Retrieved April 11, 2008, from http://crs.org/how/.

20. CHANGE website. Retrieved April 10, 2008, from http://www.genderhealth.org/Mission.php?TOPIC=ABT.

21. Christian Children's Fund website. Retrieved April 11, 2008, from http://www.christianchildrensfund.org/content.aspx?id=144.

22. Episcopal Relief and Development website. Retrieved April 11, 2008, from http://www.er-d.org/programs.htm?menupage=36744.

23. Human Rights Watch website. Retrieved April 11, 2008, from http://www.hrw.org/about/whoweare.html.

24. International Committee of the Red Cross website. Retrieved April 17, 2008, from http://www.icrc.org/web/eng/siteeng0.nsf/htmlall/68ee39?opendocument.

25. MSF website. Retrieved April 8, 2008, from http://www.msf.org/.

26. Oxfam website. Retrieved April 10, 2008, from http://www.oxfam.org/en/about/what/.

27. Partners in Health website. Retrieved April 8, 2008, from http://www.pih.org/youcando/join/District_Project_Manager.pdf.

28. Pathfinder International website. Retrieved April 11, 2008, from http://www.pathfind.org/site/PageServer?pagename=About_Mission.

29. Relief International website. Retrieved April 11, 2008, from http://ri.org/mission.php.

30. Rotary Club International website. Retrieved March 28, 2008, from http://www.rotary.org/en/Pages/ridefault.aspx.

31. Salvation Army website. Retrieved April 11, 2008, from http://www.salvationarmy.org/ihq/www_sa.nsf/vwdynamic-arrays/21F009A3B2E7354C80256F6B004FE9DB?openDocument.

32. World Vision website. Retrieved March 28, 2008, from http://www.worldvision.org.

33. OzGREEN website. Retrieved April 5, 2008, from http://www.ozgreen.org.au.

34. Indigenous Community Volunteers website. Retrieved April 5, 2008, from http://www.icv.com.au.

35. 2006 Consolidated Financial Statement and Supplemental Schedule for Samaritan's Purse. Retrieved April 11, 2008, from http://www.samaritanspurse.org/glossyIncludes/pdf_files/AnnualRep_Finance.pdf.

36. Samaritan's Purse website. Retrieved April 7, 2008, from Available at http://www.samaritanspurse.org.

37. Khana website. Retrieved March 27, 2008, from http://www.khana.org.

38. Canadian Diabetes Association website. Retrieved April 2, 2008, from http://www.diabetes.ca.

39. Coaching Association of Canada website. Retrieved April 2, 2008, from http://www.coach.ca.

40. Barrett WP. 12.08.03 Investment Guide. Genuinely Needy Our annual survey of 200 large charities picks 10 that shine. Retrieved March 21, 2008, from http://www.forbes.com/maserati/246.html.

41. IRC international Rescue Committee website. Retrieved April 2, 2008, from http://www.theirc.org.

42. Africare website. Retrieved April 2, 2008, from http://www.africare.org.

43. Deutscher Musikrat website. Retrieved April 24, 2008, from http://www.musikrat.de.

44. Deutchland Portal website. Retrieved April 24, 2008, from http://www.deutschland.de/home.php?lang=2&.

45. Komen Foundation website. Retrieved April 20, 2008, from http://www.komen.org.

46. Komen Deutchland website. Retrieved April 20, 2008, from www.komen.de.

47. International Trachoma Initiative website. Retrieved April 9, 2008, from http://www.trachoma.org.

48. Oxfam website. Retrieved April 9, 2008, from http://www.oxfam.org/en/programs/development/wafrica/ghana_water.

49. International Planned Parenthood Association website. Retrieved April 19, 2008, from www.ippf.org/en.

50. Wiser Earth website. Retrieved April 19, 2008, from http://www.wiserearth.org/organization/view/c9c598e5a4604ec61085c71725aaa2d0.

51. International Coral Reef Action Network website. Retrieved April 9, 2008, from http://www.Icran.org.

52. Heifer Foundation Annual Report 2007. Retrieved March 23, 2008, from http://www.heiferfoundation.org/download/pdf/HF_2006_annual_report.pdf.

53. Heifer Foundation website. Retrieved April 8, 2008, from www.heiferfoundation.org.

54. Operation Smile website. Retrieved April 24, 2008, from http://www.operationsmile.org/aboutus/history/.

55. Operation Smile website. Retrieved April 24, 2008, from http://www.operationsmile.org/missions/reports/?-country=IN.

56. COPE website. Retrieved April 9, 2008, from http://www.cope.ie.

57. Irish Kidney Association website. Retrieved April 9, 2008, from http://www.ika.ie.

58. Kokkyo naki Kodomotachi website. Retrieved April 16, 2008, from http://knk-network.org/.

59. Engineering and Consulting Firms Association website. Retrieved April 16, 2008, from http://www.ecfa.or.jp/english/index.html.

60. Refugees International website. Retrieved April 17, 2008, from http://www.refugeesinternational.org/.

61. Islamic Relief website. Retrieved April 16, 2008, from http://islamic-relief.com.

62. Wiser Earth website. Retrieved April 17, 2008, from http://www.wiserearth.org/organization/view/0618dbf1c79b9134c9f87ce7cff3bf86.

63. Korean Association for Suicide Prevention website. Retrieved April 23, 2008, from http://www.med.uio.no/iasp/.

64. CORECTO website. Retrieved April 15, 2008, from www.laneta.apc.org/coreco/English%20information.htm.

65. Project HOPE website. Retrieved April 9, 2008, from http://www.projecthope.org.

66. Fred Hollows Foundation website. Retrieved April 23, 2008, from http://www.hollows.org.

67. Rotorua Adventura Therapy Aotearoa Inc. website. Retrieved April 28, 2008, from http://www.adventuretherapy.org.nz.

68. Direct Relief International website. Retrieved April 10, 2008, from http://www.directrelief.org.

69. Girls Power Initiative website. Retrieved April 10, 2008, from http://www.gpinigeria.org.

70. ProWorld website. Retrieved April 10, 2008, from http://www.proworldsc.org.

71. Partners in Health website. Retrieved April 19, 2008, from http://www.pih.org/where/Peru/Peru.

72. SPAIC website. Retrieved April 11, 2008, from http://www.spaic.pt/textos/?imr=69&imc=70n.

73. Portugal Ministry of Health, 2003 Contributions to the Establishment of a National Health Plan Guidelines, Lisbon. January 2003, p. 40. Retrieved April 20, 2008, from http://www.dgs.pt/upload/membro.id/ficheiros/i005877.pdf.

74. Stop TB website. Retrieved April 18, 2008, from http://www.stoptb.org/.

75. Moscow Helsinki Watch Group website. Retrieved April 12, 2008, from http://www.mhg.ru/english.

76. NAN website. Retrieved April 18, 2008, from http://www.civilsoc.org/nisorgs/russwest/moscow/nanmoscw.htm.

77. Buddhist Lotus Hospice Care Foundation website. Retrieved April 17, 2008, from http://www.lotushcf.org.tw/english.htm.

78. Garden of Hope Foundation website. Retrieved April 17, 2008, from http://www.goh.org.tw/english/index.htm.

79. Mother Child Education Foundation website. Retrieved April 3, 2008, from http://www.acev.org/english/index.html.

80. TEMA website. Retrieved April 3, 2008, from http://www.tema.org.tr.

81. Gates Malaria Partnership website. Retrieved April 4, 2008, from http://www.lshtm.ac.uk/gmp/.

82. Parkinson's Disease Society website. Retrieved April 3, 2008, from http://www.parkinsons.org.uk.

83. American Red Cross website. Retrieved April 4, 2008, from http://www.redcross.org.

84. March of Dimes website. Retrieved April 9, 2008, from http://www.marchofdimes.com.

85. Grameen Foundation website. Retrieved April 9, 2008, from http://www.grameen-info.org.

86. Vietnam Assistance for the Handicapped website. Retrieved April 9, 2008, from http://www.vnah-hev.org.

87. Duke University NGO Directory website. Retrieved March 28, 2008, from http://library.duke.edu/research/subject/guides/ngo_guide/.

CHAPTER 23

Comparative Global Challenges and Opportunities

James A. Johnson and
Carleen H. Stoskopf

INTRODUCTION

Health systems in the 21st century are facing many new challenges as they seek to provide health care for growing populations with increasingly complex medical conditions. There is a global labor shortage of skilled professionals, especially nurses and physicians. Facilities are in need of repair or upgrading; improvements in efficiency, effectiveness, and equity remain elusive in many cases; and financial resources are often in short supply. Several overarching challenges that affect the systems described in this book are described later here.

INTERNATIONAL HEALTH POLICY, GLOBALIZATION, AND PRIVATIZATION

It is the policy of most international funding organizations, such as the World Bank and the International Monetary Fund, to encourage developing countries to move to privatization of their healthcare systems. The World Bank furthers this agenda by having privatization as an objective of many of their funded projects in developing countries, by funding priorities of the Inter-

national Funding Corporation, and by providing investment guarantees through the Multilateral Investment Guarantee Agency. The International Funding Corporation invests only in the private sector and is targeting areas such as water, transportation systems, education, health care, and the environment. The Trade-Related Aspects of Intellectual Property Rights group works actively on a global scale to ensure that pharmaceutical companies and their patents are protected in developing countries, keeping the cost of drugs high worldwide, contributing to the profits of those countries, and preventing countries from making their own drugs and providing them at cost to their own citizens. The International Monetary Fund has as its policy to privatize public services, including healthcare systems, a condition of their loans.

Second, the multinational corporations are marketing to developing countries. The World Trade Organization has spent a decade promoting privatization of healthcare systems as well. Through the General Agreement on Trade in Service, privatization is promoted as a core principle of the World Trade Organization. Adding to this trend is the role that NAFTA (North American Free Trade Agreement) and the European Union are playing. Both work to open the markets of developing counties to private companies of the developed world. These groups are seen as treating health care worldwide as a marketing opportunity. What is being promoted in developing countries is an expansion of their sales for diagnostic and therapy services such as dialysis, blood products, and magnetic resonance imaging scans, among others. Also, these treaties work to open markets to Health Maintenance Organizations and other insurers to operate in developing countries.[1–3]

The policies of the organizations outlined previously are consistent with that of creating competition in economies and consistent with their push for free-trade across countries. These policies are also consistent with the belief that competition provides the best product or service at the lowest price. It also creates an environment conducive to innovation in what services are provided and how they are delivered. In regard to healthcare organizations, a privately financed healthcare system would rely on a third-party payer and health insurance premiums paid by individuals or paid in conjunction with employers. When services are delivered, the healthcare practitioner would be reimbursed for his or her services by the health insurance plan. There have been some attempts by U.S. groups to move their financing and delivery services for health care into other countries, but so far, this effort has been weak. Also, U.S. hospitals have not been successful in expanding into other countries. What has been successful is the expansion and privatization of such healthcare services as cleaning, laundry, and food service; however, as we move further into the 21th century, it is believed that multinational companies and their subsidiaries will try to continue their expansion and hope that, as more free-trade agreements emerge, profitable opportunities will grow.

There are several problems with privatization and competition in healthcare services. First, most people do not want to purchase this service. Second, persons purchasing health care do so with a serious information inequality (information asymmetry) regarding the services they are purchasing. How does a patient know whether he or she has purchased the best appendectomy? Comparison shopping is not easily done for most healthcare services, especially emergency services. Third, where individual healthcare services are concerned, no one wants a "bargain." Everyone wants premium services, whereas in other services, the purchaser may not actually buy the most expensive product for a variety of rational reasons. Consumers are irrational when it comes to purchasing health services. Fourth, other services are not bought through a third-party payer, a situation that removes the

individual from the purchasing process. Finally, outcomes are difficult to measure. A quote from the Public Services International Research Unit at the University of Greenwich is this: "Health care industry goods and services differ significantly from those of other industries in one very particular way: The product or output of the industry is not often as tangible or measurable. From a producer's perspective, and even more so from that of a consumer, health care is an unpredictable industry with a hard-to-define output."[4]

Although it is understandable that governments want and need employers to assist in paying for healthcare services, this type of system can lead to inequities in healthcare access and services, as well as leading to a two-tiered system of care—those with insurance and those without. In some countries described in this book, that is, Portugal, Russia, and Turkey, those without health insurance partially paid by an employer are left to access a public healthcare system that often has limited resources and substandard government facilities. Not only are these systems poorly funded, but healthcare practitioners migrate to the private systems that serve the privately insured, as the potential for increased incomes is much greater, especially in high-tech, specialized medicine. This leaves only a few practitioners in public systems that often are not specialized, with limited equipment and administrative support, poor infrastructure, limited resources such as laboratories and pharmacies, and reduced nursing care, to care for "the other half of society"; therefore creating a government network available for those without employment-based insurance often forces the most vulnerable (older and poor) to use only safety net providers and have little access to higher-quality care.

Some of the barriers to privatization of healthcare systems in developing countries include putting in advanced information systems and maintaining them. Privatization with insurance companies or Health Maintenance Organizations requires that health information is collected on patients, access and utilization information is captured, billing information can be made available, and financing can be tracked. There are also issues of unionized workers in countries where unions have been a tradition, understanding local and cultural-specific healthcare needs and marketing to those groups, providing high-tech equipment and maintaining it while making a profit, and providing pharmaceuticals at a price that can be afforded in these markets.[5]

One solution to this problem can be seen when those who are not working have their health insurance premiums paid by the government. This places these vulnerable populations in the health insurance risk pool with the entire population and gives them access to the same quality of health services the working population has. It also allows for privatization. This approach reduces the probability of creating a two-tiered system and promotes the concept of a true risk pool, where risk is truly spread across entire population. South Korea is a country that engages in this type of health insurance coverage for all of its population.

DECENTRALIZATION

Most countries are attempting to decentralize their healthcare systems. By "decentralization" we mean "a political reform, designed to reduce the extent of central influence and promote local autonomy."[6] The level of decentralization used in healthcare systems is a continuous issue of concern. Decentralization is praised as an instrument for improving efficiency and quality. Theoretically, when decisions are made locally, people who have more knowledge of local conditions will have better input for the services needed, can give more immediate feedback on the quality of care, and are more attuned to what actual healthcare services cost. This approach is good from the perspective that those making decisions are closer to the problems in their jurisdiction. Local administrators and politicians do tend to have a better understanding of local problems and populations and therefore should be able to use resources in the most efficient manner for that locale. Local officials can be held accountable for poor quality by the people who live in their communities. The downside of decentralization is that the needed funding and other resources do not necessarily accompany the responsibility or mandate for providing appropriate health care in local areas. Rather, a noticeable trend is for central governments to put demands on local governments to provide part of the funding for the healthcare system, something that many are not prepared to do. The local governments now have the responsibility, but not the money. They have the authority to raise money, but a population who cannot afford to be further taxed. The health system in Congo, for example, has given much responsibility to regional and local governments for the provision of health care, but without providing the means to do so. The local governments are unable to raise the money from their poor populations to provide quality health care, and thus, the demand for health goes unmet.

Some of the other issues that are raised, especially in developing countries, are information asymmetry, local politics, capability of local officials, poor local tax base, keeping the same values between the central and local administrations (congruence), and difficulty in coordinating services. Perhaps the biggest hurdle to successful decentralization is ensuring that local leaders, especially healthcare leaders, have the training necessary to carry out the complex activities of finding resources, deciding on their use, and providing a range of health services while meeting the hugely diverse needs of the population being served. Should resources be spent on preventive care, primary care, or care of older persons? A major difference seen between the United States and some other developed countries and less-developed countries is the use of specially trained healthcare management professionals, educated specifically in business. To be successful at all levels of healthcare systems management, the people doing the "administering" must understand financing, work design, information systems, policy, and human resources, to name a few, as well as the basics of medicine and science. The melding of the skills of business managers, politicians, and medical practitioners is not easy to achieve at any level, but especially in small, local arenas.

The quality of decision making at these lower levels of the healthcare system may not be as good. The complexities of providing health care at a local level result in healthcare systems that are ineffective and often wasteful. The person making the healthcare decisions must work within the framework of local politics. Local politicians may have their own reasons for providing certain types of healthcare services, such as owning hospitals or long-term care facilities. Local healthcare administrators may actually work for the politicians. Unfortunately, in developing countries, funds that are put into the hands of local administrators or officials are not always used for the purpose they were intended. The issues of graft in developing countries among government officials at all levels of government are serious contribute to ongoing poverty.

HEALTH CARE AS AN INCREASING PORTION OF GDP

Nearly all countries are reporting that their healthcare expenditures are continuing to increase as a percentage of GDP. The question is how high can these percentages go before the opportunity costs are too high? Although this trend is seen virtually everywhere, this situation is a problem primarily for the developed countries where the percentage is inching over 10% for many countries.

Countries such as Japan, South Korea, Germany, Switzerland, the United Kingdom, and certainly the United States are struggling to control their healthcare expenditures as the percentage of the GDP that they represent continues to creep upward. The United States is seeing its healthcare costs as the highest percentage of its GDP, topping 16%. The crucial question is what could we be spending our money on instead? Could it be infrastructure, education, or manufacturing? Should some of this money be better directed toward eliminating, or at least addressing, poverty, inequity, and social injustices?

Is there such a thing as too much health care? On the other hand, the healthcare industry itself is very desirable for many communities. In the United States, for example, small hospitals in rural areas are oftentimes the major employers in that community. The majority of jobs in healthcare systems are well paid, and for those that are not (food service, custodial care), there are good benefits with the job. Healthcare workers as a group are perhaps the best overall educated as an industry. The jobs are often highly technical and highly credentialed and require a fair amount of education, even in supporting roles such as administrative jobs. These healthcare workers have higher salaries, pay more taxes, own more homes, purchase more, and make major contributions to their communities. The future appears to promise continuing increases in healthcare expenditure, especially among the developed countries.

INJURIES AND VIOLENCE

There is an increase in injuries, trauma, and death caused by violence globally. Violence is defined as "the intentional use of physical force or power, threatened or actual, against oneself, another person, or against a group or community; that either results in injury, death, psychological harm, mal-development or deprivation."[7] Although vital statistics and surveillance are inadequate in so many areas of the world, there is still evidence that there are increases in injuries and violence. Injuries increase as more people in developing countries purchase automobiles, whereas safety laws lag behind. Inadequate preparation of new drivers, poorly maintained vehicles, and a lack of traffic signs and laws make roads in many parts of the world unsafe. Second, there are areas where violence from cartels, smuggling, and gangs (Latin America) is common, and other areas of the world experience violence caused by wars and political/tribal unrest (sub-Saharan Africa and Middle Eastern crescent). In our chapters on Mexico, Congo, and Nigeria, these concerns are voiced.

In the later part of the 20th century, death caused by violence emerged as a serious threat to the public's health. Using data from the Global Burden of Disease, over 1.8 million people died of violence (35 per 100,000). Death from violence included suicide, homicide, and deaths caused by war[8] (Table 23-1). Homicides were highest in sub-Saharan Africa, followed by Latin American countries, whereas suicide was the highest in China and countries whose economies were formerly socialist. Death from wars was highest in sub-Saharan Africa, followed by the Middle Eastern crescent.[9]

In addition to deaths from the three previously mentioned causes, there is a tremendous amount of violence that does not end in death but instead results in extensive injury and disability. Included in this category are spousal and child abuse, neglect by caregivers, older person abuse, sexual violence, self-directed abuse, and collective violence.

Acts of violence and their consequences put considerable strain on healthcare systems and divert resources from other pressing healthcare needs. Incidents

TABLE 23-1 Global Causes of Violent Death

Causes of Violent Death	Estimated Number of Deaths	Percentage of Deaths by Cause	Deaths per 100,000	Deaths per 100,000 (range)
Worldwide	1,851,000	100	35	
Suicide	786,000	42.5	15.5	3.4–30.4
Homicide	563,000	30.4	10.5	1.0–44.8
War	502,000	27.1	9.3	0–52.9

Data are from Reza A, Mercy JA, Krug E. Epidemiology of violent deaths in the world. *Injury Prevention,* 2001;7: 104–111.

of violence often have long-term consequences, not only physically, but for mental health as well. In fact, psychological violence can cause extensive disruption to individuals, families, and communities. Another type of violence is deprivation, where individuals can be deprived of basic needs such as shelter, food, and water, or deprived of emotional support. Violence is often enabled by the presence of alcohol and drugs, availability of firearms, or social and economic inequities or injustices. Consequences of violence include behavioral problems, depression and/or anxiety, drug and alcohol abuse, and reproductive health problems.[10] Causes of violence can be categorized into four levels: (1) personal/biological factors, (2) close relationships, (3) community, and (4) broad societal factors (see Table 23-2 for a summary of these levels).

In response to violence, countries provide adequate and appropriate services to the victims of violence, engage in legislative reform, perform better data collection and research on the causes of violence and successful interventions, and have organizations responsible for monitoring violence. Most needed to carry out these activities as a commitment to funding nationally, empowering communities so that they have ownership of the behavior in their communities, and a global commitment to reducing wars and conflicts.

MENTAL ILLNESS

Necessary to health and well-being is good mental health. Currently, 14% of the burden of illness is from mental illness, the most prevalent of these being depression, substance abuse, and anxiety disorders. Also of importance is that mental illness is closely associated with a variety of physical illness, both chronic and communicable, as well as increasing injury. Depression is of special concern as social and economic conditions worsen such as overcrowding, an increase in war and refugees, decreased access to food and water due to climate change, competition for fuel, and greater disparity between the world's rich and poor.[11]

The challenge for the future is for healthcare providers, insurers, and policy makers to put mental health on the same par as physical illnesses in terms of both early and correct diagnosis, as well as treatment. More importantly is that the causes of mental illness, in particular the causes of depression and substance abuse, must be recognized and addressed. Once again, the conversation turns to social determinants of health status, especially those associated with mental illness. Such factors as socioeconomic development, educational attainment, technological advances, environmental hazards,

TABLE 23-2 Causes of Violence: Four Levels

Level 1: Personal or Biological Factors	Level 2: Close Relationships (Family and Friends)
Demographics (age, income, education)	Marital conflict
Personality disorders	Stress in present and past relationships
Substance abuse	Overcrowded living conditions
History of experience/witnessing violence	
Level 3: Community (schools, workplaces, neighborhoods)	**Level 4: Broad Societal Factors**
Local drug trade	Responsiveness of the criminal justice system
Decreased social networks poverty	Cultural norms relating to gender roles and parent/child relationships
	Income inequity
	Strength of the social welfare system
	Acceptability of violence
	Availability of firearms
	Mass media exposure to violence
	Political instability

Data are from Krug EG, Mercy JA, Dahlberg LL, Zwi AB. The world report on violence and health. *The Lancet.* 2002;360(9339):1083–1088.

and how they are distributed in populations continue to be a major contributor to morbidity and mortality.[12]

Globally, resources for mental health are well below those provided for other types of illness, in both developed and developing countries. The least developed countries put the fewest resources in mental health, and the care that is available is usually institutionally based. Coupled with cultural views of the mentally ill among many populations, services are poorly funded and provided and not considered a priority.

Most countries lack qualified health practitioners in numbers adequate to diagnose, treat, and care for the mentally ill. The inability to address mental illness will impact treatment of other illnesses. Given that today many mental illnesses are treatable, this is difficult to witness. Even in developed countries, where identification and treatment of mental illness is more advanced, there is inequity in access, treatment, and outcomes among varying groups in these populations.[13] Furthermore, those who are mentally ill face many difficulties in their communities where mental illness may be associated with "bad spirits," the supernatural, or an embarrassment to family and friends and the community as a whole.

AGING POPULATION

All developed countries, and to a lesser extent developing countries, are facing the issues of an aging population. These issues include (1) increasing healthcare costs/fewer young people to spread the risk, (2) an inability to replace the elderly in the workforce, (3) inadequate planning for long-term care solutions/facilities, (4) how to finance health care and pensions, and (5) end-of-life costs. The older population is generally defined as those persons aged 65 and older. Since 1950, the numbers of older persons have increased from 4% of the world population to nearly 7% in 2000. This trend is expected to continue, especially as the "baby boomers" enter this age group. In addition, those in the 65-and-older category are aging as well, as more people are living to age 85 and older. Europe and North America lead the way in the percentage of older persons, but all countries, including developing countries, are experiencing an aging of their populations.

Although in some areas of the world aging is not occurring as fast, it is nevertheless occurring. In some of the world, such as in sub-Saharan Africa, the governments are the least able to deal with these shifting demographics. As populations age, the need for more healthcare

services rises, and those services needed by the older population are often different from the ones provided to the younger part of the population, such as chronic disease management versus immunizations and infectious disease management. Aging also puts more strain on other types of services provided by caregivers, case managers, and other groups that support finding adequate shelter, food, protection, and support/social networks for older persons.[14]

A second problem that arises with an increase in the percentage of the older population is that there are fewer individuals in the workforce to support pensions, to share in the risk pool of health insurance, and to provide a tax base for all government functions. Fertility has declined worldwide, even in developing countries, and the aging of the population will be a problem. At the same time, those who reach age 60 have a longer predicted life span from that time forward than ever before. This is especially true in developed countries where modern medicine and improvements in lifestyle have created the highest proportions of older persons. As less developed countries continue to move forward in the world economy, the life expectancy of their older persons will grow as well. The rate of older people grows at a rate of 2.6% per year, whereas the population as a whole grows at a rate of 1.1% per year. In developing countries, the fastest growth among those 65 and older is among those in the lowest social economic groups, who are already vulnerable due to many other factors. Table 23-3 shows the changes in age demographics between 1950, 2000, and estimated for 2050. The ratio of those in the workforce to older person declines. The median age increases. The absolute numbers of those 60 and older increases dramatically, and among the older population, the number of those 85 and older in relation to those aged 50 to 64 increases.[15] All of these demographic changes have many consequences on many levels, and much work is needed to ensure that those 65 and older have quality health care available, adequate pensions, affordable housing and food, social networks and support, and quality of life and well-being.

ENVIRONMENTAL IMPACT/CLIMATE CHANGE

As climate change proceeds, there is considerable evidence that the world is getting warmer and drier. This has resulted in an increase in droughts in North America, Africa, and China. The overall impact of climate change contributes to food scarcity and political destabilization.

TABLE 23-3 Demographic Changes from 1950 to 2050

Statistic	1950	2000	2050
Support ratio: number in the workforce per person age 65 and older	12:1	9:1	4:1
Median age	—	28	38
Number of persons age 60 and older	200 million	600 million	2 billion
Ratio of number of persons aged 85 and older to 100 persons aged 50–64	2/100	4/100	12/100

Data are from United Nations Department of Economic and Social Affairs, Population Division. "Executive Summary: World Population Aging 2007."

Unfortunately, despite the efforts of many international groups and the high-profile work of people like Nobel Laureate Al Gore, there still is no grand consensus on how to best deal with an impending global crisis. Some countries such as Germany have worked hard to reduce carbon emissions, whereas others like the United States have a mixed approach. The recent Olympics in China underscored the need for it and other rapidly developing countries to control air and water pollution better. An increasing incidence of respiratory disorders furthers the urgency of addressing this problem. Furthermore, the United Nations–sponsored Intergovernmental Panel on Climate Change issued a report in 2007 concluding that without a dramatic reduction in human-induced carbon-dioxide emissions, climate change may bring "abrupt or irreversible" effects on air, oceans, glaciers, land, coastlines, and species.[16]

Climate change has also been associated with changes in weather patterns that have resulted in an increase in storms and floods. Hurricane Katrina in the United States provided a glaring example of how ill prepared even the wealthy nations are in dealing with such disasters. As we have seen, health systems are often vulnerable during times of disaster, thus leaving people unserved at a time of greatest need. Many health systems are functioning on limited budgets and are currently understaffed. The extra stressors of natural disaster is often enough to cause a serious disruption in even the most basic services.

There is a slow, but vibrant, movement to create sustainable health systems (Boxes 23-1, 23-2, and 23-3) that can generate their own electricity and be independent of local power grids. Others have ongoing disaster training exercises and contingency plans to address the challenges of natural disaster.

In conclusion, it can be said that health systems around the globe will be challenged in ways never before considered. The governments and private sectors in these countries will have to work in partnership to ensure the sustainability of vital health services. Additionally, health systems will need to realize their interconnectedness with the rest of the world as we face global pandemics and macro problems such as climate change. Likewise, at the micro level, health systems will need to reduce bureaucracy by streamlining management, increasing cost-effectiveness, improving efficiency through reorganized services, decentralizing services, and allocating resources to better address the needs of the population.

Box 23-1   Sustainability in Health Systems

George Velez

Sustainability uses the "triple bottom line" of financial viability, social responsiveness, and environmental responsibility and applies systems thinking to the strategic development of sustainability efforts. This is a critical component for health systems to integrate holistic strategic processes to support sustainability efforts of initiatives, services, and the mission of the organization on a whole. Healthcare organizations are a microcommunity living within a larger community. Hence, the sense and culture of community, stewardship, and neighbor are essential components of most healthcare system sustainability strategies. Healthcare systems in the near future will confront several critical issues on multiple levels. These issues are not unique to health care, but certainly will drive urgencies and opportunities in the years to come. Some examples of these critical issues are significant changes in the aging of the population, changes in family structure and employment patterns that will influence reimbursement schemes, and change traditional healthcare benefits. In view of these challenges, health systems cannot be sustained without addressing the tradeoff between restricted resources (financial, people, environmental) and reaching overall health policy goals within the context of community and environmental stewardship. It will be crucial to generate new strategies for controlling the complex mechanisms that affect expenditure and performance of healthcare sustainability while striving for the achievement of core objectives of healthcare policies such as universal access, high-quality standards, efficiency and effectiveness, adequate funding, and satisfaction of patients.

Box 23-2   Community Health Centers

Neil Steven Gardner

The community health center (CHC) movement in the United States began in the mid-1960s, an outgrowth of the neighborhood health clinics that were part of the early social programs of that period. The CHC model reflects the pioneering work done in South Africa in the 1940s by Drs. Sidney and Emily Kark. The early centers in the United States were sometimes established more on social/political considerations than with the objective of delivering primary health care. This was also the case in the Community Health Program (CHP) centers established in South Australia. The current CHC model in the United States, more specifically the Federally Qualified Health Center, provides primary healthcare services to persons who otherwise would not have access to them. Many CHCs are housed in state-of-the-art clinical facilities providing professional and pleasant family-oriented health care. In the case of South Australia, the CHP centers have been used as part of a national program to provide universal access to health care. The Australian model was initially supported by the Commonwealth government, but with subsequent revisions to the program, the centers became the responsibility of the Australian states.

India has a three-tiered system of public healthcare delivery that includes community health centers. In that nation, the CHCs receive cases from the basic primary health centers, which are the foundation of health services serving some 25,000 in the rural areas of India. The CHCs refer cases to the 30-bed hospitals and higher-level hospitals at the district level as necessary.

In the United States, there is collaboration between the federal government and the communities that are being served. The federal funding to a CHC never represents the total budget. There is the expectation for the CHC to leverage the federal dollars through enhanced Medicaid reimbursement, additional sources of funding, and private insurance reimbursements, as well as self-payment by users of the center based on a sliding fee scale that determines an individual's ability to pay.

In both the United States and Australia, there has been an emphasis on community involvement; an aspect that may be a factor contributing to the sustainability of the CHC model. This community involvement includes a U.S. requirement of 51% user representation on the governing board of the center.

(continues)

Box 23-2 Community Health Centers (continued)

In addition to well visits, specialty care services are often available in the community health center or through a paid referral for services. The model has emphasized wellness and prevention. Under the current models, no one is denied access to care. After care is sought, there is the opportunity to promote wellness and prevention through the services offered by the center. Although most of the current users in the United States are below 200% of the federal poverty level and are without health coverage, there are a number of center users who have private commercial health insurance coverage. In the United States, especially in rural areas where there are no other healthcare facilities available, insured and self-paying users make up a significant portion of the patient mix of the CHC. This is also the case in centers that are established around a culturally specific community, the attraction being culturally sensitive care.

Box 23-3 Health Systems Designs for the 21st Century

Glenn Croxton

A series of papers related to the design of hospitals for the 21st century were presented by the Center for Health Design and Health Care Without Harm at a conference sponsored by the Robert Wood Johnson Foundation, September 2006. The Center for Health Design is a nonprofit research and advocacy organization. Its mission is to transform healthcare settings into healing environments. The healing environment is seen as a vital part of therapeutic treatment and where design of healthcare setting contributes to health rather than adding to the burden of stress.

Health Care Without Harm is an international coalition of 440 groups in 55 countries working to transform the healthcare industry so that it is ecologically sustainable and no longer of harm to people and the environment.

First, Do No Harm

Gary Cohen discussed how healthcare institutions that support the Hippocratic Oath have a special responsibility to ensure that their operations are not major sources of chemical exposure and environmental harm. Until recently, healthcare professionals and hospital administrators were unaware of their contributions to chemical contaminants and broader societal disease burdens according to Cohen.

Chronic diseases and disabilities now affect more than 90 million men, women, and children in the United States alone. In spite of much advancement in medical practice, the best available data show an increase in the incidence of asthma, autism, birth defects, childhood brain cancer, acute lymphocytic leukemia, endometriosis, Parkinson's disease, and infertility. The economic costs of these diseases by 2020 will exceed $1 trillion yearly in healthcare cost and lost productivity.

The field of environmental health is attempting to link each of these diseases and disorders to exposure to toxic chemicals. The old way of looking at chemical risk and safety would have missed these links, as they are not as simple as single cause and single effect. Through the new lens of science, we have learned that exposure to toxic chemicals, at levels thought to have been safe, is increasing the chronic disease burden of millions of Americans.

Green Hospitals

The second paper, titled "Values-Driven Design and Construction: Enriching Community Benefits through Green Hospitals," was presented by Robin Guenther, Gail Vittori, and Cynthia Atwood. They discussed how many hospitals are successfully reaching beyond measures that have economic payback and are achieving community benefits beyond their four walls. Healthcare leaders recognize the high costs of inaction on matters of the environment—such as climate change and chemical contamination on the health of our families, neighbors, and communities at hand and globally. By embedding sustainable design in a broader vision of leadership and mission, these projects and organizations are succeeding in delivering the first generations of sustainable healthcare projects.

(continues)

Box 23-3   Health Systems Designs for the 21st Century (continued)

Ted Schettler, MD, MPH, identified three tiers of operational environmental performance evolving in hospitals.

- Tier 1: minimum local, state, and national environmental
- Tier 2: beyond compliance to measures that save money
- Tier 3: informed by inextricable link between environment and human health and moving beyond both compliance and monetary savings with a long-term plan to reduce environmental footprints

He contended that applying "triple bottom-line" approaches to pollution-prevention initiatives—that is, measuring economic, social, and environment benefits—would deliver significant benefits for healthcare organizations and the communities they serve. Early tier 3 hospitals supported this notion. Named one of the state's top four recyclers, the University of Michigan Health System described its program's social benefit as an institution-wide initiative that engages everyone.

As building initiatives accelerate, it is clear that we can apply the same system tiered performance to organizations engaged in sustainable building. Tier 1 organizations will not undertake green building until they are mandated to do so through legislative policy initiatives. They will not make the link or the organizational leap between the health of their facilities and the patients they serve.

Creating Safe and Healthy Spaces: Selecting Materials that Support Healing

Mark Rossi, PhD, and Tom Lent outlined the relationship of the materials and products used in healthcare facilities to the chemicals to which our communities are exposed. Rossi and Lent further described the opportunities available to healthcare organizations to help society break from its dependence on toxic materials and define the path to healthier, sustainable materials that benefit patients, communities, nature, and the organizational bottom line.

Kaiser Permanente, for example, framed its environmental goals for building design in terms of community health in March 2002 in the "Kaiser Permanente Position Statement on Green Buildings."

Kaiser Permanente's mission is to improve the health of the communities we serve. In recognition of the critical linkages between environmental health and public health, it is Kaiser's desire to limit adverse impacts upon the environment resulting from the siting, design, construction, and operation of our health facilities. We will address the life cycle impacts of facilities through design and construction standards, selection of material and equipment, and maintenance practices. Additionally, KP will require architects, engineers, and contractors to specify commercially available, cost-competitive materials, products, technologies, and processes, where appropriate, that have a positive impact, or limit any negative impact on environmental quality and human health.

Preventive Medicine for the Environment: Developing and Implementing Environmental Programs that Work

Laura Brannen suggested moving from the theoretical aspects of why healthcare facilities should adopt green principles to how to do it. According to Brannen, healthcare facilities alone generate a tremendous variety and quantity of waste—at least 2 millions tons of waste per year—that may represent real occupational and environmental health threats. Healthcare facilities are the fourth largest consumer of energy, spending $6.5 billion on energy cost alone and accounting for 11% of all commercial energy use. Water consumption and discharge to public sewer systems are excessive. Wastewater contains toxic laboratory and cleaning chemicals and pharmaceutical compounds, many of which are not broken down in sewage treatment plants and are disposed of in landfills, resulting in sewage sludge applied to farmland, or released in rivers and streams.

Finally, Brannen sees healthcare facilities of the future that are high-performance buildings that use less energy and less water, require fewer chemicals to maintain, and are designed for maximum operational waste management systems: where materials are purchased with health and the environmental considerations; where

(continues)

Box 23-3   Health Systems Designs for the 21st Century (continued)

materials are used efficiently and staff take responsibility for and participate in waste minimization programs; where end-of life considerations are maximized; and where reuse and recycling are effective.

Redefining Healthy Food: An Ecological Health Approach to Food Production, Distribution, and Procurement

The fifth paper in this series was presented by Jamie Harvie, who discussed the ecological health approach to food production. According to Harvie, food production, distribution, and procurement intersect a wide variety of issues. Economics, immigration policy, spirituality, agriculture and trade, culture, environment, and nutrition are but several of the myriad concerns associated with the food we grow and eat. There is perhaps no issue that has such a wide depth of actively involved interest. The complexity of interest requires a system, or ecological approach. Such an approach is challenging because it is not linear and requires observation of the whole context, while seeking to understand the connections between their parts.

Hospital food is big business. In 2004 alone, the top healthcare group purchasing organizations purchased approximately $2.75 billion worth of food. Although patient food receives considerable attention in the media, it is cafeteria and catered food that make up the largest percentage of the food budget, accounting for approximately 55% to 70% of hospital volume.

Hospital and health systems are not only changing procurement practices to support a healthy food system, they are explicitly identifying the link between a healthy food system and healthy patients, communities, and the planet in their policies and programs. These systems are pioneers in an ecological approach to preventive medicine.

Toward an Ecological View of Health: An Imperative for the 21st Century

The final paper presented at the conference was by Ted Schettler, MD, MPH. Schettler began by discussing the relationship between human and environmental health. In 2005, the United Nations released the largest assessment of the health of the earth's ecosystems ever undertaken. More than 1,000 experts from 95 countries prepared the report, which was then reviewed by a large independent board of editors and commented on by hundreds of experts and governments before being released.

The Green Building Council of Australia's environmental rating system Green Star has now developed tools to assess buildings in the education, retail, and healthcare sectors. The Green Star—Healthcare rating tool, in particular, aims to address the unique qualities, constraints, and opportunities within hospitals and other medical facilities.

It remains, however, much harder to measure the true value of a green hospital, because the productivity and operation have different measures and often different management. The majority of hospitals will look at patient recovery time, bed turnover, and staff retention to estimate their attributes and performance. The truly "green" hospital can look at benefits in all of these areas and more, but the situation requires true, holistic investment in people's health.

Finally, Changi General Hospital is Singapore's first purpose-built, multidisciplinary regional hospital, providing healthcare services to approximately 750,000 people in the eastern and northeastern parts of Singapore. Changi General Hospital instilled several green practices within these grounds. Some of these were waste composting from water conservation (the first hospital to use NewWater), increased energy efficiency of their hospital building and installations, waste-minimization methods to control the generation of unnecessary waste in both the administration and day-to-day running of the hospital, and participation in community grassroots education and staff-enrichment programs.

Reference: http://161.142.92/penerbitan/buletin/khas99/narimah.html.

REFERENCES

1. Hall D. *Globalization, Privatization and Healthcare—A Preliminary Report.* Public Services International Research Unit, School of Computing and Mathematical Sciences, University of Greenwich, January 2001. Greenwich: University of Greenwich; 2001.

2. Pollock AM, Price D. Rewriting the regulations: how the World Trade Organization could accelerate privatization in the health care system. *Lancet.* 2000;356(9246):1995–2000.

3. OXFAMAmerica. Retrieved June 23, 2008, from http://www.oxfamamerica.org/whatwedo/issues we work on/trade/news publications/trips/art5391.html.

4. AMEinfo. 2nd Annual Global Healthcare Expansion Congress, Dubai, UAE, 2007. Retrieved from http://www.ameinfo.com/126097.html.

5. Lethbridge J. *A Global Review of the Expansion of Multinational Healthcare Companies.* Public Services international Research Unit, University of Greenwich; September 2007. Retrieved from www.psiru.org.

6. Retrieved from http://go.worldbank.org/MUFMCLWJR1.

7. La Vecchia C, Lucchini F, Levi F. Worldwide trends in suicide mortality, 1955–1989. *Acta of Psychiatry Scandinavia.* 1994;90:53–64.

8. Murray CJL, Lopez AD, eds. *The Global Burden of Disease.* Cambridge, MA: Harvard University Press; 1996.

9. Reza Q, Mercy JA, Krug E. Epidemiology of violent deaths in the world. *Injury Prevention.* 2001;7:104–111.

10. Krug EG, Mercy JA, Dahlberg LL, Zwi AB. The world report on violence and health. *Lancet.* 2002;360(9339):1083–1088.

11. Prince M, Patel V, Saxena S, et al. Global mental health 1: no health without mental health. *Lancet.* 2007;307(9590):859–878.

12. Murray CJL, Lopez AD. Alternative projections of mortality and disability by cause 1990–2020: the global burden of disease study. *Lancet.* 1997;349(9064):1498–1504.

13. Saxena S, Thorniroft G, Knapp M, Whiteford H. Global mental health 2: resources for mental health: scarcity, inequity, and inefficiency. *Lancet.* 2007;370(9590):878–890.

14. Rand Corporation. Preparing for an Aging World. Retrieved from http://www.rand.org/pubs/research_briefs/RB5058/index1.html.

15. United Nations Department of Economic and Social Affairs, Population Division. Executive Summary: World Population Aging 2007. New York: UN; 2007, pp. xxv–xxix.

16. Friedman T. *Hot, Flat, and Crowded.* New York: Farrar, Strauss, and Giroux; 2008.

Glossary of Common Terms[1]

Access   An individual's ability to obtain appropriate healthcare services. Barriers to access can be financial (insufficient monetary resources), geographic (distance to providers), organizational (lack of available providers), and sociological (e.g., discrimination, language barriers). Efforts to improve access often focus on providing/ improving health coverage.

Accreditation   A process whereby a program of study or an institution is recognized by an external body as meeting certain predetermined standards. For facilities, accreditation standards are usually defined in terms of physical plant, governing body, administration, and medical and other staff. Accreditation is often carried out by organizations created for the purpose of assuring the public of the quality of the accredited institution or program. The state or federal government can recognize accreditation in lieu of, or as the basis for, licensure or other mandatory approvals. Public or private payment programs often require accreditation as a condition of payment for covered services. Accreditation may either be permanent or may be given for a specified period of time.

Activities of daily living (ADL)   An index or scale which measures a patient's degree of independence in bathing, dressing, using the toilet, eating, and moving from one place to another.

Acute care   Medical treatment rendered to individuals whose illnesses or health problems are of a short-term or episodic nature. Acute-care facilities are those hospitals that mainly serve persons with short-term health problems.

Acute disease   A disease that is characterized by a single episode of a relatively short duration from which the patient returns to his or her normal or previous level of activity. Although acute diseases are frequently distinguished from chronic diseases, there is no standard definition or distinction. It is worth noting that an acute episode of a chronic disease (e.g., an episode of diabetic coma in a patient with diabetes) is often treated as an acute disease.

Adverse event   In a medical context, an injury resulting from a medical intervention.

Adverse selection A tendency for utilization of health services in a population group to be higher than average. From an insurance perspective, adverse selection occurs when persons with poorer than average health status apply for, or continue, insurance coverage to a greater extent than do persons with average or better health expectations.

Affiliation An agreement (usually formal) between two or more otherwise independent entities or individuals that defines how they will relate to each other. Affiliation agreements between hospitals may specify procedures for referring or transferring patients from one facility to another, joint faculty and/or medical staff appointments, teaching relationships, sharing of records or services, or provision of consultation between programs.

Agency for Healthcare Research and Quality
The Agency for Healthcare Research and Quality (AHRQ) was created in December 1989 as the Agency for Health Care Policy and Research (AHCPR), a Public Health Service agency within the U.S. Department of Health and Human Services reporting to the Secretary. The agency was reauthorized December 1999, as the Agency for Healthcare Research and Quality. AHRQ's mission is to support research designed to improve the outcomes and quality of health care, reduce its costs, address patient safety and medical errors, and broaden access to effective services. The research sponsored, conducted, and disseminated by AHRQ provides information that helps people make better decisions about health care.

All patient diagnosis-related groups (APDRG)
An enhancement of the original DRGs designed to apply to a population broader than that of Medicare beneficiaries, who are predominately older individuals. The APDRG set includes groupings for pediatric and maternity cases as well as services for HIV-related conditions and other special cases.

Allied health personnel Specially trained and licensed (when necessary) health workers other than physicians, dentists, optometrists, chiropractors, podiatrists, and nurses. The term has no constant or agreed-on detailed meaning; it is sometimes used synonymously with paramedical personnel, sometimes meaning all health workers who perform tasks that must otherwise be performed by a physician, and at other times referring to health workers who do not usually engage in independent practice.

Allowable costs Items or elements of an institution's costs that are reimbursable under a payment formula. Both Medicare and Medicaid reimburse hospitals on the basis of only certain costs. Allowable costs may exclude, for example, luxury accommodations and costs that are not reasonable expenditures or that are unnecessary for the efficient delivery of health services to persons covered under the program in question.

All-payer system A system in which prices for health services and payment methods are the same, regardless of who is paying. For instance, in an all-payer system, federal or state government, a private insurer, a self-insured employer plan, an individual, or any other payer could pay the same rates. The uniform fee bars healthcare providers from shifting costs from one payer to another (see cost shifting).

Ambulatory care All types of health services that are provided on an outpatient basis, in contrast to services provided in the home or to persons who are inpatients. Although many inpatients may be ambulatory, the term ambulatory care usually implies that the patient must travel to a location to receive services that do not require an overnight stay (see also ambulatory setting and outpatient).

Ambulatory payment classification (APC) The basis for payment for care in the Outpatient Prospective Payment System. The APC is used in a fashion similar to the way Diagnosis-Related Groups (DRGs) are used for payment for inpatients. Both APCs and DRGs are intended to represent groups of patients that are similar clinically and that also have roughly the same resource consumption. The significant difference between them is that APCs depend on the procedures performed, whereas DRGs depend on the diagnoses treated.

Ambulatory setting A type of institutional organized health setting in which health services are provided on an outpatient basis. Ambulatory care settings may be either mobile (when the facility is capable of being moved to different locations) or fixed (when the person seeking care must travel to a fixed service site).

American Association of Health Plans (AAHP)
The AAHP, located in Washington, DC, represents

more than 1,000 HMOs, PPOs, and other network-based plans. Together they care for close to 140 million Americans nationwide. AAHP was created by the merger of the Group Health Association of America (GHAA) and the American Managed Care and Review Association (AMCRA). The merger of the two groups created a new organization that delivers a unified message about the modern style of healthcare delivery pioneered by HMOs, PPOs, and similar health plans.

Ancillary services   Supplemental services, including laboratory, radiology, physical therapy, and inhalation therapy, that are provided in conjunction with medical or hospital care.

Antitrust   A legal term encompassing a variety of efforts on the part of government to ensure that sellers do not conspire to restrain trade or fix prices for their goods or services in the market.

Any willing provider laws   Laws that require managed care plans to contract with all healthcare providers that meet their terms and conditions.

Appropriateness   Appropriate health care is care for which the expected health benefit exceeds the expected negative consequences by a wide enough margin to justify treatment.

Assignment   A process in which a Medicare beneficiary agrees to have Medicare's share of the cost of a service paid directly ("assigned") to a doctor or other provider and the provider agrees to accept the Medicare approved charge as payment in full. Medicare pays 80% of the cost and the beneficiary 20%, for most services.

Assisted living   A broad range of residential care services that includes some assistance with activities of daily living and instrumental activities of daily living but does not include nursing services such as administration of medication. Assisted-living facilities and in-home assisted-living care stress independence and generally provide less intensive care than that delivered in nursing homes and other long-term care institutions.

Association   A term signifying a relationship between two or more events or variables. Events are said to be associated when they occur more frequently together than one would expect by chance. Association does not necessarily imply a causal relationship. Statistical signif-

icance testing enables a researcher to determine the likelihood of observing the sample relationship by chance if in fact no association exists in the population that was sampled. The terms "association" and "relationship" are often used interchangeably.

Average wholesale price (AWP) of prescription drugs   The average wholesale price of a drug relates to the price that wholesalers charge pharmacies and is often used by pharmacists to price prescriptions. Drug manufacturers and labelers commonly publish suggested wholesale prices for their products. Price surveys of wholesalers are also available.

Bad debts   Income lost to a provider because of failure of patients to pay amounts owed. Bad debts may sometimes be recovered by increasing charges to paying patients. Some cost-based reimbursement programs reimburse certain bad debts. The impact of the loss of revenue from bad debts may be partially offset for proprietary institutions by the fact that income tax is not payable on income not received.

Balance billing   In Medicare and private fee-for-service health insurance, the practice of billing patients for charges that exceed the amount that the health plan will pay. Under Medicare, the excess amount cannot be more than 15% above the approved charge.

Behavioral health   An umbrella term that includes mental health and substance abuse and frequently is used to distinguish from "physical" health. Healthcare services provided for depression or alcoholism would be considered behavioral health care, whereas setting a broken leg would be physical health.

Behavioral Risk Factor Surveillance System (BRFSS)   The BRFSS, the world's largest telephone survey, tracks risk behaviors related to chronic diseases, injuries, and death in the United States. Administered and supported by the Division of Adult and Community Health, National Center for Chronic Disease Prevention and Health Promotion, Centers for Disease Control and Prevention, the BRFSS is an ongoing data-collection program. By 1994, all states, the District of Columbia, and three territories were participating in the BRFSS.

Benchmark   A level of care set as a goal to be attained. Internal benchmarks are derived from similar processes or services within an organization. Competitive benchmarks are comparisons with the best external competitors in the field. Generic benchmarks are drawn from the best performance of similar processes in other industries.

Beneficiary An individual who receives benefits from or is covered by an insurance policy or other healthcare financing program.

Biased selection The market imperfection that results from the uneven grouping of risks among competing subscribers. Biased selection includes favorable selection (attracting good risks and repelling bad ones) as well as adverse selection (the reverse). Biased selection can occur naturally, according to historical or accidental patterns, or it can occur strategically, according to conscious choices by either subscribers or insurers.

Bioterrorism The unlawful use, or threatened use, of micro-organisms or toxins derived from living organisms to produce death or disease in humans, animals, or plants. The act is intended to create fear and/or intimidate governments or societies in the pursuit of political, religious, or ideological goals.

Board certified Status granted to a medical specialist who completes a required course of training and experience (residency) and passes an examination in his or her specialty. Individuals who have met all requirements except examination are referred to as "board eligible."

Capital Fixed or durable nonlabor inputs or factors used in the production of goods and services, the value of such factors, or the money specifically allocated for their acquisition or development. Capital costs include, for example, the buildings, beds, and equipment used in the provision of hospital services. Capital assets are usually thought of as permanent and durable as distinguished from consumables such as supplies.

Capital costs Expenditures for land, facilities, and major equipment. They are distinguished from operating costs, which include such items as labor, supplies, and administrative expenses.

Capital expenditure An expenditure for the acquisition, replacement, modernization, or expansion of facilities or equipment that, under generally accepted accounting principles, is not properly chargeable as an expense of operation and maintenance.

Capitation A method of payment for health services in which an individual or institutional provider is paid a fixed amount for each person served, without regard to the actual number or nature of services provided to each person in a set period of time. Capitation is the characteristic payment method in certain health maintenance organizations. It also refers to a method of Federal support of health professional schools. Under these authorizations, each eligible school receives a fixed payment, called a "capitation grant," from the Federal government for each student enrolled.

Carrier A private organization, usually an insurance company, that finances health care.

Carve out Regarding health insurance, an arrangement whereby an employer eliminates coverage for a specific category of services (e.g., vision care, mental health/psychological services, and prescription drugs) and contracts with a separate set of providers for those services according to a predetermined fee schedule or capitation arrangement. Carve out may also refer to a method of coordinating dual coverage for an individual.

Case based Refers to a single patient or case.

Case management The monitoring and coordination of treatment rendered to patients with specific diagnoses or requiring high cost or extensive services.

Case mix A measure of the mix of cases being treated by a particular healthcare provider that is intended to reflect the patients' different needs for resources. Case mix is generally established by estimating the relative frequency of various types of patients seen by the provider in question during a given time period and may be measured by factors such as diagnosis, severity of illness, utilization of services, and provider characteristics.

Case severity A measure of intensity or gravity of a given condition or diagnosis for a patient.

Catastrophic health insurance Health insurance that provides protection against the high cost of treating severe or lengthy illnesses or disability. Generally, such policies cover all, or a specified percentage of, medical expenses above an amount that is the responsibility of another insurance policy up to a maximum limit of liability.

Catchment area A geographic area defined and served by a health program or institution such as a hospital or community mental health center that is delineated on the basis of such factors as population distribution, natural geographic boundaries, and transportation accessibility. By definition, all residents of the area needing the services of the program are usually eligible for them, although eligibility may also depend on additional criteria.

Causality Relating causes to the effects they produce. Most of epidemiology concerns causality, and several types of causes can be distinguished. A cause is termed "necessary" when a particular variable must always precede an effect. This effect need not be the sole result of the one variable. A cause is termed "sufficient" when a particular variable inevitably initiates or produces an effect. Any given cause may be necessary, sufficient, neither, or both.

Centers for Disease Control and Prevention (CDC) The Centers for Disease Control and Prevention, based in Atlanta, Georgia, is charged with protecting the nation's public health by providing direction in the prevention and control of communicable and other diseases and responding to public health emergencies. Within the U.S. Public Health Service, the CDC is the agency that led efforts to prevent such diseases as malaria, polio, smallpox, toxic shock syndrome, Legionnaire's disease and, more recently, acquired immunodeficiency syndrome (AIDS), and tuberculosis. The CDC's responsibilities evolve as the agency addresses contemporary threats to health, such as injury, environmental and occupational hazards, behavioral risks, and chronic diseases.

Centers for Medicare and Medicaid Services (CMS) The government agency within the Department of Health and Human Services that directs the Medicare and Medicaid programs (Titles XVIII and XIX of the Social Security Act) and conducts research to support those programs. It was formerly the Health Care Financing Administration (HCFA).

Charity care Generally refers to physician and hospital services provided to persons who are unable to pay for the cost of services, especially those who are low income, uninsured, and underinsured. A high proportion of the costs of charity care is derived from services for children and pregnant women (e.g., neonatal intensive care).

Chronic care Care and treatment rendered to individuals whose health problems are of a long-term and continuing nature. Rehabilitation facilities, nursing homes, and mental hospitals may be considered chronic care facilities.

Chronic disease A disease that has one or more of the following characteristics: (1) is permanent, (2) leaves residual disability, (3) is caused by nonreversible pathological alternation, (4) requires special training of the patient for rehabilitation, or (5) may be expected to require a long period of supervision, observation, or care.

Clinic A facility, or part of one, devoted to diagnosis and treatment of outpatients. "Clinic" is irregularly defined. It may either include or exclude physicians' offices, may be limited to describing facilities that serve poor or public patients, and may be limited to facilities in which graduate or undergraduate medical education is done.

Clinical condition A diagnosis (e.g., cerebral–vascular hemorrhage) or a patient state that may be associated with more than one diagnosis (such as paraplegia) or that may be as yet undiagnosed (such as low back pain).

Clinical event Services provided to patients (items of history taking, physical examination, preventative care, tests, procedures, drugs, advice) or information on clinical condition or on patient state used as a patient outcome.

Clinical performance measures Instruments that estimate the extent to which a healthcare provider: (1) delivers clinical services that are appropriate for each patient's condition; (2) provides them safely, competently, and in an appropriate time frame; and (3) achieves desired outcomes in terms of those aspects of patient health and patient satisfaction that can be affected by clinical services.

Clinical practice guidelines Systematically developed statements to assist practitioners and patients' decisions about health care to be provided for specific clinical circumstances.

Coinsurance A cost-sharing requirement under a health insurance policy. It provides that the insured party will assume a portion or percentage of the costs of covered services. The health insurance policy provides that the insurer will reimburse a specified percentage of all, or certain specified, covered medical expenses in excess of any deductible amounts payable by the insured. The insured is then liable for the remainder of the costs until their maximum liability is reached.

Community-based care   The blend of health and social services provided to an individual or family in their place of residence for the purpose of promoting, maintaining, or restoring health or minimizing the effects of illness and disability.

Community rating   A method of calculating health plan premiums using the average cost of actual or anticipated health services for all subscribers within a specific geographic area. The premium does not vary for different groups or subgroups of subscribers to reflect their specific claims experience or health status. Under modified community rating (the most common form), rates may vary based on subscribers' specific demographic characteristics (such as age and gender), but rate variation based on individuals' health status, claims experience, or policy duration is prohibited. "Pure" community rating prohibits rate variation based on demographic as well as health factors, and all subscribers in an area pay the same rate.

Community rating by class (class rating)   For federally qualified HMOs, the community rating by class (CRC) is the adjustment of community-rated premiums on the basis of such factors as age, gender, family size, marital status, and industry classification. These health plan premiums reflect the experience of all enrollees of a given class within a specific geographic area, rather than the experience of any one employer group.

Co-morbidities   Conditions that exist at the same time as the primary condition in the same patient (e.g., hypertension is a co-morbidity of many conditions such as diabetes, ischemic heart disease, and end-stage renal disease).

Competition   A characteristic of market economics in which buyers choose from among alternative goods and services made available in the market by two or more sellers. In a classic competitive market, there are many buyers and many sellers.

Computerized Needs-oriented Quality Measurement Evaluation System (CONQUEST) CONQUEST was developed by the Agency for Health-care Research and Quality (AHRQ) as a tool that permits users to collect and evaluate healthcare quality measures to find those suited to or adaptable to their needs. CONQUEST has interlocking databases describing "Measures" and clinical "Conditions." The Measure Database contains information on clinical performance measures-tools to assess the quality of the health care delivered by providers. The Condition Database contains information on incidence, prevalence, cost and utilization, co-morbidities, risk factors, treatments, and guidelines. These databases link by codes for clinical services and health outcomes related to specific measures and conditions.

Confidence interval   A range within which an estimate is deemed to be close to the actual value being measured. In statistical measurements, estimates cannot be said to be exact matches but, rather, are defined in terms of their probability of matching the value of the thing being measured.

Consumer   A person who purchases or receives goods or services for personal needs or use and not for resale.

Continuum of care   Clinical services provided during a single inpatient hospitalization or for multiple conditions over a lifetime. It provides a basis for evaluating quality, cost, and utilization over the long term.

Contractual allowance   The difference between what hospitals bill and what they receive in payment from third-party payers, most commonly government programs. Also known as contractual adjustment.

Coordination of benefits (COB)   Procedures used by insurers to avoid duplicate payment for losses insured under more than one insurance policy. A coordination of benefits, or "nonduplication," clause in either policy prevents double payment by making one insurer the primary payer, and assuring that not more than 100% of the cost is covered. Standard rules determine which of two or more plans, each having COB provisions, pays its benefits in full and which becomes the supplementary payer on a claim.

Co-payments   A fixed amount of money paid by a health plan enrollee (beneficiary) at the time of service. For example, the enrollee may pay a $10 co-pay at every physician office visit and $5 for each drug prescription filled. The health plan pays the remainder of the charge directly to the provider. This is a method of cost-sharing between the enrollee and the plan and serves as an incentive for the enrollee to use healthcare resources wisely. An enrollee might be offered a lower price benefit package in return for a higher co-payment.

Cost Expenses incurred in the provision of services or goods. Many different kinds of costs are defined and used (see allowable, direct, indirect, and operating costs). Charges, the price of a service or amount billed an individual or third party, may or may not be equal to service costs.

Cost-based reimbursement Payment made by a health plan or payer to healthcare providers based on the actual costs incurred in the delivery of care and services to plan beneficiaries. This method of paying providers is still used by some plans; however, cost-based reimbursement is being replaced by prospective payment and other payment mechanisms.

Cost–benefit analysis An analytic method in which a program's cost is compared with the program's benefits for a period of time, expressed in dollars, as an aid in determining the best investment of resources. For example, the cost of establishing an immunization service might be compared with the total cost of medical care and lost productivity that will be eliminated as a result of more persons being immunized. Cost–benefit analysis can also be applied to specific medical tests and treatments.

Cost center An accounting device whereby all related costs attributable to some "financial center" within an institution, such as a department or program, are segregated for accounting or reimbursement purposes.

Cost-effectiveness analysis A form of analysis that seeks to determine the costs and effectiveness of a medical intervention compared with similar alternative interventions to determine the relative degree to which they will obtain the desired health outcome(s). Cost-effectiveness analysis can be applied to any of a number of standards such as median life expectancy or quality of life after an intervention.

Cost of illness analysis An assessment of the economic impact of an illness or condition, including treatment costs.

Cost sharing Any provision of a health insurance policy that requires the insured individual to pay some portion of medical expenses. The general term includes deductibles, co-payments, and co-insurance.

Cost-shifting Recouping the cost of providing uncompensated care by increasing revenues from some payers to offset losses and lower net payments from other payers.

Coverage The guarantee against specific losses provided under the terms of an insurance policy. Coverage is sometimes used interchangeably with benefits or protection and is also used to mean insurance or insurance contract.

Covered entity Refers to three types of entities that must comply with Federal health information privacy regulations (i.e., HIPAA Privacy Rule): healthcare providers, health plans, and healthcare clearinghouses. For these purposes, healthcare providers include hospitals, physicians, and other caregivers, as well as researchers, who provide health care and receive, access, or generate individually identifiable healthcare information.

Covered services Healthcare services covered by an insurance plan.

Credentialing The recognition of professional or technical competence. The credentialing process may include registration, certification, licensure, professional association membership, or the award of a degree in the field. Certification and licensure affect the supply of health personnel by controlling entry into practice and influence the stability of the labor force by affecting geographic distribution, mobility, and retention of workers. Credentialing also determines the quality of personnel by providing standards for evaluating competence and by defining the scope of functions and how personnel may be used.

Critical access hospital (CAH) A rural hospital designation established by the Medicare Rural Hospital Flexibility Program (MRHFP) enacted as part of the 1997 Balanced Budget Act. Rural hospitals meeting criteria established by their State may apply for critical access hospital status. Designated hospitals are reimbursed based on cost (rather than prospective payment), must comply with Federal and State regulations for CAHs, and are exempt from certain hospital staffing requirements.

Crowd out A phenomenon whereby new public programs or expansions of existing public programs designed to extend coverage to the uninsured prompt some privately insured persons to drop their private coverage and take advantage of the expanded public subsidy.

Cultural competence A practitioner or institution's understanding of and sensitivity to the cultural background and primary language of patients in any component of service delivery, including patient education materials, questionnaires, office or healthcare organization setting, direct patient care, and public health campaigns.

Current population survey (CPS) A national survey conducted annually by the U.S. Department of Commerce, Bureau of the Census, the CPS gathers information on the non-institutionalized population of the United States. The CPS is the most commonly reported source for the number of persons without health insurance and other information about this population.

Current Procedural Terminology, 4th Edition (CPT-4) A manual that assigns five digit codes to medical services and procedures to standardize claims processing and data analysis.

Customary charge One of the factors determining a physician's payment for a service under Medicare. Calculated as the physician's median charge for that service over a prior 12-month period.

Debt service Required payments for interest on and retirement of a debt. The amount needed, supplied, or accrued for meeting such payments during any given accounting period. A budget or operating statement heading for such items.

Deductible The amount of loss or expense that must be incurred by an insured or otherwise covered individual before an insurer will assume any liability for all or part of the remaining cost of covered services. Deductibles may be either fixed-dollar amounts or the value of specified services (such as 2 days of hospital care or one physician visit). Deductibles are usually tied to some reference period over which they must be incurred, for example, $100 per calendar year, benefit period, or spell of illness.

Defined benefit Funding mechanisms for pension plans that can also be applied to health benefits. Typical pension approaches include: (1) pegging benefits to a percentage of an employee's average compensation over his or her entire service or over a particular number of years; (2) calculation of a flat monthly payment; and (3) setting benefits based upon a definite amount for each year of service, either as a percentage of compensation for each year of service or as a flat dollar amount for each year of service.

Deidentification A process whereby information that could identify the clinician, the reporter, the healthcare institution, or another organization involved in a medical error are removed from an error report after it is received. This process is used to maintain records of factors that could cause errors, but assure those who report errors that their reports will not be used in civil lawsuits against them.

Deinstitutionalization Policy that calls for the provision of supportive care and treatment for medically and socially dependent individuals in the community rather than in an institutional setting.

Demand In health economics, the amount of a good or service consumers are willing and able to buy at varying prices, given constant income and other factors. Demand should be distinguished from utilization (the amount of services actually used) and need (which has a normative connotation and relates to the amount of goods or services that should be consumed based on professional value judgments).

Denominator For a performance measure, the sample of cases that will be observed (e.g., the number of patients discharged alive with a confirmed diagnosis of acute myocardial infarction, excluding patients with bleeding or other specified conditions).

Diagnosis-related groups (DRGs) Groupings of diagnostic categories drawn from the International Classification of Diseases and modified by the presence of a surgical procedure, patient age, presence or absence of significant co-morbidities or complications, and other relevant criteria. DRGs are the case-mix measure used in Medicare's prospective payment system.

Direct cost A cost that is identifiable directly with a particular activity, service, or product of the program experiencing the costs. These costs do not include the allocation of costs to a cost center that are not specifically attributable to that cost center.

Direct patient care   Any activities by a health professional involving direct interaction, treatment, administration of medications, or other therapy or involvement with a patient.

Disability   Any limitation of physical, mental, or social activity of an individual as compared with other individuals of similar age, gender, and occupation. Frequently refers to limitation of a person's usual or major activities, most commonly vocational. There are varying types (functional, vocational, learning), degrees (partial, total), and durations (temporary, permanent) of disability. Public programs often provide benefits for specific disabilities, such as total and permanent.

Discharge   The release of a patient from a provider's care, usually referring to the date at which a patient checks out of a hospital.

Disease   May be defined as a failure of the adaptive mechanisms of an organism to counteract adequately, normally, or appropriately to stimuli and stresses to which it is subjected, resulting in a disturbance in the function or structure of some part of the organism. This definition emphasizes that disease is multifactorial and may be prevented or treated by changing any or a combination of the factors. Disease is a very elusive and difficult concept to define, being largely socially defined. Thus, criminality and drug dependence are presently seen by some as diseases when they were previously considered to be moral or legal problems.

Disease management   The process of identifying and delivering within selected patient populations (e.g., patients with asthma or diabetes) the most efficient, effective combination of resources, interventions, or pharmaceuticals for the treatment or prevention of a disease. Disease management could include team-based care where physicians and/or other health professionals participate in the delivery and management of care. It also includes the appropriate use of pharmaceuticals.

Drug risk-sharing arrangements   Healthcare provider organizations may be at partial, full, or no risk for drug costs. Provider groups at partial risk share in a proportion of savings and/or cost overruns. The group

can share in savings if it prescribes less than the budgeted amount ("upside risk"), and it may also share in any over-expenditures ("downside risk"). Groups at full risk realize all of the savings or absorb all of the losses. Groups at no risk absorb none of the losses and profits (typically, risks are absorbed by the HMO or other managed care organization).

Drug utilization review (DUR)   A formal program for assessing drug prescription and use patterns. DURs typically examine patterns of drug misuse, monitor current therapies, and intervene when prescribing or utilization patterns fall outside pre-established standards. DUR is usually retrospective but can also be performed before drugs are dispensed. DURs were established by the Omnibus Budget Reconciliation Act (OBRA) in 1990 and are required for Medicaid programs.

Electronic claim   A digital representation of a medical bill generated by a provider or by the provider's billing agent for submission using telecommunications to a health insurance payer.

Emergency medical services (EMS)   Services used in responding to the perceived individual need for immediate treatment for medical, physiological, or psychological illness or injury.

Epidemic   A group of cases of a specific disease or illness clearly in excess of what one would normally expect in a particular geographic area. There is no absolute criterion for using the term epidemic—as standards and expectations change, so might the definition of an epidemic (e.g., an epidemic of violence).

Epidemiology   The study of the patterns of determinants and antecedents of disease in human populations. Epidemiology uses biology, clinical medicine, and statistics in an effort to understand the etiology (causes) of illness and/or disease. The ultimate goal of the epidemiologist is not merely to identify underlying causes of a disease but to apply findings to disease prevention and health promotion.

Etiology   Cause. This term is used by epidemiologists.

Evidence-based decision making   In a health policy context, evidence-based decision making is the application of the best available scientific evidence to policy decisions about specific medical treatments or changes in the delivery system. The goals of evidence-based decision making are to improve the quality of care, increase the efficiency of care delivery, and improve the allocation of healthcare resources.

Evidence-based medicine   Evidence-based medicine is the conscientious, explicit, and judicious use of current best evidence in making decisions about the care of individual patients. This approach must balance the best external evidence with the desires of the patient and the clinical expertise of healthcare providers.

Exclusive provider arrangement (EPA)   All indemnity or service plans that provide benefit only if care is rendered by the institutional and professional providers with which they contract (with some exceptions for emergency and out-of-area services).

Experience rating   A method of adjusting health plan premiums based on the historical utilization data and distinguishing characteristics of a specific subscriber group.

Family practice   A form of specialty practice in which physicians provide continuing comprehensive primary care within the context of the family unit.

Favorable selection   A tendency for utilization of health services in a population group to be lower than expected or estimated.

Federal poverty level (FPL)   The amount of income determined by the federal Department of Health and Human Services to provide a bare minimum for food, clothing, transportation, shelter, and other necessities. FPL is reported annually and varies according to family size. Public assistance programs usually define income limits in relation to FPL.

Fee-for-service   Method of billing for health services under which a physician or other practitioner charges separately for each patient encounter or service rendered. It is the method of billing used by the majority of U.S. physicians. Under a fee-for-service payment system, expenditures increase if the fees themselves increase, if more units of service are provided, or if more expensive services are substituted for less expensive ones. This system contrasts with salary, per capita, or other prepayment systems, where the payment to the physician is not changed with the number of services actually used.

Fee schedule   An exhaustive list of physician services in which each entry is associated with a specific monetary amount that represents the approved payment level for a given insurance plan.

Financial feasibility   The projected ability of a provider to pay the capital and operating costs associated with the delivery of a proposed healthcare service.

Formulary   A list of drugs, usually by their generic names, and indications for their use. A formulary is intended to include a sufficient range of medicines to enable physicians, dentists, and, as appropriate, other healthcare practitioners to prescribe all medically appropriate treatment for all reasonably common illnesses. An "open" formulary allows coverage for almost all drugs. A "closed" formulary provides coverage for a limited set of drugs. A "managed" formulary includes a list of preferred drugs that the health plan prefers to use because they cost less or are more effective or for other reasons. A "tiered formulary" financially rewards patients for using generic and formulary drugs by requiring the patient to pay progressively higher co-payments for brand-name and nonformulary drugs. For example, in a three-tiered benefit structure, co-payments may be $5 for a generic, $10 for a formulary brand product, and $25 for a nonformulary brand product.

Gatekeeper   The primary care practitioner in managed care organizations who determines whether the presenting patient needs to see a specialist or requires other non-routine services. The goal is to guide the patient to appropriate services while avoiding unnecessary and costly referrals to specialists.

General practice   A form of practice in which physicians without specialty training provide a wide range of primary healthcare services to patients.

Generic substitution   In cases in which the patent on a specific pharmaceutical product expires and drug manufacturers produce generic versions of the original branded product, the generic version of the drug (which is theorized to be identical to the product manufactured by a different firm) is dispensed even though the original product is prescribed. Some managed care organizations and Medicaid programs mandate generic substitution because of the generally lower cost of generic products. There are State and Federal regulations regarding generic substitutions.

Genomics The study of genomes, which includes gene mapping, gene sequencing, and gene function.

Global budgeting A method of hospital cost-containment in which participating hospitals must share a prospectively set budget. Method for allocating funds among hospitals may vary but the key is that the participating hospitals agree to an aggregate cap on revenues that they will receive each year. Global budgeting may also be mandated under a universal health insurance system.

Global fee A total charge for a specific set of services, such as obstetrical services that encompass prenatal, delivery, and postnatal care.

Globalization[2,3] The process whereby national and international policy makers promote domestic deregulation and external liberalization; the removal of barriers to international trade, foreign direct investments, and short-term financial flows. Globalization impacts health in many ways as world markets are opened. Access to world markets affects national economies and politics, which in turn, affect the health-related sectors of the economy. These changes then affect each country's healthcare system, population level health, and individual risks. Globalization also has an impact on the economies of countries and the economies of households. In turn, the wealth of individuals and countries are highly correlated with the health status of populations.

Graduate medical education (GME) Medical education after receipt of the Doctor of Medicine (MD) or equivalent degree, including the education received as an intern, resident (which involves training in a specialty), or fellow, as well as continuing medical education. CMS partly finances GME through Medicare direct and indirect payments.

Gross domestic product (GDP) The market value of all goods and services produced by labor and property within the United States (or other country) during a particular period of time. Income from overseas operations of a domestic corporation would not be included in the GDP, but activities carried on within U.S. borders by a foreign company would be. The GDP measures how the U.S. economy is doing.

Group practice A formal association of three or more physicians or other health professionals providing health services. Income from the practice is pooled and redistributed to the members of the group according to some prearranged plan (often, but not necessarily, through partnership). Groups vary a great deal in size, composition, and financial arrangements.

Guaranteed issue Requirement that insurance carriers offer coverage to groups and/or individuals during some period each year. HIPAA requires that insurance carriers guarantee issue of all products to small groups (2–50). Some state laws exceed HIPAA's minimum standards and require carriers to guarantee issue to additional groups and individuals.

Guaranteed renewal Requirement that insurance carriers renew existing coverage to groups and/or individuals. HIPAA requires that insurance issuers guarantee renewal of all products to all groups and individuals.

Handicapped As defined by Section 504 of the Rehabilitation Act of 1973, any person who has a physical or mental impairment that substantially limits one or more major life activity, has a record of such impairment, or is regarded as having such an impairment.

Health The state of complete physical, mental, and social well-being and not merely the absence of disease or infirmity. It is recognized, however, that health has many dimensions (anatomical, physiological, and mental) and is largely culturally defined. The relative importance of various disabilities will differ depending on the cultural milieu and the role of the affected individual in that culture. Most attempts at measurement have been assessed in terms or morbidity and mortality.

Health consumer One who may receive or is receiving health services. Although all people at times consume health services, a consumer, as the term is used in health legislation and programs, is usually someone who is not associated in any direct or indirect way with the provision of health services.

Health education Any combination of learning opportunities designed to facilitate voluntary adaptations of behavior (in individuals, groups, or communities) conducive to health.

Health facilities Collectively, all physical plants used in the provision of health services—usually limited to facilities that were built for the purpose of providing health care, such as hospitals and nursing homes. They do not include an office building that includes a physician's office. Health facility classifications include hospitals (both general and specialty), long-term care facilities, kidney dialysis treatment centers, and ambulatory surgical facilities.

Health insurance   Financial protection against the healthcare costs arising from disease or accidental bodily injury. Such insurance usually covers all or part of the costs of treating the disease or injury. Insurance may be obtained on either an individual or a group basis. Although the term is often used by policy makers to refer to comprehensive coverage, insurers and regulators use it also to refer to other forms of coverage such as long-term care insurance, supplemental insurance, specified disease policies, and accidental death and dismemberment insurance.

Health maintenance organization (HMO)   An entity with four essential attributes: (1) an organized system providing health care in a geographic area, which accepts the responsibility to provide or otherwise assure the delivery of (2) an agreed-upon set of basic and supplemental health maintenance and treatment services to (3) a voluntarily enrolled group of persons and (4) for which services the entity is reimbursed through a predetermined fixed, periodic prepayment made by, or on behalf of each person or family unit enrolled. The payment is fixed without regard to the amounts of actual services provided to an individual enrollee. Individual practice associations involving groups or independent physicians can be included under the definition.

Health manpower shortage area (HMSA)   An area or group which the U.S. Department of Health and Human Services designates as having an inadequate supply of healthcare providers. HMSAs can include: (1) an urban or rural geographic area, (2) a population group for which access barriers can be demonstrated to prevent members of the group from using local providers, or (3) medium and maximum-security correctional institutions and public or nonprofit private residential facilities.

Health personnel   Collectively, all persons working in the provision of health services, whether as individual practitioners or employees of health institutions and programs, whether professionally trained, and whether subject to public regulation. Facilities and health personnel are the principal health resources used in producing health services.

Health plan   An organization that provides a defined set of benefits. This term usually refers to an HMO-like entity, as opposed to an indemnity insurer.

Health planning   Planning concerned with improving health, whether undertaken comprehensively for a whole community or for a particular population, type of health service, institution, or health program. The components of health planning include: data assembly and analysis, goal determination, action recommendation, and implementation strategy.

Health policy   An insurance contract consisting of a defined set of benefits.

Health promotion   Any combination of health education and related organizational, political, and economic interventions designed to facilitate behavioral and environmental adaptations that will improve or protect health.

Health-related quality of life (HRQL)   In public health and in medicine, the concept of health-related quality of life refers to a person or group's perceived physical and mental health over time. Physicians have often used health-related quality of life indicators to measure the effects of chronic illness in their patients in order to better understand how an illness interferes with a person's day-to-day life. Similarly, public health professionals use health-related quality of life indicators to measure the effects of numerous disorders, short- and long-term disabilities, and diseases in different populations. Tracking health-related quality of life in different populations can identify subgroups with poor physical or mental health and can help guide policies or interventions to improve their health.

Health risk factors   Chemical, psychological, physiological, or genetic factors and conditions that predispose an individual to the development of a disease.

Health service area   Geographic area designated on the basis of such factors as geography, political boundaries, population, and health resources for the effective planning and development of health services.

Health services research   Health services research is the multidisciplinary field of scientific investigation that studies how social factors, financing systems, organizational structures and processes, health technologies, and personal behaviors affect access to health care, the quality and cost of health care, and ultimately our health and well-being. Its research domains are individuals, families, organizations, institutions, communities, and populations.

Health status   The state of health of a specified individual, group, or population. It may be measured by obtaining proxies such as people's subjective assessments of their health, by one or more indicators of mortality and morbidity in the population, such as longevity or maternal and infant mortality, or by using the incidence or prevalence of major diseases (communicable, chronic, or nutritional). Conceptually, health status is the proper outcome measure for the effectiveness of a specific population's medical care system, although attempts to relate effects of available medical care to variations in health status have proved difficult.

Healthcare cost and utilization project quality indicators (HCUP QIs)   HCUP QIs comprise a set of 33 clinical performance measures that inform hospitals' self-assessments of inpatient quality of care as well as state and community assessments of access to primary care. Developed by the Agency for Healthcare Research and Quality (AHRQ) as a quick and easy-to-use screening tool, HCUP QIs are intended as a starting point in identifying clinical areas appropriate for further, more in-depth study and analysis. HCUP QIs span three dimensions of care: (1) potentially avoidable adverse hospital outcomes, (2) potentially inappropriate utilization of hospital procedures, and (3) potentially avoidable hospital admissions.

Healthcare paraprofessional   Home health aides, certified nurses aides, and personal care attendants who provide direct care and personal support services in hospitals, nursing homes, other institutions, as well as home-based care to the disabled, aged, and infirm.

High-risk pool   A subsidized health insurance pool organized by some states as an alternative for individuals who have been denied health insurance because of a medical condition or whose premiums are rated significantly higher than the average because of health status or claims experience. Commonly operated through an association composed of all health insurers in a state. HIPAA allows states to use high-risk pools as an "acceptable alternative mechanism" that satisfies the statutory requirements for ensuring access to health insurance coverage for certain individuals.

Holism   Refers to the integration of mind, body, and spirit of a person and emphasizes the importance of perceiving the individual (regarding physical symptoms) in a "whole" sense. Holism teaches that the healthcare system must extend its focus beyond solely the physical aspects of disease and particular organ in question to concern itself with the whole person and the interrelationships between the emotional, social, spiritual, as well as physical implications of disease and health.

Home- and community-based services (HCBS)   Any care or services provided in a patient's place of residence or in a noninstitutional setting located in the immediate community. Home- and community-based services may include home health care, adult day care or day treatment, medical equipment services, or other interventions provided for the purpose of allowing a patient to receive care at home or in their community.

Home health care   Health services rendered in the home to the aged, disabled, sick, or convalescent individuals who do not need institutional care. The services may be provided by a visiting nurse association (VNA) home health agency, county public health department, hospital, or other organized community group and may be specialized or comprehensive. The most common types of home health care are the following nursing services: speech, physical, occupational, and rehabilitation therapy; homemaker services; and social services.

Horizontal integration   Merging of two or more firms at the same level of production in some formal, legal relationship (see vertical integration).

Hospice   A program that provides palliative and supportive care for terminally ill patients and their families, either directly or on a consulting basis with the patient's physician or another community agency. Originally a medieval name for a way station for crusaders where they could be replenished, refreshed, and cared for, hospice is used here for an organized program of care for people going through life's "last station." The entire family is considered the unit of care, and care extends through their period of mourning.

Hospital   An institution whose primary function is to provide inpatient diagnostic and therapeutic services for a variety of medical conditions, both surgical and nonsurgical. In addition, most hospitals provide some outpatient services, particularly emergency care. Hospitals may be classified by length of stay (short- or long-term), as teaching or nonteaching, by major type of service (psychiatric, tuberculosis, general, and other specialties, such as maternity, pediatric, or ear, nose, and throat), and by type of ownership or control (federal, state, or local government; for-profit and nonprofit). The hospital system is dominated by the short-term, general, nonprofit community hospital, often called a voluntary hospital.

Iatrogenic Caused by medical treatment such as a drug side effect or a postoperative infection.

Incidence In epidemiology, the number of cases of disease, infection, or some other event having their onset during a prescribed period of time in relation to the unit of population in which they occur. Incidence measures morbidity or other events as they happen over a period of time. Examples include the number of accidents occurring in a manufacturing plant during a year in relationship to the number of employees in the plant or the number of cases of mumps occurring in a school during a month in relation to the number of pupils enrolled in the school. It usually refers only to the number of new cases, particularly of chronic diseases.

Incurred but not reported (IBNR) Claims that have not been reported to the insurer as of some specific date for services that have been provided. The estimated value of these claims is a component of an insurance company's current liabilities.

Indemnity Health insurance benefits provided in the form of cash payments rather than services. An indemnity insurance contract usually defines the maximum amounts that will be paid for covered services.

Independent practice association (IPA) An organized form of prepaid medical practice in which participating physicians remain in their independent office settings, seeing both enrollees of the IPA and private-pay patients. Participating physicians may be reimbursed by the IPA on a fee-for-service basis or a capitation basis.

Indicator A quantitative or statistical measure or gauge for monitoring clinical care.

Indigent care Health services provided to the poor or those unable to pay. Because many indigent patients are not eligible for federal or state programs, the costs that are covered by Medicaid are generally recorded separately from indigent care costs.

Indirect cost A cost that cannot be identified directly with a particular activity, service, or product of the entity incurring the cost. Indirect costs are usually apportioned among an entity's services in proportion to each service's share of direct costs.

Individually identifiable health information Information that is a subset of health information, including demographic information collected from an individual, and is created or received by a healthcare provider, health plan, employer, or healthcare clearinghouse; and relates to the past, present, or future physical or mental health or condition of an individual; the provision of health care to an individual; or the past, present, or future payment for the provision of health care to an individual; and that identifies the individual or with respect to which there is a reasonable basis to believe the information can be used to identify the individual.

Inpatient A person who has been admitted at least overnight to a hospital or other health facility (which is therefore responsible for his/her room and board) for the purpose of receiving diagnostic treatment or other health services.

Institutional health services Health services delivered on an inpatient basis in hospitals, nursing homes, or other inpatient institutions. The term may also refer to services delivered on an outpatient basis by departments or other organizational units of, or sponsored by, such institutions.

Instrumental activities of daily living (IADL) An index or scale that measures a patient's degree of independence in aspects of cognitive and social functioning, including shopping, cooking, doing housework, managing money, and using the telephone.

Integrated services network (ISN) A network of organizations, usually including hospitals and physician groups, that provides or arranges to provide a coordinated continuum of services to a defined population and is held both clinically and fiscally accountable for the outcomes of the populations served.

Intermediate care facility (ICF) An institution that is licensed under state law to provide on a regular basis, health-related care and services to individuals who do not require the degree of care or treatment that a hospital or skilled nursing facility is designed to provide. Public institutions for care of the mentally retarded or people with related conditions are also included in the definition. The distinction between "health-related care and services" and "room and board" has often proven difficult to make but is important because ICFs are subject to quite different regulations and coverage requirements than institutions that do not provide health-related care and services.

International Classification of Diseases (ICD) A publication of the World Health Organization (WHO), revised periodically and now in its 10th revision, dated 1994. The full title is *International Statistical Classification of Diseases and Related Health Problems.* This classification, which originated for use in deaths, is used worldwide for that purpose. In addition, it has been used widely in the United States for hospital diagnosis classification since about 1955 through adaptations and modifications made in the United States of the 7th, 8th, and 9th revisions.

International medical graduate (IMG) A physician who graduated from a medical school outside of the United States, usually Canada. U.S. citizens who go to medical school abroad are classified as international medical graduates, as are foreign-born persons who are not trained in a medical school in this country. U.S. citizens represent only a small portion of the IMG group.

Internist A physician who focuses his or her practice on the care of critically ill and injured patients. After initial training in internal medicine, anesthesiology, or surgery, additional training in critical care is required to become board certified as an internist.

Intervention strategy A generic term used in public health to describe a program or policy designed to have an impact on an illness or disease. Hence, a mandatory seat belt law is an intervention designed to reduce automobile-related fatalities.

Inventory A detailed description of quantities and locations of different kinds of facilities, major equipment, and personnel that are available in a geographic area and the amount, type, and distribution of services these resources can support.

Joint Commission on Accreditation of Healthcare Organizations (JCAHO) A national private, nonprofit organization whose purpose is to encourage the attainment of uniformly high standards of institutional medical care. Establishes guidelines for the oper-

ation of hospitals and other health facilities and conducts survey and accreditation programs.

License/licensure A permission granted to an individual or organization by a competent authority, usually public, to engage lawfully in a practice, occupation, or activity. Licensure is the process by which the license is granted. It is usually granted on the basis of examination and/or proof of education rather than on measures of performance. A license is usually permanent but may be conditioned on annual payment of a fee, proof of continuing education, or proof of competence.

Long-term care A set of healthcare, personal care, and social services required by persons who have lost, or never acquired, some degree of functional capacity (e.g., the chronically ill, aged, disabled, or retarded) in an institution or at home on a long-term basis. The term is often used more narrowly to refer only to long-term institutional care such as that provided in nursing homes, homes for the retarded, and mental hospitals. Ambulatory services such home health care and assisted living, which can also be provided on a long-term basis, are seen as alternatives to long-term institutional care.

Magnetic resonance imaging (MRI) This relatively new form of diagnostic radiology is a method of imaging body tissues that uses the response or resonance of the nuclei of the atoms of one of the bodily elements, typically hydrogen or phosphorus, to externally applied magnetic fields.

Major depressive disorder To be diagnosed with major depressive disorder, a patient must exhibit a depressed mood or loss of interest in most daily activities, plus at least five of nine major symptoms during a 2-week period. Major symptoms include significant weight gain or loss, insomnia or hypersomnia, psychomotor agitation or retardation; fatigue or loss of energy, feelings of guilt or worthlessness, indecisiveness or impaired ability to concentrate, and recurrent thoughts of death or suicide.

Malpractice Professional misconduct or failure to apply ordinary skills in the performance of a professional act. A practitioner is liable for damages or injuries caused by malpractice. For some professions such as medicine, malpractice insurance can cover the costs of defending suits instituted against the professional and/or any damages assessed by the court, usually up to a maximum limit. To prove malpractice requires that a patient demonstrate some injury and that the injury be caused by negligence.

Managed behavioral health organization An organization that assumes the responsibility for managing the behavioral health benefit for an employer or payer organization under a "carve-out" arrangement. The management may range from utilization management services through its own organization or provider network. Reimbursement may be on a fee-for-service, shared risk, or full-risk basis. This is a specialty managed care organization (MCO).

Managed care The body of clinical, financial, and organizational activities designed to ensure the provision of appropriate healthcare services in a cost-efficient manner. Managed care techniques are most often practiced by organizations and professionals that assume risk for a defined population (e.g., health maintenance organizations).

Management services organization Management services organizations provide administrative and practice management services to physicians. An MSO may typically be owned by a hospital, hospitals, or investors. Large group practices may also establish MSOs to sell management services to other physician groups.

Mandatory reporting A system under which physicians or other health professionals are required by law to inform health authorities when a specified event occurs (e.g., a medical error or the diagnosis of a certain disease).

Maximum allowable actual charge (MAAC) A limitation on billed charges for Medicare services provided by nonparticipating physicians. For physicians with charges exceeding 115% of the prevailing charge for nonparticipating physicians, MAACs limit increases in actual charges to 1% per year. For physicians whose charges are less than 115% of the prevailing, MAACs limit actual charge increases so they may not exceed 115%.

Measure set A collection of measures with a common purpose and developer (see clinical performance measures).

Medicaid (Title XIX) A federally aided, state-operated and administered program that provides med-ical benefits for certain indigent or low-income persons in need of health and medical care. The program, authorized by Title XIX of the Social Security Act, is basically for the poor. It does not cover all of the poor, however, but only persons who meet specified eligibility criteria. Subject to broad federal guidelines, states determine the benefits covered, program eligibility, rates of payment for providers, and methods of administering the program.

Medical audit Detailed retrospective review and evaluation of selected medical records by qualified professional staff. Medical audits are used in some hospitals, group practices, and occasionally in private, independent practices for evaluating professional performance by comparing it with accepted criteria, standards, and current professional judgment. A medical audit is usually concerned with the care of a given illness and is undertaken to identify deficiencies in that care in anticipation of educational programs to improve it.

Medical error An error or omission in the medical care provided to a patient. Medical errors can occur in diagnosis, treatment, preventative monitoring or in the failure of a piece of medical equipment or another component of the medical system. Often, but not always, medical errors result in adverse events such as injury or death.

Medically indigent Persons who cannot afford needed health care because of insufficient income and/or lack of adequate health insurance.

Medical informatics The systematic study, or science, of the identification, collection, storage, communication, retrieval, and analysis of data about medical care services that can be used to improve decisions made by physicians and managers of healthcare organizations.

Medically necessary A treatment or service that is appropriate and consistent with a patient's diagnosis and that, in accordance with locally accepted standards of practice, cannot be omitted without adversely affecting the patent's condition or the quality of care.

Medically needy Persons who are categorically eligible for Medicaid and whose income, less the accumulated medical bills, is below state income limits for the Medicaid program.

Medically underserved population A population group experiencing a shortage of personal health services. A medically underserved population may or may not reside in a particular medically underserved area or be defined by its place of residence. Thus, migrants, American Indians, or the inmates of a prison or mental hospital may constitute such a population. The term is defined and used to give priority for federal assistance (e.g., the National Health Service Corps).

Medical management information system (MMIS) A data system that allows payers and purchasers to track healthcare expenditure and utilization patterns.

Medical review criteria Systematically developed statements that can be used to assess the appropriateness of specific healthcare decisions, services, and outcomes.

Medical savings account (MSA) An account in which individuals can accumulate contributions to pay for medical care or insurance. Some states give tax-preferred status to MSA contributions, but such contributions are still subject to Federal income taxation. MSAs differ from medical reimbursement accounts, sometimes called flexible benefits or Section 115 accounts, in that they need not be associated with an employer. MSAs are not currently recognized in federal statute.

Medicare (Title XVIII) A U.S. health insurance program for people aged 65 and over, for persons eligible for Social Security disability payments for 2 years or longer, and for certain workers and their dependents who need kidney transplantation or dialysis. Monies from payroll taxes and premiums from beneficiaries are deposited in special trust funds for use in meeting the expenses incurred by the insured. It consists of two separate but coordinated programs: hospital insurance (Part A) and supplementary medical insurance (Part B).

Medicare+Choice A new Medicare program created by the 1997 Balanced Budget Act. Medicare+Choice allows the Centers for Medicare and Medicaid Services (CMS) to contract with a variety of different managed care and fee-for-service entities offering greater flexibility to Medicare participants. Persons eligible for Medicare parts A and B are also eligible for Medicare+Choice (Medicare Part C).

Medicare Payment Advisory Commission (MedPAC) MedPAC is an independent federal body that advises the U.S. Congress on issues affecting the Medicare program. It was established by the Balanced Budget Act of 1997 (P.L. 105-33), which merged the Prospective Payment Assessment Commission (ProPAC) and the Physician Payment Review Commission (PPRC).

Medicare Rural Hospital Flexibility Program (MRHFP) A limited service hospital program created by the Balanced Budget Act of 1997 and modified by the Balanced Budget Refinement Act in 1999. Under the MRHFP, rural hospitals meeting criteria specified by their state can apply to become critical access hospitals. The program provides regulatory relief and a cost-based payment option for smaller, low-volume facilities that lack the resources needed to meet hospital staffing and other requirements under Medicare.

Medigap policy A private health insurance policy offered to Medicare beneficiaries to cover expenses not paid by Medicare. Medigap policies are strictly regulated by federal rules. This is also known as Medicare supplemental insurance.

Mental health The state of being of the individual with respect to emotional, social, and behavioral maturity. Although the term is often used to mean "good mental health," mental health is a relative state, varying from time to time in the individual, with some people more mentally healthy than others.

Morbidity The extent of illness, injury, or disability in a defined population. It is usually expressed in general or specific rates of incidence or prevalence.

Mortality Death. This is used to describe the relation of deaths to the population in which they occur. The mortality rate (death rate) expresses the number of deaths in a unit of population within a prescribed time and may be expressed as crude death rates (e.g., total deaths in relation to total population during a year) or as death rates specific for diseases and sometimes for age, gender, or other attributes (e.g., number of deaths from cancer in white males in relation to the white male population during a given year).

National Committee for Quality Assurance (NCQA) A national organization founded in 1979 composed of 14 directors representing consumers, purchasers, and providers of managed health care. It accredits quality assurance programs in prepaid managed healthcare organizations and develops and coordinates programs for assessing the quality of care and service in the managed care industry.

National Health Service Corps (NHSC) A program administered by the U.S. Public Health Service that places physicians and other providers in health professions shortage areas by providing scholarship and loan repayment incentives. Since 1970, the corps members have worked in community health centers, migrant centers, and Indian health facilities and in other sites targeting underserved populations.

National Pharmaceutical Stockpile (NPS) Program The mission of the Centers for Disease Control and Prevention's (CDC) National Pharmaceutical Stockpile (NPS) Program is to ensure the availability and rapid deployment of lifesaving pharmaceuticals, antidotes, other medical supplies, and equipment necessary to counter the effects of nerve agents, biological pathogens, and chemical agents. The NPS Program stands ready for immediate deployment to any U.S. location in the event of a terrorist attack using a biological toxin or chemical agent directed against a civilian population.

Network An affiliation of providers through formal and informal contracts and agreements. Networks may contract externally to obtain administrative and financial services.

Numerator For a performance measure, the cases in the denominator group that experience events specified in a medical review criterion (e.g., the number of patients discharged alive with a confirmed diagnosis of acute myocardial infarction, excluding patients with bleeding or other specified conditions, who were discharged on aspirin) (see denominator).

Nurse An individual trained to care for the sick, aged, or injured. A nurse can be defined as a professional qualified by education and authorized by law to practice nursing. There are many different types, specialties, and grades of nurses.

Nurse practitioner A registered nurse qualified and specially trained to provide primary care, including primary health care in homes and in ambulatory care facilities, long-term care facilities, and other healthcare institutions. Nurse practitioners generally function under the supervision of a physician but not necessarily in his or her presence. They are usually salaried rather than reimbursed on a fee-for-service basis, although the supervising physician may receive fee-for-service reimbursement for their services.

Nursing home Includes a wide range of institutions that provide various levels of maintenance and personal or nursing care to people who are unable to care for themselves and who have health problems that range from minimal to very serious. The term includes freestanding institutions or identifiable components of other health facilities that provide nursing care and related services, personal care, and residential care. Nursing homes include skilled nursing facilities and extended care facilities but not boarding homes.

Occupancy rate A measure of inpatient health facility use, determined by dividing available bed days by patient days. It measures the average percentage of a hospital's beds occupied and may be institution-wide or specific for one department or service.

Occupational health services Health services concerned with the physical, mental, and social well-being of an individual in relation to his or her working environment and with the adjustment of individuals to their work. The term applies to more than the safety of the workplace and includes health and job satisfaction. In the United States, the principal federal statute concerned with occupational health is the Occupational Safety and Health Act administered by the Occupational Safety and Health Administration (OSHA) and the National Institute of Occupational Safety and Health (NIOSH).

Office of Public Health Preparedness (OPHP) The OPHP directs the Department of Health and Human Services' (HHS) efforts to prepare for, protect against, respond to, and recover from all acts of bioterrorism and other public health emergencies that affect the civilian population, and it serves as the focal point within HHS for these activities. OPHP is headed by a director, who reports directly to the secretary, and serves as the secretary's principal advisor on HHS activities relating to protecting the civilian population from acts of bioterrorism and other public health emergencies. The office was created in January 2002.

Open enrollment A method for ensuring that insurance plans, especially prepaid plans, do not exclusively select good risks. Under an open enrollment requirement, a plan must accept all who apply during a specific period each year.

Operating cost   Necessary to operate an activity that provides health services. These costs normally include costs of personnel, materials, overhead, depreciation, and interest.

Operating margin   Revenues from sales minus current cost of goods sold. A measure of operating efficiency that is independent of the cost flow assumption for inventory. Sometimes called "current (gross) margin."

Opportunity cost   The cost of foregone outcomes that could have been achieved through alternative investments.

Outcome   Refers to the "outcome" (finding) of a given diagnostic procedure. It may also refer to cure of the patient, restoration of function, or extension of life. When used for populations or the healthcare system, it typically refers to changes in birth or death rates, or some similar global measure.

Outcomes research   Research on measures of changes in patient outcomes, that is, patient health status and satisfaction, resulting from specific medical and health interventions. Attributing changes in outcomes to medical care requires distinguishing the effects of care from the effects of the many other factors that influence patients' health and satisfaction.

Outpatient   A patient who is receiving ambulatory care at a hospital or other facility without being admitted to the facility. Usually, it does not mean people receiving services from a physician's office or other program that also does not provide inpatient care.

Overhead   The general costs of operating an entity that are allocated to all the revenue producing operations of the entity but that are not directly attributable to a single activity. For a hospital, these costs normally include maintenance of plant, occupancy costs, housekeeping, administration, and others.

Parity   Equality or comparability between two things. Parity legislation, usually applicable to mental health conditions such as depression or schizophrenia, requires that health insurers adhere to a principle of equal treatment when making decisions regarding mental health benefits compared with medical benefits. Data parity is a term used by researchers to describe the degree to which different data measures are equivalent.

Participating physician   A physician who agrees by contractual arrangement to accept the rules, terms, and fee schedule of a given health plan or provider network. In Medicare, a physician who signs an agreement to accept assignment on all Medicare claims for 1 year (see assignment).

Pathological   Indicative of or caused by a disease or condition.

Peer review   Generally, the evaluation by practicing physicians or other professionals of the effectiveness and efficiency of services ordered or performed by other members of the profession (peers). Frequently, peer review refers to review of research by other researchers.

Performance measures   Methods or instruments to estimate or monitor the extent to which the actions of a healthcare practitioner or provider conform to practice guidelines, medical review criteria, or standards of quality.

Per member per month (PMPM)   A unit of measure referring to health plan costs, revenues, hospital days, or patient visits.

Pharmaceutical assistance program   A public program to provide pharmaceutical coverage to those who cannot afford or have difficulty obtaining prescription drugs. Several states operate state-funded pharmaceutical assistance programs, which primarily provide benefits to low-income older persons or persons with disabilities who do not qualify for Medicaid.

Pharmaceutical care system   A strategy that attempts to use drug therapy more efficiently to achieve definite outcomes that improve a patient's quality of life. A pharmaceutical care system requires a reorientation of physicians, pharmacist, and nurses toward effective drug therapy outcomes. It is a set of relationships and decisions through which pharmacist, physicians, nurses, and patients work together to design, implement, and monitor a therapeutic plan that will produce specific therapeutic outcomes.

Pharmacoeconomics   The study of the costs and benefits associated with various pharmaceutical treatments.

Pharmacy benefit manager (PBM)   Many insurance companies, HMOs, and self-insured employers contract with PBMs to manage drug benefit coverage for employees and health plan members. Common tools employed by PBMs to manage drug benefits include management of pharmacy networks, implementation of generic substitution and mail-order programs, negotiation of rebates with drug manufacturers, formulary management, and clinical programs such as disease management.

Physician assistant (PA)   Also known as a physician extender, a PA is a specially trained and licensed or otherwise credentialed individual who performs tasks that might otherwise be performed by a physician, under the direction of a supervising physician.

Physician-hospital organization (PHO)   A legal entity formed by a hospital and a group of physicians to further mutual interests and to achieve market objectives. A PHO generally combines physicians and a hospital into a single organization for the purpose of obtaining payer contracts. Doctors maintain ownership of their practices and agree to accept managed care patients according to the terms of a professional services agreement with the PHO. The PHO serves as a collective negotiating and contracting unit. It is typically owned and governed jointly by a hospital and shareholder physicians.

Point of service   A health insurance benefits program in which subscribers can select between different delivery systems (i.e., HMO, PPO, and fee-for-service) when in need of healthcare services, rather than making the selection between delivery systems at time of open enrollment at place of employment. Typically, the costs associated with receiving care from HMO providers are less than when care is rendered by PPO or noncontracting providers.

Population   A set of individual persons, objects, or items from which samples are taken for statistical measurement—for example, all of the patients with a disease or condition that are of interest for a particular study, such as all of the cases of myocardial infarction occurring within a given year.

Population-based services   Health services targeted at populations of patients with specific diseases or disorders (e.g., patients with asthma or diabetes). The concept that the health care can be better administered if patients are examined as populations as well as spe-

cific cases is one basis for disease management and managed care.

Portability   Requirement that health plans guarantee continuous coverage without waiting periods for persons moving between plans.

Postacute care (also called subacute care or transitional care)   Type of short-term care provided by many long-term care facilities and hospitals that may include rehabilitation services, specialized care for certain conditions (such as stroke and diabetes), and/or postsurgical care and other services associated with the transition between the hospital and home. Residents on these units often have been hospitalized recently and typically have more complicated medical needs. The goal of subacute care is to discharge residents to their homes or to a lower level of care.

Potentially preventable adverse outcomes   Complications of a condition that may be modified or prevented with appropriate treatment (e.g., permanent hearing loss as an outcome of otitis media with effusion).

Practice guidelines, parameters   Standards used to guide providers based on accepted clinical treatment protocols for typical cases.

Preadmission certification   A process under which admission to a health institution is reviewed in advance to determine need and appropriateness and to authorize a length of stay consistent with norms for the evaluation.

Preexisting condition   A medical condition developed prior to issuance of a health insurance policy. Some policies exclude coverage of such conditions for a period of time or indefinitely.

Preferred drug list (or drug formulary)   A list of prescription drugs which are covered by a health plan (or other payer, e.g., Medicaid). Some drugs may be subject to a prior authorization mechanism, whereby the physician or other prescriber must justify why the patient would need a particular brand-name product (see prior authorization).

Preferred provider arrangement (PPA)   Selective contracting with a limited number of healthcare providers, often at reduced or prenegotiated rates of payment.

Preferred provider organization (PPO) Formally organized entity generally consisting of hospital and physician providers. The PPO provides healthcare services to purchasers, usually at discounted rates, in return for expedited claims payment and a somewhat predictable market share. In this model, consumers have a choice of using PPO or non-PPO providers; however, financial incentives are built in to benefit structures to encourage utilization of PPO providers.

Prepayment Usually refers to any payment to a provider for anticipated services (such as an expectant mother paying in advance for maternity care). Sometimes prepayment is distinguished from insurance as referring to payment to organizations that, unlike an insurance company, take responsibility for arranging for and providing needed services as well as paying for them (such as health maintenance organizations, prepaid group practices, and medical foundations).

Prevailing charge One of the factors determining a physician's payment for a service under Medicare, set at a percentile of customary charges of all physicians in the locality.

Prevalence The number of cases of disease, infected persons, or persons with some other attribute, present at a particular time and in relation to the size of the population from which drawn. It can be a measurement of morbidity at a moment in time (e.g., the number of cases of hemophilia in the country as of the first of the year).

Preventive medicine Care that has the aim of preventing disease or its consequences. It includes healthcare programs aimed at warding off illnesses (e.g., immunizations), early detection of disease (e.g., Pap smears), and inhibiting further deterioration of the body (e.g., exercise or prophylactic surgery). Preventive medicine developed after the discovery of bacterial diseases and was concerned in its early history with specific medical control measures taken against the agents of infectious diseases. Preventive medicine is also concerned with general preventive measures aimed at improving the healthfulness of the environment. In particular, the promotion of health through altering behavior, especially using health education, is gaining prominence as a component of preventive care.

Primary care Basic or general health care focused on the point at which a patient ideally first seeks assistance from the medical care system. Primary care is considered comprehensive when the primary provider takes responsibility for the overall coordination of the care of the patient's health problems, be they biological, behavioral, or social. The appropriate use of consultants and community resources is an important part of effective primary care. Such care is generally provided by physicians but is increasingly provided by other personnel such as nurse practitioners or physician assistants.

Primary care case management (PCCM) The use of a primary care physician to manage the use of medical or surgical care. PCCM programs usually pay for all care in a fee-for-service basis.

Primary care provider (PCP) A generalist physician (family practice, general internal medicine, general pediatrics, and sometimes obstetrics/gynecology for women patients) who provides primary care services.

Primary payer The insurer obligated to pay losses before any liability is assumed by other, secondary insurers. Medicare, for instance, is a primary payer with respect to Medicaid.

Prior authorization A formal process requiring a provider to obtain approval to provide particular services or procedures before they are done. This is usually required for nonemergency services that are expensive or likely to be abused or overused. A managed care organization will identify those services and procedures that require prior authorization, without which the provider may not be compensated.

Probability (*P* value) The likelihood that an event will occur. When looking at differences between data samples, statistical techniques are used to determine whether the differences are likely to reflect real differences in the whole group from which the sample is drawn or whether they are simply the result of random variation in the samples. For example, a probability (or *P* value) of 1% indicates that the differences observed would have occurred by chance in one out of a hundred samples drawn from the same data.

Proprietary Profit making. Owned and operated for the purpose of making a profit, whether or not one is actually made.

Prospective payment Any method of paying hospitals or other health programs in which amounts or rates of payment are established in advance for a defined period (usually a year). Institutions are paid these amounts regardless of the costs they actually incur. These systems of payment are designed to introduce a degree of constraint on charge or costs increases by setting limits on amounts paid during a future period. In some cases, such systems provide incentives for improved efficiency by sharing savings with institutions that perform at lower than anticipated costs. Prospective payment contrasts with the method of payment originally used under Medicare and Medicaid (as well as other insurance programs) where institutions were reimbursed for actual expenses incurred.

Provider   Hospital or licensed healthcare professional or group of hospitals or healthcare professionals that provide healthcare services to patients. This may also refer to medical supply firms and vendors of durable medical equipment.

Public good   A good or service whose benefits may be provided to a group at no more cost than that required to provide it for one person. The benefits of the good are indivisible and individuals cannot be excluded. For example, a public health measure that eradicates smallpox protects all, not just those paying for the vaccination.

Public health   The science dealing with the protection and improvement of community health by organized community effort. Public health activities are generally those that are less amenable to being undertaken by individuals or are less effective when undertaken on an individual basis and do not typically include direct personal health services. Public health activities include immunizations; sanitation; preventive medicine, quarantine, and other disease-control activities; occupational health and safety programs; assurance of the healthfulness of air, water, and food; health education; epidemiology; and others.

Quality-adjusted life years (QALYs)   Years of life saved by a medical technology or service, adjusted according to the quality of those years (as determined by some evaluative measure). QALYs are the most commonly used unit to express the results in some types of cost-effectiveness analysis.

Quality improvement   The sum of all the activities that created a desired change in quality. In the healthcare setting, quality improvement requires a feedback loop that involves the identification of patterns of the care of patients (or of the performance of other systems involved in care), the analysis of those patterns in order to identify opportunities for improvement (or instances of departure from standards of care), and then action to improve the quality of care for future patients.

Quality of care   The degree to which delivered health services meet established professional standards and judgments of value to the consumer. Quality may also be seen as the degree to which actions taken or not taken maximize the probability of beneficial health outcomes and minimize risk and other outcomes, given the existing state of medical science and art. Quality is frequently described as having three dimensions: quality of input resources (certification and/or training of providers), quality of the process of services delivery (the use of appropriate procedures for a given condition), and quality of outcome of service use (actual improvement in condition or reduction of harmful effects).

Rate   A measure of the intensity of the occurrence of an event. For example, the mortality rate equals the number of those who die in 1 year divided by the number at risk of dying. Rates are usually expressed using a standard denominator such as 1,000 or 10,000 persons. Rates may also be expressed as percentages.

Rate band   The allowable variation in insurance premiums as defined in state regulations. Acceptable variation may be expressed as a ratio from highest to lowest, as a percent of the index rate (e.g., ± 20%). It is used to limit variation for individual factors (such as age, gender, occupation, or geographic region) or to limit variation for all of these factors together (called a composite rate band).

Rate review   Review by a government or private agency of a hospital's budget and financial data, performed for the purpose of determining the reasonableness of the hospital rates and evaluating proposed rate increases.

Rate setting   A method of paying healthcare providers in which the federal or state government established payment rates for all payers for various categories of health services.

Reference-based drug pricing   Reference-based pricing has been adopted both within Canada (in British Columbia and Nova Scotia) and in other countries (including the United States, Australia, New Zealand, and

Germany) as a means of limiting expenditures for drug subsidy and insurance programs. Reference based pricing limits reimbursement for a group of drugs with similar therapeutic application but different active ingredients to the price of the lowest cost drug within the group (the reference standard). Patients have the option of purchasing drugs that are partially subsidized, in which case they pay the difference between the retail price and the reference price.

Referral   The process of sending a patient from one practitioner to another for healthcare services. Health plans may require that designated primary care providers authorize a referral for coverage of specialty services.

Rehabilitation   The combined and coordinated use of medical, social, educational, and vocational measures for training or retraining individuals disabled by disease or injury to the highest possible level of functional ability. Several different types of rehabilitation are distinguished: vocational, social, psychological, medical, and educational.

Reimbursement   The process by which healthcare providers receive payment for their services. Because of the nature of the healthcare environment, providers are often reimbursed by third parties who insure and represent patients.

Reinsurance   The resale of insurance products to a secondary market, thereby spreading the costs associated with underwriting.

Relative risk   The rate of disease in one group exposed to a particular factor (e.g., a toxic spill) divided by the rate in another group which is not exposed. A relative risk of one indicates that the two groups have the same rate of disease.

Reliability   The extent to which a measurement can be replicated with low levels of random error in measurement.

Respite care   Care given to a hospice patient by another caregiver so that the usual caregiver can rest.

Retrospective reimbursement   Payment made after-the-fact for services rendered on the basis of costs incurred by the facility (see also prospective payment).

Revenue   The gross amount of earnings received by an entity for the operation of a specific activity. It does not include any deductions for such items as expenses, bad debts, or contractual allowances.

Risk   Responsibility for paying for or otherwise providing a level of healthcare services based on an unpredictable need for these services.

Risk adjustment   A process by which premium dollars are shifted from a plan with relatively healthy enrollees to another with sicker members. It is intended to minimize any financial incentives health plans may have to select healthier than average enrollees. In this process, health plans that attract higher risk providers and members would be compensated for any differences in the proportion of their members that require high levels of care compared with other plans.

Risk-based capital formula   A method of establishing the minimum amount of capital appropriate for an insurance company to support its overall business operations in consideration of its size, structure, and risk profile. It is used to assess a managed care organization's financial viability and help prevent insolvency.

Risk-bearing entity   An organization that assumes financial responsibility for the provision of a defined set of benefits by accepting prepayment for some or all of the cost of care. A risk-bearing entity may be an insurer, a health plan or self-funded employer, or a PHO or other form of PSN.

Risk or risk factor   Risk is a term used by epidemiologists to quantify the likelihood that something will occur. A risk factor is something which either increases or decreases an individual's risk of developing a disease; however, it does not mean that, if exposed, an individual will definitely contract a particular disease.

Risk selection   Occurs when a disproportionate share of high or low users of care join a health plan.

Risk sharing   The distribution of financial risk among parties furnishing a service. For example, if a hospital and a group of physicians from a corporation provide health care at a fixed price, a risk-sharing arrangement would entail both the hospital and the group being held liable if expenses exceed revenues.

Root cause analysis   A process for identifying the basic or causal factor(s) that underlies variations in performance, including the occurrence or possible occurrence of an error.

Safety net   The network of providers and institutions that provide low cost or free medical care to medically needy, low income, or uninsured populations. The healthcare safety net can include (but is not limited to) individual practitioners, public and private hospitals, academic medical centers, and smaller clinics or ambulatory care facilities.

Safety net providers   Providers that historically have had large Medicaid and indigent care caseloads relative to other providers and are willing to provide services regardless of the patient's ability to pay.

Sample   In statistical analysis, a sample is a finite subset of a statistical population whose properties are studied to gain information about the whole population or universe.

Screening   The use of quick procedures to differentiate "apparently well" persons who have a disease or a high risk of disease from those who probably do not have the disease. It is used to identify high-risk individuals for more definitive study or follow-up. Multiple screening is the combination of a battery of screening tests for various diseases performed by technicians under medical direction and applied to large groups of "apparently well" persons.

Secondary care   Services provided by medical specialists who generally do not have first contact with patients (e.g., cardiologist, urologists, dermatologists). In the United States, however, there has been a trend toward self-referral by patients for these services, rather than referral by primary care providers. This is quite different from the practice in England, for example, where all patients must first seek care from primary care providers and are then referred to secondary and/or tertiary providers, as needed.

Secondary payer   An insurer obligated to pay losses above or beyond losses that are assumed by a primary payer.

Secondary prevention   Early diagnosis, treatment, and follow-up. Secondary prevention activities start with the assumption that illness is already present and that primary prevention was not successful. The goal is to diminish the impact of disease or illness through early

detection, diagnosis, and treatment (e.g., blood pressure screening, treatment, and follow-up programs).

Self-funding/Self-insurance   An employer or group of employers sets aside funds to cover the cost of health benefits for their employees. Benefits may be administered by the employer(s) or handled through an administrative service-only agreement with an insurance carrier or third-party administrator. Under self-funding, it is generally possible to purchase stop-loss insurance that covers expenditures above a certain aggregate claim level and/or covers catastrophic illness or injury when individual claims reach a certain dollar threshold.

Sensitivity   A high rate of detection of "true positives" (i.e., the fraction of patients who actually received good care who are classified as recipients of good care).

Sentinel event   An unexpected occurrence or variation involving death or serious physical or psychological injury, or the risk thereof. Serious injury specifically includes loss of limb or function. The event is called "sentinel" because it sends a signal or sounds a warning that requires immediate attention.

Service period   Period of employment that may be required before an employee is eligible to participate in an employer-sponsored health plan, most commonly 1 to 3 months.

Severity of illness   A risk prediction system to correlate the "seriousness" of a disease in a particular patient with the statistically "expected" outcome (e.g., mortality, morbidity, efficiency of care). Most effectively, severity is measured at or soon after admission, before therapy is initiated, giving a measure of pretreatment risk.

SF-12   A shorter version of the SF-36 (one-page, 2-minute) survey form that has been shown to yield summary physical and mental health outcome scores that are interchangeable with those from the SF-36 in both general and specific populations. This shorter version of the SF-36 was published in early 1995 and is already one of the most widely used surveys of health status.

SF-36   A comprehensive short-form health status questionnaire with only 36 questions that yields an eight-scale health profile as well as summary measures of health-related quality of life. As documented in more than 750 publications, the SF-36 has proven useful in monitoring general and specific populations, comparing the burden of different diseases, differentiating the health benefits produced by different treatments, and screening individual patients. The SF-36 is a standard measure of healthcare quality used by health services researchers and others who monitor quality of care. The survey is produced by Quality Metric, Inc.

Skilled nursing facility (SNF) A nursing care facility participating in the Medicaid and Medicare programs that meets specified requirements for services, staffing, and safety.

Solo practice Lawful practice of a health occupation as a self-employed individual. Solo practice is by definition private practice but is not necessarily general practice or fee-for-service practice (solo practitioners may be paid by capitation, although fee-for-service is more common). Solo practice is common among physicians, dentists, podiatrists, optometrists, and pharmacists.

Specialist A physician, dentist, or other health professional who is specially trained in a certain branch of medicine or dentistry related to specific services or procedures (e.g., surgery, radiology, pathology), certain age categories of patients (e.g., geriatrics), certain body systems (e.g., dermatology, orthopedics, cardiology), or certain types of diseases (e.g., allergy, periodontics). Specialists usually have advanced education and training related to their specialties.

Specificity A high rate of detection of "true negatives" (i.e., the fraction of patients who actually received bad care who are classified as recipients of bad care).

Spend down The amount of expenditures for healthcare services, relative to income, that qualifies an individual for Medicaid in States that cover categorically eligible, medically indigent individuals. Eligibility is determined on a case-by-case basis.

Standard error In statistics, the standard error is defined as the standard deviation of an estimate. That is, multiple measurements of a given value will generally group around the mean (or average) value in a normal distribution. The shape of this distribution is known as the standard error.

State Children's Health Insurance Program (SCHIP) This program was enacted as part of the Balanced Budget Act of 1997, which established Title XXI of the Social Security Act to provide States with $24 billion in Federal funds for 1998–2002 targeting children in families with incomes up to 200% of the Federal poverty level.

Substance Abuse and Mental Health Services Administration (SAMHSA) The mission of SAMHSA is to provide, through the U.S. Public Health Service, a national focus for the federal effort to promote effective strategies for the prevention and treatment of addictive and mental disorders. SAMHSA is primarily a grant making organization, promoting knowledge and scientific state-of-the-art practice. SAMHSA strives to reduce barriers to high-quality, effective programs and services for individuals who suffer from or are at risk for these disorders, as well as for their families and communities.

Survey An investigation in which information is systematically collected. A population survey may be conducted by face-to-face inquiry, by self-completed questionnaires, by telephone, by postal service, or in some other way. Each method has its advantages and disadvantages. The generalizability of results depends on the extent to which those surveyed are representative of the entire population.

Supply In health economics, the quantity of services provided or personnel in a given area.

Swing-bed hospital A hospital participating in the Medicare swing-bed program. This program allows rural hospitals with fewer than 100 beds to provide skilled postacute care services in acute-care beds.

Systems approach A school of thought evolving from earlier systems analysis theory, propounding that virtually all outcomes are the result of systems rather than individuals. In practice, the systems approach is characterized by attempts to improve the quality and/or efficiency of a process through improvements to the system.

Systems error An error that is not the result of an individual's actions, but the predictable outcome of a series of actions and factors that comprise a diagnostic or treatment process.

Technology assessment A comprehensive form of policy research that examines the technical, economic, and social consequences of technological applications. It is especially concerned with unintended, indirect, or delayed social impacts. In health policy, the term has come to mean any form of policy analysis concerned with medical technology, especially the evaluation of efficacy and safety.

Telehealth The use of telecommunications technologies and electronic information to support long-distance clinical health care, patient and professional health-related education, or public health and health administration.

Telemedicine The use of telecommunications (i.e., wire, radio, optical or electromagnetic channels transmitting voice, data, and video) to facilitate medical diagnosis, patient care, and/or distance learning.

Tertiary care Services provided by highly specialized providers (e.g., neurologists, neurosurgeons, thoracic surgeons, intensive care units). Such services frequently require highly sophisticated equipment and support facilities. The development of these services has largely been a function of diagnostic and therapeutic advances attained through basic and clinical biomedical research.

Tertiary prevention Prevention activities that focus on the individual after a disease or illness has manifested itself. The goal is to reduce long-term effects and to help individuals cope better with symptoms.

Third-party administrator (TPA) A fiscal intermediary (a person or an organization) that serves as another's financial agent. A TPA processes claims, provides services, and issues payments on behalf of certain private, federal, and state health benefit programs or other insurance organizations.

Third-party payer Any organization, public or private, that pays or insures health or medical expenses on behalf of beneficiaries or recipients. An individual pays a premium for such coverage in all private and in some public programs; the payer organization then pays bills on the individual's behalf. Such payments are called third-party payments and are distinguished by the separation among the individual receiving the service (the first party), the individual or institution providing it (the second party), and the organization paying for it (third party).

Title XVIII (Medicare) The title of the Social Security Act that contains the principal legislative authority

for the Medicare program and therefore a common name for the program.

Title XIX (Medicaid) The title of the Social Security Act that contains the principal legislative authority for the Medicaid program and therefore a common name for the program.

Uncompensated care Service provided by physicians and hospitals for which no payment is received from the patient or from third-party payers. Some costs for these services may be covered through cost shifting. Not all uncompensated care results from charity care. It also includes bad debts from persons who are not classified as charity cases but who are unable or unwilling to pay their bill.

Underinsured People with public or private insurance policies that do not cover all necessary healthcare services, resulting in out-of-pocket expenses that exceed their ability to pay.

Underwriting In insurance, the process of selecting, classifying, evaluating, and assuming risks according to their insurability. Its purpose is to make sure that the group or individual insured has the same probability of loss and probable amount of loss, within reasonable limits, as the universe on which premium rates were based. Because premium rates are based on an expectation of loss, the underwriting process must classify risks into groups with about the same expectation of loss.

Uninsurables High-risk persons who do not have healthcare coverage through private insurance and who fall outside the parameters of risks of standard health underwriting practices.

Uninsured People who lack public or private health insurance.

Unit (of analysis) The unit to which a performance measure is applied (e.g., patients, clinician, group of clinicians, institution).

Usual, customary and reasonable (UCR) fees The use of fee screens to determine the lowest value of physician reimbursement based on: (1) the physician's usual charge for a given procedure, (2) the amount customarily charged for the service by other physicians in the area (often defined as a specific percentile of all charges in the community), and (3) the reasonable cost of services for a given patient after medical review of the case.

Utilization   Use. Commonly examined in terms of patterns or rates of use of a single service or type of service (e.g., hospital care, physician visits, prescription drugs). Use is also expressed in rates per unit of population at risk for a given period.

Utilization review   Evaluation of the necessity, appropriateness, and efficiency of the use of healthcare services, procedures, and facilities. In a hospital, this includes review of the appropriateness of admissions, services ordered and provided, length of a stay, and discharge practices, both on a concurrent and retrospective basis. Utilization review can be done by a peer review group, or a public agency.

Validity   The ability of a performance measure to capture what it purports to measure (e.g., a particular aspect of clinical care).

Vertical integration   Organization of production whereby one business entity controls or owns all stages of the production and distribution of goods or services.

Vital statistics   Statistics relating to births (natality), deaths (mortality), marriages, health, and disease (morbidity). Vital statistics for the United States are published by the National Center for Health Statistics.

Voluntary reporting   A medical error reporting system where the reporter chooses to report an error in order to prevent similar errors from occurring in the future. One theory of voluntary reporting systems is that they allow reporters to focus on a set of errors broader than just those that cause serious harm and that they help to detect system weaknesses before the occurrence of serious harm.

Wellness   A dynamic state of physical, mental, and social well-being. A way of life that equips the individual to realize the full potential of his or her capabilities and to overcome and compensate for weaknesses. A lifestyle that recognizes the importance of nutrition, physical fitness, stress reduction, and self-responsibility. Wellness has been viewed as the result of four key factors over which an individual has varying degrees of control: human biology, environment, healthcare organization (system), and lifestyle.

Withhold   A form of compensation whereby a health plan withholds payment to a provider until the end of a value-based purchasing period, at which time the plan distributes any remaining funds based on provider performance. Provider performance can include measures such as the number and appropriateness of referrals to specialists, or the number of patients who receive preventive screenings, i.e., measures of cost efficiency and/or quality of care. Value-based purchasing brings together information on the quality of health care, such as patient outcomes and health status, with data on the dollar outlays going towards health. It focuses on managing the use of the healthcare system to reduce inappropriate care and to identify and reward the best-performing providers. This strategy can be contrasted with more limited efforts to negotiate price discounts, which reduce costs but do little to ensure that quality of care is improved.

Working capital   The sum of an institution's short-term or current assets including cash, marketable (short-term) securities, accounts receivable, and inventories. Net working capital is defined as the excess of total current assets over total current liabilities.

World Bank[4]   The World Bank is a vital source of financial and technical assistance to developing countries around the world. Its primary focus is on helping the poorest people and countries. Two unique development institutions owned by 185 member countries—the International Bank for Reconstruction and Development (IBRD) and the International Development Association (IDA)—comprise The World Bank. The IBRD focuses on middle income and creditworthy poor countries, whereas IDA focuses on the poorest countries in the world. The World Bank provides low-interest loans, interest-free credit and grants to developing countries for education, health, infrastructure, communications and many other purposes.

World Health Organization (WHO)[5]   WHO is the directing and coordinating authority for health within the United Nations system. Established in 1948, WHO has grown to have 193 member countries. It is responsible for providing leadership on global health matters, shaping the health research agenda, setting norms and standards, articulating evidence-based policy options, providing technical support to countries and monitoring and assessing health trends.

World Trade Organization (WTO)[6]   The World Trade Organization (WTO) is the only global international organization dealing with the rules of trade between nations. Led by the General Agreement on Tariffs and Trade (GATT), WTO was created January 1, 1995. At the heart of the system, known as the multilateral trading system, are the WTO's agreements, negotiated and signed by a large majority of the world's trading nations, and ratified in their parliaments. These agreements are the legal ground rules for international commerce that covers trade in services and in traded inventions, creations, and designs (intellectual property). The goal is to help producers of goods and services, exporters, and importers conduct their business and thereby to improve the welfare of the peoples of the member countries.

FOOTNOTES

1. All terms, unless otherwise indicated, are from *Glossary of Terms Commonly Used in Health Care*, 2004 edition, AcademyHealth. A more expansive glossary is available on their website, www.academyhealth.org.

2. Cornia GA. Globalization and health: results and options. *Bulletin of the World Health Organization* 2001;79(9): 834–841.

3. Woodward D, Drager N, Beaglehole R, Lipson D. Globalization and health: a framework for analysis and action. *Bulletin of the World Health Organization* 2001;79(9):875–881.

4. http://web.worldbank.org/WBSITE/EXTERNAL/ EXTABOUTUS/0,,pagePK:50004410~piPK:36602~the SitePK:29708,00.html.
   http://siteresources.worldbank.org/EXTABOUTUS/ Resources/wbgroupbrochure-en07.pdf.

5. http://www.who.int/about/brochure_en.pdf / http://www.who.int/about/en/.

6. http://www.wto.org/english/res_e/doload_e/inbr_e.pdf.

Index

Photo Credits